DISEASES OF FOREST AND ORNAMENTAL TREES

DISEASES OF FOREST AND ORNAMENTAL TREES

D. H. PHILLIPS
(*sometime Principal Pathologist and
Chief Research Officer (South),
The Forestry Commission of
Great Britain*)

and

D. A. BURDEKIN
(*Chief Research Officer (South), and
former Principal Pathologist,
The Forestry Commission of
Great Britain*)

MACMILLAN

First published 1982
Reprinted 1985

Published by
Scientific and Medical Division
THE MACMILLAN PRESS LTD
Houndmills, Basingstoke, Hampshire RG21 2XS
and London
Companies and representatives
throughout the world

Printed in Hong Kong

ISBN 0-333-32357-2

To
T. Small, OBE, DSc (1894 – 1976)
Mycologist to the States of Jersey, 1931 – 1954
and
C. W. T. Young (1920 – 1981)
Pathology Branch, The Forestry Commission, 1955 – 1981

Contents

Preface

In recent years public interest in trees and their diseases has greatly increased, partly because attention has been drawn to them by the losses caused by Dutch elm disease. The increasing numbers of arboricultural officers, consultants and tree surgeons as well as our foresters need a new book on the tree diseases of Britain, incorporating information acquired since the publication of the late T. R. Peace's *Pathology of Trees and Shrubs with Special Reference to Britain.* Peace's comprehensive work, published by the Clarendon Press, Oxford, in 1962, is now out of date and out of print.

The present book deals with the diseases found in Britain on forest and ornamental trees. Most of these diseases also occur elsewhere, and in our account we have therefore drawn on all the available literature, though we have had to be selective, and our interpretations are inevitably coloured by the fact that our experience of tree diseases has been mainly in the British Isles. We generally comment on diseases (and pests) alien to Britain only in the section on plant health legislation. We describe diseases of fruit trees such as the apple, pear and cherry only in so far as they affect ornamental forms of the fruit tree genera and species. These diseases are already treated at greater length in texts on diseases of orchard trees.

The depth and length of the treatment given to individual diseases varies, and in general reflects both the importance of the disorders concerned and the information available about them. In many cases we have divided the diseases into those occurring mainly in the nursery and those important chiefly after the nursery stage. In other cases this has not been possible or useful, and then, for the sake of uniformity, we have grouped all under one main heading as 'nursery and post-nursery' diseases.

Our aims have been wide: we have tried to make the book useful to forest and general plant pathologists, foresters and forest managers, arboriculturists and tree surgeons, staffs of parks and gardens, staff and students of universities and other places of further education and of research stations, and to all those generally interested in trees. Where possible we have provided information on symptoms, factors affecting disease expression, host range and resistance, and brief descriptions of causal organisms. We have not provided a lengthy introduction to mycology, bacteriology and virology, but in the case of bacterial and fungal diseases have usually supplied enough bacterial or mycological detail to enable the professional pathologist to make a diagnosis based on this and the other material given. Further information must be sought in the more extensive bacterial and mycological (and virological) texts cited in the bibliographies.

Name changes of both disease organisms and their hosts cause problems in practical fields such as forestry, arboriculture and plant pathology. We have generally attempted to apply current names to pathogens and to trees. In the case of pathogens we give the better known synonyms when we use what to some may be unfamiliar names. In the case of trees we usually supply the common names now used in Britain as well as the current scientific names.

Control measures are suggested for many diseases; in some cases, however, no control measures are as yet available. A good many diseases are too minor in their effects for control measures to be required. If it appears necessary to attempt the control of any of these lesser diseases, the general measures discussed in chapter 1 may be applied. Mention is made of many fungicides and bactericides. New chemicals are continually being introduced and old ones withdrawn, however, and the reader wishing to use these materials is advised to consult the latest issue of the *List of Approved Products and Their Uses For Farmers and Growers*, which is revised annually and published for the Ministry of Agriculture, Fisheries and Food by Her Majesty's Stationery Office.

The introductory chapter on symptoms, diagnosis and control of diseases is intended mainly for the student, the beginner, and the general reader. In the rest of the book the diseases are grouped chiefly under their host genera. Most of the diseases with a wide host range (including the disorders caused by nonliving agents such as frost or air pollution), however, are described in separate chapters. In a few cases organisms affect several hosts but are far more important on one than on any of the others; they are then described under the main host. The decay fungi (many of which also have a wide host range) are also drawn together in one chapter.

Many of our colleagues have made valuable comments on the text. Among them we must especially mention the late Dr S. Batko (who helped particularly by translating literature from many languages), Dr W. O. Binns, Dr C. M. Brasier, Dr J. N. Gibbs, Mr B. J. W. Greig, Mr D. Lonsdale, Mr J. D. Low, Mr W. J. McCavish, Dr D. B. Redfern, Mr R. G. Strouts, and the late Mr C. W. T. Young. Miss Mary Trusler greatly helped by printing photographs, and Mr J. Williamson drew figure 25.

The book owes much to the decision of the publishers to illustrate many of the diseases in colour. Many of the photographs are from the collection of the Forestry Commission, to whom special thanks are therefore due. These and the other illustrations are separately listed and acknowledged elsewhere. Fuller acknowledgement of black and white illustrations from sources outside our own collections and those of the Forestry Commission are as follows. Figures 3, 4, 27, 98: B. J. W. Greig. Figures 47, 85: W. B. Grove (1913), *British Rust Fungi*, Cambridge University Press, Cambridge. Figures 51, 54, 60, 83: R. Hartig (1894), *Text-book of the Diseases of Trees*, Macmillan, London. Figure 63: D. B. Redfern. Figure 5: G. A. Salt (1974), *Trans. Br. mycol. Soc.*, **63**, 339-51. Figures 7, 8, 61, 77, 78, 81, 84: K. F. Tubeuf (1895), Pflanzenkrankheiten, Springer, Berlin. Figure 10: J. H. Western (1971), *Diseases of Crop Plants*, Macmillan, London.

Figure 48: M. Wilson and D. M. Henderson (1966), *British Rust Fungi*, Cambridge University Press, Cambridge. Figures 9, 86, 88: H. Wormald (1955), *Diseases of Fruits and Hops,* Crosby Lockwood, London. Figure 67: C.M. Braiser.

Wrecclesham, 1982   D. H. P.
                                                                       D. A. B.

The Colour Plates*

* These appear between pages 240 and 241

1 General introduction

Disease is a disorganisation of the normal physiological activity of the tree caused by some adverse agent which gives rise to characteristic symptoms. Hence a diseased tree differs from a healthy one in recognisable ways, and the pathologist must first of all become familiar with the appearance and characteristics of healthy trees. Thus in cold weather the foliage of nursery plants of western red cedar (*Thuja plicata*) may turn from green to bronze (plate 39). This colour change is normal and reversible, and the affected plants are not diseased. Nevertheless, if the temperature becomes sufficiently low, the foliage of these plants is killed, but they then become an irreversible glossy black. Similarly, the fungus *Didymascella thujina* may attack and kill the scale leaves of *Thuja* seedlings. The affected plants show the small fruit bodies of the fungus (plate 40) and are diseased, and their growth is reduced; if enough scale leaves are destroyed the plants die. Again, the bark of London plane (*Platanus* x *acerifolia*) peels off the tree in a typical pattern, but this is a normal phenomenon, whereas the breaking up of the bark in the late stages of beech bark disease (figure 56) is an indication of severe and irreparable damage by *Nectria coccinea* and other associated fungi.

CAUSES OF DISEASE

The agents that cause diseases may be nonliving or living. Among the nonliving agents are climatic factors such as high or low temperatures, drought and lightning, soil factors such as poor soil aeration and the lack of essential nutrients, and injurious chemicals such as atmospheric pollutants and misplaced herbicides. Damage by these agents is associated with some discrete event or series of events, such as an emission of some polluting chemical, or with the absence of some necessary element (as in the case of nutrient deficiency disorders). Disorders caused by nonliving agents are not infectious so they cannot spread from tree to tree.

The living pathogens include the fungi (the most important), the bacteria, and the semiparasitic mistletoes. The viruses, which are ultramicroscopic and can reproduce only in their host cells, are also included here. Some disorders formerly regarded as virus diseases now appear to be caused by mycoplasmas or by mycoplasma-like organisms. The mycoplasmas are now considered to be small bacteria. Those affecting plants are still little known. The diseases caused by these living pathogens are infectious and can spread from tree to tree by means of their own spores or other disseminules either alone or with the aid of one or more vectors.

Many fungi cause diseases of trees (and of other plants). The true fungi (excluding the slime moulds) are divided into five main subdivisions. The first two, the Mastigomycotina and the Zygomycotina, were formerly grouped together as the Phycomycetes. These fungi are microscopic, one-celled or formed of mainly nonseptate threads (*hyphae*) which in aggregate are described as *mycelium*. Most, if not all, the fungi in these groups that attack trees are classified in the Peronosporales, of the order Oomycetes, which form a class of the Mastigomycotina. Included here are species of *Phytophthora* and other downy mildews.

In the third and fourth subdivisions, the hyphae that make up both the vegetative body and the fructifications are septate (that is, they are divided into segments by cross walls). The fruit bodies are generally relatively large, and readily visible to the naked eye or with the aid of a hand lens. In the first of these two groups, the Ascomycotina (Ascomycetes), the sexual spores are borne inside sac-like or tubular *asci*. In a few the fruit body containing the asci is very simple, consisting of little or nothing more than an ascal layer (*hymenium*), as in the case of *Taphrina populina*, the cause of popular leaf blister (plate 28). In others (if we confine ourselves to those causing diseases in trees) the asci are enclosed in more or less globular, flask-shaped, saucer-shaped, or boat-shaped fruit bodies. Included here are, for example, the powdery mildews (such as the oak mildew, *Microsphaera alphitoides*), with small, globular fruit bodies (*cleistothecia*) (plate 29), the *Nectria* species (including *N. cinnabarina*, with small, bright red, flask-shaped *perithecia*) (plate 14), *Lachnellula willkommii*, the cause of larch canker (with small, disc-shaped *apothecia* with a white outer wall and a bright orange hymenial disc) (plate 23), and the *Lophodermium* species associated with needle cast in pines, with a boat-shaped *hysterothecium* opening by a slit (figure 37).

In the second of these groups, the Basidiomycotina (Basidiomycetes), the sexual spores are borne outside usually club-shaped *basidia*. Of the three classes of the Basidiomycotina, only two contain pathogens. The first, the Hemibasidio-mycetes, includes the Uredinales (the rusts), such as species of *Cronartium*, *Coleosporium* and *Melampsora*. The rusts often exhibit complex life histories, which in their most complete form involve the production of a series of spore types. Some of these spores arise on one host, while others form on a second, alternate host, which may be necessary for the completion of the life cycle. These spore forms and their associated fructifications are described below.

(1) *Spermatia*: small sex-cells produced in minute *spermogonia*, embedded in the leaves or stems.

(2) *Aecidiospores*: produced in *aecidia*, which are often cup-shaped or cylin-drical (figure 38), like those of *Coleosporium tussilaginis* on needles of pines, or blister-like, like those of *Peridermium pini* on pine stems (plate 12).

(3) *Uredospores*: produced in *uredosori*, small, often yellow or brown pustules; the uredosori of *C. tussilaginis* occur on *Senecio*, *Tussilago*, and other members of the Compositae.

(4) *Teleutospores*: produced in *teleutosori* which often resemble the uredosori and follow them on the same leaves (as they do in the case of *C. tussilaginis*). In some rusts the spores in these sori are massed together into small columns that stand up above the leaf surface like minute bristles. This is so in *Cronartium ribicola*, the white pine blister rust, the teleutosori of which occur on the leaves of the black currant and other species of *Ribes* (figure 43). In species of *Gymno-sporangium*, the teleutosori form as large, gelatinous, cushion-shaped or horn-like bodies (figure 47).

The second of these groups among the Basidiomycotina, the Hymenomycetes, includes the Agaricales (plate 17) (the toadstools, such as *Armillaria mellea* and similar forms) and the Aphyllophorales, important among which are the pore-bearing bracket fungi, with many wood-decay organisms such as *Heterobasidion annosum* (*Fomes annosus*) (plate 18).

Finally, the fifth subdivision of the fungi is the Deuteromycotina (Deutero-mycetes, the Fungi Imperfecti), an artificial assemblage consisting mainly of asexual forms of ascomycetes and of fungi with no known affinity with other groups. The fruit bodies of these fungi often superficially resemble those of ascomycetes, but they contain asexual spores instead of asci with ascospores.

For further information on the fungi, reference should be made to standard mycological texts such as those of Webster (1977) and Burnett (1977).

The few bacteria known to cause diseases of trees are species of *Agrobacterium*, *Pseudomonas*, *Erwinia* and *Xanthomonas*. Further details on these are available in the texts of Dowson (1957) and Stapp (1961).

A recent summary of the diseases caused in trees by the viruses and the mycoplasma-like organisms has been prepared by Cooper (1979).

SYMPTOMS OF DISEASE

Symptoms of disease may be found on any part of the tree, on the leaves, on the stems and branches, and on the roots.

SYMPTOMS ON LEAVES

Colour changes

Browning and death   The leaves may be partly or completely killed, when they usually turn brown (or sometimes black). This death of leaves may have many causes. It may be due to drought, or to wind damage, or frost, or sometimes to air pollution. Fungi may also sometimes destroy leaves in this way. Thus in severe attacks *Lophodermium* spp. may kill the needles of young pines in the nursery, and *Meria laricis* may similarly affect nursery plants of European larch. The leaves of broadleaved trees may also be killed and become brown. Thus secondary spread of *Ceratocystis ulmi* (the cause of Dutch elm disease) through root systems may produce rapid browning and death of the crown of the tree. Primary spread by insect vectors in its later stages also leads to leaf death. Sometimes leaf browning may be marginal only, as is often the case with leaves scorched by wind.

Other colour changes   In some cases browning and death of leaves may be replaced or preceded by other colour changes. As already noted, severely cold-damaged fronds of *Thuja plicata* die and turn glossy black.

Nursery plants (and sometimes plantation trees) may change colour when affected by mineral deficiencies (plates 5, 6, 7, 8). Thus plants deficient in nitrogen tend to be pale green, while those short of potash may become pinkish, purplish or sometimes yellow. Magnesium deficiency is indicated by a bright yellow colour which on the leaves of broadleaved trees occurs mainly between the veins. Pines on very alkaline sites often become yellow at about 10-15 years of age, and then gradually die. This is due to a complex deficiency disorder called lime-induced chlorosis. The same disease may also affect other trees (including broadleaved ones), though usually less markedly.

Virus diseases may also cause yellowing of leaves. This yellowing may take the form of a more or less regular mottle or mosaic, or it may follow the leaf veins ('vein clearing'), or appear as lines or rings (figure 76).

Some wilt diseases that block the vessels (and at least some of which produce toxins) may cause the foliage of parts of the crown to become yellow or red. Thus one of the earliest primary symptoms of Dutch elm disease, caused by *Ceratocystis ulmi*, is a yellowing of the foliage of isolated branches of the tree. Eventually (as noted above) the affected leaves die and become brown. Leaves in parts of the crown of willows affected by watermark disease (caused by the bacterium *Erwinia salicis*) turn bright red.

Some rusts may cause a yellowing of leaves; an example is provided by *Chrysomyxa* spp. which produce yellow bands on diseased spruce needles (plate 19).

Leaf distortion and reduction
A more or less general distortion of leaf shape may be caused by hormone weed killers such as 2,4,D.

Some fungi may also cause leaf distortion. Among these are the various species of *Taphrina*, including *T. deformans* which gives rise to leaf curl in peaches and almonds (plate 55), and *T. populina* which causes leaf blister in poplars (plate 28).

Many root disease fungi reduce the size of leaves. Pine trees attacked by *Heterobasidion annosum* (*Fomes annosus*) at first have short, sparse needles, which eventually fall as the tree dies.

Some virus diseases may cause the distortion of leaves and the production of small outgrowths (enations) from their surfaces.

General mould growths
Fungal attack may show itself as a more or less general mould growth. *Botrytis cinerea*, the common grey mould, appears as a greyish, sparse or more woolly growth of mould (plate 4) (often with small sporing heads and sometimes with rounded black fungal aggregates called *sclerotia*) on the leaf surface. The oidial stages of powdery mildews, such as oak mildew (*Microsphaera alphitoides*), form a powdery white (or at first yellowish or brownish) cover on the leaf surface (figures 50, 89).

Fungal fructifications
More clearly marked fungal fruit bodies may also be found on leaves (usually on spots or areas of dead or dying leaf tissue). The fungus *Rhytisma acerinum* forms large thickened black stromata ('tar spots') on the leaves of sycamore (plate 26).

Examination of the concave surfaces of the blisters on poplar leaves affected by the leaf blister disease mentioned earlier will reveal a golden-yellow lining consisting of a layer of the asci of the ascomycete *Taphrina populina* (plate 28).

Other, more distinctive ascocarps produced on leaves include, for example, the cleistothecia (cleistocarps), perithecia, hysterothecia and apothecia described above.

Among the basidiomycetes, the rusts give rise to various fructifications on leaves. These fruit bodies have also been listed above.

Finally, various small, asexual, so-called imperfect fructifications (fruit bodies of the Deuteromycotina, including asexual stages of ascomycetes) may be found on leaves. Many look like small black perithecia (when they are called *pycnidia*), but they contain asexual spores instead of asci.

SYMPTOMS ON STEMS AND BRANCHES

Splits in bark and wood

Splits in the bark and wood are often due to drought or frost damage. In the later stages of beech bark disease (associated with *Nectria coccinea*) the bark of affected trees may break into pieces and eventually fall off (figure 56).

Watery exudations

Sap may exude from cracks in tree trunks. Continuing, often foul-smelling, sap flowing from the bark of broadleaved trees may indicate the bacterial disorder wetwood (plate 11). Such exudations may also be caused by *Phytophthora* species, as in the case of the bleeding canker sometimes found on the horse chestnut (figure 82).

Exudations of bacterial slime

Wetwood exudations may often become slimy through the activities of bacteria and yeasts, and are then known as slime fluxes. In some bacterial diseases (notably in the case of bacterial canker of poplar, caused by *Xanthomonas populi*) thick bacterial slime may exude from small cracks in the bark of young stems and branches.

Resin flows

Resin may sometimes exude through the bark of conifers and flow down the trunk. Such resin flows often indicate root damage by fungi such as *Phytophthora* spp., *Armillaria mellea* or *Heterobasidion annosum* (figure 16). Resin may also exude from the stem cankers produced on pines by *Cronartium* spp. and other fungi (figure 42).

Distortions and malformations

In some seasons plant stems (including small branches of trees) may become wide, flattened and strap-like. This growth abnormality is known as *fasciation*.

Cold damage insufficient to cause death may distort the growth of tree shoots. Distortion of tree shoots may also be caused by fungi. Thus the pine twisting rust, *Melampsora pinitorqua* (a race of *M. populnea*), causes a twisting of the pine shoots (mainly of Scots pine) on which it grows (figure 40). The ends of the shoots of elms affected by Dutch elm disease often bend to form 'shepherds' crooks' which provide a useful diagnostic feature after leaf fall (figure 68).

Some fungi may cause the production of dense groups of adventitious shoots called 'witches' brooms'. An example is the witches' broom of birch caused by *Taphrina betulina* (figures 58, 59). Some viruses (and some mites) can also give rise to similar malformations on some trees.

Very marked distortions of stems of young trees may be caused by the honeysuckle (*Lonicera periclymenum*). This damage is mechanical since the honeysuckle is not a parasite.

Chemical distortion, especially of rather soft shoots, may follow applications of hormone weed killers.

Cankers

Sometimes a disease agent kills part of the cambium and the adjacent bark. The cambium around the lesion then produces new tissue which grows inwards to cover the dead area. If no further damage occurs, the canker will be occluded, and enveloped by the stem tissues. Often, however, further annual damage occurs, accompanied by further growth, and a large, swollen canker results. Such cankers are caused on poplar by the bacterium *Xanthomonas populi* (figure 75). Rough-surfaced cankers are produced on ash by another bacterium, *Pseudomonas savastanoi* f. *fraxini* (plate 31).

Other cankers are caused by fungi. Among these is the canker of larch caused by *Lachnellula willkommii* (figures 45, 46). Rusts of the genus *Cronartium* also give rise to cankers on pine trunks and branches. Among these rusts are *Cronartium ribicola*, the white pine blister rust, and *Peridermium pini* (an aecidial form of *C. flaccidum*).

General fungal growths

Grey mould (*Botrytis cinerea*), already mentioned in connection with leaves, may also produce lesions (often sunken) on twigs, and on stems of nursery plants. On these lesions it produces its mycelium, with masses of sporing heads, and sometimes its black sclerotia.

The honey fungus, *Armillaria mellea*, will often be found on dead or diseased trees as a thick sheet of creamy or whitish mycelium under the bark at the base of the trunk. At a later stage the fungus produces a network of flattened, bootlace-like *rhizomorphs*, also under the bark (figure 15). These rhizomorphs have a black outer surface, but have a white and (unlike roots) structureless tissue within. *A. mellea* also forms rhizomorphs in the soil. These are similar to those described above, but are round in section. They grow out from infested stumps and roots, and may attack the roots of surrounding trees and shrubs (and sometimes other plants).

Fungal fructifications

When these occur, they are very valuable in diagnosis. Examples among the basidiomycetes are the honey-coloured toadstools of *Armillaria mellea*, which in autumn usually grow in tufts at the bases of affected trees or on the ground around them (plate 17).

The bracket-shaped root and butt-rotting fungus *Heterobasidion annosum* also occurs at the bases of diseased trees and on infested stumps (plate 18). Another butt-rotting polypore, *Phaeolus schweinitzii* (plate 64) (the velvet-topped fungus), also usually occurs on the ground or at the stem base (but may also be found higher up the trunk), while yet another, *Polyporus squamosus* (the Dryad's saddle), causes a top rot and so fructifies near the top of the tree trunk, often on wounds caused by the loss of branches, for example.

Also among the basidiomycetes, species of *Cronartium* produce large, blister-like, cream or white aecidia filled with orange spores on the cankers caused by these rusts on the stems and branches of pines (plate 12, figure 42).

The fruit bodies of ascomycetes may also be found on trunks and branches. Sheets of the small, red, flask-shaped perithecia of *Nectria coccinea* may grow on the trunks of beech trees affected by beech bark disease.

Reddish-brown stromata containing the embedded perithecia of *Cryptodiaporthe castanea* may be found in cracks in the bark of coppice shoots of sweet chestnuts affected by Cryptodiaporthe canker.

Cup-like or disk-like apothecia of other ascomycetes also occur, like those of *Lachnellula willkommii* on the cankers caused by this fungus on larch (plate 23).

Asexual fruit bodies, imperfect stages of ascomycetes, or the fructifications of Deuteromycetes (Fungi Imperfecti) may also be found. Thus the pink, cushion-like imperfect stage of *Nectria cinnabarina* is common on twigs attacked by this fungus or colonised by it saprophytically (plate 14). Again, the pycnidial stage of *Cryptodiaporthe castanea*, *Fusicoccum castaneum*, occurs around the edges of the perithecial stroma.

Other plant growths

Algae, mosses, liverworts, ferns and lichens often grow on tree trunks and branches, but these growths are purely epiphytic. Plants of mistletoe (*Viscum album*) seen on some trees, however, are semiparasitic.

Internal symptoms

Some symptoms may be hidden inside the twigs, branches or trunks, either as stains, or rots, or as characteristic rings.

The bacterium *Erwinia salicis* causes rusty or inky stains inside the stems of cricket bat willow and other willows (plate 57). Usually after felling, various fungi cause a blue stain of the wood of pines. *Verticillium dahliae* (and the less common *V. albo-atrum*), the cause of verticillium wilt, may give rise to a brown or greenish stain in the stems of affected trees (plate 27) (as it does in the case of many other hosts, including the tomato).

In the early stages of attack many root-rot and butt-rot fungi also cause inky or rusty stains. Later the affected wood usually becomes soft and rotten, and may then occupy the centre of the stem, surrounded by a stained zone. Some of these fungi cause white rot, others a brown rot. Typical white rot fungi are *Armillaria mellea* and *Heterobasidion annosum*. The first of these causes a soft, wet, stringy rot in a conical zone usually reaching about 60 cm into the butt (figure 17). The second produces a rot with small white pockets of fungal mycelium, and the rot usually reaches much further up the trunk, to a level of about 300–400 cm (figures 29, 30, 31).

Phaeolus schweinitzii, on the other hand, is one of the brown rot fungi. It breaks the wood for a long distance up the trunk into brown, cubical blocks (figure 97), often separated by thin, yellow sheets of mycelium, and the affected wood smells of aniseed.

Rings of abnormal tissue produced by damaged cambium may be produced in twigs in the case of some disorders, and can be seen if the damaged twigs are sectioned and examined under a lens or a microscope. Such rings may be caused by frost (figure 2), drought or lightning.

A rather different type of ring may be found in the twigs of elms affected by Dutch elm disease (and occasionally by some other diseases). Here, sections of diseased twigs show a ring of brown dots in their outer wood (figure 69). If, instead of sectioning the twigs, their bark and outer wood are peeled away, these dots appear as brown streaks (figure 70).

Stem blisters

Cryptostroma corticale, the cause of the sooty bark disease of sycamore, raises the bark of affected trees into large blisters, which eventually break open to release the mass of brown, powdery spores that give the disease its common name (plate 32).

SYMPTOMS ON ROOTS

Symptoms on roots caused by root-rot and butt-rot fungi, such as *Armillaria mellea* and *Heterobasidion annosum*, are broadly similar to those caused in trunks by the same fungi. The roots of conifers attacked by *H. annosum* may exude resin (as happens with the trunks of some trees attacked by this fungus) and internally the roots show characteristic forms of rot.

The ascomycete *Rhizina undulata* (*R. inflata*) is associated with a root disease in conifers, especially in Sitka spruce. Its large, brown, hollow fruit bodies grow on the ground around diseased trees (figure 11), attached to the damaged roots, which also show characteristic lesions (figure 14).

Among the phycomycetes, *Phytophthora cambivora* and *P. cinnamomi* cause Phytophthora root rot in various broadleaved trees. In sweet chestnut the damaged roots may exude a blue, inky stain which seeps out into the soil. This stain gives rise to the name 'ink disease', but it is not in itself diagnostic.

DIAGNOSIS OF DISEASE

In the above account, the various symptoms have been isolated to draw attention to them. It must be emphasised, however, that the pathologist must usually look for symptoms as patterns or groups rather than individually, and the various symptoms added together give a picture of a given disease. The pathologist may also find clues pointing to the causes of various diseases and disorders by noting, for example, the relationships of affected trees to possible sources of air pollution or their position in frost hollows or areas of waterlogged land. He may also gain much in some cases from a study of local weather data, which will assist in the diagnosis of frost or drought damage, or damage by other adverse weather conditions. Growth changes (seen in studies of leader growth and of successive annual rings) may also provide valuable information, indicating, for example, when a decline in growth set in; it may then be possible to correlate the decline with some known adverse factor.

When dealing with diseases caused by living agents, laboratory work is usually needed to isolate and identify the organisms concerned. In the case of a new disease it is necessary to re-inoculate the isolated organism into specimens of the host plant to confirm that they do indeed produce the disease. As final confirmation they must then be re-isolated and rechecked.

Virus diseases require special techniques involving the use of test host plants and electron microscopy, for example.

LOSSES AND DAMAGE CAUSED BY DISEASE

It is usually impossible to make any precise assessment of the losses caused by tree diseases. Some diseases cause little appreciable damage, but others cause clearly visible loss of some kind or other.

Diseases such as anthracnose (*Marssonina salicicola*) (figure 79) of weeping willow make the tree look unsightly, a serious matter in the case of an ornamental tree of parks and gardens. Similarly, blue-stain fungi may give an unpleasant appearance to the wood of pine and so reduce its value and usefulness for many purposes (figure 44). The staining caused by watermark disease (*Erwinia salicis*) in the cricket bat willow (plate 57) renders the wood useless for the manufacture of cricket bats. A wood of high value then becomes virtually unmarketable.

In nurseries, species of *Phytophthora* may destroy plants; the number of dead plants may then be counted. Such a count, however, only estimates the minimum loss, as apparently healthy plants which leave an infected nursery may also be diseased. In many nurseries until recently it was impossible to grow plants of *Thuja plicata* because of the depredations of the needle blight fungus *Didymascella thujina*, though this blight may now be controlled by spraying with cycloheximide.

The stem rust *Cronartium ribicola* makes it virtually impossible to grow the valuable five-needled pine *Pinus strobus* at least on a commercial scale in Britain. So far this rust cannot be controlled (though much work on the breeding of resistant pines has been done in the USA). The fungus *Gremmeniella abietina* (*Brunchorstia pinea*), on the other hand, does not prevent the growing of

Corsican pine in Britain, but confines it to lowland areas below about 275 m.

Again, some diseases restrict the growing of susceptible varieties or clones (or of species within a susceptible group). Thus fireblight (*Erwinia amylovora*) was reduced to a commercially acceptable level in British orchards by the removal of the susceptible pear variety Laxton's Superb. Canker of larch restricts the growing of susceptible forms of European larch, and poplar canker (*Xanthomonas populi*) prevents the wide use of susceptible poplar clones.

Some diseases cause death of trees. *Heterobasidion annosum* kills pines on certain sites, though in other trees it usually causes a root rot or butt rot without killing the tree. *Armillaria mellea* may kill a wide range of garden trees and shrubs, though in conifer forests it generally causes only scattered losses. Dutch elm disease is exceptional among tree diseases in the losses it has caused in those areas (so far in North America and Europe) in which the aggressive strain of the causal fungus *Ceratocystis ulmi* and its associated vectors occur with susceptible elm populations. This fungus causes rapid death of susceptible elms, and has destroyed almost all the elms in much of southern Britain, and large numbers of the even more susceptible elms in North America.

As mentioned above, the decay fungi *Heterobasidion annosum* and *Armillaria mellea* may kill trees. They both also cause loss of wood in timber trees by rotting the interior of the trunk. Many other decay fungi also render trees dangerous by rotting roots (and so leading to windblow) or stems (leading to stem break) or branches (which may then suddenly fall).

Many diseases cause a reduction in growth, and so of increment, which is important to the forester. Thus *Heterobasidion annosum* may cause marked reduction in the growth and increment of pines on alkaline sites, due to extensive death of the roots (which eventually leads to the death of the trees).

CONTROL MEASURES

Control measures can first be divided into:
(1) Legislative measures to prevent the entry of alien diseases (and pests).
(2) Measures used to control diseases already present.

PLANT HEALTH FRONTIER LEGISLATION

The Orders designed to prevent the entry into Britain of alien organisms harmful to plants are made under the Plant Health Act, 1967, and are based on the Plant Health Directive of the European Economic Community (EEC). The principles behind the Plant Health Directive are as follows:

(1) The EEC must take all reasonable steps to protect its crops from alien organisms.

(2) At the same time the Community depends for its livelihood on trade, especially between its member states.

(3) Hence all measures used to prevent the entry of plant diseases and pests must be demonstrably justifiable on plant health grounds; it must be clear that they are not used as a means of trade protection.

(4) With only a few exceptions, the pests and diseases of Europe occur more or less throughout.

(5) Hence within the European area generally, legislation need deal only with those European pests and diseases still limited in their distribution. Only those Member States without a given European disease or pest can justifiably take steps to control its entry. Thus the United Kingdom may take steps to keep out *Ips typographus* and certain other spruce bark beetles, and *Endothia parasitica*, the cause of sweet chestnut blight, because these occur on the European mainland but not in Britain. It may not take steps against, for example, bacterial canker of poplar caused by *Xanthomonas populi*, which is already present there.

(6) In the world at large there are many potentially dangerous diseases and pests which have not yet reached Europe, and many of these are difficult to assess. Strong legislation is justifiable against these, though again it must be soundly based and justifiable on plant health grounds; and it must not be disproportionate to the risks involved.

(7) Some alien pests and diseases clearly pose a threat; these can be listed, and special measures against them can be laid down.

(8) Some crops are of particular importance, and in the case of these, more rigorous measures may be justifiable than in the case of others.

(9) In general, food crops are of special importance, and as they are grown on a wide scale in monoculture, they may be especially vulnerable to epidemics. The same applies to forest trees and a few very widely grown ornamental trees, which are also in some cases in special need of protection.

In theory, pests and diseases of trees may be carried with seeds and fruits, or with living plants, or in wood with the bark (and occasionally perhaps without it). In fact, so far, there is little evidence that important tree pests and diseases are carried with seeds or fruits, and importation of these is not subject to plant health controls in the EEC. Some pests and diseases may be carried with plants, however, and some with wood with the bark attached. Therefore, various controls are placed on these in appropriate cases.

Plant health legislation is subject to periodical revision as circumstances change and new information becomes available. The current regulation which lays down controls as far as the forest and related ornamental trees of Britain is concerned is the Import and Export of Trees, Wood and Bark (Health) (Great Britain) Order 1980. The tree genera specifically covered are *Abies, Larix, Picea, Pinus, Pseudotsuga* and *Tsuga* among the conifers, and *Castanea, Populus, Quercus* and *Ulmus* among the broadleaved trees. These genera are known to be susceptible to important identifiable alien pests and diseases. Others are covered in some other ways, however, as all 'plants, planted or intended for planting' must be inspected in the exporting country and covered by plant health certificates.

Some, including *Fagus* and *Tilia*, are covered by requirements intended to prevent the entry of San José scale, which is primarily a pest of fruit trees; these requirements effectively prevent the entry of many other pests and diseases.

The legislation lays down measures to prevent the entry of about 30 individual diseases and pests of trees, the following being the most important.

(1) On broadleaved trees.

(a) Oak wilt (*Ceratocystis fagacearum*) which occurs only in the USA.

(b) Elm phloem necrosis and its carrier the leafhopper *Scaphoideus luteolus* which are also North American.

(c) Poplar canker fungi *Mycosphaerella populorum* (occurring in North and South America) and *Hypoxylon mammatum* (which occurs in North America and, in an apparently nonaggressive form, in parts of France).

(d) Sweet chestnut blight (*Endothia parasitica*) which is present in North America, parts of Asia and Southern Europe.

(2) On conifers.

(a) Non-European bark beetles (*Scolytidae*), particularly those of North America.

(b) North American cankers of pine caused by species of *Atropellis*.

(c) Non-European dwarf mistletoes (*Arceuthobium* spp.), mostly occurring in North America.

(d) Various conifer rusts (species of *Chrysomyxa, Cronartium,* and *Melampsora*) of North America and (in a few cases) South America and Asia.

(e) Shoot blight of larch caused by *Guignardia laricina* (an Asiatic fungus).

(f) Root-rot fungus *Phellinus (Poria) weirii* from North America.

The legislation prescribes various measures to deal with these organisms, in addition to the general ones (for example, on the certification of plants planted or for planting) already mentioned. Some are broad steps to exclude the listed organisms, either in general or as contaminants of named produce (for example, conifer wood with bark). In other cases, the importation of certain plants or plant products from given areas is prohibited, or importation may be only from areas free from specified organisms, or subject to some form of treatment.

This legislation and its background, and the assessment of the potential of alien pests and diseases of trees, is further discussed by Phillips and Bevan (1966), Burdekin and Phillips (1977), Phillips (1978, 1979, 1980*a, b*, 1981) and (with regard to oak wilt) Gibbs (1978, 1979).

MEASURES FOR CONTROL OF ESTABLISHED DISEASES

Some diseases are of minor significance and need no special control measures. An example is the leaf blister of poplar caused by *Taphrina populina*. In other cases no control measures can really be taken. Thus there are no measures available to prevent infection of conifers by the decay fungus *Phaeolus schweinitzii*.

In many cases control is by *disease avoidance* of some kind. This is especially so in forestry, for the forester is concerned with populations rather than with single trees, and expenditure on disease control must be kept as low as possible.

Thus to avoid blue-stain, pines may be felled between September and February, when infection by blue-stain fungi is at a low level, and the logs quickly removed from the forest.

Nurseries may be sited to avoid frost hollows and waterlogged areas. Again, they should not be placed near mature crops which may be sources of infection by, for example, pine needle fungi such as the species of *Lophodermium*, or the larch needle fungus *Meria laricis*. Composite weeds which may act as alternate hosts of the rust *Coleosporium tussilaginis* should be kept down, for they may lead to damage to nursery pines.

Similarly, it may be necessary to destroy aspen in young pine plantations to avoid damage by the pine twisting rust *Melampsora populnea* (*M. pinitorqua*).

On suitable sites, this fungus may also be avoided by growing Corsican pine instead of Scots pine, an example of a use of differing resistance. Genetical resistance may also be used to avoid larch canker caused by *Lachnellula willkommii*, which attacks most provenances of European larch. Both Japanese larch and its hybrid with European larch, on the other hand, are generally more resistant. Again, the different forms of Douglas fir vary in their resistance to the needle cast fungus *Rhabdocline pseudotsugae*, the green form of *Pseudotsuga menziesii* being much more resistant than the others which, therefore, are no longer grown to any extent in Britain. Among the broadleaved trees, many poplar clones have been bred for resistance to the bacterial canker caused by *Xanthomonas populi*.

In some cases disease may be avoided or reduced in its effect by sanitation felling. This effectively keeps the watermark disease of willow (caused by *Erwinia salicis*) at a very low level. On sites containing many conifer stumps infested by *Heterobasidion annosum* it may in a similar manner be necessary to remove the old stumps before replanting with another susceptible crop.

Sometimes diseases may be controlled by pruning out affected parts. Removal of diseased limbs was sometimes effective in controlling the nonaggressive strain of the Dutch elm disease fungus *Ceratocystis ulmi*, though this treatment rarely inhibits the newer aggressive strain of the fungus.

Nursery plants may be protected from both frost and sunscorch by covering with overhead lath shading. Again, reasonably shade-bearing trees can be protected from frost in the establishment phase by underplanting in a mature overstorey.

Drainage (or the avoidance of wet areas) can be used to control Phytophthora root rot ('ink disease') of sweet chestnut.

Chemical control, using fungicides, is relatively little used to deal with tree diseases (except those of orchard trees). In forestry, the use of fungicides is generally too expensive except in the nursery.

In forest nurseries, thiram and captan are used to control *Botrytis cinerea*, and zineb and maneb are used if necessary to control pine needle diseases caused by species of *Lophodermium*. Colloidal sulphur is used to deal with attacks of larch needle cast caused by *Meria laricis*, and with the powdery mildews (especially the oak mildew, *Microsphaera alphitoides*). Needle blight of *Thuja plicata* may be controlled by spraying with cycloheximide. In nursery areas in which damping off occurs, the soil may be treated between crops with a soil sterilant such as formaldehyde or dazomet. A nursery crop affected by damping off may be given an emergency drench of thiram or captan to reduce the effects of the disease.

Spraying of established garden trees against various diseases such as anthracnose of weeping willow may sometimes be recommended, but it is very difficult to achieve adequate cover on a tree of any size.

The only routine chemical treatment used in the forest against a tree disease is the painting of conifer stumps with urea solution to prevent their colonisation by the root-rot and butt-rot fungus *Heterobasidion annosum*. In the case of pine stumps, a suspension of oidia of the competing fungus *Peniophora gigantea* may be substituted for the chemical to provide biological control.

In the case of ornamental trees (as well as those in fruit orchards) various chemical protectants are often applied to wounds to prevent the entry of decay fungi. So far these chemicals have had little effect, though efforts to find better materials are being made. Pruning wound protection is discussed on p.367.

Much work has been done on the injection of trees with fungicides (mainly benomyl and related materials) to control diseases, especially Dutch elm disease. Some success has been achieved but only with relatively small trees.

Some diseases are carried by insect vectors, and attempts have been made to control some diseases by dealing with these carriers. Thus sanitation felling of elms to control Dutch elm disease is primarily intended to destroy and prevent the breeding of the elm bark beetles which spread the disease. Experiments on the control of these beetles by the use of insecticides have also been done; the results have not been very encouraging, and there are environmental objections to the widespread use of many insecticides.

REFERENCES

Burdekin, D. A. and Phillips, D. H. (1977). *Some Important Foreign Diseases of Broadleaved Trees*. Forest Rec., Lond., no. 111

Burnett, J. H. (1977). *Fundamentals of Mycology*, 2nd ed., Crane-Russak Co., New York

Cooper, J. I. (1979). *Virus Diseases of Trees and Shrubs*. Institute of Terrestrial Ecology, c/o Unit of Invertebrate Virology, Oxford

Dowson, W. J. (1957). *Plant Diseases Due to Bacteria*, Cambridge University Press, Cambridge

Gibbs, J. N. (1978). Oak wilt. *Arboric. J.*, 3, 351–56

Gibbs, J. N. (1979). Measures to prevent oak wilt from reaching Europe, in D. L. Ebbels and J. E. King (Eds.), *Plant Health: The Scientific Basis For the Administrative Control of Plant Diseases and Pests*, Blackwell, Oxford

Phillips, D. H. (1978). *The EEC Plant Health Directive and British Forestry*. Forest Rec., Lond. no. 116

Phillips, D. H. (1979). British forestry: the problem of alien pests and diseases, in D. L. Ebbels and J. E. King (Eds.), *Plant Health: The Scientific Basis For The Administrative Control of Plant Diseases and Pests*, Blackwell, Oxford

Phillips, D. H. (1980*a*). *International Plant Health Controls: Conflicts, Problems and Co-operation. A European Experience.* Res. Dev. Pap. For. Commn, Lond., no. 125

Phillips, D. H. (1980*b*). Plant health legislation and forest trees in Britain. *Arboric. J.*, 4, 152–57

Phillips, D. H. (1981). Legislating for introduced species: the lessons from plant health. Discussion Paper in Conservation no. 30, BANC/University College, London, pp. 50–59

Phillips, D. H. and Bevan, D. (1966). Forestry quarantine and its biological background. *Proc. Wld For. Congr. Madrid, 1966*, 2, 1928–1934 (and Forest Rec., Lond., no. 63, 1967)

Stapp, C. (1961). *Bacterial Plant Pathogens*, Oxford University Press, London

Webster, J. (1977). *Introduction to Fungi*, 2nd ed., Cambridge University Press, Cambridge

2 Disorders caused by nonliving agents

This part of the book is concerned with damage caused to trees by a diverse range of nonliving agents. Some, including climatic and soil factors, are often (though not always) outside the direct influence of man. Others, including toxic chemicals such as atmospheric pollutants and herbicides, are produced largely as a result of man's activities. It is important in times of increasing concern about the environment to remember that plants, including trees, can be damaged by natural forces as well as by pollution in its general sense.

The identification of disorders caused by nonliving agents may sometimes be straightforward. A severe drought is likely to cause visible damage to some trees and a hard spring frost may have obvious effects on young developing shoots and foliage. In the majority of cases diagnosis is more difficult and this is particularly so when the causal event occurred some time before damage was observed. The visual symptoms may have been obscured by healthy recovery growth or the tree may be no more than a skeleton. In these circumstances examination of the internal growth patterns of the tree may yield valuable information (for example, through tree ring analysis) about the time or season at which the damage occurred.

Therefore, it is important for the pathologist to have some understanding of the physiological processes that have led to the damage so that appropriate clues may be sought. Some indication of the effects of various climatic and chemical factors have been given in this chapter. However, the interested reader who wishes to study these factors in more depth should seek information in the wide range of literature that exists on many of these subjects. Some important references are included but the list is necessarily selective and many others will surely provide valuable information.

CLIMATIC FACTORS

EFFECTS OF LOW TEMPERATURES

The damaging effect of low temperatures on trees, often broadly termed frost injury, can be particularly serious in Britain. At first sight this may seem somewhat surprising bearing in mind the oceanic conditions and the generally mild winters which characterise the British climate. However, it is precisely these conditions which have frequently persuaded foresters and arboriculturists to plant less hardy species and when periods of low temperature do occur serious damage can ensue. On the continent of Europe and in much of North America far lower temperatures are frequently recorded and frost injury may occur on more hardy trees.

Peace (1962) undertook a comprehensive review of the effect of frost on trees and more recent work has served largely to confirm and extend his observations. He pointed out that frost damage could occur both in the growing and in the dormant season and that although there would inevitably be some overlap between the seasons, the effects of autumn and spring frosts should be differentiated from that of winter cold. Not only are the trees in a different physiological condition at these times, but, as we shall see, the climatic factors that determine the low temperatures also differ.

Spring and autumn frosts
Such frosts occur primarily at night when the air is still and cloud cover is absent. Heat is lost by radiation from the plant and soil surfaces and their temperature falls. The air temperature in their vicinity also decreases and so-called 'inversion conditions' develop where the temperature of the air close to the ground is lower than that a few metres above. Such cooling may continue until the temperature falls to freezing point and below. In areas where these conditions occur the ground may be level but more frequently there are small depressions, slopes or valleys and the cold air, being heavier than the warm air above, tends to flow downhill and accumulate at the lowest points. In this way frost pockets or hollows can arise and their occurrence clearly depends on very local topographical variations. There are many localities in Britain, particularly on the eastern side, where frosts are regularly recorded in most months of the year.

The cooling of the air close to the ground during inversion conditions is influenced by a number of factors. One is the nature of the soil and its vegetation cover. Young tree crops, less than 0.5 m or so in height, are more likely to be damaged when growing in a dense grass mat than over a bare soil. When heat is lost to the atmosphere by radiation from the bare soil surface, it is replaced by heat from below, particularly when the underlying soil is moist. However, a grass cover is a poor conductor and heat lost from its surface is not replaced, and its temperature, together with that of the adjoining air mass, falls.

Overhead cover can also influence the occurrence of ground frosts. Plants established beneath an overstorey of mature trees radiate less heat than those in an open ground situation and in consequence are less liable to frost damage.

The use of artificial shade, especially under nursery conditions, has a similar effect of lessening radiation on cold, still nights and in addition may slow down the rate of thawing in the morning which may be a further advantage.

The above description of the conditions that influence temperatures at ground level applies to both autumn and spring frosts. Spring frosts tend to be damaging as the early spring growth of many species is more susceptible to frost than that formed in late autumn.

Symptoms   The nature and extent of spring frost damage depends upon the stage of growth at the time as well as on the severity of the frost. If the frost occurs before flushing but after physiological activity has begun within the tree, damage may be limited to the buds. When the buds are killed this leads to the growth of adventitious buds which, in turn, can give rise to the production of bushy plants.

Once the trees have flushed the young growth may be particularly susceptible.

The tips of the needles or peripheral parts of leaves may become necrotic or in more severe cases whole needles or leaves and often the shoots to which they are attached may be killed. In such cases the brown foliage remains attached to the shoots which themselves hang down in a characteristic, permanently bent position (plate 1). As in cases where buds are killed, adventitious growth may subsequently develop to give the tree a bushy habit. Sometimes the leader may survive repeated frosting while the lower branches are killed and the tree then assumes a columnar habit with dead branches around the base.

Figure 1. Cracking of the bark at the base of *Nothofagus*, caused by cold in the winter of 1962–63 (Forestry Commission)

Small areas of bark may be killed by spring frosts, particularly on smooth-barked species such as *Thuja plicata* and *Nothofagus*. If the stem is girdled the distal portion will die back but where damage is local, callus growth will occur. The wound may subsequently heal or if frost recurs further damage and perhaps fungal infection may follow.

On trees where external signs of damage are present and in others where they are absent, internal symptoms may be evident. Thus the cambial region is often affected and frost rings may develop (figure 2). Glerum and Farrar (1966) have studied the development of frost rings by subjecting seedlings of various conifer species to freezing temperatures. They concluded that while most cambial initials remained alive, differentiating tracheids and xylem mother cells were killed by the frost. This ring of dead cell tissues contained underlignified and crushed tracheids. Outside the ring of dead cells there was a region with abnormal tracheids and parenchyma that were formed prior to the re-establishment of normal cambial activity.

Figure 2. Frost ring formed in a young stem of *Thuja plicata* at the beginning of the 1967 growing season (D.H. Phillips)

Frost rings may be formed during both spring and autumn frosts and those produced at the end of one growing season or at the beginning of the next may be indistinguishable.

Species susceptibility   There is considerable variation within species and between species in susceptibility to frost damage. In Norway spruce (*P. abies*), for example, there are early and late flushing strains and the latter are less affected by frost. This may be as a result of the late flushing strain escaping frost at a susceptible stage of growth rather than any inherent resistance to low temperature.

Peace (1962) has categorised the susceptibility to spring frost of the commoner British trees; his assessment is given in table 2.1.

Table 2.1

Susceptibility to frost of common trees in Britain (Adapted from Peace, 1962)

	Broadleaved species	*Conifers*
Very susceptible	*Juglans* spp. *Fraxinus excelsior* *Castanea sativa* *Quercus* spp. *Fagus sylvatica*	*Abies grandis* *Picea sitchensis* *Picea abies* *Larix* spp. *Pseudotsuga menziesii* *Tsuga heterophylla* *Thuja plicata*
Moderately susceptible	*Acer pseudoplatanus* *Aesculus hippocastanum* Some *Populus* spp.	*Pinus contorta* *Pinus nigra* var. *maritima* *Picea omorika*
Hardy	*Betula* spp. *Corylus avellana* *Carpinus betulus* *Tilia* spp. *Ulmus* spp. Many *Populus* spp.	*Pinus sylvestris* *Cupressus macrocarpa*

There is less evidence available on the susceptibility of different species to autumn frosts. Japanese larch (*L. leptolepis*) frequently suffers damage perhaps because it makes active growth in the autumn. Sitka spruce (*P. sitchensis*) is sometimes damaged in the nursery, and southern provenances (for example Washington) may be more susceptible than northerly ones (such as Queen Charlotte Island).

Amelioration of spring and autumn frost damage   A number of measures can be taken to ameliorate the effects of this type of frost damage. A knowledge of the climatic conditions prevailing in an area and also of the local topography is important in order to select a suitably hardy species. Low and Greig (1973) made a detailed study of frost damage in Thetford Chase in eastern England and showed that such damage could be minimised by a variety of practices including complete cultivation, deep ploughing, underplanting and strip felling. Measurements taken in different situations indicated that temperatures were higher over bare soil and within plough furrows than over a grass cover. Similar differences were found between sites under a tree cover or within felled strips and those in the open. Marked increases in the height growth and survival of Corsican pine (*P. nigra* var. *maritima*) were recorded when such ameliorative steps were taken.

In nurseries it is clearly important to initially select a site which is free from frosts but if this is not possible artificial overhead cover may give some protection.

Winter cold

In Britain prolonged freezing conditions in winter usually occur when dry, cold, northerly or easterly air streams move over the country. Peace (1962) differentiates between damage due to low temperature alone and that due to cold, dry winds. In the former case less hardy species may be injured but in the latter the foliage of some of the more hardy evergreen species is affected.

Marginal forest species such as *Pinus radiata,* some *Nothofagus* spp. and *Cupressus macrocarpa* are damaged in severe winters. Extensive death of foliage and dieback may occur. *Nothofagus dombeyi* and *N. procera* are particularly susceptible and in addition to extensive dieback, characteristic cankers form on the main stem (figure 1). On the other hand, *N. obliqua* and *N. antartica* seem relatively resistant to winter cold damage.

Browning of evergreen foliage has been observed on a number of tree species during or following cold winters. Such discoloration may be ephemeral, as in the case of bronzing of *Thuja plicata* in the nursery (plate 39), or more permanent and followed by some defoliation in a number of other coniferous species. *Sequoia sempervirens* is perhaps one of the most frequently affected species. Browning of foliage, particularly on the eastern side of trees, has been observed in spring on various species including *Pseudotsuga menziesii, Abies grandis* and *Taxus baccata* following cold winters. Peace (1962) suggests that such damage is not primarily due to winter cold but rather to excessive loss of moisture from the foliage under freezing conditions when it cannot be replaced from below. This hypothesis is supported by more recent observations that such symptoms are found when a particularly cold spell follows a very mild period.

Another form of winter cold injury is frost crack of stems. This damage occurs more frequently on broadleaved species such as oak and poplar. The radial cracks, often on the south or southwest side of the trunk are probably caused by differential contraction of tissues during freezing. Care must be taken to distinguish frost from drought cracks which are found more frequently on conifers and in association with dry growing seasons.

Mechanism of frost damage

This controversial subject has long been the subject of discussion between plant physiologists and even now there is no single straightforward explanation. There seems to be general agreement that cells are killed if ice crystals are formed within them. However, it seems that ice crystals form more frequently in inter or extracellular spaces. Water is withdrawn from the cell during this process and the cell contents are thereby concentrated. It was thought at one time that the increased concentration of cell contents resulting from this and other cellular activities might depress their freezing point so as to avoid damage. It has now been demonstrated that this effect is small (Burke *et al.*, 1967). These authors suggest that in the more hardy species the plant tissue avoids freezing by deep supercooling to temperatures of $-20°C$ or less. Other workers, such as Levitt (1969) have placed emphasis on the structural nature of protein molecules when water is withdrawn from the cell during the formation of intercellular ice crystals. Levitt goes on to suggest that the accumulation of solutes within the cell at low temperatures may prevent the denaturing and aggregration of proteins, by osmotic retention of water. These considerations apply not only to the proteins within the cell but perhaps especially to those incorporated in the surrounding protoplasmic membrane. If proteins associated with the membrane were irreversibly damaged there would be a loss of semipermeability and consequent death of the cell.

Frost lift

Frost lift or frost heave can sometimes occur in a nursery following a severe winter frost. Layers of ice form in the nursery soil and as a result the soil surface is raised. If the soil is moist water may be drawn by capillary action from below and the volume of water frozen in the surface layers can be considerable. Small plants are firmly held by the frozen soil and rise with the soil as it expands in volume. There may be some breakage of the roots of larger plants or they may remain unmoved. Once the soil thaws the small plants remain in their uplifted position and the soil returns to its original position. The upper roots of these plants are now exposed and if repeated frosts occur they may be completely uprooted.

Maximum frost lift occurs in moist soils but soil type may also be important. Clay soils give rise to greater frost lift than sandy soils. The presence of a mulch on the soil surface may help to insulate the soil below and reduce soil freezing. These considerations have a strong bearing on methods of minimising the risk of frost lift. Nurseries are not normally established on clay soils for a variety of reasons, one of these relates to frost lift. If frost lift is likely to occur then mulches of granulated peat or stone chippings can be applied to nursery beds to reduce the damage. Raised seedbeds may also help, perhaps because they are drier than the surrounding pathways.

EFFECTS OF HIGH TEMPERATURES

Some of the symptoms that appear during or after periods of high temperature are associated more with lack of moisture in the tree than with excessive heat. Examples of this include drought crack on trunks of trees and leaf scorch on wilted trees. However, high temperatures can directly damage trees and the most commonly observed disorder is the killing of bark often referred to as sun scorch.

Direct sunlight damages the trunks of trees that have been growing under shaded conditions and are suddenly exposed to full insolation. This situation can arise, for example, when a forest is heavily thinned, when side shelter is removed from a forested area or when gaps are made in woodland for building developments and road construction.

Symptoms
The bark and sometimes also the cambium are killed in strips or patches on the south or southwest sides of the trunk. Damage is particularly severe on thin-barked species such as beech but also occurs on sycamore and other maple species. Callus tissue normally develops at the margins of the areas of necrotic bark. The dead bark and the wood which is subsequently exposed may be invaded by *Nectria* sp. and by decay fungi such as *Ganoderma applanatum*. At a much later stage the trunks may break due to the development of extensive decay within the woody tissues. Tattar (1978) differentiates between summer and winter sunscorch to the bark of trees. The symptoms are similar but Tattar suggests that winter sunscorch follows periods of rapid changes in bark temperature during cold and sunny winter days.

Mitigation of damage
Damage to bark from sunscorch often occurs following sudden exposure of trees to hot sun as, for example, when heavy thinning operations or total removal of side shelter are undertaken. However, if the operation can be staged over several years or thinning done less severely, less damage is likely to ensue. In the case of building developments where valuable trees are to be retained following the removal of immediate neighbours it may be possible to protect stems by wrapping trees with insulating material or even by painting with white paint. However, the latter technique may not be aesthetically acceptable.

DROUGHT

The term drought is defined in Britain as a period of 14 or more consecutive days without rain. When used specifically in relation to the condition of trees, or of other plants, drought has a rather different meaning. A droughted tree is one suffering from a severe lack of moisture. This arises when the rate of transpiration exceeds the rate of absorption of water through the roots over an extended period.

Peace (1962) separates soil drought, the inadequate supply of water to the roots, from atmospheric drought, the excessive loss of water from the leaves. Jamison (1956), Kramer (1962), Salter and Goode (1967) and others point out that the internal water balance in trees or other plants depends on a complex of soil, climatic and plant factors.

The absolute water content of the soil does not give a reliable measure of the availability of water to the tree. As soil dries out, the remaining water is held in the soil by increasingly greater forces until the plant roots are finally unable to extract further moisture. At this stage the plants wilt and the soil is said to be at permanent wilting point.

Different types of soil are able to withhold different quantities of water from the plant; clay soils are particularly retentive and sandy soils are not (Salter and Williams, 1969). However, the availability of soil moisture to the plants is complex and depends on a number of other factors including the absolute water-holding capacity of the soil, the nature of the layers underlying the soil (a rocky substrate may prevent the replenishment of moisture in the topsoil) and the osmotic pressure of the soil water.

Climatic factors such as net radiation, temperature, humidity and especially wind can affect the quantity of water transpired by trees. Peace (1962) draws attention to two sets of conditions where wind can cause excessive transpiration. The first is where trees previously sheltered are suddenly exposed to greater moisture loss as a result of such operations as felling, thinning or other means of removal of side shelter. Peace (1962) points out that the blast effect of wind in exposed situations is probably one of the most serious factors limiting tree growth in Britain.

Kozlowski (1964) emphasises that the ability of plants to survive moisture stress depends on their ability to absorb water, to reduce water loss and to endure dehydration. Thus the nature of a tree's root system can influence the uptake of water and deeper rooting species may have a clear advantage under drought conditions. Some tree species have special leaf characters such as thick layers of cutin or wax that limit transpiration from the leaves. Others may reduce moisture loss by abscission of leaves during dry spells.

Symptoms

No matter whether water deficits are caused by lack of soil moisture or by excessive transpiration from the tree or by some combination of the two, the symptoms on affected trees are essentially similar. Foliar symptoms include wilting followed by necrosis, usually starting at the leaf margins. Premature autumnal colorations may then appear, followed in severe cases by dieback of twigs and branches. Conifer needles turn brown, often starting at the tips, and young succulent shoots bend over and may die. In less severe cases the shoot may wholly recover its turgor or become bent near the base where some cells have been irreparably damaged. Under severe conditions symptoms may spread progressively down from the uppermost parts of a tree, dieback of shoots may develop and the tree may finally die. Where trees are subject to exposure to strong winds symptoms are more severe on the windward side and such trees may take on a permanently one-sided appearance. Small woods may also take on a characteristic wedge shape.

Young trees that have been transplanted from the nursery to their permanent site are susceptible to damage from water deficits probably because their root systems have been severed, thus rendering them less able to take up water. Semi-mature trees that have been transplanted are particularly susceptible to such damage. On young conifers a reversible discoloration may occur and needles that turn red or purple under moisture stress can become green again once normal conditions return.

There have been a number of reports of damage to the bark of trees, both coniferous and broadleaved species, as a result of water deficits. True and Tryon (1956) reported that stem cankers were found on oak following a year of severe drought and that they were unable to isolate any pathogenic organisms. Zycha (1951) suggested that drought (and winter cold) can cause death of bark and subsequent slime-fluxing on beech. He considered that these factors were causal agents of beech bark disease; however, it is now generally accepted that this disease is caused by the combined attack of *Cryptococcus fagisuga*, the beech coccus, and *Nectria coccinea* (Houston *et al.*, 1979). In this context it should be noted that death of bark in patches and subsequent slime-flux was observed in Britain on several species of broadleaved trees including birch, beech and sycamore following the severe drought in 1976. The effect of drought on the bark of trees is still largely unexplained though Bier (1959) has suggested that a lowering of the moisture content of the bark can allow weak pathogens, such as *Cryptodiaporthe salicis* on willow, to enter a weakened host.

**Figure 3. Drought crack in Sitka spruce: tree showing external crack mark
(B.J.W. Greig)**

The bark of several coniferous species cracks as a result of severe moisture stress. In Britain, this so-called drought crack has been observed during and following years of severe drought on *Abies procera, A. grandis* and *Picea sitchensis;* elsewhere in Europe it has been reported on *Picea abies.* A study of drought crack in *A. grandis* reported by Phillips (1965, 1966, 1967), indicated that this damage could be closely correlated with drought years. The cracks were usually less than 1 m in length and limited to the bark, though the longer cracks, where present, extended into the wood (figures 3, 4).

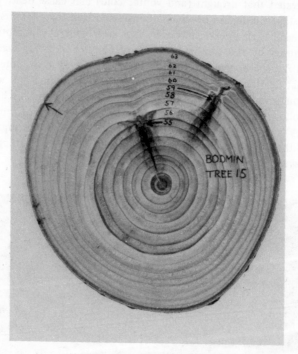

Figure 4.   Drought crack in Sitka spruce: section of tree showing cracks within the wood (B.J.W. Greig)

Abnormal morphology in the xylem has been observed in some species following a severe drought. Peace (1962) describes for Japanese larch the formation of a ring of flattened cells with smaller lumens, the radial walls of which were sometimes bowed. These drought rings are distinct from the reduction in overall ring width, also associated with drought, though the two may occur together.

Species resistant to drought
There are many cases quoted in the literature where tree species have proved particularly resistant (or susceptible) to drought; a few examples are quoted on p. 29.

Parker (1968) suggested that deep roots of *Quercus* spp. and *Pseudotsuga menziesii* seedlings contribute to the successful establishment of these trees. Albertson and Weaver (1945) reported that the deeply penetrating roots of *Quercus, Juglans, Gleditsia* and *Maclura* helped these species survive extreme drought conditions in the American prairies. Pfeffer *et al.* (1948) found in Czechoslovakia that Douglas fir was resistant and Norway spruce was susceptible to drought, particularly in competition with other trees. In Britain, Peace (1962) noted that Japanese larch was particularly susceptible to soil drought on dry sites and places with locally shallow soils.

Cadman (1953) discusses the use of tree species in shelter-belts and thus considers the resistance of trees to excessive transpiration rather than to uptake of water from the roots. He lists the following species as particularly suitable for conditions of severe exposure:

Abies procera   *Acer pseudoplatanus*
Pinus contorta   *Fagus sylvatica*
Pinus mugo
Pinus nigra
Pinus nigra var. *maritima*
Picea glauca

LIGHTNING DAMAGE

Most people recognise that trees are potential lightning conductors; few will shelter under trees during a thunderstorm because of the risk of a lightning strike. Damage to a tree when struck by lightning will vary according to the intensity of the discharge and a number of other factors such as the location, size and condition of the tree. Such damage may be limited to a single tree or small group of trees but can on occasion extend to an area covering a hectare or more. Damage often occurs on single, tall, isolated trees but it can also occur in post-thicket stage plantations and even in nurseries.

Diagnosis of lightning damage may not be entirely straightforward, particularly if the lightning has struck some months or years previously. At that stage a single dead tree or group of trees may provide little evidence of the cause. However, it is possible that the characteristic lightning scar may be evident on the trunk of one or more trees. Such lightning scars are more readily identifiable soon after the lightning strike and may take the form of superficial bark stripping or may penetrate deeper into the wood forming a rough jagged furrow. In extreme cases the trunk or parts of it may be completely shattered. The lightning scars often follow a spiral course which in some cases follows the spiral grain of the tree. Damage can sometimes extend down into the roots and the superficial soil or litter may be thrown aside to leave the roots exposed.

When lightning strikes a group of trees, most die fairly rapidly but some may survive for a year or two or longer. Where a tree remains alive there may be single dead branches in the live crown. In such cases the bark or cambium on the adjoining main stem can be killed and the whole of the upper crown may subsequently die. Lightning may also be responsible for the presence of dead tops of tall *Sequoiadendron* trees so commonly seen in Britain (plate 2).

In some recently killed small groups lightning scars may be absent but careful examination of the still fresh bark may reveal the presence of long strips of dead bark running from the roots to the upper stem. Such hidden scars, which may be discontinuous and tapering in width in the higher parts of the stem, are useful diagnostic features when trees are examined fairly soon after the suspected lightning strike.

When trees have survived a lightning strike it is often possible to find evidence of abnormal tissue in the growth rings. These abnormalities may be indistinguishable from frost rings and care must be taken in the interpretation of the available evidence. A study of the meteorological records for the area where the damage was observed should enable the investigator to determine whether the date of a thunderstorm coincided with the period of growth indicated by the abnormal tissue in the annual growth ring.

A detailed explanation of the electrical nature of lightning is beyond the scope of this book. It is often thought that a lightning discharge travels downwards from the atmosphere to the earth. However, one alternative theory which has been put forward suggests that there is a faintly luminous downward stroke, often with a number of branches; this is succeeded by a much brighter return stroke from earth to cloud which retraces the path of the leader stroke and its branches. The current in the return stroke may be up to a hundred times that in the initial leader. This explanation would fit the observation that the hidden lightning scars are wide at the base of the tree and taper in width further up the stem.

Peace (1962) reviews the susceptibility of different tree species to lightning damage. Damage is recorded more frequently amongst broadleaved species on trees such as oak, elm and poplar and among conifers on pine. This is probably because these are among the commonest genera planted as individual isolated trees. However, there may be some specific differences in susceptibility to lightning damage and these are exemplified by beech which is often grown as an isolated tree but does not appear to be damaged to the same extent as other species. Various explanations for this difference have been put forward, mainly relating to the smoothness of beech bark and the presence of a continuous film of water on the bark during thunderstorms. Further information is needed, however, before such explanations can be properly verified.

The overall damage to trees in Britain by lightning is probably small and measures are rarely taken to ameliorate the damage. Lightning conductors are very occasionally fixed to valuable amenity trees. A conductor can be seen, for example, on one of the oldest London planes in Britain found in the grounds of the old Ranelagh Club at Barn Elms in London. More significant damage has been found in some European and North American forests where large areas may be killed outright or where lightning-damaged trees can be subsequently attacked by bark beetles and perhaps decay fungi. In North America and other parts of the world lightning strikes can occur without associated rainfall and there are many reports of forest fires that have been started by lightning. Such fires have only rarely been recorded in Britain.

HAIL DAMAGE

Significant damage to trees by hailstorms occurs relatively infrequently in Britain. Symptoms of the physical damage to stems and foliage are clear enough at the time but recognition of the damage some time after the event may be a little more difficult.

Hailstones can perforate, tear or bruise the foliage of broadleaved species, especially in the early stages of growth. They can also cause small discrete lesions on young shoots of either conifers or broadleaved trees. Side shoots of conifers may be broken though leaders are less susceptible to this form of damage, perhaps because of their upright position.

Damaged foliage may be retained throughout the growing season and provide evidence of hail damage earlier in the same year. The lesions on the stems may heal over and the callus tissue that develops may provide evidence of hail damage for some time after the event. In some cases the wounds may allow entry of pathogenic or decay-causing organisms. In either case, sectioning of the lesions (which are mainly on the upper side of the stem) will indicate that they all originated at one time in the annual ring. Although hailstorms are often local, meteorological records may well provide supporting evidence of their occurrence.

Dobbs and McMinn (1973) made observations on 2 to 4-year-old research plots of *Picea glauca* and *Pinus contorta* following a ten-minute hailstorm in 1972 in British Columbia. The hailstones were 1–1½ inches (2–4 cm) in diameter, 2 per cent of the trees were killed and only 14 per cent escaped damaged. The effects were more severe on *P. contorta* than on *P. glauca* and on older trees of both species. Competing vegetation provided some degree of protection against stem lesions and defoliation but not against damage to leaders or terminal buds.

A number of experiments have been undertaken in Europe to protect crops against the damaging effects of hailstorms. Guilivo (1973), in relation to apples, pears and vines, considers that passive control by the use of plastic nets, with mesh size 4 x 8 mm, is preferable to active methods using rockets and silver oxide which are intended to precipitate the clouds in a less damaging form. No such ameliorative measures, however, have proved justified in forestry.

SOIL FACTORS

NUTRIENT DEFICIENCIES

Nutrient deficiencies can cause symptoms in nursery or planted trees which are similar to those caused by some fungal or virus pathogens. It is clearly important that the tree pathologist should be aware of the symptoms of common nutrient deficiencies in order to distinguish them from pathogenic disorders. Information on deficiency symptoms in forest nurseries and plantations is well documented (for example, Aldhous, 1972; Benzian, 1965; Binns *et al.*, 1980) and there is a large volume of literature on forest fertilisation (Baule and Fricker, 1970; Everard, 1974). However, much of this information relates to forest species (mainly conifers) and that on ornamental species is much more limited.

In this section the major concern is with methods available for the diagnosis of nutrient deficiencies. Although mention will be made of techniques for correcting deficiency symptoms it is not appropriate here to enter into a full discussion of fertiliser treatments either for nursery plants or for established trees. Symptom expression depends on a number of factors including the particular nutrient or nutrients involved, the tree species, the time of year and the local weather conditions. In general, symptoms include yellowing, purpling or withering of parts or the whole of leaves and needles. They often appear first at the tips of needles or the margin of leaves and may then progress to occupy a larger proportion of the foliage.

Symptom expression will vary on different species and may be more severe on some tree species than on others. Symptoms will also vary according to the time of year and may become more intense as the season progresses. Climatic factors such as drought or waterlogging may initiate or exacerbate deficiency symptoms. Surrounding vegetation may compete with the trees for nutrients and when competition is severe nutrient symptoms may develop.

Diagnosis of deficiencies

Nutrient deficiencies can be diagnosed in several ways, none of which alone is likely to give a conclusive result. It is important to weigh up all the evidence available before reaching any conclusion. The following diagnostic methods are available:

(1) Visual symptoms.
(2) Foliar analysis.
(3) Soil analysis.
(4) Experimental addition of nutrients.

Visual symptoms of nutrient deficiencies can be a very useful guide to determining the cause but they are rarely sufficient to provide a certain diagnosis. Severe deficiencies may cause poor overall growth including reduced height increment, small leaves or needles and perhaps shoot dieback. Leaves or needles may be discoloured or necrotic and in addition plants may become more susceptible to damage by other agents such as pests, diseases or climatic factors.

A summary of the visual symptoms of specific nutrient deficiencies is given below.

Copper   Deficiency of copper is relatively uncommon but Benzian (1965) made some interesting observations at one forest nursery on a very light sandy soil. In most seasons, withered needle tips developed on Sitka spruce seedlings; symptoms varied in intensity from season to season and from one part of the nursery to another. The symptom was referred to as 'needle tip burn' and it normally affected only the more vigorous plants. The tips of the needles turned a straw colour and were clearly demarcated from the healthy green portion of the lower part of the needle. The appearance of symptoms tended to coincide with warm sunny periods and if these conditions persisted the growing point would die and the needles turn brown or black. On the other hand if the dry conditions were only short in duration the seedlings would grow and produce healthy needles leaving a ring of affected needles lower down the stem. Benzian demonstrated experimentally that foliar applications of copper sulphate or Bordeaux mixture would remedy this deficiency. At the same nursery Benzian planted poplar cuttings and described symptoms of copper deficiency on this species. The first signs are a blackening of the leaf tips developing into a more general marginal scorch of the youngest leaves. The edges of the leaves become taut and brittle forcing the whole leaf into a cup-like shape. Soon after this the whole leaf may develop an interveinal yellowing.

Lime-induced chlorosis   Symptoms of lime-induced chlorosis are commonly found on soils formed from chalk or limestone. An excess of lime in the soil may severely limit the uptake or absorption of a number of other nutrients especially iron and manganese.

Peace (1962) refers to a serious case of lime-induced chlorosis in Scots pine growing on oolite limestone. Symptoms developed first on trees when they were twelve years old. The needles turned chlorotic and then brown, growth of needles and shoots was reduced and by the time the trees were 20 years old many had died. The most serious damage occurred where the limestone was near the surface but the relationship between soil depth and symptom severity was not entirely clear. Corsican pine is less susceptible to lime-induced chlorosis and when planted with Scots pine it was unaffected.

Lonsdale *et al.* (1979) made observations on lime-induced chlorosis in beech plantations growing on chalk downs in southern England. Chlorosis was particularly marked where evidence of patterns of ancient land-use had persisted. The beech were healthy on ancient field boundaries, where the soil had not been disturbed and symptoms of chlorosis were most severe immediately below field boundaries where the surface soil had been eroded away by ploughing and the remaining soil had been admixed with the underlying chalk.

Magnesium   In many agricultural and horticultural crops magnesium deficiency is usually seen on older leaves and the same may also be true for broadleaved tree species. Symptoms of magnesium deficiency on *Thuja plicata* include yellowing of the older needles followed by browning and death of tissues. However,

Benzian (1965) draws attention to a rather different situation in Sitka spruce seedlings. In this case a yellow discoloration first appears on the tips of the younger needles. The symptoms are sometimes referred to as 'hard yellows' as the yellow needles usually lie at a wider angle to the stem than healthy needles. On broadleaved species interveinal chlorosis and growth reductions are commonly associated with magnesium deficiency.

Nitrogen   Nitrogen is one of the three major inorganic nutrients required for all plant growth. When nitrogen is deficient (plate 5) most plants are paler green in colour overall and show reduced growth as compared with healthy plants. In nursery beds, pine and spruce seedlings may grow better on the edges of the beds than in the middle. When nitrogen deficiency is more acute, the tips of the youngest needles of Sitka spruce seedlings may turn pinkish. In broadleaved species suffering from nitrogen deficiency, reduced growth may be accompanied by premature autumn coloration.

Phosphorus   Phosphorus is the second major inorganic nutrient. In upland Britain, phosphatic fertilisers are used on iron pan, peaty-gley and deep peat soils (Mayhead, 1976), and in the lowlands Everard (1974) has recommended its use on all heathland or former heathland soils and on Hastings beds in south east England. However, visual symptoms of phosphate deficiency (plate 6) are difficult to distinguish and may only be evident by overall slow growth. In the nursery it is sometimes possible to recognise phosphate deficiency by a somewhat duller or 'lack-lustre' foliage; in young plantations poor height growth and much reduced needle length and weight are symptomatic of phosphate deficiency. In general, other techniques must be used to detect this deficiency and foliar analysis is probably the most valuable tool in this context (see Binns *et al.*, 1980).

Potassium   Potassium is the third major inorganic element required for plant growth. One of the most detailed descriptions of potassium deficiency (plate 7) has been given by Benzian (1965) for Sitka spruce seedlings. A purplish colour develops in the needles from mid-summer onwards, the symptoms are most obvious on the youngest needles and may be limited to needle tips or extend the whole length of the needle. The purple discoloration may persist through the rest of the season or may change to reddish-yellow and eventually to yellow. At this stage the whole seedling becomes yellow and, therefore, can be distinguished from magnesium deficient seedlings which are only partly yellow.

In young Sitka spruce trees on the most infertile peats there is poor development of the terminal bud, usually in the second or third year after planting (Binns *et al.*, 1980). Where the deficiency is moderate the needles at the apex of current shoots turn yellow from the tip downwards; later the tip may become purple or even brown. In more severe cases, all the needles on the current year's shoot may be affected with similar chlorosis developing from tip to base of individual needles. Potassium fertiliser is used in forestry only on deep peat or peaty-gley soils (Mayhead, 1976).

On broadleaved trees discoloration of the foliage is often followed by marginal necrosis and dieback.

POOR SOIL AERATION

Adequate soil aeration is essential for the maintenance of root growth. The concentration of oxygen in the atmosphere of well-aerated soils is somewhat lower than that in the air above ground. However, if the concentration is below 10 per cent, tree roots may be damaged and if it drops below 3 per cent, root growth stops entirely (Tattar, 1978). A number of different factors can cause poor aeration of the soil including an excess of water, compaction of the soil and sealing of the soil surface.

Few trees will survive if the ground is permanently waterlogged. However, damage to trees caused by excess water generally occurs when land becomes temporarily waterlogged due to flooding, blockage of drains or to earth-moving operations which change the natural drainage flow. The effects on tree growth will largely depend on the species present, the time of year and the duration of the inundation. The best method to deal with problems associated with the presence of excess water is to ensure that an efficient drainage system is present.

Compaction of the soil also prevents the free interchange of oxygen between soil and air. Man, animals and machines can all be causes of serious soil compaction. The increased use of forests for recreation purposes has led to soil compaction on well-used paths. Regularly used animal tracks can also cause damage to neighbouring trees. Some of this damage may be difficult to avoid but the judicious use of fencing to control access may alleviate the situation. Heavy machinery used, for example, for harvesting forest produce or for restoring mineral workings prior to forest planting, can be relieved by deep cultivation using specially designed tines (Binns and Fourt, 1980).

The commonest cause of surface sealing of the soil is the introduction of tarmac or other soil coverings around established trees in car parks and on new roads and footpaths. The extent of damage to the tree will depend on the proportion of the ground that is covered close to the trunk. Surface covers such as tarmac or paving will not only prevent gaseous interchange but also prevent free entry of water to the soil and contribute to soil compaction, thus adding to the stresses imposed on the tree roots. Nevertheless, it should be pointed out that many trees do grow successfully in paved areas. In urban areas, for example, many such trees were planted in areas largely covered by paving slabs or tarmac and therefore have been able to adapt to this situation. Most damage occurs when the soil surface around established trees is covered and roots which previously had access to well-aerated soil are suddenly deprived of adequate oxygen.

Symptoms

The symptoms of poor soil aeration are similar, regardless of the reason for the lack of oxygen (Peace, 1962). In all cases these conditions can lead to death of roots. As a result, leaf margins and needle tips become necrotic and a progressive leaf fall and dieback may follow. The severity of the symptoms will depend upon the proportion of the root system affected. Where damage is slow to develop, growth of shoots may be stunted. In severe cases the entire tree may be killed.

CHEMICAL FACTORS

AIR POLLUTION

It has long been recognised that air pollution can have damaging effects on plants. As far back as 1874, the American *Garden Chronicle* reported failure of crops and death of trees due to the adverse effects of air pollution (Cameron, 1874). During the 1930s a classic study of fume damage to vegetation, including trees, was undertaken at the Trail Smelter on the borders of the United States and Canada (Anon, 1939). More recently a large number of investigations have been made into many aspects of damage to vegetation caused by air pollution. A series of papers on air pollution damage to plants was presented to the American Phytopathological Society in August 1967 and published in *Phytopathology*, volume 58, 1968. These provide a valuable review of the subject and they will be referred to individually later in this section. Another review of the effects of air pollutants on vegetation was published a year earlier (Brandt and Heck, 1967). There is a very wide range of references to pollution damage to plants and these should be consulted for detailed information on individual pollutants.

Causal agents

There are a great many toxic gases produced by a wide range of industrial and other processes. Some, termed primary air pollutants, originate during such processes in a form which is toxic to plants. Perhaps the best-known examples are sulphur dioxide and hydrogen fluoride. Others, known as secondary pollutants have undergone chemical change after their initial production. These include the photochemical pollutants such as ozone or peroxyacetyl nitrate (PAN). The most common air pollutants causing damage to plants are those mentioned above. However, there are many others among which the following, in alphabetical order, are the most important: chlorine, hydrogen chloride, oxides of nitrogen, particulates and silicon tetrafluoride.

Chlorine and hydrogen chloride   Wood (1968) considers that chlorine and hydrogen chloride are increasing in importance as toxic agents. They originate from oil refineries, glass factories, incinerators and accidental spillages. Polyvinyl chloride (PVC) is now widely used for packaging and for wire insulation and it is often burned after its useful life is finished. PVC gives rise on combustion to a number of chemicals including hydrogen chloride and for this reason there may be an increase in the number of cases of damage caused by this pollutant. In industry efficient methods are available to remove hydrogen chloride from flue gases.

Fluorides   Fluorine compounds such as hydrogen fluoride and silicon tetra-fluoride are important air pollutants. They are found in the vicinity of a number of manufacturing industries including aluminium smelters, phosphatic fertiliser plants, brick and pottery kilns, steel manufacture, oil refineries and also in rocket fuel combustion. It is interesting to note that fluorides are toxic to plants at much lower concentrations than many other pollutants.

Oxides of nitrogen   Taylor and Eaton (1966) have demonstrated that oxides of nitrogen can act as primary air pollutants. However, they are often considered to have a more important role in the production of secondary air pollutants such as ozone and PAN and, therefore, they are discussed in more detail below.

Ozone   Ozone has been recognised as an air pollutant for at least 100 years. It can be found in the upper atmosphere, in the vicinity of electrical storms, and can also arise as the result of a photochemical reaction. During the 1950s it was discovered that ozone was present in the smog which developed over many American cities, especially during periods of very hot weather. Leighton (1961) proposed a series of chemical reactions which could lead to the production of ozone under these conditions. Oxides of nitrogen are produced by the combination of nitrogen and oxygen at the high temperatures developing in vehicle engines and some industrial processes. In the presence of sunlight, these oxides of nitrogen react with the oxygen in the air and with hydrocarbons also released by motor vehicles to produce ozone.

Peroxyacetyl nitrate   Peroxyacetyl nitrate (PAN) is also an important photo-chemical pollutant found in urban smog. It is produced in a similar manner to ozone by the reaction of oxides of nitrogen and unsaturated hydrocarbons emitted by vehicle engines, in the presence of sunlight.

Particulates   Finely divided solids, known as particulates, can also damage plants although they have been the subject of only limited study. The most important sources of particulates are coal or oil burning stoves, cement factories, lime kilns, incinerators and straw burning.

Sulphur dioxide   Sulphur dioxide is the best known and most widespread of all air pollutants. It is produced from many industrial processes including the combustion of coal, oil and gas, oil refining, the manufacture of sulphuric acid and the smelting and refining of several metal ores.

Many measures have been taken in recent years by industrialists to reduce the emissions of toxic fumes. These include the removal of pollutants before they are released into the atmosphere and the construction of high chimneys in order to disperse the fumes and reduce their concentration at ground level. Nevertheless, with ever-increasing industrial output, there is little doubt that the damaging effects of air pollution will continue for many years.

Symptoms produced by pollutants

The symptoms produced on herbaceous plants and trees by a number of air pollutants are reviewed by Heggestad (1968) and reference should be made to this article for more detailed information on the pollutants discussed below.

Chlorine   Chlorine causes widespread chlorosis and varying patterns of necrosis on the foliage and these symptoms vary on different plant species. In contrast to a number of other pollutants, older leaves seem more susceptible than young ones. Brennan *et al.* (1965) reported on the susceptibility of a range of herbaceous species and concluded that radishes and lucerne were the most susceptible. Injuries developed after exposure to 0.10 ppm chlorine for two hours. Brennan *et al.* (1966) noted that pines were damaged by a three-hour fumigation with chlorine at 1.0 ppm.

Fluorides   In some cases fluorides act as cumulative poisons although this may not always be the case. Jacobson *et al.* (1966) have demonstrated that once fluorides have entered the leaf tissue it is rapidly translocated to leaf tips and margins. As a result a tip and marginal necrosis of the foliage develops on broad-leaved trees often with a distinct narrow reddish-brown line of dead tissue separating healthy from affected parts. In conifers, tip burn is a characteristic feature with a similar well-marked differentiation between live and dead areas (plate 3). The dosage of fluoride which gives rise to damage varies according to the host species but levels of 0.5 parts per billion fluoride for prolonged periods will cause damage to plants. Brandt (1962) considers that concentrations of 50-200 ppm fluoride in the foliage will cause necrosis on susceptible plants.

Oxides of nitrogen   There is little information available on the effects of oxides of nitrogen on trees. However, Taylor and Eaton (1966) found a marked depression of growth and darker green foliage in tomato plants subjected to 0.5 ppm nitrogen dioxide for 10-12 days. At concentrations in excess of 3 ppm damage was similar to that caused by sulphur dioxide.

Ozone   Symptoms of ozone damage on broadleaved trees are frequently limited to the upper surface of the foliage which is covered with small irregular flecks varying in colour from white through yellow to reddish brown. Costonis and Sinclair (1967) give a detailed description of the development of the symptoms on *Pinus strobus*. At first, small water-soaked spots appear near the base of the needle; after 6-8 hours affected areas become yellow-pink and then purple in colour. The affected areas then coalesce to form chlorotic or necrotic bands and on highly susceptible trees damage may extend until tip necroses have developed. Concentrations of 0.02-0.05 ppm ozone will cause damage to susceptible plant species after exposures of a few hours.

Peroxyacetyl nitrate   In contrast to ozone, PAN typically produces symptoms on the undersurface of the leaves of broadleaved trees. The lower surface appears glazed or bronzed due to the collapse of the mesophyll cells around the stomata. Symptoms on coniferous needles are less characteristic and may include some chlorosis or bleaching (Brandt and Heck, 1967). Dosage rates of 0.02-0.05 ppm PAN for a few hours will cause damage to the more susceptible species.

Particulates   Deposits of genuine soot, which are distinct from sooty mould associated with honeydew secreted by aphids, are commonly found on the foliage of trees close to industrial factories burning coal or oil. It was thought at one time that sooty deposits might interfere with gaseous exchange through stomata. However, it is now considered that the most serious effect is the reduction in the amount of light reaching the foliage (Jennings, 1934). Dust deposited around cement factories may cause chlorosis and death in both broadleaved and coniferous species (Darley and Middleton, 1966).

Sulphur dioxide   On broadleaved trees sulphur dioxide causes bleaching or necrosis of the interveinal regions of the foliage, the veins remaining green. The bleached or necrotic areas are often not clearly demarcated and they are frequently surrounded by more or less chlorotic areas that merge into healthy tissue. On conifers the needles have brown necrotic tips, often with a banded appearance which is probably related to successive toxic emissions. As in the case of broadleaved trees, chlorotic areas are often found adjacent to the necrotic tissue.

Thomas (1961) reports that injury develops on susceptible species after exposure to 0.48 ppm sulphur dioxide for 4 hours or 0.28 ppm sulphur dixoide for 24 hours.

Diagnosis of air pollution damage
Whilst the symptoms of pollution injury described above are useful indicators of the nature of the injury, such damage is readily confused with that caused by other agents such as disease, insects and cultural conditions. It is also important to recognise that pollution damage may only be evident at certain seasons when the foliage is particularly susceptible and may be limited to susceptible species. Brandt (1962) discusses the wide range of factors which must be taken into account in assessing the possible role of air pollutants in causing damage to

plants. He stresses that competent observers, preferably with some previous knowledge of the local vegetation, are needed in order to make a proper assessment and interpretation of the symptoms. It is clearly important to establish that there are potential sources of pollution in an area and where possible to monitor levels of pollution at the source and at varying distances from it. The distribution of air pollution damage in relation to the source and to wind direction at the time of emissions can provide important evidence in the diagnosis of pollution damage. Foliar analysis can in some cases provide useful information on the presence of pollutants in the leaf tissues.

Relative resistance of trees to air pollution damage

Whilst there will be continuing efforts by industry to reduce the levels of pollution in the atmosphere it is important that foresters and arboriculturists recognise polluted areas and where possible plant tree species which tolerate air pollution.

The United States Department of Agriculture Forest Service has published a leaflet on trees for polluted air (Anon, 1973) and tables 2.2 and 2.3 are largely based on this information.

Table 2.2

Relative tolerance of trees to sulphur dioxide

	Tolerant	*Intermediate*	*Susceptible*
Conifers	*Cupressus lawsoniana*	*Abies* spp.	*Larix* spp.
	Juniperus spp.	*Pinus contorta*	
	Pinus nigra var. *maritima*	*Pseudotsuga* spp.	
	Thuja plicata		
	Ginkgo biloba		
Broadleaved species	*Acer campestre*		*Betula* spp.
	Carpinus betulus		*Juglans* spp.
	Fagus sylvatica		*Malus* spp.
	Platanus spp.		*Populus nigra* 'Italica'
	Populus deltoides		*Salix* spp.
	Quercus spp.		

HERBICIDE DAMAGE

A wide variety of herbicides is now used routinely in agriculture and forestry. Many are selective, that is, they kill unwanted weed species and allow the growth of crop plants or trees to continue unhindered. However, there are occasions when herbicides are applied at the wrong time, concentration or dose, or are mistakenly applied to a susceptible species and damage to crop plants and trees can follow.

Table 2.3

Relative tolerance of trees to fluorides

	Tolerant	*Intermediate*	*Susceptible*
Conifers	*Juniperus* spp.	*Thuja* spp.	*Larix* spp. *Pinus contorta* *Pinus sylvestris* *Pseudotsuga* spp.
Broadleaved species	*Alnus glutinosa* *Platanus* spp. *Salix* spp. *Sorbus aucuparia* *Tilia cordata*	*Acer campestre* *Betula pendula* *Carpinus betulus* *Castanea sativa* *Fagus sylvatica* *Fraxinus excelsior* *Juglans* spp. *Populus* spp. *Quercus* spp. *Tilia europea*	

Herbicide damage to trees can often be recognised on the basis of its distribution. Herbicides are often applied to eradicate weeds surrounding trees and if the latter are damaged it will only be those within or close to the treated area that are affected. In a tree nursery the distribution of damage may be related to the uneven application of the herbicide due to poorly adjusted spray machinery. In the case of total weedkillers, often used, for example, on paths and verges, damage to neighbouring trees may result from spray drift or from secondary distribution of the herbicide in rain water or by death of roots under the treated area.

Some herbicides can cause characteristic symptoms on susceptible plants. Such symptoms may be diagnostic on their own but, in many cases further evidence of the presence of a herbicide and of the distribution of the damage should be sought before a firm diagnosis is made as somewhat similar symptoms can be produced by other agents. Therefore, a knowledge of the symptoms is useful and a description of some of the symptoms on tree species that have been found in association with the application of a number of herbicides is given below. For convenience the herbicides have been divided into the following three main groups.

(1) Herbicides used in nurseries.
(2) Herbicides used in newly planted areas.
(3) Herbicides used for total eradication of vegetation.

Herbicides in nurseries
Herbicides are used as a pre-emergence treatment in nursery seedbeds; they are applied after sowing but before emergence of the seedlings in order to kill

rapidly germinating weed seeds. One of the chemicals sometimes used for this treatment is vapourising oil. If the application is delayed until the tree seeds have germinated and emerged, the young seedlings are likely to be killed. However, some species are rather more resistant to such damage including Scots and Corsican pines, spruces, western red cedar and Lawson cypress. Others are very susceptible including lodgepole pine, larches, Douglas fir, western hemlock and firs.

At later stages in the growth of plants in the nursery different herbicides are used. For example, simazine is commonly used to control weeds in transplant lines. If this is applied at rates or concentrations greater than those recommended, damage can ensue. Shoots and needles of Japanese larch turn white, needles of Scots pine become brown, with a reddish transition zone between healthy and affected tissues. On broadleaved species, leaves develop a marginal yellowing or browning. These symptoms appear 2-6 weeks after herbicide treatment. If the plants are not killed, normal healthy growth may appear later in the season.

Herbicides for newly planted areas
There are many different sites in which trees may be planted, ranging from forest locations with grass, herbaceous and woody weeds to urban streets or parks with predominantly grass weeds. A range of herbicides is available to deal with the varied weed species present at a planting site.

Two commonly used herbicides for the treatment of grasses and grass-herb mixtures are chlorthiamid and dichlobenil. The correct method of application is critical for these herbicides and incorrect application of the chemical can cause very characteristic symptoms. Where granules of these chemicals make contact with the stems of Scots pine, Corsican pine, Japanese larch and Douglas fir, a swelling develops at the base of the stem (plate 9). Radial growth at soil level is strongly inhibited while growth immediately above continues, giving rise to the swelling. The stem may be girdled at soil level due to complete death of cambium, in which case the plant will die. Symptoms on Norway spruce are a little different. A narrow, dead strip of tissue develops on the stem extending upwards for several centimetres, sometimes as much as 30 cm. At the same time, the needles may become chlorotic and the lower branches may die back. This is usually attributable to the uptake of the breakdown product dichlorobenzamide in excessive quantity. In extreme cases the stem may be girdled at the base.

Glyphosate is a herbicide used for killing grass, herbaceous and broadleaved woody weeds, for example in coniferous plantings. However, if applications are made during active growth of conifers or at too high a concentration many species may be damaged (plate 10). For example, larch and spruce plants turn white and then brown from the tips downwards. When damage is severe, resin-bleeding from shoots and stems may occur. Glyphosate remains within the plant and symptoms can persist throughout the season following application of the herbicide. Glyphosate is also used in agriculture, for example, for killing *Agropyron repens* in winter wheat crops. Spray drift can occur in these or other circumstances and damage to neighbouring trees, either coniferous or broadleaved has been reported. Shoot growth is severely reduced, leaves are small, often with entire margins, thus giving the whole shoot a bunched or tufted appearance. In severe cases, or on susceptible species such as beech, the trees may be killed or completely defoliated.

Hormone weedkillers such as 2,4-D and 2,4,5-T are sometimes used in forestry to eradicate woody weeds and some herbaceous weeds. They are also widely used in agriculture for killing herbaceous weeds in grass or cereal crops. On occasion, applications to agricultural crops can drift on to neighbouring trees and damage sometimes occurs. However, careful observation of the distribution and nature of the damage is needed before the proper reason for the damage can be established. Injury caused by hormone weedkillers is usually manifested by the cupping or crinkling of leaves, curling of needles and sinuous distortion of petioles and shoots in active growth; in more extreme cases dieback may occur. Broadleaved trees are generally more susceptible than conifers. On poplars, for example, growing shoots become twisted and leaf margins curl inwards. On pine the distortion of growing shoots is sometimes confused with symptoms caused by *Melampsora pinitorqua*, the pine twisting rust. However, the presence of fructifications of the fungus and the more sporadic distribution of the symptoms should enable the cause of injury to be identified.

The herbicide 2,4,5-T is sometimes applied to frill girdles on broadleaved species in order to remove unwanted trees from mixed conifer–broadleaved forests. Cuts are made into the trunk with an axe or other suitable implement and a solution of the herbicide is injected into the frill. Care must be taken when selective treatment (that is, only some trees in a plantation are treated) is undertaken as neighbouring trees of the same species can be affected by root transmission of the chemical through root grafts between trees. 2,4,5-T can also become vapourised and if applications are made on warm days, nearby untreated trees may be affected. *Cedrus* spp. are particularly susceptible and can be entirely defoliated in this manner.

Herbicides for total eradication

Total weedkillers such as sodium chlorate, bromacil or a mixture of paraquat and simazine are often used to eradicate weeds on paths or fallow ground. Damage to neighbouring trees may occur if their roots extend under the treated areas or if the herbicide seeps into untreated areas. Dead roots or withered foliage may result, particularly on that side of the tree closest to the treated area.

SALT DAMAGE

Sodium chloride is commonly used on roads and footpaths to melt ice and snow but it can also damage trees growing close by. The quantity of salt used in Britain, with its relatively mild oceanic winters, is less than that in some European countries or in the northern parts of the United States. For this reason, damage to trees and other vegetation is probably less in Britain than in some other countries. Detailed information on salt damage should therefore be sought in foreign literature (for example, Dirr, 1976; Braun *et al.*, 1978). However, damage is reported from time to time in Britain.

Roadside trees can be affected either by the presence of salt in the soil, usually introduced through run-off from treated highways, or by salt spray thrown up by passing vehicles. The most common cause of salt damage in Britain is run-off from a roadside salt dump which has been inadvertently placed close to trees.

Mode of action

The precise manner in which salt affects the growth of trees is not fully understood. However, it is generally accepted that high concentrations of salt in the soil water can prevent or reduce normal uptake of water and nutrients into the tree. Some plants are salt tolerant and they may be able to absorb greater concentrations of salt than salt-sensitive species. Nevertheless, both sodium and chloride ions can be toxic to plant growth and the ability of some plants to absorb higher salt concentrations does not necessarily enable them to avoid salt damage.

In addition, the nutrient balance in the water taken into the plant can be affected. For example, the presence of high concentrations of sodium in the soil water can result in it replacing potassium in the nutrient intake. Potash deficiency may then occur in the plant.

The other method by which salt may damage a tree is through the deposition of salt on branches and foliage following drift of salt spray from neighbouring roads. These deposits may cause damage by the withdrawal of water from the leaf or needle tissues by osmosis or the salt may be directly toxic.

Symptoms and diagnosis

As we have seen above, salt can cause damage in several different ways and can reach a tree through soil water or through aerial spray drift. It is not surprising, therefore, that symptoms of salt damage vary widely according to circumstances. In general, trees injured by excess of salt in the soil or on the foliage show small leaves, early leaf fall and dieback of twigs and branches. In addition there may be marginal necrosis on leaves or tip dieback on coniferous needles. However, the distribution of the damage is probably one of the most important factors leading to a correct diagnosis. Damage is likely to be most severe close to the roads or drain outlets and will diminish rapidly further from the highway. On individual trees affected by spray drift symptoms are likely to be more severe on the side facing the road. In some situations where snow has covered the lower branches of roadside trees, such branches may have escaped damage from spray drift. In Britain special attention should be paid to the presence of roadside deposits of salt or salted grit. Run-off from such areas may cause serious damage to roadside trees.

Confirmation of salt injury is best achieved by the chemical analysis of soil and plant tissues. It is important to analyse both soil and foliage as salt may not in some circumstances be absorbed into the plant. Much research has been undertaken on the level of salt needed in the plant to cause damage and the results of the research vary according to the species studied. In practice samples should be taken from affected trees and healthy trees of the same species growing in the vicinity. As a general guide, Williams and Moser (1975) suggested that when chloride concentrations reach about 2.7 per cent in plant tissues, visual injury was evident.

Salt damage can best be avoided by ensuring that salt run-off from roads does not occur close to trees. In order to avoid damage from salt spray it is recommended in the United States that trees should be planted at least 9 metres from the highway. In areas where these precautions cannot be avoided only species tolerant to salt injury should be planted. Various lists of species indicating relative tolerance to salt injury have been published. Braun *et al.*, (1978) give tolerances of a number of European tree species and Dirr (1976) gives that of some American tree species. A summary of the tolerance of some common European species (following Braun *et al.*, 1978) is given in table 2.4.

Table 2.4
Salt tolerance of some common trees

Tolerant	Susceptible
Alnus glutinosa	Acer campestre
Robinia pseudoacacia	Acer platanoides
Salix alba var. vitellina	Acer pseudoplatanus
	Aesculus hippocastanum
	Alnus incana
	Alnus viridis
	Picea abies
	Picea omorika
	Tilia cordata
	Tilia platyphylla

DAMAGE BY NATURAL GAS

Leaks of natural gas from underground pipes can be injurious to vegetation including trees. However, unlike coal gas, which is toxic to plants, natural gas (methane) is not directly poisonous but acts indirectly on the soil environment so that root activity is impaired. Much information on leakage of natural gas has been obtained during periods when supplies were converted from coal gas to natural gas. Holland was one of the first countries where conversion was undertaken and serious losses of street trees occurred following conversion in some areas. Investigations showed that gas leaks were likely to be responsible and it was discovered that natural gas, with a lower moisture content than town gas, had caused the drying out of certain types of joints on old cast iron mains. Other countries which converted later were able to take note of these Dutch investigations and introduce preventative measures. Damage to trees in Britain by natural gas has therefore not been severe but nevertheless reports of such damage are received on occasion.

Mode of action
The exact nature of the effects of natural gas leaks on soil and vegetation is reviewed by Pankhurst (1980) and Tattar (1978). Natural gas acts on the soil in a number of different ways. For example, it replaces other gases in the soil atmosphere including oxygen. It can also cause changes in the soil microflora and may enhance the activity of methane-oxidising bacteria. Such activity may contribute to a lack of oxygen and relative excess of carbon dioxide in the soil atmosphere. The roots of trees and other plants become deprived of oxygen and are unable to carry on normal respiration and water uptake.

Symptoms
Symptoms of damage to trees caused by leakage of natural gas are difficult to distinguish from symptoms of other conditions such as waterlogging associated with lack of soil oxygen. They are also similar to symptoms of drought. Leaves may show a marginal scorch or be subject to premature fall, a progressive die-back may develop, or buds may fail to flush if a gas leak has occurred during the dormant season.

It is probably more important in cases of suspected gas leakage to establish that underground gas pipes are present, that the characteristic smell of natural gas has been detected or that the most severe damage occurs close to the probable or known line of the gas pipe. The extent of the damage will depend on the size of the leak or leaks and to a lesser extent on the type of soil. In sandy soils, which are more porous, gas tends to move fairly rapidly upwards in the shape of an inverted cone. On the other hand in clay soils, which are more resistant to diffusing gases, gas will move more slowly and in the shape of a truncated inverted cone.

Confirmation of gas leakage is best achieved by detecting the presence of methane in the soil using a gas sampling probe. These are available either commercially or through the national gas authority. However, it should be noted that there may be a few occasions when methane gas may be present in soil for other reasons, e.g., refuse dumps incorporating decomposing vegetable material.

Treatment
Repair of gas leaks clearly takes priority for reasons of safety. Although the

sealing of leaks will prevent further escape of gas, the surrounding soil may retain excessive methane for some time afterwards. The disturbance to the soil during the repair operations will go some way to releasing any gas held in the soil but it is possible in addition to aerate the soil by introducing compressed air through soil probes.

REFERENCES

Albertson, F.W. and Weaver, J.E. (1945). Injury and death of trees in prairie climate. *Ecol. Monogr.*, 15, 393-433

Aldhous, J.R. (1972). *Nursery Practice,* Bull. For. Commn, no. 43

Anon (1939). *Effect of Sulphur Dioxide on Vegetation*, National Research Council, Canada, Ottawa, 447 pp.

Anon (1973). *Trees for Polluted Air,* U.S. Dep. Agric. Forest Service Mis. Pub., no. 1230

Baule, H. and Fricker, C. (1970). *The Fertilizer Treatment of Forest Trees*, Trans. C.L. Whittles, BLV, Munich

Benzian, B. (1965). *Experiments in Nutrition Problems in Forest Nurseries*, Bull. For. Commn, no. 37, vol. 1.

Bier, J.E. (1959). The relation of bark moisture to the development of canker diseases caused by facultative parasites. *Can. J. Bot.*, 37, 229-38

Binns, W.O. and Fourt, D.F. (1980). Surface workings and trees, in *Research for Practical Arboriculture*, Occasional Pap. For. Commn, no. 10.

Binns, W.O., Mayhead, G.J. and Mackenzie, J.M. (1980). *Nutrient Deficiencies of Conifers in British Forests; an Illustrated Guide,* Leafl. For. Commn, no. 76

Brandt, C.S. (1962). Effects of air pollution on plants, in A.C. Stern (Ed.), *Air Pollution,* 1st ed., vol. 1, Academic Press, New York, pp. 255-81

Brandt, C.S. and Heck, W. (1967). Effects of air pollutants on vegetation, in A.C. Stern (Ed.), *Air Pollution,* 2nd ed., vol. 1, Academic Press, New York, pp. 401-43

Braun, S., Schonborn, A. von and Weber, E. (1978). Untersuchungen zur resistenz von geholzen gegen auftausalz (Natriumchlorid). *Allg. Forstzg.*, 149, 216-35

Brennan, E.G., Leone, I.A. and Daines, R.H. (1965). Chlorine as a phytotoxic air pollutant. *Int. J. Air & Water Pollution,* 9, 791-97

Brennan, E.G., Leone, I.A. and Daines, R.H. (1966). Response of pine trees to chlorine in the atmosphere. *Forest Sci.*, 12, 386-90

Burke, M.J., Gusta, L.V., Quarume, H.A., Weiser, C.J. and Li, P.H. (1976). Freezing and injury in plants. *A. Rev. Pl. Physiol.*, 27, 507-28.

Cadman, W.A. (1953). *Shelterbelts for Welsh Hill Farms.* For. Rec., Lond., no. 22

Cameron, C.A. (1874). *Garden Chronicle*, 1, 274-75.

Costonis, A.C. and Sinclair, W.A. (1967). Seasonal development of symptoms of ozone injury on eastern white pine. *Phytopathology*, 57, 339

Darley, E.F. and Middleton, J.T. (1966). Problems of air pollution in plant pathology. *A. Rev. Pl. Path.*, 4, 103-18

Dirr, M.A. (1976). Selection of trees for tolerance to salt injury. *J. Arboric.*, 2, 209-16

Dobbs, R.C. and McMinn, R.G. (1973). Hail damage to a new White spruce and Lodgepole pine plantation in central British Columbia. *For. Chron.*, 49, 174-5

Everard, J.E. (1974). *Fertilizers in the Establishment of Conifers in Wales and Southern England,* Bookl. For. Commn, no. 41

Glerum, C. and Farrar, J.L. (1966). Frost ring formation in the stems of some coniferous species. *Can. J. Bot.*, 44, 879-86

Guilivo, C. (1973). Hagelschutz im obst- und weinbau mit kunststoffnetzen. *Erwerbsobstbau*, 15, 187-90

Heggestad, H.E. (1968). Diseases of crops and ornamental plants incited by air pollutants. *Phytopathology*, 58, 1089-97

Houston, D.R., Parker, E.J., Perrin, R. and Lang, K.J. (1979). Beech bark disease. A comparison of the disease in North America, Great Britain, France and Germany. *Eur. J. For. Path.*, 9, 199-211

Jacobson, J.S., Weinstein, L.H., McCune, D.C. and Hitchcock, A.E. (1966). The accumulation of fluorine in plants. *J. Air Pollution Ass.,* **16**, 412–17

Jamison, V.C. (1956). Pertinent factors in governing availability of soil moisture to plants. *Soil Sci.,* **81**, 459–71

Jennings, O.E. (1934). Smoke injury to shade trees. *Proc. 10th National Shade Tree Conf.,* pp. 44–8

Kozlowski, T.T. (1964). *Water Metabolism in Plants,* Harper, New York

Kramer, P.J. (1962). The role of water in tree growth, in T.T. Kozlowski (Ed.), *Tree Growth* Ronald Press, New York, pp. 171–82

Leighton, P.A. (1961). *Photochemistry of Air Pollution,* Academic Press, New York

Levitt, J. (1969). Dormancy and survival. *Symp. Soc. Exp. Biol,* **23**, 395–448

Lonsdale, D., Pratt, J.E. and Aldsworth, F.G. (1979). Beech bark disease and archaeological crop marks. *Nature, Lond.,* **277**, 414

Low, J.D. and Greig, B.J.W. (1973). Spring frosts affecting the establishment of second rotation crops in Thetford Chase. *Forestry,* **46**, 139–55

Mayhead, G.J. (1976). Forest fertilizing in Great Britain. *Proc. Fertil. Soc.,* **158**, 2–17

Pankhurst, E.S. (1980). The effects of natural gas on trees and other vegetation. *Landscape Design,* February 1980, 32–3

Parker, J. (1968). Drought resistance mechanisms, in T.T. Kozlowski (Ed.), *Water Deficits and Plant Growth,* vol. 1, Academic Press, New York, pp. 195–234

Peace, T.R. (1962). *Pathology of Trees and Shrubs,* Clarendon Press, Oxford

Pfeffer, A., Skoda, B. and Zlatuska, V. (1948). Uliv saucha vr. 1947 na lesni dreviny. *Lesn. Pr.,* **27**, 193–214

Phillips, D.H. (1965). Stem crack. *Rep. Forest Res., Lond., 1964,* p. 57

Phillips, D.H. (1966). Stem crack in *Abies grandis. Rep. Forest Res., Lond., 1965,* pp. 61–2

Phillips, D.H. (1967). Stem crack in *Abies grandis. Rep. Forest Res., Lond., 1966,* pp. 71

Salter, P.J. and Goode, J.E. (1967). *Crop Responses to Water at Different Stages of Growth,* Commonwealth Agricultural Bureau

Salter, P.J. and Williams, J.B. (1969). The influence of texture on the moisture characteristics of soil. V. Relationships between particle size, composition and moisture contents at the upper and lower limits of available water. *J. Soil Sci.,* **20**, 126–131

Tattar, T.A. (1978). *Diseases of Shade Trees,* Academic Press, New York

Taylor, O.C. and Eaton, F.M. (1966). Suppression of plant growth by nitrogen dioxide. *Pl. Physiol., Lancaster,* **41**, 132–36

Thomas, M.D. (1961). Effects of air pollution and plants, in *Air pollution, Wld Hlth Org. Monogr. Ser.,* **46**, 233–278, Columbia University Press, New York

True, R.P. and Tryon, E.H. (1956). Oak stem cankers initiated in the drought year 1953. *Phytopathology,* **46**, 617–21

Williams, D.J. and Moser, B.C. (1975). Critical level of airborne sea salt inducing foliar injury to bean. *Hort. Sci.,* **10**, 615–16

Wood, F.A. (1968). Sources of plant pathogenic air pollutants. *Phytopathology,* **58**, 1075–84

Zycha, H. (1951). Das Rindensterben der Buche. *Phytopath. Z.,* **17**, 444–61

3 Diseases caused by living agents on a wide range of hosts

Of the many living organisms that cause diseases, some affect a wide range of hosts, others are restricted to one or a very few host genera or species. This chapter deals with diseases caused by pathogens with many hosts. Succeeding chapters deal with those caused by organisms with a more restricted range.

DISEASES OF SEEDS

Seeds may sometimes harbour organisms that cause diseases of mature plants, though so far no seedborne diseases of trees are known in Britain. At times also, seeds may carry organisms that kill the seeds themselves, or after sowing cause the death of seedlings before or after emergence, or later give rise to root rot in older seedlings and nursery transplants.

Information on disease organisms that damage seed in this country is rather limited. Batko (1954, 1955, 1956, 1957a, 1957b), on samples of seed of a fairly wide range of conifers and some broadleaved trees, found nearly fifty species of fungi. Among these were various species of *Fusarium*, some of which cause damage to the roots of nursery plants (Buxton *et al.*, 1962; Vaartaja, 1964), but most were common saprophytes, including *Penicillium* spp., *Mucor* spp., *Rhizopus nigricans, Oedocephalum glomerulosum* and *Trichoderma viride*, many of which interfere with germination tests in the seed-testing laboratory. Similar fungi were found by Buxton *et al.* (1962).

From a detailed study of fourteen samples of seed of known percentage germination, Batko (unpublished) concluded that there was an inverse relationship between mouldiness and germinability, and that moulds were a likely cause of the reduced germination of poor seed samples.

These findings agree with those of Garbowski (1936), Huss (1952), Gibson (1957), Schubert (1960) and Shea (1960), working elsewhere. Thus Shea found that fungal contamination of seed took place in cones stored in sacks. The longer the storage period, the greater was the contamination, and the more mouldy the seeds, the lower was their germinability. In experiments, he reduced the moulds and improved the keeping qualities of conifer seeds by fungicidal treatment of the cones. Work by Huss (1952) and Gibson (1957) pointed to the importance of mechanical damage, which rendered the seed more liable to attack by normally saprophytic moulds. Schubert (1960) reduced losses through moulding by collecting only mature seed, drying to a moisture content below ten per cent, and storing at the lowest recommended temperature.

Whittle (1977) studied the mycoflora of cones and seeds of *Pinus sylvestris* from several sites in Britain. He made isolations at different stages in the development of the seed in the cone and at various stages as material passed through the seed extraction plant. He also examined seed stored at various temperatures and levels of humidity. He found that seed in the cones was contaminated at a very early stage, and for a long time the only contaminant was *Sclerophoma pithyophila* (*Dothichiza pithyophila*). During extraction, the seeds became contaminated also by various common 'storage moulds', such as *Penicillium* spp.,

Trichoderma viride and *Botrytis cinerea*. Over a storage period of 22 months, the incidence of *S. pithyophila* gradually fell, but that of the other moulds, especially the *Penicillium* spp., increased. Whittle's storage studies indicated, however, that the dry storage of seed of *P. sylvestris* at 2 °C, as normally practised, kept fungal contamination low enough to prevent significant damage.

Salt (1967), in work partly to investigate the effect of sowing seed in cold soils, found that when he kept Sitka spruce seed imported from North America at 10 °C before germinating it, germination was reduced, and the reduction was associated with the presence of seedborne *Rhizoctonia solani*, *Cylindrocarpon* sp., *Gliocladium roseum* and an unidentified endophytic fungus which, following Epners (1964), he called 'the psycrophilic seed fungus', because it caused damage only in cold conditions.

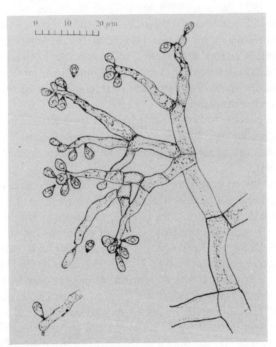

Figure 5. Conidiophores and spores of *Geniculodendron pyriforme* (G.A. Salt)

He described the fungus, naming it *Geniculodendron pyriforme* (Salt, 1974) (figure 5). Later, Paden *et al.* (1978), in Canada, found it to be the conidial stage of the orange discomycete *Caloscypha fulgens* (which so far does not appear to have been recorded in Britain). The fungus kills the seeds in the nursery beds before germination, especially when the soil temperature is at about 10 °C, which is too cool for rapid germination of the seed but warm enough for the fungus to grow. *G. pyriforme* may spread and do severe damage to infected seed given a moist stratification treatment to break dormancy, but losses can be reduced by dressing the seed with thiram or captan (Epners, 1964; Gordon, *et al.*, 1976).

Virtually all the work referred to above is concerned with seeds of conifers; most information on fungi on seeds of hardwood trees in this country is in the form of isolated records.

Thus *Stromatinia pseudotuberosa* (*Sclerotinia pseudotuberosa, Ciboria batschiana*, stat. conid. *Rhacodiella castanea*), which is known to be one of the most important of the fungi that damage acorns in eastern Europe (Urošević, 1957, 1958, 1961), is known to occur in Great Britain (Ramsbottom and Balfour-Brown, 1951; Rushton, 1977). In Italy, the same fungus causes black mould of sweet chestnuts (Voglino, 1931). *Gloeosporium quercinum* (stat. conid. of *Gnomonia quercina*), again a cause of damage to acorns in eastern Europe (Potlaychuk, 1953; Urošević, 1957), has also been recorded on oak in Great Britain (Grove, 1937; Moore, 1959), but only on the leaves.

Cryptodiaporthe castanea (*Diaporthe castanea* stat. conid. *Fusicoccum castaneum*) was isolated by Wright (1960) in North America from fruits of Chinese chestnut (*Castanea mollissima*), and also occurs in Great Britain (Grove, 1935; Moore, 1959), but again has not been found there on fruits, but only on twigs and branches. *Sclerotinia fructigena* (stat. conid. *Monilia fructigena*) causes nut drop of hazel (Wormald, 1955).

Finally, it is possible to isolate many bacteria from seeds of both conifers and broadleaved trees, but few isolates have been studied or named, though *Xanthomonas juglandis*, the cause of walnut blight, has been isolated from walnuts (Wormald, 1930).

Methods for the control of seedborne and cone-borne organisms that damage seed have in general not been worked out, and no work has been done on this problem in Britain. Elsewhere, Shea (1960), who found harmful moulds spread from Douglas fir cones to the seeds, improved the keeping qualities of the seed by dipping the cones in a fungicide, and by paying careful attention to moisture conditions and temperature in storage. Huss (1952) and Gibson (1957) both refer to attack by moulds that follow mechanical damage to seed by rough handling, dewinging, etc., and this suggests that if damage of this kind is unavoidable, subsequent mould infection might be prevented by fungicidal treatment. As already noted, conifer seed infected by *Geniculodendron pyriforme* can be successfully treated with a fungicide. According to Urošević (1958), losses of acorns through attack by *Stromatinia pseudotuberosa* may be avoided by early harvesting, reduction of the moisture content of the seed to 45 per cent, and storage at a low temperature, but protecting them from frost. Work on the protection of forest seeds from storage moulds by means of fungicides still remains to be done.

NURSERY DISEASES

DAMPING OFF AND NURSERY ROOT ROT

Once the seed has been sown, it and the resulting seedlings and transplants may be attacked not only by some of the fungi on the seed itself, but also by others present in the soil. Three forms of damage result from these attacks (Hartley, 1921). In the first, known as *pre-emergence damping off*, the seeds and seedlings die within the soil. In the second, known as *post-emergence damping off*, attack is seen in the first few weeks after the plants appear above ground, and occurs on the succulent roots and hypocotyls of the growing plants. The seedlings, mainly those in the cotyledon stage, tend to wilt, and collapse at ground level, where the tissues are brown and shrivelled, and often show extensive rotting of the roots. This is typical damping off as commonly understood. As a result of pre and post-emergence damping off, the crop may be sparse and poor, with scattered dead plants, or increasingly large bare patches may appear in the seedbed. At a later stage, a third form of damage may occur, when older, more woody seedlings and transplants do not collapse and show symptoms of damping off, but as a result of *root rot* may be stunted and sometimes killed (Warcup, 1952; Buxton *et al.*, 1962). Thus damping off and succeeding root rot may reduce both the numbers and size of the plants.

Most of the work done in Britain on damping off and nursery root rot has been done on conifers, and was reviewed by Griffin (1965), who found that in Sitka spruce (on which most of the studies described have been carried out) in unfavourable circumstances damping off may cause losses of up to 50 per cent of the plants, though they are more often of the order of 5 per cent or less.

Species of *Pythium* appear to be the main cause of damping off in nurseries in Great Britain (Warcup, 1952; Griffin, 1955; Buxton *et al.*, 1962; Salt, 1964, 1965). Buxton *et al.* isolated *Pythium* spp. mainly from damped off plants, and found them common on roots in the early part of the season. They began to disappear in July, and had gone by October. Salt (1964, 1965) found *Pythium* spp. early in the season, and in some experiments they killed all seedlings before emergence. The most important species are *P. ultimum* and *P. debaryanum* (Warcup, 1952), but *P. irregulare* and *P. mammilatum* may also cause damage on acid soils (Ram Reddy *et al.*, 1964). These fungi are commonly present in nursery soils, but have rarely if ever been isolated from seed, though Buxton *et al.* (1962) obtained indirect evidence that they might be seedborne, but were not revealed by normal isolation methods.

The cause of the later root damage and stunting are not fully understood, and appear to be complex. Griffin (1965) found three types of root damage. In one he found extensive root injury on immature tissues from which he was able to isolate pathogenic *Pythium* spp., and above which new healthy lateral roots were sometimes produced. In another, only the root tips were affected, and no pathogens could be isolated. These types occurred on heavy soils. On light soils in one nursery, the plants showed an extensive browning of the root cortex, only a small white root tip being left unaffected. Here the damage appeared to be caused by ectoparasitic eelworms. He considered that much of the damage on the heavy soils was due to adverse physical conditions. Experiments made by Vámos (1954) in Hungary support this view. Buxton *et al.* (1962) also studied plants showing leaf browning and root rot, and others showing only stunting. They found that the browning, seen mainly in July and August, was caused mostly by *Fusarium* spp., especially *F. oxysporum*. The leaf tips first became yellow, and eventually the whole plant became brown, while the root cortex became brown and eventually black; the cortex finally sloughed off, leaving the vascular cylinder, which then also turned brown, sometimes with bright red patches. In those cases in which only stunting occurred, the damage became progressively worse as the season advanced, though the affected plants remained green and their roots usually showed no lesions. It appeared that some isolates of *F. oxysporum* and *F. roseum* could cause stunting without other symptoms, but the cause of much of this stunting was obscure, and seemed to be unrelated to earlier damping off or browning. Similarly, Ram Reddy *et al.* (1964) found evidence that the cause of the stunting might be different in different nurseries. Salt (1965) carried out pathogenicity tests with isolates of *F. oxysporum, F. solani, F. sambucinum* and *Cylindrocarpon radicicola,* using seedlings in pots, and found these fungi capable of killing many of the plants after emergence.

Observations suggest that damping off is more common in Britain in heavy than in lighter soils. It is also much more frequent in old nurseries than in more newly established ones (Griffin, 1956, 1957), and is more commonly found in relatively alkaline nurseries than in those with a more acid soil reaction. Thus Warcup (1952, 1953) found that *Pythium ultimum*, one of the most important damping off fungi, was abundant in soil from three alkaline nurseries whose soil reaction ranged from 6.8 to 7.7, but rare or absent from soil with a pH of 5.3 to 5.5 from two acid ones. Similarly Griffin (1955, 1956, 1957) found damping off in the more alkaline of the nurseries he studied, but not in two with acid soils of pH 4. In experiments with *Pythium ultimum*, he found acid heathland soils did not favour the development of damping off. Ram Reddy *et al.* (1964), however, found damping off associated with *P. irregulare* and *P. mammilatum* in one acid nursery.

Information on susceptibility of tree species to damping off is rather scanty, though most species are known to be affected to some degree. Thus Griffin (1965) found damping off in Scots, Corsican and lodgepole pines, Sitka spruce, western hemlock, Douglas fir, Japanese larch and beech, but members of the Cupressaceae, including western red cedar and Lawson cypress, appeared to be resistant. These findings agree with those of Hartley (1921).

No detailed studies have been made of damping off in nursery beds of broad-leaved trees in Britain. The so-called damping off or seedling blight of beech, caused by *Phytophthora cactorum*, has sometimes been seen in nurseries and also on naturally occurring seedlings in the forest. It is dealt with further in chapter 11.

From the above, it will be seen that damping off is one of a complex of disorders, sometimes grouped together as 'soil sicknesss', and grading also into seedling and transplant root rot. Its control is dependent on individual circumstances, but its cause is not always easy to diagnose in practice. When siting nurseries, however, heavy and alkaline soils should be avoided, and alkaline grits should not be used as a covering for seedbeds. In nurseries in which damping off by fungi makes its appearance, steps may be taken against seedborne and soilborne organisms.

As an immediate step in affected beds, an emergency drench with captan may be tried, though chemical drenches have themselves sometimes been known to damage seedlings (Cram and Vaartaja, 1957).

Before resowing or replanting infested beds, further steps may be needed to protect the ensuing crop by means of seed dressings, or by soil fungicides or fumigants. Many chemicals (and also soil steaming) have been tested, though more often against 'soil sickness' in general than against damping off in particular. Hence their effectiveness has tended to vary greatly between nurseries and between seasons. Warcup (1951, 1952) and Faulkner and Holmes (1954) obtained excellent results with soil steaming, but this is expensive and difficult to use in the field. Therefore, most work has been concentrated on chemicals used on seed, or worked or watered into the soil.

Of the chemicals for use in the soil, those with a strong fumigant action have been found to be the most effective (Salt, 1964). The most useful are formaldehyde and chloropicrin, though in limited tests metham sodium and dazomet have also shown some promise (Ram Reddy *et al.,* 1964). Salt (1964, 1965) found in one season's experiments that while soil fumigants much increased plant growth, an additional seed treatment (with methoxyethyl mercury chloride) also increased the number of usable seedlings. In the following season, neither the mercury nor a thiram seed dressing produced any beneficial result. Neither soil nor seed treatments can be relied upon to give certain results. In nurseries in which damping off or 'soil sickness' are recurrent problems, tests with formaldehyde, metham sodium or dazomet, used over a small area, should be carried out. If a worthwhile improvement results, the treatment can be extended, and a seed treatment also tried.

GREY MOULD: *Botrytis cinerea* FR., STAT. CONID. OF *Sclerotinia fuckeliana* (DE BARY) FUCKEL, SYN. *Botryotinia fuckeliana* (DE BARY) WHETZEL

Grey mould, caused by *Botrytis cinerea*, has a very wide host range, occurring as both saprophyte and parasite on almost every plant of temperate regions, and causing severe damage to many horticultural crops. It may be found on trees both in the forest and the nursery, and in the cold store. A general account of the disease on forest trees is given by Pawsey (1964).

The causal fungus
On woody hosts the fungus produces a fine web of greyish or brownish mould (plate 4) with dense tufts of erect, branched conidiophores. The branches of the latter have inflated ends with minute sterigmata, each bearing subglobose or ovoid spores about 6.5-10 μm. The fungus also produces round or irregular black

sclerotia about 1 to 2 mm across. These are usually partly embedded in the host tissues. In Great Britain these sclerotia germinate to produce tufts of conidiophores, but elsewhere some strains have given rise to the stalked apothecia of *Sclerotinia fuckeliana* (Brooks, 1953). The fungus is a facultative parasite that readily colonises dead plant remains, and thence spreads to living plants. On these it often grows first as a saprophyte on dead leaves or lesions on stems caused, for example, by frost, by other fungi or similar agencies, and then in favourable conditions spreads to the living parts as an active parasite.

B. cinerea is able to grow over a very wide range of temperatures. In studies on a strain isolated from snow-smothered nursery stock, Hartley *et al.* (1919) found the fungus grew at 0 °C. A strain from *Cryptomeria japonica,* whose seedlings in Japanese nurseries are liable to mould damage under snow, grew from 1–31 °C, but not at 37 °C, and its optimum temperature was between 20 and 25 °C (Ito and Hosaka, 1951). Sato *et al.* (1959) found that the conidia germinated between 0 and 25 °C, with an optimum between 15 and 20 °C. The mycelium survived several days exposed to -7 °C, and conidia were produced under snow. It is this ability to grow at low temperatures that enables the fungus to damage plants under snow cover and in cold stores (Sato *et al.,* 1959; de Haas and Wennemuth, 1962).

Losses caused
Occasionally *B. cinerea* causes a dieback of trees in plantations, affecting the young developing twigs (Zycha, 1961/2).

In Great Britain, damage to trees is mainly confined to plants in nursery seedbeds, and even in these, attacks are sporadic. Hence the fungus rather rarely causes heavy losses, though it does give trouble in some years in a few nurseries, and Peace (1962) mentions that on occasions it has destroyed half the seedlings of Sitka spruce in some beds, and almost all those of very susceptible species such as *Sequoia* and *Cupressus.*

Important tree hosts in Great Britain
All the common conifers are known to be susceptible, though some are more often affected than others. There is no doubt that seedlings of *Sequoia* are very liable to damage, and in Great Britain more cases are recorded on this genus than on any other, in spite of the fact that it is little grown. Many attacks are also recorded on Sitka spruce, though this is probably rather because of the large nursery area under this species than because of its absolute susceptibility. Damage in recent years has also occurred in beds of Norway spruce, Japanese larch, western hemlock, Douglas fir, Scots, Corsican and lodgepole pines, grand fir, *Cupressus* spp. and *Cryptomeria japonica.* Seedlings of hardwoods may also be attacked.

Effect of age of host
Most of the damage affects young nursery stock, particularly in the summer,

autumn and winter of the first year, after which the plants become more woody and less susceptible. Transplants are seldom affected. Thus Jamalainen (1961), working in Finland, found it easier to infect one-year-old than two-year-old pine and spruce plants. Similarly, Sato *et al.* (1959) in Japan found one-year-old plants of 'Sugi' (*Cryptomeria japonica*) more susceptible than older ones.

Symptoms of disease

The symptoms on conifer seedlings commonly show as a top dieback, with a yellowing and later browning of the needles, which become covered with mycelium and conidiophores. Some of the leaves may fall, but many remain hanging on the shoots, and the black sclerotia of the fungus may develop on them. The shoots become twisted, flaccid and downward bent. Because of the loss of their tops, affected plants become bushy through the growth of side shoots from below. In some species, especially in western hemlock, and sometimes also in Japanese larch and lodgepole pine (Peace, 1962), attack may be lower down, the fungus in the seedbed spreading from the dead leaves killed by mutual shading of the plants.

On seedlings of broadleaved trees, necrotic patches occur on the leaves, and the tops of the plants wither. The characteristic grey mould develops on the damaged areas. On larger plants, dieback of shoots may take place.

When the disease affects forest trees in plantations, it attacks the young shoot tips, or if it causes lesions lower down it may girdle the young shoots, and cause secondary wilting and death of their ends (Zycha, 1961/2). Such symptoms are not easy to separate from those caused by late frosts, particularly as shoot tips damaged by frost are often later colonised by *B. cinerea* in damp weather. Dieback of this kind is unusual in Great Britain. Affected trees usually soon recover, and in a few years show no further signs of damage.

Factors affecting the disease

There is little firmly based information on conditions favouring infection and spread in forest crops, though factors usually considered important are frost damage, wet weather or generally high humidity, density of the stand, and what are vaguely called 'adverse conditions'. Little work has been done in Great Britain, but Murray (1962*a*) in studies in a number of nurseries, was unable to find any correlation between outbreaks of grey mould in seedbeds and humidity figures in the nurseries concerned. Cases of grey mould in British nurseries reach their peak in warm, humid spells in July and August, however, and a second, smaller peak occurs in October, when damage by autumn frosts tends to affect unhardened plants.

Murray, in many of his experiments with fungicides, found it difficult to induce infection, and so did Halber (1963), who worked on Douglas fir in Oregon. Halber reached the opinion that attack took place only within a relatively narrow range of conditions, and that unseasonable freezing weather, high humidities, and density of stand all contributed to infection.

Sato *et al.* (1959) found evidence that a deficiency of phosphorus and potash may render *Cryptomeria* seedlings under snow more susceptible to attack, and that this effect is enhanced if nitrogen is increased. They noted that autumn transplants were susceptible because they lost most of their root systems. On the other hand in experiments they found that root pruning seemed to impart resistance by controlling excessive late growth. Root damage as a possible predisposing factor was also suggested by Hartley *et al.* (1919).

Control

Attempts have been made to control the disease by means of fungicides, and some of these have been found to give control if applied early enough. Jamalainen (1961) in Finland found quintozene effective on pine and spruce seedlings, and zineb less so. In this country, some trials have been carried out with both quintozene and tecnazene, but neither gave any control. Magnani (1963), in experiments with several species of *Eucalyptus*, obtained control with captan. Murray (unpublished) in Great Britain tested a number of fungicides over several years. His best results were with thiram, though phenyl mercuric nitrate, griseofulvin and copper oxychloride were also effective.

Turning to chemicals other than fungicides, Japanese workers (Sato *et al.*, 1955; Sato *et al.*, 1959) controlled root growth if they treated *Cryptomeria* seedlings with the growth regulator maleic hydrazide, and found they thereby increased resistance to *B. cinerea*.

It is difficult to lay down a spray programme against *B. cinerea* in forest nurseries because outbreaks of the disease are so sporadic, and usually on most species do not cause major loss. In the case of the very susceptible genera, such as *Sequoia* and *Cupressus,* routine spraying with thiram in late summer and autumn may be necessary. Apart from this, on those nurseries in which the disease is known to be troublesome, sowing densities may be reduced to produce a more open stand, and special care should be taken to protect the plants from autumn frosts. Only the minimum shading necessary to do this should be applied, however, or the humidity of the beds may be raised, and conditions made very favourable for the fungus. If any signs of the disease are seen, the beds should be sprayed with thiram.

Pestalotia SPP. ON CONIFERS

Two species of *Pestalotia, P. funerea* Desm. and *P. hartigii* Tubeuf, have been associated with diseased conifers. The first is common on moribund leaves and twigs of trees, the second occurs on seedlings with the so-called strangling disease. At most, neither seems to be more than a weak wound parasite. They are described and discussed by Guba (1961).

The spores of *P. funerea* are five-celled, the three inner cells brown, the end cells colourless, one of them prolonged into one, the other into three or four (sometimes up to six) appendages (figure 6). They measure 21–29 x 7–9.5 μm.

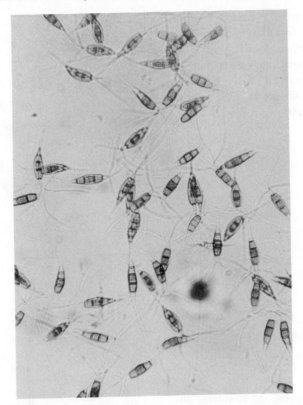

Figure 6. Spores of *Pestalotia funerea* from a culture on malt agar (Forestry Commission)

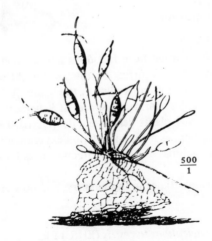

Figure 7. Spores of *Pestalotia hartigii* (K.F. Tubeuf)

The spores of *P. hartigii* are four-celled, the two middle cells brown, the end cells colourless, the apical cell prolonged into one to four appendages or into one branching appendage (figure 7). They measure 18-20 x 6 μm.

Figure 8 (opposite). Strangling disease on Norway spruce: young spruce infected near ground level by *Pestalotia hartigii*, and showing the characteristic stem swelling above the girdled zone (K.F. Tubeuf)

As noted above, *P. hartigii* has been found on nursery plants with strangling disease, a disorder most often occurring on the spruces. Affected seedlings are typically girdled at the base, with a swelling of the tissues just above the girdled zone (figure 8). Black pustules bearing the spores of *P. hartigii* are present on the diseased tissues. The affected plants yellow and die (Hartig, 1894). The cause of strangling disease is uncertain, as many inoculation experiments have shown only that the fungus may sometimes in adverse circumstances be induced to attack wounded plants.

These fungi are of no importance in this country, and no steps are needed here for their control.

SMOTHER FUNGUS: *Thelephora terrestris* (EHR.) FR.

The basidiomycete *Thelephora terrestris* is common on the soil surface in forests, and may often be found in nurseries on heathy land. It produces clusters of chocolate-brown fan-shaped fruit bodies, the tops of which are covered by radiating fibrils (plate 13). Its dark brown, angular, warty spores measure 8-9 x 6-7.5 μm (Wakefield and Dennis, 1950).

The fungus is not parasitic, but in nurseries it may grow so vigorously around the young plants that they are completely enveloped, smothered and killed (Hartig, 1894; Cunningham, 1957). Older plants may be so closely fastened together by its growth that it is difficult to separate them without causing damage (Peace, 1962). It rarely causes significant losses, and no steps for its control have been elaborated. Soil disturbance and removal of fruit bodies when weeding are likely to discourage its growth.

POST-NURSERY DISEASES

DISEASES OF SHOOTS AND STEMS

Diseases caused by *Nectria cinnabarina* (Fr.) Fr. and *N. galligena* Bres.

Some species of *Nectria* have little or no pathogenic significance. Some, like *N. ditissima*, almost confined to *Fagus*, and *N. desmazierii* on *Buxus* attack only one or very few hosts, under which they are considered here. *N. coccinea* has a rather wide host range, but is most important on *Fagus* (under which it is therefore described) as the cause of beech bark disease. It also causes cankers on *Acer* and *Populus*, and has been found on *Alnus, Carpinus, Ilex, Morus, Quercus, Rhamnus, Sambucus, Taxus* and *Ulmus* (Booth, 1959). Two species of *Nectria*, however, are particularly well known as the causes of disease on a wide range of host trees. The first of these is *N. cinnabarina*, the coral spot fungus, which causes a dieback on many woody plants. The second is *N. galligena*, which causes canker of apples and pears, and a somewhat similar canker of many broadleaved forest trees. These and other species of *Nectria* have been discussed and described by Booth (1959), and Perrin (1976) has recently published a key to the European species of the genus.

Coral spot caused by *Nectria cinnabarina* (Tode ex Fr.) Fr. (stat. conid. *Tubercularia vulgaris* Tode)

Nectria cinnabarina is a saprophytic fungus of worldwide distribution that sometimes invades living tissues as a facultative parasite. It then causes a dieback and bark necrosis in a large number of woody hosts.

It produces numerous pink, cushion-shaped conidial pustules usually up to about 1 mm across that burst through the host bark on dead and dying branches or main stems. The surface of each pustule becomes covered by a pink layer of elliptical conidia that each measure 5-7 x 2-3 μm. Later, usually in the spring, more or less globular red perithecia, up to about 0.5 mm across, arise either round the edges of the conidial pustules or on separate stromata (plate 14). The perithecia contain cylindrical to clavate eight-spored asci with thin apices. The two-celled, colourless ascospores measure 12–20 x 4.5–6.5 μm (Booth, 1959).

Optimum temperature for the growth of the fungus on agar is about 22.5 °C (van Vloten, 1943). The conidia need abundant moisture for germination, and the optimum temperature for germination is 18–20 °C (Mangin, 1894). Jørgensen (1952) and Booth (1959) found little evidence of host specialisation, though isolates vary in virulence (van Vloten, 1943; Uri, 1948; Schipper and Heybroek, 1957).

N. cinnabarina may attack by spreading from dead to living tissues, often passing in this way from small branches that have died back (Anon, 1969). It also commonly enters through wounds, including those caused by pruning, storm damage, frost and perhaps by insects (Jørgensen, 1952). Its spores may be carried on pruning tools (Uri, 1948).

It may cause dieback by growing down from wounds caused by pruning or hedge clipping, or upwards from wounds lower down. If growth is downwards from a dead stub into a larger branch or main stem, an eccentric dead area of bark develops round the stub base. Fruit bodies arise in large numbers on the dead bark. Inside affected plants, the wood may turn brown, or green (in *Acer* spp.), or violet (in *Fraxinus* spp.) (Jørgensen, 1952).

N. cinnabarina may occur on almost any broadleaved woody host, and Jørgensen (1952) lists over 100 species on which it has been found in Denmark. On trees in Great Britain it is common especially on elms and *Acer* spp., and it is found fairly frequently also on beech hedges.

Within tree genera, species differ in their susceptibility. Thus Uri (1948) found sycamore very susceptible, field maple less so, and *Acer negundo* immune to attack. In Holland, among the elms, the cultivar 'Christine Buisman', bred for resistance to Dutch elm disease (*Ceratocystis ulmi*), was found to be severely damaged by coral spot (Schipper and Heybroek, 1957).

In Great Britain, coral spot is rarely of more than minor importance, and no special steps are taken to control it on trees. Elsewhere, particularly in Holland, very detailed recommendations for its prevention and control have been put forward. They include repeated spraying with Bordeaux mixture, the cutting out of diseased tissue, the treatment of wounds with carbolineum and then with tar, and the removal and burning of plant debris (Spierenberg, 1937; Jørgensen, 1952). Such methods could be applied only to especially valuable trees in parks, gardens and arboreta.

Cankers on broadleaved trees caused by *Nectria galligena* Bres. (stat. conid. *Cylidrocarpon mali* (Allesch.) Wr.)

Nectria galligena is known in orchards in western Europe, parts of Asia, South Africa, North America, Chile, Argentina and Uruguay, New Zealand, and perhaps Tasmania, as a cause of canker of apples and pears (Anon, 1973). Apple canker has been reviewed by Swinburne (1975). To the forester, particularly in western

Europe and parts of eastern North America, it is also familiar as the cause of a canker of many broadleaved forest trees.

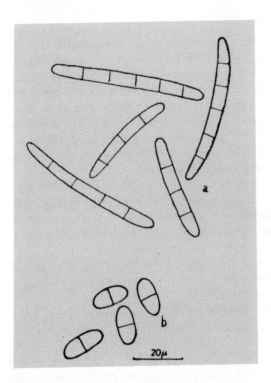

Figure 9. (a) Conidia and (b) ascospores of *Nectria galligena* (H. Wormald)

The bright red, ovate or globose perithecia of the fungus measure from 250–350 μm across, and are scattered or in small or large groups. Their club-shaped, thin-walled asci measure 75–95 x 12-15 μm, and each contains eight ascospores. These are colourless and two-celled, varying in shape from oval or ellipsoid to spindle-shaped (figure 9). They measure 14-22 x 6-9 μm. The conidia of the imperfect stage (*Cylindrocarpon mali*) form on small white pustules, and are cylindrical, slightly curved and narrow at each end (figure 9). They measure 55-65 x 5-6 μm (Booth, 1959).

N. galligena is active at very low temperatures. Small numbers of ascospores may be released and sometimes germinate at air temperatures of about 0 °C, though the optimum temperature for release is between 21 and 26.5 °C (Lortie and Kuntz, 1963; Lortie, 1964). Vegetative mycelium grows slowly at 2 °C (Munson, 1939). Different strains of the fungus vary in pathogenicity, but all have a wide host range, and most workers have found little evidence of host specificity (Lohman and Watson, 1943). In Northern Ireland, however, Flack and Swinburne (1977) found evidence that the fungus from typical ash cankers had a somewhat different host range from that from typical cankers on apple and pear, though both forms had a wide host range with many hosts in common.

Symptoms   Characteristically, the fungus causes concentric, target cankers on stems and branches. The cankers often form round branch stubs, though they may also develop around other entry points open to the fungus. Their concentric form is due to their periodic growth; the fungus grows and kills the bark in the autumn and winter, but is overgrown by host callus in spring and summer.

The symptoms show first as dark reddish-brown or black water-soaked spots around the point of entry. The canker develops to become a tumour-like swelling, and the surface bark then cracks and is then usually shed. According to Zeller and Owens (1921), however, cankers on apple and pear in Oregon and California in the USA almost always remain closed.

The mature target-like cankers are sunken and become oval or elongated up and down the stem for as much as several feet. Laterally their size is limited by the diameter of the host branch or stem, though the host tissues swell at the point of canker formation, probably because *N. galligena* produces growth-promoting substances (Lortie, 1964).

The fungus may also cause an eye rot of the fruit of apples and pears; it finally grows from the eye into the whole fruit, which eventually becomes mummified (Wormald, 1955).

Small conidial pustules and, later, small groups of red perithecia, form on the edges of the cankers and on affected fruits.

Spore production and host infection   As noted above, *N. galligena* is active at low temperatures. Its ascospores may be dispersed all through the year, and various workers have found large differences in the times of maximum discharge. Thus Lortie and Kuntz (1962, 1963) found that on hardwoods in Quebec the conidia were produced in greatest numbers in May and June, and production then quickly fell off to a minimum in August. They found that the conidial stromata later produced perithecia. These then shed ascospores at any time when the temperature rose to 0 °C or more, though the peak discharge was in August and September. The peak period in France and Germany is at about the same time, in summer and autumn (Swinburne, 1975). In Britain, Munson (1939) found that the ascospore discharge reached a maximum in February, and fell until September, and it then rose rapidly in October and November, whereas Cayley (1921) found a maximum in spring. Swinburne (1975) in Northern Ireland found a maximum in spring and early summer, and a second minor peak in the autumn. It is likely that the time of greatest discharge is much affected by local climate and weather.

The fungus may enter and establish itself through any opening that allows access to the living inner bark or cambium (Ashcroft, 1934; Brandt, 1964). Entry may be through lenticels and leaf scars, round branch stubs and dead buds, and through wounds caused by insects, weather damage by sun, frost, snow and hail, and by pruning (Marsh 1939; Brandt, 1964). *N. galligena* may also enter through openings caused by other fungi (Zeller and Owens, 1921), notably the scab fungus *Venturia inaequalis.* Wiltshire (1921) in Great Britain found that the fungus entered mainly through small cracks that appeared in the leaf scars in autumn and again in the following spring.

It was at this time, too, in October and March, that Marsh (1939) found apples in Britain were most readily infected in his inoculation experiments. Winter inoculations were much less effective. Lortie (1969), who studied the canker on hardwoods in Quebec, similarly found that inoculations made in winter from December to March were less successful than those at other times of the year. On apples in Northern Ireland, Swinburne *et al.* (1975) found that most infection took place between April and August.

Host range and susceptibility   In apple and pear, cultivars vary in their susceptibility to canker. Thus among the well-known eating and cooking apples in Britain, Cox's Orange Pippin, James Grieve and Worcester Pearmain are very susceptible, but Bramley's Seedling, and Lane's Prince Albert are more resistant. Cider apples also vary, and among these, Ellis Bitter, Royal Wilding and Silver Cup are highly resistant. Among the pears, Fertility and Marie Louise are very susceptible (Wormald, 1955).

In France, Bulit (1957) found that several local and Canadian varieties were attacked, other varieties such as Golden Delicious were less affected, and a few others, including Boskoop and La Nationale, were resistant.

In Chile, Vergara Castillo (1953) found resistance in some apple varieties, including White Water Pearmain, and the wild apple Hoover, which, however, can be used only as stock.

Such information must be used with caution, as varieties apparently resistant in one area may be found susceptible in another (Swinburne, 1975).

Information on broadleaved forest trees is less detailed, comparisons being mainly between genera and species, especially from studies in the USA and Canada. Almost all broadleaved trees may be attacked. Those most affected in North America are maples, birches, American beech, poplars and oaks (Ashcroft, 1934; Brandt, 1964; Lortie, 1969). Willows may also be attacked (Zalesky, 1968), while hickory, ash, elm and black cherry are less affected (Grant, 1937; Brandt, 1964). In Europe, Nectria cankers have been described on poplar, hawthorn, beech, ash and willow (Liese, 1931; Mooi, 1948; Booth, 1959; Flack and Swinburne, 1977).

Factors affecting the disease   Factors affecting the incidence of canker are many, and they are not fully understood.

In apple and pear, infection and development are encouraged by damp weather, impeded drainage, the presence of leaf scars, pruning wounds, and wounds made by ice and snow, over-close planting, infestation by insects such as woolly aphids, and damage by other fungi, especially scab (*Venturia inaequalis*) (Vergara

Castillo, 1953; Swinburne, 1975). Broadly similar factors affect the disease in broadleaved forest stands. In New England, Grant (1937) found cankers especially on exposed slopes at high elevations, while Brandt (1964) notes that at lower elevations they are commonest in cold pockets with poorly drained soil, and where trees have been damaged by wind, ice and snow. In forest trees, vigour may be important, the most vigorous trees recovering from canker damage (Nelson, 1940). On the other hand in apple orchards, trees with soft, vigorous growth tend to be especially prone to cankers (Swinburne, 1975).

Losses caused   On apples and pears, badly affected orchards are unprofitable, and losses through eye rot may sometimes be severe (Wormald, 1955). In the case of broadleaved forest trees, the fungus causes loss mainly by stunting growth and reducing the number of saleable trees of good form. Cankers may also allow the entry of rot fungi, and by weakening the wood give rise to breakage in the crown or main stem (Grant, 1937; Brandt, 1964).

Control   Much work has been done on the control of Nectria canker in apple and pear orchards, in which the value of the crop justifies substantial expenditure. The danger of canker can be reduced by the growing of the less susceptible varieties, by the grassing down of orchards to reduce soft, over-vigorous growth, and by the drainage of wet sites (Anon, 1971). Where canker occurs, the most effective method of control is to remove inoculum by pruning and cutting out all cankered wood (Swinburne, 1975). This is possible, however, only in the case of occasional ornamental trees and in small plantations or in orchards with only a small number of infected trees.

Various paints (the most effective based on mercury compounds and phenyl-phenol) have been formulated for use on individual cankers, but these again can be used only on a relatively small scale.

In commercial orchards of any size, therefore, control is mainly by the use of fungicidal sprays to prevent the sporulation of the fungus on the cankers and so prevent its further spread. These fungicides also control scab (*Venturia inaequalis*) which itself causes cracks that assist the entry of *N. galligena.*

Many fungicides have been used to control canker. They have generally been applied most effectively during the major infection periods. Hence in southeast England, they have been used especially in autumn (to protect fresh leaf scars) and again in spring (to prevent infection through the cracks that then develop in leaf scars and elsewhere). Good results have been obtained with organomercurial compounds, particularly phenyl mercury nitrate (PMN). More recently, in Northern Ireland, trials with carbendazim have suggested that this chemical need be applied only in autumn, when it reduces sporulation on cankers throughout the ensuing year (Swinburne, 1975).

Efforts to eradicate cankers on the wood, or to prevent sporulation on them, also prevent or reduce fruit infection. Fruit rotting may also be controlled by spraying before harvesting with a fungicide such as benomyl, captan or dinocap, or dipping freshly harvested fruit in benomyl (Swinburne, 1975).

In forest stands, chemical control of canker is impracticable. In badly affected stands in North America, it may be necessary to replace with conifers (Spaulding, 1938). Otherwise, canker-free trees should be selected to make the final crop, and the cankered trees should be removed and utilised when thinning (Roth and Hepting, 1954). As the stand increases in age, the number of new canker infections falls off sharply, and the trees in the final crop generally remain free from infection.

Phomopsis disease of conifers caused by *Phacidiopycnis pseudotsugae* (Wilson) Hahn (*Phomopsis pseudotsugae* Wilson, stat. conid. of *Phacidiella coniferarum* Hahn, syn. *Potebniamyces coniferarum* (Hahn) Smerlis).

The dieback and canker of conifers caused by the fungus first described as *Phomopsis pseudotsugae* (Wilson, 1920) is known in Great Britain, much of the rest of Western Europe, the Pacific northwest of the USA, and in New Zealand (Anon, 1968*a*).

The causal fungus   The fungus is usually found only in its pycnidial state, though a perfect stage also occurs (Hahn, 1957; Gremmen, 1959; Smerlis, 1962). The imperfect stage is not a true *Phomopsis*, and has been renamed *Phacidiopycnis pseudotsugae* (Hahn, 1957). Its one or many-chambered pycnidia grow in the bark, their apices protruding. They measure about 0.3-1 mm in diameter, and contain colourless, one-celled, fusiform spores measuring $4.5-8.5 \times 2-4 \mu m$ (Wilson and Hahn, 1928). In damp weather the spores exude as white tendrils. The same organism is known as a blue-stain fungus of pine and spruce logs under the name of *Discula pinicola* (Naumov) Petr. (*Ligniella pinicola* Naumov) (Robak, 1952).

The rarely found perfect stage forms black, disc-shaped ascocarps embedded in black stromata that develop under the bark but are later erumpent. The asci are cylindrical club-shaped, $80-135 \times 8-12 \mu m$, and contain eight colourless, one-celled elliptical or fusiform ascospores measuring $10-19 \times 3-6 \mu m$. Filamentous paraphyses occur between the asci (Hahn, 1957). The perfect stage was called *Phacidiella coniferarum* by Hahn (1957), but has since been renamed *Potebniamyces coniferarum* (Smerlis, 1962).

In culture it grows at the rate of about 5 mm per day at 25 °C, and produces pycnospores in stromata within about 3 weeks to a month. With age the mycelium turns dark olive (Gross and Weidensaul, 1967).

Mode of entry   *Phacidiopycnis pseudotsugae* is a rather weak wound parasite (van Vloten, 1952; Hahn, 1957; Gross and Weidersaul, 1967). It enters through wounds made when pruning and brashing, and occasionally those made in extraction. Its mode of attack on nursery and other small plants has not been studied, but it may perhaps enter these through leaf scars, and wounds made during cultivation and handling. Plasman (1953) suggested that in Belgium it attacked Douglas fir following frost damage.

Abundant evidence from inoculation experiments has shown that except in rare instances it can invade wounded tissues only in the dormant season.

Host range and susceptibility   In Great Britain, Phomopsis disease has been found mainly on Douglas fir, but has sometimes been known to affect Japanese larch, and occasionally also other conifers, including European larch, *Abies grandis, A. alba (A. pectinata), Cedrus atlantica* and *C. libani*, and *Tsuga alterbiana* and *T. sieboldi* (Anon, 1951; Wilson, 1925; Wilson and Hahn, 1928). Elsewhere it occurs also on pines (Hahn, 1957), on *Larix occidentalis* (Wicker, 1965), and on *Tsuga canadensis* (Gross and Weidensaul, 1967).

Of the three forms (or subspecies) of Douglas fir, the green coastal form generally appears to be more susceptible than the blue and intermediate ones (Gerlings, 1939; Hahn, 1957).

Symptoms   The symptoms of Phomopsis disease vary somewhat with the host species. On Douglas fir in Great Britain the fungus causes dieback of shoots, girdles young stems, and produces stem cankers on older trees (Anon, 1951). When leading and lateral shoots are attacked, they may die back for up to about 30 cm. Their outer tissues die, and are cut off by a cork layer from the healthy parts of the shoot below, so that the shoot suddenly narrows at the junction between the diseased tissues with the healthy, still growing part of the stem.

If the fungus succeeds in spreading down from a lateral shoot into the main stem, the latter may be girdled. The girdled zone, which may be up to about 15 cm long, then remains constricted at first, with wider healthy tissue both above and below it, until in time the stem above it also dies.

Stem cankers, found on older trees, may arise around the sites of wounds or after the passage of the fungus down a lateral shoot. Growth of the fungal mycelium is limited, and results in oval cankers up to about 15 cm long by 7.5 cm wide. The diseased bark is quickly killed, and is eventually forced off by callusing around its edges. Continued growth of the callus tissue results in the final healing of the canker.

The pycnidia of the fungus are commonly found in the bark of the dead tissues, but often they are accompanied by the fructifications of other fungi (Hahn, 1957).

On Japanese larch *P. pseudotsugae* causes cankers on stems and branches (Wilson, 1921; Anon, 1951; Hahn, 1957). The cankers may be larger than those on Douglas fir, and are often resinous round their edges. Cracks appear in the affected bark, and healing is usually slow, the diseased tissues remaining on the tree. On Western larch (*Larix occidentalis*) in the USA, Wicker (1965) described the disease as 'carrot top', because it turned the tops of the crowns of young trees bright yellow some 6 to 8 weeks before their normal autumn colour change.

Dieback of shoots occurs mainly in nurseries and young plantations not long planted out, but the stem canker form of the disease is found in older trees from about 5 to 25 years old, particularly on 10 to 11-year-old trees in the pole stage (Wilson, 1925; Anon, 1951; Hahn, 1957).

Losses caused   It is rare for Phomopsis disease to cause serious damage in Great Britain. Occasional severe losses have been known to occur locally through die-back of leading shoots of nursery transplants and in young plantation trees up to eight years old (Anon, 1951). Young Douglas fir may die if extensive dieback of the leaders takes place, and those that survive often show a bushy growth (Wilson, 1925; Hahn, 1957). Wilson (1925) found some 6 to 10-year-old plantations in which about half the trees were lost. After beating up, 20 per cent of the plants were still affected the following year. Cankers on older trees are not of major importance, though they may somewhat reduce the quality of the timber.

Control   To avoid the disease, nurseries in which Douglas fir or larch are to be grown should not be placed close to plantations of these trees, which may otherwise be a source of the fungus spores. If Phomopsis disease appears in the nursery, the affected plants should not be used for planting, but should be col-lected together and burnt. Similarly, if young plants are affected after planting out, the dead and diseased plants should be burnt before beating up, to avoid infection of the replacements in their turn.

In older trees, care should be taken when pruning to leave no stubs, and to prune and brash (especially in the case of Japanese larch) only in the active growing season when healing of wounds is rapid and infection rarely occurs. Extraction damage should also be guarded against.

WILT DISEASES

Verticillium wilt caused by *Verticillium dahliae* Kleb. and *V. albo-atrum* Reinke & Berthe.
Verticillium dahliae and *V. albo-atrum,* the most important of a number of *Verticillium* species causing wilt diseases, attack over 350 hosts, including more than 70 tree species and varieties, and many shrubs (Engelhard, 1957). They are widespread in all continents, especially in the more temperate areas (Anon, 1979a, b).

They are microfungi with erect conidiophores bearing whorls of branches that produce ovate-oblong, one-celled, colourless conidia at their ends (figure 10). The conidia accumulate in small droplets and measure $3-7 \times 1.5-3 \mu m$ (Brooks, 1953). The two species can be distinguished from one another only in culture, when *V. dahliae* produces minute black groups of cells called microsclerotia, whereas *V. albo-atrum* produces dark resting mycelium (Berkeley *et al.,* 1931; Isaac, 1949). Indeed, some prefer to regard them both as forms of *V. albo-atrum* (Ende, 1958), and they have rarely been differentiated from one another very carefully in records of wilt on trees. Their strains show little evidence of host specialisation, though they vary in pathogenicity (Donandt, 1932; Ende, 1958).

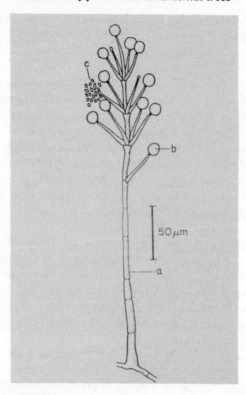

Figure 10.   *Verticillium albo-atrum*; condiophore (a) with conidia (c) in conidial
droplets (b) (J. H. Western, after Sewell)

Most of the isolates from trees in Britain (as well as in North America) are of
the microsclerotial type, and are here regarded as *V. dahliae*. In culture this
fungus will grow at 30 °C, whereas *V. albo-atrum* has a lower temperature maximum
for growth (Dochinger, 1956*a*; Caroselli, 1955*a*).

V. dahliae and *V. albo-atrum* are 'soil invading' fungi (Garrett, 1956*a*), and
spread by the contact of plant roots with the remains of previously infested root
material (Isaac, 1953; Ende, 1958). They may persist in soil infested in this way
for at least two years (Caroselli, 1954). There is also evidence that common weeds
such as groundsel (*Senecio vulgaris*) and black nightshade (*Solanum nigrum*) may
act as symptomless carriers (Ende, 1958; Matta and Kerling, 1964). In addition,
V. dahliae and *V. albo-atrum* may be wound parasites, transmitted from diseased
to healthy trees by tools such as saws, axes and increment borers (Dochinger,
1956*b*).

Symptoms   Within the plant, the fungus spreads in the sapwood, in which
mycelium and tyloses can be found (Dufrénoy and Dufrénoy, 1927). The diseased
sapwood becomes stained, and the colour of the stain varies somewhat with the

tree species. Thus the stain in *Acer* spp. (plate 27) is usually dark green, though it may be brownish or eventually turn black (Goidánich, 1932; Meer, 1926; Strong, 1936), and that in elm is brown. This staining is a helpful diagnostic feature, though it may be faint or absent in some species, and in large trees it may not occur throughout.

External symptoms are very variable, but they usually show as a wilting and yellowing of the leaves, followed by their premature fall. Death of branches may follow, and young trees often die within a year, and older ones become stag-headed (Gravatt, 1926; May and Gravatt, 1951) but may later recover, though sometimes only temporarily. Occasionally areas of bark may be killed, and a slime-flux ooze from the affected parts, from which the bark peels off (Gravatt, 1926). More commonly, however, no bark symptoms occur (Goidánich, 1934).

On maples and other *Acer* species (on which *V. dahliae* is a very important parasite), three forms of attack have been distinguished. The first is a *chronic wilt*. Progressive wilting of the foliage and crown die-back leads to death of the crown, usually within a few years, but sometimes within the season of infection. The second is an *acute wilt*, in which the foliage of the whole crown suddenly wilts and dies, generally in late summer, and hangs, dried and withered, on the tree after normal leaf fall. These forms of wilt have been described by Caroselli (1957). In the third form, described by Strong (1936), the trees are apparently healthy at the end of the season, but fail to flush in the following spring. All these forms of the disease have been observed in Britain by Pearce (1972).

Losses caused and affected species   Verticillium wilt is of no importance on forest trees in Britain but it is important as an occasional source of severe losses in nurseries raising susceptible stock such as *Acer* spp., especially the Norway maple (*A. platanoides*) and various Japanese maples. It will indeed attack a wide range of *Acer* spp. and varieties. Among other important amenity trees it is most common on *Catalpa* (in which it affects large mature trees as well as nursery stock), but the limes (*Tilia* spp.) and the sumachs (species of *Rhus* and *Cotinus*) are also very susceptible, and so is the golden rain tree (*Koelreuteria paniculata*). In the USA, the Judas tree (*Cercis siliquastrum*) is also often attacked. Recently in Britain Verticillium wilt has been found as the cause of wilt and finally the death of a young tree of *Nothofagus obliqua*. In Poland, it has caused heavy losses in oak seedlings (Lukomski, 1962).

Most information on relative susceptibility of various host trees is on trees of minor importance in Britain (Dochinger, 1956*a*; McKenzie, 1954). According to Holmes (1967), however, in the case of elms, those most resistant to wilt are also those most resistant to *Ceratocystis ulmi*.

A list of trees on which the disease has been found in Britain is given by Pearce and Gibbs (1981), who state that monocotyledonous plants and conifers are not affected, and that species of *Alnus*, *Betula*, *Carpinus*, *Fagus*, *Populus* and *Platanus* appear to be very resistant.

Factors affecting the disease   Caroselli (1955*b*, 1959) found that the severity of the disease was affected by soil moisture, and the amount of water in the sapwood, symptoms of wilt and the amount of sapwood staining both being increased in trees growing in dry soils, and in those with a low sapwood moisture level. Nitrogen levels also affect the progress of wilt. When nitrogen supplies are low, the fungus may remain in the stem bases, but when ample nitrogen is available, the vessels may be obstructed, and wilting and yellowing of the foliage may occur (Donandt, 1932). Sometimes, however, with increasing nitrogen additional growth of the tree may mask the external symptoms, and the increased extent of the vascular staining is then found only by cutting into the tissues (Dochinger, 1956*a*).

Control   Severely affected trees can only be removed and burnt (McKenzie, 1954). Attempts are sometimes made to prune out the diseased parts of slightly wilted plants, but as the fungus usually occurs widely throughout their tissues, they are often unsuccessful. Sometimes, however, if dead or wilted shoots are pruned out, the trees given fertiliser, and watered to keep the roots moist in dry weather, they may show some recovery, though the improvement is not always permanent (Strong, 1936). When pruning an infested stand, care should be taken to sterilise pruning tools when moving from tree to tree (Gravatt, 1926).

If a diseased tree has been removed and is to be replaced, one of a species or variety resistant to Verticillium wilt should be chosen.

Verticillium wilt is, however, most important as a disease of nursery stock, and a number of measures can be taken in nurseries to mitigate its effects.

In nursery beds in which Verticillium wilt has occurred, weeds should be kept down after the removal of the affected crop, and the beds either left fallow for several years, used for conifers or other resistant species (Lukomski, 1962), or treated with a soil fumigant such as chloropicrin (Wilhelm and Ferguson, 1953), metham sodium or dazomet. So far, attempts to control the disease within the plant by means of systemic fungicides such as benomyl have been only partially successful (Piearce, 1972). Growing in containers can be used to limit the disease in infested nurseries.

Fireblight caused by *Erwinia amylovora* (Burrill) Winslow

Fireblight, caused by *Erwinia amylovora,* has long been known in North America and New Zealand, and is now also widespread in northern Europe. It was first recorded in Europe in Kent, in 1957, and became established in much of southern Britain in spite of vigorous efforts to eradicate it. It has since spread to France, the Netherlands, Belgium, Germany, Denmark and Poland. A general account of the disease is given by Lelliott (1979). The causal bacterium and methods available for its isolation are described by Breed *et al.* (1948), Dowson (1957), Stapp (1961), Lelliott (1968) and Miller (1979).

E. amylovora is a gram-negative rod, measuring $0.7-1.0 \times 0.9-1.5 \mu m$, with peritrichous flagella. On meat infusion agar plates it forms convex opalescent colonies, often with white centres.

Fireblight is commercially important mainly as a disease of pome fruit trees, particularly of pears. It also affects many rosaceous ornamental trees and shrubs, and some native woodland and hedgerow trees of the same family, and these may become sources of infection to neighbouring fruit orchards.

Infection and symptoms   Primary infection takes place on the blossoms. On pears, these quickly wilt, and the bacteria spread to the shoots, which may also wilt, when the affected leaves turn dark brown or black. On very susceptible varieties (the worst affected of which is Laxton's Superb), infection quickly spreads in summer throughout the tree, which dies within six months of the initial attack.

After the killing of blossoms and leaves in summer, dark green or brown cankers develop on the branches, and from these, glistening whitish bacterial slime oozes in wet weather. The bacterium overwinters in these cankers. A reddish-brown discoloration is present in the inner bark and outer wood of the cankered areas. The brown leaves remain on affected branches after general leaf fall in autumn. So do diseased fruits, which shrivel and become dark brown or black.

In spring and summer the bacterial slime from the cankers is carried to the blossoms by insects and rain, and on the wind as dried particles, or attached to pollen grains. In Britain most infection has taken place not in the spring, when inoculum production and flowering do not usually coincide, but from mid-June to September, when on some pear varieties summer blossoming occurs when abundant inoculum is also present. Hence the frequency of infection of the variety Laxton's Superb, which produces much summer blossom.

The disease symptoms on apple are broadly similar to those on pear, but are generally less severe, and the bacterial droplets are golden yellow.

On affected hawthorn (*Crataegus* spp.) and whitebeam (*Sorbus aria*) leaves on some of the branches turn yellow, then brown, and then shrivel and fall (plate 54). In the case of the whitebeam, which is very susceptible, further rapid invasion takes place from the point of infection into the main branches and to the trunk, and the tree is commonly killed, as in the case of pear, within six months of the first attack.

Though *Sorbus aria* is so susceptible, *S. aucuparia* is more resistant, and *S. decora*, *S. intermedia* and *S. latifolia* seem to be immune under European conditions (Lelliott, 1979; Zeller, 1979). Some *Crataegus* spp. also show resistance, especially *C. coccinea* and *C. prunifolia* (Zeller, 1979).

Control   In Britain attempts at control of fireblight have concentrated mainly on the protection of fruit orchards by the destruction and replacement of the very susceptible pear variety Laxton's Superb, and the grubbing out or killing of adjacent infected hosts, especially hawthorn hedge plants. Infection of these hedge plants has also been much diminished by clipping, which reduces flowering.

Growers have also been recommended to break off secondary blossom, to remove beehives from orchards before the secondary blossom is formed (as bees may carry the causal bacteria), and to disinfect pruning tools with 3 per cent lysol between trees.

The most important measure when considering the growing of ornamental species of *Sorbus* or *Crataegus* in areas in which fireblight is prevalent is to select from among the known resistant species.

ROOT DISEASES

Phytophthora root diseases

There are at least five different species of *Phytophthora* which attack the roots of woody plants:

(1) *P. cambivora* (Petri) Buisman.
(2) *P. cinnamomi* Rands.
(3) *P. citricola* Sawada.
(4) *P. cryptogea* Pethybridge and Lafferty.
(5) *P. megasperma* var. *megasperma* (Drechsler) Waterhouse.

Other *Phytophthora* spp. have been found on trees though not necessarily on roots, including *P. cactorum* (Lebert and Cohn) Schroeter on horse chestnut (see Chapter 18) and beech seedlings (see Chapter 11) and *P. syringae* (Klebahn) Klebahn on apple. Ink disease of sweet chestnut, caused by *P. cinnamomi* is described in chapter 15.

Phytophthora root diseases, commonly and rather misleadingly called Phytophthora root rots and caused by the five species listed above, occur on a range of broadleaved and coniferous hosts in Britain (see table 3.1).

Table 3.1

Some tree species susceptible to Phytophthora root diseases
(after R. G. Strouts, 1981)

Acer spp.
Aesculus hippocastanum
Castanea sativa
Chamaecyparis lawsoniana
Eucalyptus spp.
Fagus sylvatica
Malus spp.
Nothofagus spp.
Prunus spp.
Taxus baccata
Tilia spp.

The taxonomy of *Phytophthora* spp. is a complex subject, largely because the methods of classification are based on morphological characters that do not clearly discriminate between species (Ribeiro, 1978). Only an outline of the principles of identification can be given here and the interested reader is referred elsewhere for detailed information (Newhook *et al.*, 1978; Waterhouse, 1963; Waterhouse, 1970).

The following features of the asexual spores are among those frequently used for identifying *Phytophthora* spp.

Sporangia
Caducity: sporangia separate readily from the sporangiophore.
l/b ratio: ratio of length of sporangium to breadth.
Papillae: presence or absence.
Sporangial shape: spherical, oval or elliptical.
Internal proliferation: the growth of a new sporangium within an old one.
Sexual spores
Amphigynous: antheridium growing into oogonial initials
  or
Paragynous: antheridium growing at the side of the oogonium.
Oogonium and oospore size and wall characters.
Heterothallic or homothallic reproduction.

There are many other characters including features of the hyphae, growth in culture, etc., which are used for detailed taxonomic studies.

Symptoms   The crown symptoms of Phytophthora root diseases are typical of root diseases in general (Strouts, 1981). In broadleaved species, leaves may be abnormally small, yellow or sparse over parts or all the crown. Some or all of the shoots growing in coppiced woodlands may exhibit similar symptoms, including sweet chestnut affected by ink disease. These symptoms may be followed by the ultimate death of the tree but in other cases trees may recover.

In conifers and especially in Lawson cypress, the foliage may lose its freshness or lustre and become drab, yellow and finally die.

Careful examination of the tree soon after the initial attack may reveal symptoms more specific to Phytophthora root diseases. Some or parts of the roots close to the main stem may be dead whereas more distal parts may be live, perhaps with dead areas of bark on them. *Phytophthora* spp. do not decay the roots of woody plants but kill the host tissues in the cambial region.

The dead bark may extend up the main stem for some centimetres or even metres on big trees in a characteristic strip or tongue-shaped lesion (plate 15). On some cultivars of Lawson cypress the strip of infected bark may extend to the base of a lower branch and this may also be killed. Although these lesions are indicative of Phytophthora root diseases they can also be caused by other factors such as lightning, bonfire or chemical injury and care must be taken to achieve a proper diagnosis.

Confirmation of the presence of *Phytophthora* spp. can only be obtained by culturing from recently infected tissues or (less conclusively) from the soil around infected roots. Isolation of the fungus from diseased material is notoriously difficult and a variety of techniques have been developed for the purpose. One of the best known techniques involves the use of apples, or other fruits as a bait (see, for example, Newhook, 1959). Infected material, either from the host or the soil is inserted into the apple and if *Phytophthora* spp. are present a firm rot develops in the tissues of the apple. The presence of *Phytophthora* spp. can be further substantiated by growing pieces of the infected apple tissue on a suitable medium such as potato dextrose agar. There has also been much research into the use of selective media for isolation of *Phytophthora* spp. and a number of antibiotics have proved useful (e.g., Tsao and Ocana, 1969).

Biology   Infection by Phytophthora root diseases is particularly favoured by wet and warm soil conditions. At these times large numbers of motile zoospores are released from the sporangia. The zoospores are chemically attracted to the elongation zone of young host rootlets where most infection is thought to occur (Zentmeyer, 1961). The sporangia and zoospores are relatively shortlived and it is the chlamydospores and perhaps oospores which play an important role in longer-term persistence in the soil. When suitable conditions occur the chlamydospores germinate and give rise to sporangia and zoospores. Oospores may act similarly though the proportion that germinate is often very low.

Long-distance transmission of Phytophthora root diseases can occur in drainage or irrigation water, through the transport of infected plants or in infested soil adhering to plants, vehicles, tools, footwear, etc.

These diseases are commonly found in water-retentive soils and in nurseries where very susceptible plants are grown year after year. They are also encouraged by the presence of farmyard manure and organic mulches. Low concentrations of oxygen and high concentrations of carbon dioxide produced under these conditions appear to encourage the production of zoospores.

Control   Phytophthora root diseases are difficult to control, but some measures can be taken to avoid or ameliorate them. Various methods of control in nurseries and ornamental plantings are available and these have been reviewed by Strouts (1981).

The key to the control of Phytophthora root diseases in the nursery is thorough sanitation. If an outbreak is identified in its early stages all infected plants should be destroyed and the soil sterilised. If infection is widespread it may be necessary to use only containerised material and to ensure that all planting stock and soil is clean. The containers should be isolated from infected soil by the use of raised gravel beds or standing areas over stout polythene sheeting. There are a few non-phytotoxic fungicides such as aluminium tris (ethylphosphonate), etridiazole and furalaxyl which have been developed for the control of Phytophthora root diseases. In the main, the effect of these chemicals is to suppress the production of zoospores rather than to eradicate the fungus and therefore repeated treatments with the chemical are necessary.

Control of Phytophthora root diseases in plantings of ornamental trees is largely a matter of proper site selection and aftercare. Water should not be allowed to collect around the base of woody plants, excessive irrigation or heavy applications of farmyard manure should be avoided. Livestock should not be permitted to congregate around susceptible species. Where sites are known to be infested by the disease, especially in hedge plantings, tolerant species such as Leyland cypress, western hemlock or *Chamaecyparis pisifera* cv. plumosa or cv. squarrosa can be used to replace the susceptible Lawson cypress.

Group dying of conifers caused by *Rhizina undulata* Fr. ex Fr. (*R. inflata* (Schaeff.) Quél.)

Rhizina undulata, one of the larger Ascomycetes, is sometimes known as the tea-break fungus because it grows on and round the edges of the sites of fires, many of which were at one time made by workers when brewing tea in their lunchtime breaks. It has long been known as the cause of Group dying in conifers (Hartig, 1894), and has been recorded in Great Britain (Brooks, 1910; Murray and Young, 1961), Ireland (McKay and Clear, 1953), France (Lanier, 1962), Denmark (Yde-Andersen, 1963), Finland (Laine, 1968), Holland (Gremmen, 1961) and other parts of Europe, and in the northwest and the east of the USA (Zeller, 1935; Davidson, 1935; Weir, 1915) and Canada (Ginns, 1968). A short account of Group dying is that by Phillips and Young (1976).

The causal fungus   The fruit bodies of *R. undulata* appear in June or later. Initially small, whitish and globular, they become disc shaped when about 6 mm in diameter, and deep chestnut-brown on the upper hymenial surface,

Figure 11.   Fruit bodies of *Rhizina undulata* growing on burnt ground under Scots pine trees. One fructification has been cut across to show the rootlike structures connecting the underside to the ground (D.H. Phillips)

with a creamy margin. They then develop into irregularly cushion-shaped bodies with hollow undersides connected to the ground by many thick, hollow, whitish, root-like structures (figure 11). The creamy margin of the brown fruit body disappears when growth is completed, by which time single fructifications are up to about 5 cm in diameter, and clusters may have fused in crust-like groups up to 25 cm long.

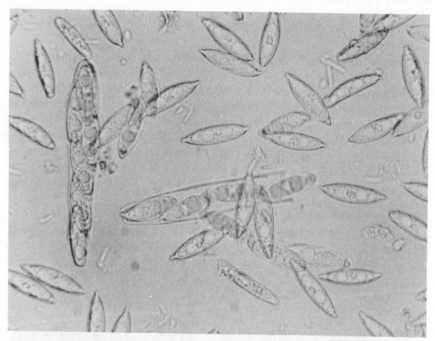

Figure 12. *Rhizina undulata:* asci and ascospores (Forestry Commission)

The asci measure about 400 x 20 μm, and contain colourless, fusiform ascospores measuring 22-40 x 8-11 μm (figure 12). They are separated by unbranched, colourless paraphyses (Dennis, 1968; Lange and Hora, 1963). The fruit bodies are annual, but old fructifications may persist until the following season, and are black or dark greenish, with a slimy surface (Ginns, 1968). Fruit bodies are common in warm summers, but not in cool ones (Murray and Young, 1961). The mycelium of the fungus bears clamp connections similar to those of Basidiomycetes.

R. undulata colonises the sites of fires made during thinning operations and those made to destroy lop and top when preparing for replanting after clear felling. Factors affecting the colonisation of fire sites were studied by Jalaluddin (1967*a*, *b*). From observations and the results of experiments Jalaluddin concluded that the fungus grew only on fire sites, and was able to colonise them only when they were made on acid soils, and when fresh conifer roots were present.

Colonisation followed the germination of ascospores, which could survive in the soil, small numbers persisting for as long as two years. The spores were stimulated to germinate by the heat of the fire, which, at its edges, heated the soil sufficiently in half an hour or more to cause germination but not to kill the spores. In Jalaluddin's laboratory experiments maximum germination occurred when the spores were heated to 37 °C for three days, followed by incubation at 22 °C. In agar culture, mycelial growth was most rapid at 25 °C, at a pH between 4.5 and 5.2, while growth at pH 7 was very slow. The rate of growth in the soil in East Anglia appeared unlikely to exceed 1 m/year.

Progress and symptoms of the disease   Epidemiology of Group dying in Great Britain was studied by Murray and Young (1961). Following colonisation of a fire site, the mycelium of the fungus ramifies outwards through the soil and attacks the roots of conifers with which it comes in contact. As a result, young newly planted trees may soon die. On pole-stage trees, the finer roots are quickly killed, and the larger roots become covered by a network of yellowish-white

Figure 13. Mycelium of *Rhizina undulata* on root of Sitka spruce, with infection cushions (arrowed) over the lenticels (Forestry Commission)

mycelium, which forms infection cushions over the lenticels (figure 13). As a reaction these fill with resin and appear white instead of their normal pink colour.

In spite of this, the fungus usually succeeds in entering, and invades the host tissues. Its progress may still be halted by the formation of a cork barrier, and a discrete rounded area of dead tissue surrounded by a dark line is then visible if the bark scales of the root are removed (figure 14). Often the mycelium advances unchecked, however, and many coalescing lesions form over the root surface, and the root soon dies. Longitudinal cracks can then often be found in the bark of

Figure 14. Lesions caused by *Rhizina undulata* on root of Sitka spruce; the bark scales have been removed (Forestry Commission)

the roots, and extensive areas of dead cortex can be found if the bark scales are stripped off.

The first symptoms seen on the tree, however, include prolific coning (which may occur from one to three years before the tree dies), and the enlargement of the lenticels on the trunk, with resin bleeding from the bark, and a thinning of the foliage (Murray and Young, 1961; McKay and Clear, 1953, 1955). The resin may exude as blobs on the bark, or sometimes a copious flow may run down the trunk, from a height of as much as 3 to 4 metres (10 to 12 feet) (McKay and Clear, 1955). Many needles may fall while still green, and complete loss of all the needles may occur suddenly in the middle of the growing season (Murray, 1953; McKay and Clear, 1955).

By the time such symptoms have become visible, however, extensive root death will have taken place. By the second year after the establishment of the fungus, the symptoms usually show on many trees close to the original fire site, and a few trees may already be dead. In favourable seasons, fruit bodies appear, sometimes on the fire site (often around fresh stumps), but commonly round its edges. The fungus advances through the soil in the manner of a fairy ring, and so fruit bodies appear in a wider and wider, complete or discontinuous circle in successive years, the central area within the ring becoming free of the fungus as it grows outwards into fresh soil. Extending rings may be partly checked by drainage ditches and similar excavations.

With time, more and more trees are killed, and individual groups may cover up to a quarter of an acre (0.1 ha). After about six years, further spread normally ceases, but groups established by *R. undulata* may later be greatly extended by windblow (Murray and Young, 1961).

Host range and age of attacked trees   *R. undulata* confines its attacks to conifers. In Great Britain it seems first to have been recorded as a cause of damage by Brooks (1910), who found it in East Anglia killing newly planted Scots and Corsican pine and European and Japanese larch. Jalaluddin (1967*a, b*) noted similar losses among newly planted trees in the same area, and found the killing of larger trees following thinning was unusual there. Deaths of young plants have also occurred in Holland (Gremmen, 1961), Finland (Laine, 1968), Sweden (Hagner, 1962), and in North America (Ginns, 1968). Davidson (1935) in Maryland, USA found the fungus killing red pines in nursery seedbeds.

In Great Britain, however, though as already noted *R. undulata* sometimes kills young plants after planting out in East Anglia (and occasionally elsewhere in the drier eastern parts of the country), this type of damage is rare, and the fungus has been important mainly as a killer of trees in the pole stage (chiefly between the ages of 22 and 32 years) in the wetter areas of the west (Murray and Young, 1961).

Group dying occurs there especially in Sitka spruce, in which it tends to be more severe than in other species, though it has also been found in Norway spruce, Scots, Corsican and lodgepole pines, and in European and Japanese larch. So far it has not been found in Douglas fir, though it has been known to kill seedlings (but not pole-stage trees) of this species in North America (Ginns, 1968). Hartig (1894), in Germany, also recorded the fungus in Douglas fir, and in *Abies alba, Tsuga mertensiana* and *Pinus strobus*, as well as on some of the species mentioned above.

Factors affecting Group dying Many of the factors affecting the development of Group dying, including its dependence on fires and the presence of fresh conifer roots, and its association with acid soils, have already been noted. The disease appears to be commoner on light, sandy soils and on peat than on the heavier mineral soils (Murray and Young, 1961).

Losses caused   In Great Britain, losses of young plants soon after planting out are uncommon and soon cease. Losses depend very much on the area of ground heated by the fires. Hence if lop and top is burnt on a few widely spaced 'spot' fires, losses remain small, but if burning is done in shallow drifts and a large area is heated, the risk of loss increases. This may be why Gremmen (1961) found that in young plantings in the Netherlands nearly all the young plants might sometimes be attacked. In older crops in Great Britain, most groups in pole-stage stands cover between about one tenth and a quarter of an acre (0.04–0.1 ha), and in groups about 30 yards (27 metres) in diameter, up to 100 trees may be killed, though losses of this order occur only in Sitka spruce (Murray and Young, 1961). On exposed sites, losses through attack by *R. undulata* may be followed by extensive windblow, which may eventually be more damaging than the fungus. Similarly, opening up of the crop, especially in the case of Norway spruce, may sometimes lead to excessive transpiration, needle fall, and death of trees previously damaged but not killed by the fungus.

Control   As *R. undulata* commonly grows on and outwards from the sites of fires, its activities in the forest can be prevented if no fires are lit in the plantations. If workers are allowed to light fires on rides or waste areas it is important to ensure that the fire sites are separated from the adjacent plantations by ditches or similar barriers, otherwise the fungus may grow out into the crops. It may perhaps also be possible to prevent the spread of newly established groups in the same way by trenching round them, but if ditches are not well maintained the fungus may succeed in crossing them.

Because the lighting of fires in forests is now usually strictly controlled, this disease has generally become uncommon in Britain. In cases where discipline has been relaxed it has quickly reappeared.

Violet root rot caused by *Helicobasidium purpureum* Pat. (stat. mycel. *Rhizoctonia crocorum* Fr., syn. *R. violace* Tul.)

Violet root rot, caused by *Helicobasidium purpureum*, which is fairly common on sugar beet, asparagus, carrots and other agricultural crops (Moore, 1959), has occasionally been reported on forest nursery stock. Its felt-like, purplish fructifications have a smooth hymenium of crozier-shaped basidia, transversely septate to form up to four cells, each with a sterigma bearing an elliptical basidiospore measuring 10–12(–15) x 6–7 μm (Wakefield and Dennis, 1950). They encrust the stems and lower parts of their host plants, spreading outwards over the soil, but usually occur only in damp weather in April. It was then that Watson (1928) found them in Scotland round the collar and lower branches of Sitka spruce seedlings, and growing over the surrounding soil. The plant roots were rotten and purple-brown, and covered with small black infection cushions. *H. purpureum* has again been found occasionally in more recent years, in 1972, 1974 and 1975, causing severe damage to Sitka spruce transplants in Scottish nurseries established on old garden or agricultural land. McKay and Clear (1958) found the same fungus in Eire destroying the root cortex and causing yellowing and browning of the branch apices of three-year-old transplants of Douglas fir and lodgepole pine growing on land four years previously cropped with sugar beet. *H. purpureum* has also been found attacking two-year-old Douglas fir plants in England.

Affected plants should be lifted and destroyed.

Root and butt rot caused by *Armillaria mellea* (Vahl. ex Fr.) Kummer (*Armillariella mellea* Karst.), the honey fungus, the bootlace or shoestring fungus

Armillaria mellea is one of the most widespread of all root disease fungi. Until comparatively recently it might have been considered to be well known and well documented. It has long been known to be a very variable fungus, but it has become increasingly clear that *A. mellea* as it was once understood is in fact a species complex (Singer, 1956; Romagnesi, 1970, 1973; Watling, 1976; Korhonen, 1978). Even in Britain there are probably five or six species within this group (including *Clitocybe tabescens* Bres., the fruit body of which has no ring). All the earlier pathological literature on *A. mellea* therefore needs careful reappraisal, and a great deal of work is now required to determine the distribution of the individual species of the complex, and to study their characteristics, including their host ranges and the extent of their pathogenicity. The account that follows therefore reviews the literature on *A. mellea sensu lato*, and will need extensive revision as important new information is acquired.

A. mellea sensu lato is distributed throughout the temperate and tropical parts of the world in North and South America, Europe, a large part of Africa, South East Asia, Japan, Australia and New Zealand (Anon, 1980*a*). It has been recorded on over 650 hosts (Raabe, 1962), causing a root, collar and butt rot in a wide range of broadleaved and coniferous trees and shrubs, and sometimes attacking herbaceous hosts also (Moore, 1959).

Although it is absent from plantations established on land that was not formerly under forest, *A. mellea* is common in forests in Great Britain. It may kill trees, or rot the timber in their butt lengths, but it causes far less overall damage than *Heterobasidion annosum* (*Fomes annosus*). Thus Peace (1938) found 80 per cent of the rotten trees he investigated were affected by *H. annosum* and only one per cent by *A. mellea*. Nevertheless, the incidence in individual stands may sometimes be considerable, and *A. mellea* is also very important as a cause of damage to many ornamental trees and shrubs in parks and gardens, and to fruit trees in orchards.

The causal fungus   The fungus may be recognised by its fruit body, by its sheets of white mycelium, and by its black, bootlace-like rhizomorphs.

The fruit body of *A. mellea* is a typical gilled toadstool (plate 17). Its cap is 5–15 cm across, yellowish or brownish with dark brown fibrillose scales that often disappear with age, at first rounded, later flattened or depressed, with a striate margin. It is the colour of the cap that gives the fungus one of its common names, the honey fungus. The gills on its underside are pinkish or pale yellowish brown, adnate or slightly decurrent. The stipe is about 10–17 cm long and about 7-12 mm across, often swollen below, yellowish or brownish, striate above its thick, white, membranous ring. The flesh is white and acrid. The spores are colourless, white in the mass, elliptical, smooth, 8-9 x 5-6 μm. They are produced in very large numbers, and can often be seen around and below the fruit bodies as a thick white dust. The fructifications commonly grow in dense tufts on stumps, at the bases of dead or sometimes dying trees, or occasionally as much as 2 or 3 metres up their trunks, or singly on the ground, connected by rhizomorphs with buried wood or rotten roots.

As noted above, a form without a ring has been called *Clitocybe tabescens* (Gibson, 1961).

Fruit bodies may be found in late summer and autumn, but with the onset of hard frosts they are reduced to a dark brown slimy mass. Hence the fruit bodies are of limited value in diagnosis, for which much more use is made of the mycelium and rhizomorphs.

The mycelium may be found under and within the bark of infested trees, appearing as thick, white or cream-coloured, washleather-like sheets, often with delicate fan-like striations.

The rhizomorphs (which provide a means of spread through the soil) are root-like, reddish-brown when young and black when older, and may be found in the soil, attached to the root collar and to root surfaces. These rhizomorphs in the soil (the *Rhizomorpha subterranea* of early authors) are round in cross section. Other, flattened, bootlace-like rhizomorphs also occur under the bark of dead

Figure 15.   Rhizomorphs of *Armillaria mellea* on stem of Sitka spruce from
which the bark has been removed (Forestry Commission)

trees, where they anastomose to form extensive networks (figure 15). They replace the white mycelial sheets in the later stages of attack, when the host bark becomes loosened. These flattened rhizomorphs (the *Rhizomorpha sub-corticalis* of the early writers), which inspired the popular names shoestring or bootlace fungus, are commonly pale yellow or reddish until exposed to light and air, when they become dark brown or black. Rhizomorphs have been known to grow at least 9 metres through the soil from infested stumps (Boughey, 1938), and Boullard (1961) calculated that they grew in soil at the rate of 2 to 3 cm/day.

Physiology of A. mellea   The optimum temperature for rhizomorph production in culture lies between about 20 and 24 °C (Bliss, 1944), and Manka (1953) found that no rhizomorphs were produced at 16 or 32 °C. In culture they grow best at the rather low pH of 4 to 5 (Manka, 1953; Benton and Ehrlich, 1941), but in soil they grow well over a wide range of type and pH, from peats with a pH of 4 to highly alkaline sands of pH 8 (Bliss, 1941*b*).

The mycelium grows over a temperature range of 7 to 28 °C (Bliss, 1946), though the optimum appears to lie between 21 and 25 °C (Benton and Ehrlich, 1941). The optimum pH for growth lies between 4.5 and 5.5 (Benton and Ehrlich, 1941; Reitsma, 1932). The optimum temperature for fruit body formation was found by Manka (1953) to be 25 °C.

Studies by Bliss (1941*b*) showed that when cultures are deprived of air they soon stop growing and die, and work by Raabe and Gold (1967) indicated that rhizomorph growth is reduced when carbon dioxide levels reach 30 per cent. At high carbon dioxide levels, rhizomorphs become flattened, like those formed under the bark of affected trees. In culture the fungus grows better in darkness than in light (Raabe, 1958). Cultures and actively growing mycelium in wood may glow in the dark (Ramsbottom, 1953).

A. mellea is a white-rot fungus, but according to Scurti (1956) for the first 6 to 12 months of its growth in wood it leaves the lignin little affected, and breaks down mainly the cellulose and hemicellulose, though Campbell (1932) concluded that after destruction of the carbohydrates in the earlier stages of attack, lignin was also destroyed. It appears that the fungus can also break down suberised cell walls (Swift, 1965).

There is some evidence (Thornberry and Ray, 1953) that in culture *A. mellea* produces a phytotoxic substance that blocks the xylem vessels of plants treated with the culture filtrates.

The above comments on the physiology of *A. mellea* are generalisations, and need to be taken with some reserve, because strains of the fungus vary in their temperature/growth relationships and other characteristics (Gibson, 1961; Rishbeth, 1978). Some strains have a wide host range (Patton and Riker, 1959), while others seem to be quite restricted (May, 1962).

Spread into and through the stand   Little is known about the mode of entry of

A. mellea into uninfested stands. It probably occurs by colonisation of stumps or wounds by airborne basidiospores, though Leach (1939) failed to infect stumps or roots by inoculation with spores, and Gibson and Goodchild (1961) similarly failed to infect fresh pine billets. However, Rishbeth (1964) obtained a few successful inoculations of both pine and hardwood stumps, and concluded that although colonisation by spores might be relatively rare, it was probably important in giving rise to new infection centres. Similarly, Molin and Rennerfelt (1959) found that mycelium of *A. mellea* developed on the surfaces of exposed sections of spruce, pine and birch, and considered that it grew following the deposition of airborne spores.

Spread within a crop is achieved by means of rhizomorphs that grow through the soil from infested trees or stumps, or by contacts between healthy and infested roots. Marsh (1952), in England, found evidence that in the tree and bush-fruit crops he studied, spread was by root contact. In Scandinavia, Molin and Rennerfelt (1959) reached the conclusion that infection of forest trees also took place mainly by root contacts. They considered that spread by means of rhizomorphs was much less important, and occurred over only short distances of less than one metre. In many parts of Africa, the fungus produces few or no rhizomorphs, probably because of high soil temperatures (Rishbeth, 1978) but the presence of inhibitors (Swift, 1968) may also be a factor and again spread is mainly by root contact (Gibson and Goodchild, 1961; Rayner, 1959; Wiehe, 1952). In Great Britain, and other temperate countries, however, infection of forest trees appears to be mainly by means of rhizomorphs (Day, 1927; Patton and Riker, 1959; Redfern, 1978; Woeste, 1956), though entry by root contacts also occurs in some stands (Prihoda, 1957).

The rhizomorphs enter through roots (Gladman and Low, 1963) or at the root collar (Day, 1927). Day found that rhizomorphs became attached to the host bark, and hyphae grew from their tips into the cork cells. They appeared to exert a toxic influence on the host cells before penetration. Small trees were often closely encircled by a web of rhizomorphs. The fungus could enter uninjured and apparently healthy trees, and often attacked some of the best and most vigorous ones, a fact confirmed by Boullard (1961). In support of this, Zeller (1926) and Thomas (1934) found that *A. mellea* could enter healthy, undamaged roots. Nevertheless, there has been much argument as to whether the fungus can in fact successfully invade healthy, unwounded trees, and Day (1929) later decided that it could enter and kill trees only if they were previously weakened by other causes, such as drought or defoliation. Results of experiments by Christensen and Hodson (1954) lend some support to this view, and Buckland (1953) in studies on Douglas fir in Canada found that when the fungus entered trees from the soil it did so only through mechanically or physiologically damaged roots. Pawsey and Gladman (1965) noted *A. mellea* commonly associated with extraction wounds on conifer roots.

Entry into tree roots may be delayed by reactions of the host tissues (Buckland, 1953), which may check its growth by laying down callus and resin barriers.

Various competing and antagonistic fungi may also hinder entry. Thus in Poland, Orloś (1954, 1957) considered that *Polyporus borealis* and other fungi sometimes competed with *A. mellea* and prevented it from colonising stumps of Norway spruce.

Relative susceptibility of common forest trees   As already noted, *A. mellea* has a very wide host range. On hardwoods in Great Britain it was considered to be the cause of the death of many oaks in the early part of this century (Osmaston, 1927). At this time, *A. mellea,* on its own or in association with other causative agents, killed many oaks in continental Europe (Georgévitch, 1926). It has been recorded also on all other common hardwood trees. In Great Britain, however, though the fungus may sometimes cause damage in cricket bat willow plantings (Anon, 1968c) and other hardwood crops, in forests it much more often causes losses in conifer crops planted on ex-hardwood sites than on hardwood crops themselves (Day, 1929).

Among the conifers, most species may be affected, but spruces (including Sitka spruce) are especially liable to attack, while Douglas fir is generally resistant. However, even the more resistant species may be killed when young. The situation is complicated, because species most often killed by *A. mellea* are not always those most liable to butt rot. Some, such as Sitka and Norway spruce, western red cedar and western hemlock, are often killed, and also among the most susceptible to rot in older trees. On the other hand, larches and Scots and Corsican pine are also frequently killed, particularly the former, yet larches are infrequently affected by butt rot, and pines hardly at all. Among the remaining species, the silver firs and Douglas fir are only occasionally killed, and are also fairly resistant to butt rot, and so are the most resistant to both aspects of the disease (Anon, 1967).

Baxter (1953), Peace (1962) and Greig and Strouts (1977) give more comprehensive lists of apparently resistant and susceptible species, but for many species the field observations on which such lists must be mainly based are difficult to interpret because of variations in the strains of the fungus and of various factors of climate and site whose effects are inadequately understood.

Redfern (1978) inoculated nine species, using one isolate of *A. mellea,* and found that of the conifers tested, Douglas fir and grand fir were more resistant than Norway spruce, Sitka spruce, Japanese larch and Scots pine.

Symptoms and forms of attack   Once the fungus has succeeded in entering and girdling a tree root, it spreads distally from the point of entry along the cambial zone between bark and wood, and there produces its characteristic sheets of mycelium. Proximally, spread takes place against the host resistance in the bark scales, and the cambium is only entered and killed behind the advancing mycelial front (Woester, 1956; Redfern, 1978). If the fungus reaches the collar, it may girdle young trees and kill them. In conifers (particularly in spruces and pines), the first sign of attack is often a flow of resin from the base of the trunk

Figure 16. Resin flow from trunk of *Picea omorika* attacked by *Armillaria mellea* (Forestry Commission)

(figure 16). The resin trickles down the bark, matting the litter on the ground at the foot of the tree into a hard mass. With time the whole root system may be colonised; the needles then yellow, and by the end of the summer they become brown and fall, and the tree dies. It is at this stage that the typical network of blackened rhizomorphs develops beneath the loosening bark.

On large trees, the fungus may progress only slowly, and for a long time may be confined to the roots. This is especially so in old hardwoods. Infections may be limited to small parts of the root systems for many years without obvious signs of infection above ground. With time and increasing root damage, however, particularly in drought conditions or following damage by defoliating insects, the trees tend to become stag-headed, and may eventually die. In many cases the fungus makes little headway until the trees are felled (Leach, 1937), but may form limited lesions on the roots, often delimited by the black zone lines described by Campbell (1934). Once the trees are felled, however, the fungus rapidly builds up in the stumps, and the latter may remain as sources of infection for at least 20 years. Though *A. mellea* may kill both coniferous and hardwood trees, and colonise their stumps in both cases, hardwood stumps rather than stumps of conifers generally appear to provide more suitable infection sources from which the fungus can grow and infect surrounding trees (Day, 1929). However, several cases have been recorded (Redfern, 1975) in which killing attacks were associated with conifer stumps alone.

Gladman and Greig (1965) have described the appearance of the decay caused by *A. mellea,* with particular reference to the butt-rot-susceptible species among the major conifers. When butt rot occurs, external symptoms, apart from occasional resin flow, are seldom seen, and infection is found only when the tree is felled, or following windblow resulting from root rot. In its earliest stages, infection shows in cross sections of the stem base as a pale brown, grey or bluish, often water-soaked stain, that later becomes dark brown or blue-black. Later still, incipient decay becomes apparent, and water-soaked brown or orange areas appear. In longitudinal sections of the stem, scattered irregular white or cream-coloured pockets are visible in the wood. Black zone lines can often be seen bounding or within the decayed area. In the final stages of decay, the centre of the stem may be reduced to a soft, stringy wet mass, often containing secondary fungi and bacteria that follow *A. mellea.* Surrounding this area, tissue as yet invaded by *A. mellea* alone usually appears as a soft, wet, orange-brown zone containing white pockets, and often also irregular black skins, the remains of the zone line tissue.

Figure 17. **Longitudinal section through butt of Norway spruce showing conical zone of central decay and stain caused by *Armillaria mellea* (Forestry Commission)**

Butt rot caused by *A. mellea* usually results in a conical zone of decayed tissue that does not ascend for more than about 60 cm from the base of the stem (figure 17).

Factors affecting progress of the disease   Factors affecting the progress of infection and attack by *A. mellea* are only partially understood. The likelihood of initial infection by rhizomorphs is much affected by inoculum potential, which is governed both by the size of the stumps from which the rhizomorphs begin their growth and the distance they have to grow before encountering a suitable host (Garrett, 1956*b*). If the nutrient status of the substrate is too low, rhizomorphs probably do not develop. As already noted, rhizomorph initiation may be hindered by the presence of various antagonistic soil fungi. In laboratory experiments, *Trichoderma viride* (Garrett, 1958) and *Pleurotus ostreatus* (Kunze, 1952–3) have been shown to exert this effect, whereas *Aureobasidium pullulans* may stimulate rhizomorph production (Pentland, 1965). In other conditions, when rhizomorphs are produced, but inoculum potential is relatively low, the fungus may make no progress against the resistance of the host, and may be overtaken by other organisms (Garrett, 1956).

The most important physical characters affecting the disease are generally considered to be soil temperature and soil moisture. In California, Bliss (1941*a*, 1944, 1946) studied the fungus in agar culture and on citrus in soil tanks. He obtained severe, moderate, and slight infection of citrus at 10, 17 and 24 °C respectively. At 31 °C the inoculum was killed. Soil temperatures are not likely to place any marked limitation on infection in Great Britain. Drought conditions have often been considered to render trees more liable to infection, however. Gladman and Low (1963) studied a crop of Sitka spruce growing on a peaty flat containing a number of dry knolls, and found *Armillaria* butt rot in the trees on the knolls but not in the wet flat.

Losses caused by A. mellea   It is difficult to assess the extent of the losses caused by *A. mellea* in forests in Great Britain, though the damage is much less than that resulting from the activities of *Heterobasidium annosum.* Greig (1962) observed that *A. mellea* frequently killed young conifers up to the first thinning when they were planted on ex-hardwood sites, but it usually caused little or no loss of saleable timber because the affected trees tended to be few and scattered. Locally the losses could be quite heavy, however, especially in the case of Sitka and Serbian spruce, western hemlock, Corsican pine and the larches, and if site conditions were unfavourable, groups of trees might be killed. On the other hand Redfern (1978) has associated group killing with other factors, such as the history of harvesting operations on the site, and variations in the pathogenicity of different clones of *A. mellea.*

Damage from butt rot is relatively low because the fungus rarely advances more than about 60 cm up the stem (though secondary fungi sometimes extend the rot further up the tree). In addition to this, rotting of roots may lead to windblow (Gladman and Low, 1963). Occasionally, large numbers of trees may show butt rot, and Greig (1962) noted one crop of Sitka spruce in which 90 per cent of the butts removed in one thinning had either butt rot or stain. As a rule, however, the fungus affects only a small proportion of the crop. Damage to ornamental and orchard trees has been mentioned above.

Control measures Few measures can be taken to control attacks by *A. mellea* under forest conditions. When dealing with valuable plantation crops in warm climates, the fungus may be eradicated by soil injection with carbon disulphide (Bliss, 1944, 1951; Darley and Wilbur, 1954). The chemical is poisonous and highly inflammable, however, and doubt has been cast on its effectiveness in Great Britain because good results are only obtained at fairly high soil temperatures (Anon, 1961). The soil fumigant methyl bromide was also found to be effective in citrus and fig plantations when tested by Larue *et al.* (1962). Other workers have suggested treatments of roots or the root zone with various fungicides, including iron sulphate (Borg, 1935; Jenkins, 1952), iodine (Guyot, 1933), copper (Rayner, 1959) and a refined creosote preparation (Pawsey and Rahman, 1976). The latter conclude from their experiments that a number of materials applied to the soil may, depending on site and perhaps climatic conditions, cause death or suppression of rhizomorphs. However, unless the source of rhizomorphs is eradicated by removal of infected stumps and roots, rhizomorphs are likely to reinvade the treated area should treatment be allowed to lapse.

Biological control methods, again intended primarily for use in plantation crops in tropical or subtropical areas, were worked out by Leach (1937) in tea plantations in Nyasaland (Malawi). Leach observed that after penetration the fungus tended to grow most rapidly on those parts of the tree richest in carbohydrates. He considered it possible that if he could reduce the carbohydrate content of the roots of trees before felling, their stumps would be less susceptible to invasion by *A. mellea* when the trees were felled, and hence they would be less likely to become sources of infection to a succeeding crop. He found experimentally that this was so, and developed a method for depleting the stump carbohydrate reserves by ring-barking them from 18 months to 2 years before felling. Other workers in Africa (Wiehe, 1952; Gibson and Goodchild, 1961) have confirmed Leach's results, and his methods have been widely used in tea and Tung plantations there. So far this method of control too has been used only in areas being cleared for crops of high value, and not in general forestry. Studies by Redfern (1968) suggest that in Great Britain girdling hardwood trees before felling, or killing them by means of 2,4,5-trichlorophenoxy acetic acid does not hinder colonisation of the stumps by *A. mellea,* though it does appear to make the stumps much less effective as food bases for the fungus within five years of treatment. It is therefore possible that girdling or poisoning could be used in this country to reduce infection in conifer plantings to be established on infested hardwood sites, provided a delay in replanting is acceptable.

The removal of infested stumps before replanting with a susceptible crop of high value has also been suggested (Bliss, 1944; Anon, 1961). This method is seldom likely to be possible in forestry, though it may be worthwhile in arboreta and gardens, and before planting orchards.

In forests, some loss from *A. mellea* is normally acceptable, but if it is necessary to replant areas of conifer in which losses through this fungus have been high, or to fill gaps caused by its activities, one of the relatively resistant species such as Douglas fir or grand fir should be chosen where silviculturally possible.

Root and butt rot caused by *Heterobasidion annosum* (Fr.) Bref. (*Fomes annosus* (Fr.) Cooke)

Heterobasidion annosum (*Fomes annosus*) is the most damaging of all the fungi that attack conifers in Great Britain. Peace (1938) found it to be the commonest cause of loss in a wide butt-rot survey, and Low and Gladman (1962*a*) found it was responsible for 90 per cent of the rot they had seen in conifers in Scotland. In some circumstances it may also kill mature trees, particularly pines, as well as young trees of this and other genera. It is widely distributed throughout the world (Anon, 1980*b*) and has an extensive host range.

The causal fungus   The basidial fruit body is perennial, usually bracket-shaped (figure 18), but often irregular and becoming resupinate when, for example, growing on the underside of roots or lining the roofs of rabbit burrows made under infected stumps. It is usually about 5 to 10 cm across but may be up to 30 cm.

Figure 18.   Typical bracket-shaped fruit body of *Heterobasidion annosum:* upper surface (D.H. Phillips)

Figure 19. Lower surface of fruit body of *Heterobasidion annosum* seen in figure 18 (D.H. Phillips)

The upper surface is covered by a bright reddish-brown crust that becomes dark brown or black with age, and is concentrically grooved. The thin, acute margin is white or cream when the fruit body is growing. The underside is white, becoming cream or biscuit coloured, and pierced by fine pores, the openings of the tubes that bear the basidial hymenium (figure 19). The tubes are formed in distinct, normally annual, layers, each from 1-10 mm deep. The flesh of the fructification is tough and leathery, and becomes hard and woody on drying. It is whitish, cream or pale wood-coloured. The basidiospores are white, globose or subglobose, 4-6 x 3-5 μm. As it grows the fruit body often encloses small objects such as small sticks and conifer needles and holes may be left as these decay and become detached (Wakefield and Dennis, 1950; Greig and Redfern, 1974). Fructifications may be found at all times of the year if the humidity is high enough. They may be killed by extreme cold, but are resistant to moderate frost and dry weather, and may shed spores even after prolonged drought and at 0 °C (Rishbeth 1951a; Haraldstad, 1962). They occur on stumps, sometimes at the bases of dying trees, and on infected roots exposed by windblow (plate 18). They generally form at or just above ground level, and are often hidden by brash and litter, or occur in deep sheltered cavities. Indeed, infected stumps may bear fruit bodies when covered with brash, or when well sheltered, but show none when more exposed, so that absence of fructifications may not indicate the absence of the fungus

(Rishbeth, 1951*a*). As already noted, resupinate fructifications may be present in rodent tunnels passing near diseased roots. They sometimes also appear in litter, and are then associated with fine infected roots, though they may then occur several metres from the stem of the tree to which the roots belong (Rishbeth 1951*a*). Small white pustules, sometimes with rudimentary pore surfaces, are frequently found, especially on cut surfaces of stumps or the base of dying trees and under roots (figure 20). Mycelium, when visible, is found only as thin, white, tissue-like sheets under the bark of dead roots (Low and Gladman, 1960).

Figure 20. *Heterobasidion annosum:* **pustules (young fruit bodies) on root of Douglas fir (Forestry Commission)**

An imperfect stage consisting of a fine turf of conidiophores with swollen heads, formed directly on the mycelium, may also occur, though it is rather rarely seen in nature and is easily overlooked. The conidia are subglobose to ovoid and hyaline, 4.5–7.5(–10.5) x 3.0–6.0 μm (Nobles, 1948), and borne on small sterigmata (figure 21). Rishbeth (1951*a*) occasionally found this stage in East Anglia round bark beetle holes at the sheltered bases of young pine trees, and under the bark of a dead pine just above ground level, and Bakshi (1950, 1952) discovered it in the tunnels of ambrosia beetles. It can often be found in damp weather when carefully sought for on the surfaces of infected stumps covered by litter and on the ends of stacked infected logs. It is readily produced in culture, and on infested wood inoculated in moist conditions, but it is usually

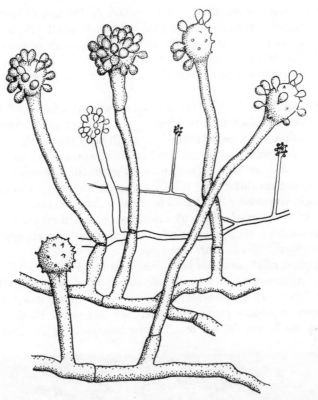

Figure 21. The microscopic imperfect stage of *Heterobasidion annosum*, showing the spores borne on the swollen heads of the conidiophores (x 500 approx.). This stage has been called *Oedocephalum lineatum* (Forestry Commission)

thought to play little part in natural dispersal. Its colonies are recognisable on incubated infested wood after 4–5 days and so often form a useful means of identifying the fungus.

The conidia are not produced in culture when the relative humidity is below 95 per cent, and they form at temperatures from 0 to 22.5 °C in light or darkness (Rishbeth, 1951a).

Rishbeth (1951a) found that growth of *H. annosum* in culture took place at temperatures from 0 to 28.5 °C, with an optimum at 22.5 °C, when he measured a growth rate of 7.8 mm/day on malt agar, and 7.3 mm/day in pine roots. Similarly, at 10 °C the fungus grew 2.5 mm/day on agar and 2.8 mm/day in roots, while in pine stumps in the field it grew 2.6 mm/day (about 1 m/year) over a period when the mean soil temperature was also 10 °C. In culture, optimum growth takes place from about pH 4.0 to 5.5 (Etheridge, 1955). Much additional information on the physiology of the fungus is given in the review by Gundersen (1962).

Spread of the fungus in the forest   Information on the rate of spread of the
fungus in British forests relates only to pine, in which Rishbeth (1951*a*) found the
growth was about 1.0 m/year. According to Fowler (1962) rate of spread through
pine plantations in northeastern USA is about the same as in Britain, though it
may be about twice as fast in some plantings of the very susceptible Red pine
(*Pinus resinosa*).

Rishbeth (1951*b*) and Gibbs (1967*b*) have shown that the roots of suppressed
trees are relatively susceptible to invasion, yet they are rarely entered under
natural conditions, perhaps because of competition by other fungi on the root
surface, and also because the fungus is not commonly present in soils.

Braun (1958) found that soil supported the growth of *H. annosum* only after
sterilisation, and concluded that the fungus could not grow freely in the soil.
When Francke-Grosmann (1962) tried to grow the fungus in nonsterilised soil, it
grew only when she provided it with a large food base, and even in these favourable circumstances it disappeared in a few weeks, apparently destroyed by other
fungi, mites, springtails and other organisms.

Basidiospores of *H. annosum* have been shown to occur in soil (Haraldstad,
1962) and may sometimes be washed down to a depth of 50 to 90 cm (Rishbeth,
1951*a*). In laboratory experiments, however, Rishbeth found it was difficult to
induce spores to produce growth on unsterilised root pieces. He therefore concluded that the fungus did not usually enter uninfested stands directly by the

Figure 22. *Heterobasidion annosum:* **transfer of disease from an old, infected,
thinning stump to a nearby Japanese larch (Forestry Commission)**

colonisation of roots by means of spores or free-living mycelium present in the soil, and sought other means by which it might enter the crop.

Hepting and Downs (1944), in a study of white pine plots in North Carolina, found root and butt rots (mainly caused by *H. annosum*) in 75 per cent of the trees in previously thinned plots, but in only 4 per cent where no thinning had been done. They suggested that butt rot was so extensive in the thinned areas because a build-up of *H. annosum* had taken place in the stumps of the thinned trees. Rishbeth (1951*a, b*) obtained experimental evidence that the fungus colonised freshly cut conifer stumps by means of airborne spores, and then grew down into the stump roots, and by root contact then invaded the healthy living roots of adjacent trees (figures 22, 23). As noted above, over a period when the mean

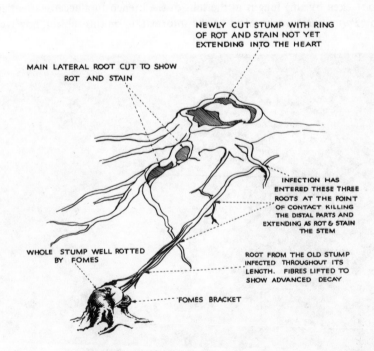

NEWLY CUT STUMP WITH RING OF ROT AND STAIN NOT YET EXTENDING INTO THE HEART

MAIN LATERAL ROOT CUT TO SHOW ROT AND STAIN

INFECTION HAS ENTERED THESE THREE ROOTS AT THE POINT OF CONTACT KILLING THE DISTAL PARTS AND EXTENDING AS ROT & STAIN THE STEM

WHOLE STUMP WELL ROTTED BY FOMES

ROOT FROM THE OLD STUMP INFECTED THROUGHOUT ITS LENGTH. FIBRES LIFTED TO SHOW ADVANCED DECAY

FOMES BRACKET

Figure 23. Diagram interpreting figure 22. *Heterobasidion annosum* has spread from the long-infected 10-year-old thinning stump (bottom left) to the 30-year-old healthy tree (top right) through the root contacts (Forestry Commission)

soil temperature was 10 °C, *H. annosum* grew in stumps at the rate of about 1 m/ year, and Rishbeth estimated that when pines were planted about 1.4 m apart, the fungus could pass down into surface-colonised stumps and along their roots, and closely approach the roots of adjacent trees within a year of initial infection. Similarly, Meredith (1960), in inoculation experiments with pine stumps, found the fungus invading from the stump surface often reached the proximal ends of lateral roots in six months, and was present in their more distal ends 12 to 18 months after inoculation. Many other workers have also found an association between thinning stumps and attack by *H. annosum*.

The surfaces of freshly cut stumps remain susceptible to invasion by *H. annosum* for only 3 or 4 weeks or even less after felling (Rishbeth 1951*a*, 1959*a*; Cobb and Schmidt, 1964), though the period of susceptibility of the subsurface tissues may be reduced or prolonged by various chemical treatments applied to the stumps (Rishbeth, 1959*a*).

Competing fungi Competing fungi often prevent the colonisation of stump surfaces by *H. annosum*. Thus Moreau and Schaeffer (1962) state that spruce is seldom attacked by this fungus in the hills of the French Jura because of antagonism by *Polyporus borealis*. Most of the information on this subject, however,

**Figure 24. Fruit body of *Peniophora gigantea* on pine stump. *P. gigantea*
competes with *Heterobasidion annosum* in the colonisation of
thinning stumps. Pine stumps may be protected from infection by
H. annosum by artificial inoculation with oidia of *P. gigantea*
(Forestry Commission)**

relates to species of pine, in which *Peniophora gigantea* is much the most important competitor (figure 24) (Rishbeth, 1951*a*; Meredith, 1959; Gremmen, 1963), though other common fungi, such as *Trichoderma* spp., *Penicillium* spp., and

Stereum sanguinolentum may also play a part (Curl and Arnold, 1964; Gooding, 1964; Meredith, 1960). Spores of *P. gigantea* are often present in the atmosphere in sufficient quantities to colonise fresh stumps and prevent the entry of *H. annosum*. At a later stage, *P. gigantea* may displace *H. annosum* in stumps already invaded by the latter (Rishbeth, 1951a; Meredith, 1960; Hodges, 1964; Towers, 1966). Meredith (1960) found that when he inoculated fresh stump surfaces with mixed suspensions of spores of *H. annosum* and *P. gigantea,* the latter became the dominant colonist even when its viable spores were outnumbered by those of *H. annosum* by as much as 10 or sometimes even 100 to 1.

The spread of *H. annosum* in stumps on ex-hardwood sites, may be restricted by *Armillaria mellea* invading either from infected roots or by means of rhizomorphs at the root collar (Low and Gladman, 1962b).

Heavy resin production by stumps also hinders invasion by *H. annosum* (Meredith, 1959). This also affects the passage of the fungus from infested to

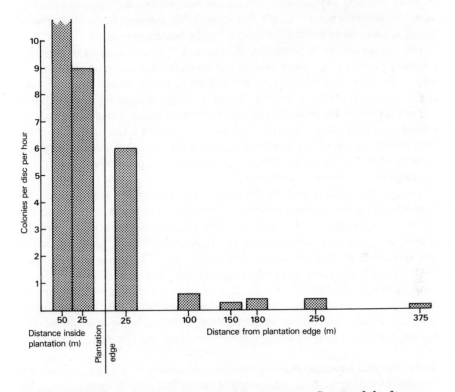

Figure 25. **Spread of spores of *Heterobasidion annosum*. Spores of the fungus were trapped on Scots pine discs in a plantation of *Thuja plicata* and at various distances from the plantation edge. The spore concentration is expressed as the mean number of colonies per exposed disc. Craig Phadrig Forest, Scotland, 1960 (data of J. D. Low and R.J. Gladman)**

healthy roots by root contact (Rishbeth, 1951*b*). Competing fungi also appear to play some part in limiting the passage of the fungus in the soil from root to root (Rishbeth, 1951*b*; Moreau and Schaeffer, 1962; Gibbs, 1967*a*)..

The likelihood of stump infection is also much affected by the distance from spore sources. This is emphasised by the figures shown graphically in figure 25, which indicate a rapid fall off in the number of spores in the air only a few hundred metres from the edge of a forest in which fruit bodies of *H. annosum* occur. Similarly, Gladman and Low (1963) sampled conifer needles from east Scotland (where conifer plantations were well established before 1900, and *H. annosum* fruit bodies were common), and found a mean count of 2652 viable spores of *H. annosum* per 10 g of needles, while on similar samples from west Scotland (where almost all conifer plantations were relatively young, with few fructifications), the counts averaged only 44 viable spores. Nevertheless, some viable spores of the fungus were found on almost every sample. Rishbeth (1959*c*), in spore trapping experiments with needle samples and with muslin square air samplers, obtained some evidence that spores of *H. annosum* could sometimes be found as far as 50 to 80 or more miles from the nearest sources.

Once colonised by *H. annosum*, stumps may remain as sources of infection for many years. Larch stumps have on one occasion been found to be infested as long as 63 years after felling (Low and Gladman, 1960), though this is unusual, and Curschmann (1960) found the fungus no longer present on land cultivated and not replanted for about 50 years after forest clearance. Large stumps, which are slow to rot and disappear, remain longer as sources of infection than do small ones. Pine stumps which are readily colonised by the fungus rot more rapidly than those of other species, so *H. annosum* does not persist in them as long as it does in stumps of, for instance, larch and spruce.

Though fresh stumps provide the main point of entry into healthy crops, the fungus has sometimes gained entry also through root contacts with fence posts made from infested wood (Jørgensen, 1955). Occasionally infection of brashing, pruning and extraction wounds also occurs (Low and Gladman, 1960). In Europe this appears to be very uncommon (Braun, 1956, 1958; Pawsey and Gladman, 1965), though it occurs more often, particularly in *Tsuga*, in parts of North America (Englerth, 1942; Hunt and Krueger, 1962; Foster, 1962). Suppressed trees appear to be rarely attacked (Anon, 1964; Meredith, 1960), but windblown trees have sometimes become infested (Anon, 1962). Singling of double leaders has also provided a place of entry in some cases (Low and Gladman, 1960).

Host range and variations in susceptibility   *H. annosum* attacks a very large number of woody hosts. Economically it causes loss only in conifer crops, but it may also attack hardwoods such as birch, beech, oak and alder (Rishbeth, 1957), which are seldom severely affected, but may pass on the fungus to a succeeding conifer crop (Low and Gladman, 1960). In conifers, symptoms of attack and the damage resulting vary with the tree species concerned (Low and Gladman 1960; Peace, 1938). Pines are very rarely subject to butt rot, except

Figure 26. A group of second-rotation Scots pine killed by *Heterobasidion annosum* **(Forestry Commission)**

in old age, but in dry areas with soils of high pH (often on limed, ex-agricultural land), many trees may be killed (figure 26). Pines are also killed on other sites with more acid soils but damage is generally less serious. However, their fresh stumps are readily colonised by *H. annosum,* and then transmit it by root contact to more susceptible species planted subsequently or in mixture. Some time before they die, the affected trees show a thinning of their foliage and a shortening of the needles (figure 27).

Trees of genera of conifers other than pines may also be killed, especially when young. As they become older, they are more usually affected by root and butt rot.

Some species of *Abies* (the silver firs) are resistant except when very young, when they may be killed by the fungus. Resistance varies very much with the species; for example, *A. alba* appears to be highly resistant on most sites, and *A. grandis* seems slightly less so (Low and Gladman, 1960), while *A. balsamea* is very susceptible (Roll-Hansen in Anon, 1962). Even *A. alba* has been severely

Figure 27. Thinning of the foliage of Scots pine trees attacked by *Heterobasidion annosum* (B.J.W. Greig)

affected on ex-agricultural sites in Italy (Bronchi, 1956), and silver firs in Britain may also be attacked particularly on alkaline soil, but the fungus is slow to advance up the stem.

All the other conifers commonly planted in Britain may be severely affected by root and butt rot, though in Douglas fir (*Pseudotsuga menziesii*) decay rarely proceeds beyond the roots, which may be extensively rotted, rendering the tree liable to windblow (Low and Gladman, 1960, 1962*b*) (figure 28).

In other species, the fungus spreads from the roots into the trunk, to cause an extensive butt rot (Gladman and Greig, 1965) (figures 29, 30, 31). At first, infection shows only as a stain, visible in the stem when the tree is felled. This stain is often eccentric in position, and can be traced down into the roots from which it originated. Its colour varies with the tree species, though in all it becomes dark brown with time. Whereas in Lawson cypress (*Chamaecyparis lawsoniana*), western hemlock (*Tsuga heterophylla*) and western red cedar (*Thuja plicata*), it is dark brown from the beginning, it is at first brownish grey in larch, and in the spruces, pink, lilac and bluish staining often mingle with the brown. Further

Figure 28. **Root system of windblown Douglas fir showing extensive decay by**
** *Heterobasidion annosum* (Forestry Commission)**

growth of the fungus results in incipient and finally advanced decay. In incipient
decay, the wood usually becomes pale in colour, and in longitudinal section begins
to show black flecks, and later small, regular, narrow, rather lens-shaped pockets
of white material. In the earlier stages the wood remains relatively firm and
sound, and the decayed zones are surrounded by bands of stained tissue. Later,
the white pockets tend to coalesce, and their white contents may disappear. The
decay may have progressed about 4 m up the stem by the time trees are 30 years
old (Low and Gladman, 1960) and in older spruces may reach more than twice
this height (Low, personal communication). Empty spaces occur in the decayed
wood, which then shows extensive breakdown, and is light, dry and fibrous (figure
32). Therefore, affected trees may become hollow and snap in high winds.

Timber showing the earliest stages of infection may be used, for example, for
fencing material, but it must then be thoroughly impregnated with creosote before
use, or it will act as a source of infection.

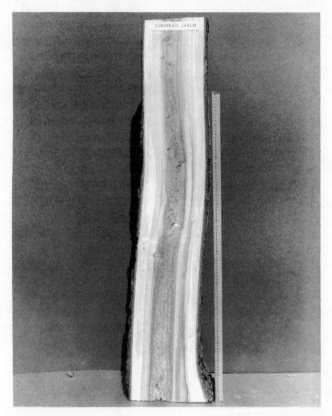

Figure 29. Longitudinal section of European larch with extensive decay caused by *Heterobasidion annosum* (scale length = 1 m) (Forestry Commission)

In one set of adjacent unreplicated 34-year-old plots, Gladman and Low (1963) found the percentage of infected trees of Scots pine, grand fir (*Abies grandis*), European larch, hybrid larch, western red cedar, Douglas fir and western hemlock to be respectively nil, 6, 25, 40, 49, 50 and 96 per cent. They considered these figures gave a fairly good general impression of the relative susceptibility of those species, though on many sites they had found losses in western red cedar relatively higher and those in Douglas fir relatively lower than those quoted here. This was partly because the figures were based only on an examination of the stump surfaces of felled trees and, therefore, gave an incomplete picture since the fungus progresses at a different rate up the trunks of trees of different species and, while in Douglas fir it normally remains mainly in the roots, in western red cedar it moves fairly quickly up the stem.

Some indications of the relative susceptibility of a number of species to butt rot caused by *Heterobasidion annosum* have also been described by Greig (1979). In a sample of 16-year-old trees from a susceptibility trial, the incidence

INCHES

Figure 30. Detail of decay of European larch by *Heterobasidion annosum*, showing pockets of white mycelium (Forestry Commission)

of infection by *H. annosum* was 21 per cent in western hemlock, 19 per cent in Leyland cypress, 11 per cent in Douglas fir, 7 per cent in western red cedar and 1 per cent in grand fir and Norway spruce. The low incidence of infection in Norway spruce was somewhat surprising and may have been related to the poor growth of the trees on the experimental site rather than any inherent resistance.

Factors affecting development of the disease   Various factors affect the development of the disease, in Britain the most important being soil conditions, former land use, the age of the trees, and the amount of thinning or other cutting carried out in the crop. Much of the available information comes from studies in pine crops, and so does not necessarily always apply fully to crops of butt-rot-susceptible species. Of the soil factors, pH, soil moisture conditions, soil texture, organic matter content, and drainage appear to have some influence. Many workers have found a relationship between high soil pH and death of pine, and Wallis (1960), showed that in the East Anglican pine stands he studied, losses were high

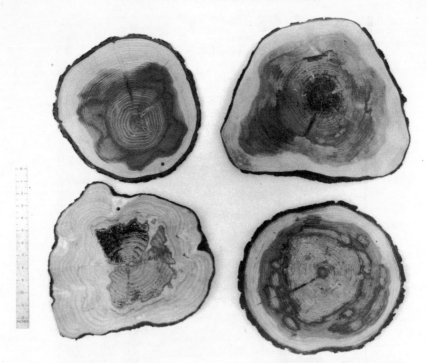

Figure 31. Cross sections of trees showing decay by *Heterobasidion annosum* in Douglas fir (top left), Sitka spruce (top right), western hemlock (bottom left) and European larch (bottom right) (Forestry Commission)

where the pH was above 6. On sites where the pH was lower than this losses were negligible. Similarly, Low and Gladman (1960) found that pines on wet acid peats were not affected by *H. annosum.* In Culbin Forest (Morayshire) established on alkaline sand dunes, they found that pines of the first rotation were killed. After planting, the sandy soil fairly rapidly became more acid, and losses in second-rotation crops appeared to be reduced. The situation in Culbin Forest is exceptional, and losses in pine crops on alkaline sites are usually long continued. Soil moisture is also important, however, and *H. annosum* may kill trees even on acid soils in very dry areas. Thus death both of lodgepole pine (*Pinus contorta*) and Sitka spruce (*Picea sitchensis*) has been recorded even in acid areas in Tentsmuir Forest (Fife), where the rainfall is low and the soil light and well-drained, as well as in similar areas in East Anglia (Rishbeth, 1957). Other workers have also noted more severe attack on light than heavy soils (Jørgensen *et al.,* 1939; Anon, 1963). This may also be because the lighter soils tend to dry out, and the trees are then more liable to invasion. In this connection, Rishbeth (1951*b*) in pot experiments obtained some evidence that well-watered plants were less readily attacked than those with a poor water supply. Jørgensen (1962) got similar

Figure 32. Rot caused by *Heterobasidion annosum* in Scots pine: the final stage, when the wood has become light, dry and fibrous (D.H. Phillips)

experimental results, and also concluded from field observations that lack of soil moisture in dry summers may predispose the trees to attack. Similarly, Rishbeth (1951*b*) also found more diseased trees on sites with soils low in organic matter, and pointed out that in the dry area in which he was working, the organic material may help to keep up the soil moisture level. The situation is complex, however. Maraite and Mayer (1966) found some evidence that in spruce crops in Belgium attack by *H. annosum* is more severe on well-drained sites than on those that are only moderately or poorly drained, while Peace (1938) in Britain found most rot in spruce on well-drained sites but most on larch where the drainage was poor.

Former land use is of major importance. In general, *H. annosum* appears first and develops most rapidly on sites previously occupied by conifer crops because on these the fungus is usually already established in stumps of the previous crop by the time planting takes place. For the same reason the incidence of the disease and the height reached by the fungus in the affected trees tends to increase with the number of conifer rotations (Jørgensen, *et al.*, 1939; Low and Gladman, 1960). On the other hand, attack by *H. annosum* tends to be delayed on ex-hardwood sites, though it develops on these in time (Greig, 1962).

On sites other than those previously under conifers, *H. annosum* is most severe on those previously under agriculture (Anon, 1930, 1963; Bronchi, 1956; Cantiani, 1960; Driver and Dell, 1961). Here there may sometimes be a strong connection with pH and former liming, as Wallis (1960) was able to show that in East Anglia many pines were killed on ex-agricultural land with a pH above 6, but where the soil reaction was lower, losses were no greater than on ex-*Calluna* heath, for example. In other parts of Britain, however, pines may be killed where the pH is considerably lower than 6 (Low, unpublished). Soil pH appears to affect the killing of trees more than it does butt rot, which may develop extensively on relatively acid soils.

Information on the effect of age of the individual trees is sparse. As the fungus takes time to spread, it is clear that there will be a tendency for older crops to be more affected than younger ones. Thus in larch crops studies by Gothe (1957), infection was most prevalent in the oldest trees. On the other hand, on sites on which killing of trees takes place, death may be more rapid in the younger trees (Anon, 1930), no doubt partly because when small the stems are rapidly girdled. Rishbeth (1951*b*) in inoculation experiments on pines, found the fungus penetrated the roots of young trees more readily than those of old ones, causing more infections, and achieving a deeper penetration of the tissues in a given time.

Losses caused   As already mentioned, Hepting and Downs (1944) noted an association between thinning and attack by *H. annosum,* and since then many other workers have confirmed this connection, which is associated with the method of entry of the fungus by the infection of fresh stumps by airborne spores. Thus in pine in East Anglia, Rishbeth (1957) found a mean loss of 0.3 per cent in volume after the first thinning, and losses of 5.9 and 19.5 per cent after subsequent thinnings.

Turning to losses from butt rot, Dowden, in an unpublished study dealing partly with Norway but mainly with Sitka spruce aged 35 to 40 years, found loss in volume caused by *H. annosum* amounted to between 2 and 24 per cent.

Most, though not all, accounts of losses caused by *H. annosum* in Britain do not give figures for loss in volume or value, however, but only for numbers or percentage of affected trees, with sometimes additional information on the distance rot had progressed up the trunk of the trees examined. Thus Low and Gladman (1960) in three Sitka spruce crops found between 20 and 80 per cent of the stems affected, and in the worst affected trees in one 28-year-old planting, the fungus had progressed nearly 5 metres up the stem. In two crops of western red cedar, 35 and 60 per cent of the trees were rotted, and they found 50 per cent affected in Douglas fir and western hemlock. In a number of plantations of larch, between 10 and 60 per cent of the trees showed decay, and in some trees rot had reached a height of nearly 4 metres. In another study, Gladman and Low (1963) found 96 per cent of the trees decayed in a plot of 34-year-old western hemlock.

Pratt (1979*a*, *b*, *c*) made a detailed study of butt rot in 484 trees in 27 stands of Sitka spruce in Great Britain. On average 9 per cent of the volumes of the trees were occupied by incipiently decayed or decayed wood. If whole butt lengths of decayed trees were rejected after felling, losses in volume were 33 per cent and in value, 43 per cent. On the other hand a computer-simulated saw-milling study indicated that losses in value would amount to about 10 per cent if such lengths were not rejected but were converted to pallet boards.

Similar losses have been recorded in many other countries, and in some cases evidence has been gained that loss has resulted not only through death of trees and through decay, but also because of loss of increment in diseased trees (Arvidson, 1954; Henriksen and Jørgensen, 1954). Further damage may result because gaps in the crop and rotten roots may lead to windblow. Loss may also be incurred because on some infested sites it may be impossible to replant with high-yielding but susceptible species, or it may be necessary to shorten the ro-tation of a crop infested by the fungus (Murray, 1962*b*).

H. annosum is therefore a great potential cause of loss, and one whose activi-ties should be controlled as effectively as possible.

Control   A large proportion of the conifer forests in Britain are relatively young, and *H. annosum* has had little time to enter and spread through them. Therefore, much of the work to find control measures has sought means to keep the fungus out of plantations that so far remain uninfested. It has been based on the finding of Rishbeth (1951*a*, *b*, 1952, 1959*a*) and others that *H. annosum* initially enters crops mainly by means of airborne spores that colonise the surfaces of freshly cut stumps, and that much of this colonisation can be prevented by thoroughly painting the fresh stump surfaces immediately after felling with creosote, a mixture of this with tar, or with titanium white and zinc oxide paints. Following this work, creosote, which is cheap and easily procured, was widely used as a stump protectant.

Creosote, however, is unpleasant to handle and variable in constitution, and was found to give rather erratic results in the field (Rishbeth, 1957; Driver, 1963*a*, *b*; Berry, 1965). To be effective it must be applied very thoroughly, and immediately after felling. It acts as a general fungicide, forming a thin barrier that for a long time keeps all fungi from colonising the stump surfaces. Treated stumps are slow to die and decay, and the tissues just below the creosote layer remain susceptible to colonisation by *H. annosum* for an abnormally long period if the protective layer is broken (Rishbeth, 1959*a*). Hence if treated stumps are later damaged, for example by brash-chopping machines, the fungus may enter through the scars. Stumps treated with creosote are only very slowly colonised by *Peniophora gigantea* and other competing fungi, so if *H. annosum* is already established in the stump roots it may grow freely through the woody tissues (Rishbeth, 1957, 1959*a*, *b*).

Therefore, other chemicals have been tested to find materials without the dis-advantages of creosote (Rishbeth, 1959*b*; Phillips and Greig, 1970). Several have been found to give better control than creosote, particularly those that do not exclude all fungi from the treated stumps, but allow the entry of some fungi antagonistic to *H. annosum* (Rishbeth, 1959*b*; Gundersen, 1963, 1967). The most generally effective of those so far most thoroughly tested are sodium nitrite,

Figure 33. Treatment of conifer stumps to prevent the entry of *Heterobasidion annosum*, using a plastic bottle with brush attachment (Forestry Commission)

urea and disodium octaborate; other promising materials are ammonium sulphamate, and the herbicides diquat and paraquat (Phillips and Greig, 1970).

Sodium nitrite was used in Britain for routine stump treatment in the 1960s but due to its toxicity to man and domestic animals it was withdrawn in 1972 and replaced by urea. A 20 per cent solution of urea, together with a marker dye, is applied copiously to the freshly cut stump surface. A variety of applicators have been used; the most satisfactory is a plastic bottle with a brush attached to the screw-cap lid (figure 33). The brush is used to remove the sawdust and debris from the stump surface so that the entire surface is effectively treated. A 10 per cent solution of disodium octaborate may be used as an alternative to urea.

As noted above, in natural conditions competing fungi may prevent the entry of *H. annosum* through the surface of fresh stumps. Their action is erratic, however, for when felling occurs, their spores may be too few in numbers compared with those of *H. annosum* for them to be effective. Following work by Rishbeth (1963), in the case of pine it is now possible to ensure the presence of a suitable competing fungus by inoculating fresh stumps with oidia of *Peniophora gigantea*. This fungus can be grown in culture and the oidia thereby produced can be made up in a sealed plastic sachet. These sachets, which are commercially available in

Britain, can be kept in a cool store for several months without serious loss of viability. For use in the forest, the contents of a sachet are added to water according to the directions on the label and a marker dye is added. The spore suspension obtained in this way is applied to freshly cut pine stumps in the same manner as a solution of urea (Greig and Redfern, 1974).

Once *H. annosum* has entered a crop, it begins to spread, and by the end of the rotation many stumps may be infested and so present sources of infection to a succeeding conifer crop. In Thetford Forest in eastern England, extensive death of pine has occurred in second rotation pine crops where these have replaced crops seriously attacked by the disease. Greig and Burdekin (1970) report a series of experiments to test treatments which might overcome this problem. These treatments included removal of stumps of the first rotation crop, delayed replanting after clear felling and treatment of stumps with *P. gigantea*. The most successful treatment was removal of stumps and this reduced infection in the second rotation after 11 years from 54 per cent in control to 20 per cent in stump removal plots.

Extensive surveys were undertaken in Thetford Forest (Greig, 1971) in order to identify those areas where serious losses from *H. annosum* were likely to occur in the second rotation. Approximately one fifth of the area due to be clearfelled in a five-year programme was severely affected and following a thorough economic evaluation, stump removal was introduced as a routine treatment for these areas (figure 34).

Figure 34. Control of *Heterobasidion annosum* by removal of pine stumps prior to replanting a second rotation (Forestry Commission)

Stump removal may have other advantages, as once the stumps are removed soil cultivation is possible, and in frosty sites may give better establishment with less beating up of some species, and reduce later weeding costs. There is also some evidence that in the case of pine, inoculation of the stumps with *Peniophora gigantea* may be beneficial, as this fungus grows down and occupies a large part of the stump body and limits the growth of *H. annosum* present in the roots (Rishbeth, 1963).

Finally, the relative susceptibility of species may be taken into account when replanting an infested site. Thus, except on alkaline or old arable sites, Scots or other pines may safely be used to follow a species that has suffered from this butt rot, though account has to be taken of possible reductions in total volume production resulting from such a change of species. For suitable sites, *Abies grandis* is a high-yielding alternative, though we still need more information on the degree of resistance of this species in conditions of heavy infestation.

Little work has yet been done on breeding or selecting for resistance to *H. annosum,* though screening of southern pines has been started in North America by Driver and Ginns (1966), and there is considerable interest in variation in Norway spruce in Europe.

MISCELLANEOUS DISEASES

Bacterial wetwood
Though wetwood (plate 11) has been described in some conifers, at least in this country it occurs in its typical form mainly in broadleaved trees. It is very fully described and discussed by Hartley *et al*. (1961).

In typical wetwood, the wood is exceptionally wet, with an abnormally high pH, and a high gas pressure commonly occurs within the trunk. As a result of the pressure, water, which usually smells of fermentation, may ooze out of the trunk, forming a slime-flux as further fermentation takes place. It soaks and kills considerable areas of bark as it runs down the stem. Some dieback in the tops of affected trees sometimes occurs. Indeed, Hartley *et al.* (1961) regard Watermark disease of willow, caused by *Erwinia salicis* and described in Chapter 17, as a form of wetwood. This disease, however is much more extreme in its symptoms, and is usually regarded as a true bacterial wilt.

Wetwood and slime-flux have so far been little studied here, but Ogilvie (1924) found the disorder in elm, willow and horse chestnut as well as in apple. Peace (1962) found it also in poplar. Elsewhere it has been noted in many other broad-leaved trees, and in a few conifers.

The cause of wetwood is not yet certainly known, though there is some evidence that weakly parasitic bacteria, possibly followed by other saprophytic ones, may be involved. Among those apparently implicated is *Erwinia numi-pressuralis* Carter (Carter, 1945).

Little can be done to control wetwood and slime-fluxes. In the case of trees in parks and gardens, the bark killed by a flux is sometimes removed, and the wound dressed with tar, and excess water is sometimes drawn off by tapping the trunk with a tube.

REFERENCES

Anon (1930). Chronique forestière. La maladie du rond. *Bull. Soc. Centr. For. Belg.*, **36**, 522–26
Anon (1951). *Phomopsis Disease of Conifers*, Leafl. For. Commn, no. 14
Anon (1961). *Armillaria Root Rot*, Advis. Leafl. Minist. Agric. Fish. Fd. No. 500
Anon (1962). Field excursions. *Conference and Study Tour on Fomes annosus, Scotland, 1960*, IUFRO, Firenze
Anon (1963). *Forest disease research. 1962 at the Southern Forest Experiment Station*, pp. 43–44. U.S. Dep. Agric. Forest Service
Anon (1964). *Fomes annosus* root rot. *Ann. Rep. N.E. For. Exp. Sta., 1963*, pp. 58–9
Anon (1967). *Honey Fungus*, Leafl. For. Commn, no. 6
Anon (1968*a*). *Phacidiella coniferarum* Hahn. *Distrib. Maps Pl. Dis.*, no. 320
Anon (1968*b*). *Cultivation of the Cricket Bat Willow*, Bull. For. Commn, no. 17, 37 pp.
Anon (1969). *Coral Spot*, Advis. Leafl. Minist. Agric. Fish. Fd., no. 23
Anon (1971). *Apple and Pear Canker*, Advis. Leafl. Minist. Agric. Fish. Fd., no. 100
Anon (1973). *Nectria galligena* Bres. *Distrib. Maps Pl. Dis.*, no. 38
Anon (1979*a*). *Verticillium albo-atrum* Reinke & Berth. *Distrib. Maps Pl. Dis.*, no. 365
Anon (1979*b*). *Verticillium dahliae* Kleb. *Distrib. Maps Pl. Dis.*, no. 366
Anon (1980*a*). *Armillaria mellea* (Vahl ex Fr.) Kummer. *Distrib. Maps Pl. Dis.*, no. 143
Anon (1980*b*). *Heterobasidion annosum* (Fr.) Bref. *Distrib. Maps Pl. Dis.*, no. 271
Arvidson, B. (1954). En studie av granrötrotans (Polyporus annosus Fr.) ekonomiska Konsekvenser. *Svenska Skogs. Tidskrift.*, **52**, 381–412
Ashcroft, J. M. (1934). *European Canker of Black Walnut and Other Trees*, Bull. W. Va. agric. Exp. Sta., no. 261, 52 pp.
Bakshi, B. K. (1950). Fungi associated with ambrosia beetles in Great Britain. *Trans. Br. mycol. Soc.*, **33**, 111–120
Bakshi, B. K. (1952). *Oedocephalum lineatum* is a conidial stage of *Fomes annosus*. *Trans. Br. mycol. Soc.*, **35**, 195
Batko, S., in G. D. Holmes and G. Buszewicz (1954, 1955, 1956, 1957*a*, *b*). Forest tree seed investigations. *Rep. For. Res., Lond., 1953*, pp. 14–17; *1954*, pp. 1–4; *1955*, pp. 13–14; *1956*, pp. 15–17; *1957*, pp. 17–19
Baxter, D. V. (1953). *Observations on Forest Pathology as Part of Forestry in Europe*, Univ. Mich. Sch. For. & Cons. Bull., no. 2, 39 pp.
Benton, V. L. and Ehrlich, J. (1941). Variation in culture of several isolates of *Armillaria mellea* from western white pine. *Phytopathology*, **31**, 803–811
Berkeley, G. H., Madden, G. O. and Willison, R. S. (1931). Verticillium wilts in Ontario. *Scient. Agric.*, **11**, 739–59
Berry, F. H. (1965). Treat stumps to prevent *Fomes annosus* in shortleaf pine plantations. *U.S. For. Serv. Res. Not.*, CS-34
Bliss, D. E. (1941*a*). Relation of soil temperature to Armillaria root rot in California. *Phytopathology*, **31**, 3 (abstract)
Bliss, D. E. (1941*b*). Artificial inoculation of plants with *Armillaria mellea*. *Phytopathology*, **31**, 859 (abstract)
Bliss, D. E. (1944). *Controlling Armillaria Root Rot in Citrus*, California Agric. Exp. Sta., 7 pp.
Bliss, D. E. (1946). The relation of soil temperature to the development of Armillaria root rot. *Phytopathology*, **36**, 302–18
Bliss, D. E. (1951). The destruction of *Armillaria mellea* in citrus soils. *Phytopathology*, **41**, 665–83
Booth, C. (1959). *Studies of Pyrenomycetes: IV. Nectria (Part 1)*, Mycol. Pap, no. 73
Borg, P. (1935). Report of the plant pathologist. *Rep. Insp. Agric. Malta, 1933–34*, pp. 43–6

Boughey, A. S. (1938). Honey fungus as a disease of Rhododendron. *Gdnrs' Chron.*, **104**, 84

Boullard, B. (1961). Etude d'une attaque de 'l'Armillaria mellea' (Vahl) Quél. sur l'Epicea de Sitka. *Rev. for. fr.*, **1**, 16–24

Brandt, R. W. (1964). *Nectria Canker of Hardwoods*, Forest Pest Leafl. no. 84

Braun, H. J. (1956). Zur frage der Infektion von Schäl -und Schurfwunden durch den Wurzelschwamm *Fomes annosus*. *Forst- u. Holzwirt*, **11**, 430–31

Braun, H. J. (1958). Untersuchungen über den Wurzelschwamm *Fomes annosus* (Fr.) Cooke. *Forstwiss. Centralb.*, **77**, 65–88

Breed, R. S., Murray, E. G. D. and Hitchins, A. P. (1948). *Bergey's Manual of Determinative Bacteriology*, Williams and Wilkins, Baltimore

Bronchi, P. (1956). Origine dell' abetina pura artificiale nella Foresta Demaniale di Badia Prataglia in relazione ai recente danni da *Fomes annosus* su 'Abies alba'. *Monti Boschi*, 7, 368–373

Brooks, F. T. (1910). *Rhizina undulata* attacking newly planted conifers. *Q. Jl. For.*, **4**, 308–9

Brooks, F. T. (1953). *Plant Diseases*, Oxford University Press, London

Buckland, D. C. (1953). Observations on *Armillaria mellea* in immature Douglas fir. *For. Chron.*, **29**, 344–7

Bulit, J. (1957). Contribution à l'étude biologique du *Nectria galligena* Bres., agent du chancre du pommier. *Ann. Inst. Rech. agron.*, *Sér. C. (Ann. Epiphyt.)*, 8, 67–89

Buxton, E. W., Sinha, I. and Ward, V. (1962). Soil-borne diseases of Sitka spruce seedlings in a forest nursery. *Trans. Br. mycol. Soc.*, **45**, 433–48

Campbell, A. H. (1934). Zone lines in plant tissues. II. The black lines formed by *Armillaria mellea* (Vahl) Quél. *Ann. appl. Biol.*, **21**, 1–22

Campbell, W. G. (1932). The chemistry of the white rots in wood. III. *Biochem. J.*, **26**, 1829–38

Cantiani, M. (1960). Note sulla diffusione del Marciunne radicale nelle abetine di Vallombrosa. *Italia for. mont.*, **15**, 122–4

Caroselli, N. E. (1954). Verticillium wilt of maple. *Diss. Abstr.*, **14**, 2186–7

Caroselli, N. E. (1955*a*). Investigations of toxins produced *in vitro* by the maple wilt fungus *Verticillium* sp. *Phytopathology*, **45**, 183 (abstract)

Caroselli, N. E. (1955*b*). The relation of soil-water content and that of sapwood-water to the incidence of maple wilt caused by *Verticillium* sp. *Phytopathology*, **45**, 184 (abstract)

Caroselli, N. E. (1957). Verticillium wilt of maples. *Rhode Island Exp. Sta. Bull.*, **335**, 1–84

Caroselli, N. E. (1959). The relation of sapwood moisture content to the incidence of maple wilt caused by *Verticillium albo-atrum*. *Phytopathology*, **49**, 496–8

Carter, J. C. (1945). Wetwood of elms. *Bull. Ill. Nat. Hist. Survey*, **23**, 401–48

Cayley, D. M. (1921). Some observations on the life history of *Nectria galligena* Bres. *Ann. Bot.*, **35**, 75–92

Christensen, C. M. and Hodson, A. L. (1954). Artificially induced senescence of forest trees. *J. For.*, **52**, 126–9

Cobb, F. W. Jr. and Schmidt, R. A. (1964). Duration of susceptibility of Eastern White pine stumps to *Fomes annosus*. *Phytopathology*, **54**, 1216–18

Cram, W. H. and Vaartaja, O. (1957). Toxicity of eight pesticides to spruce and caragana seed. *For. Chron.*, **31**, 247–9

Cunningham, G. H. (1957). Thelephoraceae of New Zealand. Parts XII & XIII. *Trans. R. Soc. N.Z.*, **84**, 479–96

Curl, E. A. and Arnold, M. M. (1964). Influence of substrate and microbiological interactions on growth of *Fomes annosus*. *Phytopathology*, **54**, 1486–7

Curschmann, O. H. (1960). Über die sogenannte 'Ackersterbe' der Kiefer und ihre waldbaulichen Auswirkungen. *Forst. Jagd*, **10**, 464–5

Darley, E. F. and Wilbur, W. D. (1954). Some relationships of carbon disulfide and *Trichoderma viride* in the control of *Armillaria mellea*. *Phytopathology*, **44**, 485 (abstract)

Davidson, R. W. (1935). Forest pathology notes. *Pl. Dis. Reptr.*, **19**, 94–7

Day, W. R. (1927). The parasitism of *Armillaria mellea* in relation to conifers *Q. Jl. For.*, **21**, 9–21

Day, W. R. (1929). Environment and disease. A discussion on the parasitism of *Armillaria mellea* (Vahl) Fr. *Forestry*, **9**, 60–61

Dennis, R. W. G. (1968). *British Ascomycetes,* J. Cramer, Lehre

Dochinger, L. S. (1956a). Maple wilt progress report. *Shade Tree,* 29, 1–3

Dochinger, L. S. (1956b). New concepts of the Verticillium wilt disease of maple. *Phytopathology,* 46, 467 (abstract)

Donandt, S. (1932). Untersuchungen über die Pathogenität des Wirtelpilzes *Verticillium alboatrum* R. u. B. *Zeitschr. Parasitenkunde,* 4, 653–711

Dowson, W. J. (1957). *Plant Diseases Due to Bacteria,* Cambridge University Press, Cambridge

Driver, C. H. (1963a). Effect of certain chemical treatments on colonisation of slash pine stumps by *Fomes annosus. Pl. Dis. Reptr.,* 47, 569–71

Driver, C. H. (1963b). Further data on borax as a control of surface infection of slash pine stumps by *Fomes annosus. Pl. Dis. Reptr.,* 47, 1006–9

Driver, C. H. and Dell, T. R. (1961). *Fomes annosus* root-rot in slash pine plantations of the Eastern Gulf Coast States. *Pl. Dis. Reptr.,* 45, 38–40

Driver, C. H. and Ginns, J. H., Jr. (1966). A method of mass screening of Southern pines for resistance to a root-rot induced by *Fomes annosus* (Fr.) Cke, in H. D. Gerhold, E. J. Schreiner, R. E. McDermott and J. A. Winieski (Eds.), *Breeding Pest-Resistant Trees,* Pergamon Press, London, pp. 421–2

Dufrénoy, J. and Dufrénoy, M. L. (1927). Hadromycoses. *Annls Epiphyt.,* 13, 195–212

Ende, G. van den (1958). Untersuchungen über den Pflanzenparasiten *Verticillium albo-atrum* Reinke et Berthe. *Acta bot. neerl.,* 7, 665–740

Engelhard, A. W. (1957). Host index of *Verticillium albo-atrum* Reinke & Berthe. (including *Verticillium dahliae* Kleb.). *Suppl. Pl. Dis. Reptr.,* 244, 24–49

Englerth, G. H. (1942). *Decay of Western Hemlock in Western Oregon and Washington,* Bull. Sch. For. Yale, no. 50, pp. i and 53

Epners, Z. (1964). A new psychrophilic fungus causing germination failure of conifer seeds. *Can. J. Bot.,* 42, 1589–1604

Etheridge, D. E. (1955). Comparative studies of North American and European cultures of the root-rot fungus *Fomes annosus* (Fr.) Cooke. *Can. J. Bot.,* 33, 416–28

Faulkner, R. and Holmes, G. D. (1954). Experimental work in nurseries. *Rep. Forest Res., Lond., 1953,* pp. 17–31

Flack, N. J. and Swinburne, T. R. (1977). Host range of *Nectria galligena* Bres. and the pathogenicity of some Northern Ireland isolates. *Trans. Br. mycol. Soc.,* 68, 185–192

Foster, R. E. (1962). *Fomes annosus* in British Columbia. *Conference and Study Tour on Fomes annosus, Scotland, 1960* IUFRO, Firenze, pp. 19–20

Fowler, M. E. (1962). *Fomes annosus* in North Eastern United States. *Conference and Study Tour on Fomes annosus, Scotland, 1960,* IUFRO, Firenze, pp. 20–22

Francke-Grosmann, H. (1962). Under what conditions can *Fomes annosus* grow in non-sterilised soil? *Conference and Study Tour on Fomes annosus, Scotland, 1960,* IUFRO, Firenze, pp. 22–8

Garbowski, L. (1936). Przyczynek do znajomości mikroflory grzybrej nasion drzew lesnych. *Prace Wydz. Chor. Rośl państw. Inst. Nauk Gosp. wiejsk Bydgoszczy,* 15, 5–30; abstract in *Rev. appl. Mycol.,* 16, 147, 1937

Garrett, S. D. (1956a). *Biology of Root-Infecting Fungi,* Cambridge University Press, Cambridge

Garrett, S. D. (1956b). Rhizomorph behaviour in *Armillaria mellea* (Vahl) Quél. II. Logistics of infection. *Ann. Bot.,* 20, 193–209

Garrett, S. D. (1958). Inoculum potential as a factor limiting lethal action by *Trichoderma viride* Fr. on *Armillaria mellea* (Fr.) Quel. *Trans. Br. mycol. Soc.,* 41, 157–164

Georgevitch, P. (1926). Sušenje hrastovich šuma u Slavoniji. Abstract in *Rev. appl. Mycol.,* 6, 5, 1927

Gerlings, J. H. J. (1939). Herkomstonderzoek van den Douglasspar aan de afdeeling houtteelt van het Instituut voor Boschbouwkundig Onderzoek. *Ned. BoschbTijdschr.,* 12, 405–32

Gibbs, J. N. (1967a). A study of the epiphytic growth habit of *Fomes annosus. Ann. Bot.,* 31, 755–74

Gibbs, J. N. (1967b). The role of host vigour in the susceptibility of pines to *Fomes annosus. Ann. Bot.,* 31, 803–815

Gibson, I. A. S. (1957). Saprophytic fungi as destroyers of germinating pine seeds. *E. Afr. agric. J.,* 22, 203–6

Gibson, I. A. S. (1961). A note on variation between isolates of *Armillaria mellea* (Vahl ex Fr.) Kummer, *Trans Br. mycol. Soc.*, **44**, 123–8

Gibson, I. A. S. and Goodchild, N. A. (1961). *Armillaria mellea* in Kenya tea plantations. *Rep. 6th Commw. mycol. Conf.*, pp. 39–48

Ginns, J. H. Jr. (1968). *Rhizina Root Rot of Douglas Fir in British Columbia*, For. Pest Leafl. Victoria, 5 pp.

Gladman, R. J. and Greig, B. J. W. (1965). *Principal Butt Rots of Conifers*, Bookl. For. Commn, no. 13.

Gladman, R. J. and Low, J. D. (1963). Conifer heart rots in Scotland. *Forestry*, **36**, 227–44

Goidánich, G. (1932). La verticilliosi dell' 'Acer campestre' L. e alcuni altri casi di tracheo-micosi in Italia. *Boll. R. Staz. Pat. Veg., N.S.*, **12**, 285–97

Goidánich, G. (1934). La verticilliosi dell' '*Acer platanoides* L., dell' *Acer pseudoplatanus* L., e della *Maclura aurantiaca* L. *Boll. R. Staz. Pat. Veg., N.S.*, **14**, 268–72

Gooding, G. V. (1964). Effect of temperature on growth and survival of *Fomes annosus* in freshly cut pine bolts. *Phytopathology*, **54**, 893–4 (abstract)

Gordon, A. G., Salt, G. A. and Brown, R. M. (1976). Effect of pre-sowing moist-chilling treatments on seedbed emergence of Sitka spruce seed infected by *Geniculodendron pyriforme* Salt. *Forestry*, **49**, 143–51

Gothe, H. (1957) Beobachtungen über stockfäule in Schlitzer Lärchen-bestanden. 2 Mitteilung. *Forst- u. Holzwirt*, **12**, 70–74

Grant, T. J. (1937). *Reduction of Nectria Canker in Hardwood Forests of the Northeast*, U.S. Dep. Agric. NEast Forest Exp. Stn. Occasional Pap., no. 6

Gravatt, G. F. (1926). *Maple Wilt*, U.S. Dep. Agric. Circ., no. 382

Greig, B. J. W. (1962). *Fomes annosus* (Fr.) Cke and other root-rotting fungi in conifers on ex-hardwood sites. *Forestry*, **35**, 164–182

Greig, B. J. W. (1971). Death and decay caused by *Fomes annosus*. *Rep. Forest Res., Lond.*, pp. 77–8, 1971

Greig, B. J. W. (1979). Species susceptibility to Fomes butt rot. *Q. Jl. For.*, **73**, 21–25

Greig, B. J. W. and Burdekin, D. A. (1970). Control and eradication of *Fomes annosus* in Great Britain. *Proc. 3rd Int. Conf. on Fomes annosus*, U.S. Dep. Agric. For Serv., pp. 21–32

Greig, B. J. W. and Redfern, D. B. (1974). *Fomes annosus*. Leafl. For. Commn, no. 5.

Greig, B. J. W. and Strouts, R. G. (1977). *Honey fungus*, Arboric Leafl. 2, HMSO, London.

Gremmen, J. (1959). Uber zwei *Phacidiaceae* von *Pinus silvestris* L. *Phytopath. Z.*, **35**, 27–30

Gremmen, J. (1961). Naaldhout aftsterving door *Rhizina undulata* in het bijzonder na takken-branden. *Ned. Boschb Tijdschr.*, **33**, 5–10

Gremmen, J. (1963). De biologiske bestrijding van de Wortzelzwam *Fomes annosus* (Fr.) Cke door middel van *Peniophora gigantea* (Fr.) Massee. *Ned. Boschb.Tijdschr.*, **35**, 356–67

Griffin, D. M. (1955). Fungal damage to roots of Sitka spruce seedlings in forest nurseries. *Rep. Forest Res., Lond., 1954*, pp. 52–3

Griffin, D. M. (1956). Fungal damage to roots of Sitka spruce seedlings in forest nurseries. *Rep. Forest Res., Lond., 1955*, pp. 75–6

Griffin, D. M. (1957). Fungal damage to roots of Sitka spruce seedlings in forest nurseries. *Rep. Forest Res., Lond., 1956*, pp. 86–7

Griffin, D. M. (1965). A study of damping-off, root damage and related phenomena in coniferous seedlings in British forest nurseries, in B. Benzian (Ed.), *Experiments on nutrition Problems in Forest Nurseries, 1*, Bull. For. Commn, Lond., no. 37, pp. 212–227

Gross, H. L. and Weidensaul, T. C. (1967). *Phacidiopycnis pseudotsugae* associated with bleeding cankers on hemlock. *Pl. Dis. Reptr.*, **51**, 807–8

Grove, W. B. (1935). *British Stem- and Leaf-Fungi (Coelomycetes)*, Vol. 1, Cambridge University Press, Cambridge

Grove, W. B. (1937). *British Stem- and Leaf-Fungi (Coelomycetes)*, vol. 2, Cambridge University Press, Cambridge

Guba, E. F. (1961). *Monograph of* Monochaetia *and* Pestalotia. Harvard University Press, Harvard

Gundersen, K. (1962). The physiology of *Fomes annosus*. *Conference and Study Tour on Fomes annosus, Scotland, 1960* IUFRO, Firenze, pp. 31–7

Gundersen, K. (1963). Nytt kemisk medel mot rotrötra. *Skogen*, **50**, 288–9

Gundersen, K. (1967). Nitrite as a nutrient for microfungi of the outer stem cortex of pine and spruce and its toxicity to *Fomes annosus*. *Studia forestal. suec.*, no. 43, 22 pp.

Guyot, R. (1933). De la maladie du rond; de l'influence des foyers ou des foyers d'incendie dans sa propagation. *Rev. gén. Sci.*, 44, 239–47.

Haas, P. G. de and Wennemuth, G. (1962). [Refrigerated storage of woody plants from nurseries. III. *Botrytis*- and *Fusarium* infection of woody plants in refrigerated storage]. *Gartenbauwissenschaft*, 27, 231–42; abstract in *Rev. appl. Mycol.*, 42, 1963, p. 323.

Hagner, M. (1962). Nagra faktorer av betydelse for rotmurklans skadegorelse. *Norrlands Skogsv. Tidskr.*, 2, 245–70

Hahn, G. G. (1957). *Phacidiopycnis (Phomopsis)* canker and dieback of conifers. *Pl. Dis. Reptr.*, 41, 623–33

Halber, M. (1963). *Botrytis* sp. on Douglas fir seedlings. *Pl. Dis. Reptr.*, 47, 556

Haraldstad, A. R. (1962). Investigations on *Fomes annosus* in Høylandskomplekset, South Western Norway. *Nyt. Mag. Bot.*, 9 (1961), 175–98

Hartig, R. (1894). *Text-book of the Diseases of Trees*, English ed., transl. W. Somerville, revised and edited H. Marshall Ward, Macmillan, London

Hartley, C. (1921). *Damping-off in Forest Nurseries*. Bull. U.S. Dep. Agric., no. 934, pp. 1–99

Hartley, C., Davidson, R. W. and Crandall, B. S. (1961). *Wetwood, Bacteria, and Increased pH in Trees* U.S. Dep. Agric. Forest Service, no. 2215, 34 pp.

Hartley, C., Pierce, R. G. and Hahn, G. G. (1919). Moulding of snow smothered nursery stock. *Phytopathology*, 9, 521–31

Henriksen, H. A. and Jørgensen, E. (1954). Rodfordoerverangreb i relation til udhugnings-grad. *Forst. ForsVaes. Danm.*, 21, 215–57

Hepting, G. H. and Downs, A. A. (1944). Root and butt rot in planted white pine at Biltmore, North Carolina. *J. For.*, 42, 119–121

Hodges, C. S. (1964). The effect of competition by *Peniophora gigantea* on the growth of *Fomes annosus* in stumps and roots. *Phytopathology*, 54, 623 (abstract)

Holmes, F. W. (1967). Resistance of certain elm clones to *Ceratocystis ulmi* and *Verticillium albo-atrum*. *Phytopathology*, 57, 1247–9

Hunt, J. and Krueger, K. W. (1962). Decay associated with thinning wounds in young-growth Western Hemlock and Douglas fir. *J. For.*, 60, 336–40

Huss, E. (1952). Skogsforskningsinstitutets metodik vid froündersökningar. *Medd. Skogs-forsken Inst. Stockh.*, 40 (1951), 1–82

Isaac, I. (1949). A comparative study of pathogenic isolates of *Verticillium*. *Trans. Br. mycol. Soc.*, 32, 137–57

Isaac, I. (1953). The spread of diseases caused by species of *Verticillium*. *Ann. appl. Biol.*, 40, 630–38

Ito, K. and Hosaka, Y. (1951). Grey mold and sclerotial disease of 'sugi' (*Cryptomeria japonica* D. Don) seedlings, the causes of the so-called 'snow moulding'. *Bull. For. Exp. Sta. Tokyo*, 51, 1–27

Jalaluddin, M. (1967a). Studies on *Rhizina undulata*. I. Mycelial growth and ascospore germination. *Trans. Br. mycol. Soc.*, 50, 449–59

Jalaluddin, M. (1967b). Studies on *Rhizina undulata*. II. Observations and experiments in East Anglian plantations. *Trans. Br. mycol. Soc.*, 50, 461–72

Jamalainen, E. A. (1961). Havupuiden taimistojen talvituhosienivauriot ja niiden kemiallinen torjunta. Reprinted from *Silva Fenn.*, 108, 15 pp.

Jenkins, P. T. (1952). Armillaria on fruit trees. *J. Dep. Agric. Vict.*, 1952, 50, 88–90

Jørgensen, C. A., Lund, A. and Treschow, C. (1939). Underøgelsen over Rodfordaervesen, *Fomes annosus* (Fr.) Cke. *K. Vet. Højeh. Aarsskr.*, 1939, 71–128; abstract in *Rev. appl. Mycol.*, 18, 772–773, 1939

Jørgensen, E. (1955). Trametes angreb i laehegn. *Dansk Skovforen. Tidsskr.*, 40, 279–85

Jørgensen, E. (1962). Fomes root rot investigations in Ontario *Conference and Study Tour on Fomes annosus, Scotland, 1960*, IUFRO, Firenze, pp. 44–7

Jørgensen, H. A. (1952). Studies of *Nectria cinnabarina*. Hosts and variations. *Årsskr. K. Vet.-Landbohøjsk.*, 1952, pp. 57–120

Korhonen, K. (1978). Interfertility and clonal size in the *Armillaria mellea* complex. *Karstenia*, 18, 31–42

Kunze, E. H. (1952–53). Uber den antagonismus zwischen *Armillaria mellea* und *Pleurotus ostreatus in vitro*. *Wiss. J. Univ. Jena*, 2, 97–9

Laine, L. (1968). Kuplamörsky (*Rhizina undulata* Fr.) uusi metsän tuhosieni maasamme. *Fol. For., Helsinki*, 44, 11 pp.

Lange, M. and Hora, B. (1963). *Collins Guide to Mushrooms and Toadstools,* Collins, London

Lanier, L. (1962). Contribution à l'étude des maladies du rond. *Note Technique Forestière, Nancy,* 9, 7 pp.

Larue, J. H., Paulus, A. O., Wilbur, W. D., O'Reilly, H. J. and Darley, E. F. (1962). Armillaria root rot fungus controlled with methyl bromide soil fumigation. *Calif. Agric.,* 16, 8–9

Leach, R. (1937). Observations on the parasitism and control of *Armillaria mellea. Proc. R. Soc., Ser. B,* 131, 561–73

Lelliott, R. A. (1968). The diagnosis of fireblight (*Erwinia amylovora*) and some diseases caused by *Pseudomonas syringae. Rep. Eur. Medit. Pl. Prot. Orgn., Conf. Fireblight 1967,* 45, 27–34

Lelliott, R. A. (1979). *Fireblight of Apple and Pear.* Leafl. Min. Agric. Fish. Fd., no. 571

Liese, J. (1931). Starke Schaden dürch den Pappelkrebs. *Dt. Forstz.,* 46, 465–6

Lohman, M. L. and Watson A. J. (1943). Identity and host relations of *Nectria* species associated with diseases of hardwoods in the Eastern States. *Lloydia,* 6, 77–108

Lortie, M. (1964). Pathogenesis in cankers caused by *Nectria galligena,* in 'Symposium on cankers of forest trees, *Phytopathology,* 54, 250–78

Lortie, M. (1969). Inoculations of *Nectria galligena* on northern hardwoods. *Contr. Fonds. Rech. for. Univ. Laval.,* 13, 31 pp.

Lortie, M. and Kuntz, J. E. (1962). Studies on spore discharge of *Nectria galligena. Phytopathology,* 52, 740 (abstract)

Lortie, M. and Kuntz, J. E. (1963). Ascospore discharge and conidium release by *Nectria galligena* Bres. under field and laboratory conditions. *Can. J. Bot.,* 41. 1205–10

Low, J. D. and Gladman, R. J. (1960). *Fomes annosus in Great Britain.* Forest Rec., Lond., no. 41

Low, J. D. and Gladman, R. J. (1962*a*). Butt-rot of conifers in Scotland. A brief account of its distribution and occurrence. *Conference and Study Tour on Fomes annosus, Scotland, 1960,* IUFRO, Firenze, pp. 48–50

Low, J. D. and Gladman, R. J. (1962*b*). Present day research on *Fomes annosus* in Britain by the Forestry Commission. *Conference and Study Tour on Fomes annosus, Scotland, 1960,* IUFRO, Firenze, pp. 56–65

Łukomski, S. (1962). *Verticillium alboatrum* moze byc grozne. *Las Polski,* 2, 10–11

McKay, R. and Clear, T. (1953). Association of *Rhizina inflata* with group dying of Sitka spruce. *Ir. For.,* 10, 58–9

McKay, R. and Clear, T. (1955). A further note on group dying of Sitka spruce and *Rhizina inflata. Ir. For.,* 12, 58–63

McKay, R. and Clear, T. (1958). Violet root rot (*Helicobasidium purpureum*) on Douglas Fir (*Pseudotsuga taxifolia*) and *Pinus contorta. Ir. For.,* 14, 90–97

McKenzie, M. A. (1954). Maple wilt. *Trees, Cleveland, Ohio,* 14, 19–20

Magnani, G. (1963). Necrosi su piantine di Eucalitto causate da *Botrytis cinerea* Pers. *Pubbl. Cent. Sper. Agric. For. Roma,* 6, 211–23

Mangin, L. (1894). Sur la maladie du rouge dans les pépinières et les plantations de Paris. *C. r. hebd. Séanc. Acad. Sci., Paris,* 119, 735–756

Manka, K. (1953). *Badania terenowe i laboratoryjne nad Opienka miodowa.* Inst. Bad. Lesnictwa (Warsaw)., Pr. no. 94, 96 pp.

Maraite, H. and Meyer, J. A. (1966). Incidence de quelques facteurs du milieu sur la pourriture rouge de l'épicea. *Bull. Soc. Roy. For. Belg.,* 73, 493–509

Marsh, R. W. (1939). Observations on apple canker. II. Experiments on the incidence and control of shoot infection. *Ann. appl. Biol.,* 26, 458–69

Marsh, R. W. (1952). Field observations on the spread of *Armillaria mellea* in apple orchards and in a black currant plantation. *Trans. Br. mycol. Soc.,* 35, 201–7

Matta, A. and Kerling, L. C. P. (1964). *Verticillium albo-atrum* as a parasite of *Senecio vulgaris. Neth. J. Pl. Path.,* 70, 27–32

May, C. and Gravatt, G. F. (1951). Vascular diseases of hardwoods (caused by *Verticillium albo-atrum* and *Dothiorella* ulmi). From *Important Tree Pests of The Northeast,* Committee on tree pest leaflets, New England Section, Society of American Foresters, New Hampshire, Tree Pest Leafl. No. 19

May, Luiza C. (1962). Unna armillariose em *Pinus elliottii* Engel. *Silvicult., S. Paulo,* 1, 71–84

Meer, J. H. H. van der (1926). Verticillium-wilt of maple and elm seedlings in Holland. *Phytopathology,* 16, 611–14

Meredith, D. S. (1959). Infection of pine stumps by *Fomes annosus* and other fungi. *Ann. Bot.*, **23**, 454–76

Meredith, D. S. (1960). Further observations on fungi inhabiting pine stumps. *Ann. Bot.*, **24**, 63–78

Miller, H. J. (1979). A review of methods used in the laboratory diagnosis of fireblight. *Eur. Medit. Pl. Prot. Orgn. Bull.*, **9**, 7–11

Molin, N. and Rennerfelt, E. (1959). Honungsskivlingen, *Armillaria mellea* (Vahl) Quél., som parasit pa barrträd. *Medd. Skogsforsken Inst., Stockh.*, no. 48, 26 pp.

Mooi, J. C. (1948). Kanker en takinsterving van der Wilg veroorzaakt door *Nectria galligena* en *Cryptodiaporthe salicina*. Thesis, University of Amsterdam, 119 pp. Abstract in *Rev. appl. Mycol.*, **28**, 92–4, 1949

Moore, W. C. (1959). *British Parasitic Fungi*, Cambridge University Press, Cambridge

Moreau, R. and Schaeffer, R. (1962). *Fomes annosus* in the French jura. *Conference and Study Tour on Fomes annosus, Scotland, 1960*, IUFRO, Firenze, pp. 66–69

Munson, R. G. (1939). Observations on apple canker. 1. The discharge and germination of spores of *Nectria galligena* Bres. *Ann. appl. Biol.*, **26**, 440–56

Murray, J. S. (1953). Group dying of spruce in Eire. *Ir. For.*, **10**, 55–7

Murray, J. S. (1962*a*). Forest pathology. *Rep. Forest Res., Lond., 1961*, pp. 57–9

Murray, J. S. (1962*b*). *Fomes annosus*. Its importance in Britain. *Conference and Study Tour on Fomes annosus, Scotland, 1960*, IUFRO, Firenze, pp. 69–71

Murray, J. S. and Young, C. W. T. (1961). *Group Dying of Conifers*, Forest Rec., Lond., no. 46, 19 pp.

Nelson, R. M. (1940). Vigorous young poplar trees can recover from injury by Nectria cankers. *J. For.*, **38**, 587–8

Newhook, F. J. (1959). The association of *Phytophthora* spp. with mortality of *Pinus radiata* and other conifers. *N.Z. J. agric. Res.*, **2**, 808–43

Newhook, F. J., Waterhouse, G. M and Stamps, D. J. (1978). *Tabular key to the species of Phytophthora de Bary*. Mycol. Pap., no. 143

Nobles, M. K. (1948). Studies in forest pathology. VI. Identification of cultures of wood-rotting fungi. *Can. J. Res.*, C, **26**, 28–431

Ogilvie, L. (1924). Observations on the 'slime-fluxes' of trees. *Trans. Br. mycol. Soc.*, **9**, 167–82

Orloś, H. (1954). Proba zwalczania opieńki w świerczynach górskich w skali pólgospodarczej. *Las Polski*, **28**, 9–11

Orloś, H. (1957). Badania nad zwalczaniem opieńki miodowej (*Armillaria mellea* Vahl) metoda bioloziczna. *Roczn. Nauk. lesn.*, **15**, 195–236

Osmaston, L. S. (1927). Mortality among oaks. *Q. Jl. For.*, **21**, 28–30

Paden, J. W., Sutherland, J. R. and Woods, T. A. D. (1978). *Caloscypha fulgens* (Ascomycetidae, Pezizales): the perfect state of the conifer seed pathogen *Geniculodendron pyriforme* (Deuteromycotina, Hyphomycetes). *Can. J. Bot.*, **56**, 2375–9

Patton, R. F. and Riker, A. J. (1959). Artificial inoculations of pine and spruce trees with *Armillaria mellea*. *Phytopathology*, **49**, 615–622

Pawsey, R. G. (1964). *Grey Mould in Forest Nurseries*, Leafl. For. Commn, no. 50, 7 pp.

Pawsey, R. G. and Gladman, R. J. (1965). *Decay in Standing Conifers Developing from Extraction Damage*, Forest Rec., Lond., no. 54.

Pawsey, R. G. and Rahman, M. A. (1976). Chemical control of infection by honey fungus, *Armillaria mellea*: a review. *Arboric. J.*, **2**, 468–79

Peace, T. R. (1938). Butt rot of conifers in Great Britain. *Q. Jl. For.*, **32**, 81–104

Peace, T. R. (1962). *Pathology of Trees and Shrubs*, Clarendon Press, Oxford

Pentland, G. D. (1965). Stimulation of rhizomorph development of *Armillaria mellea* by *Aureobasidium pullulans* in artificial culture. *Can. J. Microbiol.*, **11**, 345–50

Perrin, R. (1976). Clef de détermination des Nectria d'Europe. *Bull. trimest. Soc. mycol. Fr.*, **92**, 335–347

Phillips, D. H. and Greig, B. J. W. (1970). Some chemicals to prevent stump colonisation by *Fomes annosus* (Fr.) Cooke. *Ann. appl. Biol.*, **66**, 441–52

Phillips, D. H. and Young, C. W. T. (1976). *Group Dying of Conifers*, Leafl. For. Commn, no. 65, 7 pp.

Piearce, G. D. (1972). Studies on Verticillium wilt in maples. Ph.D. Thesis, University of Cambridge

Piearce, G. D. and Gibbs, J. N. (1981). Verticillium wilt of trees and shrubs. *Arboric. Leafl.*, no. 9, HMSO, London

Plasman, A. (1953). Note sur la découverte en Belgique de *Phomopsis pseudotsugae* Wilson sur *Pseudotsuga taxifolia* (Lam) Britt. *Parasitica*, 9, 1–5

Potlaychuk, V. I. (1953). Vrednajà mikroflora želudei i ee razvitie v zavisimosti ot uslovi proizvastanija i khranenija. *Bot. Z.*, 38, 135–142; abstract in *Rev. appl. Mycol.*, 33, 1954, p. 57

Pratt, J. E. (1979a). *Fomes annosus* butt rot of Sitka spruce. I. Observations on the development of butt rot in individual trees and in stands. *Forestry*, 52, 11–29

Pratt, J. E. (1979b). *Fomes annosus* butt rot of Sitka spruce. II. Loss of strength of wood in various categories of rot. *Forestry*, 52, 31–45

Pratt, J. E. (1979c). *Fomes annosus* butt rot of Sitka spruce. III. Losses in yield and value of timber in diseased trees and stands. *Forestry*, 52, 113–27

Přihoda, A. (1957). Nakaza živých smrku václavkou. *Les (Bratislava)*, 13, 5

Raabe, R. D. (1958). The effect of light upon growth of *Armillaria mellea* in culture. *Phytopathology*, 48, 397

Raabe, R. D. (1962). Host list of the root-rot fungus *Armillaria mellea*. *Hilgardia*, 3, 25–88

Raabe, R. D. and Gold, A. H. (1967). Effects of different levels of carbon dioxide on the growth of *Armillaria mellea* in culture. *Phytopathology*, 57, 101 (abstract)

Ram Reddy, M. A., Salt, G. A. and Last, F. T. (1964). Growth of *Picea sitchensis* in old forest nurseries. *Ann. appl. Biol.*, 54, 397–414

Ramsbottom, J. (1953). *Mushrooms and Toadstools*, Collins, London

Ramsbottom, J. and Balfour-Brown, F. L. (1951). List of discomycetes recorded from the British Isles. *Trans. Br. mycol. Soc.*, 34, 38–137

Rayner, R. W. (1959). Root rot of coffee and ring-barking of shade trees. *Kenya Coffee*, 24, 361–5

Redfern, D. B. (1968). The ecology of *Armillaria mellea* in Britain: biological control. *Ann. Bot.*, 32, 293–300

Redfern, D. B. (1975). The influence of food base on rhizomorph growth and pathogenicity of *Armillaria mellea* isolates, in G. W. Bruehl (Ed.), *Biology and Control of Soil-borne Plant Pathogens*, American Phytopathological Society, St. Paul, Minnesota, pp. 69–73

Redfern, D. B. (1978). Infection of *Armillaria mellea* and some factors affecting host resistance and the severity of disease. *Forestry*, 51, 121–35

Reitsma, J. (1932). Studien über *Armillaria mellea* (Vahl) Quél. *Phytopath. Z.*, 4, 461–522

Ribeiro, O. K. (1978). *A Source Book of the Genus Phytophthora*, J. Cramer, Lehre

Rishbeth, J. (1951a). Observations on the biology of *Fomes annosus*, with particular reference to East Anglian pine plantations. II. Spore production, stump infection, and saprophytic activity in stumps. *Ann. Bot.*, 15, 1–21

Rishbeth, J. (1951b). Observations on the biology of *Fomes annosus*, with particular reference to East Anglian pine plantations. III. Natural and experimental infection of pines, and some factors affecting severity of the disease. *Ann. Bot.*, 15, 221–46

Rishbeth, J. (1952). Control of *Fomes annosus*. *Forestry*, 25, 41–50

Rishbeth, J. (1957). Some further observations on *Fomes annosus* Fr. *Forestry*, 30, 69–89

Rishbeth, J. (1959a). Stump protection against *Fomes annosus*. I. Treatments with creosote. *Ann. appl. Biol.*, 47, 519–28

Rishbeth, J. (1959b). Stump protection against *Fomes annosus*. II. Treatments with substances other than creosote. *Ann. appl. Biol.*, 47, 529–41

Rishbeth, J. (1959c). Dispersal of *Fomes annosus* Fr. and *Peniophora gigantea* (Fr.) Massee. *Trans. Br. mycol. Soc.*, 42, 243–60

Rishbeth, J. (1963). Stump protection against *Fomes annosus*. III. Inoculation with *Peniophora gigantea*. *Ann. appl. Biol.*, 52, 63–77

Rishbeth, J. (1964). Stump infection by basidiospores of *Armillaria mellea*. *Trans. Br. mycol. Soc.*, 47, 460

Rishbeth, J. (1978). Effects of soil temperature and atmosphere on growth of Armillaria rhizomorphs. *Trans. Br. mycol. Soc.*, 70, 213–20

Robak, H. (1952). *Phomopsis pseudotsugae* Wilson – *Discula pinicola* (Naumov) Petr. as a saprophyte on coniferous woods. *Sydowia*, 6, 378–82

Romagnesi, H. (1970). Observations sur les *Armillariella* (1). *Bull. Soc. mycol. Fr.*, 86, 257–68

Romagnesi, J. (1973). Observations sur les *Armillariella* (2). *Bull. Soc. mycol. Fr.*, 89, 195–206

Roth, E. R. and Hepting, G. H. (1954). Eradication and thinning tests for Nectria and Strumella canker control in Maryland. *J. For.*, 52, 253–6

Rushton, B. S. (1977). Artificial hybridization between *Quercus robur* L. and *Quercus petraea* (Matt.) Liebl. *Watsonia*, 11, 229–36

Salt, G. A. (1964). Pathology experiments on Sitka spruce seedlings. *Rep. Forest Res., Lond., 1963*, pp. 83–7

Salt, G. A. (1965). Pathology experiments on Sitka spruce seedlings. *Rep. Forest Res., Lond., 1964*, pp. 89–95

Salt, G. A. (1967). Pathology experiments on Sitka spruce seedlings. *Rep. Forest Res., Lond., 1966*, pp. 104–8

Salt, G. A. (1974). Etiology and morphology of *Geniculodendron pyriforme* gen. et. sp. nov., a pathogen of conifer seeds. *Trans. Br. mycol. Soc.*, 63, 339–51

Sato, K., Ota, N. and Shoji, T. (1955). Influence of MH-30 treatment upon the control of overgrowth of 'sugi' seedlings. Especially on the effects of the frost damage and grey mould control. *J. Jap. For. Soc.*, 37, 533–37

Sato, K. Shoji, T. and Ota, N. (1959). Studies on the snow moulding of conifer seedlings. I. Grey mould and sclerotial disease. *Bull. Govt Forest Exp. Stn Meguro*, 110, 1–153

Schipper, M. A. A. and Heybroek, H. M. (1957). Het toetsen van stammen van *Nectria cinnabarina* (Tode) Fr. op levende takken *in vitro*. *Tijdschr. PlZiekt.*, 63, 192–4

Schubert, G. H. (1960). Fungi associated with viability losses of sugar pine seed during cold storage. *Proc. Soc. Amer. For.*, 1960, pp. 18–21

Scurti, J. C. (1956). Sulla degradazione dei legni delle piante forestali e da fruitto per azione dell' *Armillaria mellea*. *Ann. Sper. agr. N.S.*, 10, 495–512

Shea, K. R. (1960). Mold fungi on forest tree seed. *For. Res. Note Weyerhaeuser Co. Centralia, Wash.*, no. 31, 10 pp.

Singer, R. (1956). The *Armillariella mellea* complex. *Lloydia*, 19, 176–87

Smerlis, E. (1962). Taxonomy and morphology of *Potebniamyces balsamicola* sp. nov. associated with a twig and branch blight of balsam fir in Quebec. *Can. J. Bot.*, 40, 351–9

Spaulding, P. (1938). A suggested method of converting some heavily Nectria-cankered hardwood stands in Northern New England to soft-woods. *J. For.*, 36, 72

Spierenburg, D. (1937). Bestrijding van het 'vuur' in Eschdoorns. *Tijdschr. PlZiekt.*, 43, 150–51

Stapp, C. (1961). *Bacterial Plant Pathogens*, Oxford University Press, London

Strong, F. C. (1936). Maple wilt. *Q. Bull. Mich. agric. Exp. Sta.*, 18, 225–7

Strouts, R. G. (1981). *Phytophthora Root Rots*, Arboric. Leafl. no. 8, HMSO, London

Swift, M. J. (1965). Loss of suberin from bark tissue rotted by *Armillaria mellea*. *Nature, Lond.*, 207, 436–7

Swift, M. J. (1968). Inhibition of rhizomorph development by *Armillaria mellea* in Rhodesian forest soils. *Trans. Br. mycol. Soc.*, 51, 241–7

Swinburne, T. R. (1975). European canker of apple (*Nectria galligena*). *Rev. Pl. Path.*, 54, 787–99

Swinburne, T. R., Cartwright, J., Flack, N. J. and Brown A. E. (1975). The control of apple canker (*Nectria galligena*) in a young orchard with established infections. *Ann. appl. Biol.*, 81, 61–73

Thomas, H. E. (1934). Studies on *Armillaria mellea* (Vahl) Quél., infection, parasitism, and host resistance. *J. agric. Res.*, 48, 187–218

Thornberry, H. A. and Ray, B. R. (1953). Wilt-inducing protein-like pigment from *Armillaria mellea* (Vahl) Quél. isolated from peach roots. *Phytopathology*, 43, 486 (abstract)

Towers, B. (1966). Effect of induced soil moisture stress on the growth of *Fomes annosus* in inoculated loblolly pine stumps. *Pl. Dis. Reptr.*, 50, 747–9

Tsao, P. H. and Ocana, G. (1969). Selective isolation of species of *Phytophthora* from natural soils on an improved antibiotic medium. *Nature, Lond.*, 223, 636–8

Uri, J. (1948). Het parasitisme van *Nectria cinnabarina* (Tode) Fr. *Tijdschr. PlZiekt.*, 54, 29–73

Urošević, B. (1957). Mykoflora skladovaných žaludu. *Práce výzk. Úst. lesn. ČSR*, 13, 149–200

Urošević, B. (1958). Mumifikace semen našich listnáču. *Lesn. prace*, 37, 320–4

Urpšević, B. (1961). Mykoflora žaludu v období dosrávání, sběru a skladování. *Prace výzk. Úst lesn. ČSR*, 21, 81–203

Vaartaja, O. (1964). Chemical treatment of seedbeds to control nursery diseases. *Bot. Rev.*, 30, 1–91

Vámos, R. (1954). A Fenyöcsemete dölése. *Erdö*, 3, 34–40

Vergara Castillo, C. (1953). Un aporte al estudio de campo y de laboratorio del hongo *Nectria galligena* Bres. *Agricultura Técnica, Santiago*, 13, 62–85

Vloten, H. van (1943). Verschillen in virulentie bij *Nectria cinnabarina* (Tode) Fr. *Tijdschr. PlZiekt.*, 49, 163–71

Vloten, H. van (1952). Evidence of host-parasite relations by experiments with *Phomopsis pseudotsugae* Wilson. *Scott. For.*, 6, 38–46

Voglino, P. (1931). Il nerume delle Castagne. *La Difesa delle Piante*, 8, 1–4

Wakefield, E. M. and Dennis, R. W. G. (1950). *Common British Fungi*, Gawthorn, London

Wallis, G. W. (1960). Survey of *Fomes annosus* in East Anglian pine plantations. *Forestry*, 33, 203–14

Warcup, J. H. (1951). The effect of partial sterilisation on the occurrence of fungi in the soil. *Rep. Forest Res., Lond., 1950*, pp. 107–10

Warcup, J. J. (1952). Effect of partial sterilization by steam or formalin on damping-off of Sitka spruce. *Trans. Br. mycol. Soc.*, 35, 248–62

Warcup, J. H. (1953). Effect of partial sterilisation by steam or formalin on damping-off of Sitka spruce in an old forest nursery. *Rep. Forest Res., Lond., 1952*, p. 108

Waterhouse, G. M. (1963). *Key to the species of Phytophthora de Bary*, Mycol. Pap. no. 92

Waterhouse, G. M. (1970). *The genus Phytophthora de Bary*, Mycol. Pap. no. 122

Watling, R. (1976). A pilot scheme. *Bull. Br. mycol. Soc.*, 10, 43–4

Watson, H. (1928). Notes on attack by *Rhizoctonia crocorum* on Sitka spruce (*Picea sitchensis*). *Scott. For. J.*, 42, 58–61

Weir, J. R. (1915). Observations on *Rhizina inflata. J. agric. Res.*, 4, 93

Whittle, A. M. (1977). Mycoflora of cones and seeds of *Pinus sylvestris. Trans. Br. mycol. Soc.*, 69, 47–57

Wicker, E. F. (1965). A Phomopsis canker on western larch. *Pl. Dis. Reptr.*, 49, 102–5

Wiehe, P. O. (1952). The spread of *Armillaria mellea* (Fr.) Quél. in Tung orchards. *E. Afr. agric. J.*, 18, 67–72

Wilhelm, S. and Ferguson, J. (1953). Soil fumigation against *Verticillium albo-atrum. Phytopathology*, 43, 593–5

Wilson, M. (1920). A new species of *Phomopsis* parasitic on the Douglas fir. *Trans. bot. Soc. Edinb.*, 28, 47–9

Wilson, M. (1921). A newly-recorded disease on Japanese larch. *Trans. R. Scott. arboric. Soc.*, 35, 73–4

Wilson, M. (1925). *The Phomopsis Disease of Conifers*, Bull. For. Commn, Lond., no. 6, 34 pp.

Wilson, M. and Hahn, G. G. (1928). The identity of *Phoma pitya* Sacc., *Phoma abietina* Hart. and their relation to *Phomopsis pseudotsugae* Wilson. *Trans. Br. mycol. Soc.*, 13, 261–78

Wiltshire, S. P. (1921). Studies on the apple canker fungus. 1. Leaf scar infection. *Ann. appl. Biol.*, 8, 182

Woeste, U. (1956). Anatomische untersuchungen über die infektionswege einiger Wurzelpilze. *Phytopath. Z.*, 26, 225–72

Wormald, H. (1930). Bacterial 'blight' of walnuts in Britain. *Ann. appl. Biol.*, 17, 59–70

Wormald, H. (1955). *Diseases of Fruits and Hops*, Crosby Lockwood, London

Wright, W. R. (1960). Storage decays of domestically grown chestnuts. *Pl. Dis. Reptr.*, 44, 820–5

Yde-Andersen, A. (1963). Plantedød i naletraekulturer som følge af kvasbraending. *Dansk Skovforen. Tidsskr.*, 48, 112–23

Zalesky, J. (1968). Penetration and initial establishment of *Nectria galligena* in aspen and peachleaf willow. *Can. J. Bot.*, 46, 57–60

Zeller, S. M. (1926). Observations on infections of apple and prune roots by *Armillaria mellea. Phytopathology*, 16, 479–84

Zeller, S. M. (1935). Some miscellaneous fungi on the Pacific Northwest. *Mycologia*, 27, 449–66

Zeller, S. M. and Owens, C. E. (1921). European canker on the Pacific Slope. *Phytopathology*, 11, 464–8

Zeller, W. (1979). Resistance and resistance breeding in ornamentals. *Bull. Eur. Medit. Pl. Prot. Orgn.*, 9, 35–44

Zentmeyer, G. A. (1961). Chemotaxis of zoospores for root exudates. *Science,* **133**, 1595–6

Zycha, H. (1961/2). Trieb- und Nadelschäden an jungen Lärchen im Bestand. Reprinted from *Allg. Forstz.*, 27/28, 2 pp.

4 Diseases of spruce (*Picea* spp.)

Two spruces, Norway spruce (*Picea abies*) and Sitka spruce (*P. sitchensis*), are important forest trees in this country. Sitka spruce, a very fast growing tree introduced from the west coast of North america, is now the most commonly planted of all our forest trees. Norway spruce, from continental Europe, is now less important in the forest, but is produced in large numbers for the Christmas tree trade. The Serbian spruce (*P. omorika*), a fast growing species from Jugoslavia, has been grown experimentally by foresters, but has not become established in forest use. Many other species of *Picea*, particularly various cultivars of the blue spruce (*P. pungens*) are grown in parks and gardens.

NURSERY DISEASES

GENERAL

Damping-off caused by species of *Pythium* is common in beds of first-year seedlings of Sitka spruce in the more northerly parts of Britain.

The grey mould *Botrytis cinerea* mainly affects nursery stock, and is commonly reported in beds of Sitka and less often in those of Norway spruce. It is described in chapter 3.

SEEDLING AND SHOOT BLIGHTS

Seedling blight associated with *Phomopsis occulta* (Sacc.) Trav.

Phomopsis occulta is a common saprophyte on dead leaves and stems and fallen cones of many conifers. In Great Britain it has been found on Norway and Sitka spruce, Scots and Corsican pines and *Pinus radiata*, the larches, Douglas fir and *Abies alba* (*A. pectinata*). Though its pathogenicity has not been proved on the two spruces it has sometimes been associated with a seedling blight. The affected plants have been girdled at the base, which was covered by white mycelium, and the seedlings died back from the tops (Peace, 1962). The stems of the dead seedlings bore black, rounded pycnidia of *P. occulta*. The pycnidia of this fungus measure up to 1 mm across, and contain colourless A, B and C spores that exude as a white or yellowish tendril. The A spores are ellipsoid–oblong and curved, and measure 8-11 x 2-2.5 µm, the B spores are hairlike, straight or walking-stick shaped, 20-27 x 1 µm, while the C spores are intermediate (Grove, 1935). The fungus appears to be the imperfect stage of *Diaporthe conorum* (Grove, 1935; Hahn, 1930), which Wehmeyer (1933) regards as a form of *D. eres*. According to Peace (1962) it has sometimes caused severe damage in spruce seedbeds, but attacks have been infrequent.

Shoot blight caused by *Sirococcus strobilinus*

Shoot blight caused by *Sirococcus strobilinus* is a minor disease which affects both Norway and Sitka spruce in both nurseries and plantations. It is described on p.130.

ROOT ROTS

Root rot caused by *Rosellinia aquila* (Fr.) De Not

A root rot of two-year-old seedlings of Norway spruce found once in south

Scotland and apparently caused by *Rosellinia aquila* was described by Wilson (1922) from notes by Borthwick. The attack was severe, almost all the Norway spruce plants in the seedbed being affected. The upper parts of the root systems, the stem bases and the lower leaves were covered with grey mycelium bearing colourless oval conidia measuring 8 x 4 μm. On incubation, Borthwick obtained black, round perithecia up to 1 mm across, containing asci each with eight dark brown, boat-shaped ascospores measuring 18-20 x 7-8 μm. He controlled the disease by destroying the affected plants and soaking the ground with copper sulphate solution.

In recent years the disease has been found in southeast England on Norway spruce seedlings, and once also on *Picea omorika*, but so far it has been of minor significance.

Violet root rot caused by *Helicobasidium purpureum*

Violet root rot (described in chapter 3) has sometimes been found causing severe damage to Sitka spruce transplants in nurseries in Scotland.

POST-NURSERY DISEASES

NEEDLE DISEASES

Needle cast caused by *Lophodermium piceae* (Fuckel) Höhnel

Lophodermium piceae, a weak parasite, is occasional on needles of Sitka and Norway Spruce in Scotland and northern England, mainly on nursery plants. It occurs also in other parts of Europe and in North America (Tehon, 1935). The diseased needles turn reddish brown, often with dark transverse bands like those caused by *L. pinastri* on pine. The black, elongated, boat-shaped ascocarps of the fungus form in longitudinal rows on the needles, between the dark bands, and are up to about 2 mm long and ½ mm wide. The asci within each contain eight hairlike, colourless, nonseptate ascospores, each measuring 85-115 x 1.5-2 μm, and embedded in a thick gelatinous matrix. A spermogonial stage, with brown, elliptical pycnidia (spermogonia) about ⅓ mm across also occurs. The pycnidia contain oval spermatia measuring 3-4 x 0.8 μm. Both the ascocarps and spermogonia open by a slit.

The ascocarps ripen in summer, and the ascospores are then shed and infect the needles, which soon show pale green bands. The spermogonia and ascocarps develop in the succeeding spring, sometimes on needles still attached to the tree, but more often on those fallen to the ground (Ferdinandsen and Jørgensen, 1938-39).

According to Campbell and Vines (1938), *L. macrosporum* (Hartig) Rehm, whose ascospores measure 81-168 μm (Terrier, 1953), has also been known to attack Norway spruce in Scotland, though if this is so it appears to be uncommon.

Needle cast associated with *Rhizosphaera kalkhoffii* Bubák

Rhizosphaera kalkhoffii is a common and widespread fungus recorded in Great Britain (Moore, 1959) and throughout much of Europe (Bubák, 1914; Schönhar, 1959), in North America (Hawksworth and Staley, 1968) and Japan (Kobayashi, 1967). It is very common on the blue spruce (*Picea pungens*) and its varieties, and on Norway and Sitka spruces, and has also been recorded on *Abies nobilis* (*A. procera*), *A. alba*, Douglas fir, Austrian pine and *Pinus mugo* (Wilson and Waldie, 1926).

Elsewhere in some circumstances it appears to be an important cause of needle cast of blue spruce (Hawksworth and Staley, 1968; Waterman, 1947). In general both in Great Britain and in other areas, however, it is considered to be doubtfully pathogenic, and at most to be a minor secondary parasite (Moore, 1959). As noted in connection with top dying of Norway spruce, neither Went (1948, 1949) nor Murray (1957) succeeded in inoculating Norway spruce with this fungus.

According to Wilson and Waldie (1926), however, it may sometimes attack spruces. In May the affected needles become discoloured and soon turn a purple-brown, and contain large amounts of fungal mycelium. The fungus later produces rows of small, black, stalked pycnidia, the stalks of which emerge through the stomata on the needle surfaces. As they grow, the pycnidia carry up with them from the stomatal opening a small, shining white plug of wax, which may later disappear (Wilson and Waldie, 1926). The pycnidia contain ovoid, colourless, one-celled spores, measuring 7–10 x 3–4 μm (Bubák, 1914).

Waterman (1947) reported that she successfully controlled needle cast on ornamental trees by spraying with Bordeaux mixture.

Needle rusts: *Chrysomyxa abietis* Unger, and *C. rhododendri* de Bary.

The needle rusts *Chrysomyxa abietis* and *C. rhododendri* both occur sporadically on the foliage of spruce in Great Britain. The first is autoecious, and produces only pustules of teleutospores on infected needles. The diseased needles remain on the tree over the winter. The second is a heteroecious rust whose alternate host is rhododendron, on which it produces uredospores and teleutospores. Its spermogonia and white, columnar aecidia occur on spruce needles. The affected needles fall in the autumn of the season of infection.

C. abietis is fairly common, and in some seasons causes epidemics in Scotland and northern England; it has also been found in Northern Ireland, South Wales, and in southwest England. It occurs mainly on Norway spruce, but has also been found on Sitka spruce, and on *Picea rubens*, *P. pungens* and *P. engelmannii* (Murray, 1955). Sporidia infect the young developing needles in the spring. In June and July the infected needles show conspicuous, lemon-coloured, transverse bands, which become a deeper yellow as the season advances (plate 19). The mycelium of the fungus is hyaline with orange granules, and can be found in sections of the tissues of the discoloured zones (Delforge, 1930). In late summer, teleutosori begin to appear on the undersides of the needles, but they do not complete their development until the following spring. In May and June they then finally erupt by a slit through the lower epidermis of the diseased needles to form elongated yellow or orange pustules up to 10 mm long. The pustules consist of chains of orange or red-brown teleutospores that individually measure about 20-30 x 10-15 μm (Wilson and Henderson, 1966). The teleutospores germinate to produce the sporidia (basidiospores) that infect the new foliage. Soon after the germination of the teleutospores, the affected needles die and fall off, so that the branches have their current needles, but those of the previous year are partly or completely lost. A degree of natural control of *C. abietis* may sometimes be exercised by the parasitic fungus *Darluca filum*, which attacks the teleutosori (Murray, 1953).

C. rhododendri is much less common than *C. abietis*. From time to time it has appeared in Scotland and Northern Ireland on Norway spruce and occasionally also on Sitka spruce. The alternate hosts are various species and varieties of *Rhododendron*, and on these it has been found not only in Scotland (and in Northern Ireland), but also quite widely in southern England, though Moore (1959) has suggested that the fungus in the south may not be the same as the one found in Scotland.

Sporidia produced on *Rhododendron* leaves infect the young, current spruce needles in early summer, and the infected needles soon show yellow bands similar to those caused by *C. abietis*, In the case of *C. rhododendri*, however, infection is followed by the development of spermogonia, which appear as small, reddish-brown spots. Later, white, cylindrical aecidia develop (plate 20), and burst open in August to shed yellow aecidiospores. The infected leaves fall in the autumn.

Both the spermogonia and the aecidia may be found on both leaf surfaces. The aecidiospores measure 24-28 x 20-22 μm (Wilson and Henderson, 1966). They infect leaves of *Rhododendron* and the resulting mycelium overwinters in the leaves. The following spring it gives rise at first to uredosori, which form as small orange spots on the undersides of the leaves. The uredospores spread the disease further among the rhododendrons. The uredosori are succeeded, also on the undersides of the leaves, by teleutosori, which form as laccate, brownish-red areas under the epidermis. In the early part of the summer, the epidermis ruptures over the teleutosori, and the teleutospores give rise to the sporidia that complete the cycle and reinfect the young spruce needles.

As both *C. abietis* and *C. rhododendri* cause severe loss of the current year's needles, they are potential causes of marked loss of increment, but their actual effect is greatly reduced because they give rise to epidemics only in occasional years, and then usually fairly locally. In the case of both these fungi this appears to be due to the fact that the spruce needles are susceptible in only the early stages of their growth (Hartig, 1894), and epidemics occur only when sporidia are produced during the period when the needles are still liable to infection (Fischer, 1933). There is evidence that at least in the case of *C. abietis*, cold spring weather delays flushing of spruce needles to the time when maximum production of sporidia is taking place. In more normal years, flushing is earlier, and the sporidia are shed when most of the needles are no longer susceptible (Murray, 1953). According to Delforge (1930), *C. abietis* is commonest and most severe in Belgium in warm, humid conditions.

As these needle rusts are so sporadic in occurrence, and so cause relatively little damage, no measures for their control have been worked out, though it is likely that much could be done to prevent attacks of *C. rhododendri* by eradicating rhododendrons in and around spruce plantations.

DIEBACKS AND SHOOT BLIGHTS

Spring frost damage
The developing shoots of many spruces, especially Sitka spruce, are liable to damage by spring frosts. Young Sitka spruce planted in frosty sites may in their early years be trimmed annually by frost until they assume a bush-like form. In such places their growth is slow until they reach a height above the general frost level, after which their leading shoots are able to grow without further damage. Norway spruce crops are less affected because their populations form a mixture of early and late-flushing individuals, some of which escape the frosts. Frost damage is further considered in chapter 2.

Bud blight caused by *Cucurbitaria piceae* Borthwick
This disease was first described and the causal fungus named from Scottish material of *Picea pungens* (Borthwick, 1909). It has since been found in England and Wales (where, as in Scotland, it appears to be commoner than was at one time supposed), and in Switzerland (Müller, 1950; Bazzigher, 1956), Denmark (Ferdinandsen and Jørgensen, 1938-9), Germany (Mehlisch, 1938), and in Austria, Finland and Russia (Shoemaker, 1967).

Cucurbitaria piceae attacks the buds, which usually then die soon after the start of elongation. The buds often become curved or twisted, claw-like (Ferdinandsen and Jørgensen, 1938-39) or 'snail-like' (Mehlisch, 1938) (plate 21). When the damaged buds are not killed, they may produce thin, deformed shoots bearing short needles that may soon die (Müller, 1950), though some often survive. If attacks are repeated and severe, affected parts of the crown may become sparsely branched and irregular in shape.

Some time after infection, the fungus forms a black granular stromatic crust on the surface of the buds. The granulations are due to the presence of densely clustered fruit bodies embedded in and emerging from the stroma. The perfect fructifications are black, spherical perithecia about 1 mm across (plate 22), with cylindrical asci measuring $180-250 \times 25-30$ µm, each containing eight broadly spindle-shaped, yellow or brownish muriform ascospores measuring $36-50 \times 13-15$ µm (Müller, 1950). Two pycnidial forms have also been described; both outwardly resemble the perithecia, but the first (*Megaloseptoria mirabilis*) contains long, colourless, more or less curved, threadlike, multiseptate conidia measuring about 250 x 8-10 μm, and the second (*Camarosporium strobilinum*) contains brown, oval to pear-shaped, muriform spores measuring 25-30 x 15-17 μm (Ferdinandsen and Jørgensen, 1938-39).

Little is known about the epidemiology of the disease. Ferdinandsen and Jørgensen (1938-39) in Denmark have suggested that infections by conidia and ascospores may take place in winter, and that the mycelium at first grows saprophytically on the bud scales before penetrating and killing the elongating buds. A long time seems to elapse between infection and the development of symptoms of disease (Müller, 1950), but the dead buds and the fungal stroma may persist for as long as 9 or 10 years (Young, unpublished).

Bud blight has been recorded on *Picea pungens* (Borthwick, 1909), *P. alba* (*P. glauca*) (Ferdinandsen and Jørgensen, 1938-39), Norway spruce and *Picea engelmannii*. There is little or no information on variations in susceptibility between tree species and varieties, though there is some observational evidence that Norway is much more susceptible than Sitka spruce (Young, unpublished).

In Great Britain, the disease has recently been found on pole-stage Norway spruce at a number of sites widely scattered over the country. In some crops it has been present for up to ten years. It was also found in a 2.5 ha stand of 13-year-old *Picea engelmannii* in North Wales. In this case about 90 per cent of the trees were infected, some were severely damaged, and about 10 per cent had been killed by a combination of the effects of *C. piceae* and the Green spruce aphid *Elatobium abietinum*. In Denmark it has been recorded on 30 to 60-year-old Norway spruce and on 20 to 25-year-old *Picea pungens* trees (Ferdinandsen and Jørgensen, 1938-39). In Germany it has damaged nursery stock (Mehlisch, 1938).

Bud blight has attracted little attention, and appears to cause only slight loss. In Great Britain, even heavily diseased trees appear to grow with little loss of vigour, although Ferdinandsen and Jørgensen (1938-39) found that in a few affected Norway spruce crops in Denmark bud blight had almost stopped growth in up to 25 per cent of the affected trees. The disease could be troublesome if it attacked Christmas tree crops, because of the deformation it causes, but so far it has not been recorded in these.

Shoot blight caused by *Sirococcus strobilinus* Preuss (*Ascochyta piniperda* Lindau)
Sirococcus strobilinus may sometimes cause defoliation and dieback of the current year's shoots of both Norway and Sitka spruce in nurseries and plantations. It has also been recorded on seedlings of lodgepole pine (Peace, 1962) (Figures 35, 36), and on *Picea pungens* (Schneider and Paetzholdt, 1964). So far in this country it has been of only minor importance, though it continues to be recorded from time to time.

Infection shows first of all in the early part of the summer at the base of the current shoots, where the needles turn brown. For a time the shoot tips remain green, but later wilt, droop, and finally die (Lagerberg, 1933) (figures 35, 36). Later in the summer the fungus produces pycnidia on the dead bark. Whitish

Figure 35. Drooping of the needles of seedling one-year-old lodgepole pine caused by *Sirococcus strobilinus* (Forestry Commission)

tendrils of sticky, colourless, two-celled spores, each measuring $10-15 \times 2-3\,\mu m$ emerge from the openings of these fructifications. The needles fall from the affected shoots, and the pith of the diseased stems may become brown (Laing, 1929).

According to Riižička (1938), Alpine provenances of Norway spruce are susceptible to attack by *S. strobilinus*, but those from the lower mountains of Czechoslovakia are not affected by it.

BARK AND TRUNK DISEASES AND DISORDERS

Drought crack
Under forest conditions, drought crack is rather common in Sitka spruce (see chapter 2).

Spruce bark necrosis associated with *Nectria fuckeliana* Booth
Occasional cases of bark necrosis of spruce have been reported widely over Great Britain as well as in many other European countries. In this country the disease

Figure 36. Pycnidia of *Sirococcus strobilinus* on needles of lodgepole pine. These pycnidia also occur on the bark of affected shoots (Forestry Commission)

has been found mainly in Sitka spruce. Various fungi have been isolated from the damaged tissues, and of these *Nectria cucurbitula* has most often been considered to be the cause, though Zycha (1955), in inoculation experiments in Germany, was unable to prove the pathogenicity of this organism. Day (1950) considered that the symptoms on Norway spruce in Great Britain were caused by frost. In recent years, several cases of bark necrosis in Sitka spruce in this country have been traced back to the winters of 1946–47, 1954–55 and 1961–62, all of which were generally cold or contained exceptionally bitter spells.

Further study of the disorder is needed, for little is known about it. There has been some confusion as to the identity of the *Nectria* sp. that has so often been found on the lesions, and in this country no study has been made of other fungi present.

The name *N. cucurbitula* is a *nomen confusum*, and the fungus on spruce appears to be that renamed *N. fuckeliana* by Booth (1959). This fungus has a *Cephalosporium* stage with colourless, oval microconidia measuring 6–9 x 3–9 μm, a second imperfect stage, sometimes called *Cylindrocarpon cylindroides*, with curved, colourless, three-septate, *Fusarium*-like conidia measuring 33–40 x 4–5 μm, and red perithecia with cylindrical asci each containing eight 2-celled, colourless or pale brown ascospores measuring 13–16 x 5–6 μm (Booth, 1959).

The symptoms of the disease as he found it in Sitka spruce in Scotland were described by Laing (1948). The trees he studied were about 33 years old, and damage in them had first been noted about 9 years previously, after the trees had been brashed and pruned. In the early stages, sunken patches of dead bark (resembling those occurring in Norway spruce following invasion by *Stereum sanguinolentum*) appeared round the brashing wounds or round the bases of dead branches. Death of the bark often continued until long, narrow, vertical dead strips were produced. Mycelium, conidial pustules, and the perfect fruit bodies of the *Nectria* were present on and in the dead tissues. Growth of the stem continued between strips, so that in severe cases the stems became conspicuously fluted. A few of the affected trees had died or were dying, others had become ill-shaped, while resin was exuding from the bark of most of the remainder.

Crops affected to this degree have been rarely seen, and overall losses through this disease have been small. The diseased stems are best removed when thinning.

ROOT DISEASES

Group dying caused by *Rhizina undulata*

Group dying caused by the ascomycete *Rhizina undulata*, which affects a range of conifers, is commoner and more severe on Sitka spruce than on any other tree. Norway spruce is sometimes also attacked. The disease is described in chapter 3.

DECAY FUNGI

Most of the information on the susceptibility of the spruces to attack by the common decay fungi concerns Sitka spruce, Norway spruce and *Picea omorika*. All of these are very susceptible to damage by *Armillaria mellea*. Sitka spruce is also especially liable to attack by *Heterobasidion annosum (Fomes annosus)*, *Phaeolus schweinitzii*, *Sparassis crispa* and *Stereum sanguinolentum*. Norway spruce is also very susceptible to damage by *H. annosum* and *S. sanguinolentum*, and also by *Tyromyces stipticus*. *P. omorika* is more resistant to most of these fungi, but is very susceptible to attack by *S. sanguinolentum*. These fungi are described in chapter 3 *(Armillaria mellea* and *Heterobasidion annosum)* and chapter 19 *(Phaeolus schweinitzii, Sparassis crispa, Stereum sanguinolentum* and *Tyromyces stipticus)*.

CONE RUSTS

Pucciniastrum areolatum (Fr.) Otth (*Thekopsora areolata* (Fr.)P.Magn)

This is a rather uncommon heteroecious rust that in Great Britain has been known to attack the cone scales of Norway spruce in Yorkshire and a few places in Scotland.

In spring its sporidia infect the female spruce flowers, and whitish, flat, crust-like spermogonia exuding a strong smelling, sugary secretion soon form on the undersides of the developing cone scales. Later, from August to November, many small, brownish, hemispherical aecidia form, usually on the upper sides of the scales. They are about 1 mm across and 1 mm high, and split open at the top to release clouds of aecidiospores that measure 20-30 x 16-22 μm (Wilson and Henderson, 1966). In wet weather, scales of healthy cones close up, but those of affected ones remain open (Murray, 1955).

The aecidia infect the alternate hosts, the bird cherry (*Prunus padus*) and the cultivated *Prunus virginiana* and *P. serotina*. On the leaves of these arise brown uredosori, followed by dark brown teleutosori, the spores of which germinate in the following spring to produce the sporidia that reinfect the spruce flowers.

Roll-Hansen (1965) in Norway has described terminal and sometimes lateral shoot infection of Norway spruce and *Picea engelmannii* by the same fungus. The affected shoots were usually bent towards the attacked side, and died back to the point of entry of the fungus. No such shoot infection has been seen in Great Britain.

A second heteroecious cone rust of spruce, *Chrysomyxa pirolata* (*C. pyrolae*) occurs rarely on the leaves of its alternate hosts, which are species of *Pyrola* (Wintergreen). On these it produces its uredosori and teleutosori. Its large, whitish aecidia occur on the outside of Norway spruce cone scales, usually only one or two to each scale, but the aecidial stage has so far not been seen in Great Britain (Wilson and Henderson, 1966).

VIRUS DISEASES

Spruce virosis
What appears to be a virosis, which was described on Norway spruce in Czechoslovakia (Čech *et al.*, 1961), has been found on Sitka spruce in Great Britain (Biddle and Tinsley, 1968). The affected trees show shortening of the needles, which at first become yellowish green, and later fall.

Čech *et al.* (1961) inoculated seedlings by aphid transmission by *Adelges abietis* and by grafting, and observed hexagonal, rod-shaped particles 49 ± 3 mμm wide and 200-300 mμm long, with a mean length of 625 mμm. Biddle and Tinsley (1968) found similar particles in exudates from twigs of affected Sitka spruce in this country. Available information on this disorder has been summarised by Cooper (1979).

MISCELLANEOUS DISEASES

Top dying of Norway spruce
'Top dying', which occurs almost exclusively on Norway spruce (though one case has been recorded on *Picea glauca*, and one on *P. omorika*) (Murray, 1957), appears to be a complex physiological disorder, related in part to the suscepti-

bility of Norway spruce to water stress and exposure. Typically it affects trees in the pole stage and beyond, though occasionally it has been found in young plantations in the thicket stage. Since 1950 it has been reported in all parts of Great Britain, on a wide variety of sites, as well as in other areas along the coasts of northern Europe in Denmark, Germany, Ireland, the Netherlands, Norway and Sweden (Diamandis, 1978*a*).

The first symptoms have been recorded both in late summer and late winter. The initial damage appears as a spectacular browning or reddening of the foliage in parts or over the whole of the crowns of the trees (plate 16). On individual current and second year shoots this browning progresses downwards from the shoot tip. Affected needles fall, and thereafter the crowns decline or recover at varying rates according to the severity of the initial damage. Trees in decline bear sparse, sickly foliage, and they usually die within two or three years from the tops downwards, the roots being the last parts to succumb. Sometimes only edge trees are affected, and trees in the interior of the stand are always less affected than those on the edges.

The dead and dying needles are often invaded by *Rhizosphaera kalkhoffii*, but the evidence does not suggest that this fungus is the cause of top dying. Went (1948, 1949) and Murray (1957) both failed to inoculate spruce trees with *R. kalkhoffii*, which at most seems to be only a weak parasite that causes no more than a minor leaf cast, and never leads to the progressive decline and death of trees under British conditions. Similarly Diamandis (1978*b*) was unable to show that this fungus (or any other he isolated) was the cause of the disorder.

Careful study of affected crops has shown, however, that the needle browning is preceded by a disorganisation of the growth pattern of the tree. The effects on growth are associated with mild winters, which tend to be followed by a reduction in growth in the following season. The growth reduction may be accompanied or followed within the next few years by needle browning and needle loss in a proportion of the trees.

Young (reported by Phillips, 1965, 1967) suggested that two factors or groups of factors might be involved. The first, which could be called a *conditioning factor*, operated during relatively mild winters, and caused the growth reduction in the following season. The intensity of the conditioning factor, and hence the extent of the reduction in growth, varied from site to site. If the effect of the conditioning factor was sufficiently marked, part of the crop became susceptible to one or more *precipitating factors*, and if one of these operated near the time of the fall in growth, top dying might follow. There was evidence that top dying could be precipitated in this way by various factors that give rise to increased air movement through the crop, and so to an increase in transpiration and water loss. Among such factors were brashing, thinning and removal of side shelter. Top dying is also liable to occur where there is usually considerable air movement, as in exposed situations or where gaps and uneven growth in crops make for turbulence. Summer drought also seems to be involved in some cases (Young, reported by Phillips, 1963).

In the last of a series of six papers, Diamandis (1979) summarised the results of studies of the disorder in a number of forests in northeast Scotland, in which he attempted to elucidate the factors responsible. He confirmed earlier suggestions that top dying was associated with mild winters and exposure, and sometimes with drought in the early part of the growing season. From a study of weather data in the area of his investigation, he concluded that when mild winters were accompanied by long windy periods between December and March, the trees became water deficient. The water deficit caused a growth reduction in the following season and, if severe, needle browning and loss also occurred. Drought in the period from May to August intensified the effect. Presumably operations such as brashing and thinning were similar intensifying factors. The disorder therefore resulted from the combined effects of atmospheric and soil drought.

In some crops of Norway spruce, top dying has caused severe losses, but in most cases the proportion of affected trees has been relatively small. Nevertheless, partly because the onset of the disorder has been so unpredictable, forest managers in Britain and Denmark have tended to reduce the planting of Norway spruce (Diamandis, 1978a).

So far, little can be done to prevent top dying, though it may be suggested that sudden changes in the environment of the crop should be avoided. Thus, particularly following mild winters, heavy thinnings and sudden removal of side shelter should not be carried out.

REFERENCES

Bazzigher, G. (1956). *Pilzkrankheiten in Auf-forstungen.* Kurzmitt. Schweiz Anst. forstl. Versuchsw, no. 12, 3 pp.

Biddle, P. G. and Tinsley, T. W. (1968). Virus diseases of forest trees. *Rep. Forest Res., Lond., 1968*, pp. 148–51

Booth, C. (1959). *Studies of pyrenomycetes: IV. Nectria (Part 1),* Mycol. Pap., no. 73

Borthwick, A. W. (1909). A new disease of *Picea. Notes R. bot. Gdn Edinb.,* 20, 259–61

Bubák, F. (1914). Eine neue *Rhizosphaera. Ber. dt. bot. Ges.,* 32, 188–190

Campbell, A. H. and Vines, A. E. (1938). The effect of *Lophodermellina macrospora* (Hartig) Tehon on leaf-abscission in *Picea excelsa* Link. *New Phytol.,* 37, 358–69

Čech, M, Králík, O. and Blattný, C. (1961). Rod-shaped particles associated with virosis of spruce. *Phytopathology,* 51, 183–5

Cooper, J. I. (1979). *Virus Diseases of Trees and Shrubs,* Institute of Terrestrial Ecology, c/o Unit of Invertebrate Virology, Oxford

Day, W. R. (1950). *Cambial Injuries In a Pruned Stand of Norway Spruce,* Forest Rec., Lond., no. 4, 11 pp.

Delforge, P. (1930). Le *Chrysomyxa abietis* (rouille des aiguilles de l'Epicéa). *Bull, Soc. Centr. For. Belg.,* 37, 419–23

Diamandis, S. (1978a). 'Top-dying' of Norway spruce, *Picea abies* (L.) Karst., with special reference to *Rhizosphaera kalkhoffii* Bubák. I. Development of foliar symptoms. *Eur. J. For, Path.,* 8, 337–45

Diamandis, S. (1978b). 'Top-dying' of Norway spruce, *Picea abies* (L.) Karst., with special reference to *Rhizosphaera kalkhoffii* Bubák. II. Status of *R. kalkhoffii* in 'top-dying' of Norway spruce. *Eur. J. For. Path.* 8, 345–56

Diamandis, S. (1979). 'Top-dying' of Norway spruce, *Picea abies* (L.) Karst., with special reference to *Rhizosphaera kalkhoffii* Bubák. VI. Evidence related to the primary cause of 'top-dying'. *Eur. J. For. Path.*, 9, 183–191

Ferdinandsen, C. and Jørgensen, C. A. (1938–39). *Skovtraernes Sygdomme*, Gyldendalske Boghandel, Copenhagen

Fischer, E. (1933). Die Rostepidemie der Rottane in den Alpen in Herbst 1932. *Mitt. Naturforsch. Ges. Bern, 1932*, 20–21

Grove, W. B. (1935). *British Stem- and Leaf-Fungi (Coelomycetes)*, vol. 1, Cambridge University Press, Cambridge

Hahn, G. G. (1930). Life history studies of the species of *Phomopsis* occurring on conifers. *Trans. Br. mycol. Soc.*, 15, 32–93

Hartig, R. (1894). *Textbook of the Diseases of Trees*, Macmillan, London

Hawksworth, F. G. and Staley, J. M. (1968). *Rhizosphaera kalkhoffii* on spruce in Arizona. *Pl. Dis. Reptr.*, 52, 804–5

Kobayashi, T. (1967). Critical revision of the genera *Rhizosphaera* Mangin et Hariot and *Rhizophoma* Petrak et Sydow, a little known fungus group associated with needle disease of conifers. *Bull. Tokyo Govt. For. Exp. Sta.*, 204, 91–112

Lagerberg, T. (1933). *Ascochyta parasitica* (Hartig), en Skadesvamp på Granplantor. *Svenska SkogsvFör. Tidskr.*, 3, 1–10

Laing, E. V. (1929). Notes from the forestry department, Aberdeen University. *Scott. For. J.*, 43, 48–52

Laing, E. V. (1948). Preliminary note on a disease of Sitka spruce in Cairnhill Plantation, Durris, Kincardineshire. *Forestry*, 21, 217–20

Mehlisch, K. (1938). Eine pilzlicher schädling an *Abies. Blumen -u PflBau ver. Gartenwelt*, 42, 92

Moore, W. C. (1959). *British Pathogenic Fungi*, Cambridge University Press, Cambridge

Müller, E. (1950). Eine Knospenkrankheit der Stechfichte. *Schweiz Beitr. Dendrol.*, 2, 69–72

Murray, J. S. (1953). A note on the outbreak of '*Chrysomyxa abietis* Unger' (spruce needle rust) in Scotland, 1951. *Scott. For.*, 7, 52–4

Murray, J. S. (1955). *Rusts of British Forest Trees*, Bookl. For. Commn, no. 4

Murray, J. S. (1957). Top dying of Norway spruce in Great Britain. Reprinted from *Proc. 7th Br. Commonw. For. Conf., 1957*

Peace, T. R. (1962). *Pathology of Trees and Shrubs*, Clarendon Press, Oxford

Phillips, D. H. (1963). Forest pathology. *Rep. Forest Res., Lond., 1962*, pp. 60–65

Phillips, D. H. (1965). Forest pathology. *Rep. Forest Res., Lond., 1964*, pp. 57–60

Phillips, D. H. (1967). Forest pathology. *Rep. Forest Res., Lond., 1967*, pp. 96–102

Riižička, J. (1938). Doklad o škodlivosti nesprávného původu Smrhového semene. *Lesn. Pr.*, 17, 553–9

Roll-Hansen, F. (1965). *Pucciniastrum areolatum* on *Picea engelmannii*. Identification by spermogonia. Repr. from *Meddr norske SkogforsVes.*, 20, 391–7

Schneider, R. and Paetzholdt, M. (1964). Ascochyta piniperda als Erreger eines Triebsterbens an Blaufichten in Baumschulen. *NachrBl. dt. PflSchutzdienst, Braunschweig*, 16, 73–5

Schönhar, S. (1959). Eine Nedelerkrankung der Fichte. *Allg. Forstz.*, 49, 1

Shoemaker, R. A. (1967). *Cucurbitaria piceae* and associated Sphaeropsidales parasitic on spruce buds. *Can. J. Bot.*, 45, 1243–8

Tehon, L. R. (1935). *A Monographic Rearrangement of Lophodermium*. Illinois biol. Monogr., 13, 151 pp..

Terrier, C. (1953). Note sur *Lophodermium macrosporum* (Hartig) Rehm. *Phytopath. Z.*, 20, 397–404

Waterman, A. M. (1947). *Rhizosphaera kalkhoffii* associated with a needle cast of *Picea pungens. Phytopathology*, 37, 507–11

Wehmeyer, L. E. (1933). *The Genus* Diaporthe *Nitschke and its Segregates*, Univ. Mich. Studies Scientific Series, no. 9, 349 pp.

Went, J. C. (1948). Verslag van de onderzoekingen over de iepenziekte en andere boomziekten, 1974. *Meded. Iepenziektecomité, Baarn*, 43, 15 pp.

Went, J. C. (1949). Verslag over 1948. *Meded. Iepenziektecomité, Baarn*, 44, 15 pp.

Wilson, M. (1922). Studies in the pathology of young trees and seedlings. I. The Rosellinia disease of the spruce. *Trans. R. Scott. arboric. Soc.*, 36, 226–35

Wilson, M. and Henderson, D. M. (1966). *British Rust Fungi*, Cambridge University Press, Cambridge

Wilson, M. and Waldie, J. S. L. (1926). *Rhizosphaera kalkhoffii* Bubák as a cause of defoliation of conifers. *Trans. R. Scott. arboric. Soc.*, 40, 34–6

Zycha, H. (1955). Eine Krebserkrankung der Sitke-Fichte (*Picea sitchensis* [Bong.] Carr.) *Forstwiss. ZentBl.*, 74, 293–304

5 Diseases of pine (*Pinus* spp.)

Pinus sylvestris (Scots pine), *P. nigra* var. *maritima* (Corsican pine) and *P. contorta* (lodgepole pine) are the major species of pine grown in British forests. Many other introduced pines are grown in parks and gardens.

Pines are subject to a number of disorders caused by nonliving agencies such as frost and lime-induced chlorosis, and these are discussed in detail in chapter 2. Some of the pathogens that infect pines, including *Heterobasidion annosum* (*Fomes annosus*), *Armillaria mellea* and *Rhizina undulata*, are described in chapter 3.

A number of important diseases, including rusts, root diseases, cankers and needle casts, attack pines in Britain. Some, such as Brunchorstia or Scleroderris dieback and Lophodermium needle cast, are equally or even more important in mainland Europe and North America. Others are seldom found in Britain, but may be common elsewhere; an example is Dothistroma needle blight, which has rarely been found in Britain, but has caused much damage in plantations of *Pinus radiata* in many other parts of the world.

NURSERY DISEASES

NEEDLE DISEASES

Needle cast caused by *Lophodermium seditiosum* Minter, Staley and Millar

Prior to 1978, most published references to pathogenic *Lophodermium* spp. refer to *L. pinastri* as the species causing damage to Scots pine. However, as will be seen below, it now appears that a new species, *L. seditiosum*, is the likely cause of Lophodermium needle cast.

Peace (1962) indicates that, in Britain, Lophodermium needle cast can cause serious defoliation of Scots pine in the nursery but rarely causes significant damage in plantations. Melchior (1975) reports that no new plantations of Scots pine have been established in northern Schleswig-Holstein, West Germany because of the severe losses which have occurred there. The first serious outbreak in North America, attributed at the time to *L. pinastri*, was reported in 1966 and severe damage has subsequently been reported in nurseries of both Scots and red pine and in Christmas tree plantations of Scots pine (Skilling and Nicholls 1975).

Since 1978, Minter and others (Minter *et al.*, 1978; Minter and Millar, 1980) have undertaken detailed studies into the taxonomic ecology and biology of *Lophodermium* spp. on Scots pine. Minter *et al.* (1978) identified four species of *Lophodermium* on Scots pine needles:

L. pinastri (Schrad. ex Hook) Chev.
L. conigenum Hilitzer
L. pini-excelsae Ahman
L. seditiosum Minter, Staley and Millar

The four species can be distinguished on the manner in which the ascocarps are embedded in the host tissue and on their ability to produce stromatic lines of different sorts across the needle.

Minter and Millar (1980) studied the ecology and biology of three of these species (*L. pinastri*, *L. conigenum* and *L. seditiosum*) on Scots pine; *L. pini-excelsae* occurs only rarely on this host and is found more commonly on five-needled pines. They found that each of the three species occupied a distinct habitat: *L. pinastri* occurred on senescent needles in litter; *L. conigenum* on needles that had died in consequence of live branches cut off or broken, or of roots being killed; and *L. seditiosum* as a parasite on second year needles of nursery plants, in which role it appeared to be causing death of plants. It therefore seemed that in many of the earlier reports of outbreaks the disease had been incorrectly diagnosed and that the fungus responsible could well have been *L. seditiosum*. Other studies of *Lophodermium* on pines, for example those including records of ascospore dispersal, could relate to different species. Therefore, the interpretation of much of this research may need reappraisal.

Minter (private communication) later found instances of needles on lop and top being colonised by *L. seditiosum*, and not by *L. conigenum*. Such colonisation could account for the association of disease with debris from thinning and pruning recorded by Murray and Young (1956).

The boat-shaped ascocarps of *L. seditiosum* are 800–1500 μm long and are sometimes accompanied by a few diffuse brown stromatic lines across the needle. This contrasts with *L. pinastri* where many thin, black lines are found in this situation (Figure 37). The ascocarp of *L. seditiosum* is entirely covered by the host epidermis and none of the epidermal cells can be found at the base of the ascocarp. The asci are cylindrical, eight-spored, 140–170 μm long and 11–13 μm wide, and filiform paraphyses are present. The ascospores are filiform and measure 9–120 μm long.

The pycnidia are subepidermal, often coalescing, 300–500 μm long and the bacillar conidia are 6–8 μm long.

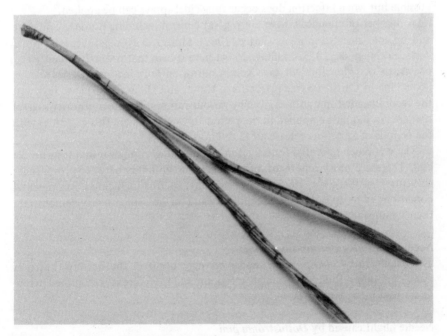

**Figure 37.   Fruit bodies of *Lophodermium pinastri* in Scots pine needles
(Forestry Commission)**

A full description of the fruiting structures of *L. seditiosum* and other *Lophodermium* spp. on Scots pine needles is given by Minter *et al.* (1978).

The first symptoms of the disease appear in summer as pale spots on the needles and these gradually enlarge and merge so that the whole needle turns brown. Needles are often infected in groups and when infection is severe the whole of the previous year's needles turn brown and fall in winter or early spring.

Infection occurs through the stomata and appears to be solely due to asco-spores. Millar (1978) reviewed the periods of ascospore release reported by various authors. Peak periods of release varied greatly and it is now apparent that records were probably taken from a range of *Lophodermium* spp. *In vitro* studies of sporulation periods of *L. seditiosum* by Minter and Millar (1980) indicated that ascospore release started in July and reached a peak between September and December. This corresponded well with the appearance of opened ascocarps on infected needles.

Many serious outbreaks of needle cast have occurred in nurseries which are sited within or very close to pine plantations. Such plantations may not them-selves be seriously affected by the disease but they may harbour sufficient inoculum to act as sources of infection for nearby seedlings or transplants. In North America, outbreaks of the disease have occurred in Christmas tree plan-tations of Scots pine following the introduction of plants from an infected nursery (Skilling and Nicholls, 1975). Such situations should be avoided wherever possible but when infection does occur fungicidal sprays can be applied.

A number of chemicals have given good control including Bordeaux mixture and organic zinc compounds (Peace, 1962). More recent experiments in North America (Nicholls, 1973; Skilling, 1974) have shown that properly timed sprays of maneb or chlorothalonil gave good control on red pine in nurseries and on Scots pine in Christmas tree plantations. Minter and Millar (1980) have reviewed the recommended spray times given by various authors. The great majority suggest that sprays should be applied in the period July–September. This coincides with the periods of ascospore release by *L. seditiosum*.

There is much potential for selection and breeding of pines resistant to needle cast. There are many reports of differences in susceptibility between provenances of Scots pine (Stephan, 1975). However, other factors including environmental conditions can also influence susceptibility and further research may demonstrate their significance.

Needle rust *Coleosporium tussilaginis*
The needle rust *Coleosporium tussilaginis* may occur in the nursery, but it is more commonly found in young plantations, and therefore it is described below under post-nursery diseases.

Needle blight caused by *Dothistroma pini*
In Britain *Dothistroma pini* was found for a few years causing quite severe damage to pine transplants in one nursery, but has since been of no importance.

In other countries, however, this fungus has caused heavy losses in pine plantations. Therefore, it is described below under post-nursery diseases.

POST-NURSERY DISEASES

NEEDLE DISEASES

Needle cast caused by *Lophodermium seditiosum*
Lophodermium seditiosum occurs in pine plantations, but as a cause of disease it is important only in nurseries. Therefore, it is discussed above under nursery diseases.

Minor needle casts
Lophodermium seditiosum, *L. pinastri*, *L. conigenum* and *L. pini-excelsae* have been described above in relation to needle cast in nurseries. They also occur in plantations where they are of little significance in Britain.

A number of minor needle casts occur on pines, mainly in the post-nursery stage. They are caused by the hypodermataceous fungi *Lophodermella sulcigena* (Rostr.) Höhnel and *L. conjuncta* Darker, and the deuteromycetes *Hendersonia acicola* Münch & Tub. and *Sclerophoma pithyophila* (Corda) Höhnel. The Hypodermataceae occurring on conifers have been well described by Darker (1932, 1967).

Lophodermella sulcigena (*Hypodermella sulcigena*) infects first year needles of both *P. sylvestris* and *P. nigra* var. *maritima* causing severe browning of foliage, defoliation and subsequent reduction of growth (Watson and Millar, 1971). These authors indicate that *Hendersonia acicola* and also *L. pinastri* infect pine needles previously infected by *L. sulcigena*. Needles infected by *H. acicola* turn a pale whitish grey.

Millar (1970) reports that needles of *P. nigra* var. *maritima* which remain healthy during their first year may become infected in their second year by *Lophodermella conjuncta*. This fungus causes brown lesions with a conspicuous yellow margin.

Sclerophoma pithyophila is commonly found as a saprophyte on dead pine needles but Jahnel and Junghans (1957) observed a definite association between infection by *S. pithyophila* and damage by the pine gall midge *Cecidomyid baeri* on first year needles of *P. sylvestris*. Batko *et al.* (1958) confirmed this observation and also the finding of Robak (1952) that, in culture, *S. pithyophila* was a form of *Pullularia pullulans*.

The needle rust *Coleosporium tussilaginis* (Pers.) Lév.
Several rusts of the genus *Coleosporium* occurring in central and northern Europe have been treated as separate species, largely based on the generic identity of the alternate host (for example, *C. tussilaginis*, *C. senecionis*, *C. campanulae*). How-

ever, it is not possible to distinguish these species on the basis of morphological characters and it is now considered best, as far as Europe is concerned, to include them as races or race groups of one species (Wilson and Henderson, 1966). The spermogonia and aecidia occur on two-needled pines and the uredosori and teleutosori chiefly on members of the Compositae, Campanulaceae and Scrophulariaceae.

The sporidia, which are sometimes called basidiospores, infect the current year's pine needles in the autumn and spermogonia and aecidia appear during the following summer. Spermogonia develop as small yellowish spots and spermatia are exuded in a sticky fluid. Soon afterwards aecidia appear, initially as white columnar blisters 1–5 mm high, whose covering membrane breaks to release orange coloured aecidiospores (figure 38). These can infect the leaves and stems of a number of herbaceous species, the commonest of which are probably *Senecio* spp. and *Tussilago* spp.; other hosts include *Campanula* spp., *Melampyrum* spp., *Petasites* spp. and *Sonchus* spp. On groundsel, uredosori can be found throughout the year as orange-yellow spots on stems or the undersides of leaves. Several generations of the orange uredospores may be produced during the summer months and also during the winter so that the fungus can maintain itself on a herbaceous host without necessarily returning to a pine host. During the autumn teleutosori may appear on the undersides of the groundsel leaves or on the stem; these develop as dark red-brown waxy crusts.

Figure 38. Aecidia of *Coleosporium tussilaginis* on needles of Scots pine (Forestry Commission)

The aecidiospores vary in shape from globoid to obovoid, 20–40 x 16–27 μm (Wilson and Henderson, 1966), and have a colourless wall 2–3 μm thick which is densely verrucose. Uredospores are similar in shape and size to the aecidiospores and measure 20–40 x 16–25 μm (Wilson and Henderson, 1966), but they have a thinner, verruculose wall, 1–1.5 μm thick. The teleutospores are clavoid to cylindric, smooth-walled and measure 60–105 x 15–24 μm (Wilson and Henderson, 1966). They are at first unicellular but later become four-celled and greatly thickened and gelatinous at the apex. This rust is quite commonly found on young pine plants either in the nursery or in the early years of establishment in the forest. In Britain it occurs on both *P. sylvestris* and *P. nigra* var. *maritima* though it has not so far been recorded on *P. contorta*. The conspicuous white aecidia sometimes give rise to concern but damage is rarely serious and no control measures are normally required. Good weed control in the nursery and its environs should eliminate the alternate hosts.

Needle blight caused by *Dothistroma pini* Hulbary

Dothistroma blight is largely a disease of pines although *Pseudotsuga menziesii* and *Larix decidua* are also slightly susceptible to attack. It has caused serious defoliation in plantations of *Pinus radiata* in several parts of the world and this is by far the most important susceptible species from an economic viewpoint. The disease has been found on many pine species and is widely distributed throughout the world, having been recorded in Europe, South and East Africa, North and South America and New Zealand. In Britain, the disease caused severe damage to pine transplants in nurseries at Wareham Forest, Dorset, during the 1950s. Extensive beds of *Pinus nigra* var. *maritima* and small beds of *P. ponderosa* and *P. bungeana* were notably affected while *P. contorta* was moderately damaged and *P. sylvestris* appeared immune. The disease was not found in plantations of pine at Wareham, nor has it been recorded elsewhere in Britain.

Hulbary (1941) was the first to name *Dothistroma pini* and he described it on *P. nigra* in Illinois. In a comprehensive review of Dothistroma blight of *P. radiata*, Gibson (1972) discusses the somewhat confused early history of the nomenclature of the pathogen. Several authors, including Siggers (1944) and Murray and Batko (1962), re-examined a range of material that had previously been disposed to fungi such as *Actinothyrium marginatum* and concluded that they corresponded most closely to *D. pini*.

The lesions on the pine needles are band-like and bear 1–12 stromata which are black, hypodermal in origin and erumpent when mature. The stromata vary in size from 300–750 x 150–400 μm, usually with one locule. The substromatal hyphae are septate, many-branched and are found only in the host mesophyll. Conidia are hyaline, filiform, one to five mainly three-septate when mature, often nonseptate when immature. The size of conidia varies and three varieties have been distinguished. Thyr and Shaw (1964) described *D. pini* var. *pini* with conidia 22.4 (15.4–28.0) x 3.2(2.6–4.0) μm and var. *linearis* 31.9(23.0–42.0) x

2.4(1.8–2.9) µm. Ivory (1967) added a third variety, *keniensis*, which measured 28.7(15.0–47.5) × 2.6(1.5–3.5) µm. This variety has been found only in Africa whereas the other two varieties have been found in North America only (var. *linearis*) or in all continents except Africa (var. *pini*). However, there is still some doubt concerning the validity of these varieties; Gadgil (1967), for example, considers that the characters used for differentation are insufficiently reliable.

The perfect stage of *D. pini* va. *pini* has been identified as *Scirrhia pini* on a range of pine hosts including *P. radiata* on Vancouver Island.

Infection appears as a chlorosis and necrosis of needles on the main stem and base of lower branches. Under favourable conditions and on a susceptible host, defoliation may be so severe that only needles at the extremities of the branches remain (Gibson *et al.*, 1964). Needle infections are first evident as yellow flecks which extend to become bands around the needle. As necrosis develops, these bands take on a characteristic red tinge and this has led to common names such as 'red band' being applied to the disease in some parts of the world. The black stromata develop within these bands and necrosis often extends throughout the needle followed by needle cast.

In his review of the factors affecting dispersal and infection Gibson (1972) indicates that research in Chile, East Africa, New Zealand and USA has shown the need for light rain or heavy mist in the effective dispersal of conidia. The conidial germ tube penetrates the needles through a stroma, a process taking 3 days or longer, depending on temperature and humidity. Macroscopic symptoms do not appear on the needles for 5–10 weeks. This relatively slow rate of growth is also a feature of the fungus in culture.

The first trials to test fungicides for the field control of the disease were undertaken in East Africa (Gibson *et al.*, 1966) and they demonstrated that fungicides based on copper compounds were particularly effective. These results have now found practical application in New Zealand where adequate protection can be achieved by three or four aerial applications with copper based fungicides at 2.24 kg per hectare copper equivalent spread over the first fifteen years' life of a *P. radiata* plantation (Bassett and Zondag, 1968). After this period the crop develops sufficient resistance for further spraying to be unnecessary. Successful control by the use of copper sprays has also been reported by Peterson (1967) on *P. ponderosa* and *P. nigra* in the United States.

The planting of *P. radiata* in East Africa ceased soon after the disease was first recognised and its place was taken by *Cupressus lusitanica* and *P. patula*. The latter species had proved immune to attack by *D. pini*. Ivory (1968) has compiled a comprehensive list which shows the relative susceptibility to *D. pini* of pines growing in East Africa (Ivory and Patterson, 1969). Gibson (1972) points out that field resistance to *D. pini* appears to take two different forms; some species such as *P. radiata* become increasingly resistant with age whilst others like *P. ponderosa* remain equally susceptible to all ages. This is an important consideration which needs to be taken into account in the selection of resistant cultivars or species.

SHOOT BLIGHTS AND DIEBACKS

Brunchorstia dieback caused by *Gremmenniella abietina* (Lagerb.) Morelat (*Scleroderris lagerbergii* Gr., *Crumenula abietina* Lagerb.; stat. conid. *Brunchorstia pinea* Karst)

In Britain Brunchorstia dieback occurs mainly on *Pinus nigra* var. *maritima* and occasionally on *P. sylvestris*. It was reported to have devastated Austrian pine (*P. nigra* var. *austriaca*) in Scandinavia in about 1880 and to have severely attacked *P. cembra* in Switzerland and young *P. sylvestris* in Sweden in more recent times. It was first identified in North America in 1962 and has subsequently caused serious damage to red pine (*P. resinosa*) and to *P. sylvestris* in the United States (Skilling *et al.*, 1979). Although mainly found on pine species Brunchorstia dieback has also been found on *Pseudotsuga menziesii*, *Picea* spp. and *Larix leptolepis*.

Gremmen (1968*b*) established that initial infection by *G. abietina* occurs on developing shoots in the spring. However, the first symptoms, at least in Britain and Holland, do not appear until the following winter when resin bleeding can be observed on the buds. Brown necrotic areas develop at the base of the buds and in the cortex of the current year's shoot. In the spring many infected buds fail to flush and the one-year-old needles turn brown at the base and eventually die. A characteristic yellow coloration of the xylem tissues can be seen (Read, 1967). When the bud is only partially infected, a poor distorted shoot may be produced. Infected shoots may also survive, in which case areas of depressed necrotic tissue may be found. At this stage affected trees have many dead shoots in the crown and if the attack is severe some trees will die. However, trees often survive and adventitious buds develop below the point of dieback to provide new growth.

Somewhat different symptoms of the disease have been described in Scandinavian countries and in the United States. In Norway, Roll-Hansen (1964) reported the presence of girdling cankers on small Scots pine 0.5–2 m in height. Ohman (1966) described the formation of elongated cankers at the base of stems of *P. banksiana* in the United States which girdled and killed the trees. On *P. resinosa*, also in the United States, Benzie (1958) mentions dead branches, cankers and dead tops as the commonest symptoms. In a more general description of the symptoms in the United States, Skilling *et al.* (1979) mention death and dieback of shoots (plate 37), rapid girdling and death of young trees and deforming cankers on the branches of older trees. The European strain of the fungus (see below) causes more severe symptoms than the so-called 'Lake States' strain.

Black, spherical pycnidia, up to 1 mm diameter, emerge through the surface of infected stems, needle bases and buds. The conidia are hyaline, sickle-shaped, mostly three-septate and measure 25–40 x 3–3.5 μm (Punithalingam and Gibson, 1973). Black apothecia occur in groups on stems and in the axis of the needles. They are about 1 mm in diameter and have short stipes. The asci are inoperculate, eight-spored and measure $100-120 \times 8-10 \mu m$; ascospores are hyaline, ellipsoidal, three-septate and measure $15-22 \times 3-5 \mu m$. Apothecia have rarely been seen in Britain but are frequent in some parts of Europe and in North America.

At least three strains of the fungus, from Europe, North America and Asia, have been identified using immunological and other methods (Dorworth and Krywienczyk, 1975). In 1977 the 'European strain' was reported for the first time in New York State (Skilling, 1977) and is more virulent and has a wider host range than the North American 'Lake States strain' (Skilling *et al.*, 1979). In addition it appears that the European strain produces very few apothecia or ascospores in the field. In spore-trapping studies in the United States there was a marked absence of ascospores in areas where the European strain was prevalent. This contrasted strongly with areas occupied by the Lake States strain where ascospores can be trapped in large numbers during May and June. Long-distance dispersal of the fungus is thought to occur largely via the windborne ascospores and their absence in the European strain clearly has implications for disease spread. Transport of infected nursery stock or movement of infected Scots pine Christmas trees may provide alternative means of long-distance dispersal.

Serious outbreaks of Brunchorstia dieback occur from time to time in European countries and often appear to be related to climatic conditions. Butin and Hackelberg (1978) considered that a series of wet spring and summer months, over a period of six years, favoured the development of the epidemic. In the United States, on the other hand, greater emphasis is placed on the identity of the fungal strain in relation to the severity of outbreaks.

Experiments in the United States (Skilling and Waddell, 1974) have shown that the disease may be controlled in the nursery using the fungicide chlorothalonil applied about seven times from late May to mid-August. The use of chemicals is not practicable in plantation crops where careful selection of planting sites at some distance from affected plantations is an important consideration. In Britain the planting of Corsican pine is not recommended in upland regions in the north and west of the country where serious outbreaks have occurred in the past.

The pine twisting rust *Melampsora pinitorqua* Rostr.

The pine twisting rust *Melampsora pinitorqua* produces its aecidial stage on two needled pines and uredial and telial stages principally on aspen (*Populus tremula*) and less abundantly on white and grey poplars (*P. alba* and *P. canescens*). Wilson and Henderson (1966) consider that this rust is indistinguishable morphologically from several other rusts which occur on poplars but which have different alternate hosts such as *Larix* spp. (see chapter 6) and *Mercurialis* spp. They are all considered to be different forms of *M. pupulnea* but the name *M. pinitorqua* will be retained here for the form on pine.

Pale yellow patches appear in June on the developing shoots of the current year. Spermogonia appear as small yellow flecks on these patches and are followed by golden yellow aecidia which soon have no covering membrane (figure

Figure 39. Aecidium of *Melampsora pinitorqua* (the pine strain of *M. populnea*) on stem of Scots pine (Forestry Commission)

39). Shoots girdled by the fungus hang down and wither, but if the lesion is confined to one side, normal growth on the opposite side results in a bending over of the shoot (figure 40). Subsequently the tip turns upward again, thus causing a characteristic twist in the stem. These symptoms might superficially be confused with damage caused by the pine shoot moth (*Rhyacionia buoliana*) where the shoot is hollowed out by the insect or with damage by hormone weedkillers which can also deform the shoot. However, the presence of aecidia on the shoot is a useful diagnostic character of infection by the pine twisting rust.

The spermogonia are subcuticular, yellow and up to 130 μm wide and 15 μm high. The aecidia are erumpent through the cortex of young shoots, golden yellow in colour and reach 20 x 3 mm in size. Aecidiospores are globoid or ovoid, pale reddish yellow, 14-20 x 13-17 μm and with a finely verruculose wall about 2 μm thick (Wilson and Henderson, 1966). Details of the uredial and telial stages on poplar are described in chapter 16.

In Britain *M. pinitorqua* has been recorded on a number of pine species,

Figure 40. Twisting of stem of Scots pine caused by *Melampsora pinitorqua*
(Forestry Commission)

commonly on *P. sylvestris. P. pinaster* is also very susceptible, even more so than
Scots pine. Corsican and lodgepole pine are practically immune and can safely
be planted with aspen.

The damage done by the fungus can be quite serious as it causes deformations
of the main stem and multiplication of leaders. Outbreaks, however, are sporadic
and only occur where pine and aspen are growing in close proximity. This may
happen when pines are planted in an area previously occupied by broadleaved
species including aspen and the latter suckers following clear-felling (Murray,
1955).

It is clearly prudent to avoid planting susceptible pines on old aspen sites.
Control would involve the eradication or constant weeding out of aspen and
would rarely be justified since appreciable damage ceases once pine reaches the
late-thicket stage, and as a rule any economic loss is confined to some reduction
of revenue from first thinnings.

BRANCH AND STEM RUSTS

Resin-top caused by *Peridermium pini* (Pers.) Lév.

Peridermium pini is a nonalternating form of the rust fungus *Cronartium flac-cidum* (Alb. and Schw) Wint. and causes the disease known as resin-top of Scots pine. *C. flaccidum* occurs on a range of hosts; in Britain it has been found infrequently as a rust on *Paeonia* spp. and the aecidial stage on *Pinus* was first proved in France in 1895 and many subsequent reports have demonstrated the relation between aecidia and other spore forms on a range of hosts (Wilson and Henderson, 1966).

Infection of pine by aecidiospores occurs mainly through needles (van der Kamp, 1970). Infected needles turn brown as the fungus invades the tissues and spreads down into the stem. Browning of foliage on individual branches in otherwise healthy crowns is frequently the first sign of disease. A black lesion develops at the base of the dieback, branches below that point remaining healthy. At a later stage the disease progresses into the main stem, which is then girdled, with consequent dieback of the crown. The lower crown remains healthy for a time but eventually the whole tree may die. Girdling lesions on the main stem appear as blackened cankers, one foot or more in length. The black appearance of the cankers is due to copious production of resin from infected parts, and this symptom gives rise to the name resin-top. During May and June creamy-white aecidia appear as blisters at the edge of the cankers. Cankers are often found at the base of branch whorls on the main stem but are sometimes intercalary. The development of large cankers on the main stem usually results in the death of the whole tree.

The spermogonia are flat, irregular in shape and form blisters up to 3 mm in diameter. They are followed by the aecidia which erupt through the bark to form groups of creamy-white bladders each 2–7 mm long and 203 mm diameter (plate 12). The pale orange aecidiospores which they contain are globoid–ellipsoid or polyhedroid and measure 24–31 x 16–23 μm (Wilson and Henderson, 1966). The spore walls are hyaline, verrucose and 3–4 μm thick.

The uredosori of *Cronartium flaccidum* occur in the leaves of *Paeonia* spp. and *Tropaeolum* spp. from July to October. The uredospores are ovoid or ellipsoid and measure 18–30 x 14–20 μm with a hyaline wall, sparsely echinulate and 1.5–2.5 μm thick. Teleutosori appear on the site of the uredosori, emerging as a straight or curved waxy mass. The teleutospores are ellipsoid 20–60 x 10–16 μm with a smooth wall up to 1 μm thick (Wilson and Henderson, 1966).

In a survey of Scots pine plantations in northeast Scotland, the disease was found in about half the stands over 30 years of age (Murray *et al.*, 1969). Disease incidence was low in crops less than 30 years old but nearly 2 per cent of 40 to 50-year-old trees had stem cankers. The proportion of infected trees declined in crops older than this although approximately 4 per cent of trees over 100 years old, including remnants of old Caledonian pinewoods, were diseased.

Observations in Europe have indicated that susceptibility to infection by *P.*

pini is closely linked with genetic factors (van der Kamp, 1968). The progeny from infected trees is more susceptible to the disease than that from healthy trees and marked differences in susceptibility may occur between crops of different provenances.

The hyperparasite *Tuberculina maxima* has been found in several locations in Britain and van der Kamp (1970) reports that it caused a one-third reduction of aecidiospore production in one stand.

No control measures are at present recommended against this disease. Some loss of produce may, however, be prevented in severely affected stands by more frequent thinning or by the selective removal of diseased trees during routine thinning operations. Timber in those trees killed by the disease rapidly deteriorates as a result of beetle infestations and the activity of blue-stain and other fungi (Pawsey, 1964).

The white pine blister rust *Cronartium ribicola* J. C. Fisher

White pine blister rust is one of the best-known diseases caused by rust fungi and it has caused extensive damage to five-needled pines in Europe and North America.

Figure 41.   Canker on main stem of *Pinus strobus* attacked by *Cronartium ribicola* which has killed the upper crown (Forestry Commission)

It is a heteroecious rust whose alternate hosts are *Ribes* spp., on which it produces uredospores and teleutospores. Spermogonia and aecidia are produced on infected pine stems which are often girdled, resulting in the death of a branch or whole tree (figure 41).

Cronartium ribicola is considered to be an asiatic fungal species with *Pinus cembra* perhaps being the original host (Wilson and Henderson, 1966). The fungus was first found in Europe on *Ribes* in 1854 and on *P. strobus* in 1887 though the alternate host relationship was not established until a year later. The first record in Britain was made at King's Lynn on *Ribes* in 1892. It is generally agreed that the disease was introduced into the United States about 1900 on young plants of *P. strobus* from Germany and that a single shipment of the same species from France was responsible for its introduction into eastern Canada in 1910.

C. ribicola occurs on a number of five-needled pines in Britain including *P. strobus* and *P. monticola*. It alternates on a wide range of wild and cultivated

Figure 42. Tree of *Pinus strobus* attacked by *Cronartium ribicola*. Aecidial blisters of the fungus have erupted from the trunk of the tree, which also shows resin bleeding (Forestry Commission)

Ribes spp. including blackcurrant, which may be severely defoliated, and red-currant and gooseberry, which are more resistant to the disease.

The first symptoms appear on pine needles as small discoloured spots, some three months after initial infection. A year or more later, the bark at the base of the needles turns a yellow-orange colour. This coloration spreads and the bark becomes swollen. Two to four years after initial infection, the white aecidial blisters (figure 42) erupt through the surface releasing their orange aecidiospores into the atmosphere. The fungus is perennial on pine, quickly girdling and killing small shoots; the needles turn reddish brown and are readily visible on dying shoots. At a later stage, the main stem is invaded and girdled, leading to the death of the whole tree.

The sporidia infect pine needles through their stomata and the mycelium grows down into the shoot where small, yellow spermogonia, 2-3 mm diameter, are produced beneath the bark. Aecidia, 2-4 x 1-3 mm across and up to 3 mm high, are formed and exposed following rupture of the bark. The aecidiospores are globoid, ellipsoid and polyhedroid, orange in colour and measure 22-29 x

**Figure 43. Teleutospore horns of *Cronartium ribicola* on leaf of *Ribes*
(Forestry Commission)**

18-20 μm (Wilson and Henderson, 1966). These spores are airborne and can travel for great distances (over 100 miles) before germinating on the undersurface of *Ribes* leaves. Uredosori then develop within a few weeks as small yellow pustules. Several generations of uredospores can be produced before teleutospores appear on the lower leaf surfaces of the *Ribes* spp. Unlike the aecidiospores, the uredospores can travel only short distances of up to a mile. The teleutosori (figure 43) are brownish, bristle-like structures which bear the teleutospores, in their turn giving rise to the sporidia which can infect only the pine host.

The effects of climatic conditions on the epidemiology of white pine blister rust and a number of other North American pine rusts have been reviewed by Peterson and Jewell (1968). Temperature requirements for the formation and germination of basidiospores on pine hosts appear to be particularly important. Limited formation of basidiospores occurs above 13°C and Van Arsdel *et al.* (1956) have found that at 16°C basidiospores take 36 hours to germinate and 48 hours to infect the pine host. Such information can be useful in the prediction of rust distribution and intensity and under field conditions an average July temperature of 70°F seems optimal for the disease. Variations in the local topography and small openings in the forest canopy can have important effects on temperature and moisture and therefore on the development of the disease.

One of the reasons that white pines have not been planted on any scale in Britain is the serious risk of rust infection. *Ribes* spp., both native and cultivated, are very widely distributed and it is difficult to find sites where they are not growing close by. In the USA where there are large natural forests of susceptible pines *Ribes* eradication campaigns have been undertaken in an attempt to control the disease. This control method has been reviewed by Peterson and Jewell (1968) and they conclude that, while this technique can effectively control the disease, it is expensive and complete eradication is essential.

Other methods of control, including chemical treatment by aerial spraying, and pruning of infected branches, have also been attempted with only limited success. Research into the possible use of a hyperparasite of *C. ribicola*, *Tuberculina* spp., to control the pathogen has not so far met with success. Perhaps the most promising approach to control is through the selection and breeding of resistant pines. A large programme of work is being undertaken in the United States on this subject with the aim of producing stocks of seed of resistant material. The possible development of races of the pathogen, able to attack previously resistant selections of pine, must always be borne in mind in such programmes.

STEM AND BRANCH CANKERS

Cankers caused by *Crumenula sororia* Karst.

Crumenula sororia was first recorded by Karsten (1871) on *Pinus sylvestris* in Finland where it has also more recently been found on *P. contorta* by Kujala (1950). The first record in Britain was on *P. nigra* var. *maritima* in Wales and it has subsequently been found on *P. sylvestris* and *P. contorta* at various locations (Batko and Pawsey, 1964; Hayes, 1973).

Van Vloten and Gremmen (1953) have reviewed the literature on the nomenclature of *C. sororia* and concluded that it is specifically distinct from *C. pinicola*, a fungus with which it had been previously confused. The two fungi show great similarities in their apothecial structures but only *C. sororia* has a pycnidial stage, *Digitosporium piniphilum* Gremmen. In addition Gremmen (1968a) reports that *C. sororia* has been observed in close association with stem and twig cankers on *P. sylvestris* and *P. nigra* var. *maritima* whereas *C. pinicola* has been found mainly on stems of *P. nigra* var. *maritima* killed by other agents. Gremmen (1968a) also found that cankers are formed following wound inoculations with *C. sororia* but not with *C. pinicola*.

The first symptom of the disease is the production of small resin pustules in the bark of stems and branches. Other agents, including insects, can cause similar symptoms but in the case of infection by *C. sororia* resin bleeding may occur, fungal mycelium penetrates the cambium and wood, and canker formation follows. On poorly grown *P. nigra* var. *maritima* the cankers are irregular in appearance and the area of bark in which the fungus is active is rather indeterminate (Batko and Pawsey, 1964). Well-established cankers usually cause a marked flattening on one side of the stem and on young trees this may lead to a complete girdling of the stem and consequent death. On more vigorous *P. nigra* var. *maritima* copious resin flow can be observed below the initial area of infection, which may either be nodal or internodal (Manap and Hayes, 1971). Longitudinal splits appear in the bark, resin production continues and canker development soon becomes evident. The subsequent flattening of infected stems usually takes four to five years to become obvious. The nodal cankers always possess a recently dead or moribund branch projecting from the area of infection. In both *P. sylvestris* and *P. nigra* var. *maritima*, with cankers of all ages and sizes, sections through the stem show a distinctive blackening of the bark and wood.

In *P. contorta* canker development is somewhat similar to that on *P. nigra* var. *maritima*, but the black discoloration of the bark and wood is absent (Hayes, 1973). On recently infected *P. contorta*, cankers are found only at nodes on the main stem but at a later stage internodal cankers may appear. In contrast to *P. nigra* var. *maritima*, nodal cankers are not associated with dead or moribund branch stubs.

The black apothecia of *C. sororia* are irregularly round or oval in outline, 1-1.5 mm across and are found on the surface of the canker. When fresh there is a black raised margin at the periphery of the grey hymenium but they tend to shrivel and distort on drying out. They are often difficult to recognise against a background of blackened resin on broken cankered surfaces. The mature asci are $90-140 \times 11-13\,\mu m$ and the ascospores, which are commonly three-septate, measure $17-23 \times 5-6\,\mu m$ (Batko and Pawsey, 1964). The pycnidia are black and measure 0.4-0.7 mm across, and forked or fingerlike, multicelled conidia show a considerable size range (Gremmen, 1968a).

A number of observations have been made on the anatomy of cankers and the underlying wood in *P. nigra* var. *maritima* (Batko and Pawsey, 1964; Manap and Hayes, 1971). Fungal hyphae are abundant in the blackened bark tissue and extend both into the medullary rays of the wood and to a lesser extent into the tracheids. The black discoloration of the woody tissues is due to the deposition of dark granular bodies in the resin ducts, their surrounding epithelial cells and tracheids. There are conflicting reports as to the presence of fungal mycelium in association with the dark stained cells. Manap and Hayes (1971) studied a number of morphological characters in wood associated with cankers and concluded that xylem tracheids were shorter and rays and resin ducts were more numerous than in healthy wood. Similar though not identical observations were made on *P. contorta* (Hayes, 1973).

No measures have been developed so far for the control of this disease. Apart from the three pine species already mentioned, *C. sororia* has also been recorded as a pathogen on *P. nigra* var. *nigra* and on *P. cembra*. Hayes (1975) indicates that provenances of *P. contorta* differ in their susceptibility to artificial inoculation and to natural infection by *C. sororia*.

ROOT ROTS

The root rot fungi *Heterobasidion annosum* and *Armillaria mellea* affect pines as as well as many other trees. They are considered in chapter 3.

HEART ROTS

The most important heart-rot fungus affecting pines is *Phellinus pini*, but *Phaeolus schweinitzii* also causes a heart rot of pine. These decay fungi are described in chapter 19.

MISCELLANEOUS DISEASES

Blue stain caused by *Ceratocystis* spp. and other fungi

The sapwood of pine is subject to a discoloration known as blue stain (figure 44) which can be caused by a number of different fungi. It can be differentiated from other stains by its bluish-grey colour and by the presence of fungi which discolour the wood without decomposing it. It occurs in logs, sawn timber and sometimes in standing trees. Although blue-stain fungi do not decay wood, they can reduce its value particularly when the appearance of the product is important. Thus in sawn timber used for packing cases, or in logs to be converted into chips or wood wool, the presence of blue stain is often unacceptable. On the other hand, in sawn timber which is to be painted or used for carcassing in buildings, blue stain may not be important.

Several species of *Ceratocystis* and the related imperfect genera *Leptographium*

Figure 44. **Blue stain on the cut ends of billets of Corsican pine (Forestry Commission)**

and *Graphium* are commonly found associated with blue stain. The following species were found in pine logs by Dowding (1970) in Britain:

Ceratocystis pilifera
Ceratocystis piceae
Ceratocystis coerulescens
Ceratocystis minor
Graphium aureum
Leptographium lundbergii

Many of these fungi have been found in association with blue stain in pine in Europe and North America (Lagerburg *et al.*, 1927; Davidson, 1935). Rumbold (1936) draws attention to another species, *Ceratocystis ips*, which is important in the USA.

There has been discussion in the literature for many years about the no-menclature of *Ceratocystis* and related genera. Hunt (1956) made a thorough study of the genus and he provided a detailed key for the identification of species.

In addition to *Ceratocystis* and related genera there are a number of Fungi Imperfecti which can cause blue stain, usually limited to a surface discoloration. In this context, Butin (1965) mentions *Cladosporium* spp., *Aureobasidium pullulans*, *Alternia* spp., *Epicoccum nigrum* and *Sclerophoma pithyophila*. Superficial staining is in general due to the growth of fungi over the surface of the exposed wood, the colour coming mainly from the dark mycelium or spores.

Those fungi, particularly *Ceratocystis* spp., which penetrate into the rays and tracheids, have dark hyphae that sometimes produce pigments that diffuse into the xylem but more frequently produce a visual appearance of stain by diffraction of light from the pigmented hyphae. Much research has been undertaken in many parts of the world on blue stain in pine but it should be noted that similar discolorations have been reported on many other hosts, both coniferous and broadleaved.

In a review of the methods by which blue-stain fungi enter host tissues, Dowding (1970) indicated that many research workers in both Europe and America have proposed wind and insects as the main agents for distribution. Airborne infections occurred mainly at the cut ends of logs, on parts of logs from which the bark has been removed, or on sawn timber. Other infections, particularly those by *Ceratocystis* spp., were closely associated with the breeding galleries of bark beetles. Dowding (1973) made a special study of these associations and found that although *Tomicus piniperda* carried spores of *C. piceae*, colonisation of the tunnels was limited by prior establishment of basidiomycetes. Following secondary invasion by dipterous larvae, other *Ceratocystis* spp. were introduced and they became successfully established in the well-developed larval galleries where basidiomycetes were absent. In the USA, Rumbold (1936) described *Ceratocystis* spp. disseminated by *Dendroctonus* spp. and correlated the incidence of *C. ips* with infestations by *Ips* spp.

Both moisture content of the wood and temperature can influence the growth of blue-stain fungi. Findlay (1959a) indicates that the moisture content of the sapwood in a live vigorous tree is too high to permit the growth of these fungi. However, if the tree should lose vigour as a result of attack by insects or other agents, the moisture content of the wood may be sufficiently reduced for infection to occur. The minimum moisture content of wood for the growth of most staining fungi is 27-28 per cent and this is clearly an important consideration in relation to the development of blue stain in felled logs or timber.

Blue stain fungi grow very much more rapidly under warm conditions than cool (Findlay, 1959a). Lindgren (1942) reports that the optimum temperature for growth of most *Ceratocystis* spp. in Canada is about 25°C.

Protection against infection by blue-stain fungi, where this is required, can be achieved in a number of ways. Sawlogs should be extracted from the forest and transported to the sawmill as rapidly as possible, thereby reducing the opportunity for the airborne and insect-borne infection and subsequent development of blue stain. Where bark beetles are involved, a knowledge of their life cycle will indicate the period when eggs are laid in the bark of sawn logs and the time of adult emergence. Felling and subsequent forest operations may be organised so as to avoid the presence of saw logs in the forest at egg-laying times or 'hot logging' may be practised and this will additionally ensure the removal of produce from the forest before adults emerge. The total bark beetle population may thereby be kept under control. An alternative practice is to store logs under water or beneath a water sprinkler so as to maintain a high moisture content which blue stain fungi cannot withstand (Findlay, 1959*b*).

Savory *et al.* (1970), in a study of chemical control of blue stain in Scots pine logs stored in the forest, reported that appreciable blue stain occurred only between March and August. The most effective control was achieved by a single application, between April and August, of a mixture of 0.75 per cent lindane and 5 per cent tribromophenol in a light mineral oil. Findlay (1959*b*) reports similar experiments from North America and other parts of Europe.

In the case of sawn timber, the moisture content can be reduced to 20 per cent by kiln drying immediately after sawing, thereby preventing the growth of many blue-stain fungi. Thorough air drying of sawn timber can achieve similar results though severe staining may develop during a favourable summer. Where appropriate, timber can be chemically treated immediately after sawing with aqueous solutions of sodium pentachlorophenate and borax. The concentrations required depend on a number of factors including species and geographic areas (Findlay, 1959*b*).

REFERENCES

Bassett, C. and Zondag, R. (1968). Protection against fungal and insect attack in New Zealand forests. *Pap. 9th Commonw. For. Conf., India, 1968*, no. 357

Batko, S., Murray, J. S. and Peace, T. R. (1958). *Sclerophoma pithyophila* associated with needle-cast of pines and its connection with *Pullularia pullulans*. *Trans. Br. mycol. Soc.*, 41, 126–8

Batko, S. and Pawsey, R. G. (1964). Stem canker of pine caused by *Crumenula sororia*. *Trans. Br. mycol. Soc.*, 47, 257–61

Benzie, J. W. (1958). A red pine plantation problem in Upper Michigan. *Lake St. Forest Exp. Stn Tech. Note*, no. 524

Butin, H. (1965). Untersuchungen zur Ökologie einiger Blaupilze an verarbeiten Kiefernolz. *Flora, Jena*, 155, 400–440

Butin, H. and Hackelberg, L. (1978). Uber den Verlauf einer *Scleroderris lagerbergii* Epidemie in einem Schwarzkiefernbestand. *Eur. J. For. Path.*, 8, 369–79

Darker, G. D. (1932). The Hypodermataceae of conifers. *Contr. Arnold Arbor.*, 1. 1–13

Darker, G. D. (1967). A revision of the genera of the Hypodermataceae. *Can. J. Bot.*, 45, 1399–1444

Davidson, R. W. (1935). Fungi causing stain in logs and lumber in the southern states including five new species. *J. agric. Res.*, 50, 789–807

Dorworth, C. E. and Krywienczyk, J. (1975). Comparisons among isolates of *Gremmeniella abietina* by means of growth rate, conidia measurement and immunogenic reaction. *Can. J. Bot.*, 53, 2506–25

Dowding, P. (1970). Colonisation of freshly bared pine sapwood surfaces by staining fungi. *Trans. Br. mycol. Soc.*, 55, 399–412

Dowding, P. (1973). Effects of felling time and insecticide treatment on the interrelationships of fungi and arthropods in pine logs. *Oikos*, 24, 422–9

Findlay, W. P. K. (1959*a*). Sap stain of timber. *For. Abstr.*, 20, 1–7

Findlay, W. P. K. (1959*b*). Sap stain of timber. *For. Abstr.*, 20, 167–74

Gadgil, P. D. (1967). Infection of *Pinus radiata* needles by *Dothistroma pini*. *N.Z. Jl. Bot.*, 5, 499–503

Gibson, I. A. S. (1972). Dothistroma blight of *Pinus radiata*. *A. Rev. Phytopathol.*, 10, 51–72

Gibson, I. A. S., Christensen, P. S. and Munga, F. N. (1964). First observations in Kenya on a foliage disease of pines caused by *Dothistroma pini* Hulbary. *Commonw. For. Rev.*, 43, 31-48

Gibson, I. A. S., Kennedy, P. and Dedan, J. K. (1966). Further observations in Kenya on a foliage disease of pines caused by *Dothistroma pini* Hulbary. *Commonw. For. Rev.*, 45, 67-76

Gremmen, J. (1968a). Stem cankers van groveden en Corscaanse den veroorzaakt door *Crumenula sororia* Karst. *Ned. BoschbTijdschr.*, 40, 176-82

Gremmen, J. (1968b). Bijdrage tot de biologie van *Brunchorstia pinea* (Karst.) Höhn., de oorzak van het taksterven bij Oostenrijkse en Corsicaanse. *Ned. BoschbTijdschr.*, 40, 221-31

Hayes, A. J. (1973). The occurrence of *Crumenula sororia* Karst. on Lodgepole pine in the United Kingdom. *Forestry*, 46, 125-38

Hayes, A. J. (1975). The mode of infection of Lodgepole pine by *Crumenula sororia* Karst. and the susceptibility of different provenances to attack. *Forestry*, 48, 99-113

Hulbary, R. L. (1941). A needle blight of Austrian pine. *Illinois Nat. Hist. Survey Bull.*, 21, 231-6

Hunt, J. (1956). Taxonomy of the genus *Ceratocystis*. *Lloydia*, 19, 1-56

Ivory, M. H. (1967). Spore germination and growth in culture of *Dothistroma pini* var. *keniensis. Trans. Br. mycol. Soc.*, 50, 563-72

Ivory, M. H. (1968). Reaction of pines in Kenya to attack by *Dothistroma pini* var. *keniensis. E. Afr. agric. For. J.*, 33, 236-44

Ivory, M. H. and Patterson, D. N. (1969). Progress in breeding *Pinus radiata* resistant to Dothistroma needle blight in East Africa. *Silvae Genet.*, 19, 38-42

Jahnel, H. and Junghans, R. (1957). Uber eine wenig bekannte Kiefernkrankheit (*Sclerophoma pithyophila*). *Forstwiss. ZentBl.*, 76, 124-32

Karsten, P. A. (1871). *Mycologica Fennica*. I. *Discomycetes*, p. 211

Kujula, V. (1950). Uber die Kleinpilze der Koniferen in Finland. *Metsatiet. Tutkimuslait Julk.*, 38, 4

Lagerburg, T., Lundberg, G. and Melin, E. (1927). Biological and practical researches into blueing in pine and spruce. *Svenska SkogsvFör. Tidskr.*, 25, 145-272

Lindgren, R. M. (1942). Temperature, moisture and penetration studies of woodstaining *Ceratostomellae* in relation to their control. *U. S. Dep. Agric. Tech. Bull.*, no. 807

Manap Ahmad, A. and Hayes, A. J. (1971). *Crumenula sororia* Karst. associated with cankering and dieback of Corsican pine. *Q. Jl. For.*, 25, 185-200

Melchior, G. H. (1975). Research in resistance in *Pinus sylvestris* to *Lophodermium pinastri*, in *Lophodermium in Pines*, pp. 5-10, Reinbek, no. 103

Millar, C. S. (1970). Role of *Lophodermella* spp. in premature death of pine needles in Scotland. *Rep. Forest Res., Lond., 1970*, pp. 176-8

Millar, C. S. (1975). Deposition of ascospores of *Lophodermium* from pines, in *Lophodermium in Pines*, pp. 11-20, Reinbek, no. 103

Minter, D. W. and Millar, C. S. (1980). Ecology and biology of three *Lophodermium* spp. on secondary needles of *Pinus sylvestris. Eur. J. For. Path.*, 10, 169-181

Minter, D. W., Staley, J. M. and Millar, C. S. (1978). Four species of *Lophodermium* on *Pinus sylvestris. Trans. Br. mycol. Soc.*, 71, 295-301

Murray, J. S. (1955). *Rusts of British Forest Trees*. Bookl. For. Commn, no. 4

Murray, J. S. and Batko, S. (1962). *Dothistroma pini* Hulbary: a new disease of pine in Great Britain. *Forestry*, 35, 57-65

Murray, J. S., Miller, C. S. and van der Kamp, B. J. (1969). Incidence and importance of *Peridermium pini* (Pers.) Lév. in north-east Scotland. *Forestry*, 42, 165

Murray, J. S. and Young, C. W. T. (1956). The effect of brashing and thinning on the incidence of *Lophodermium pinastri. Q. Jl. For.*, 50, 75-6

Nicholls, T. H. (1973). Fungicide control of *Lophodermium pinastri* on red pine seedlings. *Pl. Dis. Reptr.*, 57, 263-6

Ohman, J. H. (1966). *Scleroderris lagerbergii* Gremmen: the cause of dieback and mortality of red and jack pine in Upper Michigan plantations. *Pl. Dis. Reptr.*, 50, 402-5

Pawsey, R. G. (1964). *Resin-top Disease of Scots Pine*, Leafl, For. Commn, no. 49

Peace, T. R. (1962). *Pathology of Trees and Shrubs*, Clarendon Press, Oxford

Petersen, G. W. (1967). Dothistroma needle blight of Austrian and Ponderosa pines: epidemiology and control. *Phytopathology,* 57, 437–41

Petersen, R. S. and Jewell, F. F. (1968). Status of American stem rusts of pine. *A. Rev. Phytopathol.,* 6, 13–40

Punithalingam, E. and Gibson, I. A. S. (1973). *Gremmeniella abietina.* Descriptions of Pathogenic Fungi and Bacteria, no. 369, CMI, Kew

Read, D. J. (1967). Brunchorstia dieback of Corsican pine. *Forest Rec., Lond.,* no. 61

Robak, H. (1952). *Dothichiza pithyophila* (Cda) Petr., the pycnidial stage of a mycelium of the type *Pullularia pullulans* (de B.) Berkh. *Sydowia,* 6, 361–2

Roll-Hansen, F. (1964). *Scleroderris lagerbergii* Gremmen (*Crumenula abietina*) and girdling of *Pinus sylvestris* L. *Meddr. norske SkogsforsVes.,* 68, 159–87

Rumbold, C. (1936). Three blue staining fungi including two new species associated with bark beetles. *J. agric. Res.,* 52, 419–37

Savory, J. G., Nash-Wortham, J., Phillips, D. H. and Stewart, D. H. (1970). Control of blue stain in unbarked pine logs by a fungicide and an insecticide. *Forestry,* 43, 161–74

Siggers, P. V. (1944). *The Brown-Spot Needle Blight of Pine Seedlings.* U. S. Dep. Agric. Tech. Bull., no. 370

Skilling, D. D. (1974). Control of *Lophodermium* needlecast in Scots pine Christmas tree plantations. *Pl. Dis. Reptr.,* 58, 853–6

Skilling, D. D. (1977). The development of a more virulent strain of *Scleroderris lagerbergii* in New York State. *Eur. J. For. Path.,* 7, 297–302

Skilling, D. D. and Nicholls, T. H. (1975). The development of *Lophodermium pinastri* in conifer nurseries and plantations in North America. *Eur. J. For. Path.,* 5, 193–7

Skilling, D. D., O'Brien, J. T. and Bell, J. A. (1979). *Scleroderris Canker of Northern Conifers,* U. S. Dep. Agric. Forest & Insect Leafl., no 130

Skilling, D. D. and Waddell, C. D. (1974). Fungicides for the control of Scleroderris canker. *Pl. Dis. Reptr.,* 58, 1097–1100

Stephan, B. K. (1975). Resistance in pine species to *Lophodermium pinastri,* in *Lophodermium in Pines,* pp. 105–112, Reinbek, no. 103

Thyr, B. D. and Shaw, C. G. (1964). Identity of fungus causing red band disease of pines. *Mycologia,* 56, 103–9

Van Arsdel, E. P., Riker, A. J. and Patton, R. F. (1956). The effects of temperature and moisture on the spread of white pine blister rust. *Phytopathology,* 46, 307–18

van der Kamp, B. J. (1968). *Peridermium pini* (Pers.) Lév. and the resin-top disease of Scots pine. I. A review of literature. *Forestry,* 41, 189–98

van der Kamp, B. J. (1970). *Peridermium pini* (Pers.) Lév. and the resin-top disease of Scots pine. III. Infection and lesion development. *Forestry,* 43, 73–88

Van Vloten, H. and Gremmen, J. (1953). Studies in the discomycete genera *Crumenula* De Not. and *Cenangium* Fr. *Acta bot. neerl.,* 2, 226–241

Watson, A. R. and Millar, C. A. (1971). Hypodermataceous needle-inhabiting fungi in pines in Scotland. *Trans. Proc. bot. Soc. Edinb.,* 41, 250

Wilson, M. and Henderson, D. M. (1966). *British Rust Fungi,* Cambridge University Press, Cambridge

6 Diseases of larch (*Larix* spp.)

Two larches, the European larch (*Larix decidua*) and the Japanese larch (*L. leptolepis*), together with the hybrid between them (*L.* x *eurolepis*), are still important forest trees in Great Britain. As European larch is very susceptible to canker (caused by *Lachnellula willkommii* (*Trichoscyphella willkommii*)) and dieback, it is now little planted. Therefore, it has been overtaken in importance by the Japanese and hybrid larches. Hybrid larch would be more often planted if sufficient seed could be obtained. More European larch would also be planted in some areas if seed of the Sudeten provenances resistant to canker was more readily available.

NURSERY DISEASES

NEEDLE DISEASES

Needle cast caused by *Meria laricis* Vuill. (*Allescheria laricis* Hartig, *Hartigiella laricis* (Hartig) Sydow)
Needle cast caused by *Meria laricis* is widely distributed throughout Europe, in-

cluding Great Britain and the Republic of Ireland, and into the USSR (penetrating into Asia), and occurs also in the Pacific northwest of the USA and in New Zealand (Anon, 1970; Batko, 1956; Peace and Holmes, 1933). In Great Britain the disease is important mainly in north and west Scotland and sometimes in west Wales, though it sometimes appears elsewhere.

The causal fungus   M. *laricis* was considered by Vuillemin (1893) to be a simple member of the Basidiomycetes, because its spore-bearing hyphae resemble those of the smuts and rusts (and of some other Heterobasidiomycetes). The fungus also has thick gelatinous hyphae, and produces secondary conidia (Hiley, 1921; Peace and Holmes, 1933), both of which are characteristic of the Heterobasidiomycetes, but most later authors have preferred to place it in the Deuteromycetes (Fungi Imperfecti) (Batko, 1956).

M. *laricis* enters the host needles through the stomata (Biggs, 1957). Within the plant it at first produces branched septate hyphae, some of which have mucilaginous walls (Hiley, 1921). Soon, however, knots of hyphae form in the substomatal spaces, and from these, usually only on the lower sides of the leaves, bundles of conidiophores emerge through the stomata. Under a low magnification these bundles of conidiophores look like small, white, pustular spots, not unlike the white waxy plugs on the stomata, but they stain characteristically with cotton blue. Under a higher magnification they can be seen at first to be made up of groups of cylindrical or club-shaped hyphae, which later become transversely one to three-septate. A sterigma develops on each of the segments so formed, and spores measuring $8-10 \times 2-3$ μm (Batko, 1956) are cut off from the sterigmata. The conidiophores then resemble the basidia of some of the Heterobasidiomycetes.

The spores themselves are colourless and slightly constricted at the centre. Just before germination, a transverse septum is laid down across the middle of the spore, and one end of the spore then puts out a germ tube which may then cut off many small secondary conidia (Peace and Holmes, 1933).

M. *laricis* exists in at least four strains, but these all appear to be equally pathogenic, and are unstable within the host. The fungus grows over a temperature range of $0-25°C$, with an optimum between 17 and $20°C$. Spore germination also takes place from $0-25°C$, with the optimum at $17°C$. Mycelial growth occurs within a pH range from 3.1 to 10, with an optimum between 5 and 7 (Biggs, 1957). The spores cannot survive drying (Peace and Holmes, 1933) and they germinate only when the relative humidity is higher than 90 per cent (Biggs, 1959).

Infection of the crop   The fungus survives on infested needles that remain attached to nursery plants over the winter. Spores are produced in spring on these needles, and quickly infect the new developing leaves. Fructification also takes place on fallen needles, but on most of these the fungus dies out before the spring.

Infection appears to enter nurseries almost entirely on infested transplants, and spread by airborne spores does not seem to take place for more than a few hundred metres (Peace and Holmes; 1933).

Host range   The host range of *M. laricis* is narrow. As a cause of significant damage the fungus is important only on European larch, though it has sometimes also severely affected hybrid larch. On rare occasions it has attacked and caused minor damage to Japanese larch, and it has also been recorded in this country on Western larch (*Larix occidentalis*) (Batko, 1956), and in Norway and the USSR on *L. sibirica* (Robak, 1946; Shafranskaya, 1960).

Schöber and Fröhlich (1967) studied a number of provenances of European larch, and found that all those susceptible to *Meria laricis* (as well as to larch canker and to frost) were those originating in high altitudes, at 1400 metres or above.

Symptoms   When larch is infected by *M. laricis*, the leaves become discoloured and finally brown. On current year's needles on already established nursery plants, the symptoms may first be seen in May, but on first-year seedlings, which are infected from the plants around, signs of disease are not evident until June or later. Infection may take place at any point on a needle, which then dies from the tip down, as far as the infected zone. In cold weather, growth of the fungus is slowed down, however, and then for a time only isolated brown spots may be visible on the diseased needles (Peace and Holmes, 1933).

Damage by *M. laricis* has often been confused with that caused by frost, but the presence of the minute fructifications already described confirms the diagnosis of needle cast. Certain other differences between needle cast and frost damage may also be detected. Frost usually kills all the needles on the frosted shoot, the needles being much shrivelled, with those at the shoot tip particularly badly affected, whereas *M. laricis* first attacks only a proportion of the needles, usually leaving those at the tip undamaged. Needles affected by *M. laricis* are browned rather than shrivelled, and at first they are attacked towards the middle or base, and only later die back from the tips. Needles affected by frost usually remain long on the plant, but needles on shoots with needle cast mostly fall early, leaving relatively few on the plant as further sources of infection.

Factors affecting the disease   *Meria* needle cast is of importance mainly in the wetter highland zone of Great Britain, and its progress is favoured by warm, damp weather (Peace and Holmes, 1933; Biggs, 1959). In dry seasons it is of little significance. The age of the plants is also important, for although the fungus may occur on quite large trees, it has not been known to cause serious damage on trees more than eight years old (Peace and Holmes, 1933), and is usually of concern only in the nursery. There it does most damage to second-year plants, which are early infected by spores from diseased needles persisting on them (or on nearby plantation trees) from the previous season, First-year plants are very susceptible, but suffer badly only in wet seasons, if infected early.

Losses caused   As a rule *M. laricis* does not kill plants, but weakens and stunts them so that a high proportion of the stock may be classed as culls, and so rejected when lifting for planting.

Control of the disease   Needle cast may be largely avoided if larch is raised only from seed in nurseries sited away from larch plantations from which initial infection may come. If the disease appears in a nursery, it may be controlled by spraying, and its carry-over into the following year is known to be reduced by transplanting the affected stock.

Various spray materials may be used. Those most commonly used in Great Britain are colloidal and wettable sulphur preparations (Phillips, 1963), several of which were tested by Peace (1936). Elsewhere, good results have been obtained with captan, zineb, phygon, and copper oxychloride (Schönhar, 1958; Shafranskaya, 1960), though the last of these caused some needle-scorch.

POST-NURSERY DISEASES

NEEDLE DISEASES

Needle rusts

A number of needle rusts have their aecidial stages on larch in Great Britain, but they are of minimal significance on it. They have been little studied, and for the most part they are difficult to differentiate one from another. All are heteroecious, and are better known and more important on their alternate hosts. Indeed, in some cases it is not known whether or not the stage on larch occurs in this country.

Of the four certainly known here on larch, *Melampsoridium betulinum* (Fr.) Kleb. produces spermogonia and aecidia from April to June on the needles of European and Japanese larch. The aecidia, which are borne on the undersides of the needles, are fairly prominent, with a white peridium up to 1.5 mm wide by 1 mm long and 0.5 mm high. The spores measure 16–24 × 12–18 μm (Wilson and Henderson, 1966). The stage on larch appears to be rare, but the uredosori and teleutosori are common on birch.

The other three known needle rusts are species of *Melampsora*, and on larch they produce yellow spermogonia and yellow or orange aecidia. The latter are small and inconspicuous, and of the pustular type lacking a well-marked peridium, and known as caeomata. They are described by Wilson and Henderson (1966).

M. populnea (Pers.) Karst. (syn. *M. tremulae* Tul.) exists in a number of races, one of which, variously called *M. larici-tremulae* Kleb., *M. laricis* Hartig, and *M. tremulae* f. *laricis* Hartig, has been recorded on European larch in Scotland. It has pale yellow spermogonia and caeomata, and its uredosori and teleutosori occur on poplar. The race of this rust that occurs on pine (the pine twisting rust, *M. pinitorqua* Rostr.) is more important than that on larch.

The other two *Melampsora* species have their uredosori and teleutosori on willows, and have both been found here on European and Japanese larch. One of them is *M. caprearum* Thüm. (syn. *M. larici-caprearum* Kleb.) and the other is *M. epitea* var. *epitea* Thüm.

Two other species of *Melampsora*, *M. larici-populina* Kleb. and *M. larici-pentandrae* Kleb. may perhaps also occur here on larch. These both have orange caeomata, and the uredosori and teleutosori of the first are on poplars and those of the second are on willows.

A further *Melampsoridium* sp., *M. hiratsukanum* Ito, the spermogonia and caeomata of which elsewhere occur on larches, is known here only by its uredosori and teleutosori on alders.

DIEBACKS

Phomopsis disease caused by *Phacidiopycnis pseudotsugae*

Phomopsis disease, caused by *Phacidiopycnis pseudotsugae* (which is more common on Douglas fir) sometimes attacks Japanese and occasionally European larch. This disease is described in chapter 3.

STEM AND BRANCH CANKERS

Larch canker caused by *Lachnellula willkommii* (Hartig) Dennis (*Trichoscyphella willkommii* (Hartig) Nannf., *Dasyscypha willkommii* (Hartig) Rehm, *Lachnella willkommii* Hartig)

Apart from butt rot caused by *Heterobasidion annosum*, the most damaging disease of larch is the canker caused by *Lachnellula willkommii*. This discomycete is known in Great Britain and Ireland, and throughout the rest of Europe eastward into Russia, as well as in Japan (Ito *et al.*, 1963). In 1927 it was found in the USA, but attempts to eradicate it there seem to have succeeded (Fowler and Aldrich, 1953).

The perfect fructifications of the fungus, which occur only on cankers, are small, stalked, white, hairy apothecia, with an orange or buff hymenial disc usually up to 4 mm across (plate 23). The hymenium contains club-shaped asci mostly measuring 135-165 x 9.5-11 μm, and filiform paraphyses scarcely swollen at the tip and extending beyond the asci. Each ascus contains eight 1-celled, colourless, elliptical ascospores mostly measuring 15-23 x 5-7 μm. The apothecia may be found more or less throughout the year, and differ only slightly from those of the related saprophyte *Lachnellula hahniana* (Seaver) Dennis. They are preceded, usually in the first half of the year, by an imperfect stage in which colourless spermatia measuring 2-8 x 1-2 μm are produced in a white, waxy stroma (Hahn and Ayers, 1934; Manners, 1953; Ito *et al.*, 1963). *L. willkommii* on cankers may be followed by *L. hahniana*, which also grows on fallen larch material, and on dead branches affected by dieback. *L. willkommii* itself, however, will grow only on cankers on living trees (Hahn and Ayers, 1943).

The two fungi have been much confused, and accounts of the growth and physiology of *L. willkommii* given in the earlier literature are therefore difficult to interpret. The fungus grows slowly in agar culture (Manners, 1953). Its ascospores germinate between 0 and 30°C, with an optimum at 20°C, and will not germinate when the relative humidity falls to 92 per cent or below (Ito *et al.*, 1963). The fungus is resistant to freezing, and the ascospores are resistant to drying (Gaisberg, 1928; Plassmann, 1927).

The avenue by which *L. willkommii* enters the tree has been much discussed. Cankers often begin on young stems and branches from 2 to 5 years old (Hopp, 1957; Zycha, 1959), but many are initiated after seven or more years of stem growth (Pawsey and Young, 1969; Buczacki, 1973*a*). Most of the cankers are centred round short shoots, while some arise round the bases of long shoots and around dormant buds (Zycha, 1959; Ito *et al.*, 1963). Zycha (1959) has suggested that the fungus may enter through leaf scars whilst Buczacki (1973*c*), on the other hand, studied the morphology of dwarf shoots and suggested that, when moribund, these could be infection courts for *L. willkommii*.

The cankers first appear as small, round or oval depressions, mostly around a branch or a dead twig or short shoot, and they usually begin in winter. Once within the bark, the fungus kills the cortex and the cambium. Hence in the following season the affected cambium forms no new wood or bark, but the surrounding tissues grow with increased vigour, so that in transverse section subsequent annual

Figure 45.   Cross section of canker on European larch, caused by *Lachnellula willkommii* (Forestry Commission)

rings appear eccentric, and some inward growth may take place over the edges of the diseased area (Pawsey and Young, 1969) (Figure 45).

The fungus is contained by corky tissue during the growing season, but in the following winter it usually penetrates or bypasses the cork layer, and kills a further zone of cambium round the edges of the original diseased area. This process continues, and usually results in a perennial oval, stepped canker with a depressed centre, surrounded by deformed, swollen tissues. Resin often exudes from the cankers, and runs down the stem and branches of diseased trees. The surfaces of the cankers in time become blackened, and fruit bodies of *L. willkommii* grow around their edges (figure 46). Development of cankers is sometimes checked, and the diseased areas become covered by callus tissue. Such old healed cankers remain as pockets of damaged tissue within the tree.

Cankers may appear on the main stem of the tree (when they cause the greatest damage) or on the branches, when they sometimes cause girdling and subsequent

Figure 46. Canker on European larch, caused by *Lachnellula willkommii*. The disc-like apothecia of the fungus can be seen on the cankered tissues (Forestry Commission)

dieback, though dieback of larch is caused not only by *L. willkommii* but also, for example, by winter cold and windchill and apparently also by aphids (Pawsey and Young, 1969).

The range of hosts affected by larch canker is small. In Great Britain, as in most other parts of the world, it is usually severe enough to cause serious damage only on European larch, but it has occasionally caused some loss in hybrid larch, and occurs also on Japanese larch, on which its effects are normally slight. In fairly recent years, however, it has caused severe losses in stands of Japanese larch in Japan (Ito *et al.*, 1963). Margus (1959) in Esthonia found *Larix sukaczevii* susceptible and *L. kurilensis* resistant, while according to Plassmann (1927) *L. sibirica* is immune. Within European larch, different provenances vary greatly in their susceptibility to the disease. It has long been known that most alpine larch provenances from high elevations are very susceptible, and the Carpathian larches are more resistant. Of the Carpathian larches, certain Sudeten provenances show a good combination of canker resistance and good growth (Plassmann, 1927; Edwards, 1952; Schober and Fröhlich, 1967; Pawsey and Young, 1969).

Factors affecting the severity of the disease on susceptible larches have not been clearly defined. Berkeley (quoted by Hiley, 1919) as long ago as 1859 suggested that canker occurred particularly in damp places. This suggestion receives some support from Hiley's observation that cankers are more frequent inside plantations than on their edges. The possible importance of frost has been stressed by Day (1931), though it has been shown (Hahn and Ayers, 1943; Manners, 1957; Zycha, 1959; Ito *et al.*, 1963) that *L. willkommii* may attack without prior damage by frost, and symptoms ascribed to frost by Day (1931) and Latour (1950) occur also in trees not affected by frost, but attacked only by *L. willkommii*, or even wounded mechanically (Manners, 1957). The theory that spring and perhaps autumn frosts were responsible for the annual extension of canker lesions (Day 1931) has now been discounted. Buczacki (1973*b*) found no evidence to support this theory but suggested that alternating cold and warm temperatures during the winter encouraged canker extension. Canker epidemics tend to occur in certain years (Ito *et al.*, 1963; Leibundgut *et al.*, 1964). The factor or factors common to these 'canker years' is not known, though Leibundgut *et al.* considered that high March temperatures were involved. Some recent evidence in Great Britain suggests that these 'canker years' are those in which heavy adelgid infestations occur.

The amount of damage caused by the disease varies greatly, depending partly on the susceptibility of the species or provenance, partly on the as yet obscure environmental factors mentioned above, so that the effects even on the same provenance may vary greatly from site to site. It depends also whether most of the cankers are on the branches, in which case the losses caused may be small, or whether many cankers occur on the main stems, in which case the stand may be almost worthless.

If European larch is to be grown, canker is best avoided by growing a silviculturally suitable Sudeten provenance of known high resistance to the disease.

ROOT DISEASES

Group dying caused by *Rhizina undulata*

Larches are among the conifers affected by Group dying caused by *Rhizina undulata*, which is described in chapter 3.

ROOT AND BUTT ROTS

Diseases of larch that also affect a wide range of other trees are described in chapter 3. The larches are rather susceptible to the major butt-rot fungus *Heterobasidion annosum (Fomes annosus)*. *Armillaria mellea* may kill young trees, but rarely causes butt rot in larch, which, however, may be rotted by *Phaeolus schweinitzii (Polyporus schweinitzii)*.

MISCELLANEOUS DISORDERS

Frost and drought damage

Much has been made of the susceptibility of larches to damage by frost, though in fact observations in Britain show that larch is less liable to spring frost damage than many other conifers. Japanese larch, however, is often damaged by autumn frosts.

Japanese larch is particularly susceptible to drought damage, and young trees on thin soils or planted over a thick grass mat may be killed or badly affected in hot dry summers.

REFERENCES

Anon (1970). *Meria laricis* Vuill. *Distrib. Maps Pl. Dis.*, no. 379.

Batko, S. (1956). *Meria laricis* on Japanese and hybrid larch in Britain. *Trans. Br. mycol. Soc.*, 39, 13–16

Biggs, P. (1957). Studies on *Meria laricis*, needle cast disease of larch. *Rep. Forest Res., Lond., 1957*, pp. 102–4

Biggs, P. (1959). Studies on *Meria laricis*, needle cast disease of larch. *Rep. Forest Res., Lond., 1958*, pp. 112–13

Buczacki. S. T. (1973a). Some aspects of the relationship between growth vigour, canker and dieback of European larch. *Forestry*, 46, 71–9

Buczacki, S. T. (1973b). Factors governing mycelial establishment in the larch canker disease. *Eur. J. For. Path.*, 3, 39–49

Buczacki, S. T. (1973c). Observations on the infection biology of larch canker. *Eur. J. For. Path.*, 3, 228–32

Day, W. R. (1931). The relationship between frost and larch canker. *Forestry*, 5, 41–56

Edwards, M. V. (1952). Provenance studies. *Rep. Forest Res., Lond., 1951*, pp. 38–43

Fowler, M. E. and Aldrich, K. F. (1953). Resurvey for European larch canker in the United States. *Pl. Dis. Reptr.*, 37, 160–161

Gaisberg, E. v. (1928). Studien uber den Larchenkrebspilz, *Dasyscypha willkommii*, insbesondere uber die Keimung seiner sporen. *Centralb. fur Bakt., Ab.* 2, 73, pp. 206–33

Hahn, G. G. and Ayers, T. T. (1934). Dasyscyphae on conifers in North America. I. The large-spored, white excipled species. *Mycologia*, 26, 73–101

Hahn, G. G. and Ayers, T. T. (1943). Role of *Dasyscypha willkommii* and related fungi in the production of canker and dieback of larches. *J. For.*, 41, 483-95

Hiley, W. E. (1919). *The Fungal Diseases of the Common Larch*, Clarendon Press. Oxford

Hiley W. E. (1921). The larch needle cast fungus, *M. laricis. Q. Jl. For.*, 15, 57-62

Hopp, P. J. (1957). Zur Kenntnis des Larchenkrebses (*Dasyscypha willkommii*) an *Larix decidua. Forstwiss, Zbl.*, 76, 334-54

Ito, K., Zinno, Y. and Kobayashi, T. (1963). Larch canker in Japan. *Bull. Govt. Forest Exp. Sta. Tokyo*, 155, 23-47

Latour, J. M. (1950). Intervention de la gelée dans la formation du chancre du melèze d'Europe (*Larix decidua* Mill.). *Bull. Soc. cent. for. Belg.*, 53, 239-241

Leibundgut, H., Dafis, S. and Bezancon, M. (1964). Etudes sur diverses provenances de melèze européen (*Larix decidua* L.) et la variabilité de leur infection par le chancre du melèze (*Dasyscypha willkommii* Hart.). *Schweiz. Z. Forstwes.*, 115, 255-60

Manners, J. G. (1953). Studies in larch canker. I. The taxonomy and biology of *Trichscyphella willkommii* (Hartig) Nannf. and related species. *Trans. Br. mycol. Soc.*, 36, 362-74

Manners, J. G. (1957). Studies on larch canker. II. The incidence and anatomy of cankers produced experimentally either by inoculation or by freezing. *Trans. Br. mycol. Soc.*, 40, 500-508

Margus, M. (1959). Lehisekultuuridest ja nende tervislikust seisundist Eesti NSV-s. *Eesti NSV teadur, Akad. Toimet., Ser. biol.*, 8, 204-215; abstract in *Rev. appl. Mycol.*, 39, 197, 1960

Pawsey, R. G. and Young, C. W. T. (1969). A reappraisal of canker and dieback of European larch. *Forestry*, 42, 145-64

Peace, T. R. (1936). Spraying against *Meria laricis*, the leaf cast disease of larch. *Forestry*, 10, 79-82

Peace, T. R. and Holmes, C. H. (1933). *Meria laricis. The Leaf Cast Disease of Larch*. Oxf. For. Mem., no. 15, 29 pp.

Phillips, D. H. (1963). *Leaf Cast of Larch Meria laricis*. Leafl. For. Commn, no. 21, 4 pp.

Plassmann, E. (1927). *Untersuchungen uber den Larchenkrebs*, J. Neumann, Neudamm, 88 pp.

Robak, H. (1946). Tre skogsykdommer som hittil har vaert lite kjent eller piaktet i Norge. *Tidsskr. Skogbr. 1946*, 10-11, 323-34

Schober, R. and Frohlich, H. J. (1967). Der Gahrenberger Larchen-Provenierengversuch. *Schr. Forst. Foh. Univ. Gottingen*, 37/38, 208 pp.

Schonhar, S. (1958). Bekampfung der durch *Meria laricis* verursachten Larchenschutte. *Allg. Forstz.*, 13, 100

Shafranskaya, V. N. (1960). Regul'taty ispytanu novykh slozhnovrqonicheshikh preparator protiv boleznei khvoi Listvemnitsy. *Sborn. Rab. les. Khoz. vaes. n.-i Inst. Lesovod Mekhan. les. Khoz. 1960*, 43, 141-153; abstract in *Rev. appl. Mycol.*, 41, 1962, pp. 66-67

Vuillemin, P. (1893). Les Hypostomacées. *Comptes rend.*, 122, 543

Wilson, M. and Henderson, D. M. (1966). *British Rust Fungi*, Cambridge University Press

Zycha, H. (1959). Zur frage der Infektion beim Larchenkrebs. *Phytopath Z.*, 37, 61-74

7 Diseases of Douglas fir (*Pseudotsuga* spp.)

Species of *Pseudotsuga* occur in North America south to Mexico, and in China and Japan. The only species extensively grown in Britain (and in the rest of northwest Europe) is the Douglas fir, *P. menziesii*, a native of western North America. *P. menziesii* exists in three main forms or varieties, sometimes separated (though intermediates may be found), as var. *viridis* (the coastal or green Douglas fir), var. *caesia* (the Fraser River, intermediate or grey Douglas fir), and var. *glauca* (the Colorado or blue Douglas fir). The green Douglas fir is a fairly important forest species, which grows well on suitable sites. The blue Douglas fir is grown in some large parks and gardens, but is not extensively planted because of its slower growth and susceptibility to the needle-cast fungus *Rhabdocline pseudotsugae*.

NURSERY DISEASES

GENERAL

Nursery plants of Douglas fir are among those sometimes attacked by the grey mould, *Botrytis cinerea*. Young plants have also been found with basal swellings ('carrot root'), resembling those said to be associated with *Pestalotia hartigii* in some species. This disorder is known in spruces as 'strangling disease' (figure 8).

Douglas fir plants in the nursery are also very susceptible to Phytophthora root rot caused by *Phytophthora cinnamomi.*

Douglas fir is also one of the trees affected by Phomopsis disease, caused by *Phacidiopycnis pseudotsugae.* This disease, which occurs both in the nursery and on older trees, also attacks Japanese larch and many other trees. All the above diseases are discussed in chapter 3.

POST-NURSERY DISEASES

NEEDLE DISEASES

Douglas fir is affected by two well-known needle-cast diseases, the first caused by *Rhabdocline pseudotsugae,* and the second by *Phaeocryptopus gaumannii.* Neither of these diseases is of great importance in Britain.

Needle cast caused by *Rhabdocline pseudotsugae* Syd.

The needle cast caused by *Rhabdocline pseudotsugae* occurs throughout Britain, and is widespread on the continent of Europe, as well as in Canada and the USA (in the western parts of which it originated) (Anon, 1976a).

R. pseudotsugae has caused serious damage in many areas, but it has been important mainly because it has greatly restricted the growing of the blue and grey varieties of Douglas fir, which are very susceptible to its attack.

It rarely occurs in nurseries, but causes damage mainly on relatively young stands between the ages of 10 and 30 years (Rohde, 1932; Jančařík, 1964). In North America, however, it is a problem to growers of Douglas fir for Christmas trees (Brandt, 1960; Collis, 1971).

The fungus The fruit bodies of the fungus are elongated ascocarps up to about 3 x 0.3 mm, embedded below the epidermis on each side of the mid-rib, usually only on the undersides of the needles (plate 24). In North America (Brandt, 1960) and in Europe (Peace, 1962), a form with larger ascocarps, up to 10-15 mm long, has also been found. When the ascocarps ripen, the overlying epidermis splits open and folds back as a lid to reveal the orange-brown (later brown) interior which contains the club-shaped asci. These, which are interspersed by slender, often forked paraphyses, measure up to 130 x 20 μm, and each contains eight elliptic-cylindric, colourless, one-celled ascospores, which may be slightly swollen at each end, and measure 15-20 x 6-9 μm. Each spore is surrounded by a thick gelatinous sheath (Parker and Reid, 1969). After discharge the spores become two-celled, one cell becoming dark brown with a thickened wall (Dennis, 1968).

Symptoms and disease development The ascocarps ripen and shed their ascospores in May and June (and in some areas into July), when the sticky spores adhere to the needles of the newly developing shoots. Spore discharge and infection take place only when the humidity is high (with an optimum of

100 per cent) and when the temperature is between 1 and 15°C (with an optimum of 10°C) (Parker, 1970; Collis, 1971). Only the young, developing leaves are subject to infection.

After infection, the fungus grows within the needles which, however, show no obvious external symptoms until the autumn. Then pale yellow blotches 1-2 mm across become visible, usually on the undersides. These blotches darken, and by the following spring become red-brown or purple-brown, and on them the new fructifications arise again in May and June to complete the cycle. The more severely affected needles quickly fall, but others remain on the tree and are slowly shed throughout the year.

Host range and varietal susceptibility   *R. pseudotsugae* affects only species of *Pseudotsuga*. It is of importance only on *P. menziesii*, but in Canada it has also been recorded on *P. macrocarpa* (Collis, 1971).

In the case of *P. menziesii*, the green variety *viridis* is much less susceptible than the grey and blue varieties *caesia* and *glauca* (van Vloten, 1930; Liese, 1932; Collis, 1971) (though it is the most susceptible of the three varieties to attack by *Phacidiopycnis pseudotsugae* (Hahn, 1957)). Indeed, the effects of *R. pseudotsugae* on the grey and blue forms may be so severe that in many parts of Europe these varieties cannot be extensively grown (Fischer, 1938), and only the green variety is grown in British forests.

Nevertheless, resistant individuals can be found even in populations of the susceptible varieties (Liese, 1932; Anon, 1956; Collis, 1971) though as yet little attempt has been made at systematic selection or breeding for resistance.

Factors affecting the disease   Experiments and observations in Canada suggest that spread within susceptible stands is greatest during periods of high humidity and at relatively low temperatures at or below 13°C (though the humidity is more important than the temperature) (Parker, 1970; Collis, 1971).

Damage caused   In North America, *R. pseudotsugae* is very important as a cause of damage to Christmas trees (Brandt, 1960; Collis, 1971). At best, affected trees grow slowly and take longer to reach a marketable size. In more severe cases, trees may lose all needles except those of the current year and they then become useless for the Christmas tree trade. Large forest trees, however, are usually little affected.

In Europe, older trees from about 10 to 30 years of age may be affected, especially in dense stands (Anon, 1956). Trees heavily infested for several successive years may lose almost all their needles, cease to grow, and eventually die. Because of the disease, the growing of the susceptible grey and blue forms of Douglas fir on any scale is prevented. In Britain, although the disease may be found all over the country, it is of little importance because only the Green Douglas fir is grown to any extent, except in parks and gardens.

Control   The only practicable way of controlling the disease on a forest scale is to grow the more resistant green variety of *P. menziesii*. Fungicides could be applied only to small trees of high value, and so are likely to be of use only in nurseries (where, however, the disease hardly ever occurs) and in North American Christmas tree plantations. Among the fungicides tested, lime sulphur and Bordeaux mixture have given promising results (Fischer, 1938; Collis, 1971). Results with phytoactin and cycloheximide have been conflicting, and these chemicals both caused some damage to the test plants (Weir, 1963; Weir and Jonhson, 1967).

Needle cast caused by *Phaeocryptopus gäumannii* (Rohde) Petr. (*Adelopus gäumannii* Rohde)

Needle cast caused by *Phaeocryptopus gäumannii* occurs in Britain (mainly in the wetter, more westerly parts), and throughout the rest of Europe, in western Canada, in both western and eastern parts of the USA, in New Zealand, and in Tasmania (Anon, 1976*b*).

In Britain, the overall effect of the disease is slight, in spite of the fact that the fungus can be found in a large number of stands of Douglas fir in the west of the country.

The disease generally affects trees between the ages of 10 and 40 years (Gaisberg, 1937; Buchwald, 1939). It may be found on younger and older trees, but on these it seems to cause little damage (Liese, 1939; Krampe and Rehm, 1952).

The fungus   The minute black, smooth, rounded perithecia of the fungus emerge from stromata on the undersides of the needles, and when numerous give the needle surface a sooty appearance. They measure up to about 80 μm across, and contain club-shaped asci measuring up to 40 x 15 μm, each containing eight spores. The ascospores are colourless, two-celled, rather club-shaped, and measure 10–15 x 3.5–5 μm (Dennis, 1968).

Symptoms and disease development   The asci ripen and shed their spores in May and June and into July, when the young shoots are developing (Gaisberg, 1937; Anon, 1956). After infection of the young needles, the fungus grows within the needle tissues, and towards the end of the summer the affected needles become yellowish green. Over the winter, dark plugs of fungal mycelium form below the guard cells of the stomata. From these plugs the perithecia develop outwards and eventually form on the outside of the leaf above the stomatal pores, until in May they produce ripe asci and shed their spores to complete the life cycle (Krampe and Rehm, 1952; Anon, 1956).

Infected needles may bear many fruit bodies and yet remain green and apparently little harmed, while in other cases, on more susceptible trees, they may become more and more yellow with age and finally die, turn brown and fall.

Host range and varietal susceptibility P. *gäumannii* affects only species of *Pseudotsuga*. It attacks all the main forms of P. *menziesii*, though different provenances as well as individual trees within the species show differences in resistance (Gaisberg, 1937; Liese, 1939). In Germany, Krampe and Rehm (1952) found apparently resistant trees in stands of the green Douglas fir (var. *viridis*) which retained their needles for several years while adjacent susceptible trees were almost bare. Some of these resistant individuals were tolerant, and retained their needles in spite of a dense covering of fructifications, while others appeared to be resistant to the fungus and showed only slight infection.

Factors affecting the disease Infection by P. *gäumannii* seems to be encouraged by high summer rainfall and high humidity (Gaisberg, 1937; Merkle, 1951).

Damage caused In Britain, P. *gäumannii* can easily be found in a high proportion of the stands of Douglas fir in the western parts of the country, but it rarely causes any significant damage. Elsewhere it appears to be of greater importance. In Germany it may sometimes cause almost complete defoliation (Gaisberg, 1937; Krampe and Rehm, 1952). Liese (1939) and Merkle (1951), however, both indicate that the fungus rarely kills trees, but may render them liable to attack by *Armillaria mellea* and other secondary invaders. It has recently been suggested that attack by P. *gäumannii* has been one factor in a decline of Douglas fir in New Zealand (Anon, 1975).

Control This disease is not generally sufficiently severe to merit any special control measures. If control were needed, the best method would appear to be by selection and breeding from resistant trees. In New Zealand, promising experimental results were obtained by spraying with copper sprays and with benomyl, but lasting control was not achieved (Anon, 1975).

DISEASES OF SHOOTS

Phomopsis disease caused by *Phacidiopycnis pseudotsugae*
As noted earlier, Douglas fir is one of the trees susceptible to Phomopsis disease (caused by *Phacidiopycnis pseudotsugae*), which because of its wide host range is dealt with in chapter 3.

DISEASES OF THE TRUNK

Resin bleeding
From time to time Douglas fir trees in Britain may be affected by a profuse resin bleeding, the cause of which is still unknown. Although numerous fungi have

been found on the lesions, which occur on the trunk and at branch bases, they all appear to be saprophytes. It has sometimes been considered that the disorder is caused by drought or some other climatic factor, but insect damage has also sometimes been suspected as either a main cause or as a contributory factor.

ROOT DISEASES AND ROOT AND BUTT ROTS

Douglas fir is rather resistant to attack by *Armillaria mellea* and *Rhizina undulata. Heterobasidion annosum (Fomes annosus)* rarely penetrates the butt, though it may kill young trees, and kill and rot the roots of older trees to such an extent that they readily become victims to windblow. Douglas fir is one of the conifers that may be severely affected by *Phaeolus schweinitzii (Polyporus schweinitzii).* These fungi are discussed in chapters 3 and 19.

REFERENCES

Anon (1956). *Two Leaf-cast Diseases of Douglas Fir.* Leafl. For. Commn, no. 18
Anon (1975). Plant pathology, in *Report of Forest Research Institute for 1974,* New Zealand Forest Service, Wellington, New Zealand, pp. 44−8
Anon (1976a). *Rhabdocline pseudotsugae* Syd. *Distrib. Maps Pl. Dis.,* no. 52, 4th ed.
Anon (1976b). *Phaeocryptopus gaeumannii. Distrib. Maps Pl. Dis.,* no. 42, 4th ed.
Brandt, R.W. (1960). The Rhabdocline needle cast of Douglas fir. *Tech. Publ. N.Y. St. Coll. For.,* no. 84.
Buchwald, N.F. (1939). Douglasiens Sodskimmel *(Phaeocryptopus gaumannii).* En ny svamp paa Douglasgran i Danmark. *Dansk. Skovforen. Tidsskr.,* 1939, 357−82
Collis, D.G. (1971). *Rhabdocline Needle Cast of Douglas Fir in British Columbia.* For. Insect and Dis. Survey Pest Leafl., no. 32
Dennis, R.W.G. (1968). *British Ascomycetes,* J. Cramer, Lehre
Fischer, H. (1938). Die Douglasienschütte. *Blumen-u PflBau ver. Gartenwelt,* 62, 331−2
Gaisberg, E. v. (1937). Über die Adelopus-Nadelschütte in Württembergischen Douglasienbeständen mit Hinweis auf die bisher hier bekanntgewordene Verbreitung von Rhabdocline. *Silva,* 25, 37−42, 45−8
Hahn, G.G. (1957). *Phacidiopycnis (Phomopsis)* canker and dieback of conifers. *Pl. Dis. Reptr.,* 41, 623−33
Jančařík, V. (1964). Skotská sypavka Douglasky. *Lesn. Pr., Czechoslovakia,* 43, 420−23
Krampe, O. and Rehm, H.J. (1952). Untersuchungen über den Befall von *Pseudotsuga taxifolia viridis* mit *Adelopus gäumannii* Rohde. *NachrBl. dt. PflSchutzdienst, Berl.,* 6, 208−12
Liese, J. (1932). Zur Biologie der Douglasiennadelschütte. *Zeitsch. für Forst- u Jagdwesen,* 64, 680−93
Liese, J. (1939). The occurrence in the British Isles of the Adelopus disease of Douglas fir. *Q. Jl. For.,* 33, 247−52
Merkle, R. (1951). Über die Douglasien-Vorkommen und die Ausbreitung der Adelopus-Nadelschütte in Württemberg-Hohenzollern. *Forst- u- Jagdztg,* 122, 161−91
Parker, A.K. (1970). The effect of relative humidity and temperature on needle cast disease of Douglas fir. *Phytopathology,* 60, 1270−73
Parker, A.K. and Reid, J. (1969). The genus *Rhabdocline* Syd. *Can. J. Bot.,* 47, 1533−45
Peace, T.R. (1962). *Pathology of Trees and Shrubs,* Clarendon Press, Oxford
Rohde, T. (1932). Das Vordringen der Rhabdocline-Schütte in Deutschland. Die Folgen des Rhabdocline-Befalls in deutschen Douglasienbeständen. Welche Douglasien sind in Deutschland durch Rhabdocline gefährdet? *Forstarchiv.,* 8, 247−9

Vloten, H. van (1930). Aantasting van *Pseudotsuga taxifolia* Britton (Douglasspar) door *Rhabdocline pseudotsugae* Sydow en *Chermes cooleyi* Gillette. *Nederl. BoschbTijdschr.*, 3, 283‑98

Weir, L.C. (1963). Control of needle cast of Douglas fir by antibiotics. *For. Chron.*, 205‑211

Weir, L.C. and Johnson, A.L.S. (1967). Use of phytoactin in the treatment of Rhabdocline needle-cast of Douglas Fir. *Phytoprotection*, 48, 74‑77

8 Diseases of minor forest conifers: *Abies, Cupressus* and *Chamaecyparis, Thuja* and *Tsuga*

SILVER FIR: *Abies* SPP.
  NURSERY DISEASES
    SPRING FROST DAMAGE, DAMPING OFF AND 'CARROT ROOT'
  POST-NURSERY DISEASES
    NEEDLE DISEASES
      Needle blights caused by *Acanthostigma parasiticum* **and** *Rehmiellopsis abietis*
    NEEDLE RUSTS
      Milesina blechni
      Milesina kriegeriana
      Pucciniastrum epilobii
      Melampsorella caryophyllacearum
    DISEASES OF THE TRUNK
      The rust *Melampsorella caryophyllacearum*
      Drought crack
    DECAY FUNGI
CYPRESS AND 'FALSE' CYPRESS: *Cupressus* SPP. AND *Chamaecyparis* SPP.
  NURSERY DISEASES
    GREY MOULD (*Botrytis cinerea*) AND PHYTOPHTHORA ROOT ROTS
    CANKER AND DIEBACK CAUSED BY *Kabatina* SPP.
  POST-NURSERY DISEASES
    DISEASES OF TRUNKS AND BRANCHES
      Resin bleeding and canker caused by *Seiridium cardinale* (*Coryneum cardinale*)
    ROOT DISEASES
      Phytophthora **root rot**
WESTERN RED CEDAR (*Thuja plicata*)
  NURSERY DISEASES
    WINTER BRONZING AND WINTER COLD DAMAGE
    NEEDLE BLIGHT CAUSED BY *Didymascella thujina*

POST-NURSERY DISEASES
  STEM DISEASES
    Cambial damage by spring frosts
    Cankers caused by *Seiridium cardinale* (*Coryneum cardinale*)
  ROOT AND BUTT ROTS
WESTERN HEMLOCK: *Tsuga heterophylla*
NURSERY AND POST-NURSERY DISEASES
  NEEDLE DISEASES
    Needle blight caused by *Didymascella tsugae*
  ROOT AND BUTT ROTS

REFERENCES

SILVER FIR: *ABIES* SPP.

There are about 50 species of *Abies*, but in Britain only one, *A. grandis*, has shown marked promise as a forest tree. It is a very high yielding species, and shows considerable resistance to attack by *Heterobasidion annosum* (*Fomes annosus*). The quality of the timber is relatively low, however, and so far *A. grandis* has remained only a minor species in British forests. On the European mainland, the native silver fir, *A. alba* (*A. pectinata*), is a forest species. In Britain, a good many *Abies* species are grown in parks and gardens, the commonest being grand fir, noble fir (*A. procera*) and the Caucasian fir (*A. nordmanniana*).

NURSERY DISEASES

SPRING FROST DAMAGE, DAMPING OFF AND 'CARROT ROOT'

Nursery beds of *Abies* plants are liable to damage by spring frost and damping off, and young plants have also been found with basal swellings like those associated with *Pestalotia hartigii* in spruce, Douglas fir, and some other conifers. This disorder is sometimes described as strangling disease or 'carrot root'. These diseases are described in chapter 3.

POST-NURSERY DISEASES

NEEDLE DISEASES

Needle blights caused by *Acanthostigma parasiticum* (Hartig) Sacc. (*Trichosphaeria parasitica* Hartig and *Rehmiellopsis abietis* (E. Rostrup) O. Rostrup (*R. bohemica* Bubak & Kabat)

Two needle blights occasionally affect silver firs in Britain. The first is caused by *Acanthostigma parasiticum*, the second by *Rehmiellopsis abietis*.

Acanthostigma parasiticum has been found in west Scotland and east England causing a needle blight in *Abies alba* (Watson, 1933; Batko, 1974). It also occurs, mainly on *A. alba*, in alpine parts of Europe and in the Black Forest and Bavaria (Viennot-Bourgin, 1949). Reports on *Picea* and *Tsuga* need confirmation.

The fungus produces minute, dark brown perithecia, from 100-200 μm across, on small mycelial cushions on the undersides of affected needles. The perithecia bear brown, bristle-like, septate hairs on the upper half, and contain hairlike paraphyses, and asci each containing eight ascospores. These are colourless or later greyish or brownish, ovoid, usually four-celled, and measure 15-20 x 4-5 μm (Hartig, 1894; Viennot-Bourgin, 1949; Batko, 1974).

The ascospores are shed, and germinate and cause infection in the autumn (Watson, 1933). The mycelium is white at first, but later brownish, and grows in and over the tissues of the undersides of the branches and needles. The fungus growing within the needles kills many of them, and they become brown, but remain matted together by the mycelium, and so do not at first fall from the tree.

The mycelium, which becomes perennial, remains dormant over the winter, but grows and spreads in the following spring to attack further shoots and leaves. It forms minute cushions on the undersides of infected leaves, and it is on these cushions that the superficial perithecia arise (Hartig, 1894).

The fungus may sometimes cause severe defoliation and dieback, and may destroy all the needles except those of the leading shoot (Watson, 1933). It is fortunate, therefore, that the disease is uncommon.

It is generally considered to be encouraged by moist conditions and dense planting. Hence if control measures are needed, it is usually suggested that the effects of the disease can be reduced by thinning to open up the stand to admit more air and light and render the atmosphere drier.

Rehmiellopsis abietis, the second cause of needle blight, has been found in Scotland, Denmark (Wilson and Macdonald, 1924; Boyce, 1927), Norway (Nedkvitne, 1966) and British Columbia (Waterman, 1945).

The fungus produces small, black, globose perithecia, mainly on the upper surfaces of the needles. The perithecia are at first immersed but later emerge to appear on the leaf surface, and measure up to 200 μm across. They contain a few club-shaped, thick-walled asci measuring up to 90 x 22 μm, each containing about 16-24 ascospores. These are colourless, two-celled, rather club-shaped, and measure 11-21 x 4-6.5 μm (Dennis, 1968).

Infection takes place soon after expansion of the young needles, which then shrivel and turn red, and later become dark brown or grey-black, and finally deep black. In the case of *Abies nobilis*, the diseased shoots become twisted (Wilson and Macdonald, 1924).

In Scotland, Wilson and Macdonald (1924) recorded *R. abietis* on *Abies alba*, *A. procera* (*A. nobilis*), *A. pinsapo*, *A. pindrow* and *A. cephalonica*. The fungus has also been found on *A. alba* in Norway (Nedkvitne, 1966) and Denmark (Boyce, 1927), and on *A. lasiocarpa* in British Columbia (Waterman, 1945).

The disease is most severe on young trees, and on the lower branches of older ones (Wilson and Macdonald, 1924; Nedkvitne, 1966). Wilson and Macdonald found that 50 to 80-year-old trees of *A. alba* appeared to remain healthy even when exposed to infection from nearby diseased plantations.

In Norway, Nedkvitne (1966) found the disease was most severe on sites exposed to low late spring temperatures. However, infection could occur in the absence of injury by frost or other factors.

Though *R. abietis* may sometimes kill trees (Nedkvitne, 1966), and in the 1920s appeared to be spreading rapidly in Scotland, where *A. alba* was badly attacked (Wilson and Macdonald, 1924; Boyce, 1927), it has since been of only minor significance.

If an attack should occur, severely affected young trees should be removed and burnt. Diseased lower branches of older trees should be treated in the same way if this can reasonably be done. Waterman (1945) found that attack by the related *R. balsameae* in North America could be controlled by three applications of Bordeaux mixture at 12-day intervals, beginning as the new growth first emerged.

NEEDLE RUSTS

The following rusts found in Britain are known to have stages on species of *Abies*:

> *Uredinopsis americana* Syd. (*U. mirabilis* Magn.)
> *U. filicina* Magn.
> (1) *Milesina blechni* Syd.
>   *M. scolopendrii* (Faull) Henderson
> (2) *M. kriegeriana* (Magn.) Magn.
>   *M. vogesiaca* Syd.
>   *M. dieteliana* (Syd.) Magn.
>   *Hyalopsora aspidiotus* (Magn.) Magn.
> (3) *Pucciniastrum epilobii* Otth.
>   *P. goeppertianum* (Kühn.) Kleb.
> (4) *Melampsorella caryophyllacearum* Schroet.
>   *M. symphyti* Bub.

Of these, many are known here only on their alternate hosts, many being scarce or rare, and it is doubtful if *Pucciniastrum geoppertianum* in fact occurs here at all (Wilson and Henderson, 1966). The only species known to be present in Britain on *Abies* spp. are those numbered 1–4 in the above list, that is, *Milesina blechni*, *M. kriegeriana*, *Pucciniastrum epilobii* and *Melampsorella caryophyllacearum*. All produce their spermogonia and aecidia on species of *Abies*, and their other stages on various alternate hosts. The first three are needle rusts, while the fourth causes the production of witches' brooms and cankers on branches and trunks.

Milesina blechni Syd.

Though *M. blechni*, which is known throughout Europe, produces its spermogonia and aecidia on *Abies* spp., on these it is rare and of little pathological importance.

Its uredosori and teleutosori are produced on the common fern *Blechnum spicant*, on which it appears to be frequent, though commonly overlooked.

The flask-shaped spermogonia are embedded in the surface of the current needles, usually on the underside. The white, cylindrical aecidia, which are also on the current needles, in two rows, one on each side of the midrib, are about 0.3-0.4 mm across, and rupture at the top to shed the white, ellipsoid, ovoid or globose aecidiospores. These measure 27-36 x 21-27 μm, and are covered in coarse warts over most of their surface, but on one side the warts are minute (Wilson and Henderson, 1966).

Milesina kriegeriana (Magn.) Magn.

The spermogonia and aecidia of *M. kriegeriana*, which also occurs throughout Europe, have been found abundantly on *Abies* spp. in Britain on a few occasions, notably on *A. alba* in Scotland in 1932 and on *A. grandis* in Northern Ireland in 1952. They have also been found in Britain on *A. cephalonica* and *A. nordmanniana* (Wilson and Henderson, 1966). The rust is of little pathological importance. The uredosori and teleutosori occur on ferns of the genus *Dryopteris*.

The spermogonia are found beneath the cuticle, mainly on the upper sides of the current needles. The aecidia, also on the current needles, appear mainly on the undersides, on yellowish areas in two irregular rows. They are whitish and cylindrical, measuring 0.3-0.8 mm across and 0.5-1.3 mm high. They rupture at the apex to release the white aecidiospores. These measure 22-48 x 20-36 μm, and are covered with fine warts.

Pucciniastrum epilobii Otth. (*P. pustulatum* (Pers.) Diet.)

Pucciniastrum epilobii is known in Europe, Asia, North America and New Zealand (Kupevich and Transhel', 1957). Its spermogonia and aecidia occur on the undersides of the needles of *Abies* spp. in June and July. The uredosori and teleutosori are frequent on species of *Chamaenerion* and *Epilobium* (the willow herbs).

The spermogonia are under the cuticle. The aecidia are whitish, cylindrical, about 1 mm high and 0.25 mm wide, opening at the top or sides and soon disappearing. The aecidiospores are more or less rounded, ovoid or ellipsoid, covered in small spines but with a smooth spot on one side, and measure 14-21 x 10-14 μm (Wilson and Henderson, 1966).

P. epilobii is of little pathological importance, though in Germany it has been reported as an occasional cause of needle cast and sometimes of dieback of trees up to 2 metres in height. Schönhar (1965) found that it was most severe following warm, moist, spring weather. It does not spread to *Abies* more than about 50 metres from its alternate hosts.

Melampsorella caryophyllacearum Schroet. (*M. cerastii* (Pers.) Schroet.)

Melampsorella caryophyllacearum occurs almost wherever *Abies* is found across Eurasia and in North America, and elsewhere also on the alternate hosts, in eastern Canada, Alaska, Siberia, China and Japan. It is also said to have been introduced into South America (Ziller, 1974). In Britain it has been recorded mainly in Scotland and Ireland, especially in the west (Wilson and Henderson, 1966).

The spermogonia and aecidia occur on *Abies* spp. and the uredosori and tele-utosori on chickweeds and related species of *Cerastium* and *Stellaria*.

The minute, honey-coloured spermogonia are embedded under the cuticle, mainly on the upper sides of the needles, while the hemispherical or shortly cylindrical aecidia occur on the undersides in two rows, one on either side of the midrib. The aecidiospores form a reddish-yellow mass and are subgloboid, ellipsoid or polygonoid, measuring 16-30 x 14-20 μm. Their walls are densely covered with minute points (Wilson and Henderson, 1966).

Once established, the fungus becomes systemic in both *Abies* and in the alternate hosts, and on the former gives rise to witches' brooms.

Basiodiospores from *Cerastium* and *Stellaria* infect *Abies* in May and June. The rust mycelium grows in the *Abies* shoots and by the autumn these show elongated swellings. Early in the following summer, buds on these swollen areas give rise to erect shoots bearing spirals of pale soft needles. These needles carry the spermogonia and aecidia (the spores from which infect *Cerastium* and *Stellaria*), and then by the end of the summer become yellow and fall.

The perennial mycelium continues to grow and enlarge the swollen tumour, the buds on which produce further pale green erect shoots to enlarge the broom. So each year the broom and the tumour tend to increase in size, and the needles on the broom produce further crops of spermogonia and aecidia. As the tumour grows it tends to crack and become canker-like, and may be invaded by decay fungi. The brooms are susceptible to frost damage, and may be killed and fall, but while live buds remain on the tumours, fresh brooms arise, and some may persist for 15-20 years or more (Viennot-Bourgin, 1949; Peterson, 1964; Wilson and Henderson, 1966).

Peterson (1965) in western parts of the USA found that though some infection could take place in almost any year, there were certain peak years when many infections occurred.

Host range　　M. caryophyllacearum will attack many species of *Abies*. In Britain it has been found on *A. alba*, *A. cephalonica*, *A. concolor* var. *lowiana* and *A. pinsapo* (Wilson and Henderson, 1966). Elsewhere, in Europe, the USSR and North America, it has been found also on *A. concolor*, *A. magnifica*, *A. lasiocarpa*, *A. religiosa*, *A. grandis*, *A. sibirica* (*A. pichta*), *A. sachalinensis*, *A. balsamea* and *A. procera* (*A. nobilis*). (Mielke, 1957; Viennot-Bourgin, 1949; Peterson, 1964; Kupevich and Transhel', 1957).

Factors affecting the disease　　According to Viennot-Bourgin (1949) the rust is encouraged by moist atmospheric and soil conditions, and as conditions tend to become less humid with distance from the soil surface, it occurs mainly at the base of the tree and decreases with height. Suitable moisture (and temperature) conditions, however, are not the only factors involved. Peterson (1964) found that abundant infection took place only when the basidiospores were released in numbers at the time when the young fir shoots had developed to a suitable stage. Hence in some parts of the USA many basidiospores might be present in the atmosphere but no infection took place because the fir shoots had not reached a receptive stage.

Damage caused   In Britain, *M. caryophyllacearum* is of only minor significance. Elsewhere its importance varies, but in some areas it may cause serious damage by reducing growth and volume, and sometimes, when many brooms form in the crown, by killing trees. The wood becomes brittle around burls and cankers, and trees may break at these points as a result of wind, or the weight of snow and ice. Cankered areas may also be invaded by secondary rot fungi.

According to Peterson (1964), broom rust commonly infects between 2 and 15 per cent of the trunks of silver firs in Central Europe. In some parts of Europe cankered sections must be cut from the logs when marketing, and a loss of 5 per cent of the wood may result. Nevertheless, overall losses in the forests there are usually fairly small (Viennot-Bourgin, 1949).

In North America, the rust is of little or no importance in the eastern states, but in the west, in the Rocky Mountains and the Great Basin in the USA, almost every tree in *Abies* stands may be infected and many bear dozens of brooms. Disfigurement and loss of growth is of particular concern to growers of *A. concolor* for Christmas trees (Peterson, 1964).

Control   At one time in Europe intensive efforts were made to cut out brooms from affected trees. This is no longer economically possible on a forest scale, and it is doubtful whether it is necessary (Heck, 1927) except in small stands grown for Christmas trees (Peterson, 1964). Neither does the economic situation allow the control of alternate hosts. Growth of these is in any case restricted as the trees close canopy, but infection can still take place from plants on adjacent open land. The only practicable control measure in forest stands is the removal of diseased trees when thinning takes place. Special attention should then be paid to cankered trees and those with brooms on or near the trunk (Peterson, 1964).

DISEASES OF THE TRUNK

The rust *Melampsorella caryophyllacearum*
As noted above, *Melampsorella caryophyllacearum* not only produces its spermogonia and aecidia on the needles, but also gives rise to witches' brooms and cankers on branches and trunks.

Drought crack
Trunks of *Abies* may develop large cracks which result from drought in hot, dry summers. A survey has indicated, however, that overall losses from this cause are small. Drought crack is further discussed in chapter 2.

DECAY FUNGI

Abies is one of the few conifers showing resistance to attack by *Heterobasidion annosum (Fomes annosus)*, though the degree of resistance appears to vary with the species. *H. annosum* is considered in chapter 3.

CYPRESS AND 'FALSE' CYPRESS: *CUPRESSUS* SPP. AND *CHAMAECYPARIS* SPP.

Of the many species of *Cupressus* and *Chamaecyparis*, only Lawson cypress, *Chamaecyparis lawsoniana*, has been grown in Britain as a forest tree, and then only as a minor species. Many cultivars of *C. lawsoniana* with a great range of form and colour are grown in parks and gardens, where *C. nootkatensis* and cultivars of *C. pisifera* are also common. The hybrid Leyland cypress. x *Cupressocyparis leylandii*, is also much planted in parks, gardens and shelter belts. Of the true cypresses, *Cupressus macrocarpa* is common in lowland parks and gardens, especially in coastal areas in the west.

Species of *Cupressus* and *Chamaecyparis* (especially *Cupressus macrocarpa*) tend to be susceptible to frost and damage by winter cold, though x *Cupressocyparis leylandii* is resistant to both cold and exposure. *Cupressus macrocarpa* is resistant to sea winds, and this is almost the only reason it is so much grown in coastal districts. Some clones of Leyland cypress, especially 'Stapehill 20', are liable to defoliation in times of drought.

NURSERY DISEASES

GREY MOULD (*Botrytis cinerea*) AND PHYTOPHTHORA ROOT ROTS

The cypresses are among the conifers most often damaged in nursery beds by the common grey mould, *Botrytis cinerea*. *Phytophthora* spp. (especially *P. cinnamomi*) are also very damaging to nursery beds of cypress trees, particularly to the various forms of Lawson cypress. Phytophthora root rots may cause such heavy losses in beds of Lawson cypress that the grower is forced to change to container growing. These *Phytophthora* spp. may also attack and kill trees after planting out. Both *Botrytis cinerea* and the Phytophthora root rots are further considered in chapter 3.

CANKER AND DIEBACK CAUSED BY *Kabatina* SPP.

In 1971 young nursery plants of Leyland cypress in southern England were found with short girdling cankers on the shoots. A species of *Kabatina* was isolated from the cankers and from similar lesions on older juniper plants from Gloucestershire (Young and Strouts, 1971). The same fungus was isolated the same year from cankers associated with a dieback of Leyland cypress and *Chamaecyparis noot-*

katensis in Scotland. In one research plot of Leyland cypress, nearly all the trees, which were up to one metre tall, were affected, and some were killed. The cankers were often at branchlet bases, and dieback occurred most often on the wind-ward side of the trees, which suggested that the fungus may be a wound parasite. Inoculation tests showed it to be pathogenic (Redfern, 1971). The fungus has also sometimes been found in southern Britain on other species of cypress, in-cluding *C. macrocarpa* 'lutea'. Only one-year-old shoots have been affected. No subsequent spread has taken place, and although the attack has made the plants unsightly, recovery has generally been good (Young and Strouts, 1971).

In 1975, *Kabatina thujae* (Sutton and Gibson, 1976) was found causing die-back of Lawson cypress in an Aberdeen nursery. The fungus, which was first described on *Thuja occidentalis* in Germany, forms black acervuli appearing as scattered spots at the bases of the dead shoots. The spots measure about 50–170 μm across, and bear colourless, one-celled, egg-shaped conidia measuring 4.8–8.0 × 2.3–3.5 μm (Schneider and von Arx, 1966).

POST-NURSERY DISEASES

DISEASES OF TRUNKS AND BRANCHES

Resin bleeding and canker caused by *Seiridium cardinale* (Wagener) Sutton & Gibson (*Coryneum cardinale* Wagener)
Seiridium cardinale (*Coryneum cardinale*), first described by Wagener (1928, 1939) as the cause of a highly destructive resin bleeding and canker of *Cupressus macro-carpa* in California, USA, is now known also on many other *Cupressus* spp. and on various other members of the Cupressaceae. It is still important in California, and is now present also in Argentina, Australia, England, France, Georgia (USSR), Greece, Italy, Northern Ireland and Spain (Strouts, 1973). In Britain it has been found only on *Cupressus macrocarpa* (on which in some places it has caused severe damage), and only in the southern half of the country (where most of the trees of *C. macrocarpa* occur).

The causal fungus   *Seiridium cardinale* produces irregularly rounded to lens-shaped, erumpent, black acervuli about 0.3–1.5 mm across on the dead host bark. The acervuli contain rather spindle-shaped conidia each divided by five transverse septa into six cells. These conidia usually measure from 21–26 × 8–10 μm. The four inner cells are olive brown, and the two end cells are colourless, with rounded ends (Wagener, 1939). A recent description of the fungus is that by Sutton and Gibson (1972).

The fungus grows at temperatures from just below 5°C to about 34°C, with an optimum at 26°. In dry, protected conditions, the spores remain alive for many months, and even on exposed leaves they have been found to show 29 per cent germinability after 48 days (Wagener, 1948).

In culture, the reverse of colonies grown on 2 per cent Bacto malt extract + 2 per cent Bacto agar is Salmon or Saffron (or occasionally Buff) coloured, with a Pale Olivaceous zone near the margin (Strouts, 1973).

In California, a perfect stage of the fungus, a species of *Leptosphaeria*, has been found (Hansen, 1956), but so far this does not appear to have been described, and it has not been recorded elsewhere.

Symptoms   S. cardinale causes strongly resinous, girdling cankers on branches and sometimes on the trunks, when they may be up to 20–30 cm long (Barthelet and Vinot, 1944; Strouts, 1970). The acervuli of the fungus appear on the dead bark of the cankers.

The most conspicuous symptom is a browning and death of the foliage in the parts of the crown beyond the girdled areas (Wagener, 1939) (plate 38). Grasso (1969) in Italy found the fungus on cypress cones.

Within the host, the fungus grows vigorously in the outer tissues as far as the cambium and less abundantly also in the wood (Moriondo, 1972).

Spread of the disease   Seiridium cardinale is probably spread mainly by wind and rain, and perhaps by birds and insects. It may also possibly be spread on nursery stock and on pruning tools (Wagener, 1939). Frankie and Parmeter (1972) found some evidence that in the USA the moth *Laspeyresia cupressana* may play some part in the spread of the fungus, while Grasso (1969) in Italy considered that seedborne spread might take place because he had found *S. cardinale* on cones.

Host range and susceptibility   On trees in the field, *S. cardinale* is found most widely and causes the greatest damage on *Cupressus macrocarpa* and some of its cultivars. It is also damaging in Italy and California on *C. sempervirens*. In Italy too, Grasso (1952) found that *C. arizonica* was very susceptible.

Field observations and inoculation experiments have indicated that a great many species of *Cupressus* are to some degree susceptible, as are some species of *Thuja* (including *T. plicata* and *T. orientalis*), species of *Juniperus*, and of *Libocedrus*, though they are not often much affected in the field (Edson, 1938; Smith, 1938; Wagener, 1948; Strouts, 1973; and others). In his inoculation trials in Britain, Strouts (1973) produced severe and perennating cankers on x *Cupressocyparis leylandii* and *Chamaecyparis nootkatensis* (though Coryneum canker has not been found here on either of these in the field). He failed to induce canker formation on *Cupressus lawsoniana*, and most of the evidence available (which he reviews) indicates that this species is immune to the disease.

Damage caused   A tree affected by *S. cardinale* often shows so many brown, dead branches that it quickly becomes too unsightly to have any ornamental value. Though spread throughout the tree is rather slow, the fungus eventually kills even large specimens of susceptible species such as *Cupressus macrocarpa*.

Control of the disease   Several workers have attempted to control the disease with various fungicides. Thus Wagener (1948) found that Bordeaux mixture had some controlling effect. In Italy, thiophanate, benomyl, captan, dichlofluanid, dodine and some other materials prevented infection (though they would not eradicate it) if applied several times to small trees (Govi *et al.*, 1975; Govi and Tunioli, 1977; Parrini and Panconesi, 1977). In general, however, the affected trees can only be removed and replaced by other, more resistant ones. Of these, the most obvious replacements for *C. macrocarpa* in Britain are *Chamaecyparis lawsoniana* and *Thuja plicata*; x *Cupressocyparis leylandii* is also a possible choice, as it has not been found affected in the field, although it has proved to be susceptible on inoculation, as noted above. Outside the Cupressaceae, any silviculturally suitable species may be chosen.

ROOT DISEASES

Phytophthora root rot

As noted above, Phytophthora root rot may affect cypresses beyond the nursery stage. Indeed, attack by *Phytophthora* spp. is one of the commonest causes of the death of Lawson cypress trees of all ages, and sometimes also of that of other cypresses.

WESTERN RED CEDAR (*THUJA PLICATA*)

The introduced western red cedar (*Thuja plicata*) is one of the minor species in British forests. It is commonly grown as a specimen tree in parks and gardens, and as a hedge plant. Other *Thuja* spp. especially cultivars of the white cedar, *T. occidentalis*, are also grown as garden trees.

NURSERY DISEASES

WINTER BRONZING AND WINTER COLD DAMAGE

In winter, western red cedar, particularly in nursery beds, may turn a striking bronze colour, but in the spring, with warmer weather, the plants turn green again (plate 39). In very severe winters, however, the foliage may be killed, and it then turns a deep glossy black (Day and Peace, 1934).

NEEDLE BLIGHT CAUSED BY *Didymascella thujina* (DUR.) MAIRE (*Keithia thujina* DUR.)

Needle blight caused by *Didymascella thujina* (*Keithia thujina*) affects *Thuja* trees of all ages, but causes serious damage only on nursery plants, on which its effects are so severe that in Great Britain it has for long been a limiting factor in the production of *Thuja* nursery stock. The disease occurs in Great Britain, Northern Ireland and the Irish Republic, and in France, Belgium, Holland, Norway, Denmark, Italy, Canada and the USA (Anon, 1966), and in Germany (Burmeister, 1966).

Needle blight as it affects *Thuja plicata* in Great Britain has been described by Alcock (1928) and Pawsey (1960). The fungus occurs almost entirely on the foliage, producing its small ascocarps embedded in the leaf tissue below the epidermis, which eventually splits, and round the edges of the apothecium curls back to form a scale-like flap (plate 40). The apothecia are red-brown (dull brown when dry), cushion-like, oval or irregular in shape, 0.5 to 1.25 mm across, and one, or sometimes two or three form in each diseased scale leaf. The hymenium contains asci and unbranched paraphyses (Pawsey, 1960; Soegaard, 1969). The asci each contain two oval, pitted ascospores that become dark brown when mature, though they may be almost colourless when shed. The ascospores measure 15–24 x 15–16 μm, and when shed are surrounded by a sticky layer of mucilage 2 or 3 μm thick. They are two-celled, but one cell is minute and represented by little more than a mark at one end of the spore. No imperfect stage has been discovered, and the fungus has not been grown successfully in culture. When ascospore discharge has been completed, the ascocarps dry up, and appear as oval or rounded depressions and later as holes in the leaves.

It has been suggested that the fungus may be carried with seed in small pieces of leaf debris (Alcock, 1928), though this should be easily prevented by proper cleaning of the seed. The disease normally enters the crop by means of airborne ascospores from previously infested trees or nursery beds. These spores may be found in the air in Great Britain from May to October, with peaks usually in June and July and in September (Phillips, 1967*b*; Burdekin, 1968). In Denmark Soegaard (1969) found similar peaks, in June and July, August and September, and sometimes also in mid-October.

Needle blight is not often seen in first-year seedlings, but when found on these it usually occurs on the juvenile leaves low on the stem (Anon, 1967). Older nursery plants, both in seedbeds and transplant lines, may be severely affected, and at first show browning of scattered leaflets. The fungus usually grows only in the mesophyll and the epidermis, and it cannot as a rule spread from one leaflet to another (Pawsey, 1960), but through multiple infections large areas of the fronds, particularly at the bases of the plants, may become brown and die. In recent years in a few cases severe damage has also been observed in which death of tissues through girdling of stems and shoots was closely associated with prior infection of a leaflet on the girdled zone, on which fruit bodies were present. Whether the fungus directly caused the girdling was not determined, but it was evident that in some circumstances severe damage could result when the number of leaflets infected was relatively small (Burdekin, 1970).

In the brown leaflets one to three of the oval, elongated or irregular apothecia may develop. Much of the early infection seems to take place near the clefts between the leaflets, and is usually first seen in April, with an abundant development of the fructifications in May and June (Pawsey, 1960) and again in the autumn.

Pawsey also found evidence that incipient apothecia were formed in autumn, and these completed their development in the following spring. Hence they could be a means by which the fungus survived the winter and continued its spread within the crop. He considered, however, that overwintering was mainly by means of spores shed in autumn and remaining attached by their mucilage to the surface of the *Thuja* leaves.

In a severe attack, much of the lower foliage may be destroyed, dry up and fall, and the plants remain small and stunted, and many may die.

D. thujina is important only on *Thuja plicata*, though it was first recorded on *T. occidentalis* (Durand, 1913), and it has recently been reported in Germany on *Chamaecyparis lawsoniana* (Burmeister, 1966). *Thuja standishii*, and its F_1 hybrids with *T. plicata* are resistant to the disease (Soegaard, 1969). In *T. plicata*, the plants become more resistant with age, and cuttings struck from adult trees are little affected (Soegaard, 1969).

Little is known about the factors that control the incidence of needle blight. Pawsey (1960) found that at 20°C infection became visible about three weeks after inoculation, but at 13 and 5°C no effects could be seen at the end of 12 weeks. Porter (1957), in Canada, noted that heavy spore discharge took place when relative humidity exceeded 90 per cent, and the temperature was about 12°C. Phillips and Burdekin (unpublished) also found that spores were discharged in damp periods following rain.

Much can be done to prevent *D. thujina* from entering and building up in a crop, if *Thuja plicata* is grown only in nurseries isolated by 2 to 3 kilometres from other *Thuja* plants. Isolation alone is rarely effective for long, however, unless a rotation sowing system is also practised (Pawsey, 1963). Such a system can be used only if a number of scattered isolated sites is available that can be linked into groups each designed to produce plants for a large area. Only one nursery in the group supplies plants for the whole district in any one year, and is then completely cleared of all *Thuja* stock before resowing. In the succeeding year a second nursery supplies the plants, is cleared of *Thuja* and resown. Clearance of the *Thuja* must be carefully carried out, otherwise any infected stock remaining will provide a source of infection for the next sowing. Sufficient nurseries are maintained in the group to provide a supply of stock every year. No *Thuja* transplants must be brought into the rotation nurseries, but other tree species can be freely moved in and out.

Even in isolated nurseries run on a rotation, *D. thujina* may sometimes enter and begin to build up to epidemic proportions. It is therefore very important to keep careful watch on *Thuja* beds. If the disease is found, spraying with cycloheximide, the only fungicide known to be effective against it, should be carried out. This gives excellent control (Pawsey, 1965). In most parts of Great Britain, one application, in late March, or two, the second in late April, are almost always adequate, but in the wetter west, a third spray in June may occasionally also be necessary (Phillips 1967*a*; Burdekin and Phillips, 1970). The spray (marketed as Actidione) is made up to give a dilution of about 90 ppm of the active ingredient, and applied at 1100 litres/ha (100 gallons/acre).

POST-NURSERY DISEASES

STEM DISEASES

Cambial damage by spring frosts
Young plantation trees before the thicket stage are liable to cambial injury by spring frosts.

Cankers caused by *Seiridium cardinale*
Strouts (1973) succeeded in inducing large stem cankers in young plants of *Thuja plicata* by inoculation with *Seiridium cardinale*. The cankers healed, however, and did not persist into the second year.

ROOT AND BUTT ROTS

Western red cedar is susceptible to butt rot by *Heterobasidion annosum* (*Fomes annosus*), and *Armillaria mellea* may kill young trees and cause butt rot in older ones (chapter 3).

WESTERN HEMLOCK: *TSUGA HETEROPHYLLA*

Western hemlock (*Tsuga heterophylla*) is another of the minor forest species in Britain, and because of its ability to withstand shade is sometimes used to underplant other conifers. Other species of *Tsuga*, especially *T. canadensis*, may be found in parks and gardens.

NURSERY AND POST-NURSERY DISEASES

NEEDLE DISEASES

Needle blight caused by *Didymascella tsugae* (Farlow) Maire (*Keithia tsugae* (Farlow) Durand)
Needle blight caused by *Didymascella tsugae* (*Keithia tsugae*) has occasionally been found on *Tsuga canadensis* (eastern hemlock) in Scotland (Wilson, 1937; Foister, 1948), but so far has been of no importance. Its rounded or elliptical apothecia develop below the epidermis on the undersides of the leaves, and measure 0.3–0.5 mm across. The epidermis eventually splits to form a scale. The

hymenium consists of paraphyses with brown, club-shaped tips, and asci that each contain four oval, greenish-brown (at first colourless) ascospores with two unequal cells. The spores measure 13–16 x 6–8 μm (Stevens, 1925).

ROOT AND BUTT ROTS

T. heterophylla is very susceptible to butt rot by *Heterobasidion annosum* (*Fomes annosus*) and *Armillaria mellea*, which may also kill young trees.

REFERENCES

Alcock, N. L. (1928). Keithia thujina, Durand: a disease of nursery seedlings of Thuja plicata. *Scott. For. J.*, **42**, 77–9

Anon (1966). *Didymascella thujina* (Durand) Maire. *Distrib. Maps Pl. Dis.*, no 149, 2nd ed

Anon, (1967). *Keithia Disease of Western Red Cedar*, Leafl. For. Commn, no. 43, 7 pp.

Barthelet, J. and Vinot, M. (1944). Notes sur les maladies des cultures méridionales. *Ann. Epiphyt., N.S.*, **10**, 11–23

Batko, S. (1974). Notes on new and rare fungi on forest trees in Britain. *Bull. Br. mycol. Soc.*, **8**, 19–21

Boyce, J. S. (1927). Observations on forest pathology in Great Britain and Denmark. *Phytopathology*, **17**, 1–18

Burdekin, D. A. (1968). Forest pathology. *Rep. Forest Res., Lond., 1968*, pp. 108–15

Burdekin, D. A. (1970). Forest pathology. *Rep. Forest Res., Lond.*, 1969, pp. 114–19

Burdekin, D. A. and Phillips, D. H. (1970). Chemical control of *Didymascella thujina* on western red cedar in forest nurseries. *Ann. appl. Biol.*, **67**, 131–6

Burmeister, P. (1966). Beobachten über einige wichtige Pilzkrankheiten an Zierkoniferen im oldenburgischen Baumschulgebiet. *Gartenbauwissenschaft*, **31**, 469–506

Day, W. R. and Peace, T. R. (1934). *The Experimental Production and the Diagnosis of Frost Injury on Forest Trees*, Oxf. For. Mem. no. 16

Dennis, R. W. G. (1968). *British Ascomycetes*, J. Cramer, Lehre.

Durand, E. J. (1913). The genus *Keithia*. *Mycologia*, **5**, 6–11

Edson, H. A. (1938). United States of America: bark canker of Monterey cypress. *Int. Bull. Pl. Prot.*, **12**, 98

Foister, C. E. (1948). Report of the annual conference of the cryptogamic section, 1946. *Trans. bot. Soc. Edinb.*, **34**, 392–6

Frankie, G. W. and Parmeter, Jr., J. R. (1972). A preliminary study of the relationship between *Coryneum cardinale* (Fungi Imperfecti) and *Laspeyresia cupressana* (Lepidoptera: Tortricidae). *Pl. Dis. Reptr.*, **56**, 992–5

Govi, G., Taglioni, F. and Tunioli, F. (1975). Ricerche biologiche e prove di lotto sul 'Coryneum cardinale' Wag. *Inftore fitopatol.*, **25**, 11–17

Govi, G. and Tunioli, F. (1977). Interventi chimici contro il Coryneum cardinale. *Inftore fitopatol.*, **27**, 11–13

Grasso, V. (1952). Conifere suscettibili ed immuni al *Coryneum cardinale* Wag. *Italia for. mont.*, **7**, 148–9

Grasso, V. (1969). Attachi di *Coryneum cardinale* Wag. su galbule di cupressi. *Italia for. mont.*, **24**, 181–3

Hansen, H. N. (1956). The perfect stage of *Coryneum cardinale*. *Phytopathology*, **46**, 636–7 (abstract).

Hartig, R. (1894). *Textbook of the Diseases of Trees* (English translation), Macmillan, London

Heck (1927). Muss man die Hexenbesen der Weisstanne verfolgen? *Forstwiss. ZentBl.*, **49**, 132–140

Kupevich, V. F. and Transhel', V. G. (1957). *Cryptogamic plants of the USSR* IV. *Fungi*. (1). *Rust fungi*. Transl. Israel Programme for Scientific Translations

Mielke, J. L. (1957). The yellow witches' broom of subalpine fir in the Intermountain region. *Res. Note Intmtn For. Exp. Sta.*, no 47, 5 pp.

Moriondo, F. (1972). Il cancro del cipresso da *Coryneum* cardinale Wag. 1° contributo: La progressione del processo infettivo nei tessuti cauliari. *Annali Accad. ital. Sci. for.*, 21, 399-426

Nedkvitne, K. (1966). Dyrkning av Edelgran *Abies alba* Müll., i Vest-Norge. *Meddr. Vestland. forstl ForstStn* (40), 12, 8 pp. unnumbered, plus pp. 135-219

Parrini, C. and Panconesi, A. (1977). Lotta contro il corineo del cipresso in Toscana. 1. *Inftore fitopatol.*, 27, 5-9

Pawsey, R. G. (1960). An investigation into *Keithia* disease of *Thuja plicata*. *Forestry*, 33, 174-186

Pawsey, R. G. (1963). Rotation sowing of *Thuja* in selected nurseries to avoid infection by *Keithia thujina*. *Q. Jl For.*, 56, 206-9

Pawsey, R. G. (1965). Cycloheximide fungicide trials against *Didymascella thujina* on western red cedar, *Thuja plicata*. *Rep. Forest Res., Lond., 1964*, pp. 141-150

Peterson, R. S. (1964). Fir Broom Rust, U.S. Dep. Agric. For. Pest Leafl., no. 87, 7 pp.

Peterson, R. S. (1965). Notes on western rust fungi. IV. *Mycologia*, 57, 465-71

Phillips, D. H. (1967a). Forest pathology. *Rep. Forest Res., London, 1966*, pp. 70-74

Phillips, D. H. (1967b). Forest pathology. *Rep. forest Res., Lond., 1967*, pp. 96-102

Porter, W. A. (1957). Biological studies on western red cedar needle blight caused by *Keithia thujina* Durand. *Can. Dep. Agric., Forest Biol. Div., Interim Rep.*, 25 pp.

Redfern, D. B. (1971). In Forest pathology. *Rep. Forest Res., Lond., 1971*, p. 83

Schneider, R. and Arx, J. A. von (1966). Zwei neue, als Erreger von Zweisterben nachgewesene Pilze: *Kabatina thujae* n.g., n.sp. *Phytopath. Z.*, 57, 176-182

Schönhar, S. (1965). Schäden an Jungtannen durch Rostpilzbefall. *Allg. Forstz.*, 20, 120

Smith, C. O. (1938). Inoculation on conifers with the cypress Coryneum. *Phytopathology*, 28, 760-2

Soegaard, B. (1969). Resistance studies in *Thuja*. *Det. Forstl. Forsøgsv Danm.*, no. 245, 31, 287-396

Stevens, F. L. (1925). *Plant Disease Fungi*, Macmillan, New York

Strouts, R. G. (1970). Coryneum canker of Cupressus. *Pl. Path.*, 19, 149-150

Strouts, R. G. (1973). Canker of cypresses caused by *Coryneum cardinale* Wag. in Britain. *Eur. J. For. Path.*, 3, 13-24

Sutton, B. C. and Gibson, I. A. S. (1972). *Seiridium cardinale*. Decriptions of Plant Pathogenic Fungi and Bacteria, CMI, Kew, no. 326

Sutton, B. C. and Gibson, I. A. S. (1976). *Kabatina thujae*. Descriptions of Plant Pathogenic Fungi and Bacteria, CMI, Kew, no. 489

Viennot-Bourgin, G. (1949). *Les Champignons Parasites des Plantes Cultivées*, Masson, Paris

Wagener, W. W. (1928). Coryneum canker of cypress. *Science, N.S.*, 47, 1745, p. 584

Wagener, W. W. (1939). The canker of *Cupressus* induced by *Coryneum cardinale* n. sp. *J. agric. Res.*, 58, 1-46

Wagener, W. W. (1948). Diseases of cypress. *El Aliso*, 1, 255-321

Waterman, A. M. (1945). Tip blight of species of *Abies* caused by a new species of *Rehmiellopsis*. *J. agric. Res.*, 70, 315-37

Watson, H. (1933). Diseases attacking common silver fir (*Abies pectinata*). *Scott. For.*, 47, 71-2

Wilson, M. (1937). The occurrence of *Keithia tsugae* in Scotland. *Scott. For.*, 51, 46-7

Wilson M. and Henderson, D. M. (1966). *British Rust Fungi*, Cambridge University Press, Cambridge

Wilson, M. and Macdonald, J. (1924). A new disease of the silver firs in Scotland. *Trans. R. Scott. arboric. Soc.*, 38, 114-18

Young, C. W. T. and Strouts, R. G. (1971). In Forest pathology. *Rep. Forest Res., Lond., 1971*, p. 82

Ziller, W. G. (1974). *The Tree Rusts of Western Canada*, Can. For. Serv. Publ., no. 1329

9 Diseases of other minor conifers

MONKEY PUZZLE: *Araucaria araucana*
CEDAR: *Cedrus* SPP.
'SUGI' OR JAPANESE CEDAR: *Cryptomeria japonica*
JUNIPER: *Juniperus* SPP.
  NURSERY DISEASES
    GREY MOULD *Botrytis cinerea*
  POST-NURSERY DISEASES
    NEEDLE DISEASES
      Needle cast caused by *Lophodermium juniperinum*
      Needle blight caused by *Didymascella tetraspora*
    DIEBACKS AND TWIG BLIGHTS
      Shoot dieback caused by *Kabatina juniperi*
      Shoot dieback caused by *Seiridium cardinale* (*Coryneum cardinale*)
      Twig blight caused by *Phomopsis* sp.
      Leaf and shoot death caused by *Coniothyrium fuckelii*
    STEM RUSTS
      The stem rusts *Gymnosporangium clavariiforme, G. confusum, G. fuscum* **and** *G. cornutum*
    ROOT AND BUTT ROTS
THE DAWN REDWOOD: *Metasequoia glyptostroboides*
REDWOOD: *Sequoia sempervirens* **AND WELLINGTONIA:** *Sequoiadendron giganteum*
  NURSERY DISEASES
    GREY MOULD: *Botrytis cinerea*
  POST-NURSERY DISEASES
    NEEDLE DISORDERS
      Winter browning
    DIEBACKS
      Phomopsis disease caused by *Phacidiopycnis pseudotsugae*
    BRANCH GALLS
      Branch galls caused by *Agrobacterium tumefasciens*
    ROOT AND BUTT ROTS
    MISCELLANEOUS DISORDERS
YEW: *Taxus baccata*
  NURSERY AND POST-NURSERY DISEASES
    NEEDLE DISEASES

Needle casts caused by *Sphaerulina taxi*, *Physalospora gregaria* **var.**
foliorum **and** *Diplodia taxi*
BRANCH CANKER AND DIEBACK
Canker and branch girdling of unknown cause
ROOT DISEASES
HEART ROT
REFERENCES

MONKEY PUZZLE (*ARAUCARIA ARAUCANA*)

The only species of *Araucaria* hardy in this country is *A. araucana*, the monkey puzzle. This tree, introduced from South America is common in parks and gardens.

The monkey puzzle is singularly little affected by disease, though it is susceptible to damage by *Armillaria mellea*, which sometimes kills quite large trees (see chapter 3).

The Chilean needle rust *Micronegeria fagi* Diet. & Neger (the alternative host of which is *Nothofagus*) has been found once on *Araucaria* in Britain (Butin, private communication).

CEDAR (*CEDRUS* SPP.)

Three cedars are common in parks and gardens here. They are the cedar of Lebanon (*Cedrus libani*), from Asia Minor and the Lebanon, the atlas cedar (*C. atlantica*), from North Africa, and the Deodar (*C. deodara*), from the Himalayas.

Cedars in this country are sometimes affected by needle fall, the cause of which is unknown.

The common rot fungi *Armillaria mellea* and *Heterobasidion annosum* (*Fomes annosus*) have both been recorded here on cedars, and so has the 'Phomopsis disease' caused by *Phacidiopycnis pseudotsugae* (Peace, 1962). These diseases are described in chapter 3.

'SUGI' OR JAPANESE CEDAR (*CRYPTOMERIA JAPONICA*)

The '*Sugi*' or Japanese cedar, *Cryptomeria japonica*, a native of Japan and China, is grown here as an ornamental in parks and gardens.

Nursery plants are sometimes damaged by autumn frosts (MacDonald *et al.*, 1957), and by the grey mould, *Botrytis cinerea*, which is described in chapter 3.

JUNIPER (*JUNIPERUS* SPP.)

The common juniper, *Juniperus communis*, a bush or sometimes a small tree, is one of our few native conifers. In addition, many introduced species of *Juniperus* are grown here in parks and gardens, but most are low-growing shrubs.

NURSERY DISEASES

GREY MOULD (*Botrytis cinerea*)

Nursery plants of juniper may sometimes be attacked by the grey mould, *Botrytis cinerea*.

POST-NURSERY DISEASES

NEEDLE DISEASES

Needle cast caused by *Lophodermium juniperinum* (Fr.) de Not.
Lophodermium juniperinum has been known on both living and dead needles of *Juniperus communis* for about 150 years, and has also been recorded on *J. nana* (Moore, 1959; Dennis, 1968). It is a fairly common fungus, but of little importance as a cause of disease. Its prominent, black, elliptical, blister-like hysterothecia develop under the cuticle, usually on the upper sides of the leaves, and may be up to 1 mm long by 0.4 mm wide. They open by a slit to show a whitish hymenium of paraphyses that curl at the tips, and long asci each containing eight threadlike ascospores measuring 60–100 x 2 μm (Dennis, 1968).

Needle blight caused by *Didymascella tetraspora* (Phillips & Keith) Maire
In 1880, needle blight caused by *Didymascella tetraspora* was recorded in Scotland on the upper leaves of *Juniperus communis*, but the fungus appears to be uncommon (Moore, 1959). Dark brown apothecia are embedded in the upper surfaces of the leaves, and measure about 1 mm across. The hymenium is made up of paraphyses with swollen, olive-coloured tips, and asci each containing four oval, olive brown, unequally two-celled spores that measure 21–24 x 13–16 μm (Dennis, 1968).

DIEBACKS AND TWIG BLIGHTS

Shoot dieback caused by *Kabatina thujae* Schneider & von Arx
A shoot dieback of juniper associated with *Kabatina thujae* has been found once in southern Britain. The fungus was first described from Germany by Schneider

and von Arx (1966). The colourless, one-celled, ellipsoid conidia measure 3.5 x 2 μm (Sutton, 1980).

Shoot dieback caused by *Seiridium cardinale* (*Coryneum cardinale*)

When Strouts (1973) inoculated small plants of *Juniperus communis* with *Seiridium cardinale*, the fungus girdled and killed small twigs. *S. cardinale* has not been found in Britain on junipers in the field. It is further discussed under *Cupressus*, on which it causes severe damage.

Twig blight caused by *Phomopsis* sp.

A disease causing the death of shoots and twigs, and less often of larger branches of *Juniperus communis* and of various ornamental species of juniper in widely separated localities in Great Britain is currently under investigation (Young and Strouts, 1971). The cause is a species of *Phomopsis* that attacks the bark, girdling small twigs and producing perennial cankers on larger branches before eventually killing them also. The fungus may also attack the needles.

On recently killed bark, immersed pycnidia ooze slimy, grey to creamy or golden tendrils of conidia. The a-spores are boat-shaped, colourless, 6-12 x 3-4.5 μm. The b-spores are colourless, filiform, usually strongly curved, walking-stick or almost U-shaped, or occasionally shaped like a boomerang.

The fungus appears to be *Phomopsis juniperova* Hahn (Hahn, 1926), though it differs from Hahn's description in minor particulars.

The disease can severely disfigure ornamental plants. Spraying with benomyl appears to give some control (Otta *et al.*, 1980).

Leaf and shoot death caused by *Coniothyrium fuckelii* Sacc.

Humphreys-Jones (1977) has described serious damage to cuttings of *Juniperus communis* var. *compressa* caused by *Coniothyrium fuckelii*. Sometimes only a few leaves were destroyed, but many of the affected plants were killed. Pycnidia of *C. fuckelii* (which is better known as the cause of cane blight of the raspberry) were present on the diseased cuttings. The brownish, elliptical spores measure about 4-5 x 3 μm.

STEM RUSTS

The stem rusts *Gymnosporangium clavariiforme, G. confusum, G. fuscum* and *G. cornutum*

Four rusts, all species of *Gymnosporangium*, that occur on juniper in Great Britain are described by Wilson and Henderson (1966), but only one, *G. clavariiforme*, is generally common, though *G. cornutum* is also frequent in central Scotland when juniper and *Sorbus aucuparia* (the alternate host of this rust) grow together.

In all these *Gymnosporangium* spp., the mycelium is perennial in gall-like swellings on the juniper stems, and on these galls their teleutosori are produced, usually in April and May. When dry, the sori are hard, brownish, cushion-shaped, cylindrical or tongue-like bodies formed of masses of two-celled teleutospores with long pedicels. In moist conditions, the pedicels and the mycelium of the fungus swell and gelatinise to form yellow or orange mucilaginous masses, on the surface of which the teleutospores germinate as soon as they mature, and produce basidiospores on four-celled basidia. All these rusts are heteroecious, and the basidiospores therefore infect the alternate hosts, on which spermogonia and aecidia arise from July to September or October. The aecidiospores reinfect juniper plants.

G. clavariiforme (Pers.) DC is frequent in Great Britain and Ireland, and causes large elongated swellings on the branches of *Juniperus communis*. On these it produces cylindrical or tongue-like teleutosori 5-10 mm long (figure 47). These

Figure 47. **Masses of teleutospores of** *Gymnosporangium clavariiforme* **on swollen stem of** *Juniperus communis* **(× 845) (W.B. Grove)**

are yellow-brown and horny when dry, but in damp weather gelatinise to a soft, orange-yellow mass. They contain long, narrow teleutospores (figure 48a), some of which are pale yellow, and measure 100-120 × 10-12 μm, and some of which are brown and smaller, measuring only 50-60 × 15-21 μm. According to Bernaux (1956), the pale spores appear first, in cold weather at the start of the

season. The spermogonial and aecidial stage of *G. clavariiforme* occurs on hawthorns (*Crataegus monogyna* and *C. oxyacanthoides*).

These two hawthorns (as well as *Cydonia oblonga*, *Mespilus germanica*, and
sometimes *Pyrus communis*) are also aecidial hosts of the much rarer *G. confusum*
Plowr. This has been found on a few occasions in England on cultivated *Juniperus
sabina* and its var. *prostrata*, and very locally in Sussex and Kent on *J, communis*
(Moore, 1959). The teleutospore masses of *G. confusum* when dry are chocolate-
brown and cushion-shaped, and swell when moist. Again two kinds of spore are
present, some dark brown with thick walls and orange contents, and some colour-

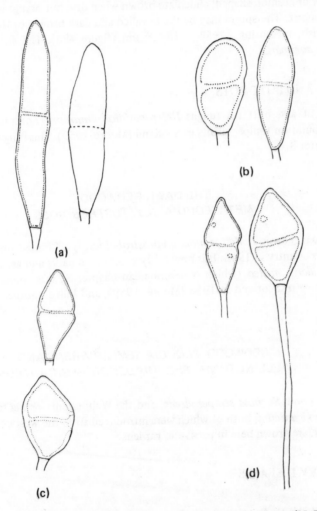

(a)

(b)

(c)

(d)

Figure 48. Teleutospores of *Gymnosporangium* spp. on *Juniperus* (M. Wilson
and D.M. Henderson) (a) *G. clavariiforme*, (b) *G. confusum*, (c)
G. fuscum and (d) *G. cornutum*

less with thin walls. The brown spores measure 30–50 x 20–25 μm, and the colourless ones are rather longer and narrower (figure 48b).

Also uncommon, on cultivated *J. sabina*, is *G. fuscum* DC (*G. sabinae* (Dicks.) Wint.), the teleutosori of which are at first cushion-shaped, later conical and up to 10 mm high, and yellow-brown when they gelatinise. The teleutospores (figure 48c) have pale brown walls, and measure 34–40 x 20–30 μm. The alternate host is *Pyrus communis*.

Finally, *G. cornutum* Kern, on *J. communis*, has been seen occasionally in England and Wales, and much more often in Scotland. Its teleutospore masses are flat or cushion-shaped, chocolate-brown when dry, but orange and gelatinous when moist. The spores may be thick-walled and dark brown, or thin-walled and yellowish, measuring 32–52 x 18–28 μm (figure 48d). The alternate host is *Sorbus aucuparia*.

ROOT AND BUTT ROTS

The root and butt rot fungus *Heterobasidion annosum* (*Fomes annosus*) has been found on juniper plants in Scotland (Moore, 1959). This fungus is described in chapter 3.

THE DAWN REDWOOD: *METASEQUOIA GLYPTOSTROBOIDES*

The dawn redwood, *Metasequoia glyptostroboides*, is a Chinese tree introduced into this country in 1948. It is now fairly common in parks and gardens.

Armillaria mellea (which is described in chapter 3) was found attacking a young tree in Scotland in 1956 (Moore, 1959), and killed another in Surrey in 1970.

REDWOOD: *SEQUOIA SEMPERVIRENS* AND WELLINGTONIA: *SEQUOIADENDRON GIGANTEUM*

The redwood, *Sequoia semperivirens*, and the Wellingtonia or big tree, *Sequoiadendron giganteum*, both of which were introduced from the west coast of North America, are grown here in parks and gardens.

NURSERY DISEASES

GREY MOULD: *Botrytis cinerea*
Nursery stock of both redwood and Wellingtonia is very susceptible to damage by grey mould (*Botrytis cinerea*), which is described in chapter 3.

POST-NURSERY DISEASES

NEEDLE DISORDERS

Winter browning
Redwood trees are very liable to a winter browning of the foliage due to winter cold.

DIEBACKS

Phomopsis disease caused by *Phacidiopycnis pseudotsugae*
According to Peace (1962), *Sequoiadendron giganteum* is one of the hosts of *Phacidiopycnis pseudotsugae*, though this fungus (described in chapter 3) has so far caused it little damage.

Figure 49. Galls caused by *Agrobacterium tumefasciens* on *Sequoia sempervirens* (Forestry Commission)

BRANCH GALLS

Branch galls caused by *Agrobacterium tumefasciens* (Smith & Townsend) Conn
Large galls up to 20 cm across have sometimes been found on the branches of *Sequoia sempervirens*, both in this country (Bull, 1951; Peace, 1962) and in France (Dufrénoy, 1922) and Germany (Martin, 1957) (figure 49). There is evidence that at least in some cases the crown gall organism, *Agrobacterium tumefasciens*, is associated with these tumours. *A. tumefasciens*, which has a very wide host range, is fully described by Stapp (1961). A soil saprophyte and wound parasite, it is rod-shaped, 1–3 x 0.4–0.5 μm, with one (rarely two) polar flagella.

ROOT AND BUTT ROTS

The most important cause of damage to Wellingtonia is the honey fungus, *Armillaria mellea*, which is described in chapter 3.

MISCELLANEOUS DISORDERS

The tops of large Wellingtonia trees are often killed. Lightning is the cause of this damage at least in some cases (plate 2).

YEW: *TAXUS BACCATA*

Like Scots pine and the common juniper, the yew is one of our few native conifers. It is widespread in England and Wales, but rare in Scotland. Yew woodland and scrub occurs especially on chalk and limestone soils, and yew is also grown as an ornamental in churchyards, parks and gardens, and as a hedge plant.

NURSERY AND POST-NURSERY DISEASES

NEEDLE DISEASES

Needle casts caused by *Sphaerulina taxi, Physalospora gregaria* var. *foliorum* and *Diplodia taxi*
These three needle fungi have all been recorded on yew in Great Britain, though all are of very small importance.

Sphaerulina taxi (Cooke) Massee (stat. conid. *Cytospora taxifolia* Cooke & Massee em. Pilat & Macal. apud Callen) causes a leaf scorch and twig blight, particularly on yew hedges (Anon, 1951). It is widespread in Scotland, and is also known in southern England (Moore, 1959; Dennis, 1968). Its black perithecia are embedded in the upper sides of the leaves, and measure 140–186 x 125–165 μm, with a short projecting ostiole. The eight-spored asci are club-shaped with a thickened tip, and measure 57–75 x 10–13.5 μm. The colourless, narrowly elliptical ascospores are 3- (sometimes 5-) septate when mature, and measure 20–37.5 x 6.5–9 μm.

The imperfect state is a multilocular, rounded or irregular pycnidium (*Cytospora taxifolia*) measuring 418–435 x 243–352 μm, and containing colourless, rod-shaped conidia measuring 3–5 x 1 μm (Callen, 1938; Dennis, 1968).

Physalospora gregaria Sacc. var. *foliorum* Sacc. (stat. conid. *Phyllostictina hysterella* (Sacc.) Petr.) was found in the Forth and Clyde area in Scotland by Callen (1938), and has also been recorded in Scotland, at Insch, on golden yew (*Taxus baccata* var. *stricta*) by Moore (1959). The black, globose perithecia are embedded in the leaves, mostly in the upper sides, and measure 183–234 x 138–202 μm, with a small projecting ostiole. The eight-spored asci are club-shaped, and measure 52–90 x 13–25 μm. The colourless, one-celled, ovate-oblong or egg-shaped ascospores are narrower at one of the two rounded ends, and measure 15–23 x 7–12 μm.

The dark brown pycnidia of the imperfect state (*Phyllostictina hysterella*) are embedded in the leaf, mostly on the upper side, and are spherical or ovoid bodies measuring 185–208 x 140–179 μm, containing colourless, one-celled, egg-shaped or elliptical, round-ended conidia measuring 10–16 x 8–10 μm (Callen, 1938).

Diplodia taxi (Sow.) de Not. is widespread on the leaves of yew (Moore, 1959), and according to Grove (1937), in Germany it has been found on branches as well as on leaves, and has there been known to kill trees. The black pycnidia are embedded in the leaves, and contain elliptical spores with rounded ends. The spores are at first one-celled and colourless, but finally become two-celled and smoky brown, when they measure 20–25 x 8–10 μm (Grove, 1937).

BRANCH CANKER AND DIEBACK

Canker and branch girdling of unknown cause
The cause of a sometimes extensive cankering and girdling of twigs and branches found in southern England on *Taxus baccata* and its cultivars is under investigation. The symptoms suggest a parasitic bark-invading organism (Strouts, personal communication).

ROOT DISEASES

Phytophthora root rot is the commonest cause of death of yew in nurseries, and also affects established ornamental trees.

HEART ROT

The commonest heart rot fungus of standing yews is *Laetiporus sulphureus* (*Polyporus sulphureus*), which causes a slow, red-brown, cubical rot. It is more important on other trees (especially oak) than it is on yew, and is briefly described in chapter 19.

REFERENCES

Anon (1951). Hedges defoliated at Huntley. *Phytopath. Intell. Rep.*(*Scot.*), No. 13

Bernaux, P. (1956). Contribution a l'étude de la biologie des Gymnosporangium. *Ann. Inst. Rech. agron., Ser. C (Ann. Epiphyt.)*, 7, 1–210

Bull, R. A. (1951). A new gall disease of *Sequoia sempervirens*. *Gdnrs' Chron.*, ser. 3, 130, 110–11

Callen, E. O. (1938). Some fungi on yew. *Trans. Br. mycol. Soc.*, 22, 94–106

Dennis, R. W. G. (1968). *British Ascomycetes*, J. Cramer, Lehre

Dufrenoy, J. (1922). Tumeurs de *Sequoia sempervirens*. *Bull. Soc. Path. veg. France*, 9, 277–281

Grove, W. B. (1937). *British stem- and leaf-fungi (Coelomycetes)*, vol II, Cambridge University Press, Cambridge

Hahn, G. G. (1926). *Phomopsis juniperova* and closely related strains on conifers. *Phytopathology*, 16, 899–914

Humphreys-Jones, D. R. (1977). Leaf and shoot death (*Coniothyrium fuckelii* Sacc.) of *Juniperus communis* L. var. *compressa* Carr. *Pl. Path.*, 26, 47–8

MacDonald, J., Wood, R. F., Edwards, M. V. and Aldhous, J. R. (1957). *Exotic Forest Trees in Great Britain*, Bull For. Commn, no. 30

Martin, E. I. (1957). Neoplastisches Wachstum bei *Sequoiadendron giganteum* Buchholz. *Phytopath. Z.*, 30, 342–3

Moore, W. C. (1959). *British Parasitic Fungi*, Cambridge University Press, Cambridge

Otta, J. D., Fiedler, D. J. and Lengkeek, V. H. (1980). Effect of benomyl on *Phomopsis juniperova* infection of *Juniperus virginiana*. *Phytopathology*, 70, 46–50

Peace, T. R. (1962). *Pathology of Trees and Shrubs*, Clarendon Press, Oxford

Schneider, R. and von Arx, J. A. (1966). Zwei neue, als Erreger von Zweigterben nachgewiesene Pilze: *Kabatina thujae* n.g., n. sp. und *K. juniperi* n. sp. *Phytopath. Z.*, 57, 176–182

Stapp, C. (1961). *Bacterial Plant Pathogens*, Oxford University Press, London

Strouts, R. G. (1973). Canker of cypresses caused by *Coryneum cardinale* Wag. in Britain. *Eur. J. For. Path.*, 3, 13–24

Sutton, B. C. (1980). *The Coelomycetes*, Commonwealth Mycological Institute, Kew

Wilson, M. and Henderson, D. H. (1966). *British Rust Fungi*, Cambridge University Press, Cambridge

Young, C. W. T. and Strouts, R. G. (1971). In Forest pathology. *Rep. Forest Res., Lond.*, 1971, 77–84

10 Diseases of oak (*Quercus* spp.)

The two British native oaks are *Quercus robur* and *Q. petraea*, the pedunculate and sessile oak respectively. Both are widespread in woodland and in hedgerows, parks and gardens throughout the country. Hybrids between the two are common. The introduced species *Q. cerris* (the Turkey oak) and *Q. ilex* (the evergreen or holm oak) are both common and naturalised in many areas in the south of the country.

Many other introduced oaks are grown in parks and gardens, though most are uncommon or rare. *Q. borealis*, the red oak, and *Q. coccinea*, the scarlet oak (both from North America) are both frequent, however, though more so in the south than in the north. The Lucombe oak, one of the forms of *Q.* x *hispanica*, a hybrid between *Q. cerris* and *Q. suber* (the European cork oak) is also commonly planted in parks in southern England.

Oaks in Britain are generally relatively free of serious diseases. Their fungus diseases have been reviewed by Murray (1974).

NURSERY DISEASES

LEAF DISEASES

Oak mildew: *Microsphaera alphitoides* Griffon & Maublanc

The oak mildew *Microsphaera alphitoides* may be very damaging, particularly on nursery stock, on young trees not long planted out and on young coppice regrowth.

The fungus and the symptoms   The oidial stage of a powdery mildew described as *Oidium quercinum* was first recorded in Portugal in 1877 but the first undoubted record of the fungus now generally called *Microsphaera alphitoides* was made in France in 1907. The fungus was at least almost unknown until the French report, after which it spread rapidly throughout Europe (Woodward *et al.*, 1929). The perfect stage was first described by Griffon and Maublanc (1912), who considered it to be a new species to which they applied the name *M. alphitoides*. However, the fungus has been regarded by some (Foëx, 1941) as a form of *M. alni,* or of the American species *M. quercina* (which is itself considered by Gardner *et al.* (1972) to be synonymous with *M. alni*). The situation is further complicated by the existence in Europe of at least one other species of *Microsphaera* on oak. This is *M. hypophylla (M. silvatica),* which is known in Norway, Sweden, Austria and Switzerland. What is almost certainly a third of these mildews is *Calocladia (=Microsphaera) penicillata* f. *quercus,* known only from Italy (Luisi and Grasso, 1973; Roll-Hansen, 1966).

M. alphitoides attacks the young leaves and sometimes the young shoots of the plants, and appears first from May onwards as small cinnamon coloured spots. These increase in size, and soon the whole leaf may be covered by a layer of white mycelium and a thick white powder of oidia (figure 50). In severe attacks the leaves shrivel, become brown and fall. Occasionally (usually after hot, dry summers), cleistothecia of the perfect stage may be found in the autumn, mainly on the upper sides of the leaves. They are yellow at first, but when mature become dark brown or black (plate 29). In Britain they were first found in 1945 (Robertson and Macfarlane, 1946; Batko, 1962).

The oidia are borne singly on three-celled conidiophores, and are elliptical or barrel-shaped, measuring $25-37 \times 15-22\,\mu m$. The cleistothecia measure about $180-200\,\mu m$ across. They contain several asci, and bear up to about 20 append-

Figure 50. Leaves of young oak covered by the white mycelium and white powdery spore masses of the oak mildew *Microsphaera alphitoides* (D.H. Phillips)

ages, the ends of which carry several repeatedly dichotomous branches. The colourless, ellipsoid ascospores, of which there are up to eight in each ascus, measure 18-24 x 6-13 μm (Robertson and Macfarlane, 1946).

Host range and host susceptibility   *M. alphitoides* is found occasionally on beech *(Fagus sylvatica)*, and (on the European mainland) on the sweet chestnut *(Castanea sativa)* as well as on oak. It is an important pathogen only on the latter, however. Of the oaks, *Q. robur* is especially susceptible; under field conditions *Q. petraea* is less so, though it may be badly affected in the nursery (Anon, 1956). In Italy, Luisi and Grasso (1973) list a number of oaks in decreasing order of susceptibility as follows: *Q. pedunculata (Q. robur), Q. pubescens, Q. farnetto, Q. cerris, Q. ilex, Q. suber, Q. coccifera.*
   Provenance trials with *Q. robur* and *Q. petraea* have shown that different

provenances may vary somewhat in resistance to the mildew, but that these differences are too small to have much practical importance (Leibundgut, 1969; Rack, 1957*a*).

Overwintering of the fungus   The oidia spread the disease rapidly throughout the summer, but are short-lived. Overwintering is by means of mycelium in a small percentage of the buds (Woodward *et al.*, 1929; Kerling, 1966). Petri (1923) found evidence that overwintering in Italy was by means of chlamydospores, but this has not been demonstrated elsewhere. Likewise so far there seems no evidence that the cleistothecia play any part in overwintering.

Factors affecting mildew   Hewitt (1974) found that the oidia germinated best at temperatures between 20 and 23°C, at a relative humidity between 76 and 96 per cent. Many authors have suggested that there is an association between hot, dry summers and the production of the cleistothecia (Batko, 1962), though Dobbs (1951) found the fruit bodies in North Wales after one notably cool, wet summer.

Observations (supported in part by experiment) have suggested that ultra-violet light at high elevations (Bolli, 1943), and gaseous sulphur compounds in industrial areas (Köck, 1935) may play some part in mildew control.

The parasitic fungus *Cicinnobolus cesati* De By. may to some extent suppress mildew attacks in late summer (Woodward *et al.*, 1929).

Importance of mildew   In the nursery if mildew is left uncontrolled it may kill young seedlings or by the destruction of shoots reduce the young tree to a bush-like shape. Nimmo (unpublished), from the results of spray trials on newly-planted stock, concluded that the disease could reduce height growth by 30 per cent over three years, and reduce the number of straight, single leaders by about the same percentage. Viney (1970) considered that in France and Belgium mildew was the main reason for the lack of natural regeneration of stands of *Q. robur*.

On older trees mildew generally causes less injury, though at times, particularly in the earlier part of this century, it has formed part of a complex involving also drought and frost, and various insects and fungi which has given rise to dieback and death of many trees over large areas. This complex is briefly considered below under general oak dieback.

Control of oak mildew   Viney (1970) has suggested that in France and Belgium it may be necessary to replace stands of *Quercus robur* with the less susceptible *Q. petraea* where mildew is troublesome. This is not always easy, however, as many seed lots contain a mixture of the two species and the hybrid between them.

Other methods of control can be applied only in the nursery. Under conditions in Eastern Europe it has been found that shading seedlings with oats and sunflowers or lupins protects them from mildew (Kartavenko, 1958; Orlos, 1951).

Control in the nursery is generally achieved by the use of fungicides. Bordeaux mixture and other copper sprays have been found to be effective, but generally the best control has been obtained with colloidal and wettable sulphur and dinocap (Woodward *et al.*, 1929; Müller-Kögler, 1954; Rack, 1957*b*; Jagielski, 1969; Mamedov, 1974). Guseinov (1976) obtained good results with benomyl, but Rack (1957*b*) found dithane ineffective.

Spraying should be begun at the first signs of infection, and to keep the disease under control it may be necessary to spray several times at intervals of two to three weeks.

Another mildew, *Phyllactinia corylea*, which is much better known on hazel and ash, has also been recorded on oak (Batko, 1962), on which, however, it causes no significant damage. It is described under Hazel in chapter 18.

ROOT DISEASES

Root rot caused by *Rosellinia quercina* Hartig
Rosellinia quercina has been found occasionally on *Quercus robur, Q. petraea* and *Q. cerris* in all parts of Great Britain, causing a root rot of young seedling oak in nurseries. It appears to be commoner and more damaging on the European mainland (Woeste, 1956; Urošević and Jančařik, 1957). It has been studied in Britain by Waldie (1930) and in Germany by Woeste (1956).

Symptoms and development of the disease   It usually shows as spreading patches of seedlings which yellow downwards from the tops. Fine hyphae growing through the soil in spring, and arising directly from resting mycelium, from small black sclerotia or from germinating ascospores, enter the young roots mainly through lenticels. The roots (especially the tap roots) are then rotted (figure 51). The mycelium develops into anastomosing rhizomorphic strands which form a dense mass. This is at first white but finally becomes dark brown or black, and spreads under and over the bark, over the root surface, and on the soil surface around the root collar. Small verticillately branched conidiophores form on the mycelium and produce short conidia, and small black sclerotia about the size of a pin's head arise on the root surfaces. Later, in September, short-necked black perithecia measuring 0.8-1 mm across develop in the mycelium on the plant stems just above the soil, and on the soil surface itself. The perithecia contain asci separated by septate paraphyses, and each ascus contains eight spindle-shaped, brown, one-celled ascospores each measuring $17-32 \times 7.5-10 \mu m$ (Waldie, 1930; Brooks, 1953). These ascospores are shed in the following spring.

Factors affecting the disease   Factors affecting Rosellinia root rot are little understood, though poor drainage is said to favour the disease. The sclerotia may persist in the soil for a long time, though infection of a nursery is not necessarily followed by persistent attacks (Peace, 1962).

Control   As the disease is so sporadic, little work has been done on its control. Waldie (1930) reported that he gained control by burning the soil to a depth of 6 in (approximately 15 cm) with a powerful blowlamp, and then watering with a 5 per cent solution of carbolic acid. Other, more recent soil sterilants might be tried if necessary. On general grounds, diseased plants should not be transplanted, but should be destroyed. Apparently healthy plants from the same beds should not be transplanted elsewhere in the same nursery or moved to other nurseries. As the disease does not attack plants more than two or three years old, however, they may be planted out in the forest or in parks or gardens.

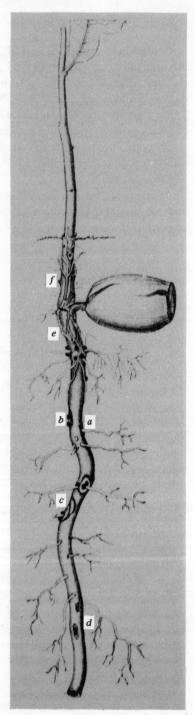

Figure 51 (opposite). Seedling oak attacked by *Rosellinia quercina*. Infection tubercles can be seen at a and b, and the cortical tissue around them has been destroyed. Near the acorn, strands of the fungus ramify over the surface of the plant, at e (R. Hartig)

POST-NURSERY DISEASES

LEAF DISEASES

Oak mildew: *Microsphaera alphitoides*

The oak mildew, *Microsphaera alphitoides*, may occur on trees of any age, and in woodland it is most important on young trees not long planted, and on coppice shoots. It is most important, however, on nursery stock and, therefore, it is covered above under nursery diseases.

Leaf blister caused by *Taphrina caerulescens* (Mont. & Desm.) Tul.

Taphrina caerulescens has been found occasionally in Great Britain and Ireland (Henderson, 1954; Brooks, 1953), across the mainland of Europe from France to the Caucasus, and in North Africa and Japan (Viennot-Bourgin, 1949) and in North America (Goode, 1953). In most of these areas it is of only minor significance, but in the southern states of the USA it has caused occasional epidemics following cool, wet springs. Some trees have then been killed by repeated loss of leaves, while the growth of others has been reduced (Wedgeworth, 1926; Goode, 1953).

The fungus causes slightly swollen, pale green, yellowish or pinkish, rounded or irregular spots up to 12 mm cross and concave below. A layer of asci forms in the concave surface, which hence becomes silvery grey and later velvety brown. The blisters may cause curling and twisting of the leaves of narrow-leaved oak species (Weber, 1941; Viennot-Bourgin, 1949).

The ascospores produce primary conidia as soon as they are formed, and these conidia themselves bud off secondary spores, so that the asci quickly fill with small 'sprout cells' (Goode and Parris, 1954; Henderson, 1954; Brooks, 1953). The asci vary in size and form with the oak species on which the fungus is growing. They are further described by Mix (1949).

The conidia infect the young leaves as the buds open. Older leaves are not susceptible (Goode and Parris, 1954).

In Great Britain *T. caerulescens* seems to have been recorded only on *Quercus petraea* and the introduced *Q. borealis (Q. rubra)* (Henderson, 1954), while in Ireland it has been found on *Q. robur* (Brooks, 1953). In the USA Weber (1941) noted it on almost all the many North American oak species, with *Q. borealis* and *Q. nigra* being especially susceptible, but *Q. phellos* showing resistance to the disease. Also in the USA, Goode and Parris (1954) found almost all the oaks they studied were severely damaged by *T. caerulescens*, only *Q. stellata*, *Q. palustris* and *Q. shumardii* being resistant.

Control of the disease   Control measures against leaf blister are necessary only in the southern states of the USA, where spraying the dormant buds before they swell and burst may be required to kill overwintering spores. Good control has been obtained with one application of Bordeaux mixture, zineb, maneb, manzate, captan and several other fungicides (Goode, 1953).

Leaf spot caused by *Sclerotinia candolleana* (Lév.) Fuckel (*Ciborinia candolleana* (Lév.) Whetzel)

Sclerotinia candolleana, which is common and usually regarded as no more than a saprophyte, has sometimes been found in Britain associated with a leaf blotch on *Quercus robur, Q. petraea* and *Q. borealis (Q. rubra)*. In the summer of 1925 and in 1926 it gave rise to an epidemic all over Scotland south of Inverness, and over much of England and Wales (Wilson and Waldie, 1927).

From July onwards, affected oak leaves develop circular brown spots, which sometimes spread over the whole leaf. Small, black, hemispherical or lens-shaped sclerotia up to 3 mm across are produced over the winter on the fallen leaves. From these sclerotia stalked apothecia arise in the following summer from May to July. The slender apothecial stalk grows until the apothecium is clear of the litter surface, and so its length varies with the depth of the sclerotium in the litter. The yellowish-brown apothecial disc is up to 4 mm across, and is flat when mature. The outer wall of the apothecium is smooth. The eight-spored asci measure up to 100 x 7 μm, and narrow paraphyses occur between them. The ascospores are colourless, more or less elliptical, and measure 6-10 x 3-4 μm (Dennis, 1968).

The same fungus is sometimes said to occur on *Castanea* (Brooks, 1953), though Dennis (1968) states that the fungus on sweet chestnut is *S. hirtella* Boud., which has long hairs on the stalk and cup of the apothecium.

The oak rust: *Uredo quercus* Duby

The rare leaf rust, *Uredo quercus*, has been found a few times in southern England on *Quercus petraea*, as well as on *Q. ilex* in Devon and Guernsey (Moore, 1959).

The yellow uredosori appear as pustules on the undersides of the leaves, and the orange-yellow, obovoid or broadly ellipsoid uredospores measure 15-25 x 10-17 μm; they are covered by minute echinulations. No other stage is known in Britain, though in France, where the rust is also known, teleutosori have been found (Wilson and Henderson, 1966).

Leaf spot caused by *Phyllosticta maculiformis* Sacc.

Phyllosticta maculiformis has been found from time to time on fading and dead leaves (and once on living leaves) of *Quercus robur* in England and Scotland (Moore, 1959). The fungus also occurs in mainland Europe, North Africa and North America (Grove, 1935). It is of negligible importance on oak.

The black pycnidia of *P. maculiformis* appear on the leaf spots on the undersides of the leaves. The cylindrical, straight or curved, colourless spores, which are found on the fallen leaves in May, measure 4-6 x 1-1.5 μm (Grove, 1935).

The fungus is said to be one of the imperfect states of *Mycosphaerella maculiformis,* which is better known on the European mainland on the sweet chestnut.

DISEASES OF LEAVES AND SHOOTS

Leaf spot and dieback caused by *Gloeosporium quercinum* West.
The leaf spot and dieback (sometimes called anthracnose) caused by *Gloeosporium quercinum* is probably not uncommon in Britain. It is well known throughout mainland Europe and in North America (Grove, 1937; Neely and Himelick, 1967).

On oaks in Britain the fungus produces irregular or angular, brownish-black leaf spots with a brown margin, and measuring up to about 15 mm across (Grove, 1937). In North America, symptoms on the very numerous oaks vary with the species, the leaf spots on some species being light brown with a yellow border (Parris and Byrd, 1962). In severe attacks, the tips of the leaves may die and wither, and the tissues curl and break into irregular shot-holes. Sometimes the disease may spread to the shoot tips, which then curl, shrivel and die.

Rounded, brown conidial pustules, about 250 µm across, form on the spots on both sides of the leaves. The one-celled, more or less colourless, oblong to spindle-shaped spores measure 10-15 x 3-5 µm (Grove, 1937). The perfect stage, *Gnomonia quercina,* does not seem to have been found in Britain, though it is well known elsewhere.

The fungus has often been considered identical with another *Gnomonia* species, *G. platani,* which attacks plane (*Platanus* spp.), Neely and Himelick (1967) reviewed previous work and carried out their own investigations with both fungi, and concluded (in agreement with several earlier workers) that the two fungi were morphologically and pathologically distinct. On potato dextrose agar *G. quercina* produced a yellow diffusible pigment, whereas *G. platani* did not. Normally *G. quercina* will not attack plane and *G. platani* will not attack oak. In cross-inoculation studies, however, they successfully grew isolates from oak on leaves of plane and *vice versa.*

The disease appears to be favoured by cool, wet weather (Neely and Himelick, 1967; Shishkina, 1969), rainfall being the most important single factor (Fergus, 1953).

DISEASES OF BARK AND SHOOTS

Dieback caused by *Diaporthe taleola* (Fr.) Sacc. and *D. leiphaemia* (Fr.) Sacc.
Diaporthe taleola and *D. leiphaemia* (figures 52, 53) are both common saprophytes on small branches of oak both in Britain and the rest of Europe and in parts of North America (Wehmeyer, 1932; Reid and Cain, 1960). Occasionally, on trees weakened by drought or other causes they may become minor parasites, giving rise to bark cankers, and even to the death of small trees (Moore, 1959).

Figure 52. **Cankers caused by** *Diaporthe taleola* **on an oak stem (Forestry Commission)**

The perithecia of *D. taleola* are embedded in a whitish to blackened stroma under the bark. The stroma is surrounded by a distinct black zone which is often visible on the bark surface (Munk, 1957), or may be seen if the outer bark is cut away. The asci each contain eight (or sometimes four) ascospores. The colourless ascospores are two-celled, constricted at the septum, and measure 17–25 x 7–9.5 μm. At first they bear cylindrical appendages at the apex and radiating from around the septum, but these growths soon disappear. Various conidial stages also occur (Wehmeyer, 1932).

The stroma of *D. leiphaemia*, which is also embedded under the bark surface, is at first orange-yellow or brown but may later blacken. The perithecia develop in the stroma. The colourless, two-celled ascospores are rather spindle-shaped to ellipsoid, slightly curved or inequilateral, and constricted at the septum. They measure 15–20 x 2.5–5.5 μm. Pycnidial locules may occur round the edges of the stroma, with cylindric, rather curved spores measuring 6–12 x 1.5–2 μm and spindle-shaped spores measuring 14–22 x 3–4 μm (Wehmeyer, 1932).

Figure 53. Stromata of *Diaporthe leiphaemia* on an oak stem (Forestry Commission)

Dieback caused by *Colpoma quercinum* (Pers.) Wallr. (*Clithris quercina* (Pers.) Rehm)

Colpoma quercinum is a common fungus on dead twigs and branches of oak trees, and at times it may cause a minor dieback (Twyman, 1946). It has been said to be a wound parasite, often following insect damage (Brooks, 1953). Its dark, narrow, leathery ascocarps develop below the bark, and at maturity split open by a longitudinal slit to reveal a light yellow hymenium measuring up to 15 x 2 mm. The club-shaped asci each contain eight threadlike, colourless ascospores that measure 80–95 x 1.5 μm and finally become multiseptate. Slender paraphyses with curled tips occur between the asci. The ascospores are found in May, June and July (Dennis, 1968).

DECAY FUNGI

Many rot fungi have been recorded on standing oaks. The most damaging appear to be *Inonotus dryadeus* (which causes a white butt rot, and which is important as a cause of root decay leading to windthrow or dieback and death), *Laetiporus sulphureus, Ganoderma resinaceum* and *Grifola frondosa*. These and other fungi affecting oak are described in chapter 19.

MISCELLANEOUS DISEASES

Spring frost damage
In some seasons spring frosts defoliate oaks, which then usually produce a new crop of leaves. This second crop may itself then be especially susceptible to attack by powdery mildew (*Microsphaera alphitoides*), which is further described on p.208 under Nursery diseases

General oak dieback
In the earlier part of this century oak forests in various parts of Europe (including Britain) (Day, 1927; Osmaston, 1927; Young, 1965; Marcu, 1966) and North America (Staley, 1965) were from time to time affected by a dieback that often killed many trees over large areas. Those who studied this phenomenon have all concluded that this dieback, which mainly affected *Q. robur,* was the result of a complex of factors varying in detail from time to time and place to place, but generally including drought, sometimes accentuated by drying winds (Young, 1965), together with attacks by various defoliating insects and a range of fungi, particularly the oak mildew *(Microsphaera alphitoides)* and *Armillaria mellea.* Oak mildew is further discussed above. *A. mellea* (chapter 3) is common on the roots of oak, and on its own may infest the roots for many years without causing serious damage.

Stag-headedness
Old, mature oaks on the English clays often become stag-headed, as do others subjected to malpractices such as the covering of their roots with asphalt or concrete.

Shakes
Oaks may also be subject to the internal cracking of the stem known as 'shakes'. These shakes appear as serious defects in the sawn timber.

Twig dieback caused by *Fusicoccum noxium* Ruhl.
In 1967, *Fusicoccum noxium* was found on 10 to 12-year-old trees of *Quercus robur* on a nursery near Lymington, Hants. The plants had been imported from the Netherlands, and showed discoloured patches on the twigs (Batko, 1974). The affected twigs were carefully pruned out and burnt, and the plants kept under observation, and the fungus does not seem to have become established. The perfect stage, *Dothidea noxia,* was not found.

REFERENCES

Anon (1956). *Oak Mildew*, Leafl. For. Commn, no. 38, 6 pp.

Batko, S. (1962). Perithecia of oak mildew in Britain, in 'New or uncommon plant diseases and pests'. *Pl. Path.*, 11, 184

Batko, S. (1974). Notes on new and rare fungi on forest trees in Britain. *Bull. Br. mycol. Soc.*, 8, 19–21

Bolli, M. (1943). Influenza dei raggi ultra-violetti sull'oidio della quercia. *Ann. Fac. Agr. Perugia*, 2, 65–8

Brooks, F.T. (1953). *Plant Diseases*, Oxford University Press, London

Day, W.R. (1927). The oak mildew *Microsphaera quercina* (Schw.) Burrill and *Armillaria mellea* (Vahl) Quél. in relation to the dying back of oak. *Forestry*, 1, 108–112

Dennis, R.W.G. (1968). *British Ascomycetes*, J. Cramer, Lehre

Dobbs, C.G. (1951). Fruiting of the oak mildew *(Microsphaera alphitoides)*. *Nature, Lond.*, 167, 357

Fergus, C.L. (1953). Relation of weather to the severity of white oak anthracnose. *Phytopathology*, 43, 103–5

Foëx, E. (1941). L'invasion des chênes de l'Europe par le blanc ou oidium *(Microsphaera alphitoides* Griffon et Maublanc). *Rev. Eaux For.*, 79, 338–49

Gardner, M.W., Yarwood, C.E. and Duafala, T. (1972). Oak mildews. *Pl. Dis. Reptr.*, 56, 313–7

Goode, M.J. (1953). Control of oak leaf-blister in Mississippi. *Phytopathology*, 43, 472 (abstract)

Goode, M.J. and Parris, G.K. (1954). Additions to our knowledge of the life cycle of *Taphrina caerulescens*. *Phytopathology*, 44, 332 (abstract)

Griffon, E. and Maublanc, A. (1912). Les *Microsphaera* des chênes. *Bull. Soc. mycol. Fr.*, 28, 88–103

Grove, W.B. (1935). *British Stem- and Leaf-Fungi (Coelomycetes)*, vol. 1, Cambridge University Press Cambridge

Grove, W.B. (1937). *British Stem- and Leaf-Fungi (Coelomycetes)*, vol. 2, Cambridge University Press, Cambridge

Guseinov, E.S. (1976). [Benomyl against powdery mildew of oak] . *Zashchita Rastenii*, 5, 32; abstract in *Rev. Pl. Path.*, 50, 1976, no. 5363

Henderson, D.M. (1954). The genus *Taphrina* in Scotland. *Notes R. bot. Soc. Edinb.*, 21, 165–180

Hewitt, H.G. (1974). Conidial germination in *Microsphaera alphitoides*. *Trans. Br. mycol. Soc.*, 63, 587–9

Jagielski, A. (1969). [Investigations on the effectiveness of some fungicides against *Microsphaera alphitoides* on oak] . *Biul. Inst. Ochr. Rośl., Poznań*, 45, 45–50; abstract in *Rev. Pl. Path.*, 50, 1971, no. 1403

Kartavenko, N.T. (1958). [The significance of shading in the control of oak mildew] . *Bot. Z.*, 43, 399–400; abstract in *Rev. appl. Mycol.*, 38, 341, 1959

Kerling, L.C.P. (1966). The hibernation of the oak mildew. *Acta bot. neerl.*, 15, 76–83

Köck, G. (1935). Eichenmehltau und Rauchgasschäden. *Z. PflKrankh.*, 45, 44–45

Leibundgut, H. (1969). Untersuchungen über die Anfälligkeit verschiedener Eichenherkünfte für die Erkrankung an Mehltau. *Schweiz. Z. Forstwes.*, 120, 486–93

Luisi, N. and Grasso, V. (1973). Biologia delle erysiphaceae di alcune cupolifere nell'Italia meridionale. *Ann. Acc. It. Sc. For.*, 22, 211–67

Mamedov, K.D. (1974). [Chemical and biological preparations against powdery mildew of oak] . *Lesnoe Khozyaistvo* (1974), 7, 83–84; abstract in *Rev. Pl. Path.*, 54, 1975, no. 1890

Marcu, G. (coordinator) *et al.* (1966). *Studiul cauzelor si al metodelor de provenire si combatere a uscarii stejarului*. Centrul de Documentare Tehnica Pentu Economia Forestiera, Romania

Mix, A.J. (1949). A monograph of the genus *Taphrina. Kans. Univ. Sci. Bull.*, 33, 3–167

Moore, W.C. (1959). *British Parasitic Fungi*, Cambridge University Press, Cambridge

Müller-Kögler, E. (1954). Bekämpfung des Eichenmehltaus. *Forstsch. Merkbl. niedersächs. forstl. VersAnst.*, Abt. B, 5, 4 app.

Munk, A. (1957). Danish pyrenomycetes. A preliminary flora. *Dansk. bot Ark.,* 17, 1–491

Murray, J.S. (1974). The fungal pathogens of oak, in M.G. Morris and F.H. Perring (Eds.), *The British Oak,* Classey, Faringdon, for the Botanical Society of the British Isles

Neely, D. and Himelick, E.B. (1967). Characteristics and nomenclature of the oak anthracnose fungus. *Phytopathology,* 57, 1230–6

Orłos, H. (1951). Zwalczanie maczniaka *Microsphaera alphitoides* Griff. et Maubl. w szkółkach debowych. *Inst. Bad. Lesn. Prace,* no. 67

Osmaston, L.S. (1927). Mortality among oaks. *Q. Jl. For.,* 21, 28–30

Parris, G.K. and Byrd, J. (1962). Oak anthracnose in Mississippi. *Pl. Dis. Reptr.,* 46, 677–81

Peace, T.R. (1962). *Pathology of Trees and Shrubs,* Clarendon Press, Oxford

Petri, L. (1923). Sur la formation des chlamydospores chez l'oidium des chênes. *Congrès Path. vég. (Centenaire de Pasteur), Strasbourg, 1923,* pp. 36–7

Rack, K. (1957a). Untersuchungen über die Anfalligkeit verschiedener Eichenprovenienzen gegenüber dem Eichenmehltau. *Allg. Forst- u. Jagdztg,* 128, 150–6

Rack, K. (1957b). Versuche zur Bekämpfung der Eichenmehltaus. *Forst. u. Holz,* 12, 5–6

Reid, J. and Cain, R.F. (1960). Additional Diaporthales on twigs from Ontario. *Can. J. Bot.,* 38, 945–50

Robertson, N.F. and Macfarlane, I. (1946). The occurrence of perithecia of the oak mildew in Britain. *Trans. Br. mycol. Soc.,* 29, 219–20

Roll-Hansen, F. (1966). Some notes on *Microsphaera hypophylla* Nevodovskij. *Meddr. norske SkogsforsVes.,* 78 (21), 19–22

Shishkina, A.K. (1969). Étiologia usykhania pobegov í list'a Gruzinskogo Duba v ranne-vesennïi period. *Mikol. i Fitopatol.,* 3, 365–7

Staley, J.M. (1965). Decline and mortality of red and scarlet oaks. *Forest Sci.,* 11, 9–17

Twyman, E.S. (1946). Notes on the dieback of oak caused by *Colpoma quercinum* (Fr.) Wallr. *Trans. Br. mycol. Soc.,* 29, 234–41

Urošević, B and Jančařík, V. (1957). [Some important diseases of oak saplings in our nurseries]. *Práce výzk. Ust. lesn. Č.S.R.;* abstract in *Rev. appl. Mycol.,* 37, 423, 1958

Viennot-Bourgin, G. (1949). *Les Champignons Parasites des Plantes Cultivées,* Masson, Paris

Viney, R. (1970). L'oidium du chêne. *Revue for. fr.,* 22, 365–9

Waldie, J.S.L. (1930). An oak seedling disease caused by *Rosellinia quercina. Forestry,* 4, 1–6

Weber, G.F. (1941). Leaf blister of oaks. *Pr. Bull. Fla. agric. Exp. Sta.,* no. 558, 2 pp.

Wedgeworth, H.H. (1926). Leaf blister of oak. *Q. Bull. State Pl. Board Mississippi,* 6, 10–12

Wehmeyer, L.E. (1932). The British species of the genus *Diaporthe* Nits. and its segregates. *Trans. Br. mycol. Soc.,* 17, 237–95

Wilson, M. and Henderson, D.M. (1966). *British Rust Fungi,* Cambridge University Press, Cambridge

Wilson, M. and Waldie, J.S.L. (1927). An oak leaf disease caused by *Sclerotinia candolleana* (Lév.) Fuckel. *Ann. appl. Biol.,* 14, 193–6

Woeste, U. (1956). Anatomische Untersuchungen über die Infektionswege einiger Wurzelpilze. *Phytopath. Z.,* 26, 225–72

Woodward, R.C., Waldie, J.S.L. and Steven, H.M. (1929). Oak mildew and its control in forest nurseries. *Forestry,* 3, 38–56

Young, C.W.T. (1965). *Death of Pedunculate Oak and Variations in Annual Radial Increment Related to Climate,* Forest Rec. Lond., no. 55, 15 pp.

11 Diseases of beech (*Fagus sylvatica*)

The native beech, *Fagus sylvatica*, still makes up about 5 per cent of the forest area in Britain, and among the hardwoods is exceeded in area only by oak. It is one of the few timber trees that grows successfully on chalk and limestone soils. Various copper, cut-leaved, and weeping varieties are common in parks and gardens, and beech is also used for hedging.

NURSERY DISEASES

DAMPING OFF

Beech seedling blight caused by *Phytophthora cactorum*
Beech seedling blight is caused by a fungus now usually considered to be *Phytophthora cactorum* (Lebert and Cohn) Schröter, though it has also been described as *P. fagi* Hartig and *P. omnivorum* de Bary (Fitzpatrick, 1930). It is soil-borne, and may give rise to both pre and post-emergence damping off (Hartig, 1900). Characteristically, in its post-emergence phase, it causes dark green lesions

on the stems of young seedlings, and large blotches on their cotyledons and first leaves (figure 54). In damp weather it spreads rapidly, and the affected plants become brown and shrivelled. According to Hartig, the fungus may persist as oospores on the soil for at least four years.

Attack on young seedlings takes place in spring following germination of the oospores, but older, more woody plants are not affected. If the disease appears in seed beds, the plants may be sprayed with Bordeaux mixture (Manshard, 1927); other fungicides effective against *Phytophthora* spp., such as zineb and maneb, might also be tried. Infested land should be fumigated with formaldehyde. Avoiding the resowing of beech in the infested soil for five or more years to give time for the disappearance of live oospores of the fungus has also been suggested, and may be an effective control measure, though *P. cactorum* has a wide host range and, therefore, it may be insufficient to confine the avoidance to beech.

Other forms: *Phytophthora citricola* and *Pythium mammilatum*
In one case of severe post-emergence damping off, the cause was found to be *Phytophthora citricola*, and in another, both pre and post-emergence damage was caused by *Pythium mammilatum* (Strouts, personal communication).

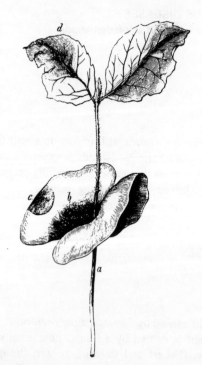

Figure 54. Beech seedling attacked by *Phytophthora cactorum*. The cotyledons at b and c and the first foliar leaves at d show blotches caused by the fungus (R. Hartig)

POST-NURSERY DISEASES

LEAF DISEASES

Leaf spot caused by *Gloeosporium fagi* Westend. (syn. *Labrella fagi* Desm. & Rob.)

Leaf spot caused by *Gloeosporium fagi* Westend. has been recorded in Essex, Buckinghamshire, Kent, Surrey and Yorkshire as well as in many parts of Scotland (Moore, 1959). Elsewhere it is known in Belgium, Holland, Denmark, Germany, Austria and Italy (Grove, 1937). *G. fagi* is often abundant on leaves infested by the beech leaf aphid (*Phylaphis fagi*). This combination may cause spectacular browning, especially on the windward side of beech crowns, and the resultant damage is sometimes wrongly attributed to salt-laden winds, windchill and the like (Young, personal communication).

G. fagi causes rounded or irregular spots that are brownish on the upper side of the leaf and olive green below (plate 30). On the undersides of the spots it produces small, honey-coloured or brown pustules with oblong–ovoid spores measuring 13–20 x 6–8 μm (Grove, 1937). The fungus is sometimes considered to be *G. fagicolum* Passer., which differs from *G. fagi* only in its smaller spores that measure 12.5 x 4 μm (Allescher, 1903). According to Ritschl (1937), *G. fagicolum* is the imperfect stage of the fungus he named *Gnomonia fagi* but regarded as only a form of *G. veneta* (Sacc. & Speg.) Kleb. (*G. platani* Kleb.). No perfect stage of such a fungus has been found on beech in Great Britain.

Gloeosporium leaf spot causes only minor damage.

Powdery mildews

The powdery mildews *Microsphaera alphitoides* (the oak mildew), and *Phyllactinia corylea* (*P. guttata*) (the hazel mildew) have been recorded on beech in Britain, but are of no importance on this host (Burchill, 1978).

CANKER, DIEBACK AND BARK DISEASE

Eight or nine species of *Nectria* have been recorded on beech in Great Britain (Booth, 1959). Most are known to be no more than saprophytes, but two, *N. ditissima* Tul. and *N. coccinea* (Pers. ex Fr.) Fr., are associated with diseases, the first with a canker and dieback, the second with a dieback and bark necrosis. These and other *Nectria* spp. have been much confused, however, and the literature on these diseases is difficult to interpret.

Canker caused by *Nectria ditissima* Tul.

The canker caused by *Nectria ditissima* Tul. was described and figured by Hartig (1900). Hartig considered that this fungus was the cause of canker of many hardwood trees. Later studies have suggested that *N. ditissima* as it is now interpreted is virtually confined to beech (Booth, 1959) although in 1972 it was found on *Sorbus aucuparia*. In Great Britain the fungus is widespread, but it occurs especially on the South Downs in Hampshire (Peace and Murray, 1956), in the Cotswolds (Brown, 1953) and in the Forest of Dean. Elsewhere it is known in Germany (Langner, 1936), France (Perrin, 1980*a*) and in Hungary (Györfi, 1957).

Its smooth-walled, dark red perithecia form clusters of from 5 to 30 on the bark, and measure about $\frac{1}{4}$ to $\frac{1}{3}$ mm across. The club-shaped asci have a thin, undifferentiated apex, and measure 85-95 x 15-18 μm, and each contains eight oval or elliptical, colourless, two-celled ascospores that measure 14-21 x 5-8 μm.

Pustules of colourless microconidia and macroconidia are also formed. The microconidia are oblong to sausage-shaped, 2-2.5 x 0.8-1 μm, and the macroconidia are long, cylindrical, four to seven-septate, 50-90 x 3-6 μm (Booth, 1959; Dennis, 1968).

The fungus attacks twigs, branches and stems of beeches, and causes deeply sunken cankers that may lead to severe twisting and distortion of the stem (figure 55). Girdling of the trunk may result in dieback of the crown (Peace, 1962).

Figure 55. Cankers on beech caused by *Nectria ditissima* (Forestry Commission)

N. ditissima may gain entry through natural openings such as leaf scars, or following damage by insects or honeysuckle, or by rubbing (Peace, 1955; Peace and Murray, 1956), or by pruning (Brown, 1953).

As a rule the disease causes little damage, though in occasional stands it may affect many trees. As far as possible the affected trees should be removed when thinning.

Bark disease associated with *Nectria coccinea* (Pers. ex Fr.) Fr.

Beech bark disease is a necrotic disorder which, unlike the canker and dieback described above, is initiated on the main stem and has a complex etiology. Various forms of this necrosis are known in parts of eastern North America (affecting *Fagus grandifolia*), Great Britain, France and Germany (Houston *et al.,* 1979) and other European countries, including Belgium (Piraux, 1980), Luxembourg (Lies, 1980), Denmark (Thomsen, *et al.,* 1949), Switzerland (Leibundgut and Frick, 1943) and Hungary (Szántó, 1948).

Symptoms   Descriptions of the symptoms include those given by Peace (1962), Shigo (1963), Parker (1974*a*), Perrin (1977) and Schütt and Lang (1980). The early symptoms of the disease complex are varied and seem to relate to factors which precede the appearance of the characteristic feature of the disease: necrotic zones in the bark and outermost sapwood.

The development of necrosis is often made externally visible by the exudation of sap which soon darkens and forms a black congealing patch ('tarry spot') on the bark surface (plate 33). Excision of the bark reveals orange-brown necrotic tissue which has a characteristic smell. Old necroses tend to become dark brown or black and friable (figure 56). The necrosis may be confined to localised patches or vertical strips which are delimited by wound periderm and/or callus (Ehrlich, 1934; Shigo, 1963). Rapid, unchecked necrosis may, however, frequently occur, followed by death of the tree. Trees which do not rapidly die show cankering and/or bark roughening of a variable appearance, often together with current exudation of sap from recently formed necroses (Ehrlich, 1934; Lonsdale, 1980*b*; Perrin, 1980*a*).

Another symptom is the development of foliar chlorosis and/or the production of small, sparse leaves. Although this symptom is characteristic of the disease in North America, the chalky soil conditions under which many British beeches grow may give rise to confusion owing to the development of lime-induced chlorosis (Lonsdale and Pratt, 1981).

Although sap exudation from necrotic bark is the main outward symptom of beech bark disease, there is another feature of many diseased trees which may be more conspicuous. This is the presence of a white, fibrous wax on the bark surface, being the secretion of a minute sap-sucking insect, *Cryptococcus fagisuga* Lind. (beech scale or felted beech coccus) (plate 34). The intensity of infestation may range from a few isolated colonies to complete coverage of much of the stem. Trees may thus appear whitewashed, although the wax tends to blacken

Figure 56. Beech bark disease: breaking up of the bark in the final stages of
the disease (D.H. Phillips)

with age. The effects of the insect infestation on the tree are not fully known,
but young trees often show a stem dimpling symptom (plate 35). Another effect
of the infestation on young stems is gall formation within the bark tissues (Hartig,
1878, 1880). The presence of the insect alone is not considered to constitute
beech bark disease, but its probable role as a causal agent is mentioned below.

Once the bark tissues have become necrotic, they usually yield a species of
Nectria on isolation. This fungus frequently fruits over older lesions, in which
the tissues are dark and friable. In Europe the species of *Nectria* is usually
considered to be *N. coccinea* (Lyr, 1967; Parker, 1974*a*; Perrin, 1977), the
imperfect state of which is *Cylindrocarpon candidum*, while in North America
N. coccinea var. *faginata* is usually isolated (Ehrlich, 1934). *Nectria galligena* has
reportedly been isolated from necroses in Denmark (Thomsen *et al.*, 1949) and
in North America, where it has been shown capable of causing the necrosis
(Cotter, 1977).

Nectria coccinea has bright red, oval or subglobose perithecia $\frac{1}{4}$ to $\frac{1}{3}$ mm in diameter, scattered or in groups of 5-30 on a stroma. Its asci are cylindrical with an apical pore surrounded by a 'chitinoid' ring. They measure 75-100 μm and each contains eight colourless (becoming pale brown), elliptical, two-celled asco-spores that measure 12-15 x 5-6 μm. Colourless cylindrical microconidia and macroconidia are also formed. The microconidia measure 4-9 x 1.5-3 μm and the macroconidia, which are nought to seven-septate, measure 20-80 x 5-7 μm (Booth, 1959; Dennis, 1968).

Other fungi soon invade the wood beneath the dead bark, sometimes on live as well as on completely dead stems, and these, particularly white-rotting poly-pores, quickly rot the trunk and often lead to snap (Shigo, 1964; Thomsen *et al.*, 1949; Parker, 1974*a*; Perrin, 1977). Hence at this stage the disease is sometimes called 'beech snap' (figure 57).

Suggested causes of beech bark disease   The cause of beech bark disease has been much debated. In North America Ehrlich (1934) concluded that the primary

Figure 57. Beech bark disease: in the final stages, secondary decay fungi have caused 'beech snap' (Forestry Commission)

cause of the disease was attack by *Nectria coccinea* var. *faginata*, following infestation by *Cryptococcus fagisuga*. In Ehrlich's experience, whenever the disease
appeared, both these organisms were present and in the absence of either, beech
bark disease failed to develop. The fungus could always be isolated from the
affected tissues and it could only attack tissues previously damaged by the insect.
These views have generally been accepted in Canada and the USA (Forbes *et al.*,
1965; Shigo, 1964) and their applicability to European beech stands has been
proposed by Houston *et al.* (1979).

The North American situation is more clear-cut than that in Europe, since it
involves a distinct front of invasion of the insect which overshadows local
variations in disease development. The insect was accidentally introduced from
Europe around 1890 to the eastern seaboard. The fungus which appears in its
wake is of unknown geographic origin. In Europe, where both insect and fungus
are endemic, their presence in diseased stands is sometimes no more obvious a
cause of disease than are abiotic factors such as drought and extreme frost. Some
European workers (for example, Perrin, 1977; Parker, 1974*b*; Houston *et al.*,
1979) have confirmed the insect–*Nectria* association while others have variously
favoured the fungus without the insect, the insect without the fungus and abiotic
factors as primary causes.

Ehrlich (1934) found that *N. coccinea* var. *faginata* could cause the disease in
the absence of the insect if artificially introduced into bark by wound-inoculation.
He suggested that the role of the insect was limited to producing wounds through
which fungal entry could occur. However, it seems likely that only small lesions
were produced in his experiments. Small, rapidly delimited lesions were produced
in inoculation experiments by Leibundgut and Frick (1943) with *N. coccinea* on
European beech and similar results were obtained by Parker (1974*b*) and Perrin
(1979) in their inoculation of young trees. Zycha (1951*a*) cited the results of
Leibundgut and Frick and suggested that *N. coccinea* was merely one of a
variety of saprophytic colonists of lesions produced not by any organism (save
possibly a virus) but by drought or extreme frost. His evidence for this abiotic
origin of the lesions was the correlation between the timing of their appearance
and the occurrence of the abnormal weather conditions (Zycha 1951*a*, *b*, 1959).
Schwerdtfeger (1963) and Peace and Murray (1956) have also found correlations
between the disease and extremes of weather, thus supporting Zycha's view that
the beech coccus and *N. coccinea* are secondary colonists and part of a succession
that finally includes the white rot fungi that cause decay of the wood. Dimitri
(1967) and Paucke (1968) have lent support to the 'abiotic theory' by the artificial induction of necroses through the application of extreme heat or cold.

Other factors thought to be important have included sunscorch (Leibundgut
and Frick, 1943), shallowness of the soil and neglected thinning (Peace, 1955)
and predisposition of the trees by lime-induced chlorosis (Day, 1946). Another
factor may be the age of the crop, several authors (Leibundgut and Frick, 1943;
Zycha, 1951*b*; Peace, 1955) having found that most damage occurs in older trees.
Perrin (1979) was able to produce undelimited, exuding lesions only on older

trees following wound inoculation with *N. coccinea*. Ehrlich (1934), on the other hand, found trees of all ages to be susceptible in North America, while in Britain severe outbreaks have occurred from the 1960s onwards on pole-stage crops (Parker, 1974*a*).

Combinations of *C. fagisuga* and/or *Nectria* together with abiotic or unknown factors have been suggested by other authors. Thus, Lyr (1967) found that the fungus could produce typical beech bark disease on beech logs, but much more effectively at 15–25°C than at 3–5°C, this effect being largely attributable to water stress at the high temperature. Rhumbler (1922) claimed that the insect and the *Nectria* (then included in *N. ditissima*), together with wood boring insects, were both involved, but that the first stage in disease development was a slime-flux of unknown origin.

The insect on its own has been regarded as capable of causing death of the entire tree (Hartig, 1878) or extensive bark necrosis (Kunkel, 1968) and this idea was supported by Braun (1976, 1977) who described a process whereby the peculiar anatomical structure of beech bark leads to the progressive development of necrosis following initial, rather superficial, damage by the insect. Braun suggested that *N. coccinea* was not essential in this necrotic breakdown of the tissues, but could accelerate the process.

The above views on the etiology of beech bark disease seem largely contradictory, but there is some evidence that they all possess some measure of validity. Lonsdale (1980*a*) found that wound inoculation of pole stage beech with *N. coccinea* resulted in extensive necrosis only when a heavy coccus infestation was present. He also found typical *Nectria* lesions on drought-stressed older trees which had little or no insect infestation. And on young insect-infested trees he found a positive correlation between the incidence of sap exudation and the presence of chalky soil conditions (Lonsdale, 1980*b*). From these data Lonsdale suggested that the invasive ability of *N. coccinea* depended largely on stress in the host and that heavy coccus infestation, drought and nutritional disorders were examples of potentially interchangeable stress factors. He pointed out that Hartig (1900) had long ago observed the role of the coccus in increasing the rate of invasion of bark tissues by '*N. ditissima*', the taxon which then included *N. coccinea*. Conditions under which one source of stress predominated would clearly favour the emergence of an incomplete understanding of etiology. However, the concept of variable etiology may raise questions about the integrity of 'beech bark disease'. The restriction of that name to the *Cryptococcus-Nectria* complex has indeed been adopted by Perrin (1980*a*).

Losses caused   In North America, beech bark disease has sometimes killed more than half the trees (Ehrlich, 1934) and many of the remaining stems have been made almost useless (Shigo, 1963). Similar heavy losses have sometimes been recorded in Europe (Thomsen *et al.*, 1949).

Control   Infestation of stems by *C. fagisuga* can be controlled by physical removal (for example, scrubbing) or by insecticide sprays (tar-oil winter wash in December to January or diazinon in May or November). There is some evidence that this may quite rapidly reduce susceptibility to the formation of *Nectria* lesions (Perrin, 1980*b*). As far as forest trees are concerned, these controls are uneconomic and further work is needed before rational control measures can be worked out. At present it can only be recommended that salvage fellings of infected trees should be made quickly before rot fungi can enter and destroy the wood.

DECAY FUNGI

Many decay fungi affect beech. *Bjerkandera adusta* (*Polyporus adustus*) is common on trees damaged by beech bark disease. It causes a white rot which breaks up the stem and so leads to the syndrome called 'beech snap'. *Ganoderma applanatum* and *G. adspersum* both give rise to a butt and branch rot of over-mature beeches. Another *Ganoderma* sp., *G. pfeifferi*, may decay roots, stems and branches and kill the whole tree. *Pleurotus ostreatus* (the oyster mushroom) may also cause extensive decay of stems and branches, while *Meripilus giganteus* (*Polyporus giganteus*) decays and kills the smaller roots. The ascomycete *Ustulina deusta* rots the stem base and major roots, which often leads to windblow. These fungi are described in chapter 19.

MISCELLANEOUS DISEASES

Spring frost damage
Beech leaves are sometimes destroyed by spring frosts, and the foliage of trees near the coast may also be scorched by salt-laden gales.

Sunscorch
Like other thin-barked trees, beeches may be affected by sun scorch, which causes the death of areas of bark on the south-facing sides of the trunks.

REFERENCES

Allescher, A. (1903). *Die Pilze Deutschlands, Oesterreichs und der Schweiz*, 7 Abt., Kummer, Leipzig
Booth, C. (1959). *Studies of Pyrenomycetes: IV. Nectria (Part 1)*, Mycol. Pap., no. 73, 115 pp.
Braun, H. J. (1976). Das Rindensterben der Buch, *Fagus sylvatica* L., verursacht durch die Buchenschildlaus *Cryptococcus fagi* Bär. I. Die Anatomie der Buchenrinde als Basis-Ursache. *Eur. J. For. Path.*, 6, 136–46
Braun, H. J. (1977). Das Rindensterben der Buche, *Fagus sylvatica* L., verursacht durch die Buchenschildlaus *Cryptococcus fagi* Bar. II. Ablauf der Krankheit. *Eur. J. For. Path.*, 7, 76–93
Brown, J. M. B. (1953). *Studies in British Beechwoods*, Bull. For. Comm, Lond., no 20, iv, 100 pp.

Burchill, R. T. (1978). In D. M. Spencer (Ed.), *The Powdery Mildews*, Academic Press, London

Cotter, H. van T. (1977). *Beech Bark Disease: Fungi and Other Associated Organisms*. M. S. Thesis, University of New Hampshire, 138 pp.

Day, W. R. (1946). The pathology of beech on chalk soils. *Q. Jl. For.*, 40, 72–86

Dennis, R. W. G. (1968). *British Ascomycetes*, J. Cramer, Lehre

Dimitri, L. (1967). Untersuchungen über die Ätiologie des 'Rindensterbens' der Buche. *Forstwiss. ZentBl.*, 257–76

Ehrlich, J. (1934). The beech bark disease, a *Nectria* disease of *Fagus* following *Cryptococcus fagi* (Baer). *Can. J. Res.*, 10, 593–692

Fitzpatrick, H. M. (1930). *The Lower Fungi*, McGraw-hill, New York and London

Forbes, R. S., Stone, G. L. and Moran, G. V. (1965). The beech disease in the Maritime Provinces. *Bi-mon. Prog. Rep. Div. For. Biol., Ottawa*, 21, 1

Grove, W. B. (1937). *British Stem- and Leaf-Fungi (Coelomycetes)*, vol. 2, Cambridge University Press, Cambridge

Györfi, J. (1957). Az erdei fák rácos niegbetegedései. *Erdész. Kutat.*, 1–2; 83–94; abstract in *Rev. appl. Mycol.*, 37, 559, 1958

Hartig, R. (1878). Die krebsartigen Krankheiten der Rotbuche. *Z. Forst-und Jagdwesen*, 9, 377–83

Hartig, R. (1880). Die Buchen-Wolllaus, *Chermes fagi* Kltb. In *Untersuchungen aus dem forstbotanischen Institut zu München*. *I*, Springer, Berlin, pp. 156–62

Hartig, R. (1900). *Lehrbuch der Pflanzenkrankheiten*, 3rd ed., Springer, Berlin

Houston, D. R., Parker, E. J., Perrin, R. and Lang, K. J. (1979). Beech bark disease: a comparison of the disease in North America, Great Britain, France and Germany. *Eur. J. For. Path.*, 9, 199–211

Kunkel, H. (1968). Untersuchungen über die Buchenwollschildlaus *Cryptococcus fagi* (Baer.) (Insecta, Coccina), einen Vertreter der Rinden parenchymsauger. *Z. Ang. Ent.*, 61, 373–80

Langner, W. (1936). Untersuchungen über Lärchen-, Apfel- und Buchenkrebs. *Phytopath. Z.*, 9, 111–45

Leibundgut, H. and Frick, L. (1943). Eine Buchenkrankheit im schweizerischen Mitteland. *Schweiz. Z. Forstw.*, 94, 297–306

Lies, E. (1980). La dépérissement du hêtre au Grand-Duché de Luxembourg. *Ann. Sci. forest.*, 94, 297–306

Lonsdale, D. (1980a). *Nectria* infection of beech bark in relation to infestation by *Cryptococcus fagisuga* Lind. *Eur. J. For. Path.*, 10, 161–8

Lonsdale, D. (1980b). *Nectria coccinia* infection of beech: variations in disease in relation to predisposing factors. *Ann. Sci. forest.*, 37, 307–17

Lonsdale, D. and Pratt, J. E. (1981). Some aspects of the growth of beech trees and the incidence of beech bark disease on chalk soils. *Forestry*, 54, 183–95

Lyr, H. (1967). Über die Ursachen der Buchenrindennekrose (beech bark disease). *Arch. Forstw.*, 16, 803–7

Manshard, E. (1927). Der Buchenkeimlingspilz *Phytophthora omnivora* de Bary und seine Bekämpfung. *Forstarchiv*, 3, 84–6

Moore, W. C. (1959). *British Parasitic Fungi*, Cambridge University Press, Cambridge

Parker, E. J. (1974a). *Beech Bark Disease*, Forest Rec., Lond., no. 96

Parker, E. J. (1974b). Some investigations with beech bark disease *Nectria* in southern England. *Eur. J. For. Path.*, 5, 118–24

Paucke, H. (1968). Frostungen an Buchen zur Unduktion von Rindennekrosen. *Arch. Forstw.*, 17, 565–70

Peace, T. R. (1955). Forest pathology. *Rep, Forest Res., Lond., 1954*, pp. 31–3

Peace, T. R. (1962). *Pathology of Trees and Shrubs*, Clarendon Press, Oxford

Peace, T. R. and Murray, J. S. (1956). Forest pathology. *Rep. Forest Res., Lond., 1955*, pp. 52–7

Perrin, R. (1977). Le dépérissement du hêtre. *Rev. for. fr.*, 29, 100–129

Perrin, R. (1979). Contribution à la connaissance de l'étiologie de la maladie de l'écorce du hêtre. I. Etat sanitaire des hêtraies françaises. Role de *Nectria coccinea* (Pers. ex Fries) Fries. *Eur. J. For. Path.*, 9, 148–66

Perrin, R. (1980a). Les infections chez le hêtre. *Rev. for. fr.*, 32, 269–78

Perrin, R. (1980*b*). Contribution à la connaissance de l'étiologie de la maladie de l'écorce du hêtre. II. Etude experimentale de l'association *Cryptococcus fagisuga* Lind-*Nectria coccinea* (Pers. ex Fries) Fries. Rôle respectif des deux organismes. *Ann. Sci. forest.*, **37**, 319-31

Piraux, A. (1980). Observations relatives à la maladie de l'écorce du hêtre dans les Ardennes belges. Bilan d'une epidemie. *Ann. Sci. forest*, **37**, 349-56

Rhumbler, L. (1922). In Nusslin, O. and Rhumbler, L., Die Buchen-Wollschildlaus (*Coccus* [*Cryptococcus*] *fagi*) Bärenspr, in *Forstinsektenkunde*, Paul Paray, Berlin, pp. 125-39

Ritschl, A. (1937). Untersuchungen über *Gloeosproium fagicolum* Passerini, den Erreger der Blattfleckenkrankheit der Buche. *Z. PflKrankh.*, **47**, 486-91

Schütt, P. and Lang, K. J. (1980). Buchen-Rindennekrose, *Waldschutz-Merkblatt*, no. 1, Paul Paray, Hamburg and Berlin

Schwerdtfeger, F. (1963). Eine wetterbedingte Baumkrankheit. *Die Umschau in Wissenschaft und Technik.*, **15**, 476-8

Shigo, A. L. (1963). *Beech Bark Disease*, U. S. Dep. Agric. Forest Service For. Pest Leafl., 75, 8 pp.

Shigo, A. L. (1964). Organism interactions in the beech bark disease. *Phytopathology*, **54**, 263-69

Szántó, I. (1948). A Bükkfa rákja mint éghajlati betegség. *Erdész. Kisérl.*, **48**, 10-31; abstract in *Rev. appl. Mycol.*, **29**, 234, 1950

Thomsen, M. Buchwald, N. F. and Hauberg, P. A. (1949). *Angreb af* Cryptococcus fagi, Nectria galligena, *og andre parasiter paa bøg i Danmark 1939-43*, Kendrup and Wunsch, København

Zycha, H. (1951*a*). Das Rindensterben der Buche. *Phytopath. Z.*, 444-61

Zycha, H. (1951*b*). Das Buchensterben Ursache und Prognose. *SchReihe forstl. Fak. Univ. Gottingen*, 2, 72-8

Zycha, H. (1959). Stand unserer Kenntnis vam Rindensterben der Buche. *Allg. Forstz.*, **14**, 786-9

12 Diseases of ash (*Fraxinus* spp.), birch (*Betula* spp.) and alder (*Alnus* spp.)

ASH (*Fraxinus* SPP.)
  NURSERY AND POST-NURSERY DISEASES
    LEAF DISEASES
      The powdery mildew *Phyllactinia corylea*
      Minor leaf spots caused by *Phyllosticta fraxinicola* and *Fusicladium fraxini*
    DISEASES OF BARK AND SHOOTS
      The violet root-rot fungus *Helicobasidium purpureum*
      Bacterial canker caused by *Pseudomonas savastanoi* **f. sp.** *fraxini*
      Fungal cankers caused by *Nectria galligena*
      Minor cankers associated with *Phomopsis* **spp. and** *Hysterographium fraxini*
    VIRUS DISEASES
    DECAY FUNGI
    MISCELLANEOUS DISORDERS
      Crown dieback
BIRCH (*Betula* SPP.)
  NURSERY DISEASES
    LEAF DISEASES
      The leaf rust *Melampsoridium betulinum*
    POST-NURSERY DISEASES
    LEAF DISEASES
      Leaf spot caused by *Taphrina betulae*
      Minor leaf spots caused by *Phyllosticta betulina, Gloeosporium betulae, G. betulinum, Marssonina betulae* and *Melanconium betulinum*
    DISEASES OF SHOOTS
      Witches' brooms caused by *Taphrina betulina*
      Black knot caused by *Plowrightia virgultorum*
    DISEASES OF FRUITS AND SEEDS
    VIRUS DISEASES
      Cherry leaf roll virus and 'flamy' birch
    DECAY FUNGI
    MISCELLANEOUS DISORDERS
      Summer heat and drought

ALDER (*Alnus* SPP.)

 NURSERY AND POST-NURSERY DISEASES

  LEAF DISEASES

   The powdery mildew *Phyllactinia corylea*

   Taphrina **spp. on leaves**

   The alder rust *Melampsoridium hiratsukanum*

  DISEASES OF INFLORESCENCES' FRUITS AND SEEDS

   Catkin blight caused by *Taphrina amentorum*

  DECAY FUNGI

  MISCELLANEOUS DISORDERS

   Dieback of unknown cause

REFERENCES

ASH (*FRAXINUS* SPP.)

The common ash, *Fraxinus excelsior*, is widespread throughout Britain, especially on calcareous sites. The manna ash, *F. ornus*, from Southern Europe and Western Asia, is often planted in parks and gardens, in which a few other introduced ash species may also sometimes be found.

NURSERY AND POST-NURSERY DISEASES

LEAF DISEASES

The powdery mildew *Phyllactinia corylea*

The powdery mildew *Phyllactinia corylea* sometimes produces its sparse mycelium on ash leaves, as well as on those of hazel (under which it is described in chapter 18), and other trees and shrubs.

Minor leaf spots caused by *Phyllosticta fraxinicola* Curr. and *Fusicladium fraxini* Aderh.

Phyllosticta fraxinicola has been recorded as fairly widespread and common on ash as a cause of rounded or irregularly oval brown leaf spots with a reddish-brown margin. A few black pycnidia occur on the spots on the upper leaf surface, and may contain mostly ellipsoid, colourless, one-celled spores measuring 4–6 x 1.5 μm (Grove, 1935).

Fusicladium fraxini was found in 1966 on living leaves of *Fraxinus excelsior* at Kilmun, near Dunoon, Argyll (Phillips, 1967). The diseased leaves showed purple or violet areas that later turned brown and necrotic. The two-celled spores measured 15–26 x 5 μm (Batko, 1974).

DISEASES OF BARK AND SHOOTS

The violet root-rot fungus *Helicobasidium purpureum*

The perfect stage of the violet root rot fungus, *Helicobasidium purpureum*, has been found on the bark of ash (Moore, 1959). This fungus is further considered in chapter 3.

Bacterial canker caused by *Pseudomonas savastanoi* (Smith) Stevens f. sp. *fraxini* Dowson

Bacterial canker, which may greatly reduce the value of the wood, is the most damaging disease of ash in Britain, and it has been recorded in almost the whole of Europe, including the USSR (anon, 1966).

The symptoms of the disease have been described in detail by Dowson (1957), Riggenback (1956), and van Vliet (1931). The cankers (plate 31) are very variable in size, from about 0.5 cm to over 30 cm across (Oganova, 1957), with the largest cankers, which may persist for many years, on the older branches and occasionally on the trunks.

Cankers are first noticeable as small longitudinal cracks. These may progress only to form small rough protuberances, but usually widen and develop into sunken cavities. The affected tissues are at first filled with layers of corky tissue parallel to the cambium, but in time the corky material is extruded, and replaced by mucillage containing bacteria. The edges of the cankers are raised, rough and irregular, and often yellowish or reddish in colour.

The bacterium present in the cankers, *Pseudomonas savastanoi* f. sp. *fraxini*, is morphologically and biochemically indistinguishable from *P. savastanoi* (Smith) Stevens, which is well known as a parasite of olive. The form species *fraxini*, however, will generally attack only species of *Fraxinus*, and (by inoculation) has been induced to form tubercles on a few related plants such as *Forsythia* (Dowson, 1957). It forms gram negative motile rods that measure 0.4-0.8 x 1.2-3.3 μm and bear 1-4 polar flagella. It produces a green fluorescent pigment in culture (Breed *et al.*, 1948).

Various fungi have been found associated with bacterial cankers. Thus Riggenbach (1956) in Switzerland found *Fusarium lateritium*, *Pleospora herbarum* and *Plenodomus rabenhorstii* as well as *Pseudomonas savastanoi*; in the presence of *P. savastanoi*, the growth of the fungi, particularly *F. lateritium*, was stimulated. In the USSR Oganova (1957) isolated *Auricularia mesenterica* from rotting tissues in bacterial cankers. In Britain a species of *Nectria* often occurs with the bacteria in the larger cankers, which Dowson (1957) considered could not be produced by the bacteria alone.

In many countries, both in Europe and North America, however, a distinct fungal canker of many broadleaved trees (including ash), caused by *Nectria galligena*, also occurs. This is separately discussed below and in chapter 3.

According to Dowson (1957), *P. savastanoi* f. sp. *fraxini* enters young shoots through wounds caused by hailstones. It may also enter through leaf scars.

Škorić (1938) considered that the bacteria were spread by rain, and insects played no important part in dissemination. However, Oganova (1957) in the USSR and Tubeuf (1936) in Germany believed that the bark beetle *Leperisinus fraxini* (*Hylesinus fraxini*) damaged the trees and transmitted the disease.

So far ash canker seems to have caused greater loss on the mainland of Europe than in Britain. In Jugoslavia Škorić (1938) found that young trees affected by bacterial canker grew to no more than 1 to 2 m. According to Tubeuf (1936) canker sometimes caused severe damage in Germany, where many diseased trees had to be felled.

Control   Little can be done to control bacterial canker of ash, though Oganova (1957) in the USSR recommended the cutting out of affected branches, and the complete removal of severely diseased trees. She also suggested that wounds should be avoided, and any found should be treated with an antiseptic. As she considered that *Leperisinus fraxini* played a part in the spread of the disease, she recommended the disinfection of the soil around the trees to kill bark beetles. These measures, apart from the removal of diseased trees when thinning, are not practicable on a forest scale.

Fungal canker caused by *Nectria galligena* Bres.
In the Netherlands van Vliet (1931) found two distinct types of canker on ash. The cankers of the first type were bacterial in origin, like those already described, and occurred on both trunks and branches. The second, caused by *Nectria galligena* var. *major* (the perithecia of which were often present on them) were verrucose, and occurred only on the trunks of young trees. The diseased cortex on these cankers became reddish brown. D'Oliveira (1939) in Portugal also found cankers of both bacterial and fungal origin, and on the latter found *Cylindrocarpon mali* or its variety *flavum*, the imperfect stages of *Nectria galligena* and its variety *major*, respectively. Similar bacterial and fungal cankers, the latter associated with *Nectria ditissima* or *N. galligena*, were described in Germany by Tubeuf (1936), who also found cankers, mainly on small shoots, caused by frost.

These cankers have been extensively studied on apple, especially in Europe and North America, and on many broadleaved trees, mainly in eastern North America. Characteristically, as the fungus in the cankers grows and causes damage when the tree is dormant and is delayed and partly overgrown by callus tissue in the growing season, the cankers show a target-like form. As these cankers occur (especially in North America) on a wide range of broadleaved trees, they are discussed further in chapter 3, and under *Malus* in chapter 18. Booth (1959) considered that the fungus on the ash cankers was *N. galligena* (from which the variety *major* was not separable). The fungus forms bright red perithecia, usually in groups of two to five, on a stroma. The two-celled, colourless ascospores may be oval, ellipsoid or spindle-shaped, and measure 14–22 x 6–9 μm.

Minor cankers associated with *Phomopsis* spp. and *Hysterographium fraxini* (Pers. ex Fr.) de Not.

Grove (1935) stated that *Phomopsis controversa* Trav. occurred as a saprophyte on dry branches of *Fraxinus excelsior*, while *P. scobina* von Höhn. was rather common in England and Scotland on twigs and leaf stalks of *F. excelsior* and *F. ornus*. He considered it likely, however, that these two *Phomopsis* species were one and the same fungus. Wehmeyer (1932) took the same view, regarding them as conidial stages of *Diaporthe eres* Nits.

The two fungi were studied in Scotland by Macdonald and Russell (1937), who concluded that they should be regarded as two species, both on their cultural characteristics and their pathogenicity. They found that *P. controversa* grew rapidly in culture to form a white woolly mycelium, produced no pycnidia when inoculated into plum and apple fruits, and scarcely entered the tissues when inoculated into ash twigs. Its colourless a-spores measured 5.5–9 x 1.5–4 μm, and no b-spores were to be found. There were dark zone lines round the pycnidia.

P. scobina grew slowly in culture to form a white, sometimes later pinkish, tufted mycelium, produced many pycnidia when inoculated into plum and apple fruits, and entered the tissues when inoculated into ash twigs. Colourless a and b-spores occured, the a-spores measuring 7–13 x 2–4 μm and the b-spores measuring 16.5–25 x 1 μm. No zone lines were present round the pycnidia.

Parallel studies in the field indicated that *P. scobina* could cause lesions up to 25 cm long completely encircling large branches, and many pycnidia occurred in the brown sunken bark, which cracked and fell away on older lesions. Young twigs might be induced to form small witches' brooms.

P. controversa was generally only weakly parasitic. It sometimes killed small twigs but on larger branches and trunks it was associated only with small cankers which soon ceased to develop.

Hysterographium fraxini is known in Britain though it appears to be rare except in West Wales (Dennis, 1968). It is normally only a saprophyte on the bark of ash and sometimes other deciduous trees and shrubs, but Zogg (1943) concluded that in Switzerland in damp conditions and on waterlogged soils it could act as a wound parasite. It could then cause elongated, canker-like depressions in stems and branches, and produce dieback of shoots, resulting in considerable damage, though without reinfection the lesions did not persist from year to year.

The black, rather elliptical hysterothecia occur on the lesions, and open by a slit. The club-shaped asci contain up to eight ascospores. These are ellipsoid, golden or chestnut-brown, divided into many cells by about five to ten transverse and one to three longitudinal septa, often constricted at the central septum, and measuring 30–50 x 12–20 μm (Dennis, 1968).

VIRUS DISEASES

Two virus diseases of the foliage of ash have been recorded in Britain (Cooper,

1979). In the first the symptoms are erratic, and may be only partially expressed. They show as a chlorotic vein banding, oak leaf patterns and chevrons, or a mild mottle. Arabis mosaic virus was found in leaves with symptoms, but may not be the cause of the disease.

In the second of these diseases, which has been found on root stocks of *Fraxinus americana* and *F. excelsior*, affected leaves are distorted, and show chlorotic ring and line patterns. In this case, Arabis mosaic virus was isolated and produced the symptoms of the disorder in inoculated plants.

DECAY FUNGI

Of the rot fungi, the commonest on ash is *Inonotus hispidus*, and *Daldinia concentrica* often causes a branch rot. *Armillaria mellea* may also attack ash, and *Fomitopsis cytisina* (*Fomes fraxineua*) has been found on it causing a basal rot. These rot fungi are further discussed in chapter 19.

MISCELLANEOUS DISORDERS

Older ash trees, especially on clay soils, frequently show severe dieback of the crowns. The cause of this damage is unknown, though it is suspected that scale insects may be implicated.

BIRCH (*BETULA* SPP.)

Of the three birches native to Britain, one, *Betula nana*, is only a shrub that grows locally on moorlands in the Scottish mountains. The other two, *B. pubescens* and *B. pendula*, both occur commonly throughout the country, the former generally on damper soils, the latter on the drier ones. A good many introduced birches are occasionally to be found in parks and gardens, and the variety 'Dalecarlica' of *B. pendula* is quite common.

NURSERY DISEASES

LEAF DISEASES

The leaf rust *Melampsoridium betulinum* (Fr.) Kleb.
The leaf rust *Melampsoridium betulinum* occurs widely throughout Europe, Asia and North America. It is common on the leaves of birches of any age, but it causes significant damage only on nursery stock and occasionally on young natural regeneration. In Britain it is known mainly on *Betula pubescens* and *B. pendula*, but it has been found also on various introduced species, though Peace (1962) observed *B. ermanii* and *B. utilis* to be very resistant.

The orange uredosori appear in late summer as very small orange pustules up to about 0.5 mm in diameter on the undersides of the leaves, showing as pale yellow spots on the upper leaf surfaces. The uredospores are ellipsoidal or sub-clavate, with a spiny wall, and measure 22-38 x 9-15 μm. They are formed in long chains (Roll-Hansen and Roll-Hansen, 1980). Orange to yellow-brown teleutosori appear on the undersides of the leaves in late summer and early autumn, and may cover the whole leaf surface. The prismatic teleutospores form below the epidermis, have smooth walls, and measure 30-52 x 8-16 μm (Wilson and Henderson, 1966).

There is evidence that the fungus may overwinter in birch buds (D'Oliveira and Pimento, 1953) and in fallen leaves, on which new uredosori may arise in the spring to reinfect the young expanding leaves (Weir and Hubert, 1918).

The spermogonia and aecidia, which occur on larch, appear to be rare, and the fungus can certainly be found on birches far from any affected larches.

Control meaures for birch rust have not been worked out. If the disease should prove troublesome in the nursery, general control measures could be applied, including the clearing up and destruction of any affected fallen leaves and the application of one of the fungicides known to be effective against the other leaf rusts.

POST-NURSERY DISEASES

LEAF DISEASES

Leaf spot caused by *Taphrina betulae* (Fuckel) Johansen
Taphrina betulae is known as the cause of pale green to yellow, later reddish-brown leaf spots on birch over much of northern Europe (Mix, 1949), including Scotland (Henderson, 1954). The spots may be up to 1 cm across, and in mid-summer bear a layer of asci that may be on either or both leaf surfaces. The asci measure 20-24 x 11-13 μm, and contain eight elliptical or ovate ascospores. These measure 4-6 x 3.5-5 μm, but may bud in the ascus to produce many smaller spores. The fungus has been recorded on *B. pendula* and *B. pubescens*, and in other parts of Europe also on *B. intermedia, B. medwediewi* and *B. turkestanica* (Mix, 1949).

A second species of *Taphrina, T. betulina* Rostrup, also attacks birch and fruits on its leaves. Since it also gives rise to witches' brooms, it is described below under diseases of shoots.

Minor leaf spots caused by *Phyllosticta betulina* Sacc., *Gloeosporium betulae* Fuckel, *G. betulinum* Westd., *Marssonina betulae* Magn. and *Melanconium betulinum* Schm. and Kunze
A number of fungi have been associated with leaf spots on birch. They have gen-

erally caused little damage, and in many cases little is known about their pathogenicity.

Grove (1935) reported that the black, globose pycnidia of *Phyllosticta betulina* were not uncommon in Britain scattered on living leaves of birch, usually on the upper side. The colourless, one-celled spores measured about 4–7(–10) x 1–2.5 μm. Affected leaves sometimes became brown and withered.

Grove (1935) also described two species of *Gloeosporium* associated with leaf spots on birch in Britain and throughout the rest of Europe. *G. betulae* produced pustules on spots on the upper or on both sides of the leaves. Its colourless, one-celled spores measured 13–16 x 2 μm. *G. betulinum* formed rounded brown spots on both sides of the leaves, but its small pustules were on the undersides only. Its colourless, one-celled spores generally measured 4–10 x 2.5 μm. Of these two fungi, *G. betulinum* appears to be common on birch leaves, and in some seasons may cause premature defoliation moving upwards from the base of the tree (Young and Strouts, personal communication).

Marssonina betulae has been found forming pustules on irregular or stellate, brownish-black spots with a dentate margin (Grove, 1937). The colourless spores, which are finally two-celled, and then occasionally constricted at the septum, measure 17–22 x 5–6 μm (Batko, unpublished).

Melanconium betulinum, which was recorded by Grove (1937) on dead birch bark, was reported on birch leaves by Redfern *et al.* (1973). The dark, smoky-brown, one-celled, narrowly ellipsoid or almond-shaped spores measure 13–18 x 5–6.5 μm. *M. betulinum* is an imperfect state of *Melanconis stilbostoma* (Fr.) Tul.

DISEASES OF SHOOTS

Witches brooms caused by *Taphrina betulina* Rostr. (*T. turgida* Sadeb.)
Witches' brooms, formed of dense masses of adventitious twigs (figures 58, 59), are very common in Britain on *Betula pubescens* and *B. pendula* (especially the former), and occur elsewhere in Europe also on *B. nana*, *B. aurata*, *B. carpatica* and *B. intermedia* (Henderson, 1954; Mix, 1949). They are caused by the fungus *Taphrina betulina* (though very similar brooms are caused by the mite *Eryophes rudis*). The leaves on the affected shoots may become yellow, and on their undersides they bear a layer of asci that measure 41–75 x 15–21 μm. The ascospores, which measure 4.5–6.5 x 4–5.5 μm, quickly bud in the ascus to produce many smaller spores. The fungus becomes perennial in the brooms. The infected twigs are susceptible to frost, and many of them may be destroyed in autumn and winter (Blomfield, 1924; Henderson, 1954).

Black knot caused by *Plowrightia virgultorum* (Fr.) Sacc.
Massee (1914) described growths on birch somewhat like witches' brooms but associated with the fungus *Plowrightia virgultorum*. Small black lesions formed round the points of infection, sometimes girdling the stems. Below the girdled

Plate 1. Spring frost damage

Plate 2. Lightning damage

Plate 3. Damage by fluorine

Plate 4. Grey mould (*Botrytis cinerea*)

For fuller captions, see pp. xiii–xv.

Plate 5. Nitrogen deficiency

Plate 6. Phosphorus deficiency

Plate 7. Potassium deficiency

Plate 8. Healthy plant
(cf. plates 5, 6, 7)

Plate 9. Damage by the herbicide chlorthiamid

Plate 10. Damage by the herbicide glyphosate

Plate 11. Wetwood and slime flux

Plate 12. Aecidia of *Peridermium pini*

Plate 13. *Thelephora terrestris*

Plate 14. Coral spot (*Nectria cinnabarina*)

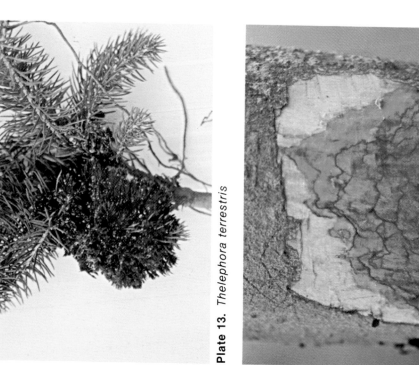

Plate 15. Damage by *Phytophthora cactorum*

Plate 16. Top dying of Norway spruce

Plate 18. *Heterobasidion annosum*

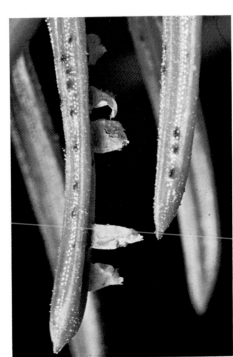

Plate 20. Spermogonia and aecidia of *Chrysomyxa rhododendri*

Plate 17. Fruit bodies of *Armillaria mellea*

Plate 19. *Chrysomyxa abietis*

Plate 21. *Cucurbitaria piceae* on spruce

Plate 22. Perithecia of *Cucurbitaria piceae*

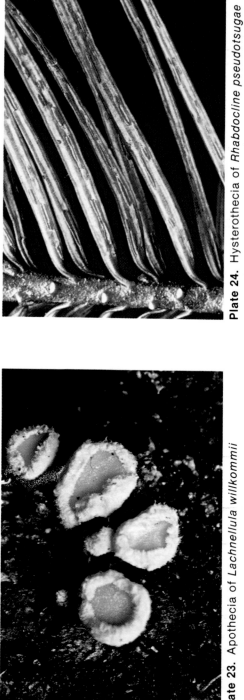

Plate 23. Apothecia of *Lachnellula willkommii*

Plate 24. Hysterothecia of *Rhabdocline pseudotsugae*

Plate 26. Tar spot (*Rhytisma acerinum*)

Plate 28. Poplar leaf blister

Plate 25. *Uncinula aceris*

Plate 27. Verticillium wilt: internal symptoms

Plate 29. Oak mildew

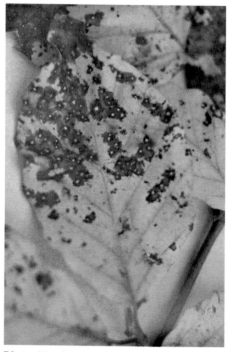

Plate 30. *Gloeosporium fagi:*
leaf spots on beech

Plate 31. Bacterial canker of ash

Plate 32. Sooty bark disease
of sycamore

Plate 33. Beech bark disease: 'tarry spots'

Plate 34. Beech bark disease: beech scale infestation

Plate 35. Beech bark disease: 'dimpling'

Plate 36. *Platychora ulmi* on elm

Plate 37. *Gremmeniella abietina* on pine

Plate 38. *Seiridium cardinale:* damage on *Cupressus*

Plate 39. Winter bronzing of *Thuja plicata*

Plate 40. *Didymascella thujina* on *Thuja plicata*

Plate 41. Symptoms
of Dutch elm disease

Plate 42. Dutch elm disease:
wilting of shoots

Plate 43. Anthracnose of London plane

Plate 44. *Sclerotinia laxa*
on *Prunus avium*

Plate 45. *Venturia tremulae* on *Populus*

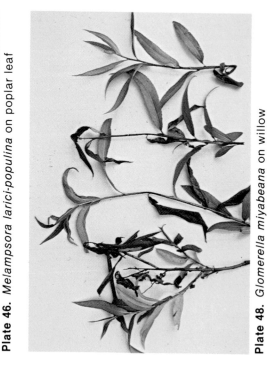

Plate 46. *Melampsora larici-populina* on poplar leaf

Plate 47. *Marssonina brunnea*: leaf spots on poplar

Plate 48. *Glomerella miyabeana* on willow

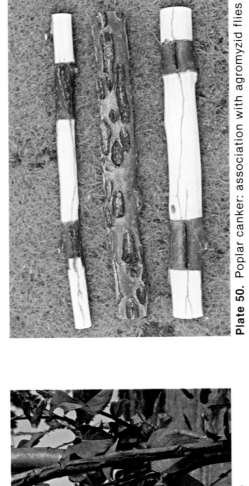

Plate 49. Poplar canker: wilting of foliage

Plate 50. Poplar canker: association with agromyzid flies

Plate 51. Box damaged by *Pseudonectria rousseliana*

Plate 52. *Podosphaera leucotricha* on apple bud

Plate 53. Watermark disease of willow: crown symptoms

Plate 54. Fireblight on *Sorbus aria*

Plate 55. Leaf curl on almond

Plate 56. Leaf blotch of horse chestnut

Plate 58. *Fomes fomentarius*

Plate 60. *Inonotus hispidus*

Plate 57. Watermark disease of willow: stain in wood

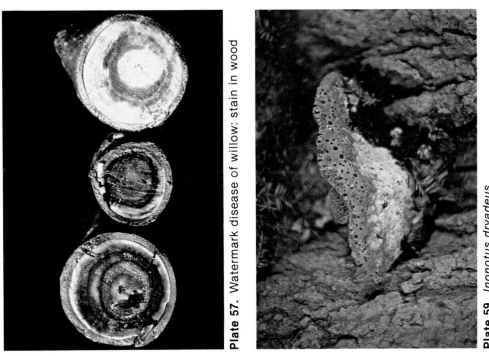

Plate 59. *Inonotus dryadeus*

Plate 61. *Ganoderma resinaceum*

Plate 62. *Phaeolus schweinitzii*

Plate 63. *Coriolus versicolor*

Plate 64. *Laetiporus sulphureus*

Figure 58. Witches' brooms on birch caused by *Taphrina betulina* (D.H. Phillips)

Figure 59. Witches' broom on birch caused by *Taphrina betulina* (D.H. Phillips)

point adventitious shoots like those of witches' brooms grew out. Some of these shoots were themselves killed and replaced by others. The fungus forms a black stroma on the branches, erumpent from the wood. The perithecia are embedded in the stroma, and contain eight-spored asci measuring 45–66 x 12 μm. The unequally two-celled, egg or club-shaped ascospores are colourless or greenish, and measure about 12 x 6 μm (Winter, 1887).

DISEASES OF FRUITS AND SEEDS

Batko (unpublished) found the minute discomycete *Ciboria betulae* (Woronin) White (*Sclerotinia betulae* Woronin) on fruits of birch.

VIRUS DISEASES

Cherry leaf roll virus (CLRV) and 'flamy' birch

Cherry leaf roll virus (CLRV), which has been found on *Prunus avium*, *Sambucus nigra* and other hosts (Cropley and Tomlinson, 1971), has been isolated from *Betula pendula* (*B. verrucosa*) by Cooper and Atkinson (1975). Schmelzer (1972) found the same virus on *B. pendula* in East Germany.

Cooper and Atkinson (who fully describe the virus) found that birches affected by the virus become bushy, with small leaves on affected branches. From July onwards the leaves showed mild chlorotic blotches, rings and line patterns. These symptoms became more clearly defined with time and by October the lines and rings were yellow. The virus seems to be transmitted by seed, and perhaps by pollen.

A stem grooving and pitting and figuring of wood known as 'flamy' birch (Gardiner, 1965) is also thought to be caused by a virus (Cooper 1979).

DECAY FUNGI

Birch is one of the least durable of woods, and the bracket fungus *Piptoporus betulinus* (*Polyporus betulinus*) is common on standing trees. Birch is very frequently attacked and killed by the root rot fungus *Armillaria mellea* and sometimes by *Heterobasidion annosum* (*Fomes annosus*). Other decay fungi, including *Fomes fomentarius* and *Inonotus obliquus*, may also affect it. These fungi are described in chapter 19.

MISCELLANEOUS DISORDERS

Summer heat and drought

Birch is resistant to winter cold and frost and tolerates a wide range of site conditions. However, it may be badly affected (though less so than beech) by summer heat and drought, and in Britain was the first tree to show conspicuous damage in the phenomenally hot dry summers of 1975 and 1976. Affected trees showed varying degrees of premature browning and defoliation, death of bark with dark exudations, and ultimately death.

ALDER (*ALNUS* SPP.)

The native common alder, *Alnus glutinosa*, is widespread in damp woods and by lakes and streams throughout Britain. The introduced grey alder, *A. incana*, is sometimes planted, especially in small woods in Scotland and on reclaimed tips. The American red alder. *A. rubra*, is occasionally found in parks and gardens, and so far to a very limited extent in forest plantings.

NURSERY AND POST-NURSERY DISEASES

LEAF DISEASES

The powdery mildew *Phyllactinia corylea*
The powdery mildew *Phyllactinia corylea* sometimes forms a sparse mycelium on alder leaves. It is commoner, however, on hazel under which it is described in chapter 18.

Taphrina spp. on leaves
Alders are attacked by three species of *Taphrina*, two of which, *T. tosquinetii* and *T. sadebeckii*, affect the leaves, the first and commonest causing a distortion of the leaves and the second a leaf spot. The third is *T. amentorum*, which gives rise to outgrowths on the catkin scales.

Leaf curl caused by Taphrina tosquinetii (Westend.) P. Magn. (T. alnitorqua Tul., Exoascus alnitorquus (Tul.) Sadeb.) The ascomycete *Taphrina tosquinetii* causes a distortion of the leaves (usually called leaf curl) and of the twigs of *Alnus glutinosa* in Britain, and of other species of alder, including *A. crispa* and *A. hybrida*, in other parts parts of Europe (Mix, 1949).

Leaf curl as it affects alders in Britain has been described by Henderson (1954), and Bond (1956). The fungus is most common on sucker shoots at the bases of trees, though sometimes on trees in crowded, damp conditions, twigs in the crown up to 20 feet (6.5 metres) from the ground may also be affected.

The cortex of diseased shoots is thick and wrinkled, and on these affected shoots the leaves, which are late in unfolding, at first appear reddish and crumpled. Parts of an affected leaf may become swollen, or the whole leaf may become enlarged, thickened, brittle and distorted. A bloom of developing asci appears on the swollen areas on one or both leaf surfaces.

The asci of the fungus are more or less cylindrical, and arise from basal cells which form below the cuticle and partly between the epidermal cells. They measure 17–40 x 7–13 μm (Mix, 1949). At first they contain eight ovate or elliptical, colourless ascospores which measure 2.5–5.5 x 2.5–5 μm. The ascospores may be discharged through an apical slit or may bud to form many smaller cells which are passively liberated (Bond, 1956).

The infected shoots may die after one or two seasons, but may persist for as long as ten or twelve years.

Leaf spot caused by Taphrina sadebeckii Johansen   *Taphrina sadebeckii* causes bright yellow, unthickened spots up to 1 cm across on the leaves of *Alnus glutinosa* (Henderson, 1954). Elsewhere in Europe and in Japan it occurs also on *A. hirsuta* and its variety *sibirica*, and on *A. rugosa* (Mix, 1949).

The cylindrical asci arise from the subcuticular mycelium and measure 17–65 x 10–21 μm. They contain eight ovate or elliptical ascospores which measure 4–6 x 3.5–5 μm and often bud in the ascus (Mix, 1949).

The alder rust *Melampsoridium hiratsukanum* Ito
Melampsoridium hiratsukanum is a rust that has occasionally been found on *Alnus glutinosa*, *A. cordata* and *A. incana* in Scotland and Ireland (Wilson and Henderson, 1966). It occurs also in Japan and North America. The fungus is heteroecious, with the spermogonia and aecidia on *Larix* and the uredosori and teleutosori on *Alnus*. In Britain, however, it persists on *Alnus* alone, as the stages on *Larix* have not been found.

The uredosori form as small orange-yellow pustules up to 0.4 mm across on the undersides of the leaves, showing as reddish-yellow spots on the upper surface. The ovoid or ellipsoid uredospores measure 21–34 x 10–18 μm and are sparsely covered by minute spines. The small teleutosori, also on the undersides of the leaves, are up to 0.5 mm across, at first yellow, later darkening to blackish-brown. The teleutospores are prismatic or club-shaped, yellow, smooth-walled, and measure 32–45 x 10–16 μm (Wilson and Henderson, 1966). The fungus is not a cause of significant damage.

DISEASES OF INFLORESCENCES, FRUITS AND SEEDS

Catkin blight caused by *Taphrina amentorum* (Sadeb.) Rostrup (*T. alni-incanae* (Kühn.) Sadeb.)
Taphrina amentorum sometimes affects the female catkins of *Alnus glutinosa* and *A. incana* in Britain (Henderson, 1954), and elsewhere in Europe and in Japan and Alaska occurs also on *A. hirsuta*, *A. hybrida* and *A. rubra* (Mix, 1949). The fungus causes conspicuous, red, tongue-like outgrowths up to about 2 cm long and 0.5 cm wide to develop on the catkin scales (figure 60).

The cylindrical asci emerge from between the epidermal cells on both sides of the outgrowths. Mix (1949) found that the asci measured 26–53 x 10–23 μm.

Figure 60. Catkin blight of alder caused by *Taphrina amentorum* (R. Hartig)

Each contains eight colourless, ovate or elliptical ascospores. These measure 4.5–6 x 4–5 μm, but may bud in the ascus to form other smaller spores.

DECAY FUNGI

Probably the commonest cause of rot in standing alders is *Inonotus radiatus* (*Polyporus radiatus*).

MISCELLANEOUS DISORDERS

Dieback of unknown cause

Alders, especially *A. rubra*, but sometimes also *A. glutinosa*, may be affected by dieback. In Britain this disorder has not been investigated, though it is suspected that scale insects may be involved. In Hampshire such dieback of *A. rubra* followed an infestation by the willow scale (*Chionaspis salicis*), which had passed unobserved because it was rendered inconspicuous by algae and lichens (Young and Carter, unpublished). In Germany and Holland various fungi that appear to be at most weak parasites have been found associated with it (Truter, 1947).

REFERENCES

Anon (1966). *Pseudomonas savastanoi* var. *fraxini* (Brown) Dowson. *Distribu. Maps Pl. Dis.*, no. 134, 2nd ed.

Batko, S. (1974). Notes on new and rare fungi on forest trees in Britain. *Bull. Br. mycol. Soc.*, 8, 19–21

Blomfield, J. E. (1924). Witches-brooms. *J.R. micr. Soc., Lond.*, 1924, 190–94

Bond, T. E. T. (1956). Notes on *Taphrina. Trans. Br. mycol. Soc.*, 39, 60–66

Booth, C. (1959). Studies of Pyrenomycetes. IV. *Nectria* (Part 1). *Mycol. Pap.*, 73.

Breed, R. S., Murray, E. G. D. and Hitchins, A. P. (1948). In *Bergey's Manual of Determinative Bacteriology*, 6th ed., Williams and Wilkins, Baltimore

Cooper, J. I. (1979). *Virus Diseases of Trees and Shrubs*, Institute of Terrestrial Ecology, c/o Unit of Invertebrate Virology, Oxford

Cooper J. I. and Atkinson, M. A. (1975). Cherry leaf roll virus causing a disease of *Betula* spp. in the United Kingdom. *Forestry*, 48, 193–203

Cropley, R. and Tomlinson, J. A. (1971). *Cherry Leaf Roll Virus.* CMI/AAB Descr. Pl. Viruses, no. 80

Dennis, R. W. G. (1968). *British Ascomycetes*, J. Cramer, Lehre

D'Oliveira, A. L. B. and Pimento, A. A. L. (1953). Infecçöes latentes de *Melampsoridium betulinum* (Pers.) Kleb. em gomos de *Betula celtiberica* Rothm. et Vasc. *Estud. Inform Serv. flor. aqüíc. Portugal*, no. 9-C3, 3pp., abstract in *For. Abstr.*, 15, no. 2646

D'Oliveira, M. de L. (1939). Inoculacaões experimentais com o *Bacterium savastanoi* E. F. Smith e o *Bacterium savastanoi* var. *fraxini* N. A. Brown. *Agron. lusit.*, 1, 88–102

Dowson, W. J. (1957). *Plant Diseases Due to Bacteria*, 2nd ed., Cambridge University Press, Cambridge

Gardiner, A. S. (1965). 'Flamy' birch and its frequency in some highland populations. *Scott. For.*, 19, 180–84.

Grove, W. B. (1935). *British Stem- and Leaf-Fungi* (*Coelomycetes*), vol. 1, Cambridge University Press, Cambridge

Grove, W. B. (1937). *British Stem- and Leaf-Fungi* (*Coelomycetes*), vol. 2, Cambridge University Press, Cambridge

Henderson, D. M. (1954). The genus *Taphrina* in Scotland. *Notes from the Royal Botanic Garden, Edinburgh*, 21, 165–80

Macdonald, J. A. and Russell, J. R. (1937). *Phomopsis scobina* (Cke) v. Höhn. and *Phomopsis controversa* (Sacc.) Trav. on ash. *Trans. bot. Soc. Edinb.*, 32, 341–52

Massee, G. (1914). Black knot of birch. *Kew Bull.*, pp. 322–3

Mix, A. J. (1949). A monograph of the genus *Taphrina. Univ. Kansas Sci. Bull.*, 33, 3–167

Moore, W. C. (1959). *British Parasitic Fungi*, Cambridge University Press, Cambridge

Oganova, E. A. (1957). [On bacterial canker of ash]; abstract in *Rev. appl. Mycol.*, 38, p. 281, 1959

Peace, T. R. (1962). *Pathology of Trees and Shrubs*, Clarendon Press, Oxford

Phillips, D. H. (1967). Forest pathology. *Rep. Forest Res., Lond.*, 1967, 96–102

Redfern, D. B., Gregory, S. C. and Low, J. D. (1973). In 'Forest pathology'. *Rep. Forest Res., Lond.*, 1973, 102–3

Riggenbach, A. (1956). Untersuchungen über den Eschenkrebs. *Phytopath. Z.*, 27, 1–40

Roll-Hansen, F. and Roll-Hansen, H. (1980). Uridiniospore chains in *Melampsoridium betulinum. Eur. J. For. Path.*, 10, 382–4

Schmelzer, K. (1972). Das Kirschenblattroll-virus aus der Birke (*Betula pendula* Roth.). *Zentbl. Bakt. ParasitKde*, Abt. II, 127, 10–12

Škorić, V. (1938). Jasenov rak i njegov uzrocnik. *Ann. appl. for., Zagreb*, 6, 66–97

Truter, S. J. (1947). Een voorlopig onderzoek naar de insterving van *Alnus glutinosa* (L.) Gaertner, Thesis, University of Utrecht; abstract in *Rev. appl. Mycol.*, p. 576, 1947

Tubeuf, C. v. (1936). Tuberkulose, Krebs und Rindengrind der Eschen- (*Fraxinus*) Arten und die sie veranlassenden Bakterien, Nectria-pilze und Borkenkäfer. *Z. PflKrankh.*, 46, 449–83

Vliet, J. I. van (1931). *Esschenkankers en hun bouw.* Thesis, University of Utrecht; abstract in *Rev. appl. Mycol.*, 11, 12–13, 1932

Wehmeyer, L. E. (1932). The British species of the genus *Diaporthe* Nits. and its segregates. *Trans. Br. mycol. Soc.*, 17, 237–95

Weir, J. R. and Hubert, E. E. (1918). Notes on the overwintering of forest tree rusts. *Phytopathology*, 8, 55–9

Wilson, M. and Henderson, D. M. (1966). *British Rust Fungi*, Cambridge University Press, Cambridge

Winter, G. (1887). In Rabenhorst's *Kryptogamenflora von Deutschland, Ostereich und der Schweiz*

Zogg, H. (1943). Untersuchungen über die Gattung *Hysterographium* Corda insbesondere über *Hysterographium fraxini* (Pers.) de Not. *Phytopath. Z.*, 14, 310–84

13   Diseases of sycamore and maple (*Acer* spp.)

Sycamore, *Acer pseudoplatanus*, introduced four or five hundred years ago, and now naturalised here, is the only *Acer* sp. grown in Great Britain as a forest tree. The native *A. campestre*, the field maple, is a small tree common in woodland and scrub and in hedgerows. Many *Acer* species are extensively grown as ornamental trees, especially the Norway maple *(A. platanoides)* and its varieties, and numerous introduced maples from the Far East and from North America.

NURSERY AND POST-NURSERY DISEASES

LEAF DISEASES

The powdery mildew *Uncinula aceris* (DC) Sacc. (*U. bicornis* (Fr.) Lév.)
The common powdery mildew *Uncinula aceris* forms a usually sparse, incon-

spicuous white covering on one or both sides of the leaves of sycamores and field maples (plate 25). In mainland Europe it has also been recorded on Norway maple and *Acer rubrum* (Winter, 1887).

The mycelium first produces chains of colourless, barrel-shaped oidia. Later, black , subglobose ascocarps measuring up to about 0.2 mm across are formed. On their upper halves they bear many short, colourless, spreading appendages that fork at the tip to two (sometime three) recurved hooks (figure 61). Within are four to twelve pear-shaped asci measuring 70-95 x 45-55 μm, each containing from six to eight colourless, elliptical ascospores that measure 22-26 x 13-15 μm (Dennis, 1968). The ascocarps are formed towards the end of the season, mature over the winter, and shed their ascospores in the following spring.

The fungus is of no practical importance, and often passes unnoticed.

Giant leaf blotch disease of sycamore caused by *Ophiognomonia pseudoplatani* (von Tubeuf) Barrett & Pearce (*Gnomonia pseudoplatani* von Tubeuf)

The giant leaf spot disease of sycamore caused by *Ophiognomonia pseudoplatani (Gnomonia pseudoplatani)*, described from Germany some 50 years ago and since found in Denmark, has been known in the Oxford area since 1973 (Barrett and Pearce, 1981).

Symptoms of the disease first appear in mid-June. The fungus quickly causes large, radially spreading lesions which most often originate at the junction with the petiole and appear dark brown above and pale greyish-brown below, with infected leaf veins blackish in colour.

Figure 61. Cleistocarps of *Uncinula aceris* showing the bifurcated appendages, and (in a dissected cleistocarp) the asci and ascospores (K.F. Tubeuf, after Tulasne)

By early September the lesions may occupy up to 70 per cent of the leaf surface, and on some trees as many as 75 per cent of the leaves may be affected. Such trees are severly disfigured and their amenity value is much impaired. Affected leaves fall prematurely, from the early part of September.

The perithecia of *O. pseudoplatani* are found on the lesions on overwintered infected leaves, beginning in March. Tubeuf (1930) found these perithecia mainly on the upper sides of the leaves, but Barrett and Pearce (1981) found them chiefly on the leaf surface closest to the ground. The numerous necks of the perithecia project from the leaf surface like small black bristles. The perithecia embedded in the leaf tissues measure 150–320 μm across. Their necks are laterally attached, and measure 260–330 μm, but of this length only 160–220 μm projects above the leaf surface. The asci, which measure 60–90 x 6–10 μm, each contain eight elongated, two-celled ascospores measuring 45–65 x 0.5–1 μm.

Tar spot caused by *Rhytisma* spp.

By far the commonest cause of tar spot of sycamore and some other *Acer* spp. in Great Britain and the rest of Europe, as well as in North America, is *Rhytisma acerinum* (Pers.) Fr. (plate 26). In Great Britain this fungus is common wherever the sycamore is grown, except in the polluted atmosphere of large industrial towns (Jones, 1944) and in very remote upland areas (Maxwell, 1933a,b).

Development of the disease   The disease has been described by Bracher (1924) and Jones (1923, 1925). Ascospores produced on fallen leaves in April and May infect the new foliage, their germ tubes entering through the stomata. Water-soaked spots appear at the sites of infection, and enlarge and become yellow. The fungus grows in the leaf, and within and just below the epidermal cells gives rise to a thick stroma with a shining black exterior, so that the yellow areas become transformed into rounded black, slightly raised spots, usually up to about 15 mm across.

In summer, what appear to be spermogonial cavities (*Melasmia acerina* Lév.) form in the stroma, and open by round pores to extrude numerous colourless, slender, slightly curved spermatia that measure 6–9 x 0.5–1 μm (Grove, 1937), and the function of which remains uncertain (Jones, 1925).

Over the winter, on the fallen leaves, ascocarps form in cavities in or around the edges of the spermogonial stromata. The ascocarps are elliptical, and open by long, narrow, sometimes forked slits. They contain club-shaped asci that measure up to 130 x 10 μm, each containing a bundle of eight long, narrow, colourless ascospores slightly thicker at the upper end, measuring 60–80 x 1.5–2.5 μm. Between the asci are slender paraphyses with curled and sometimes forked tips (Dennis, 1968). The young ascocarps may be found in February, and the ascospores are shed in April and May as the host leaf buds open and the leaves expand (Grove, 1937). The ascospores have a gelatinous sheath (Bracher, 1924) and stick to the leaves after ejection. As they germinate they become bicellular before the production of a germ tube (Jones, 1925).

Host range   In Great Britain *R. acerinum* is commonest on sycamore, but is occasional on the field maple. Elsewhere in Europe it has been found also on the Norway maple and the box elder (Grove, 1937; Laubert, 1933). In North America it affects many *Acer* spp., and the related *R. punctatum,* which is discussed briefly below, attacks the bigleaf maple, *Acer macrophyllum* (Anon, 1967).

Variation in R. acerinum: other tar spot fungi   Cross inoculation studies have suggested that *R. acerinum* exists in several stains. One of these, which affects only sycamore, has sometimes been separated as *R. pseudoplatani* Müller (Müller, 1912). This has been listed as occurring in Great Britain (Ramsbottom and Balfour-Browne, 1951).

Also recorded here on sycamore leaves is *R. punctatum* Müller (Ramsbottom and Balfour-Browne, 1951). This also causes large spots on the leaves, but the larger spots are made up of groups of smaller spots each up to about 1-5 mm across, and the asci are described as measuring 70-80 x 9-10 μm, each containing eight colourless ascospores measuring 30-36 x 1.5-2 μm (Rehm, 1896). The fungus is certainly much less common than *R. acerinum,* and Grove (1937) was of the opinion that it and its spermogonial state *Melasmia punctata* Sacc. & Roum. were only stages in the development of the better-known fungus. These tar spot fungi of sycamore need further study.

Damage caused   Though in severe attacks *R. acerinum* causes some premature defoliation, and some may regard its black stromata as unsightly on trees grown for ornament, its effects are rarely serious. It has sometimes been known to cause appreciable damage to seedlings and young trees in Germany (Wagner, 1927), but has so far been of little significance in Great Britain.

Control of tar spot   As the disease is of so little importance, control measures are not usually employed against it, but sources of infection may be reduced by the collection and burning or burial of infected leaves in autumn and winter. Young stock can be sprayed at intervals from bud burst with copper or other fungicides (Wagner, 1927; Anon, 1967).

Leaf spot caused by *Cristulariella depraedans* (Cooke) Höhnel (*Polyactis depraedans* Cooke, *Illosporium diedickeanum* Sacc.)

Christulariella depraedans, which occurs in Europe and North America, causes spotting and withering of the leaves of sycamores and other *Acer* spp. (Bowen, 1930; Moore, 1959).

The fungus, one of the Deuteromycetes (Fungi Imperfecti), causes grey spots on the green leaf. The spots are at first water-soaked and only about 1 mm across, but enlarge somewhat, and become greyish brown, and may join together to cover large areas (figure 62). Fungal fruit bodies arise on the spots on one or both sides of the leaf, sometimes particularly on the leaf veins (Bowen, 1930).

Figure 62. Leaf spots on sycamore caused by *Cristulariella depraedans* (D.H. Phillips)

Under a hand lens they look like minute white pinheads. Each consists of a simple, erect, colourless, septate hypha about 100-270 µm long and 8-16 µm wide, bearing at its top a compact, flattened-globose sporing head about 100-150 µm across. The sporing head is made up of one-celled, repeatedly di- or trichotomously dividing branches that radiate from a central rounded cell. At their outer ends the outermost branches carry two or three-lobed cells somewhat resembling basidia, that produce small, globular, colourless conidia singly on the lobes. These conidia measure 2-3 or 4 µm across (Bowen, 1930; Waterman and Marshall, 1947). The fungus may also form small black sclerotia (Cooke, 1885).

With time, but often quite rapidly, the affected leaves wilt and wither, and fall early from the tree.

In Great Britain, epidemics caused by *C. depraedans* on sycamore were recorded in Norfolk about 1879, in Perthshire about 1935, on the Clyde in 1945 (Moore, 1959), and on sycamore and Norway maple in east and southeast England from August to October 1968 (Burdekin, 1969). In August and September 1980 it was widespread in South Wales and southern England and in Argyll. Attacks appear to be associated with cool, wet summers. The disease is often most severe on the lower branches, on which affected leaves are usually first found. In North America the fungus occurs on the sugar maple *(Acer saccharum)* and the silver maple *(A. saccharinum)* (Bowen, 1930).

As *C. depraedans* causes epidemics only infrequently, and when it does it attacks only late in the season, it is of no importance as a cause of damage, and no control measures have so far been required to deal with it.

Other minor leaf spots caused by species of *Phyllosticta, Diplodina, Phleospora* and *Leptothyrium*

Various species of *Phyllosticta, Diplodina, Phleospora* and *Leptothyrium* have been recorded in Great Britain associated with spotting of the leaves of *Acer* spp. Several of these fungi may occur together on the same leaf, and they form a very confused group that needs further study (Moore, 1959).

Phyllosticta aceris Sacc. produces more or less rounded, brownish spots up to about 10 mm or more across on living leaves of the field maple. Its black pycnidia, which are embedded in the leaf tissues, open by a pore usually on the upper side of the leaf, and contain colourless, ovoid spores measuring 5-7 x 2.5-3 μm. The fungus may be found from July to September in southern England and the midlands, and occurs also in continental Europe as far south as Italy (Grove, 1935). *P. campestris* Pass. in litt. apud Brun. has also been recorded here on field maple seedlings, but Grove (1935) considered that it was no more than a young stage of *P. aceris*.

P. platanoidis Sacc. has been recorded on sycamore in parts of southern England, South Wales and southern Scotland (Moore, 1959) and on young seedlings of Norway maple in Oxfordshire (Grove, 1935). It causes rather indistinct spots, and the globose, black pycnidia, which are embedded in the leaf with their openings on the underside, contain straight, cylindrical, colourless spores measuring 4-6 x 0.5-1 μm. *P. platanoidis* is often accompanied by *Phleospora aceris*, and also by *Leptothyrium platanoidis*, which Grove (1935) considered was a form of the *Phyllosticta*.

Diplodina acerum Sacc. & Br., the pycnidia of which contain colourless, two-celled spores measuring 10-20 x 3-4.5 μm, was found by Batko (unpublished) causing considerable but very local damage to leaves of Norway maple at Auchencastle, Scotland, in early September, 1957.

Phleospora aceris Sacc. is common in summer and autumn on leaves, especially of seedlings, of sycamore, and sometimes of field maple. It causes brown, rounded spots, and embedded in these are large pycnidia with a poorly developed wall. The pycnidia contain more or less cylindrical or rather narrowly club-shaped, eventually four-celled, colourless spores that measure 20-30(-45) x 2-(4-5) μm. *P. pseudoplatani* Bubák, which has also been recorded on *Acer*, was considered by Grove (1935) to be the same fungus as *P. aceris*.

Grove (1935) also described *P. platanoidis* Petr., found causing small spots on the leaves of young plants of Norway maple in Oxfordshire. The pycnidia, on the upper side of the leaf, contain long, hairlike, curved, four-celled spores measuring 60-70 x 1.5-2.5 μm.

Leptothyrium platanoidis Pass. apud Brun. was also recorded by Grove (1937) causing brown spots on leaves of seedling sycamores in South Wales and Stafford-shire. The pycnidia open on the undersides of the leaves, and contain straight or slightly curved spores measuring 4.5 x 1 μm. As noted above, in Grove's opinion *L. platanoidis* was part of the life cycle of *Phyllosticta platanoidis*.

DISEASES OF THE BARK AND TRUNK

Sun scorch

Like other thin-barked trees, *Acer* spp. may be affected by sun scorch, which leads to the death of areas of bark on the south-facing sides of their trunks.

Sooty bark disease caused by *Cryptostroma corticale* (Ell. and Everh.) Gregory and Waller

The imperfect fungus *Cryptostroma corticale* has been found in the Great Lakes region in Canada and the USA, and in England, France and Germany (Anon, 1953; Plate and Schneider, 1965). In North America and in Germany it is known almost entirely as a saprophyte and as a cause of asthma (Towey *et al.*, 1932; Plate and Schneider, 1965). In Great Britain it was first noticed in 1945 in Wanstead Park in northeast London (Waller, 1952). Within a few years it appeared in many adjacent parts of Greater London, where strong circumstantial evidence suggested that it was the cause of a devastating wilt and dieback of sycamores (Gregory *et al.*, 1949). Surveys soon revealed its presence outside Greater London in Surrey, Essex and Hertfordshire, and further afield in Norfolk (Peace, 1955), and later as far north as Kettering, Northants (Pawsey, 1962). Beyond the London area, however, it was almost invariably a saprophyte on trees killed by some other agency (Peace, 1955). Not long after the discovery of the fungus in London, it was also found to be destroying sycamores in France, first in Paris, and later in Grenoble (Moreau and Moreau, 1954).

How the fungus reached Europe is unknown, though Gregory and Waller (1951) were of the opinion that it came to Great Britain in timber imported into London docks.

The causal fungus   *C. corticale* has been most fully described by Gregory and Waller (1951). These authors considered it to be mainly an invader of the phloem and cambium, but it has more recently become apparent (Young, 1978) that the fungus first invades the woody tissues and then moves out to the cambium and bark at a later stage. It forms a thin, black stroma in the cambium, and one, or sometimes up to three, sporing stromata in the bark. The sporing stroma is at first a white mycelial sheet, but it splits parallel to the surface, to form a roof and a floor. These are separated by the growth of vertical columns, so that a shallow space arises, up to about 1 mm deep. Hence the affected area of bark is pushed up to form a blister. The roof, floor and the columns blacken as they mature. The floor is lined by a bluish-grey layer of conidiophores from the ends of which long fragile chains of spores are formed. These conidia are one-celled, smooth, oval, brown when mature, and measure 4-6.5 x 3.5-4 μm. They fill the stromatic cavity in a sooty mass, and between them run sticky, unbranched capillitial threads attached to the floor. With time, the bark breaks up and falls from the affected trees, and the spores are exposed as a velvety layer that is gradually dispersed by the wind (plate 32). In France, Moreau and Moreau (1954) found the ascomycete *Eutypa acharii* associated with *C. corticale* on affected trees. In Britain, *E. acharii* has been found growing as a saprophyte on wood under the dead bark of sycamore, and may be mistaken for the cambial stroma of *C. corticale*. However, the perithecia of *E. acharii*, about 0.5 mm in diameter and embedded in the wood beneath a black layer, are very distinctive.

Symptoms of the disease   Careful observation has shown that the first symptom of the disease is a wilting of the leaves of part of the crown of the tree. This wilting has been seen at varying times between May and September, and is followed by dieback of the affected branches (Gregory and Waller, 1951). The wilting leaves dry and their petioles droop, but they remain attached to the tree. The woody tissues inside a wilted branch are stained dark yellow or green. Later, at any time of the year, sporing lesions may be found, either as blisters or as open spore masses. The affected trees usually die within a few years. The disease is often first noticed only when the bark lesions are visible, and the affected tree fails to come into leaf in the spring. Inspection then shows dark vertical blisters on the trunk and branches. If the bark is then stripped off the blisters, a character-istic crackling sound may be heard as the stromatic columns break, and the brown spore mass is exposed.

On dead smooth-barked sycamores, the fungus may spread within the bark over the whole truck, and as the bark breaks up and falls, the spores form a sooty deposit on the vegetation around (Gregory *et al.*, 1949). Sometimes, how-ever, the sporing lesions may be high up in the crown, when they are difficult to see, and on thick-barked sycamores only small stromata a few inches across are formed (Gregory and Waller, 1951; Peace, 1955).

If a partly affected tree is cut up, a yellow or dark greenish-brown stain like that in the wilted shoots may be found in the heartwood, extending up and down the trunk, sometimes for the whole length of the stem and into the branches. Both the stain and the fungus may also be traced downward into the root system (Moreau and Moreau, 1951; Townrow, 1954). In places the stain extends into the sap wood and reaches the bark, and most of the stem blisters appear to form where the stain touches the cambium. Once the tree is dead, the stain dis-appears, leaving the wood a uniform grey colour (Gregory, *et al.*, 1949). 1949).

Host range   *C. corticale* is known as a pathogen chiefly in Great Britain and France. There it is restricted almost entirely to sycamore, though it has also been found on field maple *(Acer campestris)*, the Norway maple *(A. platanoides)* and (in France only) on the box elder *(A. negundo)* (Peace, 1955).

In North America it has occurred mainly as a saprophyte on maple logs (probably on *Acer saccharum*), though it was also recorded by Towey *et al.* (1932) on dying maples, hickories (*Carya* spp.) and basswoods (*Tilia* spp.).

Factors affecting the disease   The most severe outbreaks of Sooty bark disease have occurred in and around Greater London, the warmest region in Britain, and have developed in years following particularly hot summers. Thus in the forty years up to 1980 very high summer temperatures occurred in 1947, 1948, 1955, 1959, 1975 and 1976 and disease outbreaks developed in the subsequent season or seasons. Young (1978) studied the meteorological data related to these years and concluded that the disease was likely to become acute in seasons following those where any summer month (June, July or August) had a mean daily maximum temperature of 23°C or more.

Observations by Townrow (1954) indicated that the fungus grew three times as fast in culture at 25°C as it did at 10°C and that spore germination also increased with temperature. These observations provide some evidence to support the hypothesis that this is a temperature-regulated disease.

More recent research by Dickenson and Wheeler (1980) has shown that the fungus grows more rapidly in the wood of sycamore plants held at 25°C rather than 10°C. It seems likely that high temperatures play a very important role in the rate of fungal growth in the host and therefore in the development of serious outbreaks of the disease.

In Wanstead Park when it was first found here, *C. corticale* killed between 15 and 20 per cent of the sycamores each year from 1948-1951 (Gregory and Waller, 1951). Since that time there has been a series of outbreaks, associated with hot summers, culminating in a severe outbreak in 1976 and 1977 following the hot summer of 1975 and the record temperatures in the summer of 1976. Although no formal surveys were undertaken at this time, death of sycamore occurred over many parts of southern Britain and was particularly severe in the Greater London area.

Control   If the relationship between summer temperatures and the disease is maintained, the disease should largely be confined to southern Britain and Greater London in particular. Serious outbreaks are likely to occur only infrequently in seasons following hot summers. In summers with average or below average temperatures the disease is likely to remain quiescent. Unless there is a dramatic change in the summer temperatures in Britain active measures to control the disease would therefore seem to be unnecessary.

WILT DISEASES

Verticillium wilt

Acer spp. are among the trees most often and most severely affected by Verticillium wilt (plate 27), which is described in chapter 3.

ROOT DISEASES

Phytophthora root rot
A root rot of snake-bark maple *(Acer pensylvanicum)*, which in one case killed a number of trees in southern England, appeared to be caused by *Phytophthora cambivora*, which was quickly followed by *Armillaria mellea* (Brasier, 1971).

VIRUS DISEASES

Stunt and leaf spot of *Acer negundo* and *A. pseudoplatani*
Cooper (1979) has summarised information on a virus disease of *Acer negundo* and *A. pseudoplatanus* known from Hungary and the United Kingdom. Affected plants show a shortening of the internodes and failure of the terminal bud. The leaves change in outline, and show chlorotic spots.

DECAY FUNGI

The commonest decay fungi affecting the sycamore are *Inonotus hispidus* and *Polyporus squamosus*, which both rot the stems and branches. These fungi are described in chapter 19.

REFERENCES

Anon (1953). *Cryptostroma corticale* (Ell. & Everh.) Gregory & Waller. *Distrib. Maps Pl. Dis.*, no. 272
Anon (1967). *Maple Diseases and Their Control*, U.S. Dep. Agric. Home and Gardens Bull., no. 81, 8 pp.
Barrett, D.K. and Pearce, R.B. (1981). Giant leaf blotch disease of sycamore *(Acer pseudoplatanus)* in Britain. *Trans. Br. mycol. Soc.*, 76, 317-45
Bowen, P.R. (1930). A maple leaf disease caused by *Cristulariella depraedans*. *Bull. Conn. agric. Exp. Stn.*, 316, 625-47
Bracher, R. (1924). Notes on *Rhytisma acerinum* and *Rhytisma pseudoplatani*. *Trans. Br. mycol. Soc.*, 9, 183-6
Brasier, C.M. (1971). In Forest pathology. *Rep. Forest Res., Lond., 1971*, pp. 77-84
Burdekin, D.A. (1969). Forest pathology. *Rep. Forest Res., Lond., 1969*, pp. 106-10
Cooke, M.C. (1885). Some remarkable moulds. *J. Queckett microsc. Club, S II*, no. 12, 138-43
Cooper, J.I. (1979). *Virus Diseases of Trees and Shurbs*, Institute of Terrestrial Ecology, c/o Unit of Invertebrate Virology, Oxford
Dennis, R.W.G. (1968). *British Ascomycetes*, J. Cramer, Lehre
Dickenson, Susan and Wheeler, B.E.J. (1981). Effects of temperature, and water stress in sycamore, on growth of *Cryptostroma corticale*. *Trans. Br. mycol. Soc.*, 76, 181-5
Gregory, P.H., Peace, T.R. and Waller, S. (1949). Death of sycamore trees associated with an unidentified fungus. *Nature, Lond.*, 164, 275
Gregory, P.H. and Waller, S. (1951). *Cryptostroma corticale* and sooty bark disease of sycamore *(Acer pseudoplatanus)*. *Trans. Br. mycol. Soc.*, 34, 579-97
Grove, W.B. (1935). *British Stem- and Leaf-Fungi (Coelomycetes)*, vol. 1, Cambridge University Press, Cambridge
Grove, W.B. (1937). *British Stem- and Leaf-Fungi (Coelomycetes)*, vol. 2, Cambridge University Press, Cambridge

Jones, E.W. (1944). Biological flora of the British Isles. *Acer* L. *J. Ecol.,* **32**, 215–52

Jones, S.G. (1923). Life-history of *Rhytisma acerinum* (preliminary account). *Ann. Bot.,* **37**, 731–732

Jones, S.G. (1925). Life-history and cytology of *Rhytisma acerinum* (Pers.) Fr. *Ann. Bot.,* **39**, 41–75

Laubert, R. (1933). Mehltau und *Rhytisma* auf *Acer negundo. NachrBl. dt. Pflschutzdienst.,* **13**, 94

Maxwell, H. (1933*a*). The sycamore fungus. *Nature, Lond.,* **132**, 409

Maxwell, H. (1933*b*). The sycamore fungus. *Nature, Lond.,* **132**, 752

Moore, W.C. (1959). *British Parasitic Fungi,* Cambridge University Press, Cambridge

Moreau, C. and Moreau, M. (1954). Nouvelles observations sur le dépérissement des érables. *Bull. Soc. Linn. de Normandie,* 7, 66–67

Müller, K. (1912). Über des biologische Verhalten von *Rhytisma acerinum* auf verschiedenen Ahornarten. *Ber. dt. bot. Ges.,* **30**, 385–91

Pawsey, R.G. (1962). Resurgence of sooty bark disease of sycamore, in 'New or uncommon plant diseases and pests'. *Pl. Path.,* **11**, 138.

Peace, T.R. (1955). Sooty bark disease of sycamore – a disease in eclipse. *Q. Jl. For.,* **49**, 197–204

Plate, H.P. and Schneider, R. (1965). Ein Fall von asthmatiger Allergie, verursacht durch den Pilz *Cryptostroma corticale. NachrBl. dt. PflSchutzdienst,* **17**, 100–101

Ramsbottom, J. and Balfour-Brown, F.L. (1951). List of discomycetes recorded from the British Isles. *Trans. Br. mycol. Soc.,* **34**, 38–137

Rehm, H. (1896). *Die Pilze Deutschlands, Oesterreichs und der Schweiz,* III Abt., Kummer, Leipzig

Towey, J.W., Sweany, H.C. and Huron, W.H. (1932). Severe bronchial asthma apparently due to fungus spores found in maple bark. *J. Am. med. Ass.,* **99**, 453–9

Townrow, J.A. (1954). The biology of *Cryptostroma corticale* and the sooty bark disease of sycamore. *Rep. Forest Res., Lond., 1953,* pp. 118–120.

Tubeuf, C. von (1930). *Gnomonia pseudoplatani* n. sp., die Ursache der Riesenflecken auf den Blättern des Bergahorns *(Acer pseudoplatanus). Z. PflKrankh. PflPath. PflSchutz.,* **40**, 364–75

Wagner, K. (1927). Erkrankungen unserer Gehölze *Rhytisma acerinum* (Runzelschorf). *Gartenflora,* **76**, 81–2

Waller, S. (1952). The Wanstead fungus disease of sycamore. *Essex Nat.,* **29**, 9–13

Waterman, A.M. and Marshall, R.P. (1947). A new species of *Cristulariella* associated with a leaf spot of maple. *Mycologia,* **39**, 690–98

Winter, G. (1887). *Die Pilze Deutschlands, Oesterreichs und der Schweiz.* II Abt., Kummer, Leipzig

Young, C.W.T. (1978). *Sooty Bark Disease of Sycamore,* Arboric. Leafl., no. 3, 8 pp., HMSO, London

14 Diseases of elm (*Ulmus* spp.)

Only one species of elm, *Ulmus glabra*, the wych elm, seems to be truly native in Great Britain. Others, such as *U. procera*, the English elm, and *U. carpinifolia*, the smoothleaved elm, are thought to have been introduced in the Roman or post-Roman period. A variety of cultivars of the smoothleaved elm or of hybrids between this and the wych elm have appeared since that time. Among these are *U. hollandica* 'vegeta', the Huntingdon elm, and *U. carpinifolia* var. *sarniensis*, the Wheatley elm. Elms are widely found in town and country, in woodlands, hedgerows, in parkland and in suburban streets. All have been severely affected by the epidemic of Dutch elm disease which began in the late 1960s. As a result, in large areas of southern Britain most of the mature trees have been lost.

NURSERY AND POST-NURSERY DISEASES

LEAF DISEASES

Minor leaf fungi: *Platychora ulmi* (Duval ex Fr.) Petr., *Septogloeum ulmi* Died., *Gloeosporium inconspicuum* Cav., and *Taphrina ulmi* (Fuckel) Johans.
Several minor leaf fungi attack elm, though none is of economic importance. The

best known is *Platychora ulmi* (*Systremma ulmi* (Duval ex Fr.) Theiss. and Syd., *Dothidella ulmi* (Duval ex Fr.) Wint., *Euryachora ulmi* (Schleicher ex Fr.) Schroet., stat. conid. *Piggotia astroidea* B. & Br.). In autumn and the early part of winter this forms small rounded black bodies on living and moribund leaves, and it is therefore sometimes called tar spot (Moore, 1959) (plate 36). These bodies, which are about 2-5 mm in diameter, are the stromata of the fungus, and at first contain pycnidial cavities (*Piggotia astroidea*) producing clear brown cylindrical spores measuring 8-10 x 5-6 μm (Viennot-Bourgin, 1949). Later in the winter, perithecial cavities also arise, and produce cylindrical, eight-spored asci with ovoid, colourless, very unequally two-celled ascospores that eventually turn pale olive brown (Dennis, 1968). These spores measure 10-12 x 4-4.5 μm.

The imperfect fungus *Septogloeum ulmi* Died. (*Phleospora ulmi* (Fr.) Wallr.) causes brown (at first yellow) spots on elm leaves, and sometimes on their branches. It appears to be the asexual stage of *Mycosphaerella ulmi* Kleb. (Grove 1937) (though it has sometimes been wrongly considered to be that of *Platychora ulmi*). Its small pustules arise on the spots on the undersides of the leaves, and bear white masses of long, cylindrical or sausage-shaped spores with rounded ends. At first the spores are one or two-celled, but when mature they are three (or occasionally four) septate, and then measure 30-58 x 5-6 μm (Grove, 1937). This fungus is common on *Ulmus glabra* and *U. procera* (Moore, 1959), but its perfect stage, *Mycosphaerella ulmi*, whose two-celled, colourless ascospores measure 22-27 x 4-5 μm (Brooks, 1953), appears to be still unrecorded in Great Britain.

Another imperfect fungus, *Gloeosporium inconspicuum* Cav., which is considered by Grove (1937) to be only an early stage of *Septogloeum ulmi*, also produces small, inconspicuous brown spots on the undersides of living and moribund leaves of English elm (*U. procera*). Pustules on the spots bear small, colourless, ellipsoid spores measuring 1-2 x 0.5-1 μm.

Also inconspicuous and easily overlooked is *Taphrina ulmi* (Fuckel) Johans. (*Exoascus ulmi* Fuckel). So far in Great Britain this fungus has been recorded only in Kent, and on hedgerows in Somerset, where it is known to be common. It causes only a diffuse blotching of the leaves of the suckers and adventitious shoots. The blotches turn brown, and the dead tissues fall out so that holes remain in the leaves. The small, naked asci form palisades on the leaf surfaces, and measure 12-20 x 8-10 μm. They each contain four to eight spherical ascospores that often bud in the ascus (Bond, 1956; Viennot-Bourgin, 1949).

DIEBACKS AND CANKERS

Coral spot: *Nectria cinnabarina*

Elms are among the trees most often attacked by the coral spot fungus, *Nectria cinnabarina*, which is described in chapter 3.

Canker and dieback caused by *Plectophomella concentrica* Redfern & Sutton

An inconspicuous and apparently minor canker and dieback of elm caused by

Plectophomella concentrica has been described by Redfern and Sutton (1981). The disease is widespread on wych elm (*Ulmus glabra*) in northeastern parts of Britain from Scarborough in northeast England to Stonehaven in east Scotland. It has also been found on the same host in west Scotland and in Orkney. On one occasion the fungus was also found in Edinburgh causing a canker on lime (*Tilia* sp.). In many respects *P. concentrica* resembles *P. ulmi* (*Dothiorella ulmi*), which affects elm in North America.

Symptoms   *P. concentrica* causes swollen cankers mainly on one-year-old shoots, though infection of two- and three-year-old material may also take place (figure 63). Young affected shoots usually die during the winter after infection. The fungus then appears to die out, and in the ensuing growing season healthy recovery shoots grow out from the live shoot below the canker. When older and larger shoots are affected, the cankers usually heal, though the healing process may take several years to complete.

Inside affected shoots, black streaks similar to those caused by *Ceratocystis ulmi* may often be found in the xylem up to 5 or 6 cm above and below the cankers.

The causal fungus   *P. concentrica* forms rings of epidermal or subepidermal, dark brown or black stromata, in which the conidia are formed in locules. These

Figure 63.   Canker on elm caused by *Plectophomella concentrica* (D.B. Redfern)

locules open by several circular ostioles. The colourless, one-celled conidia are ellipsoid to cylindrical, straight or slightly curved, with smooth walls, and measure 2.4–4 × 1–1.5 μm.

The optimum temperature for the growth of the fungus in culture was found to be 20°C. Growth was still good at lower temperatures down to 5°C, but at 25°C it abruptly declined.

Infection   Infection appears to take place in the dormant season, usually on the internodes, but occasionally associated with buds and leaf scars.

WILT DISEASES

Dutch elm disease caused by *Ceratocystis ulmi* (Buism.) Moreau (*Ceratostomella ulmi* Buism., *Ophiostoma ulmi* (Buism.) Nannf., stat. conid. *Graphium ulmi* Schwarz)

Dutch elm disease is a vascular wilt caused by *Ceratocystis ulmi*. This disease is one of the most serious tree diseases known and has caused extensive losses in Europe, North America and western Asia. The first record was made in Picardy in France in 1918 and over the next decade it spread to a number of other European countries. It was first identified in Britain in 1927 at Totteridge in Hertfordshire. The status and development of the disease in Britain up to 1960 has been fully reviewed by Peace (1960). The disease was first reported from the United States in 1930, which it probably reached as a result of the shipment of infested logs from Europe and it was found for the first time in Canada in 1944. In Asia the disease has been found in Turkey, Iran, Kashmir and in Uzbekistan (Gibbs, 1978).

There was a general decline in the level of disease in Britain during the 1940s and 1950s. However, in the late 1960s there was renewed concern about the disease and several locally severe outbreaks were reported. At first it was thought that these were local flare-ups similar to those which had occurred from time to time in the previous two decades. By 1970 it was clear that a new and more severe epidemic had started and by the late 1970s over three-quarters of the original elm population of 23 million in southern England was dead or dying. At the same time serious losses were reported from many other parts of Europe.

Brasier and Gibbs (1973) demonstrated that this epidemic probably originated from the importation of diseased elm logs from North America containing a hitherto unidentified aggressive strain of *C. ulmi*. Subsequent research has indicated that there may have been two simultaneous epidemics present in Europe, one developing in western Europe from North American sources and the other spreading into Europe from Russia or western Asia (Brasier, 1979).

There are several hundred references in the literature to research on Dutch elm disease. A few of the most important of these will be noted in this section but readers may find it useful to refer to review articles including those of Brasier and Gibbs (1978), Gibbs (1978), Peace (1960), Sinclair and Campana (1978), and Stipes and Campana (1980).

Figure 64. Dutch elm disease: under surface of infested bark, showing maternal and larval galleries of *Scolytus scolytus*, one of the insect vectors of the disease (Forestry Commission)

Figure 65. Dutch elm disease: elm twig, showing feeding grooves made by the bark beetle *Scolytus scolytus* (Forestry Commission)

The fungus is carried by bark beetles that emerge in spring and summer from galleries (figure 64) under the bark of infested elm wood and feed in the tops of elms, where they form grooves in the crotches of the twigs (figure 65). The beetles bear the spores of *C. ulmi* on and in their bodies, and so infect many of the wounds they make. They later breed under the bark of dead and dying elms and in fallen or felled elm material (Gibbs *et al.*, 1977). The beetles responsible for transmission in Great Britain are *Scolytus scolytus* (figure 66) and *S. multistriatus*, but *S. laevis* is the main carrier in Sweden (Heybroek, 1967). The European *S. multistriatus* is also the most important carrier in North America, but there the native beetle *Hylurgopinus rufipes* can also transmit the disease.

C. ulmi produces its fructifications in sheltered moist places, mainly under dead bark when it begins to lift and separate from the wood, and in the galleries made by the bark beetles. The fungus has long been known to be heterothallic, so perithecia are formed only when two compatible mating types are present. The perithecia are black, with a flask-shaped base 105–135 μm across, and a long

Figure 66. *Scolytus scolytus* (actual length 5–6 mm), one of the beetles that carry Dutch elm disease (Forestry Commission)

neck measuring 263–380 μm; the eight-spored asci soon break down to a jelly in which are embedded the colourless, slightly curved ascospores that measure 4.5–6 x 1.5 μm. The spores ooze out in the jelly, and are commonly to be seen in a round droplet surmounting the perithecial neck.

There are three asexual spore forms of the fungus (Brasier, 1981). The coremiospores or synnematal spores are borne at the tips of black coremial stalks 1–2 mm in height. The single-celled spores are hyaline and measure 2–5 x 1–3 μm. Conidia of the *Cephalosporium* stage (more recently referred to *Sporothrix* (de Hoog, 1974)) are produced on short mycelial branches or conidiophores, and the hyaline single-celled spores range in size from 4–6 x 2–3 μm. Mucilaginous droplets containing a cluster of these spores can often be found. The third asexual form is the yeast stage, and budded yeast cells, very variable in size, can be found in liquid state cultures and also on agar plates and in the xylem vessels of an infected tree.

The coremia appear on newly dead material and in Great Britain coremial production takes place in all except the coldest wheather. The formation of perithecia is more restricted, and is most abundant from November to February (Brasier, 1981).

Following the onset of the severe outbreak of the disease in the late 1960s, it was established that *C. ulmi* existed as two strains: one the highly pathogenic 'aggressive' strain and the other less pathogenic 'nonaggressive' strain (Gibbs and Brasier, 1973). The aggressive strain was responsible for the later outbreak and the nonaggressive strain is thought to be a relict from the earlier epidemic of the 1920s and 1930s. The two strains can be differentiated both in the field, by their pathogenicity on English elm, and in culture by their morphology, growth rates and reduced interfertility. More recently it has been shown that the aggressive strain comprises two races, the North American strain and the Eurasian strain (Brasier, 1979) (figure 67).

Once within the tree the fungus increases mainly by a yeast-like budding process, and the bud spores so formed are distributed in the sap stream, and so spread rapidly throughout the current xylem tract. The fungus rarely succeeds in growing laterally through the living summer wood from one growth ring to the next, either of the preceding or succeeding year (Peace, 1960), though it may cross in this way in the roots and lower part of the trunk (Banfield, 1968).

In inoculation experiments, Kerling (1955) found the fungus had moved 5 cm above the inoculation point in two days, and 75 cm two days later. When Banfield (1941) inoculated trees early in the season, when transport of the spores is most rapid, he found the fungus moved from the foot to the top of tall trees in between 20 minutes and 48 hours. He also made inoculations 40 feet (12½ metres) up the trunks of trees, and the spores then moved down to the base in 15–20 minutes.

In Great Britain, the vector beetles emerge from May to October, so that they begin to transmit the disease in May, and the first external symptoms are usually visible in June. Parts of the crown then show wilting of the leaves, which turn

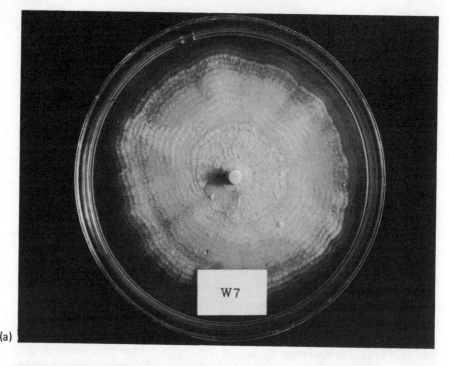

(a)

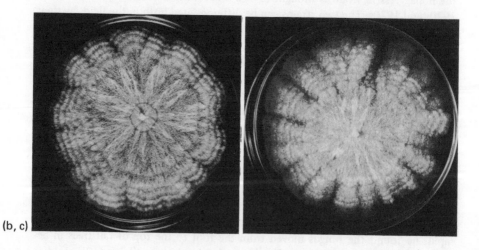

(b, c)

Figure 67. Cultures of the nonaggressive (a) and aggressive (b,c) strains of
Ceratocystis ulmi, which causes Dutch elm disease. The aggressive
strain occurs in two well-marked forms, the North American form
(NAN) (b) and the Eurasian form (EAN) (c) (Forestry Commission)

yellow and eventually brown (plates 41, 42), and dieback of twigs and branches may follow. Fast-growing twigs may curl to form 'shepherd's crooks', which are useful in the detection of diseased trees in winter (figure 68). In a severe attack, the entire tree is killed before the end of the summer; if it survives, the tree is likely to die in the following season, as a result of the fungus passing from one annual ring to the next (probably in the roots). In the earlier epidemic of the disease in Britain (Peace, 1960) trees frequently recovered from the disease, but since the arrival of the aggressive strain of the fungus recovery has become relatively rare.

Internal symptoms soon begin to appear in infected trees. Dark droplets of gum become visible in the living cells and also in some of the vessels, in which colourless bladder-like tyloses also form and fill the conducting cavities. Fungal hyphae may also sometimes be found in the vessels, tracheids, fibres and parenchyma cells (Kerling, 1955; Wilson, 1965), and some breakdown of pits and cell walls may occur as a result of their activities (Oeillette, 1961). The affected tissues show in transverse sections of the twigs and branches as rings of dark brown spots in the spring wood (figure 69). If the bark and outer wood are pared away they show as discontinuous streaks (figure 70). These spots and streaks give a good indication of years in which active infection was present.

Figure 68. Dutch elm disease: diseased twigs twisted into 'shepherds' crooks'
(D.H. Phillips)

Figure 69. Dutch elm disease: a cross section of a diseased twig showing two rings of darkly stained, infected vessels (Forestry Commission)

Wounds are necessary for primary infection to take place (Smucker, 1937), and though it has been shown (Smucker, 1935) that direct spread by airborne spores is possible, almost all transmission is by the feeding of vector beetles. Secondary spread from tree to tree along root grafts and the common root systems of suckers is especially important in hedgerows or in closely planted avenues (figure 72).

The fungus is usually considered to cause wilting and death partly by the plugging of the conducting system and partly by the production of toxins (Peace, 1960). There is no doubt that materials that can be used to induce wilting artificially are present in culture filtrates of *C. ulmi* (Kerling, 1955). In experiments, Elgersma (1967) found that the vascular system in stems of susceptible elms had become completely blocked 7 days after infection, and almost no water would pass through it, whereas blockage was only partial in resistant varieties. On the other hand Smalley (1962) controlled wilting by injecting trees with 2,3,6-trichlorophenylacetic acid (TCPA), which induced tylosis formation, and he considered that the tyloses at least in part were responsible for the limitation of the spread of infection. Pomerleau (1968) has suggested that blockage of vessels cannot be the direct cause of wilting, but that before blockage occurs the small

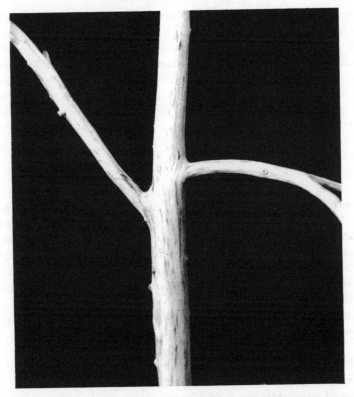

Figure 70. Dutch elm disease: infected stem stripped of its outer tissues to show longitudinal streaks (Forestry Commission)

spores of the fungus reach the leaves, and there directly give rise to the death of the leaves and shoots.

C. ulmi is the only important fungus that causes epidemic wilting of elms in Great Britain, though on very rare occasions Verticillium wilt (caused by *Verticillium albo-atrum* and *V. dahliae*) is said to have been recorded and to have caused somewhat similar symptoms, including streaking of the wood (Peace, 1960).

For practical purposes it may be said that *C. ulmi* attacks only *Ulmus* and the related genus *Zelkova*, and it has been suggested that some tropical members of the *Ulmaceae*, including *Trema*, *Celtis* and *Holoptelea*, which are very resistant to it, might be used in the production of resistant hybrids (Smalley and Riker, 1962).

All the species and hybrids of elm commonly grown in Great Britain are susceptible to Dutch elm disease, though the hybrid Huntingdon elm, *Ulmus* x *hollandica* 'vegeta', appears to show some resistance. *U. americana* and other American elms are even more susceptible than those of Europe (Beattie, 1937). Some Asian elms, including *U. pumila*, *U. japonica* and *U. parvifolia*, are resistant.

Breeding for resistance   Work on the selection and breeding of elms resistant to Dutch elm disease has been undertaken in several countries including Holland and the United States. In Holland, a number of clones have been developed which incorporate crosses between European elms and *U. wallichiana* from India. In the United States selections have been made from *U. pumila* or hybrids including this as one parent (Lester, 1978). All these selections show at least moderate resistance to the aggressive strain of *C. ulmi*. The resistant selections differ in form and vigour from the native species of North America and Europe and cannot be considered as replacements for them. However, several may be suitable for planting as windbreaks or as urban trees.

Losses caused   The losses caused by Dutch elm disease have been very great. Heybroek (1966) states that in Hilversum, in Holland, in nine years 71 per cent of the elms were killed by the disease. In the Province of Quebec in Canada it killed an estimated 16 per cent, or at least 600,000 white elms in 20 years (Pomerleau, 1961). In a campaign to eradicate the disease from the USA over 2½ million dead or dying elms were removed between 1933 and 1938 (Anon, 1938). More recently it has been stated (Hart, 1965) that in Michigan, the losses in amenity caused by *C. ulmi* amount to about 30 million dollars per annum. Losses in southern England, from 1970 to 1978, amounted to over 75 per cent of the original population of 23 million elms.

Control   A variety of measures have been suggested for the control of Dutch elm disease, ranging from attempts to eradicate the disease to chemical control by means of insecticides and fungicides and more recently with the aid of insect pheromones.

Eradication programmes were tried in the United States soon after the disease arrived there, but none succeeded. However, the felling of diseased and dead trees and the destruction of the wood and bark at an early stage of an epidemic can markedly slow down its rate of progress. The object of such sanitation felling is to eliminate the breeding grounds of the insect vector and thus reduce the beetle populations. These measures, sometimes in conjunction with other control measures such as insecticidal spraying, have been carried out over many years in parts of the United States (Neely, 1967, 1972). In the outbreak during the 1970s in Britain, many local authorities were unable to contain the spread of the disease but a few, including East Sussex and Brighton, have succeeded in markedly slowing down its progress by sanitation felling (Gibbs, 1978).

Sanitation felling is considered to be the basis of any control programme against Dutch elm disease. Other control methods, many of which involve the use of chemicals, have little hope of success unless the beetle population is brought under control.

Insecticides have long been associated with Dutch elm disease control campaigns in the United States. DDT and later methoxychlor have been used to protect trees from attack by the beetle (Doane, 1962).

More recently interest has centred on possible control of the vector beetle by the use of pheromones (Peacock, 1975). The chemical constituents of the pheromone released by the virgin female of *S. multistriatus* have been synthesised and tested in the field. It remains to be seen whether traps incorporating this pheromone can be used for mass-trapping or whether their use is limited to monitoring beetle populations within an area.

Many fungicides have also been tested and among the most promising are carbendazim and thiabendazole. Techniques for injecting solutions of these chemicals into trees have been developed either as curative or preventative treatments (Smalley, 1978) (figure 71). However, such treatments are costly and can only be justified on valuable specimen trees or groups of trees and even then there is no guarantee of success.

Root transmission of the disease is common in urban areas through root grafts and in hedgerow English elms through the common root system (figure 72). Where sanitation programmes are adopted it may be necessary to adopt measures to prevent root transmission. This can be achieved by physically breaking the

Figure 71. Dutch elm disease: injecting a tree with a curative or protective fungicide (Forestry Commission)

Figure 72. Dutch elm disease: an excavated root system of elm, showing young suckers. The causal fungus spreads along these suckers to give rise to secondary infections (Forestry Commission)

root connections using mechanical diggers or trenching machines or by the use of soil sterilants such as methyl bromide or metham sodium (Epstein, 1978).

Whatever steps are taken to control Dutch elm disease, when diseased elms are felled they become a source of vector beetles. Hence smallwood and the bark from the trunks of such trees should be removed and burnt. Legislation requiring this has been introduced in a number of countries. As the disease may be carried by trade in elm wood with bark attached, legislation controlling the movement of elm timber with bark may also be used to slow the spread of the disease.

Verticillium wilt

Elms may very occasionally be attacked by *Verticillium albo-atrum* and *V. dahliae*, the causes of Verticillium wilt. This disease is described in chapter 3.

VIRUS DISEASES

Elm mottle virus

Elm mottle virus (E Mot V) has been found in Scotland causing ring-spot and line-pattern symptoms on the leaves of wych elm (*Ulmus glabra*). Its characteristics have been described by Jones and Mayo (1973), who found that it could be seed-borne. The same virus has been found in lilac, but its economic importance is unknown.

Elm witches' broom

Available information on elm witches' broom, which seems to be a virus disease, has been summarised by Cooper (1979). The disease has been found on *Ulmus carpinifolia*, the smoothleaved elm, in Czechslovakia, the United Kingdom, and in Italy. On affected trees twigs with short internodes bear small chlorotic leaves. Sometimes the leaves at the proximal ends of affected twigs show 'cowl-formation', in which the leaf blade twists round the midrib to form a cone. Transmission has been achieved by budding.

DECAY FUNGI

The commonest decay fungi affecting the stems of elms are *Pleurotus ulmarius* and *Polyporus squamosus*, while *Rigidoporus ulmarius* and *Ustulina deusta* attack the butt. *U. deusta* also destroys the roots. These fungi are described in chapter 19.

MISCELLANEOUS DISEASES

Wetwood

Elms are among the broadleaved trees sometimes affected by wetwood. High water and gas pressure in the trees then causes sap to ooze from the bark and flow down the trunks. The water-soaked bark is killed, and the sap flow often becomes very evil-smelling through the growth in it of various bacteria and yeasts. At least in some cases wetwood appears to be associated with bacteria within the trunks, and affected trees may also become liable to dieback. Wetwood is further discussed in chapter 3.

REFERENCES

Anon (1938). Elm disease eradication in the United States. *Chron. Bot.*, 4, 429–32

Banfield, W. M. (1941). Distribution by the sap stream of spores of three fungi that induce vascular wilt diseases of elm. *J. agric. Res.*, 62, 637–681.

Banfield, W. M. (1968). *Dutch Elm Disease; Recurrence and Recovery in American Elm*. Bull. agric. exp. Stn. Massachusetts, no. 568, 60 pp.

Beattie, R. K. (1937). The Dutch elm disease in Europe. *Am. Forests*, 43, 159–62

Bond, T. E. T. (1956). Notes on *Taphrina. Trans. Br. mycol. Soc.*, 39, 60–66

Brasier, C. M. (1979). Dual origin of recent Dutch elm disease outbreaks in Europe. *Nature, Lond.*, 281, 78–80

Brasier, C. M. (1981). The pathogen, in J. Stipes and R. J. Campana (Eds.), *A Compendium of Elm Diseases*, American Phytopathological Society

Brasier, C. M. and Gibbs, J. N. (1973). Origin of the Dutch elm disease epidemic in Britain. *Nature, Lond.*, 242, 607–9

Brasier C. M. and Gibbs, J. N. (1978). Origin and development of the current Dutch elm disease epidemic, in P. R. Scott and A. Bainbridge (Eds.), *Plant Disease Epidemiology*, Blackwell, Oxford

Brooks, F. T. (1953). *Plant Diseases*, Oxford University Press, London

Cooper, J. I. (1979). *Virus Diseases of Trees and Shrubs*, Institute of Terrestrial Ecology, c/o Unit of Invertebrate Virology, Oxford

Dennis, R. W. G. (1968). *British Ascomycetes*, J. Cramer, Lehre

Doane, C. C. (1962). Evaluation of insecticide for control of the smaller European elm bark beetle. *J. econ. Ent.*, 55, 414-5

Elgersma, D. M. (1967). Factors determining resistance of elms to *Ceratocystis ulmi. Phytopathology*, 57, 641-2

Epstein, A. H. (1978). Control tactics in research and practice. Preventing root graft transmission, in W. A. Sinclair and R. J. Campana (Eds.), *Dutch Elm Disease, Perspectives After 60 Years; Search, Agriculture*, 8, 32-33

Gibbs, J. N. (1978). Development of the Dutch elm disease epidemic in southern England, 1971-1976. *Ann. appl. Biol.*, 88, 219-28

Gibbs, J. N. and Brasier, C. M. (1973). Correlation between cultural characters and pathogenicity in *Ceratocystis ulmi* isolates from Britain, Europe and North America. *Nature, Lond.*, 241, 381-3

Gibbs, J. N. Burdekin, D. A. and Brasier, C. M. (1977). *Dutch Elm Disease*, Forest Rec., Lond., no. 115

Grove, W. B. (1937). *British Stem- and Leaf-Fungi (Coelomycetes)*, vol. 2, Cambridge University Press, Cambridge

Hart, J. H. (1965). Economic impact of Dutch elm disease in Michigan. *Pl. Dis. Reptr.*, 49, 830-32

Heybroek, H. M. (1966). Dutch elm disease abroad. Reprinted (unpaginated) from *Am. Forests*, June, 1966

Heybroek, H. M. (1967). The Dutch elm disease in the old world. *Pap. 14th IUFRO Conf. Sec. 24, Munich, 1967*, pp. 447-54

Hoog, G. S. de (1974). The genera *Blastobotrys, Sporothrix, Calcarisporium* and *Calcarisporiella* gen. nov. *Stud. Mycol., Baarn*, 7.

Jones, A. T. and Mayo, M. A. (1973). Purification and properties of elm mottle virus. *Ann. appl. Biol.*, 75, 347-57

Kerling, L. C. P. (1955). Reactions of elm wood to attacks of *Ophiostoma ulmi* (Buism.) Nannf. *Acta bot. neerl.*, 4, 398-403

Lester, D. T. (1978). Control tactics in research and practice. Exploiting host variation, in W. A. Sinclair and R. J. Campana (Eds.), *Dutch Elm Disease, Perspectives After 60 Years; Search, Agriculture*, 8, 39-42

Moore, W. C. (1959). *British Parasitic Fungi*, Cambridge University Press, Cambridge

Neely, D. (1967). Dutch elm disease in Illinois cities. *Pl. Dis. Reptr.*, 51, 511-14

Neely, D. (1972). Municipal control of Dutch elm disease in Illinois cities. *Pl. Dis. Reptr.*, 56, 460-62

Oeillette, G. B. (1961). Studies in the infection process of *Ceratocystis ulmi* (Buism.) C. Moreau in American elm trees. *Can. J. Bot.*, 40, 1568-75

Peace, T. R. (1960). *The Status and Development of Elm Disease in Britain*, Bull. For. Commn, Lond., no. 33, 44 pp.

Peacock, J. W. (1975). Research on chemical and biological control of elm bark beetles, in D. A. Burdekin and H. M. Heybroek (Eds.), *Dutch Elm Disease, Proc. IUFRO Conf. Sept. 1973*, USDA pp. 76-87

Pomerleau, R. (1961). History of the Dutch elm disease in the Province of Quebec. *For. Chron.*, 37, 356-7

Pomerleau, R. (1968). Progression et localisation de l'infection par le *Ceratocystis ulmi* dans l'orme d'Amerique. *Phytopath. Z.*, 63, 301-27

Redfern, D. B. and Sutton, B. (1981). Canker and dieback of *Ulmus glabra* caused by *Plectophomella concentrica* and its relationship to *P. ulmi. Trans. Br. mycol. Soc.*, 77, 381-90

Sinclair, W. A. and Campana, R. J. (1978). Dutch elm disease, perspectives after 60 years. *Search, Agriculture*, 8 (5), 52 pp.

Smalley, E. B. (1962). Prevention of Dutch elm disease by treatments with 2,3,6-trichloro-phenyl acetic acid. *Phytopathology*, **52**, 1090–91

Smalley, E. B. (1978). Control tactics in research and practice. Systemic chemical treatments of trees for protection and therapy, in W. A. Sinclair and R. J. Campana (Eds.), *Dutch Elm Disease, Perspectives After 60 Years; Search, Agriculture*, **8** (5), 34–9

Smalley, E. B. and Riker, A. J. (1962). Tropical members of the *Ulmaceae* resistant to Dutch elm disease. *Univ. Wis. Res. Not.*, no. 77, 4 pp.

Smucker, S. J. (1935). Air currents as a possible carrier of *Ceratocystis ulmi. Phytopathology*, **25**, 442–3

Smucker, S. J. (1937). Relation of injuries to infection of American elm by *Ceratocystis ulmi. Phytopathology*, **27**, 140

Stipes, J. and Campana, R. J. (1981). *Compendium of Elm Diseases*, American Phyto-pathological Society

Viennot-Bourgin, C. (1949). *Les Champignons Parasites des Plantes Cultivées*, Masson, Paris

Wilson, C. L. (1965). *Ceratocystis ulmi* in elm wood. *Phytopathology*, **55**, 477

15 Diseases of sweet chestnut (*Castanea* spp.)

The only species of *Castanea* of any importance in Britain and the rest of Europe is *C. sativa,* the sweet or Spanish chestnut. This tree is grown in more southerly parts of Europe for its nuts as well as for its timber, though in some areas, especially in Italy, it has declined in importance because of damage by the chestnut blight fungus *Endothia parasitica.* In Britain it was formerly much grown as a coppice crop for fencing, etc., and small areas are still used for that purpose. It is now grown mainly as an ornamental in parks and gardens. Though sweet chestnut fruits ripen in southern England, they remain small, and nearly all the chestnuts sold for eating are imported.

As might be expected of a tree of Mediterranean origin, *C. sativa* is rather susceptible to damage by spring frosts.

POST-NURSERY DISEASES

DISEASES OF SHOOTS

Diebacks and cankers on sweet chestnut caused by the two fungi *Cryptodiaporthe castanea* and *Diplodina castaneae* have both been recorded in Britain. They are, however, little known, and seem to have caused only minor loss. What little is known about them is summarised below.

Dieback and canker caused by *Cryptodiaporthe castanea* (Tul.) Wehm. (stat. conid. *Fusicoccum castaneum* Sacc.)

A dieback and canker of sweet chestnut associated with *Cryptodiaporthe castanea* is known in France as *javart* disease. This popular name is due to a resemblance between the small cankers on the chestnut shoots and the ulcers sometimes formed on horses' feet between hoof and hair, a disorder known as *javart* in French, or quitter or quittor in English (Day, 1930). The disease has been found in Switzerland (Défago, 1937) and in the USA (Fowler, 1938) as well as in France and England.

Symptoms   The symptoms of the disorder show as a wilting and defoliation of coppice shoots, often on only part of a stool. Small greyish or reddish-brown fungal stromata up to 2 mm across appear in cracks in the bark of the affected shoots, from which the bark eventually peals (Moreau and Moreau, 1953). Sunken cankers may girdle the stem and cause it to collapse (Défago, 1937) (figure 73).

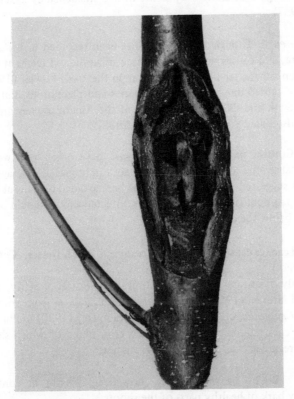

Figure 73.   **Canker on sweet chestnut coppice shoot caused by *Cryptodiaporthe castanea* (Forestry Commission)**

The causal fungus   The perithecia of the fungus are embedded usually in groups in the central part of the stroma. They measure 240-800 x 200-400 μm and their openings scarcely protrude above the stromatic surface. The perithecia contain asci that measure 50-60 x 7-8 μm. Each ascus contains eight colourless, more or less cylindrical, two-celled ascospores measuring 11-16 x 2-3 μm, each usually with a colourless, short cylindric appendage at each end (Wehmeyer, 1932). The pycnidia *(Fusicoccum castaneum)* form as irregular cavities usually round the edges of the stroma. The pycnospores are colourless, oval or spindle-shaped, measuring 4-9 x 3-5 μm. In very damp weather the outer layers of the pycnidium may break open and reveal the spores within as a gelatinous mass (Défago, 1937).

Entry into host and factors affecting the disease   *C. castanea* appears to be a rather weak wound parasite, which may also enter through dead buds. In strongly growing trees, callus formation arrests the growth of the fungus, which is able to enlarge the canker only if the host is weakened by adverse conditions (Défago, 1937).

Damage caused   Though this dieback has been recorded in Britain, it is little known there, and causes no serious damage. Elsewhere it seems at least at times to have been of greater importance. Thus in the USA, Fowler (1938) reported that it often caused damage in both nurseries and plantations, killing branches, reducing growth and deforming the trees of the American chestnut. In Switzerland it has also killed young trees (Défago, 1937).

Control   Control measures for this disease have never been worked out in Britain because the disorder has been so rarely noted. Défago (1937) in Switzerland suggested that the disease was best avoided by careful site selection and soil preparation. If the disease appears, infected shoots should be cut back at least 15 cm below the cankers.

Dieback and canker caused by *Diplodina castaneae* Prill & Delacr. (*Cytodiplospora castaneae* Oud.)

In their study of diseases of sweet chestnut in the Forest of Marly, west of Paris, Moreau and Moreau (1953) isolated *Diplodina castaneae* from wilted trees also invaded by *Cryptodiaporthe castanea*. In Britain, Day (1930) found *D. castaneae* on a sweet chestnut pole from a coppice crop much of which showed severe dieback; he regarded it as a form of *javart* disease.

Symptoms   Bright brown patches showed up clearly in contrast to the purplish-grey bark of healthy parts of the shoots.

The causal fungus   Small, black stromata formed on the brown areas. Pycnidia were produced as cavities in these stromata. They contained colourless, two-celled, spindle-shaped spores measuring 6-7 x 1-1.5 μm (Grove, 1935) or 9-12 x 2.5-3 μm (Day, 1930).

Control   Day (1930) suggested that the disease could be controlled by cutting out and destroying all the diseased shoots. He also recommended trenching round an infected area to isolate it and prevent the possible spread of the fungus from diseased to healthy roots, though there appears to be no evidence that the disease can be transmitted in this way.

DISEASES OF ROOTS

Phytophthora root rot ('ink disease') caused by *Phytophthora cinnamomi* Rands and *P. cambivora* (Petr.) Buism.

Probably the best known of the diseases of sweet chestnut in Britain is the Phytophthora root rot caused by *Phytophthora cinnamomi* and *P. cambivora*. The disease is often called 'ink disease' because a blue-black inky stain may often be found round the damaged roots. This name is not a good one, however, as this stain is not associated only with this disease, but a similar inky fluid will also seep even from fresh, undiseased chestnut wood or bark in contact with the ground (Peace, 1962); the disease, on the other hand, also occurs on other hosts (including beech), in which no such staining is induced (Day, 1938).

Distribution and the causal organism   On *Castanea*, Phytophthora root rot is known to occur throughout most of Europe, in Asia (in India and Turkey), in Australia and New Zealand, in Canada and the USA, and in Argentina (Urquijo Landaluze, 1942).

The causal fungus in Britain is most often *Phytophthora cinnamomi*, but *P. cambivora* may sometimes be involved. These fungi are further discussed in chapter 3. Both occur on other hosts, and both have often been misidentified in the past. Indeed, a survey is needed to provide more information on the relative importance of the two fungi as causes of this disease in chestnut. The world distribution of *P. cambivora* is given in CMI Distribution Map No. 70 (Anon, 1971), and that of *P. cinnamomi* in the corresponding Map No. 302 (Anon, 1978).

The host range and geographical distribution of *P. cinnamomi* are both very wide. The host range of *P. cambivora* is much narrower. Indeed, Crandall (1950) considered that the fungus occurred only on *Castanea*, but according to Waterhouse and Waterston (1966) it is now known to affect also *Acer, Fagus, Juglans, Nothofagus, Quercus* and *Ulmus*.

Symptoms on sweet chestnut   Symptoms of the disease on chestnut may vary, and sometimes quite severely affected trees may show no obvious symptoms above ground (Grente and Solignat, 1952). In the case of coppiced chestnut only some of the shoots may show symptoms, while others remain apparently healthy.

The disease primarily affects the roots, and symptoms in the aerial parts follow and are consequent upon the root infection. At first the fine roots are destroyed, and the fungus spreads inwards into the larger roots and so to the root collar. The tap roots are usually especially severely affected, and as they are destroyed the tree may react by producing further lateral roots. The diseased roots may exude a violet or blue-black inky slime, and cankers may form on the larger roots and at the bases of the trunks (Day, 1938; Dufrénoy, 1922; Milburn and Gravatt, 1932). These basal lesions are the most characteristic and useful symptoms for diagnostic purposes in the field.

The first symptoms to be observed, however, are usually those in the crown, and they arise as a result of the root damage and often the girdling of the trunk by the causal fungi. Sometimes the first visible sign of disease is the falling of unopened male catkins early in the season (Schell, 1922). Leaf symptoms may vary, and with regard to these the disease seems to take two main forms (Day, 1938; Milburn and Gravatt, 1932); these, however, are probably only stages in the same disorder, depending, for example, on the time of attack or its severity. In the first form, the leaves are very small, and after flowering the following year the tree dies. In the second form, the leaves are of normal size, but they quickly become yellow, and finally brown. On such trees fluid may exude from affected bark at the bases of their trunks. The trees may then recover, or die slowly in a few years (Day, 1938). In France, where the trees may be grown for their fruit, the nuts on affected trees are small, and may abort before they can mature; they then hang on the branches for several years (Dufrénoy, 1922).

Host variation in sweet chestnut   It has been known at least since 1922 that the Japanese chestnut *Castanea crenata* and the Chinese chestnut *C. mollissima* are immune or at least highly resistant to Phytophthora root rot (though not to the chestnut blight fungus *Endothia parasitica*) (Dufrénoy, 1922). Hence these trees have been planted to some extent, and used in crossing programmes with *C. sativa* in France (Dufrénoy, 1922), Spain (Urquijo Landaluze, 1944) and Portugal (Guereiro, 1949). In the USA, Milburn and Gravatt (1932) found that the Chinese chestnuts *C. henryi* and *C. seguinii* also showed high resistance.

Factors affecting the disease   It is the general view that the disease is encouraged by various soil factors. Day (1938) found that severe attacks occurred only on shallow, heavy, compact clay soils with poor drainage below. There is no doubt that the disease is worst on wet, poorly drained soils. According to Schell (1922) death often takes place in less than two years on poor soils, but on rich soils the affected trees may persist for four or five years or more. Dufrénoy (1922) noted that the disease developed most rapidly in those affected trees with the most abundant foliage.

Losses caused   Though Phytophthora root rot has often been found in sweet chestnut crops in Britain, in Europe it has done most damage in France and Spain. In France in the earlier part of this century it caused heavy losses in the forests of the Pyrenees, and was also damaging in other areas (Schell, 1922). In Spain, in the better areas half the trees were killed in 25 years, in others in which the trees were a valuable source of income, almost all were destroyed (Del Cañizo, 1942). Crandall *et al.* (1945) considered the disease was also the main cause of the loss of the American chestnut *(Castanea dentata)* in a large part of the eastern USA.

Control   In Britain, Day (1939) suggested that the disease could sometimes be arrested in its early stages on individual trees by cutting out patches of diseased bark and then applying a sterilant to the wound and to the surrounding soil. In general, however, it is best prevented by avoiding wet, ill-drained soils when planting chestnut.

More attention has been paid to chemical treatments in other countries in which the disease is of more importance. Sulphate of iron and various copper compounds applied to wounds on trunks or roots, or to the soil, have been tried with some success in some areas (see, for example, Schell, 1922; Del Cañizo, 1942; Urquijo Landaluze, 1963; Fernandes, 1955). Dufrénoy (1922) recommended soil disinfection with carbon bisulphide or calcium carbide. He also noted that newly affected trees might be saved by severe pruning, which slowed down the disease and also encouraged the formation of new roots. Such methods are likely to be of limited application.

Following the work on selection and breeding for resistance, mentioned above, Cristinzio (1938) in Italy advocated replacing the susceptible trees with the Japanese chestnut, *Castanea crenata*. This tree, however, does not grow well in Britain.

DECAY FUNGI

The sweet chestnut may be attacked by various decay fungi, including *Armillaria mellea*, *Fistulina hepatica* and *Laetiporus sulphureus (Polyporus sulphureus)*. These are discussed in chapter 19.

REFERENCES

Anon (1971). *Phytophthora cambivora. Distrib. Maps Pl. Dis.*, no. 70
Anon (1978). *Phytophthora cinnamomi. Distrib. Maps Pl. Dis.*, no. 302, 4th ed.
Crandall, B.S. (1950). The distribution and significance of the chestnut root rot Phytophthoras, *P. cinnamomi* and *P. cambivora. Pl. Dis. Reptr*, 34, 194-6
Crandall, B.S., Gravatt, G.F. and Ryan, M.M. (1945). Root disease of *Castanea* species and some coniferous and broadleaf nursery stocks, caused by *Phytophthora cinnamomi. Phytopathology*, 35, 162-180
Cristinzio, M. (1938). Il male dell' inchiostro del castagno nella Campania. *Ric. Ossvz. Divulg. fitopat. Campania ed Mezzogiorne (Portici)*, 7, 64-71
Day, W.R. (1930). The 'javart' disease of sweet chestnut, *Cytodiplospora castaneae* Oudemans (= *Diplodina castaneae* Prilleux et Delacroix). *Q. Jl For.*, 24, 114-17
Day, W.R. (1938). Root-rot of sweet chestnut and beech caused by species of Phytophthora. I. Cause and symptoms of disease: its relation to soil conditions. *Forestry*, 12, 101-16
Day, W.R. (1939). Root-rot of sweet chestnut and beech caused by sepcies of *Phytophthora*. II. Inoculation experiments and methods of control. *Forestry*, 13, 46-58

Défago, G. (1937). *Cryptodiaporthe castanea* (Tul.) Wehmeyer, parasite du chataignier. *Phytopath. Z.*, **10**, 168–77

Del Cañizo, J. (1942). A new method of controlling ink disease of the European chestnut. *Int. Bull. Pl. Prot.*, **16**, 2M–3M

Dufrénoy, J. (1922). Les maladies du chataignier. *C. r. Congres Regional a Brive*, 1922, 45–63

Fernandes, C.T. (1955). A luta contra a 'doenca da tinta' nos santos do norte de Portugal e ensoios diversos para a sua major eficiencia e economica. *Publ. Serv. flor. Portugal*, **22**, 53–9

Fowler, M.E. (1938). Twig cankers of asiatic chestnuts in the eastern United States. *Phytopathology*, **28**, 693–704

Grente, J. and Solignat, G. (1952). La maladie de l'encre du chataignier et son évolution. *C. r. Acad. Agric. Fr.*, **38**, 126–9

Grove, W.B. (1935). *British stem- and leaf-fungi (Coelomycetes)*, vol. 1, Cambridge University Press, Cambridge

Guerreiro, G. (1949). Estudos realizados no Castanheiro em 1948. *Bol. Jun Frut., Lisb.*, **9**, 13–40

Milburn, M. and Gravatt, G.F. (1932). Preliminary note on a Phytophthora root disease of chestnut. *Phytopathology*, **22**, 977–8

Moreau, C. and Moreau, M. (1953). Les maladies du chataignier en forêt de Marly. *Rev. for. fr.*, **6**, 411–14

Peace, T.R. (1962). *Pathology of Trees and Shrubs*, Clarendon Press, Oxford

Schell, E. (1922). Diseases of the French chestnut tree – particularly the 'ink-malady'. *J. Am. Leather Chem. Ass.*, **17**, 353–9

Urquijo Landaluze, P. (1942). La enfermedad de la 'tinta' del castano y sn tratamiento. *Agricultura Madr.*, **11**, 54–6

Urquijo Landaluze, P. (1944). Aspectos de la obtencion de hebridos resistentes a la enfermedad del castano. *Bol. Pat. veg. Ent. agric., Madr.*, **13**, 447–62

Urquijo Landaluze, P. (1949). Accion de las sales de cobre el hongo *Phytophthora cinnamomi* y difusion de aquellas en la tierra. *Bol. Pat. veg. Ent. agric., Madr.*, **16**, 295–310

Urquijo Landaluze, P. (1963). Nuevos aspectos de la produccion de Castanos resistentes a la enfermedad de la tinta'. *Bol. Pat. veg. Ent. agric., Madrid*, **26**, 163–79

Waterhouse, G.M. and Waterston, J.M. (1966). *Phytophthora cambivora*. Descr. Pl. Pathogenic Fungi and Bacteria, CMI, Kew, no. 112

Wehmeyer, L.E. (1932). The British species of the genus *Diaporthe* Nits. and its segregates. *Trans. Br. mycol. Soc.*, **17**, 237–95

16 Diseases of poplar (*Populus* spp.)

Of the many species of poplar, the aspen, *Populus tremula*, is native here, as perhaps are also the grey poplar, *P. canescens*, and the black poplar, *P. nigra*. Many introduced poplars are also grown. These include the white poplar, *P. alba*, and the Lombardy poplar, *P. nigra* var. *italica*. The forms grown for timber (mostly for the production of matches), however, are mainly clones of the balsam poplar, *P. trichocarpa*, and of the hybrid black Italian poplar, *P. x euramericana*.

NURSERY DISEASES

DISEASES OF BARK AND SHOOTS

Dothichiza **bark necrosis or trunk scab caused by** *Cryptodiaporthe populea* **(Sacc.) Butin (stat. conid.** *Dothichiza populea* **Sacc. et Briard,** *Chondroplea populea* **Kleb.)**

The ascomycete *Cryptodiaporthe populea* is found throughout Europe and into Turkey, in the eastern parts of North America, and perhaps in Argentina (Anon, 1968). It attacks both plantation trees and nursery plants, and in some areas from time to time causes a severe bark necrosis. In Great Britain it is common, but has so far been of minor importance, and has caused significant damage only in nurseries. In continental Europe, however, it has severely affected large trees and even caused their deaths (Schönhar, 1952; van der Meiden and van Vloten, 1958).

Its perfect fructifications seem to have been found only once in this country, on Lombardy poplar in Gloucestershire in January 1969 (Burdekin, 1970). They are long-necked perithecia wholly embedded in the host tissues with only the ostioles visible at the surface, and contain asci measuring 75–85 x 12–16 μm, each with eight two-celled, colourless, elliptical ascospores measuring 16–24 x 6–9 μm (Butin, 1958*a*). The imperfect stage of the fungus (*Dothichiza populea*) is very common, and consists of pycnidia up to 2 mm across, embedded in the host tissues but wide open when mature, and forming waxy masses of colourless, subglobose or egg-shaped conidia measuring 8–12 x 7–9 μm (Butin, 1958*a*; Goidànich, 1940).

The pycnidia are formed throughout much of the year, from March till late autumn, and the pycnospores can survive for five years (Gremmen, 1958; Taris, 1959), though usually under natural conditions they persist at most for not more than 10 months (Butin, 1962). The pycnidia cease to produce spores only in very dry weather (Goidànich, 1940).

In culture, *C. populea* grows well in media containing malt or yeast extracts (Butin, 1958*b*) or in poplar extracts (Hubbes, 1959). It produces an oily, partly crystalline toxin, which is partly responsible for the damage it causes (Braun and Hubbes, 1957; Butin, 1958*b*; Hubbes, 1959). The fungus grows best at a temperature of about 20°C, but growth can still take place at temperatures only a few degrees above freezing (Viennot-Bourgin and Taris, 1957). The conidia germinate when the relative humidity is 90.5 per cent or higher (Butin, 1962).

Various strains of *C. populea* exist. They differ in host specialisation, and change the colour of a poplar extract medium to various shades of yellow and brown (Braun and Hubbes; 1957; Brendel, 1965), the deepest brown colours being produced by the most pathogenic strains (Hubbes, 1959).

Mode of entry   *C. populea* is a facultative parasite that enters the tree mainly through wounds (including leaf scars and bud scale scars as well as mechanical injuries) (Viennot-Bourgin and Taris, 1957; Gremmen, 1958; Schmidle, 1953), but also through lenticels (Hubbes, 1959), and through shoot tips and buds (Braun and Hubbes, 1957; Viennot-Bourgin and Taris, 1957). It has been known to enter through leaf scars following premature defoliation caused by *Melampsora larici-populina* (van der Meiden and van Vloten, 1958).

Symptoms   The fungus gives rise to dead, oval, generally sunken, greyish, brown or black patches on the stems round the bases of twigs, particularly at the junction of one and two-year-old growth. Similar lesions may occur on branches and around buds (Butin, 1956a). On areas of active infection the black pycnidia of *C. populea* protrude through the dead bark, though older parts of lesions are often colonised by other fungi, such as *Cytospora chrysosperma* (*Valsa sordida*), *Glomerella miyabeana*, and *Chondrostereum purpureum*, and by bacteria (Gremmen, 1958; Breuel and Börtitz, 1966). As a reaction to the attack the host may produce wound periderm, and this may sometimes prevent further spread of the pathogen (Butin, 1956b).

Time of infection and factors affecting the disease   There is some disagreement concerning the time of infection and the factors affecting the disease, perhaps partly because the fungus may remain latent for as long as two years after infection (Gremmen, 1958).

Most writers have agreed that infection occurs mainly in the winter months. Thus Schönhar (1953) concluded that infection took place mostly in winter, and in spring and autumn affected only drought-weakened trees. Müller (1953b) also considered that infection took place mainly in winter, and that the trees were resistant in the growing season. Braun and Hubbes (1957) found that callusing of wounds took place only above 12°C, and wounded plants became infected only below this temperature. Later, Hubbes (1959) failed to infect plants at temperatures above 16°C. On the other hand, Aerts *et al.* (1959) found in their experiments that infection occurred only in spring and summer. According to Viennot-Bourgin and Taris (1957) there are three main periods of infection. Most infection takes place in winter (when the tree is most susceptible) and in April and May (when the buds open, and spores are first available). To a small extent, infection may also take place through wounds in the early part of the summer. In experiments with spores, Schmidle (1953) succeeded in inoculating plants at all seasons, but the percentage of successful inoculations between April and July was relatively low, and was at its highest in September and October. More recently, Gremmen (1978) has partly resolved the question of time of infection by observing that infection can occur both in the spring, through bud scale scars, and in the autumn, through leaf scars.

Factors thought to affect the disease include temperature conditions (which have been already mentioned), water loss (Müller, 1953a; Butin, 1956b), frost (Franken, 1956; Kalandra, 1962), excess nitrogen fertiliser (Gremmen, 1978), leaf diseases (Gremmen, 1978), and waterlogging (Schmidle, 1953). Most workers have concluded that these and other factors operate mainly by weakening the trees and predisposing them to attack, and that plants checked, for example, by transplanting are especially vulnerable. Peace (1962) notes that in Great Britain plants with tops two or more years old have been especially liable to attack.

Host susceptibility   Results of many tests of species and clones for resistance have been published, but in most cases they show little agreement one with another. As a general rule it appears that poplars of the *Leuce* section are least susceptible (Bavendamn, 1936; Kalandra, 1962). Of the common hybrid black poplars, *P. 'robusta'* is particularly susceptible, and *P. 'gelrica'* is resistant (Kalandra, 1962). *P. nigra* var. *italica* is very susceptible (Veldeman and Welvaert, 1960). Werner and Siwecki (1978) have demonstrated that the mechanism of resistance may be related to the ability of the host to form lignin and cork in the tissues below the infection court.

Losses caused   Among the poplar diseases found in Great Britain, bark necrosis is second in importance to bacterial canker. Occasional severe attacks have occurred on dry sites, on over-large transplants, and on plants crowded in the nursery, though the overall damage caused has been small.

In some other countries severe damage has been reported. Thus in Italy up to 95 per cent of the plants have sometimes been killed by this disease (Goidànich, 1940). Similar losses on five to eight-year-old trees were reported in Germany by Kämpfer (1931). Extensive damage has also been found on young plantation trees in the USA (Waterman, 1957).

Control   To avoid the disease, good rooting and growing conditions should be provided (Waterman, 1957; Peace, 1962; Magnani, 1963). Overcrowding in the nursery and the use of overlarge plants should both be avoided, and any pruning of nursery plants should be done before mid-August to allow some healing of pruning wounds before growth ceases (Peace, 1962).

If such steps are taken, the disease should rarely be a problem. If it is, attempts should be made to improve growing conditions, and steps taken to select suitable resistant clones. As a temporary measure, spraying may be considered, since various fungicides, especially copper compounds, have been found to reduce the spread of the disease (Bavendamm, 1936; Wettstein and Donaubauer, 1958), and its carry-over into the following season (Dahte, 1960).

Cytospora dieback and bark necrosis caused by *Valsa sordida* Nits. (stat. conid. *Cytospora chrysosperma* Fr.)

Valsa sordida, an ascomycete whose pycnidial state is *Cytospora chrysosperma*, is a saprophyte and weak wound parasite that sometimes causes a dieback and bark necrosis of poplars, mostly of nursery plants and young trees. It is a common fungus throughout most of Europe, in North America, North and South Africa,

Australasia, and Chile (Anon, 1966*a*). So far it has proved of no importance in Great Britain.

The causal fungus   The fungus grows in the bark of twigs, branches and stems, and its pycnidial stage, which may be found from May to September, erupts as scattered greyish-black stromata about 2 mm across. Masses of sausage-shaped conidia measuring 4–5 x 1 μm form in cavities in the stromata, and in damp weather emerge in numerous long, yellow or golden tendrils (Grove, 1935). The perithecia, which are seldom found in Great Britain, are also embedded in the stromata; they are black and flask-shaped, and measure 0.5 mm across. Their necks are 0.5–0.6 mm long, and their ostioles open at the stroma surface. The club-shaped asci are with or without a short stalk. They measure 26–43 x 4.3–6.4 μm, and each contain eight colourless, sausage-shaped ascospores measuring 6.6–10.9 x 1.3–1.7 μm. These perithecia occur in autumn (Schreiner, 1931*b*).

The fungus grows readily in culture, and resists temperatures well below freezing (Taris, 1956).

Entry into the plant   As noted above, *V. sordida* enters through wounds. It is common on the bark even of healthy trees (Christensen, 1940), and so is always available to enter if conditions favour it. It can also grow on dead tissue and spread thence to live parts of the plant (Stahl, 1967). It may also be able to enter through lenticels (Persson, 1955).

Symptoms and development of the disease   Within the plant, the fungus grows in the bark, kills the cambium, and enters the wood. Small twigs and branches may be girdled and dieback ensue, but on larger branches and stems sunken lesions are produced (Schreiner, 1931*a*), and on these the scattered stromata of the fungus are found. Stahl (1967) in Australia noted infection only on strips of bark about 10–15 cm wide on the sunny side of the trunk. The fungus often spread from these strips, and killed the crown above the lesions.

Viennot-Bourgin and Taris (1957) found that, like *Cryptodiaporthe populea*, *V. sordida* invaded the trees in the winter, but was then able to progress in its attack over the growing season.

Host range and variations in resistance   As a cause of disease, *V. sordida* is of importance almost solely on poplar, though it has been once reported in Great Britain as a cause of the death of young willows (Moore, 1959), and elsewhere has been recorded on species of *Juglans* and *Ulmus* (Christensen, 1940) and *Sorbus* (Peace, 1962).

There is some evidence that various poplar species and hybrids vary in resistance to attack by the fungus, though much of the information is derived only from field observations. Species or hybrids found very resistant by one worker may be recorded as highly susceptible by another, and even the same workers have sometimes noted some species as apparently almost immune in one season that in another year were the only ones attacked (Müller-Stoll and Hartmann, 1950).

Bloomberg, (1962b), however, studied a species and two hybrids that covered a range of resistance, and found evidence that the more resistant the tree the greater its water storage capacity, and resistance to water loss. Tsȳplakova (1967) found that chemical extracts from bark and wood of resistant trees inhibited the growth of cultures of V. sordida.

Factors affecting the disease　　It is generally agreed, however, that environmental factors are more important than those inherent in the tree. Those most often considered significant are moisture stress, temperature, the quality of the site and the resulting vigour of the trees, and closeness of planting.

Thus Bloomberg (1962a) found that he could inoculate plants successfully only when he subjected them to drought and low atmospheric humidity. Further, if he inoculated cuttings that had been allowed to dry out, necrosis developed, but ceased if the cuttings were put in water, while cuttings inoculated when in water only developed necrosis if removed from the water and allowed to dry out.

Stahl (1967), who found the disease developed only on the sunny side of the trunk, concluded that sunshine on the bark raised its temperature high enough at times to interfere with the formation of antibiotic substances (phytoalexins) produced by the plant in response to infection. The fungus, which is normally unable to attack, was then able to gain a hold.

Schreiner (1931a, b) found that trees of poor growth on unfavourable sites were most affected, and on vigorous trees the necrotic patches often healed over. Similarly, when he transplanted diseased trees from a poor site to a good one, they recovered, but those left in the original site were killed by the fungus. He also found that cuttings stored over the winter were very liable to infection.

Treshow and Harward (1965) reported a correlation between necrosis and earlier leaf blight caused by a *Marssonina* sp.

Losses caused by the disease　　Damage and loss caused by this disease in Great Britain have so far been negligible. Elsewhere, however, it has sometimes given rise to heavy losses. Thus in one season it killed many thickly planted poplars in the Bashkir Republic (USSR) (Ibragimov, 1957). Schreiner (1931a) regarded it as the most important disease of poplars in New England, where in one case in which 10 000 cuttings were stored over the winter, only 20 or 30 survived its attack. Also in the USA, Treshow and Harward (1965) found that the main damage caused by the disease was indirect and resulted from suckering and excessive branching, which lead to mishapen boles. Similarly, in Australia, Stahl (1967) noted that few affected trees were killed but many lost all commercial or aesthetic value and had to be removed. Epidemics were rare, but when they did occur, whole plantings could be badly damaged.

Control   To prevent *Cytospora* dieback and bark necrosis, care should be taken to provide good growing conditions in nurseries, with sufficient water and nutrients. Damage to the plants, particularly in winter, should be avoided (Müller-Stoll and Hartmann, 1950), and so should overcrowding.

Other means of control are likely to be rarely needed in Britain, though Schreiner (1931*b*) recommended that cuttings stored over the winter should be kept at 2°C to avoid infection. Trunk injection with ferric sulphate and spraying with 1 per cent Bordeaux or Burgundy Mixture gave promising results in the USSR (Ibragimov, 1964), where Kleiner (1965) also recommended spraying with 1 per cent DNOC in early spring and late autumn to prevent attack.

POST-NURSERY DISEASES

LEAF DISEASES

Leaf blister caused by *Taphrina populina* Fr. (*T. aurea* Fr.)

Taphrina populina is an ascomycete that causes large, conspicuous blisters on poplar leaves (plate 28). The blisters first appear in May and June as convex rounded or irregular projections, sometimes on both sides of the leaf, but more often on the upper side only. The upper sides of the blisters remain the same green colour as the rest of the leaf surface, but the concave underside soon becomes lined by a bright golden-yellow layer of asci. The asci measure 70–90 x 18–22 μm, and contain numerous bud spores that measure about 2 x 1 μm (Dennis, 1968).

The fungus overwinters as spores on the bud scales, and in damp weather attacks the young shoots when the buds burst in spring (Schneider and Sutra, 1969).

Servazzi (1935) has suggested that various physiologic forms of the fungus exist, and attack different poplar species.

T. populina attacks *Populus nigra* and some of its varieties, *P. deltoides*, and clones of *P.* x *euramericana* (Magnani, 1960; Servazzi, 1935). In Great Britain it occurs especially on the euramerican poplar clones, and it has also been found there on *P. alba* (Peace, 1962). It is very common and striking, but causes no significant damage in this country.

Leaf blight caused by *Venturia tremulae* Aderh. (stat. conid. *Pollaccia radiosa* (Lib.) Bald. & Cif.)

Leaf blight caused by *Venturia tremulae* (stat. conid. *Pollaccia radiosa*) is known throughout Europe and North America. In Great Britain it has been found only two or three times (Sutton, 1961; Sutton and Pirozynski, 1963).

In its imperfect stage (*P. radiosa*), the fungus produces small tufts of conidiophores, each of which bears one conidium. The conidia are ellipsoid or club-shaped with a flattened base, almost colourless or brownish, smooth, two or three-celled, and measure 14.5–19 x 6–7.5 μm (Sutton, 1961). The perithecia of the perfect stage (*V. tremulae*) are embedded in the leaf tissues, with a short, projecting neck furnished with stiff bristles, and the asci within each contain eight two-celled, ellipsoid ascospores measuring about 16 x 7 μm (Viennot-Bougin, 1949).

Dance (1961), in Canada, carried out spore trapping experiments and found most spores in the air in June, with a small later peak in August and September. The number of conidia in the air was directly related to rainfall, but the duration of the rain was more important than the total amount.

So far in Great Britain, *V. tremulae* has caused only rounded or irregular buff-coloured leaf spots up to about 2 cm across, and with a black margin (plate 45). Deep olive-coloured pustules of *P. radiosa* occur on the spots, mostly on the upper side of the leaf. The pustules are made up of the tufts of conidiophores and conidia. The perfect stage has been found only once in this country, in Scotland (Sutton, 1961).

Elsewhere, in Continental Europe and in Canada, more severe symptoms have been produced, with blackening and death of leaves, and dieback of young shoots, whose tips become characteristically hook-shaped (Gremmen, 1956; Dance, 1961).

The fungus overwinters as mycelium in the diseased shoots, and as perithecia in the withering leaves (Shavrova, 1967).

V. tremulae seems to be confined to poplars of the *Leuce* section. In Great Britain it has been found on *P. tremula* (aspen) and *P. alba* (the white poplar) (Sutton, 1961; Sutton and Pirozynski, 1963). In other parts of Europe it has also been found on these, and on hybrids between them (Servazzi, 1940; Gremmen, 1956), while in Canada it occurs on *P. tremuloides* (trembling aspen) and *P. grandidentata* (large-toothed aspen) (Dance, 1961).

In parts of the world where this leaf blight causes significant damage, larger, mature trees are little affected, but young trees, seedlings and suckers may be badly attacked, the young trees becoming malformed, nursery plants damaged, and natural regeneration delayed (Dance, 1961; Ginzburg, 1961).

In Great Britain the fungus has been of no more than mycological interest, and no control measures have been needed against it. Elsewhere, plant sanitation measures and spraying with Bordeaux mixture and other copper fungicides have been suggested (Pospíšil, 1960; Shavrova, 1967).

Poplar leaf rusts: *Melampsora* spp.

Three species of *Melampsora* attack the leaves (and to some extent the shoots) of poplar, but one is divided into three races, which are themselves sometimes regarded as species. All are heteroecious, producing their uredosori and teleutosori on poplar, and their spermogonia and aecidia on various alternate hosts. They are listed in table 16.1. All are fully described in Wilson and Henderson (1966), and only a brief account of them is given here. They occur in both the nursery and the

Table 16.1

Poplar leaf rusts

Poplar hosts	Rusts	Alternate hosts
Black and balsam poplars	(1) *M. allii-populina*	*Allium* and *Arum*
	(2) *M. larici-populina*	*Larix**
White poplars and aspen	(3) *M. populnea* including:	
	(a) *M. larici-tremulae*	*Larix*
	(b) *M. aecidioides*	*Mercurialis*
	(c) *M. pinitorqua*	*Pinus*

*Not certainly known on larch in Great Britain

plantation, and are more important in the former than in the latter. In Great Britain, though very common, they appear to be of minor importance.

M. allii-populina Kleb. produces its small uredosori and teleutosori on the undersides of the poplar leaves. The uredosori are up to about 1 mm across, round, and bright orange in colour, with oblong or broadly club-shaped uredospores measuring 24–38 x 11–18 μm. The dark brown teleutosori, which form under the epidermis, are about the same size as the uredosori, and are made up of groups of column-shaped teleutospores measuring from 35–60 x 6–10 μm.

M. larici-populina Kleb., which appears to be the commonest of these rusts in Great Britain, also produces small orange uredosori up to about 1 mm across on the lower sides of poplar leaves, with elliptical uredospores measuring 30–40 x 13–17 μm. The reddish-brown teleutosori are also small, and occur on the upper sides of the leaves. They are black when mature, and the columnar spores, which arise below the epidermis, measure from 40–50 x 7–10 μm.

In *M. populnea* (Pers.) Karst. (*M. tremulae* Tul.), both uredosori and teleutosori are again produced on the undersides of the leaves, and are very small, with the uredosori measuring only up to about $\frac{1}{2}$ mm across, and the teleutosori about twice this diameter. The uredosori (plate 46) are yellowish orange, and the uredospores are subglobose, measuring 15–25 x 11–18 μm. The dark brown, subepidermal teleutosori contain columnar teleutospores measuring 22–60 x 7–12 μm. *M. populnea* is a complex, containing *M. larici-tremulae* Kleb., *M. aecidioides* Plowr., and *M. pinitorqua* Rostr.

The three rusts, *M. allii-populina*, *M. larici-populina* and *M. populnea*, are exceedingly similar in their stages on poplar, and can be separated with difficulty, and then only by the use of minute microscopical differences (Gremmen, 1954; Hennebert, 1964). These include differences in the uredospores, which are subglobose in *M. populnea* but elongated, and so more or less elliptical, in the other two species. In these, the uredospore wall is uniformly thickened in *M. alli-*

populina, but is more thickened at the equator than elsewhere in *M. larici-populina* (Wilson and Henderson, 1966; Hennebert, 1964). These and other differences have also been noted by Pinon (1973).

Information on the biology of these rusts is limited, but Taris (1966) found that the uredospores of an unspecified *Melampsora* sp. from poplar were still alive and able to cause infection after 270 days. He found that the optimum temperature for spread of these uredospores was from 18–22°C. In Japan, *M. larici-populina* can overwinter by means of uredospores as well as by teleuto-spores (Chiba and Zinno, 1960). This is probably the case elsewhere, as this fungus often occurs on poplars when larch is absent from the vicinity. Indeed, in Great Britain it is not certainly known to occur on larch, though elsewhere it seems to have appeared on poplars only when larches were planted nearby (van der Meiden and van Vloten, 1958).

Host range   The rusts of the *M. populnea* group all attack aspen (*Populus tremula*); in addition, *M. larici-tremulae* and *M. aecidioides* both affect the white poplar (*P. alba*).

The host range of *M. allii-populina* and *M. larici-populina* is probably incompletely known, though broadly they attack black poplars and their hybrids, balsam poplars, and the hybrids between the black and balsam poplars. So far, *M. larici-populina* appears to attack members of all these groups, but *M. allii-populina* may perhaps be restricted to *P. nigra* among the black poplars and *P. trichocarpa* among the balsams.

Within species, varieties and hybrids, different poplar clones vary in resistance to the rusts (Donaubauer, 1964; Chiba, 1964), but clones resistant in one area may be susceptible in another (Schreiner, 1959), as the rusts exist as a range of physiological races each capable of attacking a different range of clones (van Vloten, 1944; Magnani, 1966).

Losses caused   Although by the end of the season these rusts are often very conspicuous, covering the leaves with sori and causing premature defoliation, their effects in Great Britain generally appear to be small, because their attack usually comes late, when growth of the trees has been completed. In parts of continental Europe, however, *Melampsora* spp. cause serious damage, and in Nordbrabant in Holland, in the years following 1948–1950, after extensive planting of larch in the area, it became impossible to establish *P. 'serotina'*, *P. 'marilandica'* and *P. 'Heidemij'* because of severe attacks by *M. larici-populina*. Financial losses were estimated to be up to 400 Dutch florins per hectare (van der Meiden and van Vloten, 1958). Further, extensive damage by *Cryptodiaporthe populea* (stat. conid. *Dothichiza populea*) often followed the rust attacks, because the rust caused premature leaf fall, and the spores of *C. populea* were then able to enter the fresh leaf scars.

Control   In Great Britain it is rarely necessary to take any steps to control these leaf rusts. If they cause trouble, a search should be made for clones resistant in the area concerned. It is seldom economically justifiable to spray poplars, though Bordeaux mixture and other copper sprays control *Melampsora* spp. (Šarič and Milatović, 1960; Nohara *et al.*, 1961), and zineb has also given good results in some cases (van der Meiden, 1964*a*) though not in all.

Leaf spot diseases caused by species of *Marssonina*

At least three species of *Marssonina* that cause leaf spots on poplars have been identified in Great Britain, and are generally considered to be the following:

M. populi-nigrae Kleb., of which *M. populi* (Lib.) Magn. is now regarded as a synonym (Zycha, 1965; Donaubauer, 1967)

M. castagnei (Desm. & Mont.) Magn.

M. brunnea (Ellis & Everh.) Magn.

All are imperfect stages of species of *Drepanopeziza*, but so far in Great Britain the perfect state has been found of only one of them, *D. punctiformis* Gremmen, the conidial stage of which is *M. brunnea* (Byrom and Burdekin, 1970).

Marssonina populi-nigrae (stat. conid. of *Drepanopeziza populorum* Desm.) Höhnel) occurs throughout Europe, as well as in Canada and the USA (Donaubauer, 1967). In Great Britain it has been described (by Grove, 1937) as *M. populi*.

The fungus produces brown spots, with irregular edges, on the upper sides of the leaves. The spots often coalesce to form blotches, on which from July to September small tawny pustules may be found. From these pustules, whitish tendrils of macroconidia emerge in damp weather. The spores are rather pear shaped, straight or curved, constricted at a septum that divides them unequally below the middle, and measure 15–20 x 7–12 μm. The fungus may also form black spots on the twigs and branches (Grove, 1937).

The perfect stage, *Drepanopeziza populorum*, is a brown apothecium with club-shaped asci measuring 80–100 x 13–14 μm, each containing eight colourless, ellipsoid, one-celled (later two-celled) ascospores measuring 16–18 x 6–8 μm (Gremmen, 1962). It has been found in Ireland (O'Riordain and Kavanagh, 1965) but not as yet in Great Britain. It occurs on dead leaves in the spring (Veldeman, 1966).

M. populi-nigrae attacks various clones of *Populus* x *euramericana* (Gremmen, 1964) and has also been recorded on *P. tacamahaca* (*P. balsamifera*) (Laubert, 1936). It also affects *P. nigra* (Magnani, 1964), and it is on *P. nigra* cv. 'italica', the Lombardy poplar, that it causes most damage in Great Britain, though it also occurs there on *P.* x *euramericana*. On the Lombardy poplar it causes premature loss of leaves from the base upwards, so that only a tuft of foliage at the top of the crown may be left alive (Peace, 1962) (figure 74). Trees thus defoliated over several seasons may be killed.

Marssonina castagnei (stat. conid. of *Drepanopeziza populi-albae* (Kleb.) Nannf.) occurs throughout much of Europe.

Figure 74. Lombardy poplars almost entirely defoliated by *Marssonina populi-nigrae* so that the only remaining live foliage forms a tuft at the top of the crown (D.H. Phillips)

The fungus, which is described by Grove (1937), causes spots and blotches much like those of *M. populi-nigrae* (but with no well-defined darker margin) on the upper sides of the leaves. Small pustules of macroconidia arise on the blotches in moist weather in summer and early autumn. The conidia, which ooze out in short whitish tendrils, are more or less pear-shaped, curved, with no constriction at the septum that divides them below the middle. According to Grove, they measure 25–26 × 9 μm, though the figures given by Magnani (1964) are 18.4–23.6 × 6.5–7.5 μm, and those by Zycha (1965) are 15.5–19.0 × 8.0–9.5 μm.

M. castagnei appears to be confined or almost confined to *Populus alba* (Laubert, 1936; Gremmen, 1964), though Magnani (1964) also recorded it in Italy on *P.* × *euramericana*. In Great Britain it does not seem to be of much importance.

Marssonina brunnea (stat. conid. of *Drepanopeziza punctiformis* Gremmen) was not found in Great Britain until 1966 (Phillips, 1967*a*), and is known also in

France, Belgium, Holland, Germany, Austria, Italy, Canada, Japan (Donaubauer, 1967) and Hungary (Gergácz, 1967).

The fungus causes very small, dark brown spots up to about 1 mm across on leaves and petioles and sometimes on the young green twigs (plate 47); when infection is severe the spots coalesce over the whole leaf surface. The macroconidia form in pustules on the spots, and are colourless, unequally two-celled, often sickle-shaped, 15– 18 x 4–6 μm. The apothecia of the perfect stage are dark brown, and occur in May on both sides of the leaves. The asci are clavate, measuring 45–84 x 9–12 μm, and each contains eight colourless, ellipsoidal ascospores measuring 6– 17 x 4–7 μm (Byrom and Burdekin, 1970).

M. brunnea has so far been most damaging on clones of *Populus x euramericana*, though it has also been found on *P. deltoides, P. nigra* and various species in the *Tacamahaca* section (Magnani, 1965). Different poplar clones vary considerably in resistance to the fungus (Donaubauer, 1965).

In Italy the fungus causes premature leaf fall and reduces growth (Castellani and Cellerino, 1964). So far in Great Britain it has not been of major importance, although one or two locally serious outbreaks have been reported.

Control of Marssonina leaf spot diseases   Few if any measures have ever been taken to control these leaf spots in Great Britain. On a small scale, any steps taken to remove, dig in or rot down the infected fallen leaves should reduce the inoculum available in the spring. Spraying with various chemicals has shown promise elsewhere, particularly with dithane M45 (Castellani and Cellerino, 1967) and maneb (Guldemond and Kolster, 1966). Spraying must begin in spring, when the first infection is taking place. The best means of control, however, lie in the growing of resistant clones, and in this connection it is known that the promising clone *P. trichocarpa* MB (*P. trichocarpa* Fritzi Pauley), which is resistant to *Xanthomonas populi,* the bacterial canker organism, is also resistant to *Marssonina brunnea.*

Leaf spots caused by *Phyllosticta populina* Sacc. and *Septoria populi* Desm.
Phyllosticta populina and *Septoria populi* have both been recorded as the cause of leaf spots on poplar in Great Britain (Grove, 1935; Moore, 1959), though neither has so far proved to be of any importance.

Phyllosticta populina, which occurs on *Populus nigra* and *P. x euramericana*, produces small rounded spots that later join to become angular or sinuous brown or grey blotches with a darker margin. Pycnidia about 150 μm across appear on the blotches, on the upper side of the leaf, and contain ellipsoid or oval conidia measuring 6– 8 x 2.5–3.5 μm (Grove, 1935).

Septoria populi has also been found in the field mainly on *Populus nigra* and its varieties and on *P. x euramericana* (especially cv. 'serotina') (Grove, 1935), though Magnani (1962) in Italy succeeded in inoculating *P. alba, P. deltoides, P. tacamahaca* (*P. balsamifera*), *P. simonii* and *P. x berolinensis*.

It produces dry, pale spots with a brownish-black margin, up to about 2 mm across, scattered over the leaf. Pycnidia about 225 μm in diameter appear on the spots, on top or on both sides of the leaf, and contain curved, wormlike, two-celled spores measuring 30–45 x 3–3.5 μm.

S. populi is the conidial stage of *Mycosphaerella populi* Schroet., but perithecia have not yet been found in Great Britain.

DISEASES OF TWIGS, BRANCHES AND STEMS

Dothichiza bark necrosis or trunk scab caused by *Cryptodiaporthe populea*
As already noted, Dothichiza bark necrosis or trunk scab may attack plantation trees as well as nursery plants, and in continental Europe may severely damage or even kill large trees. In Britain, however, it has caused serious losses only in the nursery. Therefore, it is described above under nursery diseases.

Cytospora dieback and bark necrosis caused by *Valsa sordida*
Cytospora dieback and bark necrosis, which may be found on trees in plantations, is nevertheless mainly a disease of nursery plants and young trees. Therefore, it is described in the nursery diseases section.

Bacterial canker caused by *Xanthomonas populi* (Ridé) Ridé and Ridé (*Aplanobacterium* (*Aplanobacter*) *populi* Ridé)
The bacterial canker caused by *Xanthomonas populi* (Ridé and Ridé, 1978) which is much the most important disease of poplars in Great Britain, is also of major importance in France, Belgium, Holland, Germany, Poland, the USSR, and Hungary, and appears to be present also in Rumania and Jugoslavia (Anon, 1966*b*).

   X. populi was first isolated in 1956 by Ridé, who proved that it produced typical cankers on inoculation into susceptible poplars (Ridé, 1958, 1963). It is a gram-negative rod with a single polar flagellum observable by immunofluorescence techniques (Ridé and Ridé, 1978). It has stringent nutrient requirements, but if grown on a standard medium with the addition of yeast extract, glucose and peptone it forms creamy mucoid colonies.

Symptoms of the disease   The various symptoms of the disease have been described by Sabet and Dowson (1952), Ridé (1963), Jobling and Young (1965) and others. The first visible symptom is seen in early spring, when a dense, whitish slime that swells in damp weather exudes mainly from cracks in young branches from one to two (or sometimes up to four) years old. The tissues below the cracks are greenish and translucent, because their intercellular spaces are filled with bacterial slime, and it is at this time that the bacterium is most easily isolated from the infected wood. These young branches may be girdled, and a dieback results (plate 49), but on older and larger branches and stems cankers may arise, and develop for many years (figure 75). Slime exudes also from these cankers, and sometimes from the bases of buds, and is usually easy to find on diseased

Figure 75. Canker on a poplar stem caused by *Xanthomonas populi* (D.H. Phillips)

trees of most (but not all) susceptible clones in spring and early summer. It becomes progressively scarcer as the season advances, however, and also more and more contaminated by secondary organisms, and less and less effective as an inoculum (Ridé, 1966).

The cankers may be 'closed', rough excrescences, usually up to 3 cm across, or 'open', elongated lesions with exposed wood surrounded by a raised rim of callus tissue (Sabet and Dowson, 1952). Jobling and Young (1965) have also described series of elongated and sometimes sinuous cankers arising over the tunnels made by the larvae of agromyzid flies.

When Ridé (1959) inoculated poplar leaves with *X. populi*, it produced diffuse blotches that became grey in the centre, but similar inoculations by Whitbread (1967) resulted in no symptoms.

Once cankers have arisen, they become colonised by other organisms, particularly *Pseudomonas syringae*, which was at one time considered to be the cause of the disease (Sabet and Dowson, 1952), though inoculations with pure cultures of this bacterium always fail to produce the characteristic symptoms of canker, but cause only a local necrosis of the bark, with subsequent recovery (Ridé, 1963).

Inoculation tests with *X. populi* have shown that trees infected from April to July produce cankers in the same year. If infection takes place between August and early October, slime production and necrosis of the affected branch takes place at the time of bud burst in the following season. Inoculations made at other times have given variable results (Ridé, 1959).

Entry into the plant   *X. populi* appears to enter the plant through wounds of various kinds. Infection succeeds only if the bacterium reaches the cambium (Ridé, 1966). It has been suggested that under natural conditions entry is gained through bud scale, stipule and leaf scars, and wounds made by insects, small cracks caused by virus diseases, and perhaps by frost, as well as through pruning (Ridé, 1959, 1963, 1966; Jobling and Young, 1965; Whitbread, 1967; Burdekin, 1972).

Bud scale scars and stipule scars are both present at the beginning of the season, when bacterial slime is most abundant. Fresh stipule scars were successfully inoculated by Ridé (1966). Leaf scars remain open to infection for only a few days (Ridé, 1963), and they occur mainly at the end of the season when little slime is present. Nevertheless, some slime may be found at times throughout the growing season (Burdekin, in Phillips, 1967b), and leaf scars have been successfully inoculated (Whitbread, 1967). Careful field observations have also shown them to be important infection sites (Burdekin, 1972).

When Jobling and Young (1965) found elongated cankers over the tunnels made by the larvae of agromyzid flies (plate 50), they considered that the bacterium entered the exit holes made by the insects, and grew in the parenchyma filling the tunnels. Burdekin (1966) found that the bacterium could be introduced into the tunnels, and multiplied there. Openings leading directly into tunnels within the cambium are clearly ideal entry points for *X. populi* which, as noted above, can invade the plant only if it reaches cambial tissue. Ridé and Viart (1966) were also of the opinion that a *Dendromyza* sp. played some part in the transmission of the disease, and Ridé (1963) also noticed bacterial slime emerging from galls formed by the moth *Gypsonoma aceriana* (*Semasia aceriana*).

Sabet (1953) carried out freezing experiments with poplars, but they provided no evidence that frost damage led to the establishment of bacterial canker. Cankers of purely physical origin may sometimes arise near the bases of poplars (and other trees) as a result of frost cracking, but *X. populi* is not involved in these.

Little is known about the mode of spread of the bacterium from tree to tree, though rain splash is probably involved, and carriage by insects has been suggested. In France, Ridé and Viart (1966) noticed that the disease spread rapidly in the direction of the prevailing wind.

Susceptibility of poplar species, varieties and clones Many tests have been made to test the relative susceptibility of various species, varieties and clones of poplar, but the results as a whole are difficult to interpret because until the isolation of *X. populi* they were carried out by inoculation with natural slime, which is a very variable material, containing differing concentrations of *X. populi* and other organisms (Ridé, 1963). Bacterial slime may also be difficult to obtain, particularly as late as September, the best month for inoculation tests (Ridé, 1959). To be reliable, tests must be carried out over several seasons by standard methods, using virulent cultures of *X. populi*, and parallel tests should be made with plants exposed to natural infection in the field (Ridé, 1963).

Broadly, within the *Leuce* group, the aspen (*P. tremula*) is susceptible (and indeed was a main source of bacterial slime for resistance tests), while the white and some clones of the grey poplar (*P. alba* and *P. canescens*, respectively) are resistant (Peace, 1962). Among the balsam and hybrid black poplars, which are of potential commercial importance, however, there is great variation not only between species but even between clones. Thus within *P. trichocarpa*, some clones are highly susceptible, while others are very resistant (Whitbread, 1967). Before silviculturally desirable clones can be recommended for planting, they therefore need adequate testing for resistance to bacterial canker (and also to the leaf spot fungus, *Marssonina brunnea*).

Factors affecting the disease Most of the factors known to affect the disease under natural conditions have been already mentioned. Thus of high importance is the susceptibility of the individual poplar species, variety or clone concerned. So is the presence of suitable wounds, such as bud scale, stipule and leaf scars, damage by agromyzid flies, or pruning, at a time when bacterial inoculum is available. Stipule scars are present when bacterial slime is most abundant (Ridé, 1966). Leaf scars occur mainly when slime is scarce, as the amount of available inoculum declines throughout the season. Hence the provision of early leaf scars through premature defoliation caused by *Taphrina populina* or *Marssonina brunnea* may also be important (Ridé, 1966). Already-diseased poplars are important sources of *X. populi* when planting new stands.

Losses caused The damage caused to susceptible poplars may lead to severe dieback and even death of the tree. Even a small number of cankers on the trunks of trees may make them valueless. Apart from this direct damage, the disease greatly restricts the use of available clones, as many that are otherwise silviculturally desirable cannot be grown because they are susceptible to canker.

Control measures In France (Ridé, 1963) and in some other countries, attempts have been made since 1957 to control poplar canker partly by legislation demanding the removal of diseased trees that act as sources of inoculum. It is difficult to enforce such legislation adequately, however, and the disease is controlled almost entirely by the planting of resistant clones. At the present time, in

Great Britain the most promising of these is that known as *P. trichocarpa* MB (also known as *P. trichocarpa* Fritzi Pauley) which is also resistant to the leaf spot caused by *Marssonina brunnea*, and is a fast-growing tree suitable for use both as an amenity tree and for rapid timber production (Burdekin, 1969).

DISEASES OF CATKINS

Catkin blight caused by *Taphrina johansonii* Sadeb. and *T. rhizophora* Johans.
Taphrina johansonii and *T. rhizophora* are two uncommon ascomycetes that infect catkins and cause swelling of the carpels. The swollen carpels are sterile, and become covered by a golden-yellow layer of club-shaped asci.

In Great Britain, *T. johansonii* has been recorded in Scotland on *Populus tremula* (aspen) (Foister, 1961). Elsewhere, where it occurs throughout much of Europe, in North America, and in Japan, it has sometimes been found also on *P. tremuloides*, *P. grandidentata*, *P. canescens*, *P. nigra* var. *pyramidalis*, *P. sieboldii* (Mix, 1949) and *P. fremontii* (Viennot-Bourgin, 1949). Its asci measure 60–140 x 12–27 μm, and contain numerous oval or globular bud spores measuring 4–10 x 1.5–4 μm (Dennis, 1968).

Taphrina rhizophora Johans. has also been recorded in Great Britain (Ramsbottom and Balfour-Brown, 1951). It scarcely differs morphologically from *T. johansonii*, but its asci measure 129–160 μm in length, and it is restricted to *Populus alba* (Mix, 1949; Viennot-Bourgin, 1949).

VIRUS DISEASES

Poplar mosaic
Poplar mosaic is a virus disease known in Great Britain (Tinsley, 1967; Biddle and Tinsley, 1971*a*) as well as throughout much of continental Europe in France, Holland, Germany, Denmark, Czechoslovakia, Switzerland, Italy, Jugoslavia and Bulgaria, and in Canada and the USA (Berg, 1964).

The fullest account of the disease is by Berg (1964), who found that the rod-shaped particles of the virus measured up to 735 mμm. Biddle (1969) considered that the virus in Great Britain was identical with that elsewhere in Europe, and showed no evidence of differentiation into strains. The best herbaceous test plant is *Vigna sinesis*, the cowpea (Berg, 1964), though *Nicotiana glutinosa* may also be used (Tinsley, 1967).

Symptoms of the disease   In poplars, the virus causes vein clearing and spotting, so that star-shaped or diffuse light green or yellowish spots appear scattered over the leaves (figure 76). Symptoms vary somewhat with the species or clone of poplar, and in some clones necrotic spots may be found on leaf veins and petioles. In severe infections, leaf curling may occur, and swellings appear on twigs (Berg, 1964). Infection may be very distinct on some clones, for example, *P. 'Heidemij'*,

Figure 76. Poplar mosaic virus: symptoms on leaves (Forestry Commission)

while on others, particularly at the end of the summer and into the autumn, symptoms are difficult to detect (van der Meiden, 1964*b*). Berg (1964) found that symptoms were especially clear in warm growing seasons. In Italy infection of some clones may lead to premature leaf fall, and reduction in growth may result, though in more northerly countries, including Great Britain, this applies mainly to nursery plants and not to more mature trees in plantations (van der Meiden, 1964*b*; Biddle, 1969).

Distribution of virus within the tree   Within the plant, distribution of the virus may be uneven, and symptomless cuttings taken from diseased trees usually produce symptomless plants, though cuttings from plants showing no symptoms occasionally give rise to diseased plants (Berg, 1964).

Means of spread   The virus is spread mainly by the use of diseased cuttings. Berg (1964) failed to pass the disease from poplar to poplar by pruning shears or by aphids, and succeeded in transmitting it only by grafting. He readily passed it to herbaceous hosts by sap transmission, however. Biddle and Tinsley (1968) from field observations concluded that subterranean spread of the virus probably took place, but considered that this was not to any large extent through root grafts.

Host range   Poplar mosaic affects almost all the poplars in the *Aigeiros* section, including many clones of *P.* x *euramericana*. Members of the *Tacamahaca* section and crosses between species in this and the *Aigeiros* section are also affected (Berg, 1964).

Damage caused   In Great Britain, Biddle and Tinsley (1971*b*) found that poplar mosaic could greatly reduce the growth in height and diameter of some clones in the nursery, but it had little effect on the growth of older trees in the plantation. In Holland, the growth of commerical clones is also little affected, though in Italy, where the disease is more severe and may cause early leaf fall, growth reduction may occur (van der Meiden, 1964*b*).

Apart from its effect on growth, the virus may reduce the specific gravity of the wood of affected trees, but it may cause a slight increase in the strength of the timber (Biddle and Tinsley, 1968; Biddle and Tinsley, 1971*b*).

Control of the disease   So far the disease can be controlled only by the destruction of diseased propagating stools to prevent the dissemination of diseased planting stock. Attempts by Berg (1964) to free plants of the virus by heat treatment were unsuccessful.

DECAY FUNGI

The most frequent causes of stem and branch rots in poplars are *Chondrostereum purpureum* (the silver leaf fungus) and *Pleurotus ostreatus* (the oyster mushroom), while *Pholiota squarrosa* may rot the butt. These fungi are described in chapter 19.

REFERENCES

Aerts, R., Soenen, A. and Beauduin, E. (1959). Essais de lutte contre le Dothichiza du Peuplier (*Dothichiza populea* Sacc. et Br.). *Agricultura, Louvain*, Sér. 2, 7, 269–87
Anon (1966*a*). *Valsa sordida* Nits. *Distr, Maps Pl. Dis.*, no. 416
Anon (1966*b*). *Aplanobacter(ium* sic) *populi* Ridé. *Distr. Maps Pl. Dis.*, no. 422
Anon (1968). *Cryptodiaporthe populea* (Sacc.) Butin. *Distrib. Maps Pl. Dis.*, no 344, 2nd ed.
Bavendamm, W. (1936). Der Rindenbrand der Pappeln. *Tharandt. forstl. Jb.*, 87, 177–9
Berg, T. M. (1964). Studies on poplar mosaic virus and its relation to the host. *Meded. Land-bHoogesch. Wageningen*, 64, (11), 59 pp. and appendix

Biddle, P. G. (1969). Virus diseases of forest trees. *Rep. Forest Res., Lond., 1969*, p. 150

Biddle, P. G. and Tinsley, T. W. (1968). Virus diseases of forest trees. *Rep. Forest Res., Lond., 1968*, pp. 149–51

Biddle, P. G. and Tinsley, T. W. (1971*a*). Poplar mosaic virus in Great Britain. *New Phytol.,* 70, 61–66

Biddle, P. G. and Tinsley, T. W. (1971*b*). Some effects of poplar mosaic virus on the growth of poplar trees. *New Phytol.* 70, 67–75

Bloomberg, W. J. (1962*a*). Cytospora canker of poplars: factors influencing the development of the disease. *Can. J. Bot.,* 40, 1271–80

Bloomberg, W. J. (1962*b*). Cytospora canker of poplars: the moisture relations and anatomy of the host. *Can. J. Bot.,* 40, 1281–92

Braun, H. and Hubbes, M. (1957). Sporeninfektion und Antagonismus bei *Dothichiza populea. Naturwissenschaften,* 44, 333

Brendel, G. (1965). Untersuchungen über Hybriden der Gattung *Populus*, Sektion 'Aegeiros' und ihren Einfluss auf die Biologie von *Dothichiza populea* Saccardo et Briard. *Phytopath. Z.,* 53, 1–34

Breuel, K. and Börtitz, S. (1966). Beiträge zur Ätiologie des Braunfleckengrindes, eine Rindennekrose der Gattung *Populus*. 2. Mitteilung: Untersuchungen über das pathogene Agens. *Phytopath. Z.,* 57, 59–78

Burdekin, D. A. (1966). The role of Agromyzid flies in relation to bacterial canker. *Publ. FAO Int. Poplar Commn Res. Dis. Group*, 1 p.

Burdekin, D. A. (1969). Forest pathology. *Rep. Forest Res., Lond., 1969*, pp. 106–10

Burdekin, D. A. (1970). Forest pathology. *Rep. Forest Res., Lond., 1970*, pp. 114–19

Burdekin, D. A. (1972). Bacterial canker of poplar. *Ann. appl. Biol.,* 72, 295–9

Butin, H. (1956*a*). Beobachtungen über das vorjährige Auftreten der *Dothichiza*-Krankheit der Pappel. *NachrBl. dt. PflSchutzdienst, (Braunschweig), Stuttgart,* 8, 55–58

Butin, H. (1956*b*). Untersuchungen über Resistenz und Krankheitsanfälligkeit der Pappel gegenüber *Dothichiza populea* Sacc. et Br. *Phytopath, Z.,* 28, 353–74

Butin, H. (1958*a*). Über die auf *Salix* und *Populus* vorkommenden Arten der Gattung *Cryptodiaporthe* Petr. *Phytopath. Z.,* 32, 399–415

Butin, H. (1958*b*). Untersuchungen über ein Toxin in Kulturfiltraten van *Dothichiza populea* Sacc. et Br. *Phytopath. Z.,* 33, 135–46

Butin, H. (1962). (Germination and viability of spores of *Dothichiza populea* under various atmospheric humidities). *Ber. dt. bot. Ges.,* 75, 221–32; abstract in *Rev. appl. Mycol.,* 42, 222, 1963

Byrom, N. A. and Burdekin, D. A. (1970). *Drepanopeziza punctiformis*. British records, no. 101. *Trans. Br. mycol. Soc.,* 54, 139–141

Castellani, E. and Cellerino, G. P. (1964). Una pericolosa malattia dei pioppi euramericani determinata da *Marssonina brunnea* (Ell. & Ev.) P. Magn. *Cellulosa Carta*, 15, 3–16

Castellani, E. and Cellerino, G. P. (1967). Resultati di tre anni di lotta contro la *Marssonina brunnea* del pioppo. *ExGiornate fitopatologiche 1967, Bologne*, 213–219; abstract in *Rev. appl. Mycol.,* 47, 1968, no. 2853

Chiba, O. (1964). Studies on the variation in susceptibility and the nature of resistance of poplars to the leaf rust caused by *Melampsora larici-populina* Klebahn. *Bull. For. Exp. Sta. Meguro,* 166, 86–157

Chiba, O. and Zinno, Y. (1960). Uredospores of the poplar leaf rust *Melampsora larici-populina* Kleb. as a source of primary infection. *J. Jap. For. Soc.,* 42, 406–10

Christensen, C. M. (1940). Studies on the biology of *Valsa sordida* and *Cytospora chrysosperma. Phytopathology,* 30, 459–75

Dahte, A. (1960). Vorbeugung gegen Dothichiza-befall der Baumschulpflanzen durch Chemikalienspritzung. *Holzzentralblatt,* 86, 934

Dance, B. W. (1961). Spore dispersal in *Pollaccia radiosa* (Lib.) Bald. & Cif. *Can. J. Bot.,* 39, 1429–35

Dennis, R. W. G. (1968). *British Ascomycetes*, J. Cramer, Lehre

Donaubauer, E. (1964). Untersuchungen über die Variation der Krankheitsanfälligkeit verschiedener Pappeln. *Mitt. Forstl. Bundes-Versuchsamst. Mariabrunn,* 63, pp. 121 (Vienna); abstract in *For. Abs.,* 26, 1965, no. 817

Donaubauer, E. (1965). [The Marssonina disease of poplar in Austria]. *Allg. Forstz.,* 76, suppl. (*Infomationsdienst* no. 96), 2 pp.; abstract in *For. Abs.,* 27, 1966, no. 2424

Donaubauer, E. (1967). Über die Verbreitung von *Marssonina brunnea* (Ell. & Ev.) Magn. und *M. populi-nigrae* Kleb. *Pap. IUFRO Congr. Munich 1967*, vol, 5, pp. 279–84

Foister, C. E. (1961). *The Economic Plant Disease of Scotland*. Dep. Agric. Fish. Scotl., Tech. Bull., no. 1

Franken E. (1956). Witterungsverlauf im Frühjahr 1955 und Pilzkrankheiten der Pappeln. *Holzzucht*, 9, 30

Gergácz, J. (1967). Marssonina Kárositása Nyárakon. *Erdö*, 16, 304–8; abstract in *Rev. appl. Mycol.*, 47, 1968, no. 3585

Ginzburg, M. (1961). Biologia i szkodliwość grzyba *Venturia tremulae* Aderh. w Polsce. *Prace Inst. badaw. Leśn.*, 211, 3–37

Goidànich, A. (1940). La 'necrosi coricale' del Pioppo causata da *Chondroplea populea* (Sacc. & Br.) Kleb. Repr. from *Riv. cellulosa*, 18, 5, 29 pp.

Gremmen, J. (1954). Op *Populus* en *Salix* voorkomende *Melampsora*-soorten in Nederland. *Tijdschr. PlZiekt.*, 60, 243–50

Gremmen, J. (1956). Een blad- en twijgziekte van populieren veroorzaakt door *Venturia tremulae* en *Venturia populina*. *Tijdschr. PlZiekt.*, 62, 236–42

Gremmen, J. (1958). Bijdrage tot de biologie van *Cryptodiaporthe populea* (Sacc.) Butin (*Dothichiza populea* Sacc. & Bri.). *Ned BoschbTildschr.*, 30, 251–260

Gremmen, J. (1962). De Marssonina-ziekte van de Populier. 1. Het voorkomen van apotheciën en de functie van de ascosporen voor de verspreiding van de ziekte. *Ned. Bosb. Tijdschr.*, 34, 428–32

Gremmen, J. (1964). Three poplar-inhabiting *Drepanopeziza* species and their life history. *Nova Hedwigia*, 9, 170–76

Gremmen, J. (1978). Research on Dothichiza-bark necrosis (*Cryptodiaporthe populea*) in poplar. *Eur. J. For. Path.*, 8, 362–8

Grove, W. B. (1935). *British Stem- and Leaf-Fungi (Coelomycetes)*, vol. 1, Cambridge University Press, Cambridge

Grove, W. B. (1937). *British Stem- and Leaf-Fungi (Coelomycetes)*, vol. 2, Cambridge University Press, Cambridge

Guldemond, J. L. and Kolster, H. W. (1966). De bestrijding van *Marssonina* bij populieren. *Ber. BosbProefstn Dorschk.*, 51, 6 pp.

Hennebert, G. L. (1964). L'identification des rouilles du peuplier. *Agricultura*, 12, 661–71

Hubbes, M. (1959). Untersuchungen über *Dothichiza populea* Sacc. et Briard, den Erreger des Rindenbrandes der Pappel. *Phytopath. Z.*, 35, 58–96

Ibragimov, I. A. (1957). (On the question of poplar withering in the Bashkir, A.S.S.R.); abstract in *Rev. appl. Mycol.*, 38, 1959, p. 427

Ibragimov, I. A. (1964). Tsitosporoz Topoleї i voprosў ikh ot zabolevaniya. Abstr. in *Rev. appl. Mycol.*, 44, 1965, no. 2630

Jobling, J. and Young, C. W. T. (1965). Apparent variations in the resistance of poplar clones to bacterial canker. *Rep. Forest Res., Lond., 1964*, pp. 151–7

Kalandra, A. (1962). Škodlivý výskyt korní spály na Topolech v českých krajích v ČSSR. *Práce výzk. Úst. lesn. ČSSR, 1961*, pp. 273–303

Kämpfer, M. (1931). Neue Seuche an Pappeln. *Gartenwelt*, 35, 525

Kleiner, B. D. (1965). Tsitosporoz Topoleї v Uzbekistane. Ex Sporovўe Rasteniya Sredneї Azü i Kazakhstana (133–138). Tashkent, Nauka; abstract in *Rev. appl. Mycol.*, 46, 1967, no. 449

Laubert, R. (1936). Die Blattfallkrankheit der Pappeln. *Kranke Pflanze*, 13, 196–7

Magnani. G. (1960). Bolla fogliare del pioppo. *Cellulosa Carta*, 11, 27–31

Magnani, G. (1962). Septoriosi del *Populus nigra* L. da *Septoria populi* Desm. *Pubbl. Cent. Sper. agric. for.*, Rome, 6, 7–25

Magnani, G. (1963). Prove di resistenza di alcuni Pioppi euramericani a *Dothichiza populea* Sacc. et Briard. *Pubbl. Cent. Sper. agric.*, 6, 155–78

Magnani, G. (1964). Alterazioni su foglie di pioppo causata da specie di Marssoninae. *Pubbl. Cent. Sper. agric. for.*, 7, 251–81

Magnani, G. (1965). Contributo alla conoscenza della *Marssonina brunnea* (Ell. & Ev.) P. Magn. *Pubbl. Cent. Sper. agric. for.*, 8, 123–26

Magnani, G. (1966). [Investigations on the possibility of physiological specialisation in *Melampsora allii-populina*]. *Pubbl. Cent. Sper. agric. for.*, 8, 127–33; abstract in *For. Abs.*, 28, 1967, no. 2506

Mix, A. J. (1949). A monograph of the genus *Taphrina. Univ. Kansas Sci. Bull.*, 33, 3–167

Moore, W. C. (1959). *British Parasitic Fungi*, Cambridge University Press, Cambridge

Müller, R. (1953a). Zur Frage des Pappelrindentodes. Ergebnisse und Folgerungen aus einem versuch. *Schweiz. Z. Forstwes.*, 104, 408–28

Müller, R. (1953b). Weitere Erfahrungen über den Pappelrindentod (*Dothichiza populea*). *Schweiz. Z. Forstwes.*, 104, 534–5

Müller-Stoll, W. R. and Hartmann, U. (1950). Uber den *Cytospora*-Krebs der Pappel (*Valsa sordida* Nitschke) und die Bedingungen für eine parasitäre Ausbreitung. *Phytopath. Z.*, 16, 443–78

Nohara, Y., Kodama, T. and Aoyama, Y. (1961). Studies on the control of poplar rusts. Part 1. Control tests with fungicides. *Bull. For. Exp. Sta.*, Meguro, 130, 45–50

O'Riordain, F. and Kavanagh, T. (1965). Marssonina leaf spot of poplar. *Ir. J. agric. Res.*, 4, 233–5

Peace, T. R. (1962). *Pathology of Trees and Shrubs*, Clarendon Press, Oxford

Persson, A. (1955). Kronenmykose der Hybridaspe. 1. Untersuchungen über Auftreten selektive Wirkung und Pathogenität des Erregers. *Phytopath. Z.*, 24, 55–72

Phillips, D. H. (1967a). Forest pathology. *Rep. Forest Res., Lond., 1966*, pp. 70–74

Phillips, D. H. (1967b). Forest pathology. *Rep. Forest Res., Lond., 1967*, pp. 96–102

Pinon, J. (1973). Les rouilles du Peuplier en France. *Eur. J. For. Path.*, 3, 221–8

Pospíšil, J. (1960). Houbový škůdce na Osice *Venturia tremulae* Aderh. *Lesn. Práce*, 38; abstract in *Rev. appl. Mycol.*, 39, 1960, p. 631

Ramsbottom, J. and Balfour-Brown, F. L. (1951). List of Discomycetes recorded from the from the British Isles. *Trans. Br. Mycol. Soc.*, 34, 38–137

Ridé, M. (1958). Sur l'étiologie du chancre suintant du peuplier. *C.r. Acad. Sci., Paris*, 246, 2795–8

Ridé, M. (1959). Aspects biologiques de la maladie du chancre suintant du peuplier. *Publ. FAO Int. Poplar Commn Res. Dis. Group*, 4 pp.

Ridé, M. (1963). Our present knowledge of bacterial canker on poplar caused by *Aplanobacterium populi. Publ. FAO Int. Poplar Commn Res. Dis. Group*, 9 pp.

Ridé, M. (1966). Chancre bacterien. Inoculum développement des pousses de l'année et expression des symptomes. Cycle biologique. *Publ. FAO Int. Poplar Commn Res. Dis. Group*, 1 p.

Ridé, M. and Ridé, S. (1978). *Xanthomonas populi* Ridé comb. nov. (syn. *Aplanobacter populi* Ridé), specificité, variabilité et absence de relations avec *Erwinia cancerogena* Ur. *Eur. J. For. Path.*, 8, 310–33

Ridé, M. and Viart, M. (1966). Etude de la contamination d'une peupleraie par le chancre bacterien. *Bull. Serv. Cult. & Etudes Peupl. & Saule*, 1–2, 45–61

Sabet, K. A. (1953). Studies on the bacterial die-back and canker disease of poplar. III. Freezing in relation to the disease. *Ann. appl. Biol.*, 40, 645–50

Sabet, K.A. and Dowson, W. J. (1952). Studies on the bacterial die-back and canker disease of poplar. I. The disease and its cause. *Ann. appl. Biol.*, 39, 609–16

Šarić, A. and Milatović, I. (1960). Pokus suzbijanja rde Topola u šumskom rasadniku Banova Jaruga. *Šumarski List*, 84, 290–91; abstract in *For. Abs.*, 22, 1961, p. 424

Schmidle, A. (1953). Zur Kenntnis der Biologie und der Pathogenität von *Dothichiza populea* Sacc. et Briard, dem Erreger eines Rindenbrandes der Pappel. *Phytopath. Z.*, 21, 189–209

Schneider, A. and Sutra, G. (1969). Les modalités de l'infection de *Populus nigra* L. par *Taphrina populina. C. r. hebd. Séanc. Acad. Sci., Paris, Sér. D*, 269, 1056–9

Schönhar, S. (1952). Untersuchungen über den Erreger des Pappelrindentodes. *Allg. Forstz.*, 49, 509–12

Schönhar, S. (1953). Untersuchungen über die Biologie von *Dothichiza populea* (Erreger des Pappelrindentodes). *Forstw. Zbl.*, 72, 358–68

Schreiner, E. J. (1931a). The rôle of disease in the growing of poplar. *J. For.*, 29, 79–82

Schreiner, E. J. (1931b). Two species of *Valsa* causing disease in *Populus. Am. J. Bot.*, 18, 1–29

Schreiner, E. J. (1959). Rating poplars for *Melampsora* leaf rust infection. *For. Res. notes Northwestern For. Exp. Sta. Upper Darby, Pa.*, No. 90.

Servazzi, O. (1935). Contributi alla patologia dei pioppi. II. La 'tafrinosi' o 'bolla fogliare' dei pioppi. *Difesa Piante*, 12, 48–62

Servazzi, O. (1940). Appunti di fitopatologia. *Boll. Lab. sper. Oss. Fitopat.*, **16**, 19–32

Shavrova, L. A. (1967). K biologii vozbuditelya parshi Osinÿ *Mikol. i Fitopatol.*, **1**, 321–9

Stahl, W. (1967). An investigation on the Cytospora disease of poplars in Australia. *Pap. 14th IUFRO Conf. Sec. 24, Munich, 1967*, pp. 428–44

Sutton, B. C. (1961). British records. 58. *Pollaccia radiosa* (Lib.) Bald. & Cif. *Trans. Br. mycol. Soc.*, **44**. 608–9

Sutton, B. C. and Pirozynski, K. A. (1963). Notes on British microfungi. 1. *Trans. Br. mycol. Soc.*, **46**, 505–22

Taris, B. (1956). Résistance au froid du mycélium de *Dothichiza populea* Sacc. et Briard et de *Cytospora chrysosperma* (Pers.) Fr. *C. r. Acad. Sci., Paris*, **242**, 1648–9

Taris, B. (1959). Contribution à l'étude des maladies cryptogamiques des rameaux et des jeunes plantes de peupliers. *Publ. FAO Int. Poplar Commn Res. Dis. Group*, 13 pp.

Taris, B. (1966). Etude et mise en evidence du maintien du pouvoir pathogène des urédospores de *Melampsora* sp., rouille des peupliers cultivés. *C. r. hebd. Séanc. Acad. Sci., Paris, Sér. D*, **262**, 882–5

Tinsley, T. W. (1967). Virus diseases of forest trees. *Rep. Forest Res., Lond., 1966*, p. 112

Treshow, M. and Harward, M. (1965). Preliminary investigations in the incidence of canker and decline in Utah aspen stands. *Proc. Utah Acad. Sci.*, **42**, 196–200

Tsÿplakova, O. D. (1967). O vzaimosvyazi fitonsidnÿkh svoīstv Topoleī i ikh ustoīchivosti k tsitosporozu. *Biol. Nauki*, **10**, 139–141

van der Meiden, H. A. (1964*a*). Die Bedeutung von einigen Blattkrankheiten für die Pappelwirtschaft. *Forst- u. Holzw.*, **19**, 257–60

van der Meiden, H. A. (1964*b*). Virus bij populier. *Ned. Bosb. Tijdschr.*, **36**, 269–75

van der Meiden, H. A. and van Vloten, H. (1958). Roest en schorsbrand als bedreiging van de teelt van populier. *Ned. Bosb. Tijdschr.*, **30**, 261–73

van Vloten, H. (1944). Is verrijking van de mycoflora mogelijk? (Naar aanleiding van de populierenroest). *Tijdschr. PlZiekt.*, **1**, 49–62

Veldeman, R. (1966). [Marssonina disease of poplars]. *Meded. Rijksfac. Landbouww. Gent*, **31**, 907–14; abstract in *For. Abs.*, **28**, 1967, no. 5923

Veldeman, R. and Welvaert, W. (1960). Schorsbrand bij populier. *Meded. LandbHogesch. Gent*, **25**, 1107–1115; abstract in *For. Abs.*, **23**, 1962, no. 808

Viennot-Bourgin, G. (1949). *Les champignons parasites des plantes cultivées. 1.* Masson, Paris

Viennot-Bourgin, G. and Taris, B. (1957). Les maladies cryptogamiques des peupliers (Etat des travaux réalisés en France). *6th Int. Pop. Cong. Rep. & Comm. Fr.*, pp. 75–90, Paris

Waterman, Alma M. (1957). Canker and dieback of poplars caused by *Dothichiza populea. For. Sci.*, **3**, 175–83

Werner, A. and Siwecki, R. (1978). Histological studies of the infection process by *Dothichiza populea* Sacc. et Briard in susceptible and resistant poplar clones. *Eur. J. For. Path.*, **8**, 217–26

Wettstein, W. and Donaubauer, E. (1958). Survey of *Dothichiza populea*. Austria. *Docum 14th Sess. stand. exec. Comm. int. Poplar Comm. Rome 1958*, no. FAO/CIP/16-A, 1958, 6 pp.

Whitbread, R. (1967). Bacterial canker of poplars in Britain. 1. The cause of the disease and the role of leaf scars in infection. *Ann. appl. Biol.*, **59**, 123–31

Wilson, M. and Henderson, D. M. (1966). *British Rust Fungi*, Cambridge University Press, Cambridge

Zycha, H. (1965). Die Marssonina-Krankheit der Pappel. *Forstwiss. Cbl.*, 7/8, pp. 254–9

17 Diseases of willow (*Salix* spp.)

NURSERY AND POST-NURSERY DISEASES
  LEAF DISEASES
    The powdery mildew *Uncinula salicis* (*U. adunca*)
    Leaf spots caused by *Rhytisma salicinum* and *R. symmetricum*
    Leaf spot caused by *Marssonina kriegeriana*
    Leaf spot caused by *Gloeosporium salicis*
  DISEASES OF LEAVES AND SHOOTS
    Rusts of tree willows and osiers: *Melampsora larici-pentandrae*, *M. allii-fragilis*, *M. epitea* var. *epitea*, *M. caprearum*, *M. salicis-albae*, *M. ribesii-viminalis*, and *M. amygdalinae*
    Anthracnose caused by *Marssonina salicicola*
    Black canker caused by *Glomerella miyabeana* and willow scab caused by *Fusicladium saliciperdum*
    Canker and dieback caused by *Cryptodiaporthe salicina* and dieback associated with *C. salicella*
    Twig blight caused by *Cryptomyces maximus*
  WILT DISEASES
    Watermark disease caused by *Erwinia salicis*
    Wilt caused by a fluorescent *Pseudomonas* sp.
  DECAY FUNGI
REFERENCES

Many willow species occur in Great Britain. Some are only small creeping forms, like *Salix repens*, others are only shrubs. Some, like *S. triandra* and *S. alba* var. *vitellina*, are grown as osiers. Of the tree species, *S. alba* var. *coerulea* is grown for its timber, which is used to make cricket bats. *S.* x *chrysocoma* is the common weeping willow much grown in parks and gardens. The Japanese *S. matsudana* var. *tortuosa* is among the introduced species and varieties also now planted in gardens.

Many of the diseases of willows would repay further study, for the information on them is often scanty or conflicting. Much of that so far available has been summarised by Butin (1960).

NURSERY AND POST-NURSERY DISEASES

LEAF DISEASES

Powdery mildew, *Uncinula salicis* (de Candolle ex Mérat) Winter (syn. *U. adunca* Lév.)

The powdery mildew *Uncinula salicis* is sometimes found on various *Salix* spp. in this country (Bisby and Mason, 1940; Thomas, 1974; Greenhalgh, 1976), and in other countries is said to occur also on *Populus* and *Betula*. The white mycelium forms patches on the leaves on one or both leaf surfaces. The very dark brown, rounded cleistothecia are scattered over the white patches. They have colourless, unbranched appendages that may be curved at the top (figure 77), and contain eight to twelve asci, each with four to five spores. The colourless, elliptical spores measure 25–30 × 15–19 μm (Rabenhorst, 1884).

Leaf spots caused by *Rhytisma salicinum* Fr. (stat. conid. *Melasmia salicina* Lév. apud Tul.) and *R. symmetricum* Fr.

The uncommon *Rhytisma salicinum* has sometimes been found producing irregularly rounded, thick, shining black stromatic spots on the upper sides of willow leaves in Britain. These stromata somewhat resemble the tar spots made on sycamore leaves by the related fungus *Rhytisma acerinum*, but at maturity they measure only 2–5 mm across. In the autumn, one to three pycnidia of the *Melasmia* stage form within each stroma. The pycnidia contain colourless, long–cylindric

Figure 77. Cleistocarps of *Uncinula salicis* showing the curled appendages (K.F. Tubeuf, after Tulasne)

spores 5–6 μm long (Grove, 1937). The ascocarps of the perfect stage, also embedded in the stromata, form in winter on the fallen leaves. They contain long asci each having eight colourless, threadlike ascospores measuring 60–90 x 1.5–3 μm (Viennot-Bourgin, 1949).

The rare *R. symmetricum* has also been found producing many small stromatic spots on willow leaves in Britain (figure 78). The stromata extend from one side of the leaf to the other, and the spots therefore appear on both upper and lower leaf surfaces. The fruit bodies are also embedded in the stromata on both sides of the leaves. Their asci contain threadlike ascospores that measure 30–108 μm in length (Dennis and Wakefield, 1946).

Leaf spot caused by *Marssonina kriegeriana* (Bres.) Magn.
Reports in Britain of *Marssonina kriegeriana* (Grove, 1937; and a few later unpublished records), described by Nattras (1930) as the cause of a leaf spot of willows in Egypt, need confirmation. The conidia measure 13–17 x 4–7 μm. The perfect state, *Drepanopeziza triandra* Rimpau (Rimpau, 1962), has not yet been found in Britain.

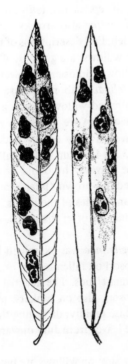

Figure 78. Willow leaf with stromatic spots caused by *Rhytisma symmetricum* (K.F. Tubeuf)

Leaf spot caused by *Gloeosporium salicis* **Westd.** (*Gloeosporidium salicis* (Westd.) **Nannf.,** *Monostichella salicis* (Westd.) **v. Arx)**

A leaf spot caused by *Gloeosporium salicis* was recorded in this country on *Salix alba, S. caprea* and *S. fragilis* by Grove (1937). In Germany the same fungus has been found on *S. americana* hort. (Butin, 1960). It is also known on *S. fragilis* in the USA (Nelson, 1965).

G. *salicis* causes dark brown or black, crowded spots, which often coalesce and may eventually cover the whole leaf. The conidial pustules form on the upper leaf surface. The ellipsoid or oblong, colourless, one-celled conidia measure 12-16 x 4-6 μm (Grove 1937).

The perfect stage, *Drepanopeziza salicis* (Tul.) var. Höhn. (*Trochila salicis* Tul., *Pseudopeziza salicis* (Tul.) Pot.), which has not yet been found in Britain, is described by Rimpau (1962).

DISEASES OF LEAVES AND SHOOTS

Rusts of the tree willows and osiers

Five species of *Melampsora* affect tree willows. They are *M. larici-pentandrae* Kleb., *M. allii-fragilis* Kleb., *M. epitea* var. *epitea* Thüm., *M. capraearum* Thüm., and *M. salicis-albae* Kleb. *M. epitea* also attacks osiers, as do *M. ribesii-viminalis* Kleb. and *M. amygdalinae* Kleb. Full descriptions of these rusts, as well as of others affecting creeping and bush willows, are given by Wilson and Henderson (1966). Their host ranges on tree willows and osiers are given in table 17.1.

The autoecious *M. amygdalinae* Kleb. may cause serious damage to the basket willow *Salix triandra* (the almond willow), making the rods useless. The bright orange aecidial pustules (caeomata) are produced with the orange spermogonia on the stems and young leaves, usually on the undersides. The globoid to ovoid aecidiospores measure 18-23 x 14-19 μm. The small orange uredosori are almost all on the undersides of the leaves. The ovoid or oblong uredospores measure 20-40 x 11-18 μm. The reddish-brown (later almost black) teleutosori occur under the epidermis on the undersides of the leaves. The teleutospores, measuring 8-15 x 7-14 μm, are very much shorter than those of any other *Melampsora* sp. on willows.

The life cycle of *M. amygdalinae* was examined by Ogilvie (1932). This rust overwinters either as teleutosori on fallen leaves, or as mycelium in the buds and as perennial uredosori on uncut rods. The aecidial stage causes cankers on the young stems in April. Uredosori, also on cankers, may be found from March to October, and spread the disease rapidly, damaging the leaves as well as the stems. The teleutosori occur on the leaves from July onwards. This rust is found locally in England.

All the other *Melampsora* spp. on willows are heteroecious, and their teleutospores are more than 20 μm in length. Both the uredosori and teleutosori are produced on the willows. In three species, *M. salicis-albae, M. allii-fragilis* and

Table 17.1

Rusts on tree willows and osiers

	Tree willow and osier hosts	Alternate hosts
(1) *Melampsora larici-pentandrae*	*S. pentandra** *S. fragilis* x *pentandra**	[*Larix* spp., but not known in this country?]
(2) *M. allii-fragilis*	*S. pentandra** *S. fragilis* x *pentandra** *S. fragilis*[+]	[*Allium* spp., but not known in this country?]
(3) *M. epitea* var. *epitea*: Euonymus strain (*M. euonymi-caprearum*)	*S. caprea** *S. cinerea** *S. alba*[+]	*Euonymus europaeus*
Larix strain (*M. larici-epitea*)	*S. alba*[+] *S. caprea* x *viminalis** *S. daphnoides** *S. fragilis*[+] *S. viminalis*[≠] *S. triandra*[≠]	*Larix* spp.
Ribes strain (*M. ribesii-purpureae*)	*S. purpurea*[≠]	[*Ribes* spp., but British records doubtful]
(4) *M. capraearum*	*S. caprea** *S. cinerea** *S. caprea* x *viminalis**	*Larix* spp.
(5) *M. salicis-albae*	*S. alba*[+] *S. alba* var. *vitellina*[+]	*Allium* spp.
(6) *M. ribesii-viminalis*	*S. viminalis*[≠]	[*Ribes uva-crispa*, but not known in this country?]
(7) *M. amygdalinae*	*S. triandra*[≠]	None; autoecious, with all stages on *Salix*

Note: all these rusts except *M. amygdalinae* are heteroecious, with the uredosori and teleutosori on *Salix* and the spermogenia and aecidia on the alternate hosts.

*   shrub or small tree
[+]   tree
[≠]   osier

M. larici-pentandrae, the uredospores are smooth at their upper ends, but otherwise echinulate.

In *M. salicis-albae* Kleb. (*M. allii-salicis-albae* Kleb.) the uredospores are oblong, or club or pear-shaped, measuring 20–36 x 11–17 µm. In spring they occur in large pustules up to 2 mm long on the young twigs. Later, throughout the summer and autumn they are present in smaller spots on the undersides of the leaves. The dark brown teleutosori are on both sides of the leaves, under the epidermis, and the teleutospores measure 24–45 x 7–10 µm.

Overwintering is by the teleutospores on the leaves or by mycelium which perennates in the branches and gives rise to uredosori in spring, before the aecidia arise on the alternate host, *Allium ursinum*. Hence, once established, it can persist in *Salix* without the further presence of the alternate host (Weir and Hubert, 1918; Wilson and Henderson, 1966).

M. salicis-albae is thought to be fairly common on *Salix alba*, and on its variety *vitellina*, the rods of which it makes too brittle for basket-making.

In *M. allii-fragilis* Kleb., which appears to be rather rare, the spermogonia and aecidia again occur on *Allium*, and are indistinguishable from those of *M. salicis-albae*. Indeed, it is not known with certainty whether they occur in this country. The small reddish-orange uredosori appear mostly on the undersides of the leaves, and the obovoid uredospores measure 22–33 x 13–15 µm. The dark brown, shining teleutosori are mainly on the upper sides of the leaves, and occur under the cuticle. The teleutospores measure 30–48 x 7–14 µm.

M. larici-pentandrae Kleb. is also scarce, and is known in Great Britain only in Scotland and Ireland. The bright orange uredosori are mostly on the undersides of the leaves, and the ovoid or ellipsoid uredospores measure 23–44 x 12–16 µm. The yellowish-brown (later almost black) teleutosori are under the epidermis, on the undersides of the leaves. The teleutospores measure 28–38 x 6–11 µm.

In the remaining three species, *M. epitea*, *M. capraearum* and *M. ribesii-viminalis*, the uredospores are spiny over the whole surface.

M. epitea Thüm. consists of several varieties or races, sometimes regarded as distinct species. The orange-yellow uredosori are on both sides of the leaves. The ellipsoid or globoid uredospores measure 12–25 x 10–18 µm. The small, yellowish-brown (later almost black) teleutosori are under the epidermis, mostly on the undersides of the leaves. The teleutospores, which are not much thickened at their tips, and have no conspicuous germ pore, measure 20–50 x 7–14 µm. *M. epitea sensu lato* is common in Great Britain and Ireland. The forms on tree willows and osiers are all races of the variety *epitea*, with *Euonymus europaeus* (*M. euonymi-caprearum* Kleb.), *Larix* spp. (*M. larici-epitea* Kleb.) and perhaps *Ribes* spp. (*M. ribesii-purpureae* Kleb.) as the alternate hosts.

M. capraearum Thüm. (*M. larici-caprearum* Kleb.) has its uredosori on the lower leaf surfaces; they show as pale yellow spots on the other side. The ovoid or ellipsoid uredospores measure 14–21 x 13–15 µm. The dark reddish-brown teleutosori are under the cuticle on the upper sides of the leaves. The teleutospores are thick-walled above, with a clearly marked germ pore, and measure 30–40 x

7-14 µm. *M. capraearum* is common in this country. Its spermogonia and aecidia are on larch.

M. ribesii-viminalis Kleb. has small, pale orange-yellow uredosori on the undersides of the leaves. Its rounded uredospores measure 15-19 x 14-16 µm. The dark brown, shining teleutosori are under the cuticle on the upper sides of the leaves. The teleutospores, like those of *M. epitea*, are unthickened above, with no clearly visible germ pore. They measure 25-40 x 7-14 µm. It is doubtful if the spermogenial and aecidial stage, on *Ribes* spp., is present in Great Britain, and the fungus on *Salix* seems to be rare.

Of these seven rusts, it will be seen that *M. allii-fragilis*, *M. larici-pentandrae* and *M. ribesii-viminalis* are uncommon. *M. amygdalinae* is locally common in England, on the basket willow *S. triandra*, and *M. epitea* is common on various willows, including the basket willows *S. viminalis*, *S. triandra* and *S. purpurea*. *M. salicis-albae* is fairly common on the basket willow *S. alba* var. *vitellina*.

Pathological information (apart from the few points on overwintering referred to above) is scanty. Ogilvie and Hutchinson (1933) found that the germination of the uredospores of *M. amygdalinae* and *M. epitea* was encouraged by cool, damp conditions, and the spread and severity of the disease was much reduced in hot weather.

Control   Control measures for rust have been proposed only in the case of basket willows, which locally at one time formed an important crop. Their acreage has now much declined, however. Ogilvie and Hutchinson (1933) suggested that the spread and development of *M. amygdalinae* on *S. triandra* could be slowed and reduced by delaying the cutting of the rods in spring to avoid the production of young, susceptible growth when the basidiospores arise from the teleutospores. If cutting cannot be delayed, young growth can be removed by grazing cattle or the use of a tar-oil winter wash to kill the young shoots. Control later in the season might be attempted by the use of copper sprays or perhaps of zineb or maneb, but frequent spraying would be necessary to ensure the covering of new growth as it arose. Such spraying so far remains experimental. Similar spraying might be tried if necessary in nursery beds. Control on established trees is not required.

Anthracnose caused by *Marssonina salicicola* (Bres.) Magn.

The anthracnose caused by the fungus *Marssonina salicicola* has for long been the most damaging disease of the weeping willow, *S. x chrysocoma*, on the shoots of which it causes very unsightly cankers. In New Zealand, Murray (1926) found trees so badly affected that they lost their weeping habit. The disease also occurs in Britain on the osier *S. purpurea* (Nattras, 1930). Elsewhere it has been found in Argentina on the cricket bat willow, *S. alba* var. *coerulea* (Jauch, 1952), and in New Zealand on *S. fragilis* (Murray, 1926), as well as on various willows in the Netherlands (van Poeteren, 1938) and Germany (Butin, 1960).

The fungus causes small, black, elliptical spots on the developing shoots; these spots spread to become elongated, irregular, sunken cankers with a dark brown or black raised rim and a paler centre (figure 79). Typically, black or purple-black spots also develop on the leaves, which in severe attacks become distorted and are shed. Similar spots may sometimes also be found on the catkins.

Whitish fruiting pustules (acervuli) of the fungus develop on the cankers and leaf spots. The acervuli may be up to 400 µm across (Nattras, 1930), but generally measure about 150–200 µm. They contain the colourless, often curved, club-shaped or pear-shaped conidia, which measure 11–19 x 3–7 µm (Nattras, 1930; Murray, 1926). The spores are two-celled, with the lower cell much smaller than the upper.

The perfect stage of the fungus is *Drepanopeziza sphaeroides* (Fr.) Nannf. (Butin, 1960; Rimpau, 1962), which so far does not appear to have been recorded in Britain.

The fungus overwinters on the cankers, and probably on the bud scales and on dead, fallen leaves. Spores formed on these early in the year infect the young leaves and the newly elongating shoots. Nattras (1930) found some evidence from

Figure 79. Willow anthracnose: leaf spots and stem cankers on weeping willow caused by *Marssonina salicicola* (Forestry Commission)

inoculation experiments that the fungus was a wound parasite. Its attacks are especially severe in wet summers.

Murray (1926) in New Zealand found that *S. fragilis* was less badly affected than the weeping willow. Rose (1970) reported that selection and breeding for resistance against willow anthracnose had begun at Long Ashton.

The growing of resistant stock would indeed appear to be the best ultimate answer to the disease. Meanwhile, spraying with a suitable fungicide remains the only practicable control method, though it can usually be done only on relatively small trees.

Spraying with a copper fungicide has often been suggested, for example, by Rose (1970), who advised applying copper at weekly intervals from budbreak until midsummer. Gaggini (1970) reported the results of spray trials with more recently developed fungicides. He obtained excellent control with captafol (as difolotan at 1 lb/100 gal (1g/litre)) and with quinomethionate (as morestan, at 1 lb of 25 per cent wettable powder/100 gal (1g/litre)). These results were achieved with two sprays in early May, the second applied about a week after the first.

Black canker, caused by *Glomerella miyabeana* (Fukushi) v. Arx & Müller (syn. *Physalospora miyabeana* Fukushi; stat. conid. *Colletotrichum gloeosporioides* Penz.) and willow scab, caused by *Fusicladium saliciperdum* (All. & Tub.) Tub. (*Pollaccia saliciperda* (All. & Tub.) v. Arx; perfect stage *Venturia chlorospora* (Ces.) Karst.)

Black canker, caused by *Glomerella miyabeana*, and willow scab, caused by *Fusicladium saliciperdum*, have often been confused, partly because their symptoms are very similar. Furthermore, inoculation experiments by some workers have indicated that *G. miyabeana* is a major pathogen, and *F. saliciperdum* at most only a secondary organism (Nattras, 1928; Dennis, 1931; Rupert and Leach, 1942; Wiejak, 1960). Alcock (1924), Clinton (1929) and Brooks and Walker (1935), however, all found good evidence, at least in the areas and under the conditions in which they were working, that *F. saliciperdum* could act as an important primary pathogen in the absence of *G. miyabeana*.

Black canker   Black canker, caused by *Glomerella miyabeana* (which has sometimes (Arx, 1957*b*) been regarded as a specialised race of *G. cingulata* (Stoneman) Spaulding and von Schrenk) is important mainly on basket willows. On these it may make the rods useless for basket making (Brooks, 1953). In Czechoslovakia, Farský and Fekete (1965) found that the disease, then recorded there for the first time, had destroyed up to 50 per cent of the first-year setts in the area affected.

As well as in Britain and Czechoslovakia, black canker is known in Japan (Fukushi, 1921), Germany (Diercks, 1959), the Netherlands (van Poeteren, 1935), Canada (Harrison, 1965; Conners *et al.*, 1941) and the USA (Rupert and Leach, 1942).

The first symptoms of the disease, which may be found as early as May, show as reddish-brown, angular spots on the leaves. The spots spread, and the leaves blacken and shrivel, but commonly remain attached to the stem (plate 48). Often the fungus spreads further through the petiole into the stem, where it produces oval, elongated, flattened cankers, which are then generally isolated by a layer of cork (Nattras, 1928; Dennis, 1931). The bark over these cankered areas dries, contracts and splits.

The fruit bodies of the fungus occur mainly on the shoot cankers. The conidial pustules (acervuli) develop first, in spring, on shoots in which the mycelium has overwintered. The acervuli, which are of a *Gloeosporium* or *Colletotrichum* type, have been described as *Colletotrichum gloeosporioides* Penz (Arx, 1957*b*). The spore mass is colourless or pale pink (Nattras, 1928) to light brick red (Brooks, 1953), and the one-celled, ellipsoid, colourless conidia measure 13–23 x 4–7 μm (Nattras, 1928; Brooks, 1953). The fungus also overwinters as perithecia which form in autumn. The one-celled, oblong–ellipsoid, colourless ascospores measure 15–17 x 5.5–7 μm, and the asci are interspersed with slender paraphyses (Brooks, 1953).

Rybak-Mikitiuk (1962) found that the optimum temperature for conidial germination and mycelial growth was 26°C, and in the field the disease spread most rapidly at a temperature of 25°C when the relative humidity was high.

In Britain, black canker has been recorded on *Salix americana* hort., *S. alba* var. *vitellina*, and *S. alba* var. *cardinalis* (and occasionally on a few other ornamental willows) (Nattras, 1928; Dennis, 1931). Elsewhere it has also been found on *S. alba* x *fragilis* (Farský and Fekete, 1965), and the grey willows (van Poetesen, 1935).

Control measures are probably necessary and feasible only in basket willow beds and in nurseries, and on young plants not long established. Spraying with Bordeaux mixture and other copper sprays has often been recommended (Brooks, 1953). Trials with more recently developed fungicides suggest that weekly spraying throughout the growing season with zineb or a mixture of captan and brestan are likely to give control (Diercks, 1959).

Willow scab   The second of these diseases, willow scab, caused by *Fusicladium saliciperdum*, may cause considerable damage in damp seasons. In England it has been found especially on *Salix decipiens* (Brooks and Walker, 1935), and in Scotland Alcock (1924) recorded it on *S. alba* var. *vitellina*. It has been found elsewhere on various willow species and varieties in Germany (Janson, 1927), the Netherlands (Arx, 1957*a*), Poland (Twarowska, 1968), Canada (Harrison, 1965), and the USA (Steinmetz and Prince, 1938).

In Canada, Bloomberg and Funk (1960) reported that one third of the crown of some trees was destroyed by the fungus. In Britain, Brooks and Walker (1935) found that in a wet season trees might lose almost all their leaves by the middle of the summer. Very severe damage has also been recorded in Germany (Appen, 1927) and Poland (Twarowska, 1968).

The symptoms of the disease (figure 80) are very similar to those of Black canker, and first become visible in early spring. Irregular spots form on the young

Figure 80. Dieback of *Salix alba* caused by *Fusicladium saliciperdum* (Forestry Commission)

leaves, and as they spread, the leaves blacken, die and fall. Black lesions may girdle shoots so that twigs and even whole branches may be killed. In conditions favourable to the fungus, the progress of the disease may be very rapid (Brooks and Walker, 1935; Bloomberg and Funk, 1960).

Small olive-brown pustules of *Fusicladium saliciperdum* develop on the affected leaves, mainly along the veins on the undersides (Brooks and Walker, 1935; Clinton and McCormick, 1929). The fungus overwinters as similar pustules on affected twigs (Brooks, 1953). The brown, rather slipper-shaped conidia measure 15–23 x 5–10 μm, and are eventually two-celled.

The perfect stage of the fungus, generally considered to be *Venturia chlorospora* (Ces.) Karst., develops in autumn and winter on the fallen leaves (Butin, 1960). It has not been found in Britain. Arx (1957*a*), in pure culture experiments, was in fact unable to link *V. chlorospora* with *F. saliciperda*, as his cultures derived from ascospores gave rise to typical perithecia of the former, while those from the *Fusicladium* conidia again produced cultures of *F. saliciperda*.

The fungus overwinters on the dead twigs infected in the previous season. In spring, pustules of the *Fusicladium* stage arise on the diseased twigs, and the conidia they produce attack the newly opening buds and young leaves (Brooks and Walker, 1935; Clinton and McCormick, 1929).

In Scotland, Alcock (1924) found *F. saliciperdum* on *Salix alba* var. *vitellina*, while Brooks (1953) noted that it occurred in Britain especially on *S. fragilis* var. *decipiens*. *S. alba* var. *vitellina* was also found to be very susceptible in eastern Canada and the USA (Clinton and McCormick, 1929; Steinmetz and Prince, 1938). A great many other willow species are known to be susceptible, the osier *S. americana* hort. being especially badly affected in Germany and the Netherlands (Appen, 1927; Arx, 1957a). In Poland, Kochman (1929) found that *S. alba*, *S. blanda* and *S. babylonica* (*S. × chrysocoma?*) were the most liable to damage. On the other hand, some clones of *S. fragilis* have shown resistance (Steinmetz and Prince, 1938), and so have *S. viminalis*, *S. purpurea*, *S. amygdalina*, *S. pentandra*, and *S. alba* var. *calva* (*S. alba* var. *coerulea*) (Appen, 1927; Harrison, 1965; Kochman, 1929).

The development of the disease is greatly encouraged by cool, wet weather (Brooks and Walker, 1935; Davidson and Fowler, 1967). A fertiliser balance high in nitrogen and low in potassium has also been said to favour the disease (Anon, 1927; Janson, 1927).

In general, control measures are probably warranted only in osier beds and in nurseries and on young trees. In view of evidence that the disease may be spread with infested stock (Anon, 1927), cuttings should be taken only from healthy material. Winter washes of copper sulphate solution, for example, may be used in stool beds (Alcock, 1924; Twarowska, 1968). Avoidance of winter pruning is said to aid in control (Pape, 1925). Various fungicides, including Bordeaux mixture and lime sulphur have been recommended (Alcock, 1924). More recently, spraying with phygon (dichlone) (Harrison, 1965), chinosol, maneb, zineb, captan and brestan (Diercks, 1959; Twarowska, 1968) has been suggested.

Canker and dieback caused by *Cryptodiaporthe salicina* (Curr.) Wehm. (stat. conid. *Discella carbonacea* (Fr.) Berk. and Br.) and dieback associated with *Cryptodiaporthe salicella* (Fr.) Wehm.

The canker and dieback of willows caused by *Cryptodiaporthe salicina* is generally of minor significance; the fungus is common as a saprophyte on dead twigs, and its pathogenicity has sometimes been doubted (Moore, 1959). Schwarz (1922) and Broekhuijsen (1934) were both able to demonstrate its pathogenicity, however, and Bier (1959) showed that it became pathogenic when the relative turgidity of the plant fell to 80 per cent or less.

The disease is known in Britain (Grove, 1937; Redfern, 1974), the mainland of Europe, especially in the Netherlands (Broekhuijsen, 1934), and in Canada (Bier, 1959).

Affected shoots die back to a node, at first appearing brownish-green. The lesions bear flat, disc-shaped pycnidia of *Discella carbonacea*, the imperfect stage of the fungus (Broekhuijsen, 1934; Schwarz, 1922), which form just within the bark. The bark eventually splits open and releases the spores. These are almost colourless or slightly greenish, spindle-shaped, two-celled, and widest at the septum. They measure 13-18 x 3.5-5 µm (Grove, 1937). The perithecia of the perfect stage later appear scattered singly or in small groups, also just beneath the bark surface, through which their small black ostioles emerge. They contain club-shaped asci each with eight colourless, ellipsoid or inequilateral, blunt-ended, finally two-celled ascospores measuring 15-20 x (3.5)-4.5-7.5 µm (Wehmeyer, 1932).

In Britain the disease has been found especially on *Salix alba, S. alba* var. *vitellina* and *S. fragilis* (Grove, 1937). On the mainland of Europe it has been found on *S. alba* var. *vitellina pendula* (the Dutch weeping willow) (Schwarz, 1922), *S. alba* and *S. alba* var. *coerulea* (Mooi, 1948), *S. viminalis* (Broekhuijsen, 1934), and most other willows (Butin, 1960). Records in Canada include *S. hookeriana* and *S. scouleriana* (Bier, 1959).

Another species of *Cryptodiaporthe, C. salicella* is also sometimes regarded as a cause of a minor dieback of willows, though it is of doubtful pathogenicity (Moore, 1959). Its perithecia resemble those of *C. salicina*, but the ascospores measure 25-50 x 9-12 µm (Wehmeyer, 1932). The nomenclature of the perfect stages of these two fungi is still a matter of dispute. The subject is discussed by Wehmeyer (1932) and Butin (1958).

Twig blight caused by *Cryptomyces maximus* (Fr.) Rehm

On rare occasions *Cryptomyces maximus* (figure 81) has been found causing dark brown or black, irregularly elongated, blister-like stromatic cushions up to 8 in (200 mm) long on the twigs and branches of willows (Alcock and Maxwell, 1925). The edges of the cushions are at first yellow at the edges. At maturity the outer tissues of the stroma break to expose a yellowish-brown hymenium. The cylindric-clavate, 8-spored asci measure up to 250 x 33 µm, and contain colourless or pale yellowish, ellipsoid to ovoid, 1-celled ascospores measuring 20-30 x 10-13 µm and covered by a thin gelatinous coating. The asci are separated by septate hyphae which unite at their tips to form a brownish gelatinous layer (Dennis, 1968). In wet weather the stromatic cushions swell and fall off, to leave elongated scars on the bark. Affected twigs may be girdled and die (Alcock and Maxwell, 1925).

C. maximus has been found in Scotland damaging *Salix fragilis* (Alcock and Maxwell, 1925), and in Norfolk attacking the cricket bat willow, *S. alba* var. *coerulea* (Anon, 1952). Elsewhere in Europe it occurs also on *S. incana* and *S. amygdalina* (Butin, 1960).

According to Alcock and Maxwell (1925) *C. maximus* may be followed by the weakly parasitic *Scleroderris fuliginosa* Karst. and *Myxosporium scutellatum* (Otth) Petrak, which then cause further damage.

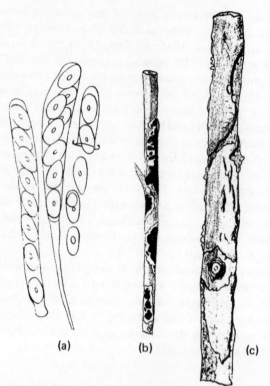

(a)   (b)   (c)

Figure 81. *Cryptomyces maximus*: (a) asci and ascospores, (b) twig of *Salix incana* with stromata of the fungus, (c) an osier twig, after the stromatic cushions have scaled off in autumn (K.F. Tubeuf)

WILT DISEASES

Watermark disease caused by *Erwinia salicis* (Day) Chester (*Bacterium salicis* Day, *Pseudomonas saliciperda* Lindeijer)

Watermark disease, caused by the bacterium *Erwinia salicis*, is particularly important as a cause of stain and degrade in the cricket bat willow, *Salix alba* var. *coerulea*. The wood of trees affected by the disease is unsaleable, partly because it is badly discoloured (plate 57) and partly because any cricket bats made from it are liable to splinter (Metcalfe, 1940).

The disease was first described in England by Day (1924). It is known to occur there in Norfolk, Suffolk, Cambridgeshire, Essex, Middlesex, Wiltshire, Gloucestershire, Bedfordshire, Hertfordshire and Yorkshire (Dowson and Callen, 1937; Bryce, 1950; Preece, 1977). A similar disease on willows in the Netherlands was originally considered to be caused by a separate bacterium, *Pseudomonas saliciperda* Lindeijer. It is now the view in the Netherlands, however, that *P. saliciperda* and *E. salicis* are the same organism (Gremmen and de Kam, 1970).

E. salicis is fully described by Dowson (1937, 1957). It is a straight, cylindrical rod, either single, in pairs end to end, or occasionally in chains. The individual cells measure 0.8 -1.7 x 0.5-0.7 μm, and move by means of five to seven long, perithrichous flagella. The bacterium produces a light yellow pigment on sterilised potato, and forms yellowish colonies on potato agar.

As noted above, *E. salicis* is important especially as the cause of watermark disease of *Salix alba* var. *coerulea*. It also affects other willows, including other varieties of the white willow, *S. alba*, such as var. *vitellina* (Day, 1924; Wong and Preece, 1973). In the Netherlands the disease has been found affecting *S. caprea*, *S. viminalis*, *S. purpurea*, *S. amygdalina* and *S. triandra* as well as *S. alba* (Lindeijer, 1931; Burger, 1932). Day (1924), and Wong and Preece (1973) failed to find it on *S. fragilis*. Wong and Preece were also unable to find it on the hybrid *S.* x *rubens* (*S. viridis*), though Dowson and Callan (1937) found this hybrid affected.

External symptoms first appear in late April or early May, when the young leaves on one or more branches turn reddish and wither (plate 53). This phase of the disease is known as the red-leaf stage. A thin, sticky liquid containing bacteria exudes from insect exit holes and other wounds on affected twigs (Dowson, 1957). Further leaf reddening, wilting and dieback may continue through the summer, though only parts of the crown are affected in any one year, and throughout the season fresh green shoots may appear on the diseased branches. These new adventitious shoots may later be attacked in their turn (Day, 1924; Metcalfe, 1940). The diseased trees rarely die, but soon become stag-headed.

Internally the wood of infected trees shows a watermarked stain. This may form complete or interrupted rings or spread widely through the wood. On exposure to the air it turns bright red and then black (Metcalfe, 1940) (plate 57). Sometimes, in recently affected trees, the staining is confined to a few shoots with withered leaves. In other cases, in long-diseased trees, it occurs almost throughout, reaching even as far as the roots. At times, however, when staining is extensive inside the tree, only a few shoots may show dieback and leaf wilting, and the severity of the external symptoms may be a poor indication of that of the deterioration within.

Once inside the tree, the bacteria persist from one year to another, and commonly spread outwards from one annual ring to the next (Dowson, 1957).

It has been suggested that the wilting and 'red leaf' symptoms are caused by obstruction of the water conducting system by the bacteria, and by the effects of toxic substances and the consequent production of tyloses (Day, 1924; Dowson, 1957).

The disease tends to spread in the direction of the prevailing wind. It has often been surmised that transmission is by various insects, and even by the willow tit, *Parus montanus* (Dowson, 1957). Callan, who made a prolonged study of insect transmission (and much of whose work remains unpublished), failed to demonstrate that it definitely took place (Callan, 1939).

Day (1924) observed that the bacteria appeared to gain entry through wounds in the branches, and Dowson (1957) noted that it was through the exit holes made in the bark by adult midges and sawflies that the bacterial ooze emerged in the summer.

Field observations support the view that watermark disease spreads into cricket bat willow plantings from other susceptible willows, especially *S. alba*, growing nearby (Dowson and Callan, 1937). Spread may also take place from the stumps of felled infected trees (Wong *et al.*, 1974). Field evidence also suggests that the disease may be distributed with the setts used in propagation (Bryce, 1950; Wong *et al.*, 1974).

Control   The disease is controlled by careful examination and roguing of pro-pagating beds to prevent the distribution of infected setts, and by the felling and destruction of infected trees. The stumps of felled diseased trees should be killed by the use of a suitable herbicide. In areas in which the cricket bat willow is an important crop the local authorities have the power under the Watermark Disease (Local Authorities) Order 1974 (S I 1974 No 768) to inspect willows and demand the destruction of any that show symptoms of the disease. Under this and similar earlier orders a vigorous campaign has been maintained against watermark disease for some 20 years, and when Wong *et al.* (1974) carried out an intensive survey in Essex in 1972 they found that only about 0.075 per cent of the trees were in-fected. In the long term it would presumably be possible to breed resistant willows to combat the disease, but the long and costly research programme that this would entail would scarcely be justified by the small losses at present experienced.

Twig and branch dieback and wilt caused by a fluorescent *Pseudomonas* sp.
Hunter and Stott (1978) have briefly described a twig and branch dieback caused by an un-named fluorescent pseudomonad which produces a nondiffusible fluorescent pigment on King's B medium. The bacterium was causing leaf-yellowing and premature leaf fall in seven-year-old cricket bat willows in Essex. Severe, slightly sunken cankers occurred on the main branches, on which narrow, longi-tudinal cracks were also present. The cracks measured up to 3.6 m long and 25–85 mm wide. The underlying tissues showed a brown stain, mainly in the vessels, for some way beyond the leading edge of the canker. A similar disease caused by a *Pseudomonas* sp. has been reported in Canada.

DECAY FUNGI

The cricket bat and weeping willows are very susceptible to attack by the honey fungus, *Armillaria mellea*, which is described in chapter 3.

REFERENCES

Alcock, N. L. (1924). A dieback, and bark disease of willows, attacking the young twigs. *Trans. R. Scott. arboric. Soc.*, 38, 128–30
Alcock, N. L. and Maxwell, I. (1925). Successional diseases on willow. *Trans. R. Scott. arboric. Soc.*, 39, 34–7

Anon (1927). Abbanerscheinungen bei der amerikanischen Weide. *Dt. Korbweidenzüchten,* Juliheft, 75–6

Anon (1952). Editorial notes. Diseases of the cricket bat willow. *Q. Jl For.,* **46,** 1

Appen, A. von (1927). Weidenschorf (*Fusicladium saliciperdum*). *Illus. Landw. Zeit.,* **47,** 67–8

Arx, J. A. von (1957*a*). Ueber *Fusicladium saliciperdum* (All. et Tub.) Lind. *Tijdschr. PlZiekt.,* **63,** 232–6

Arx, J. A. von (1957*b*). Die Arten der Gattung *Colletotrichum* Cda. *Phytopath. Z.,* **29,** 413–68

Bier, J. E. (1959). The relation of bark moisture to the development of canker diseases caused by native, facultative parasites. I. *Cryptodiaporthe* canker on willow. *Can. J. Bot.,* **37,** 229–38

Bisby, G. R. and Mason, E. W. (1940). List of pyrenomycetes recorded for Britain. *Trans. Br. mycol. Soc.,* **24,** 127–243

Bloomberg, W. J. and Funk, A. (1960). Willow blight in British Columbia. *Bi-m. Progr. Rep. Div. For. Biol., Dep., Agric. Can.,* no. 16, pp. 3–4

Brooks, F. T. (1953). *Plant Diseases,* Oxford University Press, London

Brooks, F. T. and Walker, M. M. (1935). Observations on *Fusicladium saliciperdum. New Phytol.,* **34,** 64–7

Broekhuijsen, M. J. (1934). Wilgenkanker, veroorzaakt door *Discella carbonacea* (Fries) Berk et Br. *Tijdschr. PlZiekt.,* **40,** 62–3

Bryce, J. (1950). Watermark disease of willows. *Essex Farmers' J.,* **28,** 24

Burger, F. W. (1932). Bacterieziekte van de wilg. *Ned. BoschbTijdschr.,* **5,** 75–84

Butin, H. (1958). Uber die auf *Salix* und *Populus* vorkommenden Arten der Gattung *Cryptodiaporthe* Petr. *Phytopath. Z.,* **32,** 399–415

Butin, H. (1960). *Die Krankheiten der Weide und deren Erreger,* Berlin

Callan, E. McC. (1939). *Cryptorrhynchus lapathi* L. in relation to the watermark disease of the cricket bat willow. *Ann. appl. Biol.,* **26,** 135–7

Clinton, G. P. (1929). Willow scab-blight. *Proc. Am. Meeting Fifth Nat. Shade Tree Conf., 1929,* pp. 61–3

Clinton, G. P. and McCormick, F. A. (1929). The willow scab fungus *Fusicladium saliciperdum. Connecticut Agric. Exp. Sta. Bull.,* no. 302, pp.443–69

Conners, I. L., McCallum, A. W. and Bier, J. E. (1941). Willow blight in British Columbia. *Phytopathology,* **31,** 1056–8

Davidson, A. G. and Fowler, M. E. (1967). Scab and black canker of willow, in *Important Forest Insects and Disease of Mutual Concern to Canada, the United States and Mexico,* Dep. For. rur. Dev. Can. Publ., no. 1180, pp. 201–3

Day, W. R. (1924). *The Watermark Disease of the Cricket Bat Willow,* Oxf. For. Mem., no. 3, 30 pp.

Dennis, R. W. G. (1931). The black canker of willows. *Trans. Br. mycol. Soc.,* **16,** 76–84

Dennis, R. W. G. (1968). *British Ascomycetes,* J. Cramer, Lehre

Dennis, R. W. G. and Wakefield, E. M. (1946). New or interesting British fungi. *Trans. Br. mycol. Soc.,* **29,** 141–66

Diercks, R. (1959). Zur chemischen Bekämpfung der Korbweiden-Parasiten *Fusicladium saliciperdum* (All. et Tub.) Lind. und *Glomerella miyabeana* (Fuk.) v.Arx. *Pflanzenschutz,* **11,** 125–30

Dowson, W. J. (1937). *Bacterium salicis* Day, the cause of the watermark disease of the cricket-bat willow. *Ann. appl. Biol.,* **24,** 528–44

Dowson, W. J. (1957). *Plant Diseases Due to Bacteria,* Cambridge University Press, Cambridge

Dowson, W. J. and Callan, E. McC. (1937). The watermark disease of the white willow. *Forestry,* **11,** 104–8

Farský, O. and Fekete, D. (1965). *Glomerella miyabeana* (Fukushi) Arx (*Physalospora miyabeana* Fukushi), pricinou odumiráni řizků stromovýkh Vrb na jižnúm Slovensku. *Lesn. Cas Ust. ved. Inform. MZLVH,* **10,** 745–58

Fukushi, T. (1921). A willow canker disease caused by *Physalospora miyabeana* and its conidial form *Gloeosporium. Ann. phytopath. Soc. Japan,* **1,** 1–12

Gaggini, J. B. (1970). Anthracnose of weeping willows. *Gdnrs' Chron.,* **168,** 13

Greenhalgh, G. N. (1976). Aberdeen foray. *Bull. Br. mycol. Soc.,* **10,** 55–63

Gremmen, J. and de Kam, M. (1970). *Erwinia salicis* as the cause of dieback in *Salix alba* in the Netherlands and its identity with *Pseudomonas saliciperda. Neth. J. Pl. Path.*, 76, 249–52

Grove, W. B. (1937). *British Stem- and Leaf-Fungi (Coelomycetes)*, vol. 2, Cambridge University Press, Cambridge

Harrison, K. A. (1965). Willow blight and the survival of some *Salix* species in Nova Scotia. *Can. Pl. Dis. Surv.*, 45, 94–5

Hunter, T. and Stott, K. G. (1978). A disease of *Salix alba* var. *coerulea* caused by a fluorescent *Pseudomonas* sp. *Pl. Path.*, 27, 144–5

Janson, A. (1927). Ueber den Schorf und andere Korbweidenschädlinge. *Nachricht über Schädlingsbekämpf*, 2, 161–4

Jauch, C. (1952). La 'antracnosis' de los sauces cultivados en el Delta del Paraná. *Rev. Fac. Agron. B. Aires*, 13, 285–308

Kochman, J. (1929). Studja biologiczne nad paroszytem Wierzby *Fusicladium saliciperdum* (All. et Tub.) Lind. *Mém. Inst. nat. polon. Econ. Rur. Putawy*, 10, 555–73

Lindeijer, E. J. (1931). Een bacterie-ziekte van de wilg. *Tijdschr. PlZiekt.*, 37, 63–7

Metcalfe, G. (1940). The watermark disease of willows. I. Host-parasite relationships. *New Phytol.*, 39, 322–32

Mooi, J. C. (1948). *Kanker en Takinsterving van der Wilg veroorzaakt door Nectria galligena en Cryptodiaporthe salicina*, Thesis, University of Amsterdam; abstract in *Rev. appl. Mycol.*, 28, 1949, pp. 92–4

Moore, W. C. (1959). *British Parasitic Fungi*, Cambridge University Press

Murray, B. J. (1926). Three fungus diseases of *Salix* in New Zealand, and some saprophytic fungi found on the same hosts. *Trans. N. Z. Inst.*, 56, 58–70

Nattras, R. M. (1928). The Physalospora disease of the basket willow. *Trans. Br. mycol. Soc.*, 13, 286–304

Nattras, R. M. (1930). *A Note on Two Marssonina Diseases on Willows*, Minist. Agric., Egypt (Pl. Prot. Sect.) Bull., no. 99, 19 pp.

Nelson, A. C. (1965). The morphology and cytology of three noteworthy ascomycetes. *Diss. Abstr.*, 25, 3812

Ogilvie, L. (1932). Notes on the rusts of basket willows and their control. *Rep. agric. hort. Res. Stn Univ. Bristol, 1931*, pp. 133–8

Ogilvie, L. and Hutchinson, H. P. (1933). *Melampsora amygdalinae*, the rust of basket willows (*Salix triandra*). I. Observations and experiments in 1932. II. Spore germination experiments. *Rep. agric. hort. Res. Stn Univ. Bristol, 1932*, pp. 125–38

Pape, H. (1925). Der Pilz *Fusicladium saliciperdum* (All. et Tub.) Lind. als Korbweiden-schädling. *Dt. Erwerbsgartenbau*, 24, 326–9

Poeteren, N. van (1935). Verslag over de verhzaamheden van den Plantenziektenkundigen Dienst in het jaar 1934. *Versl. PlZiekt. Dienst Wageningen*, 80, 108 pp.

Poeteren, N. van (1938). *Versl. PlZiekt. Dienst Wageningen, 1936 and 1937*; abstract in *Rev. appl. Mycol.*, 18, 1939, pp. 153–4

Preece, T. R. (1977). *Watermark Disease of the Cricket Bat Willow*, Leafl. For. Commn, no. 20, 9 pp.

Rabenhorst, G. L. (1884). *Kryptogamenflora von Deutschlands, Osterreich und der Schweiz*, vol. 1 p. 40

Redfern, D. B. (1974). In forest pathology. *Rep. Forest Res., Lond., 1974*, p. 38

Rimpau, R. H. (1962). Untersuchungen über die Gattung *Drepanopeziza* (Kleb.) v. Höhn. *Phytopath. Z.*, 43, 257–306

Rose, D. (1970). Disease resistant willows sought. *Gdnrs' Chron.*, 167, 40

Rupert, J. A. and Leach, J. G. (1942). Willow blight in West Virginia. *Phytopathology*, 32, 1095–96

Rybak-Mikitiuk, T. (1962). *Acta agrobot.*, 11, 93–129 abstract in *Rev. appl. Mycol.*, 42, 1963, p. 158

Schwarz, M. B. (1922). *Das Zweigsterben der Ulmen, Trauerweiden und Pfirsichbaume*, Thesis, University of Utrecht; abstract in *Rev. appl. Mycol.*, 2, 1923, pp. 92–4

Steinmetz, F. H. and Prince, A. E. (1938). Observations on willow blight in Maine, 1927–1938. *Pl. Dis. Reptr.*, 22, 282–3

Twarowska, I. (1968). Gospodarcze znaczenie, biologia i podstawy zwalczania grzyba *Pollaccia saliciperda* (all. et Tub.) v. Arx. *Prace Inst. Bad. Lésn.*, no. 351/353 pp. 3–54

Thomas, A. (1974). Society autumn foray, Cardiff. *Bull. Br. mycol. Soc.*, 8, 51–7

Viennot-Bourgin, G. (1949). *Les Champignons Parasites des Plantes Cultivées*, vol. 2, Masson et Cie, Paris

Wehmeyer, L. E. (1932). The British species of the genus *Diaporthe* Nits. and its segregates. *Trans. Br. mycol. Soc.*, 17, 237–95

Weir, J. R. and Hubert, E. E. (1918). Notes on the overwintering of forest tree rusts. *Phytopathology*, 8, 55–9

Wiejak, K. (1960). Obserwacje nad wystepowaniem zgorzeli pedow Wikliny powodowanej przez *Physalospora miyabeana* Fukushi. *Biul. Inst. Ochr. Rós.*, Poznan, 9, 205–13

Wilson, W. M. and Henderson, D. M. (1966). *British Rust Fungi*, Cambridge University Press, Cambridge

Wong, W. C., Nash, T. H. and Preece, T. F. (1974). A field survey of watermark disease of cricket bat willow in Essex and observations on some of the probable sources of the disease. *Pl. Path.*, 23, 25–9

Wong, W. C. and Preece, T. F. (1973). Infection of cricket bat willow (*Salix alba* var. *coerulea* Sm.) by *Erwinia salicis* (Day) Chester detected in the field by the use of a specific antiserum. *Pl. Path.*, 22, 95–7

18 Diseases of other broadleaved trees

HORSE CHESTNUT: *Aesculus* **SPP.**
  NURSERY AND POST-NURSERY DISEASES
    LEAF DISEASES
      Guignardia leaf blotch caused by *Phyllosticta paviae*
      Leaf spot caused by *Septoria hippocastani*
    DISEASES OF THE BARK AND TRUNK
      Bark necrosis or bleeding canker associated with *Phytophthora cactorum*
      Wetwood
    ROOT DISEASES
      Phytophthora root rot
    DECAY FUNGI
    VIRUS DISEASES
      Horse chestnut mosaic
BOX: *Buxus sempervirens*
  NURSERY AND POST-NURSERY DISEASES
    LEAF DISEASES
      Leaf fall caused by *Trochila buxi*
      The leaf rust *Puccinia buxi*
      Paecilomyces buxi (*Verticillium buxi*)
      Leaf spots caused by *Phyllosticta buxina* and *P. limbalis*
    DISEASES OF LEAVES AND TWIGS
      Leaf and twig blight caused by *Pseudonectria rousseliana*
    STEM DISEASES
      Stem canker associated with *Nectria desmazierii*
HORNBEAM: *Carpinus betulus*
  NURSERY AND POST-NURSERY DESEASES
    LEAF DISEASES
      Leaf spot caused by *Gloeosporium carpini*
    STEM DISEASES
      Witches brooms caused by *Taphrina carpini*
CATALPA
HAZEL: *Corylus avellana*
  NURSERY AND POST-NURSERY DISEASES
    LEAF DISEASES
      The powdery mildew *Phyllactinia corylea* (*P. suffulta, P. guttata*)
      Leaf spots caused by *Gnomoniella coryli, Phyllosticta coryli, Labrella coryli* and *Septoria avellanae*

LABURNUM
>**NURSERY DISEASES**
>>LEAF DISEASES
>>>**Brown spot caused by** *Pleiochaeta setosa (Ceratophorum setosum)*
>**POST-NURSERY DISEASES**
>>LEAF DISEASES
>>>**Powdery mildew:** *Oidium* **sp. and Downy mildew:** *Peronospora cytisi*
>>>**The rust** *Uromyces laburni*
>>>**Leaf spots caused by** *Ascochyta kabatiana* **and** *Septoria cytisi*
>>BRANCH DISEASES
>>>**Branch canker associated with** *Cucurbitaria laburni*
>>>**Branch dieback caused by** *Chondrostereum purpureum (Stereum purpureum)*
>>DECAY FUNGI

MAGNOLIA
>**NURSERY AND POST-NURSERY DISEASES**
>>LEAF DISEASES
>>>**Leaf spot caused by** *Phyllosticta magnoliae*

APPLE AND PEAR: *Malus* **AND** *Pyrus* **SPP.**
>**NURSERY AND POST-NURSERY DISEASES**
>>LEAF DISEASES
>>>**Apple scab caused by** *Venturia inaequalis* **(stat. conid.** *Fusicladium dendriticum)* **and pear scab, caused by** *V. pirina* **(stat. conid.** *F. pirinum)*
>>SHOOT DISEASES
>>>**Canker caused by** *Nectria galligena*
>>ROOT DISEASES
>>>**Honey fungus:** *Armillaria mellea*
>>OTHER DISEASES

SOUTHERN BEECH: *Nothofagus* **SPP.**

PAULOWNIA
>**NURSERY AND POST-NURSERY DISEASES**
>>LEAF DISEASES
>>>**Leaf spots caused by** *Phyllosticta paulowniae* **and** *Ascochyta paulowniae*

PLANE: *Platanus* **SPP.**
>**NURSERY AND POST-NURSERY DISEASES**
>>DISEASES OF LEAVES AND SHOOTS
>>>**Anthracnose caused by** *Gnomonia platani (G. veneta)*
>>DECAY FUNGI

ALMOND, CHERRY AND OTHER SPECIES OF *Prunus*
ALMOND: *Prunus dulcis*
>**NURSERY AND POST-NURSERY DISEASES**
>>LEAF DISEASES
>>>**Leaf curl caused by** *Taphrina deformans*

CHERRY: *Prunus avium, P. padus, P. cerasus*

NURSERY AND POST-NURSERY DISEASES

  LEAF DISEASES

    Blossom wilt and twig blight caused by *Sclerotinia laxa*

    Silver leaf caused by *Chondrostereum purpureum (Stereum purpureum)*

  DISEASES OF STEMS AND BRANCHES

    Bacterial canker caused by *Pseudomonas mors-prunorum*

  DECAY FUNGI

PORTUGAL LAUREL: *Prunus lusitanica*

BUCKTHORN: *Rhamnus cathartica* and **ALDER BUCKTHORN:** *Frangula alnus*

  NURSERY AND POST-NURSERY DISEASES

    LEAF DISEASES

      Crown rust *(Puccinia coronata)*

FALSE ACACIA OR LOCUST TREE: *Robinia pseudoacacia*

  NURSERY AND POST-NURSERY DISEASES

    LEAF DISEASES

      Leaf spot caused by *Phleospora robiniae*

    DECAY FUNGI

      Butt rot caused by *Fomitopsis cytisina (Fomes fraxineus)*

ELDER: *Sambucus nigra*

  NURSERY AND POST-NURSERY DISEASES

    LEAF DISEASES

      Leaf spots caused by *Cercospora depazeoides, Phyllosticta sambuci,*

      P. sambucicola, and *Ramularia sambucina*

    DECAY FUNGI

      Jews' ear fungus: *Auricularia auricula-judae*

MOUNTAIN ASH OR ROWAN, WHITEBEAM AND SERVICE TREE (*Sorbus* **SPP.)**

  NURSERY AND POST-NURSERY DISEASES

    LEAF DISEASES

      The powdery mildew *Podosphaera oxyacanthae*

      The rust *Gymnosporangium cornutum (G. juniperi)*

    WILT DISEASES

      Fireblight caused by *Erwinia amylovora*

LILAC *(Syringa vulgaris)*

  NURSERY AND POST-NURSERY DISEASES

    LEAF DISEASES

      Powdery mildew: *Oidium* sp.

      Leaf blotch caused by *Heterosporium syringae*

      Leaf spot caused by *Phyllosticta syringae* and *Ascochyta syringae*

    DISEASES OF LEAVES AND SHOOTS

      Leaf and twig blight caused by *Pseudomonas syringae*

    WILT DISEASES

      Wilt caused by *Phytophthora syringae*

    VIRUS DISEASES

Lilac ringspot

LIME: *Tilia* SPP.

NURSERY AND POST-NURSERY DISEASES
LEAF DISEASES
Leaf spots caused by *Phyllosticta tiliae, Ascochyta tiliae, Gloeosporium tiliae,* and *Cercospora microsora*
DISEASES OF TWIGS AND BRANCHES
Twig and branch blights caused by *Discella desmazierii (Lamproconium desmazierii)* and *Pyrenochaeta pubescens*
Shoot canker caused by *Plectophomella concentrica*
WILT DISEASES
Verticillium wilt
ROOT DISEASES
Phytophthora root rot
DECAY FUNGI
MISCELLANEOUS DISORDERS
Sooty moulds

REFERENCES

This chapter deals with broadleaved trees, the pathology of which is insufficiently known to warrant chapters of their own. Some minor native trees are included, and so are many ornamentals. Many trees receive no mention because there appear to be no authenticated records of any diseases on them in this country. Diseases of the well-known fruit tree species *Malus, Pyrus* and *Prunus* are dealt with only if they are known to be of some importance on ornamental species or varieties, as most of their diseases can be found in books on the pathology of fruit and horticultural crops.

The root rot fungi *Armillaria mellea* and *Heterobasidion annosum (Fomes annosus)*, the silver leaf fungus *Chondrostereum purpureum*, and the grey mould *Botrytis cinerea* have been found on most of these tress. These fungi are described in chapter 3. They are not further considered here, and are mentioned only if, for example, some particular tree is especially susceptible to attack by one of them.

HORSE CHESTNUT: *AESCULUS* SPP.

The horse chestnut, *Aesculus hippocastanum*, and the pink or red-flowered *A. carnea*, both of which are introduced, are common ornamental trees in this country. A few other species, especially the splendid *A. indica*, deserve to be grown more often.

NURSERY AND POST-NURSERY DISEASES

LEAF DISEASES

Guignardia leaf blotch caused by *Phyllosticta paviae* Desm.

Leaf blotch is an important disease of horse chestnut and related species of *Aesculus* in eastern North America (Stewart, 1916) and in Europe, where it has caused particular damage in Austria (Lohwag, 1962), Italy and Switzerland (Scaramuzzi, 1954), and Jugoslavia (Milatović, 1956); it occurs also in France and Belgium (Grove, 1935), and in West Germany (Schneider, 1961), as well as in Great Britain (Grove, 1935; Moore, 1959).

The fungus usually associated with the disease is *Phyllosticta paviae* Desm., which is common on affected leaves in this country. Its perfect stage is probably *Guignardia aesculi* (Peck) Stewart. This seems to have been found here only once (Moore, 1959). *P. paviae* has more or less globose black pycnidia 90–175 μm across, containing colourless, elliptical spores that measure 10–16 x 6.5–10 μm, and emerge in white tendrils. The perithecia are also black and globose, and contain asci measuring 54–70 x 15–17 μm. Each ascus contains eight colourless, subelliptical ascospores measuring 12–18 x 7–9 μm. Spermogonia containing small, colourless, more or less oblong spermatia measuring 3–9 x 0.75–3 μm also occur (Stewart, 1916).

In Great Britain, the disease first appears in June, July or August. Symptoms on affected leaves (plate 56) show as very conspicuous irregular blotches that later spread over much of the leaf surface, and as a marginal scorch that often runs from the leaf tips along their edges, and extends irregularly inwards. In colour the blotches vary from a dull light brown to a deep chestnut, and they are eventually bordered by a distinct yellow margin (Grove, 1935; Pawsey, 1962; Stewart, 1916). The pycnidia are scattered on the spots, mainly on the upper surface, and the perfect stage arises on the overwintering leaves (Schneider, 1961).

In this country and in the rest of Europe, the disease is found mainly on the horse chestnut, though the first record here was on *Aesculus parviflora* at Kew (Grove, 1935). In eastern North America it occurs mainly on horse chestnut and the Ohio buckeye *(A. glabra)* but it is found also on *A. parviflora* (Stewart, 1916). Neely and Himelick (1963) in the USA inoculated many *Aesculus* spp., most of which were severely affected.

In southern Europe, leaf blotch has sometimes caused considerable damage both to nursery plants and mature trees (Scaramuzzi, 1954; Milatović, 1956; Kišpatić, 1962; Lohwag, 1962). In Great Britain it caused premature leaf fall on nursery stock in Gloucestershire in 1953 (Moore, 1959), and Pawsey (1962) reported scattered cases on mature trees as far north as Edinburgh. In recent years the disease has been common in southern England, though damage has so far been slight.

The severity of the damage here has not justified the use of control measures. Sweeping up the fallen leaves in autumn should reduce the sources of infection. Elsewhere spraying with lime sulphur or Bordeaux mixture or dusting with sulphur (Stewart, 1916), or more recently, spraying with zerlate, parzate (Davis, 1948) or with ziram or zineb (Kišpatić, 1962) have been found to give control. Several applications at intervals of two to four weeks are needed. Therefore, if necessary, spraying could be used to control outbreaks in nurseries.

Leaf spot caused by *Septoria hippocastani* B. & Br.

A common minor leaf spot of horse chestnut is caused by the imperfect fungus *Septoria hippocastani*. The numerous small brown spots are round or rather angular. The pycnidia, which are mainly on the upper side, are lens-shaped and up to 180 μm across. They contain long, hairlike spores that are divided into four cells by three faint septa, and measure 30–57 x 2.5–3.5 μm (Grove, 1935).

DISEASES OF THE BARK AND TRUNK

Bark necrosis or bleeding canker associated with *Phytophthora* spp.

Brasier and Strouts (1976) have examined horse chestnut trees with often extensive necrotic areas of bark on the trunks (commonly on the south-facing

Figure 82.   Horse chestnut with bleeding canker caused by *Phytophthora citricola* (Forestry Commission)

sides) and on large branches (figure 82). In many cases sap oozed from the lesions and flowed down the trunk to form a slime flux. In some cases, *Phytophthora cactorum* (described in chapter 11 as the cause of seedling blight of beech) was isolated from the diseased bark. The same fungus has caused similar symptoms on horsechestnut, *Acer*, and many other broadleaved trees in North America, where because of the associated slime flux the disease has been aptly named bleeding canker (Pirone *et al.*, 1960). *P. citricola* (figure 82) and *P. syringae* have sometimes been isolated from similar cankers.

Wetwood
As noted above, slime-flux is one of the symptoms of bleeding canker. The bacterial wetwood that affects many broadleaved trees, which may then show an associated fluxing, is also fairly often found in the horse chestnut. This disorder is described in chapter 3.

ROOT DISEASES

Phytophthora root rot
Recently several cases of death of large horse chestnut trees following death of their root have been investigated in England (Brasier and Strouts, 1976). Various species of *Phytophthora*, including *P. megasperma*, have been isolated from dying roots.

DECAY FUNGI

The butt and stem of the horse chestnut may be decayed by *Ganoderma adspersum* and *G. applanatum*, while *Pleurotus ostreatus* may rot the stem and branches. These fungi are described in chapter 19.

VIRUS DISEASES

Horse chestnut mosaic
A yellow mosiac of horse chestnut leaves has been found in Czechoslovakia, East Germany and Romania as well as in the United Kingdom. The leaves of affected plants become bright yellow. The symptoms are very striking, and as the virus involved can be transmitted by budding and grafting, affected trees have been propagated by nurserymen and distributed as an ornamental form (Cooper, 1979).

BOX: *BUXUS SEMPERVIRENS*

Box, a small evergreen shrub or tree, is native in a few places on chalk and limestone in southern England, and is also widely planted, especially to form a hedge.

NURSERY AND POST-NURSERY DISEASES

LEAF DISEASES

Leaf fall caused by *Trochila buxi* Capron apud Cooke

According to Moore (1959) and Foister (1961), the fungus *Trochila buxi*, which usually grows only on dead leaves, has been associated with a leaf fall of box in many parts of Scotland. The fruit bodies of *T. buxi* are olive brown apothecia with a black hymenial disc. They are at first embedded in the upper surfaces of the leaves but later exposed by the splitting of the epidermis. The colourless, elliptical ascospores measure 10–12.5 x 4–5 μm (Rehm, 1896).

The leaf rust *Puccinia buxi* DC

The box rust, *Puccinia buxi*, is widespread and frequent, especially in Scotland. As a result of infection in spring and early summer, the young leaves become thickened. In the following spring, the fungus produces brownish pustular teleutosori on both sides of the swollen leaves. The brown, smooth-walled teleutospores are two-celled, and measure 55–90 x 20–35 μm. Their very long, persistent, colourless pedicels are up to 160 μm in length (Wilson and Henderson, 1966).

Paecilomyces buxi (Link ex Fr.) Bezerra (*Verticillium buxi Link ex Fr.*)

The fungus long known as *Verticillium buxi* but renamed *Paecilomyces buxi* by Bezerra (1963) at most seems to be only a very weak parasite (Dodge, 1944) on moribund leaves. Its erect conidiophores are up to 110 μm long, branching above to end in tapered phialides. These produce chains of colourless, elliptical or sickle-shaped spores measuring 5–8 x 2–2.5 μm (Bezerra, 1963).

Leaf spots caused by *Phyllosticta buxina* Sacc. and *P. limbalis* Pers.

Leaf spots of box caused by two species of *Phyllosticta* have been described by Grove (1935).

P. buxina has been found on Box Hill, Surrey, on pale leaf spots with a narrow purple border. The small black pycnidia are densely scattered on the upper side, and are up to 100 μm across. They contain many colourless, oblong-elliptical spores measuring 4–5 x 1.5–2 μm.

P. limbalis, which has been found occasionally in Surrey and Hampshire (Moore, 1959), causes white spots with a narrow brown border. Small numbers of dark brown pycnidia arise on the spots on both sides of the leaf. The spores measure about 5–7 x 3–4 μm.

DISEASES OF LEAVES AND TWIGS

Leaf and twig blight caused by *Pseudonectria rousseliana* (Mont.) Seaver (stat. conid. *Volutella buxi* (DC ex Fr.) B. & Br., syn. *Chaetodochium buxi* (DC ex Fr.) Hohn.)

Volutella buxi, the imperfect stage of *Pseudonectria rousseliana* (Bezerra, 1963), causes a blight of leaves, twigs and branches of box. Dieback and death of the leaves of individual branches occurs, so that large, conspicuous, brown patches of foliage appear on the plants (plate 51). The wood of affected twigs and branches shows a characteristic blackening. The pathogenicity of the fungus was demonstrated by Dodge (1944). *V. buxi* produces small pink pustules *(sporodochia)* up to 110 μm across on the surfaces of the leaves, mainly on the undersides. These pustules are made up of long, bristle-like hairs up to 190 μm long, and many shorter, branched conidiophores that produce colourless conidia at their ends. The conidia form a slimy mass, and individually are spindle-shaped, smooth, one-celled, and measure 8-12 x 2.5-3 μm (Bezerra, 1963). The perithecia of *Pseudonectria rousseliana* occur on the fallen leaves, and have been found at sites scattered over England as far north as Yorkshire. They arise in groups, and vary in colour from straw-coloured or brick-red to green. They are subglobose, and sparsely covered with stiff bristles that measure up to 100 μm in length. Their club-shaped asci contain colourless, single-celled, oval ascospores measuring 9-16 x 3-5 μm (Petch, 1938).

STEM DISEASES

Stem canker associated with *Nectria desmazierii* Beccari & de Notaris (stat. conid. *Fusarium buxi* Sacc.)

A related fungus, *Nectria desmazierii* (stat. conid. *Fusarium buxi*) has on rare occasions been found associated with a stem canker of box in Great Britain as well as in North America. Its small conidial pustules form on leaf scars and buds. The sickle-shaped conidia measure 30-55 x 4-5 μm, and are finally four to six septate. Later, yellow or orange, ovate or globose perithecia up to about 175 μm across form in groups of up to 30 over the conidial pustules. They contain cylindrical, eight-spored asci measuring 65-80 x 7-9 μm. The colourless, ellipsoid, two-celled ascospores measures 12-16 x 5-7 μm (Booth, 1959). The fungus was found in Surrey in 1932, and again, in Oxfordshire, in 1968 (Batko and Strouts, unpublished).

Pirone *et al.* (1960) recommend control of canker by the cutting out of dead parts, burning of dead leaves, and spraying four times with Bordeaux mixture or lime sulphur, beginning just before new growth begins in the spring.

HORNBEAM: *CARPINUS BETULUS*

Hornbeam is native in southeast England, where it was once managed as coppice. It has also been widely planted throughout the rest of England and Wales, and into Scotland.

NURSERY AND POST-NURSERY DISEASES

LEAF DISEASES

Leaf spot caused by *Gloeosporium carpini* Desm.

Gloeosporium carpini may cause brownish, irregular, unbordered spots on horn-beam leaves. It produces many small, brownish pustules on the undersides of the spots. The spores that form in the pustules are long and cylindrical, measuring 8–10 x 1 µm (Grove, 1937). *G. carpini* is considered to be the pycnidial stage of *Gnomonia fimbriata* Auersw. (syn. *Gnomoniella fimbriata* (Pers. ex Fr.) Sacc., *Mamiana fimbriata* (Pers. ex Fr.) Ces. and de Not.). This ascomycete produces small black stromata on the fallen leaves. Long-necked perithecia embedded in the stromata mature in the spring. Their colourless, broadly elliptical asco-spores measure 8–11 x 3–4 µm, and a single septum cuts off a very small cell at one end. The perfect stage is rare (Dennis, 1968).

STEM DISEASES

Witches' brooms caused by *Taphrina carpini* (Rostr.) Johans.

The fungus *Taphrina carpini* causes witches' brooms on hornbeam (figure 83). From May to July its asci form a whitish layer covering the surface of pale greenish leaves on the long, lax shoots of the brooms, which form bunches of

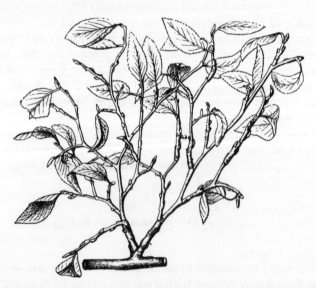

Figure 83. Witches' broom on *Carpinus* caused by *Taphrina carpini* (R. Hartig)

much-branched twigs. The individual eight-spored asci are cylindrical, and measure 20-30 x 7-14 μm. Their one-celled elliptical spores measure 5-7 x 3-4 μm. *T. carpini* appears to be uncommon, though it has been found at sites widely scattered over England and Scotland (Dennis, 1968; Reid, 1969).

CATALPA

The Indian bean tree, *Catalpa bignonioides,* is frequently found in parks and gardens, and a few other *Catalpa* species are occasionally grown.

Verticillium wilt is often the cause of death of *Catalpa bignonioides,* even of large trees. The disease is considered in chapter 3.

HAZEL (CORYLUS AVELLANA)

Hazel is a shrub or small tree, native and common almost throughout Great Britain. It is much used in hedging, and small plantings, mainly in southeast England, are managed as coppice for the production of poles and fencing materials, and others are grown for their nuts.

NURSERY AND POST-NURSERY DISEASES

LEAF DISEASES

The powdery mildew *Phyllactinia corylea* (Pers.) Karst. (syn. *P. suffulta* (Rabenh.) Sacc., *P. guttata* (Wallr.) Lév.).
The powdery mildew *Phyllactinia corylea* forms a sparse mycelium over the leaves of hazel, and sometimes of ash, birch, oak (Batko, 1962), and other trees and shrubs.

Erect conidiophores on the mycelium produce usually single oidia measuring 50-120 x 8-15 μm (Brooks, 1953). Later, mainly on the undersides of the leaves, scattered, rather flattened-globose, closed ascocarps (cleistocarps) arise. These are black when mature, and up to about 1/3 mm across. Round the equator each bears up to 15 stiff, colourless, pointed appendages with bulbous bases (figure 84). In length the appendages are up to three times the diameter of the fruit body. The top of the ascocarp is covered with a mass of short, branched outgrowths. Within each ascocarp are up to 45 ovate asci measuring 70-100 x 25-40 μm, and each ascus usually contains two ascospores that measure 30-40 x 16-25 μm (Brooks, 1953; Dennis, 1968).

By hygroscopic movements, the appendages dislodge the ascocarps so that they fall from the leaves and mature on the ground (Brooks, 1953).

Though the mildew may cause some defoliation, it is of only minor importance.

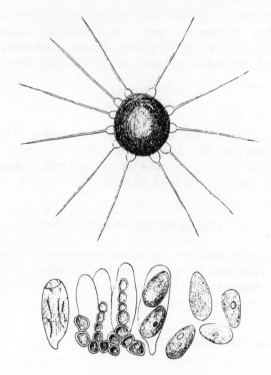

Figure 84. Cleistocarp, asci and ascospores of *Phyllactinia corylea*. The
cleistocarp shows the appendages with bulbous bases (K.F. Tubeuf)

Leaf spots caused by *Gnomoniella coryli* (Batsch ex Fr.) Sacc. (*Mamiana coryli* (Batsch ex Fr.) Ces. & de Not.), *Phyllosticta coryli* Westd., *Labrella coryli* Sacc., and *Septoria avellanae* B. & Br.

Several unimportant fungal leaf spots occur on hazel. They are caused by the ascomycete *Gnomoniella coryli* and the Deuteromycetes (Fungi Imperfecti) *Phyllosticta coryli*, *Labrella coryli* and *Septoria avellanae*.

Gnomoniella coryli produces one to several black, long-beaked perithecia in small stromata embedded in the leaves. The eight-spored asci measure 40–50 x 8–9 μm, and contain one-celled, colourless, elliptical ascospores that measure 8–9 x 3 μm (Winter, 1897).

Phyllosticta coryli causes rather large, brown, later whitish spots on the leaves. Embedded in the spots are flattened, lens-shaped, brownish pycnidia 100–150 μm across, that contain colourless, elliptical, one-celled spores measuring 7–8 x 2–3 μm. Grove (1935) considered the fungus to be only an early stage of *Labrella coryli*, which often appears on the same spots.

The brownish pycnidia of *Labrella coryli* are also lens-like, and form mostly on the undersides of the leaves on reddish-brown irregular spots. The pycnospores are oblong, club-shaped or fiddle-shaped, and measure 12–15 x 5 μm (Grove, 1937).

Septoria avellanae causes large brown spots on which groups of pycnidia form on the underside of the leaf. The pycnidia measure 80–100 μm across, and contain curved, colourless, hairlike spores measuring 14–20 x 1.5 μm (Grove, 1935).

NUT ROTS

Nut rots may be caused by the fungi *Sclerotinia fructigena*, *Botrytis cinerea* and *Gibberella baccata*.

HAWTHORN (*CRATAEGUS* SPP.)

The hawthorns are small thorny trees or shrubs. Of the two native species, *Crataegus monogyna* is common throughout Great Britain, and *C. oxyacanthoides* occurs in the midlands and the southeast. Various double-flowered and pink-flowered forms of these are grown as ornamentals.

NURSERY AND POST-NURSERY DISEASES

LEAF DISEASES

The powdery mildew *Podosphaera oxyacanthae* (DC) de Bary
The common powdery mildew *Podosphaera oxyacanthae* forms a white powdery covering over the leaves of hawthorn. It has also been found in Scotland on cherry (Moore, 1959), and also occurs on *Sorbus* spp.

The colourless, barrel-shaped oidia that arise on the mycelium measure about 26–28 x 12–15 μm. Perithecia *(cleistothecia)*, which are rarely found, are brown when mature, and up to 90 μm across. At the top they bear up to 30 stiff appendages dichotomously branched at their ends. They each contain one globose ascus with eight ovoid ascospores measuring 18 x 10 μm (Viennot-Bourgin, 1949).

The disease is common, but does appreciable damage only on soft growth on young trees and on newly planted hedges. On these, control may be obtained by spraying with dinocap, or with colloidal or wettable sulphur (Martin and Worthing, 1976).

Leaf spots and blotches caused by *Sclerotinia crataegi* Magn. and *Phleospora oxyacanthae* (Kunze & Schm.) Wallr.
The ascomycete *Scelerotinia crataegi* may grow over the surface of hawthorn leaves as a sweet-scented, powdery, grey mould. Occasionally in southeast England it has killed the leaves, the blackened remains of which at first continue

to hang on the tree (Dowson and Dillon-Weston, 1937; Wormald, 1937). Only the imperfect stage, *Monilia crataegi* Died., has been found in this country, and its one-celled, barrel-shaped spores measure about 13 x 11 µm (Lindau, 1910).

Phleospora oxyacanthae, one of the Deuteromycetes (Fungi imperfecti), causes yellowish or brown spots on hawthorn leaves. Its brown, open and cup-shaped pycnidia are mostly on the undersides of the leaves, and are up to 150 µm across. The pycnospores, which ooze out in yellowish masses, are club-shaped, have six to eight septa, and measure 50–80 x 6–8 µm (Grove, 1935). The fungus is widespread and sometimes damaging, as in favourable conditions the spots spread over the leaves, which become brown and scorched.

DISEASES OF LEAVES AND SHOOTS

The hawthorn/juniper rusts *Gymnosporangium clavariiforme* (Pers.) DC and *G. confusum* Plowr.

Two heteroecious rusts with their teleutosori on *Juniperus* have *Crataegus monogyna* and *C. oxyacanthoides* as the primary hosts on which they produce their spermogonia and aecidia (figure 85). These rusts, which are described by Wilson and Henderson (1966), are *Gymnosporangium clavariiforme* and *G. confusum*. Both cause conspicuous red or orange swellings on the leaves, twigs and fruits. The spermogonia of *G. clavariiforme* are at first yellow and finally brown. The white or yellowish aecidia are cylindrical, but later torn almost to the base. The aecidiospores are pale brown and globose or almost so, measuring 22–30 x 18–26 µm.

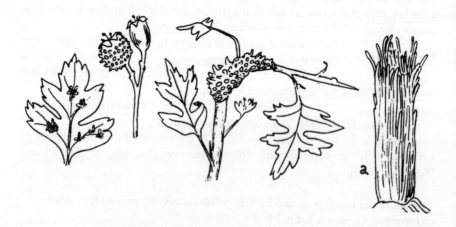

Figure 85. *Gymnosporangium clavariiforme* on hawthorn, showing the aecidia on a leaf, fruit and branch. The aecidium at *a* (x 17) shows the fringed top (W.B. Grove)

The spermogonia of *G. confusum* are orange. The yellowish or pale brown aecidia are more or less cylindrical, with an open fringed top, and the globose or ellipsoid, brown aecidiospores measure 19–26 x 19–22 μm.

According to Wilson and Henderson (1966), *G. clavariiforme* is of frequent occurrence, but neither this nor the much rarer *G. confusum* is of economic importance.

BACTERIAL WILTS

Fire blight caused by *Erwinia amylovora* (Burr.) Winsl.

Hawthorn is one of the hosts of the serious disease fireblight, caused by the bacterium *Erwinia amylovora*, and affected trees may be important sources of infection to nearby commercial pear and apple orchards (Lelliott, 1959, 1979). Hence, infected trees should be grubbed up and burnt. Hawthorns near apple and pear orchards should be cut back each year to hinder blossoming, as the disease (which is briefly described in chapter 3) enters the plant primarily by infection of the flowers.

VIRUS DISEASES

Cooper (1979) has reported a foliage disease of *Crataegus* widespread in Britain. The symptoms, chlorotic ring and vein banding patterns, seem to be caused by a form of chlorotic ring spot virus.

EUCALYPTUS

A few *Eucalyptus* spp. have been introduced into this country from Australasia as ornamental trees. The commonest is *E. gunnii*.

NURSERY DISEASES

OEDEMA

Small oedematous, blister-like swellings (intumescences) on the undersides of the leaves, caused by over-humid growing conditions and lack of ventilation, have been found on nursery plants of *Eucalyptus* in frames in west Scotland. Like those described by Pirone *et al.* (1960), they finally cracked open and became rust coloured.

FROST DAMAGE AND GREY MOULD *(BOTRYTIS CINEREA)*

Nursery plants of *Eucalyptus* are very susceptible to frost (chapter 2), and may also be attacked by grey mould, *Botrytis cinerea* (chapter 3).

POWDERY MILDEW (*OIDIUM* SP.)

Glasscock and Rosser (1958) recorded a powdery mildew (an *Oidium* sp.) on seedlings of *E. perrineana* and *E. gunnii* here. The conidia of the fungus measured about 24-30 x 15-18 μm, and control was achieved by spraying with capryl.

POST-NURSERY DISEASES

WINTER COLD

Mature trees may be killed by winter cold, and many in the eastern more continental parts of great Britain were destroyed in the hard winter of 1962-63. According to Wood (in Macdonald *et al.,* 1957) the most hardy species in this country are *E. vernicosa, E. parviflora, E. niphophila, E. gunnii* and *E. pauciflora.*

HOLLY *(ILEX AQUIFOLIUM)*

The common holly, *Ilex aquifolium,* is a small evergreen prickly tree or shrub that grows all over Great Britain. This and its many cultivars are grown also as ornamentals, often as hedging.

NURSERY AND POST-NURSERY DISEASES

LEAF DISEASES

Leaf spots caused by *Phyllosticta aquifolina* and Coniothyrium ilicis
Grove (1935, 1937) described two pycnidial fungi causing leaf spots on holly.

The spots produced by the first of these, *Phyllosticta aquifolina* Grove, which has been found in Kew Gardens, are round or irregular, greyish with a brown border, and up to 3 mm across. Black pycnidia up to 400 μm in diameter arise on the spots, and contain colourless, one-celled, oblong-ellipsoid spores measuring 6-7 x 2-2.5 μm (Grove, 1935).

A second fungus, *Coniothyrium ilicis* Smith and Ramsbottom, produces white spots in the upper side of which are embedded black, thin-walled pycnidia up to 200 μm across. The pale brown pycnospores are globose to ellipsoid, and measure 3-5 x 2-3 μm. In 1922 this fungus caused an epidemic on holly trees at Sutton Coldfield, Warwickshire (Grove, 1937).

TWIG DISEASES

Twig blight caused by *Vialaea insculpta* (Fr. em. Oud.) Sacc.
From time to time the ascomycete *Vialaea insculpta* (*Boydia insculpta* (Oud.)

Grove) has been found apparently killing the twigs of holly in Scotland and southern England (Grove, 1921; Moore, 1959). The dull black, globose or lens-shaped perithecia are up to 500 μm across. The asci within them soon deliquesce. The colourless ascospores are two-celled, and shaped like two clubs placed end to end. They measure 80–100 x 8–9 μm.

ROOT DISEASES

Violet root rot
The violet root rot fungus, *Helicobasidium purpureum* (described in chapter 3), which attacks a very wide range of herbaceous and woody hosts, has been found in this country on holly (Moore, 1959).

WALNUT (*JUGLANS* SPP.)

The walnut, *Juglans regia*, and the black walnut, *J. nigra*, are both introduced, and grown mainly as garden trees. Both species produce a valuable timber, but *J. regia* is grown chiefly for its nuts, though in Britain these ripen only in hot summers.

NURSERY DISEASES

LEAF AND SHOOT DISEASES

Graft disease caused by *Chalaropsis thielavioides* Peyronel
Walnut varieties grafted under glass have occasionally been affected by graft disease caused by *Chalaropsis thielavioides*, a fungus that also gives rise to a blackening of stored carrots. Affected grafts fail, and both stock and scion become covered by a dark brown mass of powdery spores. The spores are thick-walled, round or egg-shaped, and measure about 17 x 3 μm. On incubation under moist conditions the fungus produces white masses of cylindrical endospores that measure 16 x 3 μm (Wormald, 1955) (figure 86).

The disease is easily controlled by using formaldehyde solution to clean the propagating house before use. If necessary, material for grafting can be painted with the same chemical, which can also be used to sterilise the grafting knife (Hamond, 1931, 1935; Wormald, 1955).

Bacterial blight caused by *Xanthomonas juglandis* (Pierce) Dowson
Much more damaging, however, is the bacterial blight caused by *Xanthomonas juglandis*. This bacterium causes small black, angular spots, particularly towards the tips of the leaflets. Large, withered patches may arise as they spread over the leaf surface. Elongated black patches on the shoots may lead to girdling, and so

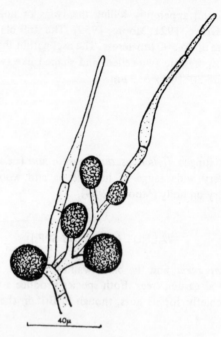

Figure 86. *Chalaropsis thielavioides*: large, dark macrospores and cylindrical endospores (H. Wormald)

to death of the tissues beyond the diseased zone. Black blotches arise on the fruits, and the male catkins may also be destroyed (Wormald, 1955).

If the diseased tissues are teased out in water, a gelatinous mass of bacteria oozes out. The bacteria are small, gram-negative, nonsporing, motile rods, each with one polar flagellum. They measure about $1.5-3 \times 0.3-0.5 \mu m$ (Dowson, 1957; Stapp, 1961).

In Great Britain, bacterial blight occurs mainly on young trees in the nursery, and is of minor importance. It is best controlled by cutting out any affected shoots well beyond the diseased tissues, frequently sterilising the pruning tools with formaldehyde. If necessary the young foliage may be sprayed with Bordeaux mixture or some similar but less phytotoxic copper spray (Wormald, 1955), or with streptomycin (Miller, 1958).

POST-NURSERY DISEASES

LEAF DISEASES

Leaf blotch caused by *Gnomonia leptostyla* (Fr.) Ces. and de Not. (stat. conid. *Marssonina juglandis* (Lib.) Magn.)

Of the fungus diseases that affect walnut leaves the best known is the leaf blotch caused by *Gnomonia leptostyla* (stat. conid. *Marssonina juglandis*). This disease occurs thoughout much of Europe, North America, parts of South America, Israel, Iran, parts of the USSR (Anon, 1961) and India (Kaul, 1962). It is common and widespread in Great Britain, particularly in England and Wales.

The fungus causes brown blotches on the leaves and the young fruits. The small, black conidial pustules *(Marssonina juglandis)* form on the dead patches, mainly on the undersides. They give rise to rather crescent or comma-shaped, colourless, two-celled conidia that measure $14-26 \times 2-3\,\mu m$ (Brooks, 1953). Black, long-necked perithecia arise on the overwintering leaves. Their eight-spored asci contain colourless, two-celled, spindle-shaped ascospores that measure $19-28 \times 2.5-3\,\mu m$ (Wormald, 1955).

Primary infection is by the ascospores liberated in the spring. Secondary spread is by the conidia. Severe attacks result in defoliation, and blackening of the young green nuts, which become useless.

Control on single trees and in nut plantings is by the raking up and burning of the fallen leaves, so removing the source of the ascospores that give rise to the spring infections (Wormald, 1955). In parts of continental Europe and North America, spraying may be needed in wet seasons. Many chemicals, including zineb and maneb, give effective control (Berry, 1964).

SHOOT DISEASES

Dieback associated with *Cytospora juglandina* Sacc.
The various minor fungi described on walnut include *Cytospora juglandina*, which has been found associated with a dieback. Its pycnidia are grouped in small stromata, and contain colourless, one-celled, cyindrical spores measuring $6-7 \times 1\,\mu m$ (Grove, 1935).

DECAY FUNGI

Inonotus hispidus and *Polyporus squamosus* both decay the stems and branches of walnut. They are described in chapter 19.

VIRUS DISEASES

Walnut chlorosis
A virus disease of walnuts occurs in Britain, especially in the south. It causes yellow spots, rings and line patterns on the leaf blade, and sometimes necrotic flecks or chrome yellow blotches on the leaves and fruits. A similar disease is known in southern Italy (Cooper, 1979).

MISCELLANEOUS DISORDERS

Frost damage

Young trees are very susceptible to frost damage, and in severe winters trunks of older trees may crack, and then often bleed copiously for long periods.

GOLDEN RAIN TREE (*KOELREUTERIA PANICULATA*)

This tree, which comes from the Far East, is sometimes grown in parks and gardens, but it flowers only in hot summers. It is very susceptible to Verticillium wilt, which is described in chapter 3.

LABURNUM

The laburnum, *Laburnum anagyroides*, is a common introduced garden tree.

NURSERY DISEASES

LEAF DISEASES

Brown spot caused by *Pleiochaeta setosa* (Kirchn.) Hughes (*Ceratophorum setosum* Kirchn.)

The imperfect fungus *Pleiochaeta setosa (Ceratophorum setosum)* has occasionally damaged cuttings and seedlings of laburnum as well as of other leguminous plants (Green and Hewlett, 1949; Moore, 1959). Black spots form on the leaves, and small groups of conidiophores on the spots produce very characteristic spores. These have a fusoid body measuring 63-98 x 13-19 μm. The body of the spore is five to nine-celled, and the central cells are brown, while the basal and apical cells are almost colourless. The more or less conical apical cell bears a long, apical, hairlike appendage, and up to four similar but shorter lateral appendages (Hughes, 1951). The fungus may defoliate affected shoots, but Green and Hewlett (1949) found that it could be controlled by spraying once or twice with colloidal copper or Bordeaux mixture.

POST-NURSERY DISEASES

LEAF DISEASES

Powdery mildew: *Oidium* sp. and Downy mildew: *Peronospora cytisi* Magn.

An undescribed powdery mildew (*Oidium* sp.) has been recorded occasionally on laburnum in this country, and there is an unconfirmed record of the downy mildew *Peronospora cytisi* on the same host (Moore, 1959).

The rust *Uromyces laburni* (DC) Fuckel

The uredosori and teleutosori of the rare rust *Uromyces laburni* have been found on laburnum in Yorkshire (Moore, 1959). Wilson and Henderson (1966) group this rust with a number of others within *U. pisi* (DC) Otth. The minute yellow uredosori occur on the undersides of the leaves, and the rounded uredospores measure about $15-32 \times 14-23 \, \mu m$. The brownish teleutosori, which occur on both sides of the leaves, bear brown, elliptical, one-celled teleutospores measuring about $20-28 \times 14-24 \, \mu m$. The spermogonia and aecidia of *U. pisi* have been found on *Euphorbia cyparisias* in Kent (Wilson and Henderson, 1966).

Leaf spots caused by *Ascochyta kabatiana* Trott. and *Septoria cytisi* Desm.

Ascochyta kabatiana (of which *Phyllosticta cytisi* is said to be an early stage) has occasionally caused a leaf spot on laburnum (Moore, 1959). The spots are up to 2 cm across, and bear subglobose, brownish pycnidia up to $150 \, \mu m$ in diameter on their upper sides. The colourless, eventually two-celled, ellipsoid pycnospores measure $7-15 \times 3-4 \, \mu m$ (Grove, 1935).

Grove (1935) also described *Septoria cytisi* Desm. as a cause of whitish spots on laburnum leaves. The brownish-black pycnidia contain long, hairlike, multi-septate measuring $90-100 \times 2.5-3.5 \, \mu m$.

BRANCH DISEASES

Branch canker associated with *Cucurbitaria laburni* (Pers. ex Fr.) de Notaris

The black perithecia of the ascomycete *Cucurbitaria laburni* emerge in crust-like groups through the bark on dead and dying twigs of laburnum. The eight-spored asci measure up to $200 \times 15 \, \mu m$, and contain yellowish-brown, elliptical, muriform ascospores measuring $24-36 \times 9-16 \, \mu m$ (Dennis, 1968). The spores are constricted at the middle transverse septum. The fungus is at most a very weak parasite, and Green (1932), who made a careful and detailed study of it, concluded that on normal, vigorous trees it was not even a wound parasite.

Branch dieback caused by *Chondrostereum purpureum* (Stereum purpureum)

Chondrostereum purpureum (Stereum purpureum), the cause of silver leaf in many broadleaved trees, has been found on laburnum, in which it causes a branch dieback, but no silvering of the leaves (Peace, 1962).

DECAY FUNGI

Fomitopsis cytisina (Fomes fraxineus), which attacks various broadleaved trees, including ash, elm and beech, may cause a white rot in standing laburnum trees (Cartwright and Findlay, 1946). This fungus is described in chapter 19.

MAGNOLIA

A good many species of *Magnolia,* all of which are introduced from North America or the Far East, are grown in this country as garden trees.

NURSERY AND POST-NURSERY DISEASES

LEAF DISEASES

Leaf spot caused by *Phyllosticta magnoliae* Sacc.
Phyllosticta magnoliae has occasionally been found in this country on magnolia leaves, causing irregular bleached spots with an indistinct brownish border. The spots bear a few lens-shaped pycnidia containing colourless, oblong-elliptical, one-celled pycnospores measuring 8–12 x 3–4.5 μm (Grove, 1935).

APPLE AND PEAR (SPECIES OF *MALUS* AND *PYRUS*)

Numerous cultivars of the apple, *Malus sylvestris,* and of the pear, *Pyrus communis,* are grown for their fruit. A few introduced apples, such as the Japanese crab, *M. floribunda,* are grown as ornamentals in streets and gardens, as is also the Asian willow-leaved pear, *P. salicifolia.*

Many diseases affect orchard apples and pears. Their disorders are dealt with in detail in books on diseases of fruit trees (for example, Wormald, 1955).

LEAF DISEASES

Apple scab caused by *Venturia inaequalis* (Cooke) Wint. (stat. conid.
***Fusicladium dendriticum* (Wallr.) Fuckel) and Pear scab, caused by *V. pirina*
Aderh. (stat. conid. *F. pirinum* (Lib.) Fuckel)
By far the commonest disease of ornamental *Malus* varieties is scab, caused by *Venturia inaequalis,* which is also the most troublesome disease of the apple fruit grower. The fungus causes brown or olive-green spots and sometimes blisters on the leaves (figure 87). The imperfect spores of the *Fusicladium* stage form on the leaf spots, and are brown, slipper-shaped, one or two-celled, measuring about 30 x 8 μm (Wormald, 1955) (figure 88a). If infection is severe, the leaves may wither and fall. The fungus also causes blister-like lesions on young shoots; these lesions burst open to reveal more pustules of the brown conidia.

In orchard apple varieties the fungus spreads from the leaves to the fruits. The affected fruits may then fall before they can enlarge, or become ill-shaped or cracked. On fully developed fruits, later infections cause unsightly dark spots (much like those on the leaves), which reduce the market value of the fruit.

Figure 87. Blisters on apple leaf caused by the scab fungus *Venturia inaequalis* (D.H. Phillips)

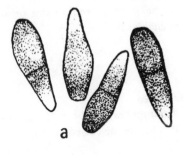

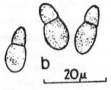

Figure 88. Slipper-shaped conidia (a) and 2-celled ascospores (b) of *Venturia inaequalis* (H. Wormald)

Sometimes fruit may appear healthy when picked, but late infections may develop and cause black spots on the apples in store.

The flask-shaped perithecia of the perfect stage of *V. inaequalis* are produced in winter on the fallen leaves. Ripe asci occur in these perithecia in the spring. The ascospores from these fruit bodies infect the young leaves, and so complete the life cycle. These ascospores (figure 88b) are pale olive green, and two-celled (with one cell longer than the other), and measure 12–15 x 6–7 μm (Wormald, 1955).

A disease very similar to apple scab also affects pears, and the pear scab fungus, *Venturia pirina,* is similar to *V. inaequalis* in all but minor details. It produces dark brown, velvety patches on the leaves, and sometimes causes leaf distortion. Like apple scab, it may also cause leaf fall, produce blister-like pustules on the shoots, and spread to the fruits, which are then deformed and scabby, and reduced in value.

Control of scab　　Some control of apple and pear scab may be obtained by cutting out and burning diseased twigs before the buds burst, and raking up and burning fallen leaves. Trees may be sprayed with captan or lime sulphur at the green bud stage, and after petal fall. Some other fungicides, such as benomyl, thiophanate-methyl and dodine may also be tried (Brooks and Halstead, 1976).

SHOOT DISEASES

Canker caused by *Nectria galligena*
Canker, caused by *Nectria galligena,* is troublesome on some ornamental *Malus* varieties. It is described in chapter 3.

ROOT DISEASES

Honey fungus: *Armillaria mellea*
The honey fungus, *Armillaria mellea,* has been found fairly often killing young ornamental crab apples. It is further discussed in chapter 3.

OTHER DISEASES

Orchard apples and pears may be affected by many other diseases. At times, some of these diseases may also be found on ornamental varieties of *Malus* and *Pyrus.* Examples are the Powdery mildew *Podosphaera leucotricha* (plate 52) (which distorts and stunts the leaves and covers them with a white, powdery growth, and which may be controlled by cutting out infected shoots and spraying with a sulphur preparation), and Fireblight (*Erwinia amylovora*), described in chapter 3. The blossom wilt and spur blight caused by *Sclerotinia laxa* may also be found, though it is commoner on flowering cherries, under which it is therefore described. The form on apple differs slightly from that on cherry, however, and is described as *S. laxa* f. *mali* (Wormald) Harrison.

SOUTHERN BEECH (*NOTHOFAGUS* SPP.)

Several species of *Nothofagus* have been introduced from South America and Australasia, and planted in parks and gardens. Two Chilean species, *N. procera* and *N. obliqua*, have shown some promise as forest trees. However, in hard winters (particularly in the very severe winter of 1962–63) both species, especially *N. procera*, have been badly affected by cold. This has caused dead patches and splits in the bark at the base of the trunks, and dieback in the tops of the trees (figure 1) (Nimmo, 1964).

So far *N. procera* and *N. obliqua* have been little affected by fungus diseases here, though plots of trees planted on land infested by *Heterobasidion annosum (Fomes annosus)* have been severely attacked and killed by that fungus. The needle rust *Micronegeria fagi* (the alternative host of which is *Araucaria*) has been found once on *Nothofagus* in Britain (Butin, private communication).

PAULOWNIA

One or two species of *Paulownia*, introduced from China, are grown here as ornamentals in parks and gardens.

NURSERY AND POST-NURSERY DISEASES

LEAF DISEASES

Leaf spots caused by *Phyllosticta paulowniae* **Sacc. and** *Ascochyta paulowniae* **Sacc. and Brun.**
The two imperfect fungi *Phyllosticta paulowniae* and *Ascochyta paulowniae* have occasionally been recorded in Great Britain as the cause of spots on paulownia leaves. Both have brownish, lens-shaped pycnidia. The colourless, oblong, one-celled pycnospores of *P. paulowniae* measure 3–7 x 1.5–3 µm (Grove, 1935). Those of *A. paulowniae* are pale olive coloured, two-celled, and spindle-shaped. They measure 14–18 x 3 µm (Allescher, 1901).

PLANE: *PLATANUS* SPP.

The London plane, *Platanus* x *acerifolia*, is much grown in streets, parks and gardens. It is usually considered to be a natural hybrid between two introduced trees, *Platanus orientalis* and *P. occidentalis*, the first of which is also sometimes found as a tree of parks and gardens.

NURSERY AND POST-NURSERY DISEASES

DISEASES OF LEAVES AND SHOOTS

Anthracnose caused by *Gnomonia platani* Kleb. (*Gnomonia veneta* (Sacc. and d Speg.) Kleb., stat. conid. *Gloeosporium nervisequum* (Fuckel) Sacc., *Discula la platani* Sacc., *Sporonema platani* Baum.)

Anthracnose caused by *Gnomonia platani* is known throughout Europe and in North America. It is fairly common on London plane trees in the southern half of England, but causes serious damage only in occasional years. It is a more severe problem on the occidental plane in North America.

Neely (1976) describes the symptoms of anthracnose in four separate phases which can be distinguished partly by the stage of growth of the host.

The first phase is bud blight. During the winter and early spring a brown area develops around the base of the bud. As a result the bud dies and fails to flush and the brownish discoloration extends up and down the neighbouring stem. When growth starts in the spring a discrete canker develops in the twig around the dead bud.

Sometimes the fungus infects the whole circumference of the twig near the bud. When this occurs the disease is in the twig blight phase. The twig is girdled and the distal parts of the twig die before the buds open. This phase develops in the early spring or perhaps during the previous winter.

The third phase of the disease, called shoot blight, occurs after the bud has opened and flushed but before the new shoot is fully extended. It appears that the host tissues neighbouring the bud have been infected but the bud has not been killed. However, as the bud opens and fresh growth starts, the fungus can invade the new tissues and shoot blight then develops. Shoot blight is the most dramatic phase of symptom expression and whole trees or boughs can be affected in certain seasons.

The final phase, leaf blight, develops on the new or expanded leaves at any time during the summer. The fungus infects the leaves and gives rise to striking tongues of dead brown tissue mainly bordering the veins (plate 43).

There are several imperfect stages of *G. platani*. The imperfect fruit bodies on the stem lesions have been called *Discula platani* (Bongini, 1939). Those on the infected leaves during the leaf blight phase of the disease are known as *Gloeosporium nervisequum*. Conspicuous black pustules appear along the veins, chiefly on the underside of the leaves. The colourless, one-celled, oblong-ovoid spores measure 12–15 x 4–6 μm (Grove, 1937). Yet another imperfect stage, described as *Sporonema platani* may be found on the brown leaves still hanging on the trees in winter. It resembles *G. nervisequum* but has a more clearly differentiated wall to the fructification.

The perithecia of the perfect stage arise in winter on the fallen leaves. They are black, with long necks, and contain club-shaped, eight-spored asci. The unequally two-celled ascospores measure $14-19 \times 4-5 \mu$m (Brooks, 1953).

The biology of *G. platani* is still far from being fully understood. Neely (1976) has studied the four phases of the disease and showed that the first three phases, bud, twig, and shoot blight develop in the spring following infections which occurred in the previous year. Climatic conditions in the spring are critical for the development of serious disease outbreaks and a mean daily temperature in the low fifties Fahrenheit (approximately 12°C) for two weeks after leaf emergence seems necessary for the shoot blight phase. The origin of the infections is not known though Neely (1976) has suggested that twigs may become infected as a result of the growth of the fungus down the petiole from an infected leaf. Even the origin of the leaf blight phase has not been elucidated as artifical inoculations, with spore suspensions, of undamaged leaves have not been successful.

Anthracnose of plane, at least the shoot blight phase, has been controlled by the application of organic mercurial fungicides when the buds begin to swell in the spring. However, these fungicides are no longer recommended for use in disease control and, to date, no alternative has been found.

Some research has been undertaken into the selection and breeding of planes resistant to anthracnose. The occidental plane or American sycamore *(Platanus occidentalis)* is relatively susceptible to the disease whereas the oriental plane *(Platanus orientalis)* is resistant. The hybrid between these two species, the London plane *(Platanus x acerifolia)* shows variable resistance. Santamour (1976) has crossed the two parent species and has made preliminary selections amongst the progeny for resistance to anthracnose.

DECAY FUNGI

Inonotus hispidus causes a decay of the stems and branches of plane. It is described in chapter 19.

ALMOND, CHERRY AND OTHER SPECIES OF *PRUNUS*

ALMOND *(PRUNUS DULCIS)*

The almond, *Prunus dulcis,* is often grown in suburban gardens for its flowers.

NURSERY AND POST-NURSERY DISEASES

LEAF DISEASE

Leaf curl caused by *Taphrina deformans* (Berks.) Tul.
The commonest disease of ornamental almonds is the leaf curl caused by *Taphrina deformans*, which is better known as a disease of the peach. The leaves of affected shoots become curled soon after they unfold, and as they grow they become increasingly distorted and thickened, and reddish in colour (plate 55). The fungus produces a layer of asci, mainly on the upper surface of the leaf, and the affected leaves then show a whitish bloom. The diseased leaves usually shrivel and fall, but are often replaced by new ones, which generally remain uninfected. The ascospores of the fungus (and secondary spores budded from them) appear to carry it over the winter in the bud scales (Wormald, 1955).

Control   Leaf curl may be controlled by spraying with a copper spray or with lime sulphur just before the leaves begin to swell in late February or early March, and again just before leaf fall in the autumn (Alford and Wiggell, 1976).

CHERRY

Cultivars of the native wild cherries *Prunus avium* (gean) and *P. padus* (the bird cherry) are common in gardens, in which the European sour cherry *P. cerasus* is also often grown. Even commoner are asiatic flowering cherries, especially *Prunus subhirtella, P. x hillierii* 'spire', *P. x yedoensis, P. sargentii*, and varieties of the Japanese cherry *P. serrulata*.

NURSERY AND POST-NURSERY DISEASES

LEAF DISEASES

Blossom wilt and twig blight caused by *Sclerotinia laxa* Aderh. and Ruhl. (stat. conid. *Monilia cinerea* (Aderh. and Ruhl.) Honey)
Like orchard trees, flowering cherries may be affected by the blossom wilt and twig blight caused by *Sclerotinia laxa* (stat. conid. *Monilia cinerea*). The same fungus causes a similar disease on plums and other related trees, and its f. *mali* causes blossom wilt and spur canker of apple. These fungi also cause brown rot of the fruits of rosaceous orchard trees (Moore, 1959).

On flowering cherries, leaves may be infected (plate 44), and the fungus then grows down into the shoots; the whole shoot then wilts. More often, flower infection occurs, and the fungus grows through the flower stalk into the spur. The flowering spur wilts, and the flowers and leaves wither.

The greyish tufts of sporophores and conidia of the *Monilia* stage of the fungus are produced on the affected twigs in the following spring. The conidia form in chains, and are ovoid and single-celled, measuring 5-19 x 4-12 μm on the overwintered leaves, but 8-23 x 7-16 μm on leaves newly infected (Wormald, 1955). The perfect stage of the fungus, which forms its stalked apothecia on mummified fruits, is very rare in Britain.

Control   The disease may be controlled by cutting out infected spurs, and spraying the trees in the dormant season with tar-oil winter wash (Anon, 1980); the trees may also be sprayed with Bordeaux mixture or lime sulphur just before flowering or as the first flowers open (Alford and Wiggell, 1976).

Silver leaf caused by *Chondrostereum purpureum* (*Stereum purpureum*)
Silver leaf is not a true leaf disease, but the earliest and most characteristic symptoms appear on the leaves, which exhibit a silvery sheen. Death of branches or of the whole tree then occurs. The causal fungus, *Chondrostereum purpureum*, sometimes attacks flowering cherries, though it has a wide host range (and is best known as the cause of silver leaf of plum trees). It also causes a wood rot, and is further described in chapter 19.

DISEASES OF STEMS AND BRANCHES

Bacterial canker caused by *Pseudomonas mors-prunorum* Wormald
The bacterium *Pseudomonas mors-prunorum* may cause a canker (and sometimes a shoot wilt) on flowering cherries (Brooks and Halstead, 1976) and also on the ornamental purple-leaved plum, *Prunus pissardii* (Wormald, 1955). Trees girdled by cankers quickly die. On ungirdled stems, sunken cankers arise. In summer, leaf and shoot infection may take place. Water-soaked spots then appear on the leaves. These spots become brown, and the central dead area falls out to leave 'shot-holes'. Shoot infection may cause the shoots to curl if it remains one-sided, but the tops of girdled shoots wither and die.

Control   Bacterial canker may be controlled by spraying with Bordeaux mixture at the end of August and again at the end of September (Brooks and Halstead, 1976).

DECAY FUNGI

Laetiporus sulphureus may rot the stems of cherries, and *Phellinus pomaceus* causes a decay of both their stems and branches. These fungi are described in chapter 19.

PORTUGAL LAUREL *(PRUNUS LUSITANICA)*

The introduced Portugal laurel is common as a shrub and hedge plant, but when left unclipped it becomes an attractive small tree.

Portugal laurel seems to be especially susceptible to silver leaf, caused by *Chondrostereum purpureum* (Strouts, personal communication).

BUCKTHORN *(RHAMNUS CATHARTICA)* AND ALDER BUCKTHORN *(FRANGULA ALNUS)*

The buckthorn and alder buckthorn are both shrubs or small trees that grow wild throughout much of England and Wales.

NURSERY AND POST-NURSERY DISEASES

LEAF DISEASE

Crown rust (*Puccinia coronata* Corda)

Buckthorn and alder buckthorn are the primary hosts on which are found the spermogonia and aecidia of the crown rust, *Puccinia coronata,* which is an important parasite of oats and various other grasses, on which it produces its uredosori and teleutosori. Its attacks on the buckthorns are of minor significance.

The spermogonia occur mostly on the upper sides of the buckthorn leaves and on their petioles. Later, the aecidia arise mainly on the undersides of the leaves, and between the spermogonia on the petioles. The affected leaves and leaf stalks become swollen. The aecidia are cylindrical or cup-shaped, with a white margin. The orange, rounded aecidiospores are 16–25 x 20 µm (Wilson and Henderson, 1966).

FALSE ACACIA OR LOCUST TREE: *ROBINIA PSEUDOACACIA*

The false acacia is an ornamental tree introduced from eastern North America. A few other *Robinia* spp. are also sometimes grown in parks and gardens.

NURSERY AND POST-NURSERY DISEASES

LEAF DISEASES

Leaf spot caused by *Phleospora robiniae* v. Höhnel

Yellowish leaf spots that later become brown, and are caused by the imperfect fungus *Phleospora robiniae* have sometimes been found on *Robinia*. The small pycnidia have thin, ill-defined walls, and from their openings emerge whitish blobs of elongated, faintly one-septate, colourless pycnospores that measure 25-28 x 2-5 μm (Grove, 1935).

DECAY FUNGI

Butt rot caused by *Fomitopsis cytisina* (*Fomes fraxineus*)

A white rot in the butt of false acacia trees is sometimes caused by *Fomitopsis cytisina*, which also effects various other broadleaved trees (Cartwright and Findlay, 1946). This fungus is described in chapter 19.

ELDER: *SAMBUCUS NIGRA*

The elder is a shrub or rarely a small tree occurring as a native throughout Great Britain.

NURSERY AND POST-NURSERY DISEASES

LEAF DISEASES

Leaf spots caused by *Cercospora depazeoides* (Desm.) Sacc. *Phyllosticta sambuci* Desm., *P. sambucicola* Kalchbr., and *Ramularia sambucina* Sacc.

Several imperfect fungi have been described as the cause of leaf spots on elder. The best known is *Cercospora depazeoides*, which gives rise to greyish spots that turn whitish or pale brown with age, and measure up to 5 mm across. The fungus produces long, colourless spores, particularly on the undersides of the spots. The spores, which have 1-6 transverse walls, measure 50-147 x 4-6 μm (Moore, 1946).

Grove (1935) also described *Phyllosticta sambuci* and *P. sambucicola* from leaf spots on elder. These both produce brownish-black pycnidia on the spots. The colourless, one-celled, oblong-ovoid spores of the former are 5-8 x 2.5-3 μm. Those of the latter are round, one-celled, and 3-4 μm across, or oval, measuring 4-5 x 3 μm.

Ramularia sambucina has also been recorded several times on elder leaves (Wakefield and Bisby, 1941). It causes small, brownish spots that later turn white with a brown border. Its two-celled, colourless, spindle-shaped conidia are formed in chains, and measure 25-35 x 4-4.5 μm (Lindau, 1907).

DECAY FUNGI

Jews' ear fungus: *Auricularia auricula-judae* (L. ex Fr.) Schröt.

The Jews' ear fungus, *Auricularia auricula-judae*, is common as a slow, weak parasite on old elders. The pale brown, gelatinous, earlike fruit bodies occur on dead branches (Wakefield and Dennis, 1950).

MOUNTAIN ASH OR ROWAN, WHITEBEAM AND SERVICE TREE (*SORBUS* SPP.)

The native mountain ash or rowan, *Sorbus aucuparia,* is common throughout Great Britain. Two other native *Sorbus* spp., *S. aria,* the whitebeam, and *S. torminalis,* the wild service tree, occur more locally, mainly in the southern half of England and Wales. Many other very local native species also occur, and various introduced species are grown in parks and gardens.

Figure 89. White mycelium and powdery spores of *Podosphaera oxyacanthae* on leaf of mountain ash (D.H. Phillips)

NURSERY AND POST-NURSERY DISEASES

LEAF DISEASES

The powdery mildew *Podosphaera oxyacanthae* (DC) de Bary

The powdery mildew *Podosphaera oxyacanthae* (figure 89), which is well known on hawthorn (under which it is described above), also occurs on mountain ash and other *Sorbus* spp.

The rowan rust *Gymnosporangium cornutum* Kern. (*G. juniperi* Link)

The rust *Gymnosporangium cornutum (G. juniperi)*, the teleutosori of which develop on *Juniperus communis*, produces its spermogonia and aecidia on mountain ash. It is common in Scotland, but much less so in England and Wales. Groups of the spermogonia, which are at first yellow, but later turn black, arise on red or orange spots on the upper surfaces of the leaves. The yellowish-brown aecidia are cylindrical or horn-shaped (rostelioid), up to about 5 mm high and about 0.5 mm across. They appear on thickened orange spots on the undersides of the leaves. The brown, two-celled teleutospores measure 20–29 x 18–25 μm (Wilson and Henderson, 1966).

WILT DISEASES

Fireblight caused by *Erwinia amylovora*

Like many other members of the Rosaceae, *Sorbus* spp. are among the hosts of *Erwinia amylovora*, the cause of fireblight. The diseased trees may therefore become a danger to adjacent plantings of apples and pears. Fireblight is described in chapter 3.

LILAC: *SYRINGA VULGARIS*

Many varieties of the common lilac, *Syringa vulgaris*, an introduced shrub or small tree, have long been grown in gardens in this country. A few other *Syringa* spp. are also sometimes grown.

NURSERY AND POST-NURSERY DISEASES

LEAF DISEASES

Powdery mildew: *Oidium* sp.

An *Oidium* sp. (perhaps the imperfect stage of *Microsphaera alni* (Wallr.) Wint.) was found on lilac leaves in southern England and South Wales in 1948 and the succeeding few years (Moore, 1952).

Leaf blotch caused by *Heterosporium syringae* Oud.

A leaf blotch of lilac caused by *Heterosporium syringae* has occasionally been found on lilac in southern England (Moore, 1959). The fungus produces a black turf of erect conidiophores on the brown leaf blotches. The brown conidia are spiny, cylindrical with rounded ends and 1 to 3 cross walls, and measure 25–30 x 7–9 μm (Lindau, 1910).

Leaf spot caused by *Phyllosticta syringae* Westend.

Grove (1935) also describes *Phyllosticta syringae* (which he considers to be a young state of *Ascochyta syringae* Bres.) as the cause of a lilac leaf spot. The spots are grey, with a darker border. The pycnidia, which grow on the upper sides of the leaves, are lens-shaped, and the colourless, one-celled spores measure 5–8 x 2–3 μm. According to Allescher (1901), the pycnidia of *Ascochyta syringae* are up to 130 μm across, and its colourless, two-celled pycnospores measure 8–10 x 3–3.5 μm.

DISEASES OF LEAVES AND SHOOTS

Leaf and twig blight caused by *Pseudomonas syringae* van Hall

The gram-negative bacterium *Pseudomonas syringae*, which attacks many hosts, is well known as a cause of leaf and twig blight of lilac. Buds may be blackened, and shoots girdled and killed. On the older shoots, elongated blackened areas may by found. Leaves may become distorted, with crinkled edges, and angular brown spots on their surfaces. The causal bacterium appears to enter through the stomata, and perhaps also through hail wounds on the young shoots (Dowson, 1957). It is rod-shaped, and motile by several polar flagella, and measures 1.6–3.2 x 0.2–0.4 μm. It produces a green fluorescent pigment in culture (Stapp, 1961).

Control may be achieved by cutting out the diseased shoots, and by spraying with a copper spray such as Bordeaux mixture or copper oxychloride (Brooks and Halstead, 1976).

WILT DISEASES

Wilt caused by *Phytophthora syringae* (Kleb.) Kleb.

Phytophthora syringae has been recorded in Scotland as a cause of a wilt of lilac (Moore, 1959). Its sympodially branched sporangiophores each carry one to seven colourless, one-celled sporangia that each measure 40–75 x 30–42 μm. Its yellowish spherical or sometimes oval oospores measure 18–36 x 17–25 μm (Brooks, 1953).

VIRUS DISEASES

Lilac ringspot

Of several virus diseases of lilac, the lilac ringspot virus has been recorded in

Great Britain. The virus causes pale green or yellow spots, or narrow lines and broad rings and bands on the leaves, which may also be distorted (Smith, 1957).

LIME: *TILIA* SPP.

Of the limes, the native small-leaved lime, *Tilia cordata*, is widely scattered throughout England and Wales, and has been planted in Scotland. The large-leaved lime, *T. platyphylla*, may be native on a few limestone soils, but has also been much planted elsewhere. The common lime, *T.* x *europaea*, a hybrid between the other two species, is almost certainly introduced, but has been very widely planted all over Great Britain.

NURSERY AND POST-NURSERY DISEASES

LEAF DISEASES

Leaf spot caused by *Phyllosticta tiliae* Sacc. and Speg, *Ascochyta tiliae* Kab. and Bub., *Gloeosporium tiliae* Oud. and *Cercospora microsora* Sacc.
Four imperfect fungi recorded as the cause of minor leaf spots on lime are *Phyllosticta tiliae*, *Ascochyta tiliae*, *Gloeosporium tiliae* and *Cercospora microsora*.

Phyllosticta tiliae, which has been fairly widely noted, causes pale yellowish-brown spots with a darker margin. Its brown, lens-shaped pycnidia are up to 130 μm across, and contain colourless, ellipsoid or oblong, one-celled spores measuring 5-7 x 3 μm (Grove, 1935).

Ascochyta tiliae, so far observed here only in Scotland, produces greyish spots up to 15 mm across, which finally drop out to leave 'shot-holes'. The rounded, brownish pycnidia are up to 150 μm in diameter, and contain colourless, two-celled, oblong spores measuring 8-10 x 2.5-3 μm (Grove, 1935).

Gloeosporium tiliae is said to be common in Scotland, and less so in England. It causes yellowish-brown, rounded leaf spots up to 2 cm across, sometimes with a darker border. Minute pustules on the undersides of the leaves contain colourless, one-celled, oblong-ovoid spores measuring 10-18 x 4-7 μm (Grove, 1937).

Cercospora microsora (the imperfect stage of the ascomycete *Mycosphaerella microsora* Syd.) causes rounded black leaf spots about 3 or 4 mm across, with a greyish centre. On this central area the fungus produces its long, narrow, colourless or slightly yellowish, one to three-septate conidia which measure 30-46 x 3-4.5 μm (Viennot-Bourgin, 1949). *C. microsora* also causes small cankers on young shoots. The perfect stage does not appear to have been found in Britain.

The fungus was long ago described by Hartig (1900) as a cause of severe defoliation in the European mainland. More recently it has been known to cause appreciable damage to young *Tilia* plants in nursery beds in Romania, where good control has been obtained by spraying with copper oxychloride or Bordeaux mixture (Poleac *et al.*, 1968).

DISEASES OF TWIGS AND BRANCHES

Twig and branch blights caused by *Discella desmazierii* B. and Br. and *Pyrenochaeta pubescens* Rostr.

Two weakly parasitic imperfect fungi have been found attacking lime twigs and branches in Great Britain. The first of these, *Discella desmazierii* (*Lamproconium desmazierii* Grove) has been found from time to time over a fairly large part of mid and southern England. Its pustules on the dead bark contain narrowly oval, grey to deep-blue spores that eventually become two-celled, and measure 30-36 x 6-10 μm (Grove, 1937).

The second, *Pyrenochaeta pubescens*, has so far been found once only, on young stock of *Tilia* x *vulgaris* 'pallida' imported from Holland (Burdekin, 1968). It forms rounded or oval, purple (finally grey) spots on the bark. The small black pycnidia that arise on the lesions are clothed with colourless, septate hairs up to 50 μm long. They contain colourless, one-celled, elliptical spores measuring 6-8 x 3-4 μm (Allescher, 1903). The disease is of minor importance, and can be controlled by pruning out the affected parts in the summer (Příhoda, 1950).

Shoot canker caused by *Plectophomella concentrica*

Shoot canker caused by *Plectophomella concentrica* has recently been found in Edinburgh causing a canker on young shoots of lime. The canker is described under *Ulmus*, on which it seems to be much more widespread.

WILT DISEASES

Verticillium wilt

Young plants of the Caucasian lime, *Tilia euchlora*, have been found with Verticillium wilt caused by *Verticillium dahliae* (which is described in chapter 3). Adjacent plants of *T.* x *europaea* were not affected (Young, personal communication).

ROOT DISEASES

Phytophthora root rot

Die-back of the common lime, *T.* x *europaea*, is often associated with root attack by *Phytophthora citricola*. The Phytophthora root rots are considered in chapter 3.

DECAY FUNGI

The commonest decay fungus on lime is *Ustulina deusta*, which rots the butt and the roots. It is described in chapter 19.

MISCELLANEOUS DISORDERS

Sooty moulds

Lime trees (especially the common lime, *T.* x *europaea*) are much infested by aphids, which cover the leaves with sticky 'honeydew'. This sugary secretion forms a substrate for the growth of various sooty moulds, particularly *Aureobasidium pullulans* (de Bary) Arn. (*Pullularia pullulans* (de Bary) Berkh.) and *Cladosporium herbarum* (Pers.) Link ex Fr. (Friend, 1965), which form a black, saprophytic coating on the leaves.

REFERENCES

Alford, D.V. and Wiggell, D. (1976). In H. Martin and C.R. Worthing (Eds.), *Insecticide and Fungicide Handbook*, 5th ed., Blackwell, Oxford

Allescher, A. (1901). *Die Pilze Deutschlands, Osterreichs, und der Schweiz*, Abt. 6, Kummer, Leipzig

Allescher, A. (1903). *Die Pilze Deutschlands, Österreichs, und der Schweiz*, Abt, 7, Kummer, Leipzig

Anon (1961). *Gnomonia leptostyla* (Fr.) Ces. and de Not. *Distrib. Maps Pl. Dis.*, no. 384

Anon (1980). *Approved Products for Farmers and Growers 1980*, HMSO, London

Batko, S. (1962). Perithecia of oak mildew in Britain, in 'New or uncommon plant diseases and pests'. *Pl. Path.*, **11**, 184

Berry, F.H. (1964). *Walnut Anthracnose*, U.S. Dept. Agric. Forest Pest Leafl., no. 85

Bezerra, J.L. (1963). Studies on *Pseudonectria rousseliana. Acta Bot. Neerl.*, **12**, 58–63

Bongini, V. (1939). Note fitopatologiche. *Boll. Lab. sper. Oss. Fitopatol.*, **16**, 54–64

Booth, C. (1959). *Studies of pyrenomycetes: IV. Nectria* (Part 1). Mycol. Pap., no. 73, 115 pp.

Brasier, C.M. and Strouts, R.G. (1976). New records of Phytophthora on trees in Britain. 1. Phytophthora root rot and bleeding canker of horse chestnut (*Aesculus hippocastanum* L.). *Eur. J. For. Path.*, **6**, 129–36

Brooks, A.V. and Halstead, A. (1976). In H. Martin and C.R. Worthing (Eds.), *Insecticide and Fungicide Handbook*, Blackwell, Oxford

Brooks, F.T. (1953). *Plant Diseases*, 2nd ed., Oxford University Press, London

Burdekin, D.A. (1968). Forest pathology. *Rep. Forest Res., London., 1968*, pp. 108–11

Cartwright, K. St. G. and Findlay, W.P.K. (1946). *Decay of Timber and Its Prevention*, HMSO, London

Cooper, J.I. (1979). *Virus Diseases of Trees and Shrubs*, Institute of Terrestrial Ecology, c/o Unit of Invertebrate Virology, Oxford

Davis, S.H. (1948). Organic fungicides in the control of certain shade and ornamental tree diseases; abstract in *Phytopathology*, **38**, 575

Dennis, R.W.G. (1968). *British Ascomycetes*, J. Cramer, Lehre

Dodge, B.O. (1944). *Volutella buxi* and *Verticillium buxi. Mycologia*, **36**, 416–25

Dowson, W.J. (1957). *Plant Diseases Due to Bacteria*, 2nd ed., Cambridge University Press, Cambridge

Dowson, W.J. and Dillon-Weston, W.A.R. (1937). Brown rot of hawthorn. *Gdnrs' Chron.*, **101**, no. 2624, 426

Foister, C.E. (1961). *The Economic Plant Diseases of Scotland*, HMSO, Edinburgh

Friend, R.J. (1965). A study of sooty moulds on lime trees *(Tilia* x *vulgaris). Trans. Br. mycol. Soc.,* 48, 367–70

Glasscock, H.H. and Rosser, W.R. (1958). Powdery mildew on *Eucalyptus,* in 'New or uncommon plant diseases and pests', *Pl. Path.,* 7, 152

Green, D.E. and Hewlett, M.A. (1949). Die-back of Cytisus cuttings. *Jl. R. hort. Soc.,* 74, 310–12

Green, F.M. (1932). Observations on *Cucurbitaria laburni* (Pers.) de Not. *Trans. Br. mycol. Soc.,* 16, 289–303

Grove, W.B. (1921). Mycological notes. *J. Bot., Lond.,* 59, 13–17

Grove, W.B. (1935). *British Stem- and Leaf-Fungi (Coelomycetes),* vol. 1, Cambridge University Press, Cambridge

Grove, W.B. (1937). *British Stem- and Leaf-Fungi (Coelomycetes),* vol. 2, Cambridge University Press, Cambridge

Hamond, J.B. (1931). Some diseases of walnuts. *Ann. Rep. East Malling Res. Sta.,* 1928, 1929 and 1930, II suppl., pp. 143–49

Hamond, J.B. (1935). A graft disease of walnuts caused by a species of Chalaropsis. *Trans. Br. mycol. Soc.,* 19, 158–9

Hartig, R. (1900). *Lehrbuch der Pflanzenkrankheiten,* 3rd ed., Springer, Berlin

Hughes, S.J. (1951). *Studies in Micro-fungi.* III. *Mastigosporium, Camposporium,* and *Ceratophorum.* Mycol. Pap., no. 36.

Kaul, T.N. (1962). Occurrence of *Gnomonia leptostyla* (F.) de Not. on walnut in India. *Curr. Sci.,* 31, 349.

Kišpatić, J. (1962). [Leaf blotch of horse chestnut]. *Šumarski List,* 86, 45–6; abstract in *Rev. appl. Mycol.,* 42, 1963, 577

Lelliott, R.A. (1959). Fireblight of pears in England. *Agriculture, Lond.,* 65, 564–69

Lelliott, R.A. (1979). *Fireblight of Apple and Pear.* Leafl. Agric. Fish. Food, 571 (amended)

Lindau, G. (1910). *Die Pilze Deutschlands, Österreichs und der Schweiz,* Abt. 9, Kummer, Leipzig

Lindau, G. (1910). *Die Pilze Deutschlands, Österreichs und der Schweiz,* 9 Abt., Kummer, Leipzig

Lohwag, K. (1962). Die Blattbräune der Rosskastanie. *Pflanzenarzt,* 15, 40

Macdonald, J., Wood, R.F., Edwards, M.V. and Aldhous, J.R. (1957). *Exotic Forest Trees in Great Britain,* Bull. For. Commn, no. 30

Martin, H. and Worthing, C.R. (1976). *Insecticide and Fungicide Handbook,* 5th ed., Blackwell, Oxford

Milatović, I. (1956). Palez lisea Divljeg Kestena. *Zasht. Bilja,* 38, 109–11

Miller, P.W. (1958). Recent studies on the effectiveness of agri-mycin 100 and agri-mycin 500 for the control of walnut blight in Oregon. *Pl. Dis. Reptr.,* 42, 388–9

Moore, F.J. (1952). Some powdery mildews on ornamental plants. *Pl. Path.,* 1, 53–5

Moore, W.C. (1946). New and interesting plant diseases. *Trans. Br. mycol. Soc.,* 29, 250–58

Moore, W.C. (1959). *British Parasitic Fungi,* Cambridge University Press, Cambridge

Neely, D. (1976). Sycamore anthracnose. *J. Arb.,* 2, 153–7

Neely, D. and Himelick, E.B. (1963). *Aesculus* species susceptible to leaf blotch. *Pl. Dis. Reptr.,* 47, 170

Nimmo, M. (1964). Winter damage in Southern beeches, *Nothofagus* species. *Rep. Forest Res. Lond., 1964,* p. 29

Pawsey, R.G. (1962). Leaf blotch of horse-chestnut, in 'New or uncommon plant diseases and pests'. *Pl. Path.,* 11, 137–38

Peace, T.R. (1962). *Pathology of Trees and Shrubs,* Clarendon Press, Oxford

Petch, T. (1938). British Hypoceales. *Trans. Br. mycol. Soc.,* 21, 243–305

Pirone, P.P., Dodge, B.O. and Rickett, H.W. (1960). *Diseases and Pests of Ornamental Plants,* 3rd ed., Ronald Press, New York

Poleac, E., Ditu, I. and Dumitru, G. (1968). (Biology and control of *Cercospora microsora).* *Stud. Cerc. Inst. Cerc. For., Bucaresti (Silv.),* 26, 235–51; abstract in *For. Abstr.,* 30, no. 4153

Příhoda, A. (1950). Keřovitý rust Lipovych sazenic jako následik nepadení houbon *Pyrenochaeta pubescens* Rostr. *Ochr. Rost.,* 23, 366–368

Rehm, H. (1896). *Die Pilze Deutschlands, Österreichs und der Schweiz*, Abt. 3, Kummer, Leipzig

Reid, D.A. (1969). New or interesting British plant diseases. *Trans. Br. mycol. Soc.*, 52, 19-38

Santamour, F.S. (1976). Resistance to sycamore anthracnose disease in hybrid *Platanus*. *Pl. Dis. Reptr.*, 60, 161-162

Scaramuzzi, G. (1954). Sul seccume delle foglie d'ippocastano. *Ann. sper. agr.*, N.S., 8, 1256-81

Schneider, R. (1961). Untersuchungen über das Auftreten der Guignardia Blattbräune der Rosskastanie *(Aesculus hippocastanum)* in Westdeutschland und ihren Erreger. *Phytopath. Z.*, 42, 272-8

Smith, K.M. (1957). *A Textbook of Plant Virus Diseases*, Churchill, London

Stapp, C. (1961). *Bacterial Plant Pathogens*, Oxford University Press

Stewart, V.B. (1916). The leaf blotch disease of horse-chestnut, *Phytopathology*, 6, 5-20

Viennot-Bourgin. G. (1949). *Les Champignons Parasites des Plantes Cultivées*, vol. 1, Masson, Paris

Wakefield, E.M. and Bisby, G.R. (1941). List of hyphomycetes recorded for Britain. *Trans. Br. mycol. Soc.*, 25, 49-126

Wakefield, E.M. and Dennis, R.W.G. (1950). *Common British Fungi*, Gawthorn, London

Wilson, M. and Henderson, D.M. (1966). *British Rust Fungi*, Cambridge University Press, Cambridge

Winter, C. (1897). *Die Pilze Deutschlands, Österreichs und der Schweiz*, Abt. 2, Kummer, Leipzig

Wormald, H. (1937). Leaf blotch of hawthorn. *Gdnrs' Chron.*, 102, 47

Wormald, H. (1955). *Diseases of Fruits and Hops*, Crosby Lockwood, London

19 Decay fungi of broadleaved and coniferous trees

This chapter does not open with a list of contents because the fungi described are arranged in the alphabetical order of their scientific names.

A great many decay fungi attack trees of both broadleaved and coniferous species and a number of those most commonly found are described in this chapter. The majority of these fungi do not seriously effect the general health of the host trees and the presence of decay is often evident only from the presence of fungal fruit bodies. However, the decay fungi here described do cause a serious reduction in the mechanical strength of the woody tissues. Decayed branches, stems and roots are all liable to break and severe damage can occur when broken limbs or uprooted trees fall on neighbouring buildings, vehicles and people. It is the duty of tree owners regularly to inspect their trees for any external signs of decay. This is an important and specialist subject and readers are referred to the leaflet by Young (1977) for further information. In contrast, there are two root and butt-rot fungi, *Heterobasidion annosum* (*Fomes annosus*) and *Armillaria mellea*, which can cause widespread death of a range of tree species and full descriptions of these fungi have been included in chapter 3.

There has been relatively little research undertaken into the biology of most of the decay fungi mentioned in this chapter. It is generally considered that these fungi enter their hosts either through wounds in above-ground parts of the tree or through the roots. Precise evidence on this and on the factors controlling invasion is generally lacking. However, some research has been undertaken into the infection of pruning wounds on mature trees and on its prevention by a variety of chemical treatments. Mercer (1979) has reviewed this subject and concluded that many treatments, though they may encourage callus production around the wound, do little to prevent infection by decay fungi.

For many years it was thought that trees showed only passive resistance to decay. However, Shigo (1977) has put forward a concept of active resistance whereby barriers to decay development are formed within a tree in response to wounding and fungal invasion. The coordinated formation of these barriers in various parts of the wood is termed compartmentalisation.

In contrast to the paucity of information on the biology of many decay fungi there is a wealth of authoritative texts on the identification of fungal fruit bodies. A list of some of the more useful references, particularly in relation to Basidiomycetes, is included at the end of this chapter. The nomenclature of these fungi is a complex and often confusing subject. As far as possible the naming of poly-pores, which are well represented among decay fungi, has followed that of Pegler (1973). For descriptions of the types of decay produced by wood rotting fungi, Cartwright and Findlay (1958) and Burdekin (1979) should be consulted for further information. Some information on the cultural characters of decay fungi is given by Cartwright and Findlay (1958) and a comprehensive description of those occurring in North America is given by Nobles (1948).

Two tables of host/pathogen relationships (one for conifer and one for broad-leaved species) are included at the end of the chapter in order to indicate, by tree species, the hosts on which the fungi are most commonly found.

Armillaria mellea: see chapter 3

Bjerkandera adusta (Willd. ex Fr.) Karst. (*Polyporus adjustus* Fr.)

Bjerkandera adusta is commonly found in Europe and North America growing on dead wood of a number of broadleaved species.

The annual fruit bodies are thinnish brackets up to 4 cm across, often imbri-cate, soft and pliable when fresh, later turning hard and brittle. The upper surface is pubescent, at first white to cream, later grey to blackish especially along the margin. The flesh is white and distinctly thicker than the short tubes which are grey to black and separated from the flesh by a thin black zone. The lower sur-face is grey to black and the pores are round to angular, 0.2 mm diameter. The hyaline spores are ellipsoid to cylindrical, thin walled and smooth, measuring 4.5 x 2.5-3 μm (Rea, 1922), and are pale straw-coloured in the mass. In culture *B. adusta* grows as a smooth white felt, it rarely fruits but the hyphae may break up into oidia.

B. adusta is commonly found on beech, often on trees that have been attacked by beech bark disease. When parts of a beech stem are killed by the disease, *Am-brosia* beetles may carry spores of this and other fungi into the dead wood where a white decay subsequently develops. The stem may eventually break giving rise to a condition referred to as beech snap (Parker, 1974).

Chondrostereum purpureum (Pers. ex Fr.) Pouz. (*Stereum purpureum* (Pers. ex Fr.)

Chondrostereum purpureum has a worldwide distribution and is found on wounds, dead branches, stumps and felled logs of many broadleaved species especially birch, beech, elm and poplar. It is an important wound pathogen on trees and shrubs in the family Rosaceae, causing the disease known as 'silver leaf' and is of major importance especially to orchard growers of plums and other top fruit, and to a lesser extent on other members of this family. The fruit bodies may be found at any time of the year and are thin, leathery brackets 2 cm or more across, sometimes entirely resupinate, often imbricate and confluent. The upper surface is whitish and greying, hairy, and the margin is sometimes lobed. The hymenium is smooth, lilac and purplish at first, soon becoming purplish brown and finally fading to pale fawn. The hyaline spores, flattened on one side, measure 6–8 x 3–4 μm (Rea, 1922) and are white in the mass.

C. purpureum commonly causes a discoloration in beech logs. Yatsenko-Khmelevky (1938) describes the formation of tyloses and dark-coloured materials as a consequence of the reaction of living cells to fungal activity. Gummy materials form in the parenchyma cells of beech wood infected by *C. purpureum* and later small whitish areas develop giving the wood a mottled appearance. *C. purpureum* does not appear to cause extensive decay and Cartwright and Findlay (1958) report only slight losses in weight in laboratory tests. Guinier (1933) suggested that *C. purpureum* can only invade wood in which the parenchyma and medullary rays are still intact and contain reserve materials. It appears to be localised in the younger, outer layers of wood and ceases growth after about a year when the reserves have been exhausted. Rayner (1977) also indicates that *C. purpureum* is a pioneer colonist of wounds or other freshly exposed surfaces. He considers that it is poor as an agent of decay and is highly susceptible to competition from other organisms.

In culture on malt agar *C. purpureum* produces a colourless, cottony growth which later becomes a smooth, felted mat with yellowish or lilac tinges (Cartwright and Findlay, 1958). Small hymenial surfaces may occasionally be formed. The colourless hyphae bear large clamp connections, often in whorls.

Although *C. purpureum* is an important pathogen of fruit trees, it does not cause serious decay at wound sites or on felled logs. It is often rather conspicuous as fruit bodies may rapidly appear on freshly exposed surfaces and infected wood may become markedly stained. As a result it is easily credited with causing more damage to timber than is actually the case.

Coriolus versicolor (L. ex Fr.) Quel. (*Polystictus versicolor* (L. Fr.)

Coriolus versicolor is commonly found in all temperate countries on dead wood of many different species of broadleaved trees and occasionally of conifers. It is normally saprophytic and attacks sapwood on felled timber or on parts of trees killed by other agents, but it is occasionally found invading heartwood or live sapwood.

The annual fruit bodies of *C. versicolor* are thin, leathery, imbricate brackets, 3–8 cm across; the upper surface is velvety, with concentric satiny zones which are greyish or brownish in colour (plate 63). The white tubes are very short and the creamy coloured pores are at first small and round, becoming irregular as they develop. The hyaline, oblong spores measure 6–8 x 3 μm (Rea, 1922).

Wood infected by *C. versicolor* turns a paler colour as decay develops and at a more advanced stage becomes white and very light in weight (figure 90). There are no markedly characteristic features of this rot but *C. versicolor* is a particularly active fungus and is able to decompose heavily lignified tropical timbers (Cartwright and Findlay, 1958).

In culture *C. versicolor* grows on malt agar as a fine, colourless mycelium closely appressed to the medium. A slightly raised margin of fluffy aerial growth

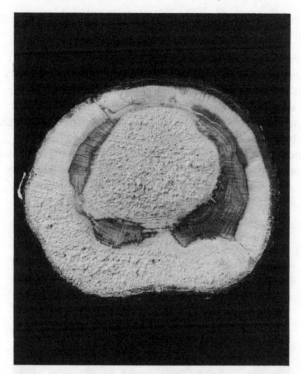

Figure 90.   Decay in oak caused by *Coriolus versicolor* (Forestry Commission)

develops around the culture and at a later stage a tough, flat, closely-felted mat is formed, white or slightly tinted in colour. Malt agar on which *C. versicolor* has been growing always becomes bleached (Cartwright and Findlay, 1958). Some chlamydospores may be formed and crystals occur in the medium.

C. versicolor is one of the commonest causes of decay in felled wood in broad-leaved species. It is frequently found growing on fence posts where they are in contact with the soil, in poorly ventilated timber stacks and in damp mining timber (Cartwright and Findlay, 1958).

Daedaleopsis confragosa (Fr.) Schroet. (*Trametes rubescens*) (A. & S.) Fr.)
Daedaleopsis confragosa is not uncommonly found in Europe, particularly on willow, birch and alder.

The annual fruit bodies are attached to the stems and are flattened, semi-circular brackets measuring 5–12 cm across. The upper surface is more or less smooth and ochraceous to red-brown in colour. The flesh is corky, zoned, white at first then turning reddish or pale brown. The tubes are up to 1 cm long, pale then reddish brown; the pores are round then elongate, white becoming greyish, turning blood-red when bruised. The hyaline spores are oblong, slightly curved and measure 10×2 μm (Rea, 1922).

D. confragosa cause an active white rot and usually occurs on severely wounded or suppressed trees (Cartwright and Findlay, 1958).

Daldinia concentrica (Bolt.) Ces. and de Not.
Daldinia concentrica has a worldwide distribution; in Britain it is very commonly found on ash and also on birch particularly after heath fires. In France it is most frequent on alder but also occurs on walnut and birch. It is usually considered to be a saprophyte on dead wood but may spread back into living tissues.

The fruit bodies of this ascomycete, which can be found at all times of year on dead branches, are almost smooth, dotted with fine pores, and hemispherical in shape, measuring 3–6 cm or more in diameter (figure 91). They are at first

Figure 91. Fruit bodies of *Daldinia concentrica* (D.H. Phillips)

reddish brown but soon become black and when mature have the appearance and consistency of charcoal. The young fruit body is covered with conidia which are borne on conidiophores resembling those of *Botrytis* (Cartwright and Findlay, 1958). Similar conidiophores arise from moistened, decayed wood and the hyaline conidia which they bear measure 6.5–8 x 5–6 μm (Panisset, 1929). The flesh is dark purplish-brown, fibrous with darker concentric zones. Perithecia form in a single layer just below the surface and narrow canals lead to tiny ostioles on the outside of the fruit body. The eight-spored asci measure 200 x 12 μm and the black ascospores are 12-17 x 6-9 μm (Dennis, 1968).

Ash wood decayed by *D. concentrica* (figure 92) was at one time termed

Figure 92. Decay in ash caused by *Daldinia concentrica*, a fruit body of which can be seen on the right (Forestry Commission)

'calico-wood' by timber merchants. The decay is a mottled rot with white patches amongst apparently healthy wood. The affected wood often contains scattered black flecks and irregular, waxy, purplish-brown or black stripes. The black flecking is due to the presence of dark fungal mycelium in the spring wood vessels. These stripes are 1-5 mm in width but in some sections they appear as circular patches or rings (Panisset, 1929).

In culture on malt agar the fungus produces a soft, powdery mat. After the mycelium is well established, the agar and hyphae change colour to dark brown and greenish black respectively. After repeated subculturing the culture may appear mainly a dirty fawn. The dark coloured hyphae sometimes become aggregated into small spherical bodies about 300 μm in diameter (Panisset, 1929). Typical conidia are borne in groups on short conidiophores.

D. concentrica probably causes decay in wood which has been killed by other agents and furthermore does not seem to spread very rapidly but it is able to resist desiccation and has been found, for example, causing decay in seasoned maple floor blocks (Cartwright and Findlay, 1958).

Fistulina hepatica Huds Fr. Beef Steak Fungus

Fistulina hepatica is commonly found in Europe and also occurs in America and Australia. It is frequently reported on oak, also on sweet chestnut and sometimes on a number of other hardwoods including ash, walnut, willow, beech, hornbeam and elm (Rea, 1922).

The sporophores vary in size from 5–30 cm across and they can be found between August and November on branches, stems or stumps. They appear at first as creamy, soft, juicy lumps which soon become tongue-shaped or semicircular brackets. They may be sessile or stipitate, the stipe when present measuring 3–7 x 2–4 cm. The mature fruit body is purplish red or brown and the flesh is marbled (like raw steak) and reddish; it exudes a blood-red juice when broken. The tubes are separate, pale yellow and very long. The individual spores are pink, ovoid, measure 4.5–5 x 4 μm and are pinkish brown in mass (Rea, 1922). Secondary spores are produced on the surface of the sporophore; these are ovoid and measure 5–10 x 4–6 μm (Bourdot and Galzin, 1927). The fruit body is edible.

Cartwright (1937) made a detailed study of *F. hepatica* in oak wood and showed that it was responsible for the condition known as 'brown oak'. In the early stages a streaky brown discoloration of the heartwood is produced and this gradually spreads to give the whole infected area a rich brown colour. In the advanced stage the wood exhibits cubical cracking but it never becomes soft and crumbly as in the case of decay caused by *L. sulphureus*.

In the wood the mycelium is rather sparse and mostly present in medullary rays though it may be difficult to observe in heavily stained cells. In culture the fungus grows best in the dark and on 5 per cent rather than 2 per cent malt agar (Cartwright, 1937). It forms a soft, woolly mat at first creamy white but later developing tints which range from pale pinkish-cinnamon to straw-yellow and later russet. Abnormal phalloid fruit bodies are often formed with rudimentary tubes bearing spores present at their apex.

Cartwright and Findlay (1958) note that *F. hepatica* is frequently found in pollarded oaks and suggest that it enters its host through wounds which extend into the heartwood.

The production of 'brown oak' by *F. hepatica* enhances the value of the timber because of its attractive appearance. Results of mechanical tests have indicated that there is no appreciable loss in strength during the early stages of infection but at a more advanced stage considerable softening occurs and the timber is rather brittle (Latham and Armstrong, 1934). The fungus does not continue its activity in converted timber as in the case of *Laetiporus sulphureus*.

Fomes annosus: see *Heterobasidion annosum* (chapter 3)

Fomes applanatus: see *Ganoderma applanatum*

Fomes fomentarius (Fries) Kickx. Tinder fungus
Fomes fomentarius occurs widely in Europe and America on beech and birch and has been reported from India and Australia. It is also common in parts of the highlands of Scotland on birch but has rarely been found in England and then only on beech. Many of the early references to this fungus on beech in England may have referred to *Ganoderma applanatum* though it could be more common than current records indicate.

The perennial fruit bodies of *F. fomentarius* are found on dead trees and stumps (plate 58). They are hoof-shaped, broadly attached, up to 40 cm across, 50 cm long and 15 cm thick at the base. The upper surface is smooth, hard and concentrically zoned; its colour varies from grey or greyish brown to almost black. The flesh is light brown, firm to spongy and up to 3 cm thick. The tubes are up to 12 cm long, distinctly stratified and cinnamon coloured. The pores measure 0.3 mm in diameter and the pore surface is beige in active growth darkening to amber brown. The hyaline spores are cylindrical to ellipsoid, thin walled and measure 15–18 x 5 μm (Rea, 1922).

Initial infection by *F. fomentarius* usually occurs through broken branches or other wounds on the stem. Decay in birch develops as creamy white rot containing small black flecks. At an early stage the decayed area is surrounded by a narrow brown invasion zone. Sheets of pale creamy-coloured mycelium may be found in cracks in the decayed wood.

In culture on malt agar a white, closely woven, tough, smooth, even mat is soon formed (Cartwright and Findlay, 1956). In the light the culture develops a light brownish coloration which darkens with age.

F. fomentarius is the commonest cause of decay in birch in parts of the highlands of Scotland. The flesh of the fruit body was once used as the basis of the tinder used in flint boxes and hence the common name tinder fungus is sometimes applied to this species.

Fomes fraxineus: see *Fomitopsis cytisina*

Fomes ignarius: see *Phellinus ignarius*

Fomes pini: see *Phellinus pini*

Fomes pomaceus: see *Phellinus pomaceus*

Fomes ulmarius: see *Rigidoporus ulmarius*

Fomitopsis cytisina (Berk.) Bond. and Sing. (*Fomes fraxineus* (Bull.) Fr.)

Fomitopsis cytisina is comparatively rare in Britain but is widely distributed in the rest of Europe and North America. The most important hosts in Britain are ash, *Robinia* and laburnum but it also occurs on elms, poplar and beech. It is found on these host species throughout Europe; in the United States it has been found on other hardwoods including oak and maple.

The bracket-shaped fruit body measures 5–40 cm across, is sometimes imbricate and is found at the base of infected trees or on stumps. The upper surface is initially whitish but darkens with age to become fuscous and then dark brown or black. The flesh is soft and yellowish at first but soon turns hard and woody. The tubes, 5–25 mm in length, are similar in colour to the flesh, in contrast to the otherwise rather similar fruit body of *Rigidoporus ulmarius* where the tubes and flesh differ in colour. The pores are small, 0.25 mm in diameter and pinkish brown. The hyaline spores are subglobose and measure 6–7 x 6 μm (Rea, 1922).

Decay is usually restricted to the basal part of the main trunk. At an early stage, infected wood tends to break readily across the grain; later the wood decomposes into a felt-like mass of white mycelium.

Montgomery (1936) and Campbell (1938) have described the fungus in culture. Growth starts with fine radiating hyphae appressed to the surface of the culture medium. A white felted mat develops on 2 per cent malt agar and pore surfaces may form over an extensive area. Normal basidiospores are produced on these surfaces. A pale buff coloration may be seen in the centre of the culture but this tends to lighten and become creamy-white in older cultures.

F. cytisina may cause a severe butt rot in ash and other species but it is not of great significance because of its limited occurrence.

Ganoderma applanatum (Pers. ex Wallr.) Pat. (*Fomes applanatus* (Pers. Wallr., *Polyporus applanatus* (Pers.) Fr.) and *G. adspersum* (Schultz) Donk (*G. australe* (Fr.) Pat.)

Ganoderma applanatum is a cosmopolitan polypore that causes heart rot in many broadleaved species. Its fructifications may appear throughout the year as large, often imbricate brackets on the trunks of the host trees. They are up to 12 in (30 cm) across with a reddish-brown, lumpy upper surface covered by a crust which is soft when young but hard and laccate when old. The pores are small, at first white, but becoming brownish with age. The tubes are reddish brown or cinnamon, and may be broken away from the flesh, which is brownish, thick and hard but felt-like. The basidiospores are cocoa-brown in the mass, measuring 6.5–8.5 x 5–6.5 μm (Ryvarden, 1976). The spores are copiously produced, and often coat the tops of the fruit bodies as a brown dust.

In Great Britain, *G. applanatum* causes root and butt rot of many broadleaved trees. It is especially damaging to old, over-mature beeches, but is also the commonest cause of rot in standing poplars, and is frequent also in elms. It also attacks oak, sycamore, horse chestnut, willow and walnut (Cartwright and Findlay, 1958).

Affected wood at first shows a white mottle, and tends to break up into rectangular pieces, eventually the wood becomes white, soft and spongy. In living wood the rotted zone is surrounded by a black line (Cartwright and Findlay, 1958).

The fungus is mainly a wound parasite that enters particularly through wounds in stems or roots.

G. adspersum (Schultz) Donk (syn. *G. australe* (Fr.) Pat.) is very closely related to *G. applanatum* but has slightly larger spores measuring 9–11.5 x 6–8 μm (Ryvarden, 1976).

Ganoderma australe: see *Ganoderma adspersum*

Ganoderma lucidum (Leyss.) Karst. (*Polyporus lucidus* Fr.)
Ganoderma lucidum causes a root and butt rot in oak and other broadleaved species in Britain and has been found worldwide on a range of broadleaved hosts. Descriptions of the sporophores of *G. lucidum* are very similar to those for *G. resinaceum* and it is possible that some records of *G. resinaceum* in Europe may be comparable to those of *G. lucidum* in Asia and America. Cartwright and Findlay (1958) report that a closely related species or variety, *G. tsugae*, grows on coniferous stumps in America.

The annual sporophores, which measure 5–28 cm across and up to 3 cm thick, are kidney-shaped, usually with a lateral stalk and can be found at the base of trunks or on stumps. The upper surface is at first light yellow becoming blood-red chestnut and varnished. The margin is white or yellow and the flesh at first white becoming reddish, spongy then corky or woody. The tubes are white then cinnamon and measure 0.4–1.2 cm in length; the minute pores are white, discolouring with age. The brown spores are elliptical, truncate at the base and measure 10–12 x 6–8 μm (Rea, 1922).

The fruit bodies are similar in many respects to those of *G. resinaceum* but *G. lucidum* is generally smaller in size and has a stalk.

In India, Bakshi *et al.* (1976) describe a root rot of *Acaciacatechu* Willd. caused by *G. lucidum*. Trees, both young and old, were killed as a result of attack by *G. lucidum* and infection could be traced back to root contacts with stumps and roots of the previous forest cover. Toole (1966) observed root infections by *G. lucidum* on several hardwood species in the Mississippi Delta and by inoculation experiments proved it pathogenic on *Albizzia julibrissin* and *Liquidambar styraciflua*.

G. lucidum causes a white rot which does not extend far up the trunk and appears less active as a decay agent than other *Ganoderma* sp.

Ganoderma pfeifferi Bres.
Ganoderma pfeifferi occurs throughout Europe; in Britain it is found mainly on beech but elsewhere in Europe it has been reported on oak.

The perennial fruit bodies are found on trunks and stumps. They are flattened or hoof-shaped brackets 30 cm or more across, 25 cm wide and 7–8 cm thick, sometimes imbricate. The upper surface is sulcate, chestnut-brown and coated with a varnished resinous crust which is sometimes covered with a brown deposit of spores. The resinous surface can easily be melted in a match flame and will on cooling become smooth and glossy (Ryvarden, 1976). The flesh is corky to firm in texture, up to 4 cm thick, dark brown in colour and zoned towards the margin. The tubes are also dark brown, 1 cm or more in length and usually stratified. The margin and lower surface are white when in active growth, becoming resinous and yellow later turning brown but retaining yellow tints in places. The similar colour of the flesh and tubes is a feature which can be used to distinguish *G. pfeifferi* from *G. resinaceum*. The pores are small and round, 5–6 per mm. The light brown spores are ellipsoid, verrucose and measure 9–11.5 x 6–9 μm (Ryvarden, 1976).

Decayed beech wood has a mottled yellow-brown appearance caused by the presence of small straw-coloured pockets of decay amongst darker brown areas of relatively sound wood. In Britain *G. pfeifferi* can cause severe root, stem and branch decay in beech. The fungus can extend out from the central wood of live trees into the cambial region, killing extensive areas of bark and ultimately killing the whole tree.

Ganoderma resinaceum Bond.

Ganoderma resinaceum is considered to be uncommon in this country (Rea, 1922) but a number of cases of severe decay in oak caused by this species have been reported (figure 93) (Young and Strouts, personal communication). It has also been recorded elsewhere in Europe on oak, beech, willow and plane.

The sporophores (plate 61), which measure 10–45 cm across and 10 cm thick, are sessile (sometimes with a rudimentary stipe), semicircular, concentrically grooved with wide primary furrows and occur at the base of trunks and on stumps. The upper surface is at first yellow and viscid then burning blood-red to chestnut-brown and varnished, although at this stage it may be covered with a brownish deposit of spores. The margin is white and the flesh pale cinnamon, thick, soft and corky. The tubes are dark cinnamon 0.5–3 cm long and the pores at first are white becoming dark cinnamon, 0.4–0.5 mm in diameter. The spores are fuscous, ovate, oblong or obovate truncate at the base, 10–12 x 8–8 μm. The fruit body of *G. resinaceum* is similar to that of *G. lucidum* (Rea, 1922), though the latter generally has a stalk and is smaller.

Bourdot and Galzin (1927) describe *G. resinaceum* as a 'dangerous parasite whose decay affects the heartwood; under the action of the mycelium the wood melts away, so to speak, and is replaced by a mycelial felt'. It causes a more serious decay on oak than *G. lucidum* (Cartwright and Findlay, 1958).

Grifola frondosa (Dicks. ex Fr.) S. F. Gray (*Polyporus frondosus* Fr.)

G. frondosa is not uncommon in Britain and the rest of Europe on oak and horn-beam and is also found in North America on a number of hardwoods including oak and elm and occasionally on coniferous species.

Figure 93. Decay in oak caused by *Ganoderma resinaceum* (Forestry Commission)

The sporophore is stipitate, the stem branching many times and giving rise to numerous overlapping pilei (Overholts, 1953). It occurs at the bases of trees, on roots and on stumps. The overall size may vary from 15–30 cm, the individual pileus measures 2–6 cm across and the stipe 10–30 x 5–10 cm. The upper surface is rough and greyish and the margin is white, spatulate, lobed and intricately relobed. The flesh is at first white and fleshy, not more than 5 mm thick and becomes discoloured and firm with age. The tubes are a similar colour, decurrent and 0.5 mm long. The pores are also white, 0.3–1.0 mm diameter, round at first and later becoming angular. The hyaline spores are subglobose and measure 6 x 5 μm (Rea, 1922).

Cartwright (1940) described various stages of butt rot in oak caused by *G. frondosa*. The first signs of decay are streaks or pockets of white rot surrounded by a water-soaked, reddish-brown invasion zone. Greig and Gulliver (1976) noted the presence of a characteristic bright orange zonation in association with the white pocket rot. At a very advanced stage the wood is severely decayed and only a soft, spongy pulp remains interspersed with white mycelium.

In culture the fungus grows moderately rapidly (8 cm in 3 to 4 weeks) as a dense, white, raised mycelial mat with irregular yellow and chamois patches (Greig and Gulliver, 1976). Numerous clamp connections, sometimes arched, and globose to ovoid chlamydospores are present in culture. The cultures often have a characteristic 'carbide' smell.

G. frondosa can cause a very severe butt rot in oaks in Britain making them unsafe and also markedly reducing the value of any timber which might be harvested. However, the fungus has so far not been found widely in Britain.

Heterobasidion annosum: see chapter 3

Inonotus dryadeus (Pers. ex Fr.) Murr. (*Polyporus dryadeus* (Pers.) Fr.)
Inonotus dryadeus is widespread and fairly common on oak in Britain and Europe and has occasionally been found in North America. Burdekin (1977) reported that it was observed in the trunks of oaks broken following a severe gale.

The annual sporophore (plate 59) can be seen from May to December usually at the base of oaks or on their stumps. It is a thick, sessile bracket, semicircular in shape, measuring from 7 to 30 cm across and up to 8 cm thick and is sometimes found in overlapping groups. The upper surface is thin, soft and yellowish at first then turning light brown. Small, round depressions at the margin of an actively growing fruit body are often filled with a very astringent watery exudate. The flesh is ferruginous in colour, soft at first and later becoming corky. The tubes are similarly coloured, 10–30 mm in length and the pores are whitish, 0.2–0.4 mm across. The spores are hyaline or pale yellow, subglobose, 1-guttulate and measure 6–8 x 6–7 μm (Rea, 1922). The cystidia are brown, thick-walled, irregular, sickle or hook-shaped.

Fruit bodies are not regular in their occurrence and several years may elapse between the appearance of consecutive sporophores on an infected tree. They often appear in early autumn and decompose during the winter.

At an early stage, infection by *I. dryadeus* causes a dark brown, water-soaked area in which appears irregular stripes of a yellowish colour (Cartwright and Findlay, 1958). These gradually expand and the decayed wood becomes lighter in colour, finally becoming a soft, white filamentous mass. The severely decayed wood is broken up into sections by thick sheets of white mycelium. Decay is largely confined to the heartwood.

In culture growth is very slow; at first it appears as a whitish, furry mycelium tinged with yellow, later becoming yellow and darkening to brown.

Decay is confined to the roots and the butt region and rarely spreads more than 2 metres up the stem. Although it may not cause serious loss of timber it is important because the decay at the base of the stem and in the roots renders oaks susceptible to windthrow.

Inonotus hispidus (Bull. ex Fr.) P. Karst. (*Polyporus hispidus* (Bull.) Fr.)
Inonotus hispidus is the most frequent cause of decay in ash (*Fraxinus excelsior* L) in Britain; it is also found on apple and plane and occasionally on sycamore, walnut and elm. It has been reported from Europe, America, Asia and Australia. In North America it has been found on a range of hosts including ash, oak, willow and walnut.

The annual sporophore (plate 60) can be found in Britain from May to

February attached to the main stem or branches of the host tree. In the United States, in Mississippi, the fruit bodies appear from July to October, the majority in September and October. They reach full size in 1 to 2 weeks and discharge their spores for 2 to 4 weeks (McCracken and Toole, 1969). They are semicircular in shape, 6-35 cm across and 2-10 cm deep. The upper surface is at first orange-rust coloured and tomentose, darkening to black and becoming hispid with age. The tubes are similarly coloured, 0.5-4.0 cm long and they open into fine pores, 0.25-0.40 mm in diameter. The yellowish, subglobose spores measure 8.3-11 x 7-9 μm (Pegler and Waterston, 1958); brown cystidia are sometimes present. The black fruit bodies may remain attached to the host during the winter months although they often fall and gradually disintegrate on the ground at the base of the tree.

Infection usually occurs through a branch wound or stub. Nutman (1929) observed that although *I. hispidus* was usually saprophytic in the heartwood in inoculation experiments it could penetrate and grow slowly in living wood. Toole (1955) found elongated cankers associated with infection by *I. hispidus* on oak and reported that once well-established in the heartwood it grows out through the sapwood to the cambium. Fruit bodies appeared on the surface of the cankers. Similar observations have been made on ash in Britain although the narrow, elongated cankers associated with the branch wounds are relatively inconspicuous.

The decay (figure 94) shows at first as white or yellow tongues of discolor-

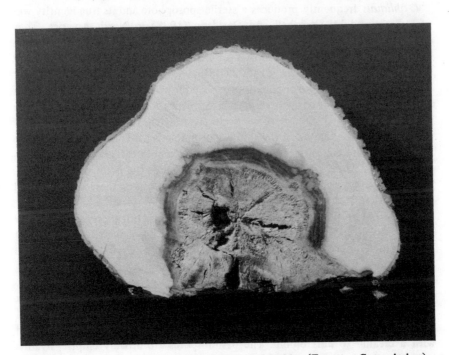

Figure 94. Decay in *Acer* caused by *Inonotus hispidus* (Forestry Commission)

ation, limited by a brown zone resulting from the formation of a gummy material (Cartwright and Findlay, 1958). In ash and walnut the more advanced decay is yellowish brown and spongy.

Cartwright *et al.* (1936) tested the strength of small sample blocks of ash and found that resistance to a sudden blow was reduced by 27 per cent two weeks after inoculation with *I. hispidus* and 90 per cent after twelve weeks.

In culture *I. hispidus* grows readily but rather slowly. On malt agar it forms a thick mat, broadly zoned and coloured yellow turning to brown. No clamp connections and no secondary spores have been observed in culture.

Burdekin (1977) reported many cases of branch and stem breakage in hedgerow ash in Britain where decay from *I. hispidus* was evident. As ash timber is used for wooden handles for a wide variety of tools and sports equipment, even slight decay could render the implement dangerous and infected wood must be rejected.

Inonotus obliquus (Pers.) Pilat (*Poria obliqua* (Pers.) Bres.)

Inonotus obliquus is common on birch in certain countries in Europe including parts of Britain, Russia, Sweden and Yugoslavia, and in North America. In Britain its distribution appears to be limited largely to parts of northeast Scotland although there are occasional records from other parts of northern England and Scotland (Batko, 1950).

I. obliquus frequently produces a sterile sporophore and its true identity was first discovered by Campbell and Davidson (1938) in North America. They demonstrated that the sterile form was associated with a fertile fruit body and that cultures derived from these two sources were identical. Reid (1976) found the fertile form of *I. obliquus* for the first time in Britain in 1975.

The sterile sporophore or conk is produced on trunks of live birch trees and it appears as a black outgrowth varying in size from 5 to 20 cm diameter with a very irregular and fissured surface. It closely resembles a partly burnt piece of coal or wood. The texture of the sterile sporophore is hard and woody and when broken the internal surfaces are rusty brown, somewhat granular and often mottled with white or cream streaks leading towards the point of attachment. No spores, either conidia or basidiospores, are produced on these structures and their function, if any, remains unknown.

In contrast to the sterile sporophore, the fertile fructification has only rarely been observed and then only beneath the bark of dead birch trees. The fruit bodies are resupinate, poria-like fructifications. They may extend over several metres and at intervals horizontal outgrowths of the fungus, measuring up to 2 cm across, develop beneath the bark and produce a pore surface on their underside. These structures may be up to 10 cm in length and they resemble pilei but there is no differentiated surface layer. The upper surface and context are golden brown, the tubes are up to 6 mm long and the pores, 2–4 per mm, are covered with a creamy to buff bloom. The basidiospores are broadly elliptic, hyaline becoming faintly coloured and measure 8.0–9.2 x 5.2–5.75 μm (Reid, 1976).

Cultures of the fungus on malt agar develop a pore surface which produces spores of similar size.

I. obliquus causes a white rot in which dark brownish-black zones may be found. The annual rings of decayed wood may separate from one another and in the later stages a weft of mycelium replaces the medullary rays (Cartwright and Findlay, 1958).

I. obliquus may cause a serious heart rot in birch leading to breakage of stems, often where the sterile fruit body is found. In Russia, it is called 'Tchaga' and an infusion from the sterile conk has been used for medicinal purposes since the sixteenth and seventeenth centuries (Reid, 1976). It is said to relieve pain and has been used in treatment of the early stages of cancer.

Inonotus radiatus (Sow. ex Fr.) Karst. (*Polyporus radiatus* (Sow.) Fr.)
Inonotus radiatus is commonly found in Europe and America and occurs frequently on alder, occasionally on birch, willow and poplar.

The fruit body is often found on the trunks of dead trees, and is annual, developing between September and April. It is a thick short bracket, 2–6 cm across, and often imbricate. The upper surface is radially grooved, velvety becoming smooth and tawny or rust-brown in colour; the margin is golden yellow when young. The flesh is hard, fibrous and yellow to rust-brown; the tubes are a similar colour and measure 5–10 mm in length. The minute pores are at first silvery and glistening finally turning rust-brown. The hyaline spores are subglobose, measuring 4.5–7 x 3–4.5 μm (Pegler, 1973), and the dark brown cystidia are fusiform, measuring 20–30 x 5–8 μm.

Decay in alder caused by *I. radiatus* is whitish or pale biscuit coloured and breaks with a flaky fracture (Cartwright and Findlay, 1958).

In culture on malt agar a velvety, slightly tufted, compact mat forms which eventually has a somewhat powdery appearance. The culture develops various yellow-brown tints, particularly when grown in the dark. The submerged mycelium and surrounding medium are rich dark brown (Cartwright and Findlay, 1958).

I. radiatus is the most important cause of decay in alder in Britain.

Laetiporus sulphureus (Bull. ex Fr.) Murr. (*Polyporus sulphureus* (Bull.) Fr.)
Laetiporus sulphureus occurs commonly in both Europe and America, attacking both hardwood and coniferous species. In Britain it is probably the most important decay fungus found in old standing oaks; it has also been found on sweet chestnut, yew, cherry and sometimes on pine, larch and beech.

The annual sporophores (plate 64) appear from May to November on the main stem of their host and often at the site of a wound. They occur in overlapping groups which measure from 10–40 cm across. The individual parts are thin and resupinate and have a wavy margin. The upper surface is a brightly coloured orange and the flesh is soft and cheesy. The lower surface is a pale sulphur-yellow at first but colours on both surfaces fade with time. Young fructifications often exude a pale yellow juice if bruised. The pores are small, 0.3–0.8

mm, sometimes absent and the tubes short, 0.5 mm. The spores are white, elliptical and measure 7–8 x 5 μm (Rea, 1922).

The first visible signs of infection are a yellow or reddish discoloration in the wood (Cartwright and Findlay, 1958). At a later stage the wood becomes a dark reddish brown and breaks up into cubical blocks (figure 95). The radial cracks

Figure 95. **Brown, cubical rot in oak caused by** *Laetiporus sulphureus* **(Forestry Commission)**

between the blocks may be filled with sheets of a pale yellowish mycelium, 2–4 mm thick, which resemble chamois leather in colour and texture.

In culture, *L. sulphureus* grows moderately rapidly, it is white to pale buff in colour, sparse and powdery. Numerous spores are produced in culture; they are thin walled, oval to round and measure 5–9 x 5–7 μm (Greig and Gulliver, 1976). Terminal and intercalary thick-walled chlamydospores are often present.

L. sulphureus is commonly found causing serious decay in open-grown oaks and also in larger structural timbers. Even small traces of infection can continue their development in sawn timber particularly if the wood remains moist. Cartwright and Findlay (1958) consider that *L. sulphureus* can only enter when the heartwood is exposed, as for example when a large branch is broken. Greig and Gulliver (1976) frequently observed sporophores of *L. sulphureus* on branch stubs of oaks but report that in some cases the decay was most extensive at ground level and likely to have entered through the roots.

Meripilus giganteus (*Polyporus giganteus* (Pers.) Fr.)

Meripilus giganteus is widely distributed throughout Europe and has been reported from North America (Cartwright and Findlay, 1958). In Britain it is found commonly on beech and also on oak and robinia.

The fruit body is annual (from July to January) and consists of a rounded mass of imbricated pilei which may be 30 cm or more across and can weigh up to 12 kg. It develops either on stumps or on decayed roots near the base of the trunk. The pileus when fresh is brownish yellow to chestnut brown on top with a yellowish margin. The upper surface is somewhat granular and fibrillose, the flesh is white, and the lower surface, with its angular or irregular pores, is creamy white. The lower surface darkens when touched, as does the whole fruit body with age. The fruit body usually deteriorates into a black, slimy mass following the first severe autumn frost. The tubes are 4–6 mm long and the spores are hyaline, subglobose or broadly elliptical and measure 6 x 5 μm (Cartwright and Findlay, 1958).

M. giganteus causes a decay in the roots and stumps particularly of beech (figure 96). Decayed roots are at first generally brown with small areas apparently

Figure 96. Decay in beech root caused by *Meripilus giganteus* (Forestry Commission)

filled with white mycelium; these gradually enlarge and the root may subsequently become hollow.

In culture the fungus produces a soft, white, cotton-woolly growth; mycelial hummocks may develop and also tubes bearing spores. The mycelium becomes more leathery and finally tawny or cinnamon-brown patches appear.

Cartwright and Findlay (1958) suggest that it is usually a pathogen of secondary importance but more recently Young and Strouts (1974) have found it commonly associated with windblown beech and sometimes with large trees showing thin and sparse foliage. Such trees may have severely decayed roots though death and decay of roots may be limited to the smaller roots at a depth of 45 cm or more.

Phaeolus schweinitzii (Fr.) Pat. (*Polyporus schweinitzii* Fr.)

Phaeolus schweinitzii is widely distributed, and is known to occur on many coniferous species throughout Europe and North America, parts of Central America and the West Indies, Japan and a few other areas in East Asia, North and South Africa, New Zealand, and perhaps Australia and South America (Anon, 1967). As a cause of loss it is far less important than *Heterobasidion annosum* (*Fomes annosus*), though it may cause considerable local damage, and was one of the more important fungi found by Peace (1938) in his butt-rot survey. In Great Britain it does not kill trees, but gives rise to an extensive rot in the tree stem.

It is found mainly in mature trees fifty or more years old (Peace, 1938; Greig, 1962), though this is often because the infection is not discovered until the tree is felled or windblown. In fact it may be already present in the stem when trees are no more than 12 to 15 years of age (Greig, unpublished). It occurs chiefly in conifer plantations following hardwoods or in second rotation conifers after pines (Greig, 1962).

The sporophores of the fungus arise annually in summer or early autumn (plate 62). They are most often found on old thinning stumps or inside the remains of wind-shattered trees. They also occur on standing infected trees (sometimes on the sites of fire scars or other wounds), or on the ground around them, often several feet from their bases. Those on the ground (apparently on the litter surface, but in fact attached below to the root system by thick, well-marked mycelial cords) are toadstool-like, with a thick, brown, velvety stalk attenuated below, and a cap about 30 cm across. Fruit bodies growing on tree trunks are bracket-like and unstalked. The upper surface of the fructification is bright brown, becoming a deep rusty-brown, with a coarsely velvety texture that gives the fungus its popular name of velvet top. The rim is thick and pale yellow, and the underside is greyish green, with irregular angular pores. The pore surface is water-soaked when fresh, and turns brown when bruised. The basidiospores are white, elliptical to oval, 7-8 x 3-4 μm. The flesh is spongy-fibrous, and at first yellowish brown, but later a deep rusty brown. The sporophores remain as described above for from 2 to 3 months, but then die, and become dark brown, corky, and light in weight. It is in this condition that they are most often seen, remaining many months before decomposing, so that they often occur alongside those of the current year (Gill, 1925; Wakefield and Dennis, 1950; Gladman and Greig, 1965; Barrett, 1968).

P. schweinitzii occurs as many strains, which vary in their cultural characters and growth rate (Childs, 1937; Barrett, 1968). Typically in culture it produces velvety cushions, at first greenish yellow, later bright yellow, becoming reddish brown, and smelling of aniseed (Cartwright and Findlay, 1958).

Mode of entry   It is usually considered that the fungus enters the tree through damaged roots and wounds on the stem. York *et al.* (1936) showed experimentally that it could enter the roots of seedlings of *Pinus strobus*. Gremmen (1961) and Greig (1962) both found the fungus in tree root systems, and the former traced it into the stem from main roots which it appeared to have killed. Most tree infections in Great Britain originate from the roots, particularly the tap roots. Barrett (1968) did pot experiments which showed that *P. schweinitzii* could invade damaged roots of young conifers, though in his trials it did not spread far beyond the damaged area. In the field he studied infested root systems, and concluded that infection took place only after injury by other agents, such as adverse physical conditions or *Armillaria mellea*. Barrett (1970) also found in laboratory experiments, that the growth of *P. schweinitzii* through sterilised wood colonised by *A. mellea* was not inhibited and indeed might have been stimulated.

Studies by Hepting and Chapman (1938) in shortleaf and loblolly pines in the USA indicated that the fungus sometimes invaded trees through the roots, but these usually gained entry through basal wounds, particularly those caused by fires. They noted that in Arkansas, where there was little fire damage, few trees were infested by *P. schweinitzii*, but in Texas fire damage was more extensive, and also more trees were attacked by the fungus. According to Harvey (1962), in young Douglas fir in the USA infection takes place mainly through the roots, but most damage is found in older trees, in which entry is through fire scars. In Great Britain, Greig (1962) obtained some evidence that infection of 60-year-old pines had taken place through fire scars.

Greig made other observations that suggested occasional entry through wounds made by snow-break, singling of double leaders, and in extraction, though this fungus was not among those found by Pawsey and Gladman (1965) in their survey of extraction damage. Boyce (1924) recorded entry through an old knot.

How far entry is by means of airborne spores and how much by mycelial growth through the soil is unknown, though some work by Barrett (1968) suggests that initial infection is by spores.

Host range   *P. schweinitzii* occurs on most of the commoner conifer species, and was found by Rhoads (1921) on charred stumps of *Eucalyptus globosus*. In Great Britain it has been noted especially on Sitka spruce and Douglas fir, but it

also attacks Scots pine and larches; it has recently been recorded there on lodgepole pines, *Pinus pinaster*, and western red cedar. Elsewhere it has also been
noted on southern pines (Hepting and Chapman, 1938), *Pinus ponderosa* (Gill,
1925), *P. strobus* (York, Wean and Childs, 1936), and *Chamaecyparis* sp. (Yde-
Andersen, 1961).

Symptoms of decay   Incipient decay may be present in trees that appear quite
healthy, and the first sign of attack may be the presence of fructifications on or
around the bases of the affected stems (Gremmen, 1961). Even at an early stage,
the wood becomes weak and useless (Kimmey and Bynum, 1961). At first the
fungus stains the wood a uniform pale yellow or yellowish brown. Later the
wood becomes dry, soft and crumbly. It soon begins to show radial cracks, and
breaks up into irregularly cubical chunks, sometimes with thin sheets of white or
yellowish mycelium between (figure 97). The rotten chunks finally become dark

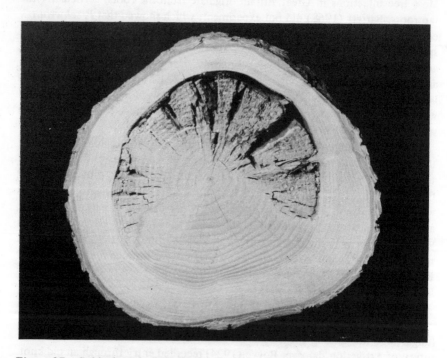

Figure 97.   Cubical rot in Douglas fir caused by *Phaeolus schweinitzii*
      (Forestry Commission)

brown in colour and very light in weight, and can be readily picked out if the
tree is felled, or shattered by wind (Greig, 1981). The infected wood smells
strongly of aniseed, and in the later stages of rot can be crushed to a smooth
powder between the fingers (Harvey, 1962).

Damage caused   The damage caused to individual trees is often severe, as the rot may progress for several metres up the stem, and affect most of its diameter. In Great Britain decay may reach a height of 2 to 3 metres or more, particularly in Sitka spruce, and because of weakening of the wood in the earlier stages, and later its complete breakdown into separate pieces, windsnap often follows infection (Gladman and Low, 1963). Losses overall are not great, however, because in spite of the high loss of timber in each affected tree, the fungus is only sporadic in its distribution (Gladman and Greig, 1965).

Measures for its control are not yet available.

Phellinus igniarius (L. ex Fr.) Quel. (*Fomes igniarius* (Linn) Fr.

Phellinus igniarius is commonly found in Europe and America and has been reported from India and Australia. It generally occurs in Britain on willow but has occasionally been found on ash. Rea (1922) describes a form of this fungus, *F. igniarius* var. *nigricans*, occurring on birch. In America, Verrall (1937) found three different types of sporophore of *P. igniarius* occurring on aspen, birch and on other hosts respectively. Ryvarden (1976) distinguishes three closely related but separate species, *P. populicola, P. nigricans* and *P. igniarius* on aspen, birch and other species respectively.

The perennial fruit body of *P. igniarius* is hoof-shaped or a thick, broadly attached bracket measuring up to 20 cm across. The upper surface is greyish black, rough, often cracked and the margin is fawn when in active growth. The flesh is dark brown and hard, the stratified tubes are cinnamon, 2–8 mm long and the pores are 0.25 mm in diameter, yellowish or greyish brown. The spores are hyaline, subglobose and measure 5–6 x 4–5 μm (Bourdot and Galzin, 1927). Dark coloured pointed setae measuring about 20 μm in length are present but sometimes rather scarce.

The fungus invades the tree through wounds, particularly dead branch stubs. A central heart rot develops which is soft and yellowish white with a distinct dark zone separating decayed from healthy wood. At a later stage fine black zone lines are formed in the spongy decayed wood (Ohman and Kessler, 1964).

Cartwright and Findlay (1958) describe the growth of *P. igniarius* in culture as thin, sparse, with appressed hyphae later developing into a smooth, brown, felted mat with only traces of zonation. Verrall (1937) found considerable variation in isolates of *P. igniarius* in the USA and distinguished three main groups which more or less corresponded with three different types of sporophore.

P. igniarius is a fairly common cause of decay in willow in Britain but it assumes far greater significance on poplars and birches elsewhere in Europe and in the USA. Ohman and Kessler (1964) claim that *P. igniarius* is the most serious cause of decay in broadleaved species in the USA.

Phellinus pini (Thore ex Fr.) Pilat (*Fomes pini* (Thore) Karst., *Trametes pini* (Thore) Fr.)

Phellinus pini is one of the most serious heart-rotting fungi in conifers in North

America; it is commonly found in Northern Europe and also reported from Asia. It is very rare in England and occasionally found in Scotland, always on pine.

Sporophores often appear on branch stubs or on the site of old injuries. They are often perennial and are variable in shape, from a thin bracket to a more ungulate form, ranging in size from 5–14 cm across. The upper surface is rough, becoming encrusted with age and is at first rusty brown darkening to almost black. The flesh is tawny-ferruginous, tough and woody. The tubes are often stratified and are a similar colour to the flesh; the pores vary in size from 0.16–0.4 mm and may be round or oblong in cross-section. The spores are pale yellow, maturing to light brown, 5.5–6 x 4.5–5.5 μm (Bourdot and Galzin, 1927). Pointed, conical, dark brown setae are present, measuring 40–65 x 6–10 μm.

Initial infection takes place through branch stubs where heartwood is present and therefore is largely restricted to older trees. In the early stage of fungal invasion, sometimes known as red-heart, a pinkish or purplish-red discoloration occurs in ring or crescent-shaped areas. There is often an abundance of resin present. At a later stage a white pocket rot develops, often in rings around the

Figure 98. Ring scale in pine caused by *Phellinus pini* (B.J.W. Greig)

stem separated by apparently healthy wood. This type of decay is often described as a ring scale (figure 98) and it is usually found in the upper parts of the tree where the original infection occurred (Cartwright and Findlay, 1958).

Phellinus pomaceus (Pers.) Maire (*Fomes pomaceus* (Pers.) Lloyd)
Phellinus pomaceus occurs throughout Europe and America and has been recorded in Australia and Japan. In Britain it is found on plum, cherry, hawthorn and other Rosaceae and on poplar. It is closely related to *Fomes igniarius*, of which some authorities (for example Bourdot and Galzin, 1927) classify *P. pomaceus* on a subspecies. The fruit bodies are found on live or dead stems and branches. They are hard and woody, either hoof-shaped or respuinate or semi-resupinate and measure about 5 cm across. The upper surface, where present, has concentric furrows and is ash or brownish grey. In active growth the rounded margin is grey and velvety, later becoming cinnamon. The flesh is light brown, the tubes are cinnamon, 4-6 mm long and stratified in older specimens. The pores are brown, with a greyish bloom at first, and measure about 0.2 mm in diameter. The pale brown or hyaline spores are almost spherical and measure 6 x 5-6 μm (Rea, 1922). Flask-shaped cystidia are abundant, dark brown at the base and hyaline at the apen and they measure 15-20 x 7-8 μm (Rea, 1922).

Decay caused by *P. pomaceus* is commonly found in old plum trees. At an advanced stage of decay the wood in the centre of the stem is white and crumbling. A dark purplish zone, 1-2 cm of apparently sound wood, surrounds the decayed region.

In culture on malt agar the mycelium is at first white but in the light it soon develops colour ranging from buff to tawny. No clamp connections have been observed in culture but crystals are numerous in older cultures (Cartwright and Findlay, 1958). *P. pomaceus* may cause serious decay in old orchards. It appears to infect trees through natural or pruning wounds.

Pholiota squarrosa (Müll. ex Fr.) Cke.
Pholiota squarrosa is commonly found in Europe and America on a range of broadleaved species including aspen, poplar, apple, cherry and occasionally on conifers (Peace, 1938).

The fruit bodies develop from July to December and are often found in clusters at the base of the trunk. The cap is 3-12 cm across, convex then flattened, and ochre yellow to yellowish rust in colour (Wakefield and Dennis, 1950). The upper surface is crowded with reddish-brown recurved shaggy scales. The flesh is light yellow and the gills are yellowish when young, then pale rust coloured, broadly adnate with a decurrent tooth. The stipe measures 6-20 x 1-2.5 cm, concolorous with cap and similarly squarrose up to the ring. The ring is small, dark brown, often torn and attached to the upper part of the stipe. The brown spores are smooth, elliptical and measure 6-8 x 3.5-4 μm (Wakefield and Dennis, 1950).

In culture on Nobles' medium after one month a golden brown mat of mycelium has developed with a white advancing zone. Yellow strands of mycelium, covered with crystals, may be present near the inoculum plug and occasional conidia may be seen.

There is little information on the nature of the decay caused by *P. squarrosa* though Peace (1938) mentions that it causes a soft brown rot in Norway spruce. Davidson *et al*. (1959) suggest that it may infect aspen poplars through the roots.

Piptoporus betulinus (Fr.) Karst. (*Polyporus betulinus* (Bull.) Fr.)
Polyporus betulinus occurs widely on birch in Europe, Asia and America.

The annual fruit bodies are frequently found on dead trees or logs but also develop on live stems and branches. They measure 5 to 30 cm across, are hoof or kidney-shaped and are attached by a narrow base which sometimes forms a thick short stalk. The upper surface is rounded, pale brown in colour, smooth when young and cracking with age. The flesh is white, soft at first then corky. The tubes are white, 2–8 mm in length and the pores, also white, are 0.3 mm in diameter. The hyaline cylindrical spores measure 4.4–5.5 x 1.4–2 μm (Macdonald 1937).

Infection appears to occur largely through stem or branch wounds. At an advanced stage of decay the wood becomes reddish brown in colour, is brittle in texture and breaks up into rectangular blocks often separated by thin sheets of whitish mycelium. Macdonald (1937) observed the appearance of dark zone lines in wood blocks artificially inoculated with the fungus.

In culture, on potato dextrose agar, growth is at first thin but soon develops a cotton wool appearance (Macdonald, 1937). The mycelium is at first white later becoming pale brown or faintly pink and often exudes drops of clear or amber coloured liquid. Numerous crystals are formed in the medium. Flat pore surfaces and roughly rounded sporophores may develop on drier parts of the culture medium.

P. betulinus is the commonest cause of decay in birch in England though its place is taken by *Fomes fomentarius* in parts of the highlands of Scotland. Although *P. betulinus* is frequently found on dead birch it also occurs on live trees which have been damaged by branch or stem breakage or by fire.

Pleurotus ostreatus (Jacq.) Fr. (The Oyster Fungus)
Pleurotus ostreatus is commonly found in Europe and America and has also been reported from Africa, Asia and Australia. It occurs on a wide range of broad-leaved species in Britain, particularly on beech and also horse chestnut and poplar. It has been reported on oak in the United States.

The annual sporophores often occur in clusters and usually appear on a wound on the trunk or at a branch stub in autumn, though they can develop at any time of year. They are thick, fleshy, fan or shell-shaped and measure 7–13 cm across. The fruit bodies are often sessile but the stipe when present is 2–4 cm long and 2 cm thick. The upper surface is smooth and moist, at first almost black, soon becoming pale grey or fawn. The white flesh is soft when young but becomes firm at a later stage. The under surface consists of gills which are white, becoming yellow with age, decurrent and said by some authorities to anastomose at the base. This fungus is very variable and this is exemplified by the range of spore sizes quoted by various authors. Rea (1922) states that the spores measure 9–11 x 4.5–6 μm whereas Romagnesi (1962) records measurements of 7.2–10 x 3.2–4.2 μm.

P. ostreatus causes a white flakey rot, decayed areas being separated from healthy wood by a narrow, dark brown invasion zone. Marked cracking across the grain has been observed in decayed poplar wood.

In culture on malt agar *P. ostreatus* grows rapidly as a white, woolly, felted mat which becomes rough and almost leathery and develops occasional creamy patches (Cartwright and Findlay, 1958). Small fruit bodies with pilei and long stipes usually appear though the pileus may be absent. If the fungus is cultured in the dark on bread the mycelium is at first white but later a central flesh-ochre coloured patch develops. In the light, drops of a yellowish-red liquid are exuded when grown on this medium. These colours help to distinguish *P. ostreatus* from other common species of *Pleurotus* which remain white when cultured on bread.

This fungus can cause extensive decay in beech and other hardwood species and its development can be particularly rapid once it has gained entry.

Pleurotus ulmarius (Bull.) Fr.
Pleurotus ulmarius is fairly common in Britain and Europe and is usually found on elm.

The annual fruit bodies are found from June to December often on wounds on trunks of elm. The pileus is 6–20 cm across, more or less circular, fleshy, convex then plane, ochraceous and often cracked (Wakefield and Dennis, 1950). The near-central stipe is stout, measuring 5–11 cm long and 1.5–4 cm thick, white becoming tinged with yellow, firm, often curved upward, the base often downy. The flesh is white and tough. The gills are broad, pale ochraceous, adnate and somewhat crowded. The spores are globose 5–6 μm in diameter (Rea, 1922). The fruit bodies are edible.

Cartwright and Findlay (1958) report that *P. ulmarius* causes a brown rot in the heartwood and that in such wood the annual rings of decayed portions become separated.

Polyporus adustus: see *Bjerkandera adusta*

Polyporus albidus: see *Tyromyces stipticus*

Polyporus betulinus: see *Piptoporus betulinus*

Polyporus dryadeus: see *Inonotus dryadeus*

Polyporus frondosus: see *Grifola frondosa*

Polyporus giganteus: see *Meripilus giganteus*

Polyporus hispidus: see *Inonotus hispidus*

Polyporus lucidus: see *Ganoderma lucidum*

Polyporus radiatus: see *Inonotus radiatus*

Polyporus schweinitzii: see *Phaeolus schweinitzii*

Polyporus squamosus (Huds.) Fr. Saddle-back Fungus, Dryad's saddle
Polyporus squamosus is commonly found in Britain and other parts of Europe and has been reported from India, Australia and from America, where it is described as rare. In Britain it occurs on a number of hardwoods particularly elm and sycamore, but also on other *Acer* species, *Pyrus* spp. and walnut. It is probably the principal cause of stem rot in elm.

The annual, fan-shaped sporophores can be found from April to December usually on pruning wounds or branch scars fairly high in the tree. They are often imbricate and when fully grown vary in size from 10 to 60 cm across. The short, thick, lateral stalk is black at its base. The upper surface is pale fawn and has numerous brown appressed scales. The tubes are white then yellowish, 5-10 mm long. The lower surface is pale cream and the angular pores are relatively large, measuring 1-2 mm across. The spores, which are produced in vast numbers, are hyaline, oblong and measure 10-12 x 4-5 μm (Rea, 1922).

Infection usually occurs through a branch wound and extensive decay may develop both up and down the heartwood. At an advanced stage the decay is spongy or stringy, and includes a mass of white mycelium. The stem may eventually become hollow and a tough brown stromatic sheet may line the cavity. Campbell and Munsun (1936) report the presence of black zone lines, particularly in decayed wood close to the sporophore. These authors describe the development of the dark, bladder-shaped cells which form the pseudosclerotial plates or zone lines.

In culture, *P. squamosus* grows relatively slowly and the mycelium tends to aggregate at the sides of agar slopes into groups of short papillae (Campbell and Munsun, 1936). A brownish skin forms over the hyaline mycelium and in some cases it has a dusty yellow appearance due to the presence of large numbers of ovoid oidia with average measurements of 18 x 8 μm (Cartwright and Findlay, 1958). Numerous rod-shaped crystals are formed in the medium, sometimes in clusters. Occasionally small fertile sporophores are formed but more frequently only the stipes develop; pore surfaces have also been observed.

Elm boughs are notoriously liable to breakage and although in some cases the wood may be free from decay, in others, heartrot, particularly that caused by *P. squamosus*, is often present. The young fruit body is said to be edible and when mature it has been used as a razor strop.

Polyporus stipticus: see *Tyromyces stipticus*

Polyporus sulphureus: see *Laetiporus sulphureus*

Polystictus versicolor: see *Coriolus versicolor*

Rigidoporus ulmarius (Sow. ex Fr.) (*Fomes ulmarius* (Sow. ex Fr.)
Rigidoporus ulmarius is commonly found in Britain and is rather less common

in the rest of Europe. It has also been reported from Asia and North Central America. Cartwright and Findlay (1958) considered that *Fomes geotropus* Cooke, found in southeastern USA was closely related to and perhaps a distinct variety of *R. ulmarius*. Lowe (1957) critically studied these species and concluded that the American species was specifically identical with *R. ulmarius*. Lombard *et al.* (1960) point out that cultures of *R. ulmarius* previously used to describe the species in the United States were incorrectly identified and this had led to some confusion in nomenclature.

The most important host of *R. ulmarius* in Britain is elm but it has also been found on lime, plane, poplar and sycamore. In the USA it occurs in large, old hardwoods especially *Magnolia grandifolia* L.

The perennial fruit bodies are bracket-shaped, measure from 7 to 30 cm across and are usually found at the base of trees or on stumps. The upper surface is white or yellowish with age, usually lumpy and sometimes the sporophore consists of irregular rounded masses. Green algae often grow on the surface of older fruit bodies. The flesh is at first white, tough and fibrous becoming yellowish, hard and woody with age. The stratified tubes are cinnamon, up to 15 mm long, and the pores are a similar colour, measuring 0.25–0.4 mm across. The spores are hyaline, smooth, thin-walled, more or less globose and measure $6-7 \times 6 \mu$m (Rea, 1922). The contrasting colours of the flesh and tubes in *R. ulmarius* afford a ready means of distinguishing this fungus from the rather similar *Fomitopsis cytisina* (*Fomes fraxineus*).

Decay is usually found at the base of the tree and at an advanced stage the wood is dark brown, friable and tends to break up into rectangular blocks. No thick mycelial sheets develop in the cracks between blocks.

The fungus makes moderate growth in culture and is difficult to isolate from the sporophores, even when active, owing to heavy contamination with bacteria. Growth on malt agar is loose and spidery; in places the hyphae become aggregated into small lumps which are white or fawn in colour.

R. ulmarius is one of the most important causes of butt rot in elm in Britain. It is particularly common in parkland and hedgerows where trees have been damaged, for example following bark stripping by deer.

Sparassis crispa (Wulf.) Fr. (*Sparassis radicata* Weir)

Sparassis crispa is commonly found causing a root and butt rot in old pine, Sitka spruce, Douglas fir, larches and cedar in Europe and has also been reported from Japan. The same fungus is known as *S. radicata* in North America (Martin and Gilbertson, 1976) where it is found on Douglas fir, spruces, pines and larches. A closely related but distinct species, *S. laminosa* Fr. is found on oak (Delatour, 1975) in Europe and North America.

The fleshy sporophores of *S. crispa* are annual, up to 30 cm across, cream or white in colour and grow annually in late summer at the base of living trees and on stumps. They form a dense mass, shaped like a cauliflower or sponge with many flattened branches or lobes, the edges of which turn brown with age (fig-

Figure 99. Fruit body of *Sparassis crispa* growing on pine (D.H. Phillips)

ure 99). Spores are pale ochraceous in mass, individually hyaline, subglobose, 6–7 μm in diameter or elliptical, 6 x 4 μm (Rea, 1922).

In Britain *S. crispa* causes a brown cubical rot in conifers over 60 years of age, especially Scots pine (Greig, 1981). The decayed wood is dry, crumbly and light brown in colour and closely resembles that caused by *P. schweinitzii*. A possible distinction can be observed in the colour of mycelium which develops in the radial cracks in advanced decay; that of *S. crispa* is always white, whereas the mycelium of *P. schweinitzii* is often yellow (Pawsey, 1971). Trees which are severely decayed frequently break during gale force winds, usually close to ground level.

Sparassis radicata: see *Sparassis crispa*

Stereum gausapatum Fr. (Stereum spadiceum Fr.)
Stereum gausapatum is commonly found in Europe and America on a range of broadleaved trees, especially on oak.

The fruit bodies may be found at any time of year on branches or stems, stumps and logs as a thin, leathery skin 5 cm or more across, often confluent, imbricate and either resupinate or reflexed. The upper surface is hirsute, greyish or brownish with a lobed margin which is white when in active growth. The hymenium is smooth, brown, darkening with age and when fresh bleeds on cutting or bruising. The hyaline spores are oblong, incurved and measure 7–8 x 4–5 μm (Rea (1922). *S. gausapatum* is somewhat similar to *S. rugosum* (see below).

Cartwright and Findlay (1958) describe the decay in small branches as a soft, yellowish-white rot. In large branches, dark brown streaks occur, in the middle of which are yellowish bands where the wood is completely decayed. The wood between decayed areas appears to be perfectly sound, though fungal hyphae may be present. Long pipes of rot may thus develop in stems or branches and the term pipe rot is often used for this type of decay (figure 100). At an advanced

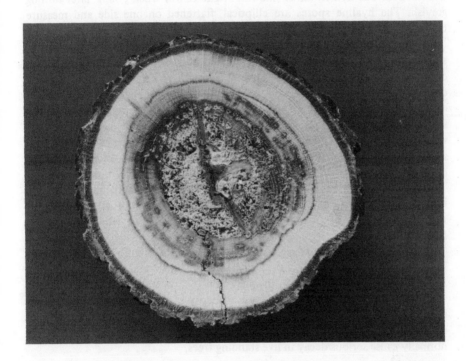

Figure 100. Pipe rot in oak branch caused by *Stereum gausapatum* (Forestry Commission)

stage of decay the whole branch may become light coloured and rotten following coalescence of the decayed areas.

In culture on malt agar the mycelium is at first white but later a wood-brown mat develops around the inoculum plug. Considerable variation in the general appearance of the cultures has been noted (Cartwright and Findlay, 1958).

S. gausapatum is an important cause of decay in the branches and stems of standing trees though it can also cause rot in the sapwood of felled trees. It has also been found causing a butt rot in oak but this is not a frequent occurrence.

Davidson *et al.* (1942) found *S. gausapatum* causing decay in oak sprouts (coppice shoots) in the USA where parent stumps were the main source of infection.

Stereum hirsutum Fr.

Stereum hirsutum is commonly found in Europe and America on wounds, dead branches and timber of a number of broadleaved trees including oak, birch and beech.

The fruit bodies occur from January to December and consist of thin leathery brackets, 2–10 cm across, sometimes entirely resupinate, often imbricate and confluent. The upper surface is hairy, yellowish or greyish in colour and somewhat zoned. The hymenium is smooth, bright yellow when young, later turning greyish. The hyaline spores are elliptical, flattened on one side and measure 6–8 x 3–4 μm (Rea, 1922).

S. hirsutum is often found decaying the sapwood of oak, the wood becoming soft and lighter in colour and weight. Cartwright and Findlay (1958) report, on occasion, that the fungus is able to invade the trunk from dead branches and cause a pipe-rot in the heartwood. However, this type of rot is more commonly caused by *S. gausapatum*, *S. hirsutum* more commonly being confined to the sapwood. In contrast to *Chondrostereum purpureum*, *S. hirsutum* can attack the wood in the absence of living tissues (Guinier, 1933). In support of this view, the same author observed the presence of *S. hirsutum* on 2-year-old fire scars on beech in France.

In culture on malt agar, *S. hirsutum* grows first as a loose aerial mycelium soon developing into a thicker mat and finally forming a tough skin over most of the mat (Cartwright and Findlay, 1958). The mycelium is at first white later becoming yellow.

The broad young hyphae bear whorled clamp connections which may be very large, sausage-shaped and loosely attached (Cartwright and Findlay, 1958). A few crystals may be produced in the medium.

S. hirsutum is a very common cause of decay in the sapwood of logs of oak and other broadleaved species. Decayed wood is paler than normal and at an advanced stage in oak it is yellowish white and very light in weight. It does not normally cause serious decay in live standing trees.

Stereum purpureum: see *Chondrostereum purpureum*

Stereum rugosum is said to occur commonly in Europe on broadleaved trees including oak and beech but it can be confused with *S. gausapatum*.

The fruit bodies of *S. rugosum* can be found at any time of year on stems or branches, stumps and logs. They are 2 cm or more across, widely effused or shortly reflexed, silky then glabrous. Where visible, the upper surface is pinkish-buff, later becoming grey, and the hymenium is similarly coloured and bleeds when bruised. The flesh is whitish, becoming discoloured and relatively rigid (in contrast to *S. gausapatum* which is thinner and softer). The spores are hyaline, oblong, incurved and measure 10–12 x 4–5 μm (Rea, 1922).

S. rugosum can cause a pipe rot in oak and Liese (1930) observed a canker on oak associated with the decay.

Stereum sanguinolentum (A & S.) Fr.

Stereum sanguinolentum is a common saprophyte on conifers, appearing on the cut surfaces of stumps and felled trees left in the forest, and sometimes causing a trunk rot in standing trees. It·is known in Europe, temperate North America, East Africa, and in New Zealand, and is variously called red rot, red heart, *sapin rouge*, or (in Douglas fir) mottled bark disease (Basham *et al.*, 1953; Hubert, 1935).

The fruit bodies are thin, resupinate crusts or small brackets (figure 101), up

Figure 101.   Fruit bodies of *Stereum sanguinolentum* on cut end of Scots pine log (Forestry Commission)

to about 8 cm across (Cartwright and Findlay, 1958), and may form in large, imbricate groups. The upper surfaces of the brackets are greyish or fawn, with silky radiating fibrils, and sometimes zoned. The hymenium is smooth, greyish or buff, and bleeds when scratched or bruised. The basidiospores are colourless (white in the mass), elliptical or cylindrical, and measure 8-9 x 2-2.5 μm (Wakefield and Dennis, 1950). Cultures of the fungus on malt agar stain the medium red, and have a characteristic sweet smell (Cartwright and Findlay, 1958).

As a saprophyte the fungus has a wide host range, occurring on stumps and brash and fallen trees of many conifers (Gladman and Low, 1963). On living trees in Great Britain it has been found causing damage mainly on Norway and Sitka spruce (particularly the former), though it has also been found on larches and sometimes on other conifers. In North America, however, it is known mainly as a cause of trunk rot of silver firs (Basham *et al.*, 1953; Risley and Silverborg, 1958). In Kenya it has rotted standing trees of *Pinus patula* and *P. radiata* (Gibson, 1966).

Mode of entry   S. *sanguinolentum* is a wound parasite, and in Great Britain enters the standing tree chiefly through carelessly made brashing and pruning wounds (Banerjee, 1955), branches broken by snow and ice, and wounds made during extraction (Gladman and Low, 1963; Pawsey and Gladman. 1965). Elsewhere it has entered also through blazes cut to mark trees (Spaulding *et al.*, 1935) and through wounds made by elephants and other game (Gibson, 1966). There is evidence that dead branches do not provide places of entry (Etheridge, 1963).

Symptoms   Growth of the fungus in the wood may be relatively fast, but rotting is fairly slow. Hence in Great Britain staining and incipient decay are much more often seen than are the later stages of rot (Cartwright and Findlay, 1958). On wound surfaces and on transverse sections of affected stems, infection shows in the earlier stages as an irregular yellow-brownish stain. Wood with incipient decay is firm and brownish yellow, and at a more advanced stage the rotted wood becomes dry, fibrous and orange-brown with longitudinal lemon-yellow streaks (Greig, 1981). Evidence of rot in standing trees sometimes shows externally as white streaks and resin flow on the lower part of the trunk (Hubert, 1935; Banerjee, 1955).

Pawsey and Gladman (1965) calculated that the average rate of growth of the fungus in the tree was 6.7 in (17 cm)/year, but in some Scottish stands it reached 16 in (39.6 cm)/year in Norway spruce, 10.5 in (26.7 cm)/year in Sitka spruce, and 9.6 in (24.4 cm)/year in Japanese larch. Rate of decay increases with the size of the wounds that permit the fungus to enter (Hunt and Krueger, 1962; Davidson and Etheridge, 1963).

Pawsey and Gladman (1965) considered that of all the fungi they found causing butt rot following extraction damage in conifers, *S. sanguinolentum* was potentially the most important. So far in this country losses caused by this fungus have been relatively small. This may be due partly to the age of many British forests, as losses have been greater in North America, where they have occurred mainly in old plantations. Thus Davidson (1951) in New Brunswick recorded no loss in Balsam fir under 40 years old, but in trees over 80 years old, decay gave rise to a loss of a quarter of the marketable volume, and in trees over 170 years old losses were three times as great as this.

To avoid infection and rot by *S. sanguinolentum*, live branches should be brashed or pruned carefully by sawing close to the stem. Wounding when extracting produce should be kept to the minimum. Steps to deal with snow and ice damaged trees can be taken only in gardens and arboreta, but in such places wounds should be trimmed and treated with stockholm tar or some similar protective covering.

Trametes pini: see *Phellinus pini*

Trametes rubescens: see *Daedaliopsis confragosa*

Tyromyces stipticus (Fr.) Kotl. and Pouz. (*Polyporus stipticus* Fr., *Polyporus albidus* Secr.)
Tyromyces stipticus is fairly commonly found associated with extraction damage to coniferous trees or on logs in Europe and has occasionally been reported from North America. The most common hosts are Norway and Sitka spruce and larch.

The sporophores occur as small brackets (5-8 cm across and 3-15 mm thick at the base) on stem wounds, or on the cut ends of logs or sometimes as irregular pads on the underside of logs (Greig, 1981). The fruit bodies are white, fleshy easily broken and the pores are clearly visible on the under surface. Older specimens are cream or grey in colour and become hard when dry. The spores are oblong-ellipsoid to subcylindrical, smooth, thin walled and hyaline, measuring 3.5-4.5 x 1.5-2.0 μm (Ryvarden, 1976).

At an early stage *T. stipticus* produces a light yellow stain in the wood and as incipient decay develops the wood becomes light brown, dry and softish. Advanced decay takes the form of a brown cubical rot, with broad radical cracks filled with white mycelium.

This decay is very similar to that caused by *P. schweinitzii* and *S. crispa*, particularly in Sitka spruce (Pawsey, 1971). However, it can usually be distinguished in the forest since only decay caused by *T. stipticus* is normally associated with damage to the stem of the host.

Ustulina deusta Fr. (*Ustulina vulgaris* Tul., *Ustulina zonata* Lev.)
Ustulina deusta causes a serious root and butt rot in lime, beech and elm (Wilkins 1934, 1936, 1939b, 1943) and is also commonly found on old hardwood stumps. Burdekin (1977) found it occurring commonly in windblown beech where severe decay had rendered the base of the main trunk or the major roots liable to breakage. In the USA Blaisdell (1939) found it frequently in hardwoods such as maple and oak. It has also been reported in the tropics on a wide range of hosts such as cocoa, rubber and tea in Asia, Australia, Africa and America (Cartwright and Findlay, 1958). *U. zonata* is the synonym which has been generally used to describe the tropical form of the fungus and *U. vulgaris* is its temperate counterpart.

Ustulina is one of the few ascomycete genera that can cause decay in standing trees; it is a pyrenomycete and a member of the family Xylariaceae. The conidia are produced on a thin disc that measures up to 5 cm across, at first bluish grey with a white margin, later becoming yellowish grey and powdery. The conidia are oval, thin-walled and hyaline and measure 7 x 3 μm (Wilkins, 1939a). The mature sexual fructification consists of a black stromatic crust, peppered with the ostioles of embedded perithecia and having the consistency of charcoal. The fructifications usually merge and form a mass that may be up to 0.5 metre long. They are often found in the clefts between buttress roots or on the surface of decayed wood and they may persist for several years. The asci are cylindrical, about 300 x 15 μm and eight-spored; the ascospores are uniseriate, fusiform, with one side somewhat flattened and measure 28–34 x 7–10 μm (Dennis, 1968).

Wilkins (1936) describes *U. deusta* in lime, noting that it may have entered the tree through a basal wound, and the same author (Wilkins, 1939*b*, 1943) studied decay in elm and beech in which it may have started in the tap root area. Campbell and Davidson (1940) observed that *U. deusta* commonly infected sugar maple stems through the parent stump and through neighbouring dead stubs. They also found infection present in roadside maples with large wounds; trees with basal infections were frequently killed by girdling. Wilkins (1939*a*) suggests that conidia may be important in the infection process.

In culture the fungus grows as a white, smooth and flat mat; it turns grey at the centre and then gradually black (Cartwright and Findlay, 1958).

Wilkins (1936, 1939*b*, 1943) gives a detailed description of the decayed wood (figures 102, 103), which is paler than healthy tissues and contains many fine, black zone lines. There may be a discoloured reaction zone marking the radial

(Text continues on p.406)

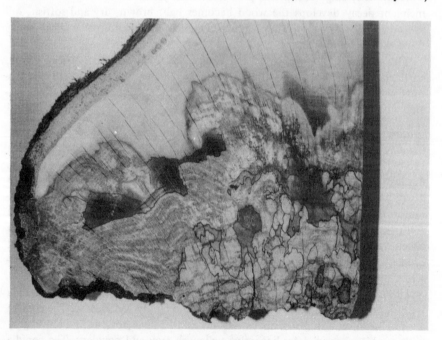

Figure 102. Decay in beech caused by *Ustulina deusta* (Forestry Commission)

Table 19.1

Summary of common broadleaved trees and their associated decay fungi

Tree species	Position of rot	Appearance of rot	Decay fungus
Alder	Stem	White rot	*Daedaleopsis confragosa*
	Stem	White flaky rot	*Inonotus radiatus*
Ash	Root and butt	White, stringy to spongy with dark zone lines	*Armillaria mellea*
	Stem and branch	White with black specks and streaks	*Daldinia concentrica*
	Butt	White, felt-like mass	*Fomitopsis cytisina*
	Stem and branch	Yellow with dark gummy reaction zone	*Inonotus hispidus*
Beech	Root and butt	White, stringy to spongy with dark zone lines	*Armillaria mellea*
	Stem and branch	White flaky rot	*Bjerkandera adusta*
	Stem and branch	Brown stain later becoming mottled decay	*Chondrostereum purpureum*
	Root and butt	White pocket rot	*Heterobasidion annosum*
	Butt, stem and branch	White mottled decay with dark reaction zone	*Ganoderma adspersum/applanatum*
	Butt, stem and branch	Yellow mottled decay	*Ganoderma pfeifferi*
	Root	Soft brown decay with white pockets	*Meripilus giganteus*
	Stem and branch	White flaky rot	*Pleurotus ostreatus*
	Root and butt	Light coloured decay with many fine zone lines	*Ustulina deusta*
Birch	Stem and branch	Brown stain, later mottled decay	*Chondrostereum purpureum*
	Stem and branch	White, flaky rot	*Coriolus versicolor*
	Root and butt	White pocket rot	*Heterobasidion annosum*
	Stem	Creamy white rot with black flecks	*Fomes fomentarius*
	Stem	White decay with dark reaction zone	*Inonotus obliquus*
	Stem	Reddish-brown, brittle, decay	*Piptoporus betulinus*

Table 19.1 continued

Tree species	Position of rot	Appearance of rot	Decay fungus
Cherry	Stem	Brown cubical rot	Laetiporus sulphureus
	Stem and branch	White crumbly decay	Phellinus pomaceus
Elm	Stem	Brown decay	Pleurotus ulmarius
	Stem	White spongy decay	Polyporus squamosus
	Butt	Brown cubical rot	Rigidoporus ulmarius
	Root and butt	Light coloured decay with many fine zone lines	Ustulina deusta
Horse chestnut	Butt and stem	Mottled decay with dark reaction zone	Ganoderma adspersum/applanatum
	Stem and branch	White flaky rot	Pleurotus ostreatus
Lime	Root and butt	Light coloured decay with many fine zone lines	Ustulina deusta
Oak	Stem and branch	White flaky rot	Coriolus versicolor
	Stem and branch	'Brown oak'	Fistulina hepatica
	Butt	White decay	Ganoderma lucidum
	Butt	Leathery white rot	Ganoderma resinaceum
	Butt	White decay with orange zones	Grifola frondosa
	Butt	Soft white rot	Inonotus dryadeus
	Stem and branch	Brown cubical rot	Laetiporus sulphureus
	Stem	Pipe rot	Stereum gausapatum
	Stem	Soft white decay	Stereum hirsutum
	Stem	Pipe rot	Stereum rugosum
Plane	Stem and branch	Yellow with dark reaction zone	Inonotus hispidus

Table 19.1 continued

Tree species	Position of rot	Appearance of rot	Decay fungus
Poplar	Stem and branch Stem and branch Butt	Brown stain, later mottled decay White flaky decay Soft brown decay	*Chondrostereum purpureum* *Pleurotus ostreatus* *Pholiota squarrosa*
Sweet chestnut	Stem and branch Stem and branch	Rich brown stain Brown cubical rot	*Fistulina hepatica* *Laetiporus sulphureus*
Sycamore	Stem and branch	Yellow with dark reaction zone Yellow spongy rot	*Inonotus hispidus* *Polyporus squamosus*
Walnut	Stem and branch Stem and branch	Yellow with dark reaction zone White spongy rot	*Inonotus hispidus* *Polyporus squamosus*
Yew	Stem and branch	Brown cubical rot	*Laetiporus sulphureus*

Table 19.2

Susceptibility of major conifer species to the six most common decay fungi. HS: highly susceptible, MS: moderately susceptible, SS: slightly susceptible, R: resistant (After B. J. W. Greig, 1981)

Conifer hosts	Armillaria mellea	Heterobasidium annosum	Phaeolus schweinitzii	Sparassis crispa	Stereum sanguinolentum	Tyromyces stipticus
Scots pine* (Pinus sylvestris)	R	R	MS	MS	SS	SS
Sitka spruce (Picea sitchensis)	HS	HS	HS	HS	HS	MS
Norway spruce (P. abies)	HS	HS	R	R	HS	HS
Omorika spruce (P. omorika)	HS	MS	MS	MS	HS	MS
Larches+ (Larix spp.)	SS	MS	MS	MS	MS	MS
Douglas fir (Pseudotsuga menziesii)	SS	SS	MS	MS	MS‖	–
Western hemlock (Tsuga heterophylla)	HS	HS	R	R	MS‖	–

Table 19.2 continued

Conifer hosts	Armillaria mellea	Heterobasidium annosum	Phaeolus schweinitzii	Sparassis crispa	Stereum sanguinolentum	Tyromyces stipticus
Western red cedar (*Thuja plicata*)	HS	HS	R	R	MS[‖]	–
Lawson cypress[‡] (*Chamaecyparis lawsoniana*)	HS	MS	R	R	MS	–
Grand fir[§] (*Abies grandis*)	SS	R or SS	R	R	MS[‖]	–

* Similar ratings for Corsican pine (*Pinus nigra* var. *maritima*) and lodgepole pine (*P. contorta*).
+ Includes European (*Larix decidua*), Japanese (*L. kaempferi*) and hybrid larch (*L. eurolepis*).
‡ Similar ratings for Leyland cypress (*Cupressocyparis leylandii*).
§ Similar ratings for noble fir (*Abies procera*) and other silver first (*Abies* spp.)
‖ The susceptibility rating is taken from studies outside Britain.

Figure 103. Fractured end of a wind-snapped lime tree decayed by *Ustulina deusta*. Black stromatic sheets of the fungus can be seen (Forestry Commission)

limit of decay. The decay column may extend for 5 metres up the tree and above this there may be a reddish-brown zone caused by infiltration of the cell walls with colouring matter.

Ustulina vulgaris: see *Ustulina deusta*

Ustulina zonata: see *Ustulina deusta*

REFERENCES

Anon (1967). *Polyporus schweinitzii* Fr. *Distrib. Maps Pl. Dis.*, no 182

Bakshi, B. K., Reddy, M. A. R. and Sujan Singh (1976). Ganoderma root rot mortality in Khair (*Acacia catechu* Willd.) in reforested stands. *Eur. J. For. Path.*, 6, 20–38

Banerjee, S. (1955). A disease of Norway spruce (*Picea excelsa* (Lam.) Link) associated with *Stereum sanguinolentum* (A. and S.) Fr. and *Pleurotus mitis* (Pers.) Berk. *Indian J. mycol. Res.*, 1, 1–30

Barrett, D. K. (1968). In Tinsley, T. N., Barrett, D. K. and Biddle, P. G., Forest pathology. *Ann. Rep. Commonw. For. Inst. Oxford, 1966–67,* pp. 23–6

Barrett, D. K. (1970). *Armillaria mellea* as a possible factor predisposing roots to infection by *Polyporus schweinitzii. Trans. Br. mycol. Soc.,* 55, 459–62

Basham, J. T., Moole, P. V. and Davidson, A. G. (1953). New information concerning balsam fir decays in Western North America. *Can. J. Bot.,* 31, 334–60

Batko, S. (1950). A note on the distribution of *Poria obliqua* (Pers.) Bres. *Trans. Br. mycol. Soc.,* 33, 105–6

Blaisdell, D. J. (1939). Decay of hardwoods by *Ustulina vulgaris* and other Ascomycetes. *Phytopathology,* 29, 2

Boyce, J. S. (1924). An unusual infection of *Polyporus schweinitzii* Fr. *Phytopathology,* 14, 588

Burdekin, D. A. (1977). Gale damage to amenity trees. *Arb. J.,* 3, 181–9

Burdekin, D. A. (1979). *Common Decay Fungi in Broadleaved Trees,* Arboric. Leafl. no. 5, HMSO, London

Bourdot, H. and Galzin, A. (1927). *Hymenomycetes de France,* Societe Mycologique de France

Campbell, A. H. and Munsun, R. R. (1936). Zone lines in plant tissues. III. The black zone lines produced by *Polyporus squamosus. Ann. appl. Biol.,* 23, 453–64

Campbell, W. A. and Davidson, R. W. (1940). *Ustulina vulgaris* decay in sugar maple and *Bot. Cl.,* 65, 31–69

Campbell, W. A. and Davidson, R. W. (1938). A Poria as the fruiting stage of the fungus causing the sterile conks on birch. *Mycologia,* 30, 553–60

Campbell, W. A. and Davidson, R. W. (1940). *Ustulina Vulgaris* decay in sugar maple and other hardwoods. *J. For.,* 38, 474–7

Cartwright, K. St. G. (1937). A reinvestigation into the cause of 'Brown oak', *Fistulina hepatica* (Huds.) Fr. *Trans. Br. mycol. Soc.,* 21, 68–83

Cartwright (1940). Note on a heart rot of oak trees caused by *Polyporus fronduses* Fr. *Forestry,* 14, 38–41

Cartwright, K. St. G., Campbell, W. G. and Armstrong, F. H. (1936). The influences of fungal decay on the properties of timber. I. Effect of progressive decay by *Polyporus hispidus* Fr. on the strength of English ash (*Fraxinus excelsior* L.). *Proc. R. Soc. B,* 120, 76–95

Cartwright, K. St. G. and Findley, W. P. K. (1958), *Decay of timber and its prevention.* H. M. S. O. London

Childs, T. W. (1937). Variability of *Polyporus schweinitzii* in culture. *Phytopathology,* 27, 29–50

Davidson, A. G. (1951). Decay of balsam fir in New Brunswick. *Bi-m. Prog. Rep. Div. For. Biol. Dep. Can.,* 7 (5), 1

Davidson, A. G. and Etheridge, D. E. (1963). Infection of balsam fir, *Abies balsamea* (L.) Mill., by *Stereum sanguinolentum. Can. J. Bot.,* 41, 759–65

Davidson, R. W. , Campbell, W. A. and Vaughan, D. B. (1942). Fungi causing decay in living oaks in the Eastern United States and their cultural identification. *U. S. Dep. Agric. Tech. Bull.,* no. 785

Davidson, R. W., Hinds, T. E. and Hawkesworth, F. G. (1959). Decay of aspen in Colorado. *U.S. Dep. Agric. Rocky Mount. Forest Range Exp. Stn Pap.,* no. 45

Delatour, C. (1975). Comportement *in vitro* du *Sparassis crispa* Wulf. ex. Fr. et du *Sparassis laminosa* Fr. *Eur. J. For. Path.,* 5, 240–47

Dennis, R. W. G. (1968). *British Ascomycetes,* J. Cramer, Lehre

Etheridge, D. E. (1963). Infection of balsam fir, *Abies balsamea* (L.) Mill. by *Stereum sanguinolentum* (Alb. and Schw. ex Fr.) Fr. *Trans. R. Soc. Can. 1, Ser. 4, Sect. 3,* pp. 357–60

Gibson, I. A. S. (1966). A note on *Stereum sanguinolentum,* a new record for Kenya forests. *E. Afr. agric. For. J.,* 32, 38–40

Gill, L. S. (1925). Notes on sporophores of *Polyporus schweinitzii* Fr. on yellow pine in California. *Phytopathology,* 15, 492–3

Gladman, R. J. and Greig, B. J. W. (1965). *Principal Butt Rots of Conifers.* Bookl. For. Commn, no. 13

Gladman, R. J. and Low, J. D. (1963). Conifer heart rots in Scotland. *Forestry*, 36, 227–44

Greig, B. J. W. (1962). *Fomes annosus* (Fr.) Cke. and other root-rotting fungi in conifers on ex-hardwood sites. *Forestry*, 35, 164–82

Greig, B. J. W. (1981). Decay in conifers. *Leafl. For. Commn*, no. 79

Greig, B. J. W. and Gulliver, C. C. (1976). Decay in oaks in the Forest of Dean. *Q. Jl. For.*, 70, 157–9

Gremmen, J. (1961). *Polyporus schweinitzii* Fr., de oorzaak van stamrot in naaldhout. *Ned. Bosb. Tijdschr.*, 33, 354–8

Guinier, P. (1933). Sur la biologie de deux champignons lignicoles. *C. R. Soc. Biol. Nancy*, 112, 1363–6

Harvey, G. M. (1962). *Heart Rots of Douglas Fir*, U. S. Dep. Agric. Pest Leafl., no. 73

Hepting, G. H. and Chapman, A. D. (1938). Losses from heart rot in two shortleaf and lob- lolly pine stands. *J. For.*, 36, 1193–1201

Hubert, F. E. (1935). A disease of conifers caused by *Stereum sanguinolentum. J. For.*, 33, 485–9

Hunt, J. and Krueger, K. W. (1962). Decay associated with thinning wounds in young-growth western hemlock and Douglas fir. *J. For.,* 60, 336–40

Kimmey, J. W. and Bynum, H. H.., Jr. (1961). Heart rot of red and white firs. *U.S. Dep. Agric. For. Pest Leafl.*, No. 52

Latham, J. and Armstrong, F. H. (1934). The mechanical strength properties of 'Brown oak'. *Forestry*, 8, 131–5

Liese, J. (1928). Verhalten holzzertörender pilze gegenüber verschiedenen Holzarten und Giftstoffen. *Angw. Bot.*, 10, 156–70

Lombard, F. F., Davidson, R. W. and Lowe, J. L. (1960). Cultural characteristics of *Fomes ulmarius* and *Poria ambigua. Mycologia*, 11, 280–94

Lowe, J. L. (1957). Polyporaceae of North America, the genus *Fomes*. N.Y. State Univ. Coll. Forestry at Syracuse Univ., Tech. Pub. no. 80

McCracken, F. I. and Toole, E. R. (1969). Sporophore development and sporulation of *Poly- porus hispidus. Phytopathology*, 59, 884–5

Macdonald, J. A. (1937). A study of *Polyporus betulinus* (Bull.) Fr. *Ann. appl. Biol.*, 24, 289–310

Martin, K. J. and Gilbertson, R. L. (1976). Cultural and other morphological studies of *Sparassis radicata* and related species. *Mycologia*, 68, 622–39

Mercer, P. C. (1979). Attitudes to pruning wounds. *Arboric. J.*, 3, 457–65

Montgomery, H. B. S. (1936). A study of *Fomes fraxineus* and its effects on ashwood. *Ann. appl. Biol.*, 23, 465–86

Nobles, M. K. (1948). Studies in forest pathology, VI. Identification of cultures of wood- rotting fungi. *Can. J. Res.*, C26, 281–431

Nutman, M. J. (1929). Studies of wood-destroying fungi. I. *Polyporus hispidus* (Fries). *Ann. appl. Biol.*, 16, 40–64

Ohman, J. H. and Kessler, K. J. (1964). White trunk rot of hardwoods. *U.S. Dep. Agric. For. Pest Leafl.*, no. 88

Overholts, L. O. (1953). *The Polyporaceae of the United States, Alaska, and Canada*, Uni- versity of Michigan Press

Panisset, T. E. (1929). *Daldinia concentrica* attacking the wood of *Fraxinus excelsior. Ann. appl. Biol.*, 16, 400–421

Parker, E. J. (1974). *Beech Bark Disease*, Forest Rec., Lond., no. 96

Pawsey, R. G. (1971). Some recent observations on decay in conifers associated with extrac- tion damage, and on butt rot caused by *Polyporus schweinitzii* and *Sparassis crispa. Q. Jl. For.*, 65, 193–208

Pawsey, R. G. and Gladman, R. J. (1965). *Decay in Standing Conifers Developing from Extraction Damage*, Forest Rec., Lond., No. 54

Peace, T. R. (1938). Butt rot of conifers in Great Britain. *Q. Jl. For.*, 32, 81–104

Pegler, D. N. (1973). *The Polypores*. Suppl., *Bull. Br. mycol. Soc.* 7, 43 pp.

Pegler, D. N. and Waterston, J. M. (1968). *Inonotus hispidus*. CMI Descriptions of Patho- genic Fungi and Bacteria, no. 193, Commonwealth Agricultural Bureau

Rayner, A. D. M. (1977). Fungal colonisation of hardwood stumps from natural sources. II. Basidiomycetes. *Trans. Br. mycol. Soc.*, 69, 303–12

Rea, C. (1922). *British Basidiomycetes*, Cambridge University Press, Cambridge

Reid, D. A. (1976). *Inonotus obliquus* (Pers. ex Fr.) Pilat in Britain. *Trans. Br. mycol. Soc.*, 67, 329–32

Rhoads, A. S. (1921). Some new or little-known hosts of wood-destroying fungi. *Phytopathology*, 11, 319–26

Risley, J. A. and Silverborg, S. B. (1958). *Stereum sanguinolentum* on living Norway spruce following pruning. *Phytopathology*, 48, 337–8

Romagnesi, H. (1962). *Petit Atlas Des Champignons*, 3 vols., Bordas, Paris and Harraps, London

Ryvarden, L. (1976). *The Polyporaceae of North Europe*, Fungiflora, Oslo

Shigo, A. L. (1977). *Compartmentalisation of Decay in Trees*, U.S. Dep. Agric. Agriculture Information Bulletin, no. 405

Spaulding, P., MacAloney, H. J. and Cline, A. C. (1935). *Stereum sanguinolentum*. A dangerous fungus in pruning wounds on northern white pine. *U.S. Dep. Agric. Tech. Note*, no. 19

Toole, E. R. (1955). *Polyporus hispidus* on southern bottomland oaks. *Phytopathology*, 45, 177–80

Toole, E. R. (1966). Root rot caused by *Polyporus lucidus. Pl. Dis. Reptr.*, 50, 945–6

Verrall, A. F. (1937). Variation in *Fomes igniarius* (L.) Gill. U.S. Dep. Agric. Tech. Bull. Minn. agric. Exp. Sta. no. 117

Wakefield, E. M. and Dennis, R. W. G. (1950). *Common British Fungi*, Gawthorn, London

Wilkins, W. H. (1934). Studies in the genus *Ustulina* with special reference to parasitism. I. Introduction, survey of previous literature and host index. *Trans. Br. mycol. Soc.*, 18, 320–46

Wilkins, W. H. (1936). Studies in the genus *Ustulina*. II. A disease of common lime (*Tilia vulgaris*) caused by *Ustulina. Trans. Br. mycol. Soc.*, 20, 133–156

Wilkins, W. H. (1939a). Studies in the genus *Ustulina*. IV. Conidia, germination and infection. *Trans. Br. mycol. Soc.*, 23, 65–85

Wilkins, W. H. (1939b). Studies in the genus *Ustulina*. V. A disease of elm caused by *Ustulina. Trans. Br. mycol. Soc.*, 23, 171–85

Wilkins, W. H. (1943). Studies in the genus *Ustulina*. VI. A brief account of heartrot of beech caused by *Ustulina. Trans. Br. mycol. Soc.*, 26, 169–70

Yatsenko-Khmelevky, A. A. (1938). Sur l'echauffure du bois de l'hetre. *C. r. Acad. Sci. U.R.S.S.*, 18, 207–12

Yde-Andersen, A. (1961). Om angreb of *Polyporus schweinitzii* Fr. i naletraebevorkinger. *Dansk Skogforen. Tidsskr.*, 46

York, H., Wean, R. E. and Childs, T. W. (1936). Some results of investigations on *Polyporus schweinitzii* Fr. *Science, N.S.*, 84, 160–61

Young, C. W. T. (1977). *External Signs of Decay in Trees*, Arboric. Leafl., no. 1, HMSO, London

Young, C. W. T. and Strouts, R. G. (1974). *Rep. Forest Res., Lond.*, 1974

Glossary

Only a short, simple, mainly mycological glossary is provided here, as most of the terms used in this book can be found readily in either a good general dictionary or a dictionary of biology, in which expanded definitions of the terms included here can also be found.

AECIDIOSPORE   A spore formed in an *aecidium*. Also called an *aeciospore*.

AECIDIUM (pl. AECIDIA)   One of the spore-producing bodies found in the rust fungi (Uredinales), usually cup-like or blister-like in form. Also called an *aecium* (pl. *aecia*).

APOTHECIUM (pl. APOTHECIA)   A usually disc-like or saucer-like fruit body found in the discomycetes, one of the groups of the Ascomycotina.

ASCOCARP   A general term for the perfect fruit body in the Ascomycotina.

ASCOMYCOTINA   The ascomycetes, a main group of the fungi, the perfect spores of which are formed in *asci*.

ASCOSPORES   The spores formed in *asci*.

ASCUS (pl. ASCI)   The cell in which the ascospores of the Ascomycotina are formed.

BASIDIOMYCOTINA   The basidiomycetes, a main group of the fungi the perfect spores of which are formed on *basidia*.

BASIDIOSPORES   The spores formed on *basidia*.

BASIDIUM (pl. BASIDIA)   The cell on which the basidiospores of the Basidiomycotina are formed.

CLEISTOCARP, CLEISTOTHECIUM (pl. CLEISTOTHECIA)   An ascal fruit body with no specialised opening for the release of the spores.

DEUTEROMYCOTINA   An artificial assemblage of fungi. Most are either forms with no perfect (sexual) stages or are the imperfect (asexual) forms of ascomycetes.

FUNGI IMPERFECTI   Deuteromycotina.

HYMENIUM   The layer of a fruit body bearing the spores.

HYPHA (pl. HYPHAE)   One of the filaments which form the *mycelium* in the fungi.

HYSTEROTHECIUM (pl. HYSTEROTHECIA)   A long, narrow ascocarp.

MASTIGOMYCOTINA   One of the main groups of fungi, in which the hyphae are generally nonseptate, the fruit bodies are simple, and the sex cells are motile. cf. ZYGOMYCOTINA.

MYCELIUM (pl. MYCELIA)   The hyphal mass forming the body of a fungus.

OIDIUM (pl. OIDIA)   Term used for the usually barrel-shaped asexual spores of the mildews, and for superficially similar spores formed by the breaking up of the hyphae of, for example, some Basidiomycotina.

PERFECT STATE The state in a fungal life cycle in which spores such as basidio-spores or ascospores are formed following nuclear fusion or by parthenogenesis.

PERITHECIUM (pl. PERITHECIA) A subglobose or flask-shaped ascocarp found in the pyrenomycetes, one of the groups of the Ascomycotina.

PHYCOMYCETES The 'lower fungi', now separated into the Mastigomycotina and the Zygomycotina.

PYCNIDIUM (pl. PYCNIDIA) A subglobose or flask-like fruit body in the Deuteromycotina. It superficially resembles a perithecium but contains asexual spores.

RHIZOMORPH A cord-like or bootlace-like body made up of fungal hyphae.

SCLEROTIUM (pl. SCLEROTIA) A generally rounded mass of fungal hyphae.

SEPTATE (of fungal hyphae) Divided by crosswalls.

SPERMATIUM (pl. SPERMATIA). A sex cell formed in some fungi (for example, the rusts and some ascomycetes).

SPERMOGONIUM (pl. SPERMOGOMIA). A walled body in which spermatia are produced.

TELEUTOSORUS (pl. TELEUTOSORI). One of the spore stages of the rusts (Uredinales), in which teleutospores ('resting spores', 'winter spores') are produced. Also called a *telium.*

TELEUTOSPORE The 'resting spore' or 'winter spore' produced in a *teleutosorus.*

UREDOSORUS (pl. UREDOSORI) One of the spore stages of the rusts, in which uredospores ('summer spores') are produced. Also called a *uredinium.*

UREDOSPORE The 'summer spore' produced in a *uredosorus.*

VECTOR An organism, usually an insect or other small animal, which carries the living agents of disease from one host to another.

ZYGOMYCOTINA One of the main groups of fungi, in which the hyphae are generally nonseptate, the fruit bodies simple, and the sex cells are nonmotile. cf. MASTIGOMYCOTINA.

Index

Pages with black and white figures are indexed in italics. Terms such as 'fungi' (which are described throughout the book under their individual names) are indexed only where they appear in the General introduction

Cherry (*continued*)
  Monilia cinerea, 354–5
  Nectria galligena, 65
  Phellinus pomaceus, 355, 389
  Pseudomonas mors-prunorum, 355
  Sclerotinia laxa, 354–5, plate 44
  silver leaf, 355
Cherry leaf roll virus (CLRV), on
  Betula, 242
Chickweeds, 185
Chinosol, 318
Chionaspis salicis, on *Alnus*, 245
Chlorine, pollution by, 36–7, 38
Chondrostereum purpureum, 367–8;
  on broadleaved trees (various), 330;
  on *Betula*, 367; on cherry, 355; on
  Fagus, 367–8; on *Laburnum*, 347;
  on *Populus*, 285, 302, 367; on
  Prunus lusitanicus, 356; on *Ulmus*,
  367
Christmas trees, 175, 176, 186
Chrysomyxa spp., 5, 13; *abietis*, on
  Picea, 127–9, plate 19; *pirolata*,
  on *Picea*, 134; *pyrolae*, see *pirolata*;
  rhododendri, on *Picea*, 127–9,
  plate 20
Ciboria batschiana, see *Stromatinia
  batschiana*
Ciboria betulae, on *Betula*, 242
Ciborinia candolleana, on *Quercus*,
  214
Cicinnobolus cesati, 210
Cladosporium spp., on *Pinus*, 158;
  herbarum, on *Tilia*, 363
Cleistocarps, 5
Cleistothecia, 3, 5
Clithris quercina, on *Quercus*, 217
Clitocybe tabescens, see *Armillaria
  mellea*
Cold damage, see Winter cold damage,
  and Frost damage
Cold stores, damage by *Botrytis
  cinerea* in, 56
Coleosporium spp., 3; *campanulae*, on
  Pinus, 143; *senecionis*, on *Pinus*,
  143; *tussilaginis*, 3, 14; on *Pinus*,
  142, 143, *144*, 145
Colletotrichum gloeosporioides, on
  Salix, 315–6
Colpoma quercinum, on *Quercus*, 217
Compartmentalisation, 366
Compositae, as alternate hosts of
  Coleosporium tussilaginis, 3, 14

Cones
  fungal contamination of, 50
  fungicidal dips for, 52
Coniothyrium fuckelii, on *Juniperus*,
  199; *illicis*, on *Ilex*, 342
Control measures, 11–15; biological,
  15; chemical, 14, 15; drainage, 14;
  for established diseases, 13–15;
  injection with fungicides, 15;
  legislation, 11–13; Plant Health
  Act, 11; removal and burning of
  plant debris, 62; sanitation felling,
  14; shading, 14; stump removal, 14;
  underplanting, 14; wound protection, 15
Copper fungicides, 91, 177, 251, 281,
  286, 293, 315, 316; colloidal
  copper, 346; copper oxychloride,
  58, 166, 362; copper sulphate, 318
Copper deficiency, on *Picea*, 33; on
  Populus, 33
Coral spot, 61, 62, plate 14; on *Acer*,
  62; on *Fagus*, 62; on *Ulmus*, 62
Coriolus versicolor, 368, *369*, plate
  63
Corylus (hazel)
  Botrytis cinerea, 339
  Gibberella baccata, 339
  Gnomoniella coryli, 338
  Labrella coryli, 338
  Mamiana coryli, 338
  Phyllactinia corylea, 337, *338*;
    guttata, 337; *suffulta*, 337
  Phyllosticta coryli, 338
  Sclerotinia fructigena, 32, 339
  Septoria avellanae, 338, 339
Coryneum cardinale, see *Seiridium
  cardinale*
Cotinus
  Verticillium wilt, 71
Crataegus (hawthorn)
  Erwinia amylovora, 73–4, 341
  fireblight, 73–4, 341
  Gymnosporangium clavariiforme,
    201, *340–41*; *confusum*, 201,
    340–41
  Monilia crataegi, 340
  Nectria galligena, 65
  Phleospora oxyacanthae, 340
  Podosphaera oxyacanthae, 339
  Sclerotinia crataegi, 339–40
  virus diseases, 341
Creosote, 91, 109